THE AFRICAN EXPERIENCE
Volume I: Essays

THE
AFRICAN
EXPERIENCE

Volume I:
Essays

Edited by
JOHN N. PADEN
and
EDWARD W. SOJA

Northwestern University Press
Evanston 1970

Library of Congress Catalog Card Number: 70–98466
Cloth Edition SBN 8101–0293–5
Paper Edition SBN 8101–0294–3
Copyright © 1970 by Northwestern University Press

JOHN N. PADEN is Assistant Professor of Political Science
at Northwestern University.
EDWARD W. SOJA is Associate Professor of Geography
at Northwestern University.

Book design by Elizabeth G. Stout.
Cover design by Edward Hughes.
Photograph by Russell Kay.
Chi-Wara antelope headdress, used by Bambara (Mali) dance society,
from the collection of Robert Plant Armstrong.

Contents

Preface   *Gwendolen M. Carter*   *vii*
Acknowledgments   *x*

Prologue
1   Introduction to the African Experience   *Edward W. Soja*   3
2   The African Setting   *Edward W. Soja and John N. Paden*   20

Part I: African Society and Culture
3   Traditional Society in Africa   *Ronald Cohen*   37
4   Traditional Economic Systems   *George Dalton*   61
5   Language Systems and Literature   *Jack Berry*   80
6   Conceptual Systems in Africa   *Ethel M. Albert*   99
7   Visual Art in Africa   *Frank Willett*   108
8   Ethnomusicology in Africa   *Klaus Wachsmann*   128

Part II: Perspectives on the Past
9   Major Themes in African History   *John A. Rowe*   154
10   Empires and State Formation   *Jeffrey Holden*   177
11   West Africa and the Afro-Americans   *Peter B. Hammond*   195
12   Race and Resistance in South Africa   *J. Congress Mbata*   210
13   The Impact of Colonialism   *Michael Crowder*   233

Part III: Processes of Change
14   Major Themes in Social Change   *Pierre L. van den Berghe*   252
15   Personality and Change   *Robert A. LeVine*   276
16   Education and Elite Formation   *Remi Clignet*   304
17   Urbanization and Change   *Akin L. Mabogunje*   331
18   Communications and Change   *Edward W. Soja*   359
19   Religion and Change   *Johannes Fabian*   381

Part IV: Consolidation of Nation-States
20   African Concepts of Nationhood   *John N. Paden*   403
21   Patterns of Nation-Building   *Aristide Zolberg*   434
22   Political Systems Development   *Crawford Young*   452
23   Legal Systems Development   *Roland Young*   473

24 Economic Systems Development   *Arnold Rivkin*   498
25 Developments in Technology   *Raymond A. Kliphardt*   522

Part V: Africa and the Modern World
26 African International Relations   *Ali A. Mazrui*   532
27 Africa and the Islamic World   *Ibrahim Abu-Lughod*   545
28 Confrontation in Southern Africa *Gwendolen M. Carter*   568
29 Contemporary African Literature   *Wilfred Cartey*   582
30 Afro-American Perspectives   *James Turner*   592

Epilogue
31 Social Science and Africa   *John N. Paden*   607

        The contributors   623
        Index   627

MAPS

Colonial Spheres of Influence — 1924   5
Patterns of Independence   6
Major Physiographic Features   22
Physical Features and Relief   *following* 20
Vegetation, Precipitation, Climate, Population   *following* 20
Distribution of Rules of Descent   45
Classification of African Languages: Greenberg, 1955   84
Classification of African Languages: Greenberg, 1963   86
Major Pre-Colonial States and Empires   178
Major Pre-Colonial Urban Centers   332
Major Contemporary Urban Centers   348
Circulation Regions   369
Islamic Areas   549
Agents of Islamization   555

Preface

AFRICAN STUDIES IN THE UNITED STATES began later than other area studies, but they developed more quickly. In a remarkably short time, a bare two decades, African studies have spread from their original concentration in the graduate schools to undergraduate curriculums and, increasingly, into the high schools. It is now unusual not to find either a course or courses on Africa in an institution of any size.

The reasons for this phenomenal growth are varied, but they have recently converged to highlight for all Americans the importance of understanding both the past and the present of a continent from which so substantial a proportion of our own population originated. Concurrently, avenues to understanding are increasingly open and varied as transport and communications technology reduce the distance between Africa and the United States.

Prior to World War II, American diplomats tended to think of Africa as an appendage to Europe, since so much of it was under colonial control. Only Liberia, Egypt, and South Africa were independent at that time; Ethiopia, by far the oldest of independent African states, had been invaded and annexed by Italy in the 1930s. But war, in particular the North African campaigns, focused strategic attention on the southern side of the Mediterranean Sea and led to a hasty scramble to collect information for military purposes and to train Americans in unfamiliar African languages. A major American air base was established in Liberia, the Free French were encouraged in their efforts to keep French African territories from falling into the hands of Pétain or other collaborators, and an anxious eye was kept on the possibility that Nazi forces would attempt a sweep south into Nigeria.

During the same period, scholars were planning means to ensure that African studies would receive the broader attention they deserved. In 1948 the Program of African Studies at Northwestern University—the first such program in the United States—was formally established with a grant from the Carnegie Corporation. Yet there were still many difficulties to be overcome. Material had to be collected, teachers trained, and, not the least of the difficulties, departments and disciplines had to be convinced of the academic respectability of this new area of study.

In the postwar period colonial Africa underwent the most rapid political evolution in history, as 37 states achieved independence from 1956 through 1969. The sheer drama of the process captured world-wide attention, and scholars had an unrivaled opportunity to observe political, economic, and social change on a wide comparative basis. Moreover, warm ties of friendship were established between many African leaders and American scholars during this critical period of transition, contacts that helped to infuse scholarly studies with insight and understanding.

In contrast to the mid-1950s, when the paucity of literature about Africa made the organization of courses a difficult process, the vast outpouring of books on an ever increasing number of African subjects has replaced scarcity with abundance. Academic disciplines, once so inhospitable to African subject matter, are now broadened through using rich data on Africa secured through field and library research. And because developing societies like those in Africa are not sharply differentiated into political, economic, and social spheres, interdisciplinary courses have multiplied both at the introductory and at the most advanced levels.

The greatest stimulus to African studies in the United States has come from belated recognition of the fact that, next to Europe, Africa is the continent from which the largest proportion of the American people draw their heritage. European history, society, art, music, and literature are so fully part of our education and ways of thinking that we hardly recognize them as "area studies." As the influence of African culture on our own society is now being recognized, we are realizing that courses about Africa, particularly African history, society, art, literature, folklore, and music, are also of particular relevance.

While Afro-American studies are not a branch of African studies, but a significant part of what is becoming a fuller, deeper, and more meaningful study of our own country's history and character, there are obvious relations between them in many fields. Moreover, both Africans and Afro-Americans are now asserting their rightful places in history and in contemporary life, and each is helping the other to do so.

African studies can be said to have come of age in 1969, twenty-one years after the founding of the first program of African Studies in this country. There are now over forty African studies programs in colleges and universities throughout the country. The number of courses offered is legion. The demand for more is omnipresent.

To meet the particular need for appropriate material for introducing African studies at the college or university level, Northwestern University, with the support of the U.S. Office of Education, prepared this comprehensive volume. The scholars chiefly responsible for its production and for the accompanying syllabus and bibliography are Dr. Edward W. Soja of the Department of Geography and Dr. John N. Paden of the Department of Political Science at Northwestern University. To the process of preparation, all members of the African Studies Program at Northwestern University, as well as colleagues from other universities, have contributed. Most of the sections providing comprehensive and analytical studies of the current state of our knowledge and understanding were written by scholars in different fields on the staff at Northwestern University, a demonstration of the fact that interdisciplinary teamwork is the hallmark of Northwestern's Program of African Studies.

No one can either expect or desire that African studies will remain at the stage presented in this volume. The special fascination of African studies is their rapid pace of development, a pace to which students and faculty contribute in their own ways but which is inherent in the ambitious and strenuous efforts being made by Africans themselves to respond to their own aspirations and needs. We are richly privileged to be able to study this process of development, to learn to appreciate the causes of its unevenness, and to look deeper into its complexities. We welcome all those who, through this volume or any other source, become intrigued with African studies. We look forward to sharing as broadly as possible the ever widening horizons of understanding which lie in store.

May 1, 1969   GWENDOLEN M. CARTER

Acknowledgments

THIS COLLECTION OF ESSAYS originated as part of the African Curriculum Development Project, sponsored by the Office of Education, U.S. Department of Health, Education, and Welfare. In 1967 USOE contracted with the Program of African Studies, Northwestern University, to develop a three-volume set of teaching materials on Africa for college use. The set was to include a syllabus for teachers, a computerized bibliography, and an anthology of original essays. Since the completion of the contract in 1968–69, and after receiving comments from readers of the privately distributed USOE edition, work was begun to revise and enlarge the three volumes with the intention of producing an interdisciplinary introduction to African studies that would be available to a wider readership. *The African Experience, Volume I: Essays* is the first product of these efforts.

The original USOE materials were accompanied by the statement that "contractors undertaking . . . projects under Government sponsorship are encouraged to express freely their professional judgment in the conduct of the project. Points of view or opinions stated do not, therefore, necessarily represent official Office of Education position or policy." In the present volume individual scholars have again been encouraged to express their professional opinions and judgments in their essays, and thus, while the content of the volume is coordinated, the essays in themselves reflect a range of value orientations. Although most of the contributors are, or have at one time been, associated with Northwestern's Program of African Studies, a remarkable diversity of academic perspectives and personal backgrounds is represented. The contributors come from the fields of anthropology, economics, political science, linguistics, history, geography, art, literature, law, sociology, music, philosophy, psychology, and industrial engineering, as well as from combinations of these fields, such as sociolinguistics, economic anthropology, and political geography. The authors also represent different national and ethnic backgrounds, including French, English, Belgian, German, Austrian, Canadian, Nigerian, Kenyan, South African, Arab, West Indian, black American, and white American. All, however, have had experience teaching some aspect of African studies at the university level in the United States. While the volume is geared primarily to an American university audience, we hope that the diversity of the contributors will prove a source of strength.

The editors are grateful to many persons for assistance in the preparation of this volume. We are especially indebted to Professors Paul Bohannan, Ronald Cohen, and Gwendolen Carter, of Northwestern University, who have read all the essays and have made important suggestions. We would also like to thank Dr. Robert P. Armstrong, Director, and Mr. John B. Putnam, Senior Editor, of Northwestern University Press, for advice on substantive aspects of the volume as well as on production matters. In addition, thanks are due Mrs. Diana Cohen and Mrs. Ruth Graf for research and administrative work from the earliest stages of the project and to Ann Paden for editorial assistance. The Program of African Studies at Northwestern has given aid and cooperation throughout the entire period of preparation.

We reserve our deepest gratitude, however, for the contributors to this volume, who have all taken time from their full schedules to meet our ever impending deadlines and to read critically the papers of other contributors in an effort to make this a truly integrated volume.

Prologue

Introduction to the African Experience

EDWARD W. SOJA

In 1956 THE FORMER ANGLO-EGYPTIAN SUDAN became independent, symbolizing the blend of old and new which has come to characterize the emergent African states. The vast Gezira irrigation scheme along the Nile was set against a background of accomplishments from the African past. In the area of Nubia contacts with Egypt had been established many hundreds of years before the beginning of the Christian era, and for more than a millennium this area was pivotal in the patterns of culture contact between the Lower Nile Valley and sub-Saharan Africa. Moreover, this culture contact was not unidirectional; it consisted of a two-way flow of innovative ideas and technology between the kingdoms of the Nile Valley and the predominantly black peoples south of the Sahara.

In 1957 the colonial territory of the Gold Coast became the independent state of Ghana, a name filled with memories of a glorious African past and imbued with hopes for an equally glorious African future. Ancient Ghana, which reached its zenith in the tenth and eleventh centuries A.D., was the earliest of a series of African states and empires which developed in the Sudanic belt—the savanna grassland region lying south of the Sahara and north of the Guinea Coast forests and stretching across the continent from the Atlantic Ocean to the Ethiopian Highlands. Contemporary Ghana lies south of the major centers of Sudanic state formation, although its gold deposits were a vital component in the trade of many of these ancient states. Its name was selected to recall the rich heritage of Africa and to symbolize the dream of future unity and achievement.

By 1969 the roster of independent African states numbered over forty. The African empire of Great Britain had completely disappeared, except for Rhodesia, which unilaterally and unconstitutionally sought to declare its independence under white minority rule in 1965—a status which no other state has recognized. The extensive French empire had dwindled to the tiny Territory of the Afars and Issas (formerly French Somaliland), while the only large remaining empire — the Portuguese-controlled territories of Angola, Mozambique, and Portuguese Guinea — was rent with rebellion and held together in large part through the presence of Portuguese armed forces (see maps on pages 5 and 6).

Thus, within less than a generation, a most remarkable series of interrelated events had taken place in Africa (and elsewhere in the former colonial world). Dozens of new and independent actors entered the international system and helped to produce major transformations in world politics. A Third World emerged to modify the bipolar power structure which prevailed in the post-World War II period. New words and phrases exploded into our vocabularies symbolizing not only the transformed contemporary context but also the radically new demands for the future: "the revolution of rising expectations," "the challenge of nation-building," "nonalignment," "negritude," "neocolonialism," "the developing countries," "modernization."

Having achieved an independent presence in world affairs, and beginning to chart its own future, Africa simultaneously has rediscovered its past. No longer is the coming of the European used to mark the beginnings of African history. A new sense of pride in past achievements is accompanied by a search for those historical continuities which shape African life and culture. The distinctively Western bias which had characterized the literature on Africa has been clearly identified, and demands have been made for an indigenously based interpretation of the African experience.

The end of the colonial era and the emergence of independent Africa have created the need for new perspectives on the contemporary world which encompass not only an understanding of current situations but a deeper knowledge of their development through space and time. The study of Africa has the additional burden and responsibility of trying to correct a previously distorted image. This volume of interdisciplinary essays is devoted to the search for new and more balanced perspectives on the African experience, to a deeper understanding of Africa's past, present, and future, and to a concern for Africa's place in the broader context of world history.

THE AFRICAN EXPERIENCE:
AN INTERDISCIPLINARY INTRODUCTION

In America, formally organized academic study of Africa dates back only a score of years. Prior to 1948, when the first program of African studies in the United States was officially established at Northwestern University, teaching about Africa was limited to particular courses at institutions like Northwestern, Columbia, and Howard universities and at a few denominational schools in-

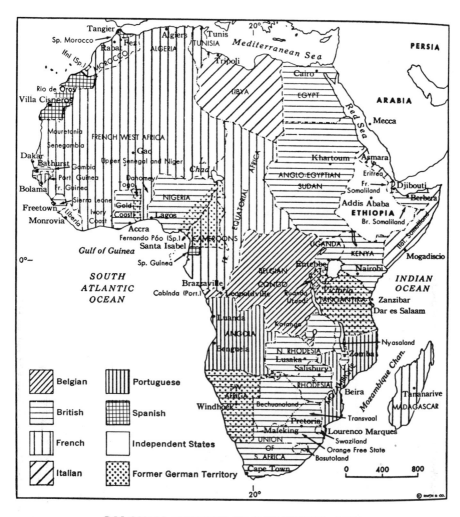

COLONIAL SPHERES OF INFLUENCE – 1924

From *Collier's Encyclopedia*, Vol. 1, 1966. Copyright by Rand McNally & Company, R.L. 69–S–91. Used with permission of Crowell-Collier Educational Corporation.

volved in missionary work. African history, when it was recognized to exist, was treated essentially as an appendage to European colonial history. The American image of Africa in and out of the schools was shaped almost entirely by the popularizing media and the vast storehouse of distortions inherited from an uninformed past. In 1951 the only African studies program among the nearly thirty non-Western area-studies programs at American universities was at Northwestern.

The rush to independence in the late 1950s and early 1960s, however, awakened world interest in Africa and was accompanied by the rapid growth of African studies in the United States. With basic financial support from private

Algiers • • Tunis
Rabat • TUNISIA
MOROCCO • Tripoli
Aiún • Benghasi • Cairo
SPANISH   ALGERIA   LIBYA   UNITED
SAHARA   ARAB REPUBLIC
MAURITANIA
Nouakchott •   MALI   NIGER   Khartoum •
SENEGAL   FRENCH TERRITORY OF
Dakar •   CHAD   SUDAN   AFARS AND ISSAS
Bathurst • GAMBIA Bamako • • Niamey   • Djibouti
Bissau •   Ouagadougou •
PORT   UPPER VOLTA   • Fort Lamy   ETHIOPIA
GUINEA   GUINEA   DAHOMEY   • Addis Ababa
Conakry • Freetown • TOGO   CENTRAL
SIERRA   IVORY GHANA NIGERIA   AFRICAN REPUBLIC   SOMALIA
LEONE   COAST Lomé • • Lagos
Monrovia •   Accra • Porto-Novo CAMEROON • Bangui
LIBERIA   Abidjan   UGANDA
           Fernando Po • Yaoundé •   Kampala • KENYA   • Mogadishu
           EQUATORIAL Rio Muni   RUANDA   • Nairobi
           GUINEA   CONGO-   Kigali •
           Libreville • GABON   BRAZZAVILLE   Bujumbura • RUANDA
                        CONGO-   BURUNDI
                        BRAZZAVILLE   CONGO-
                        Brazzaville •   KINSHASA
                                        Kinshasa •   TANZANIA   • Zanzibar
                                                                 Dar es Salaam
                        Luanda •

Before 1956   ANGOLA
1956-1959   ZAMBIA   MALAWI
1960   Lusaka •   • Zomba
1961-1969   SOUTHERN   MOZAMBIQUE
Not independent   Salisbury •   Tananarive •
                        SOUTH-WEST   RHODESIA
                        AFRICA   (ZIMBABWE)   MALAGASY
                                 BOTSWANA   REPUBLIC
                        Windhoek •
                        (NAMIBIA) Gaberones •
                                        Pretoria •
                                   Mbabane • • Lourenço Marques
                                        SWAZILAND
                        REPUBLIC   Maseru •
                        OF   • LESOTHO
                        SOUTH AFRICA

0   500   1000
Scale in Miles

PATTERNS OF INDEPENDENCE

foundations such as Ford, Carnegie, and Rockefeller, and supplementary aid in promoting language and area studies from the federal government, African studies programs were able to multiply, keeping pace with the equally rapid emergence of independent African states. In the last decade, the number of African studies programs rose from three to nearly forty, representing undergraduate as well as graduate programs. The twenty-one largest centers in 1969 had some 300 faculty members and over 1,400 associated graduate students, with many thousands of undergraduates taking courses in African studies. The African Studies Association, established with 35 members in 1957, has increased its membership (institutional and individual) to over 2,000 in just twelve years. The ASA annual meeting in October, 1969, was attended by 1,700 persons.

We can extend the analogy between developments in Africa and the growth of African studies still further. In both, the first flush of enthusiasm and expansion began to wane somewhat in the mid-1960s. After the panoply of independence was over, the new African states were faced with the enormous problems of consolidation, creating political order, stimulating economic growth, and promoting increased interaction between the relatively small national elites and the masses of the population. In this country, there was widespread disillusionment over the failure of the relatively small American foreign-aid program to produce immediate economic miracles in Africa and disappointment over the fact that political miracles did not seem to be emanating from the new leaders of Africa, resulting in a distinct leveling off of interest in African affairs.

Similarly, in the mid-1960s it appeared that the development of African studies in the United States had reached a plateau. It seemed unlikely that African studies would continue to receive financial support to match that of the period after 1957. In the early 1960s, American universities had turned out more trained Africanists than specialists in Latin America, but the prospects for further expansion relative to other area programs, such as those for East and South Asia or the Soviet Union, were not very favorable.

Furthermore, in the early 1960s, African studies were concentrated at the graduate level and were not able to successfully bridge the same "elite-mass gap" that was so prominent in the developing countries of Africa. A survey of 685 liberal arts institutions in 1964 revealed, for example, that only 5 per cent of the nearly 3,000 undergraduate courses given on non-Western areas dealt specifically with Africa. Several valuable efforts were made to introduce African subject matter into the secondary schools, but nevertheless teaching at that level rarely extended beyond a fascination with the strange, the exotic, and the unusual. Even today, much of the information on Africa conveyed in secondary schools and in many institutions of higher learning is still heavily involved with topics such as the Bushmen of the Kalahari Desert—surely one of the most widely discussed groups of its size and importance in the world.

In the late 1960s, however, another element entered the picture which has precipitated a reevaluation of African studies in American education. As black American demands for increased attention to Afro-American studies have begun to have an impact, Africa has acquired a new significance in relation to the American people, a significance which is independent of the foreign-policy perspectives of the federal government. This domestic influence has resulted in a resurgence of interest in things African and a new challenge and responsibility for existing programs of African studies in America.

These factors, especially as they are related to the role of African studies in American education, make a thorough examination of the African experience a most appropriate and relevant task. African studies, after a brief period of equilibrium, now appear to be entering a new phase of expansion. It is most important that their past accomplishments be comprehensively evaluated, their present responsibilities clearly recognized, and the range of their future alternatives broadly charted. Furthermore, African studies now find themselves in a significantly altered educational environment. Africa today is becoming a continent of more immediate concern to a very large proportion of the American population, black and white. It is still not clear how great a role Africa will play in the future of black studies in America, or whether its role will be central or supplementary. What is certain, however, is that specialists on Africa have a growing obligation to promote greater understanding of that continent and to help correct the distortions and ethnocentricities which have characterized the image of Africa in contemporary America.

Changes have also taken place within African studies over the past decade which have tended to blur the boundaries between academic disciplines and to foster the growth of interdisciplinary approaches to contemporary problems. Africa is complex. Its area is more than three times that of the United States. Its population of approximately 300 million is organized into about fifty political units (constituting more than one-third of the entire United Nations membership). The peoples of Africa identify themselves with hundreds of different ethnic groups and speak over a thousand distinct languages. The range of variations in African economies, societies, political organization, and ecology rivals that of any place on earth. This complexity and variation had hitherto discouraged generalization, to the detriment of African studies. Today, however, intellectual reorientation as well as the urgency of Africa's—and America's—problems have led to a reduction in academic compartmentalization and to the growth of the interdisciplinary cooperation and interaction necessary to handle the complex and multidimensional problems facing the student of Africa.

The primary objective of this volume is to survey, in a series of original essays, each directed to an important theme, the African experience: the African response to the challenges facing all mankind. The volume represents a wide-ranging introduction to African studies as well as to the perspectives and methods of social-science research in Africa. The contributing authors, in many cases, were asked to synthesize an enormous body of personal experience and research activity in a short essay designed to explore the subject matter and to present challenging questions and problems for future research. In addition, each author was asked to consider the interdisciplinary relevance of his theme, with the result that no single contribution stands in isolation from the others. Each is conceptually linked within the overall framework of the volume, while several groups of essays form highly interrelated sets sharing similar approaches, terminology, and conclusions.

These original essays form an integral part of a larger set of instructional materials designed for use in university courses in African studies. *The African Experience, Volume II: Syllabus* consists of 100 teaching modules, keyed into the conceptual framework of the volume of essays, which suggest and interpret major discussion points which might be presented in an introductory African studies course. Although the sequence of these topic summaries is intended to provide an integrated overview of African economic, political, and social patterns in the past and in the present, the modular construction enables the individual teacher to restructure the basic units to fit his specific requirements. *The African Experience, Volume III: Bibliography* arranges more than 3,500 selected references topically to follow the syllabus outline. To ensure the widest possible use, the references are also arranged as case studies listed by country and alphabetically by author. Introductory sources are annotated, and further basic references, foreign language publications, general theoretical works, and case-study materials are classified within each topical unit.

Because of the highly integrated nature of these materials, it is appropriate to discuss briefly the thematic framework used and the basis for its selection, particularly with respect to the essays in this volume. The focus of Part I, "African Society and Culture," is on traditional Africa, not as a historical entity or as a contemporary anachronism but as a dynamic form of human expression, identity, and organization. Traditional or ethnic Africa is viewed not simply as a base line of change but as a creative way of life which has characterized the bulk of Africa's population for the major part of its history. It is a way of life in which kinship and descent provide a primary basis of social cohesion, political behavior, economic organization, psychological attitudes, and artistic expression. Contemporary change in African societies and cultures, when viewed against the traditional context, is seen to be an accelerated and far-reaching manifestation of forces which have been operative in Africa for many centuries rather than the consequence of European-generated sparks which settled on a static and stagnant population.

The introductory essay in this section, by Ronald Cohen, presents a broad and systematic discussion of traditional African social and political organization. As such it provides an overall view of the essential components of ethnic Africa. This essay is followed by George Dalton's examination of traditional economic organization and a discussion by Jack Berry of the distribution and study of African languages and oral literature. Ethel Albert considers African conceptual systems and ethnoscience, and the achievement and orientations of African visual art and the dimensions of African music are discussed by Frank Willett and by Klaus Wachsmann respectively. In these essays the continuities of African society and culture are emphasized, and each essay is relevant not only to the study of Africa's past but also to an understanding of its present and future.

Part II is entitled "Perspectives on the Past." Although more specifically historical than Part I, the essays here are also concerned with contemporary problems. The introductory essay by John Rowe identifies a number of significant themes in African history, ranging from the evolution of man in Africa to the movements for African independence. Several of these themes are developed more intensively in the essays which follow. African state formation, for example, provides the central theme of the essay by Jeffrey Holden, which focuses on the growth of centralized political institutions in the Western Sudan from the eighth century B.C. to the sixteenth century A.D. The relevance of the West African slave trade to the growth of Afro-American culture is explored by Peter Hammond, while a form of domestic colonialism generated by racial confrontation in South Africa is traced to its roots by J. Congress Mbata. To conclude this section, Michael Crowder analyzes the imprint of colonialism on the African experience in the former colonial territories of West Africa. It is noteworthy that each of these primarily historical essays provides material which is relevant to contemporary problems in Africa and in the United States.

"Processes of Change" provides the focus for Part III. Again, this section is introduced with a wide-ranging essay. Pierre van den Berghe reviews many of the concepts and themes discussed in previous sections while at the same time providing an overview for subsequent essays. Van den Berghe mentions the problem of ethnocentrism in the study of Africa, and this topic is explored in greater detail in the essay by Robert LeVine, which discusses the concept of an African personality. LeVine's treatment of the individual personality in a changing environment is further expanded by Remi Clignet in his analysis of education and the growth of African elites. Still further expansions of scale characterize Akin Mabogunje's examination of urbanization and its impact on the individual and on the larger society, and Edward Soja's study of communications and transportation within their spatial and historical contexts. Finally, Johannes Fabian links the processes of change to the influence of Christianity, Christian missions, and the syncretisms emerging from indigenous reappraisals of proselytizing religion.

Part IV is concerned with the "Consolidation of Nation-States." John Paden introduces this section with a survey of pre-independence concepts of nationhood, including the ideas of negritude and Pan-Africanism. From the pre-independence period, the emphasis shifts to the contemporary problems of nation-building. The essay by Aristide Zolberg explores the broad dimensions of Africa's search for order and stability, particularly with respect to the difficulties growing out of interethnic relations and the mass-elite relations which evolved during the colonial period. The theme of nation-building is then broken down into some of its major components, first in an analysis of the growth of political systems by Crawford Young and then in studies of the development of legal systems by Roland Young and of economic systems by the late Arnold Rivkin. The section concludes with a discussion by Raymond Kliphardt of the role of technology in modern Africa. By emphasizing the task of integrating the traditional with the modern, each of these essays links up with materials covered in preceding sections.

Part V thematically relates to "Africa and the Modern World." The first essay, by Ali Mazrui, examines Africa's role in international relations, particularly its position within the Third World. This is followed by examinations of the Islamic factor in Africa, by Ibrahim Abu-Lughod; of white-dominated southern Africa, by Gwendolen Carter; and of contemporary African literature, by Wilfred Cartey. The final essay in this section is an analysis by James Turner of the relevance of Africa to the Afro-American experience. Taken together, these essays supply perspectives on the global implications of developments in contemporary Africa.

It is quite clear that no single collection of essays can reflect the African experience in its entirety. The contributors to this volume have attempted to identify some of the more significant dimensions of this complex subject, to examine them primarily from the perspectives of social science, and to relate these dimensions to a framework of interdisciplinary effort and methodology. The concluding essay by John Paden summarizes the fundamental concepts of social science, including its language, methodology, and types of analysis, and relates social science to the study of Africa by drawing upon examples from the contributions to this volume.

THE AFRICAN EXPERIENCE: AN OVERVIEW OF ITS CONTEMPORARY DIMENSIONS

An overview of the dynamic processes affecting Africa today would provide a further introduction to the essays which follow. But rather than attempt to cover the entire spectrum of the contemporary scene, special attention will be given here to three key forces which are shaping modern Africa. The effects of these forces—ethnicity, nationalism, and political stability—thread through the entire fabric of this volume.

Ethnicity and "Tribalism"

Human communities are organized in a variety of ways, and each individual anywhere on earth has a wide range of loyalties. The American, for example, identifies to varying degrees with such groups as his family, his religious organization, his country, and even his linguistic community (English-speakers) and his city, state, or region (Boston, California, the Midwest). The relative strength of these loyalties differs from person to person and may in fact differ in any given individual from place to place and from one time to another.

One of the most fundamental categories of human loyalties and organization is *ethnicity,* or loyalty to a group which shares a common sense of origin, real or artificially constructed. The Walloon in Belgium, the Welshman in Great Britain, the Slovak in Czechoslovakia, the Irish and the Italian in American cities, and the Yoruba in Nigeria—all identify in varying degrees of intensity with their respective ethnic groups. Most, but not all, traditional African societies were ethnically based in that they were communities primarily bound together by a belief in blood relationship, a belief that all members were descendants of a common ancestor. These beliefs were frequently reinforced by a common language, similar economic and political organizations, and a wide variety of shared characteristics and customs.

These ethnic loyalties remain very powerful in contemporary Africa and are often competitive with the growth of larger transethnic loyalties to the nation-state. The daily newspaper, however, attests to the fact that ethnicity remains a powerful factor throughout the world, affecting the outlook for political stability not only in Africa but in Western Europe, the Communist countries, and the United States as well.

In recent years, the term "ethnicity" has, for a variety of reasons, been substituted for "tribalism" when referring to African societies in which blood ties or common descent—real or assumed—provide a primary basis for human group solidarity. Similarly, such terms as "people" or "ethnic group" are being substituted for the word "tribe." The terms "tribe" and "tribalism" have assumed pejorative connotations for many indigenous Africans (as has "primitive"), but more specifically these terms have not proved to be very effective concepts for analytical purposes. It is extremely difficult, for example, to develop valid criteria for selecting the particular level at which the terms should be applied. Moreover, the changing nature of ethnic-group identity is easily overlooked by use of a term which is filled with static connotations in the literature.

"Tribe" and "tribalism" have also lacked cross-cultural applicability. What is called a tribe in Africa is often called a nation or nationality in Europe and North America. It is difficult to imagine an American presidential candidate discussing his views of the "tribal" vote in the United States. But it is equally unsound to refer to thirteen million Yoruba, eight million Ibo, and fifteen million Hausa as "tribes" and to identify conflicts between them as arising from "tribalism."

Perhaps the most critical deficiency of the concept of tribe is the tendency to view this form of ethnicity as static and unchangeable. Whatever the tribe may be, it is certainly not a constant, immutable unit. It thus becomes absurd, as Ronald Cohen points out in his essay on traditional society, to speak of Africans as "reverting to tribalism." Ethnic identity is a dynamic phenomenon which adjusts and adapts itself to external pressures and to the demands of the immediate local environment. Aristide Zolberg, in his essay on nation-building, emphasizes that "the concept of ethnicity constitutes a moving rather than a static pattern of identities; interaction between the old and the new does not occur once and for all when 'tradition' encounters 'modernity,' but continues in a process of change." This situational and adaptable quality of ethnicity is a key theme in many other essays in this volume, including those by Michael Crowder, Pierre van den Berghe, Edward Soja, John Paden, and Crawford Young.

During the colonial period, political order was maintained by a system which can be characterized as one of "ethnic pluralism." This system persisted primarily through the power of the central government, which arbitrated disputes between the ethnic units under its administration. As Crawford Young, in his essay in this volume, points out, "The elite corps of colonial administrators constituted a mandarinate whose authority was virtually unrestricted." Some residual power often remained with local African intermediaries, especially when they were the legitimate heirs of established centralized systems. "But the African chiefs, legitimate or imposed, had a restricted orbit of influence and had very little impact on decision-making at the territorial level."

Once the colonial system was removed, however, a vacuum was created at the very top which could not easily be filled by indigenous leaders because of their individual ethnicity. Whereas mechanisms were developed during the colonial period to govern relationships between ethnic groups and the colonial power, similar mechanisms for conflict resolution between ethnic groups themselves were virtually nonexistent. Independence therefore created a situation of competition for power largely between ethnic units, since other forms of group identity at the national level usually were not sufficiently developed to provide a wide basis of support.

Contemporary problems in Africa are thus not simply the result of a resurgence of traditional identities but to a greater extent reflect the struggle by, and frequently between, contemporary ethnic units to achieve some larger identity with sufficient power to maintain order and promote development within ethnically pluralistic societies. Similar struggles exist in other developing areas, as well as in many of the most developed countries of the world, including Belgium, Canada, Yugoslavia, and the United States.

One of the best summary evaluations of ethnicity in contemporary Africa has been given by Elliott Skinner, an Afro-American anthropologist who has been United States Ambassador to Upper Volta. Skinner writes:

> Some of the names which are now used as symbols for group identity do refer to distinct socio-cultural entities in the past. However, many of the so-called "tribal" groups were creations of the colonial period. But even those groups for which continuity with the past could be claimed have lost so many of their traditional characteristics that in fact they must be viewed as new entities.
>
> The various groups in contemporary African societies are not competing for ancestral rights or privileges, but for the appurtenances of modern power. In most cases they seek to control the nation-state where they find themselves, or at worst seek to prevent being dominated by other groups within the state. Even when groups do try to secede from a nation-state, it is not because they prefer small-scale organization *per se*, but because they believe that a separate organization, or unity with members of the same group across state borders, would bring with it a better life.
>
> One of the reasons why Africans rally around descent groups, fictive or otherwise, is that the colonial situation did not provide sufficient scope for the growth

and development of those secondary associations which historically have appeared in societies with complex political organizations. The social orders within the most complex traditional African polities decayed during the colonial period. And the incipient classes which began to emerge within the mainly pluralistic colonial society were not strong enough to provide the group identity around which Africans, fighting for political power, could rally. Many an African leader with universalistic values found that he had to appeal to group identity based on descent, if he would galvanize his followers to seek political power, and thus the opportunity to build a modern society.[1]

One does not attack the problem of nepotism by wiping out the family. Ethnicity still provides the basic glue which holds together most of the societies currently engaged in the exciting processes of modernization and nation-building. Ethnic units are not erasable, but must be worked with and adapted to the new situation in which Africa is involved. Hence an important place in this volume is given to the characteristics and accomplishments of ethnic Africa.

Nationalism and Nation-building

The concept of *nationalism* is the second of the broad themes which characterize contemporary Africa. Most African states are attempting to construct cohesive national communities from an amalgam of smaller scale, primarily ethnic societies which exist within the territorial boundaries inherited from the colonial period. This marks an interesting contrast to the Western experience. Whereas in classic European nationalism state boundaries evolved almost in recognition of successful integration within particular areas, the new African states started with their boundaries as given and are now struggling to develop some form of unity within them. Put in another way, in Western Europe the growth of national communities generally preceded the establishment of the national state, while in Africa the process has been reversed. Moreover, those boundaries which now shape the processes of nation-building in Africa initially were drawn with little regard for the pre-existing patterns of cultural and ethnic identity.

Political boundaries in colonial Africa were highly artificial in that they cut across ethnic divisions and grouped very diverse and often antagonistic peoples together under one administration. The people of Nigeria, for example, today speak nearly 250 different languages and dialects and present an enormous range of cultural, economic, and political forms. The forced pluralism resulting from these colonial creations has been a major source of Africa's current instability. One might ask, then, whether it would be more logical to discard the presumably artificial colonial boundaries and redraw the map of Africa to con-

1. "Group Dynamics in the Politics of Changing Societies: The Problem of 'Tribal' Politics in Africa," in *Essays on the Problem of Tribe*, ed. June Helm (Seattle: University of Washington Press for the American Ethnological Society, 1968), p. 183.

form more closely to existing ethnic communities. This is a controversial question—the range of opinion has been reflected in discussions of the secession of Biafra, the former Eastern Region of Nigeria—but it is interesting to note that one of the first steps taken by the Organization of African Unity immediately after its establishment in 1963 was to draft a resolution stating that independent Africa would respect and uphold the former colonial boundaries. And, indeed, the international boundaries of Africa have remained remarkably stable over the past ten years. Several factors can be suggested to account for the apparent paradox of this retention in the post-colonial period of boundaries which had been externally imposed upon diverse ethnic communities.

First of all, although initially artificial, the boundaries of colonial Africa assumed new significance during the colonial period. They came to outline systems or compartments within which the processes of modernization and social change were directed, coordinated, and linked together. Ethnic units were split by these boundaries, and the two segments often experienced significantly different agencies of change. They came to speak a different second language, pay taxes to different authorities, and participate in distinctly different patterns of behavior. Moreover, as is noted in the essay on "Communications and Change," the degree of divergence was accentuated as social change increased. Just as the traditional ethnic boundaries of Africa outlined distinct "circulation systems" within which the movement of people, goods, and ideas were channeled, so the colonial boundaries recompartmentalized Africa with respect to the new patterns of circulation and change which emerged from the colonial context. In short, the boundaries of modern Africa are no longer artificial.

Additional reasons for at least the temporary retention of colonial boundaries in Africa can be derived from examining some of the alternatives. As John Paden stresses in his essay on concepts of nationhood, nationalism does not preclude the existence of other loyalties, either at the subnational or supranational levels. In particular, he focuses upon the relevance of suprastate political communities (for example, Pan-Africanism, Third-Worldism, and suprastate regionalism) and concludes that, in Africa, "The three major levels of nationalism will probably turn out to be subnational ethnic loyalties, sovereign-state nationalism, and some combination of regionalism and Pan-Africanism."

The desire to build beyond the existing framework of sovereign states involves the view that this larger unity, through mutual interdependence and cooperation, could provide an organizational basis more suitable to the demands of development, more potent in the international political arena, and more expressive of the cultural identity of black people everywhere. These important themes appear again and again in the essays in this volume; they enter into discussions of the growth of communications and transport systems (Soja), Pan-Africanism and negritude (Paden), the birth of African diplomacy and international relations (Mazrui), the problems of economic development (Rivkin), contemporary African literature (Cartey), and the formation of Afro-

American perspectives on Africa (Turner). The expressed interest of most African leaders in this supranational view—whether or not they work toward it in reality—makes squabbling over boundary lines seem self-defeating.

An additional consideration is the fear that if one former colonial boundary is modified according to traditional ethnic considerations, a Pandora's box would be opened. If boundaries were adjusted along ethnic lines and if a large proportion of the over one thousand ethnic groups in Africa demanded independence, the continent would be politically and economically shattered. This frightening image—whether it is realistic or not—is best expressed in the term "Balkanization." Most political leaders do not want Africa to be further fragmented.

In summary, therefore, it appears that the boundaries of colonial Africa, despite the difficulties they have created, will not be altered in the foreseeable future. Their functions may change. International boundaries may become intranational boundaries, for example, as they have in regional federations such as Cameroon and in Somalia and Ethiopia (which has subsequently become a unitary state after the full incorporation of Eritrea). But a redrawing of national boundaries to coincide with ethnic boundaries is not likely to occur. Such pressures for rearrangement which do emerge, especially as they may provoke comparison to the secession of Biafra, will probably be resisted with the full strength of the African states.

While on the one hand trying to work with the ethnic pluralism that is likely to characterize nearly all African states for many years to come, and on the other maintaining the dream for some form of suprastate political community, the contemporary states of Africa find themselves confronted with the immediate practical problems of nation-building and social change. These themes—when coupled with a deeper understanding of traditional African society and culture and its historical continuities, and utilized as guidelines for assessing Africa's role in the modern world—encompass the conceptual framework upon which this volume is built.

Political stability

The question of *political stability* in contemporary Africa is examined in detail by Aristide Zolberg and Crawford Young in their essays on "Patterns of Nation-Building" and "Political Systems Development." Its relevance to current problems in southern Africa is discussed by J. Congress Mbata in a historical essay on racial confrontation in the Republic of South Africa and by Gwendolen Carter in her examination of the powerful domestic colonialism in the southern portions of the continent. In several other essays, the historical background or contemporary implications of political stability are assessed. At least two conclusions emerge from these discussions.

The first is that, given the enormity of the problems facing the new states of

Africa, some degree of political instability is almost to be expected. Michael Crowder in his essay on colonialism points out that the administrative system that was inherited at independence was not geared to promoting the growth of wider loyalties and interethnic interaction, nor was it geared to government by representative assembly rather than centralized authority; it did not accommodate an economy directed toward serving the local population but rather one that acted as a raw materials reservoir for the developed world.

A second conclusion is that some forms of political instability, far from being wholly unfavorable, may in fact be beneficial at this stage in the development of cohesive and prosperous African states. The shocks and reorientations introduced by *coups d'état* and military takeovers may, for example, forestall in Africa the entrenchment of social and economic inequalities such as have taken hold in Latin America, inequalities which many feel cannot be overcome short of wholesale and probably violent revolution.

It would be important to know whether general patterns can be identified in the political instability which caused major upheavals in almost half of the independent states of Tropical Africa in the period from 1963 to 1969. A good deal of research is currently being done on this subject, but any conclusions drawn now must, of necessity, be tentative. Nevertheless, some interesting relationships appear to be emerging from these studies. First, with some important exceptions, those countries which have been more unstable politically are among the more developed countries in Africa. This seems to suggest that political instability is associated in part with the attainment of a particular level in the process of economic development. Furthermore, there has as yet been no strong indication that military takeovers have curtailed the rate of economic growth. Indeed, preliminary observations suggest somewhat the opposite. Second, among several of the more developed states which have not experienced successful *coups d'état*, there are indications that external support and protection of the existing government have been most influential. In other words, these countries may have been temporarily shielded from the challenge of the new pluralistic order and may continue to survive under the protection of the former colonial authority system.

Perhaps the most interesting pattern arising from recent events in Africa is one which suggests that the continent has already entered a new phase in its post-independence existence, a conclusion which is discussed in some detail in the essay by Crawford Young. The colonial system was unsuitable and generally unresponsive to the rising demands for social, economic, and political development and participation on the part of the colonized population. This situation in large part generated the African nationalist movements which eventually led to independence. During the nationalist period interethnic unity was remarkably high in opposition to the common enemy. But the immediate post-independence political systems, in many cases, also proved inadequate to the kinds of demands which arose after the common foe was defeated, particularly with respect to reconstructing a workable framework of ethnic pluralism and the closely related problem of curtailing corruption and nepotism.

The instability of the 1960s thus appears to have marked the transition of much of Africa to a second post-independence phase which involves the painful search for new political formulas upon which to build for the future. In Tunisia and Tanzania, as Crawford Young points out, this transition involved a revitalization of the mass-party regimes which led these countries to independence. Today, both of these countries must rank very high on the list of important and imaginative political innovators in the modern world. In Kenya and Somalia a competitive-party system survived this transition, with Somalia being almost unique in Africa in that it had three peaceful constitutional changes in government after independence. It is no coincidence, however, that Somalia is one of the very few African states which approach ethnic homogeneity. During 1969, however, Somalia experienced political assassination and military takeover, while in Kenya the competitive party system virtually disappeared with the banning of the Kenya People's Union and the detaining of its leader, Oginga Odinga.

Setting these and a few other exceptions aside, however, in the majority of the states of Africa, some thirty or more, two major alternative political patterns have emerged. The first is characterized by the transformation of the dominant party at the time of independence to a more narrowly based, almost elitist, party, which Crawford Young has identified as the basis for an oligarchic party-state. This process has been associated with the monopolization of the power apparatus of the state, an increased concentration of support in a few regions and among a limited number of ethnic groups, and, particularly in such former French colonies as Senegal, Gabon, and Ivory Coast, by a dependence upon external support. The future prospects for these oligarchic party-states seem to depend largely on how responsive this direct imitation of the colonial pluralist system is to the demands of the population. If it is sufficiently responsive and is flexible enough to prevent the solidification of the inequalities which exist, then it is possible that these states can foster the growth of the common social fabric upon which national unity is based. All too often, however, the sources of power in these new systems have proved too narrow and too concentrated along regional and ethnic lines. Alternatively, economic problems have also prevented many of these regimes from fulfilling their developmental objectives. Whatever the cause, in the 1960s these situations have led to an increasing frequency of military takeovers, the second major pattern in the post-independence phase.

It is remarkable how few students of Africa, during the period immediately following independence, anticipated the military coup as a means of political change. But now, in retrospect, the reasons behind these military takeovers seem all too obvious. The oligarchic party-states which have emerged in independent Africa provide abundant opportunities for problems to arise which cannot be dealt with effectively by a government concerned largely with maintaining itself in power under increasingly limited mass support. In these circumstances, the government is likely to increase repression and security measures as a means of gaining time in which to deal with the issues. Since the mechanism of popular elections, for a variety of reasons, has not proved to be effective as a means for changing governments in most of Africa, one of the few avenues to a change in regime is the *coup d'état* executed by the military establishment, which is often the only group with sufficient power to succeed and is usually a group without an overriding ethnic image.

It is important to note that these new military regimes are not entirely staffed by the army but include many leaders of the previous government and other civilian political figures. The major alteration involves the basis of power and legitimacy—an alteration which must be interpreted with respect to the earlier discussion of ethnic pluralism. Thus, there is some element of continuity in the new regime. Moreover, military rule is not likely to continue indefinitely. In almost every case the expressed desire is to return to civilian rule as quickly as possible—although in a few areas, such as the United Arab Republic and Congo-Kinshasa, the military has become politicized into the dominant party, an interesting development which may be repeated elsewhere in Africa.

But what is most important about these military takeovers and most relevant to this discussion is that they provide an opportunity which might otherwise not be available for reevaluation and creative innovation in political organization and procedures. What is often inconceivable for a civilian government may be within the realm of possibility for a military regime. It is necessary, therefore, to view the current instability in Africa within a broader framework and to avoid the assumption that all forms of political instability are necessarily retrogressive and damaging.

There has been a tendency in recent years for the great optimism of the early period of African independence to be replaced by a sense of almost fatalistic pessimism regarding the contemporary African scene. Both of these extreme views are equally unrealistic. What is needed is a balanced perspective, rooted in historical insight and acutely aware of the complexity and context of the African experience.

The outlook for political stability is not the important question about contemporary Africa. Political stability is a valuable goal only when it is accompanied by more responsive governments and the growth of cohesive social and economic fabrics capable of sustaining further development and also of spreading the effects of this development to as large a portion of the population as possible. The more significant question is whether Africa can capitalize on the opportunities now available to it to acquire the leadership, direction, and imaginative experimentation necessary for the growth of peaceful and prosperous communities in the future.

2

The African Setting

EDWARD W. SOJA and JOHN N. PADEN

THE ESSAYS IN THIS VOLUME share a common setting: the African continent, its people, and its regions. In this chapter a brief exploration is made of several factors fundamental to the African experience. It is recognized that the factors examined — environment and ecology, population patterns, race, and region — deserve more extensive treatment than they receive here, but it is hoped that these summary comments will serve as a backdrop to the essays which follow.

ENVIRONMENT AND ECOLOGY IN AFRICA

Africa is thought to have been at one time at the core of a vast supercontinent. About two hundred million years ago this continent (called Gondwanaland) fractured into pieces which eventually drifted away to become South America, Antarctica, peninsular India, and Australia. Africa remained as a large continent of plateaus carved out by a series of huge interior drainage basins, most of which were later emptied by rivers flowing to a newly formed coast. Subsequent geologic events tilted the African block, fracturing the higher eastern half of the continent in the dramatic trenches of the Rift Valley system and further restructuring the patterns of drainage.

Today Africa is an extremely compact continent, nearly devoid of prominent peninsulas and deep inlets. Its relatively smooth coastline offers very few natural harbors, and along almost the entire periphery of the continent the coast is backed by the edge of the African plateaus. Most of the large rivers with outlets to the sea are consequently broken up with respect to their navigability, particularly at those points where they plunge over the plateau edge or where the ancient crystalline rock which composes most of Africa outcrops to the surface

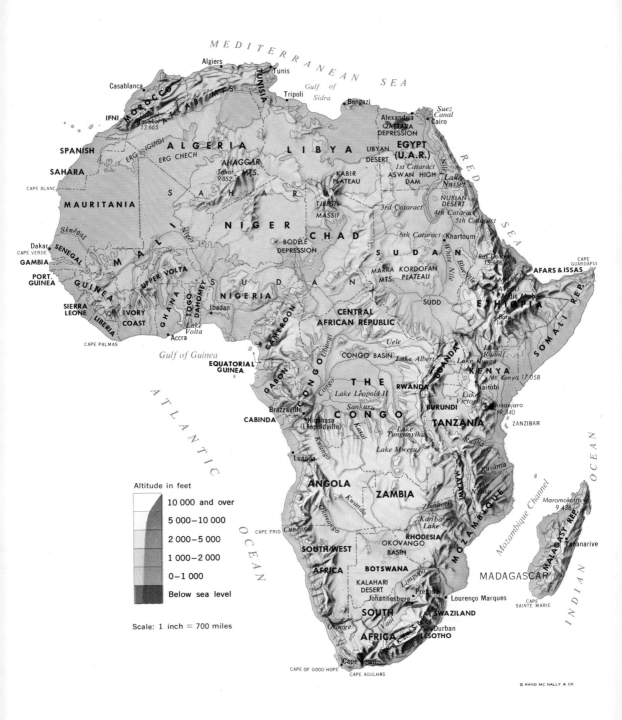

MEDITERRANEAN SEA

Algiers
Tunis
Casablanca
Tripoli
Gulf of Sidra
Bengazi

MOROCCO
TUNISIA
ATLAS MTS.
13,665
IFNI
SPANISH
SAHARA
CAPE BLANC
MAURITANIA

ERG IGUIDI
ERG CHECH
ALGERIA
AHAGGAR
Tahat
9,852
MTS.

LIBYA
LIBYAN
DESERT

Suez
Canal
Alexandria
Cairo
QATTARA
DEPRESSION
EGYPT
(U.A.R.)
1st Cataract
ASWAN HIGH
DAM
Lake
Nasser
NUBIAN
DESERT
3rd Cataract
4th Cataract
5th Cataract

S A H A R A

KABIR
PLATEAU

RED SEA

Dakar
CAPE VERDE
Sénégal
SENEGAL
GAMBIA
PORT.
GUINEA
GUINEA
SIERRA
LEONE
LIBERIA
IVORY
COAST
CAPE PALMAS

MALI
Niger
UPPER VOLTA
GHANA
TOGO
DAHOMEY
Lake
Volta
Accra

S U D A N
NIGERIA
Ibadan

NIGER
BODÉLÉ
DEPRESSION
TIBESTI
MASSIF

CHAD

6th Cataract
Khartoum
S U D A N
MARRA KORDOFAN
MTS. PLATEAU
SUDD

White Nile
Blue Nile
Ras Dashan
15,158
Addis Ababa
ETHIOPIA
Bati
14,131

CAPE
GUARDAFUI
AFARS & ISSAS
SOMALI REP.

Gulf of Guinea
EQUATORIAL
GUINEA
GABON
CONGO
CAMEROON
CENTRAL
AFRICAN REPUBLIC

Uele
Ubangi
CONGO BASIN
Lake Albert
Congo
Lake Léopold II
THE
CONGO
Sankuru
Kasai

UGANDA
RWANDA
BURUNDI

Lake
Rudolf
Lake Kioga
KENYA
Mt. Kenya 17,058
Nairobi
Lake
Victoria
Kilimanjaro
19,340
TANZANIA
ZANZIBAR

Brazzaville
Kinshasa
(Leopoldville)
CABINDA
Kwango
Luanda

Lake
Tanganyika
Lake Mweru
Ruaha

ATLANTIC OCEAN

ANGOLA
ZAMBIA

Kwanza
Kwando
Okovango
Cunene
CAPE FRIO
SOUTH-WEST
AFRICA
OKOVANGO
BASIN
RHODESIA
Zambezi
Kariba
Lake
Limpopo
BOTSWANA
KALAHARI
DESERT
Johannesburg
Pretoria
Lourenço Marques

MOZAMBIQUE
Lake
Nyasa
MALAWI
Ruvuma
Luangwa

Mozambique Channel
Maromokotro
9,436
MADAGASCAR
Tananarive
CAPE
SAINTE MARIE

INDIAN OCEAN

Altitude in feet
10 000 and over
5 000–10 000
2 000–5 000
1 000–2 000
0–1 000
Below sea level

Scale: 1 inch = 700 miles

SWAZILAND
SOUTH
AFRICA
Orange
Vaal
LESOTHO
Durban
Cape Town
CAPE OF GOOD HOPE
CAPE AGULHAS

© RAND MC NALLY & CO.

VEGETATION

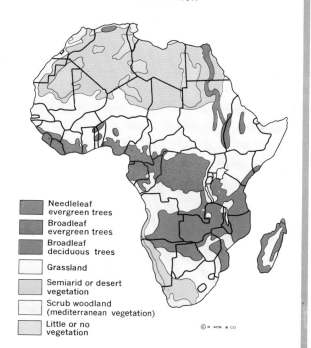

- Needleleaf evergreen trees
- Broadleaf evergreen trees
- Broadleaf deciduous trees
- Grassland
- Semiarid or desert vegetation
- Scrub woodland (mediterranean vegetation)
- Little or no vegetation

© R. MsN. & CO

PRECIPITATION

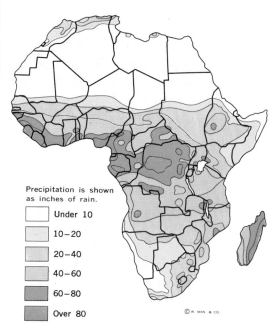

Precipitation is shown as inches of rain.

- Under 10
- 10 – 20
- 20 – 40
- 40 – 60
- 60 – 80
- Over 80

© R. MsN. & CO

CLIMATE

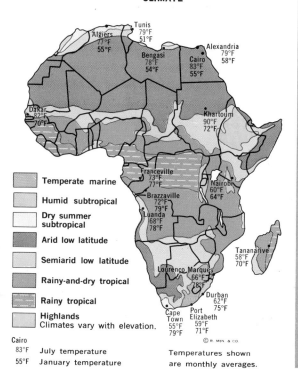

Tunis 79°F 51°F
Algiers 77°F 55°F
Alexandria 79°F 58°F
Bengasi 78°F 54°F
Cairo 83°F 55°F
Dakar 82°F 70°F
Khartoum 90°F 72°F
Franceville 73°F 77°F
Nairobi 60°F 64°F
Brazzaville 72°F 79°F
Luanda 68°F 78°F
Tananarive 58°F 70°F
Lourenço Marques 66°F 78°F
Durban 62°F 75°F
Cape Town 55°F 79°F
Port Elizabeth 59°F 71°F

- Temperate marine
- Humid subtropical
- Dry summer subtropical
- Arid low latitude
- Semiarid low latitude
- Rainy-and-dry tropical
- Rainy tropical
- Highlands Climates vary with elevation.

Cairo
83°F July temperature
55°F January temperature

Temperatures shown are monthly averages.

© R. MsN. & CO

POPULATION

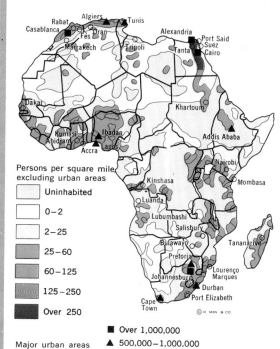

Rabat, Algiers, Tunis, Casablanca, Fes, Oran, Alexandria, Port Said, Marrakech, Tripoli, Tanta, Suez, Cairo, Dakar, Khartoum, Kumasi, Ibadan, Abidjan, Accra, Lagos, Addis Ababa, Nairobi, Kinshasa, Mombasa, Luanda, Lubumbashi, Salisbury, Bulawayo, Tananarive, Pretoria, Lourenço Marques, Johannesburg, Durban, Cape Town, Port Elizabeth

Persons per square mile excluding urban areas

- Uninhabited
- 0 – 2
- 2 – 25
- 25 – 60
- 60 – 125
- 125 – 250
- Over 250

© R. MsN. & CO

Major urban areas
- ■ Over 1,000,000
- ▲ 500,000 – 1,000,000
- ○ 200,000 – 500,000

(as in the cataracts of the Nile). Since the plateau so closely impinges on the coast, many great African rivers such as the Congo are navigable only for short distances from their ocean outlets.

The plateau surface of Africa is dominated by a series of basins surrounded by upland swells, the former filled with more recent sedimentary deposits and the latter composed primarily of the hard rock of what is called the basement complex (see map, *Major Physiographic Features,* on page 22 and map following page 20, *Physical Features and Relief*). Although four of the five major basins now have outlets to the sea, all bear evidence of having been basins of interior drainage in the distant geologic past. In the Middle Niger Basin, for example, near where the Niger River takes an abrupt right-angle turn to the southeast, is an ancient delta formed at a time when the upper section of the river emptied into an inland lake. The "Niger Bend" area with its fertile alluvial soil later became a major locus for state formation in the Western Sudanic belt.

The Sudd of the Upper Nile Valley is still another example. This vast and nearly impenetrable swamp, considered by many historians to have been a major barrier to interaction between East Africa and the Middle and Lower Nile Valley, is probably the remains of another ancient lake which was drained as the Nile began to assume its present course.

In addition to the Middle Niger and the Middle and Upper Nile, the major basins of Africa include the Chad Basin (still without an ocean outlet), the Congo Basin, and the Kalahari Basin (drained on its northern fringe by the Zambezi River and on the south by the Orange River, while retaining much of its probable former character in between). Each is ringed by a series of crystalline uplands which form the major river divides of the continent.

The uplifted eastern portion of Africa, from the Red Sea to South Africa, differs from the predominant basin-and-swell structure of the rest of the continent. Here the most prominent feature is the Rift Valley system, a complex series of troughs generally varying in width from twenty to sixty miles, with the longer eastern branch extending from north of the Dead Sea in the Middle East through eastern Africa into Natal in South Africa — a distance of some 6,000 miles. The shorter western rift extends from the southern part of the Republic of the Sudan along the eastern border of Congo-Kinshasa and joins the eastern rift near Lake Malawi (Nyasa). It has been suggested that the forces which produced the rifts were similar to those which originally split apart the supercontinent.

Volcanic activity has been closely associated with the Rift Valley system, and eastern Africa contains some of the most dramatic physical landscapes and much of the most fertile soil in Africa. The highlands of Ethiopia and Kenya, as well as the much less extensive highland areas elsewhere in eastern Africa, are primarily volcanic in origin and contain the continent's highest peaks: Mount Kilimanjaro (19,340 feet), Mount Kenya (17,040 feet), the non-volcanic Ruwenzori Mountains (reaching an elevation of 16,821 feet), and Rash Dashan in

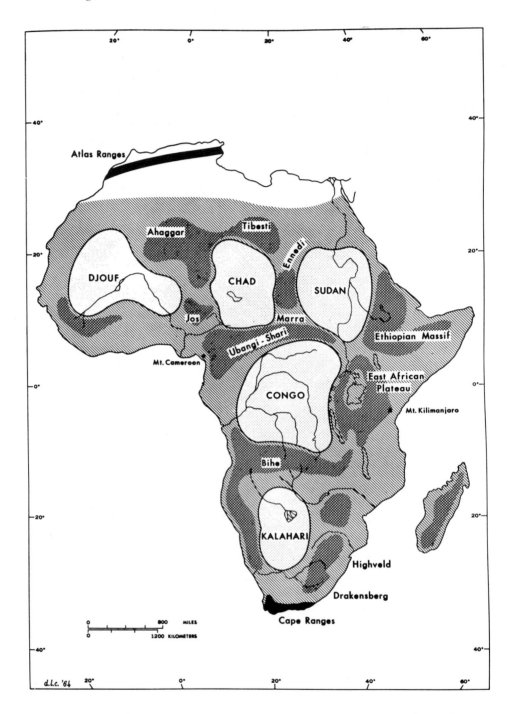

MAJOR PHYSIOGRAPHIC FEATURES

From *A Geography of Subsaharan Africa* by Harm de Blij. Copyright 1964 by Rand McNally & Company. Used with permission of Rand McNally·& Company.

Ethiopia (15,158 feet). The other major highland zone is the Drakensberg Escarpment in eastern South Africa, the steepest and highest edge of the tilted plateau surface. Only volcanic Mount Cameroon (13,354 feet) in West Africa and some peaks of the Atlas Range in northwest Africa even approach these in elevation.

The rifts themselves contain many of Africa's largest lakes, including the extremely deep Lake Tanganyika, and Lakes Malawi, Albert, Edward, Kivu, Rudolf, and Nakuru. Africa's largest lake, however, and second only to Lake Superior among the fresh-water lakes of the world, is Lake Victoria (Nyanza), which nestles in an upland basin between the two arms of the Rift Valley system. The area surrounding Lake Victoria and several other lakes in northern East Africa is commonly called the Great Lakes, or interlacustrine, region of Africa and has been another important locus for state formation throughout African history.

The climate and vegetation of Africa primarily reflect its position astride the equator, which almost exactly bisects the north-south extent of the continent. Except for the distortions caused by elevation in eastern Africa, where the climate is distinctly more temperate, ecological zones in Africa alternate in a fairly regular pattern away from the equatorial region. Perhaps the best way to grasp these ecological variations is to examine first the two extremes, the desert and the rainforest, and then consider the others as seasonal variations of these extremes.

Probably the most important determinant of African ecology is rainfall. Rainfall in Tropical Africa is closely associated with the migration of a zone of air-mass convergence, generally called the Inter-Tropical Front or the Inter-Tropical Convergence Zone (ITCZ), and with the influence of altitude and exposure to the major rain-bringing winds. These variables, combined with more localized influences and the effect of middle-latitude circulation systems impinging on the northern and southern extremities of the continent, are the most significant factors in explaining the character of the major ecological zones (see maps following page 20, *Vegetation, Precipitation, Climate*).

In the equatorial regions outside of the highlands of East Africa, the ITCZ never strays very far, and annual rainfall is consequently quite high, reaching over eighty inches in the central Congo Basin and along the coast of Gabon, Cameroon, and Nigeria. The major belt of tropical rainforest in Africa stretches from southern Nigeria through the northern half of Congo-Kinshasa to the edge of the East African highlands—in all, a relatively small portion of the continent.

Additional areas of rainforest include the western Guinea Coast (Guinea, Sierra Leone, Liberia), the eastern coast of the island of Madagascar, and occasional patches along the coast of eastern Africa. Unlike the Nigeria-Congo rainforests, where rainfall is relatively evenly distributed throughout the year, these other areas are characterized by marked seasonal variations. Distinct dry seasons alternate—usually with a regular shift of the predominant wind direction—with seasons of very heavy rainfall (for example, an August average of 40 inches in Freetown, Sierra Leone). Because of the pronounced contrasts, these areas have often been referred to as "monsoon rainforests." The monsoon circulation, however, extends well beyond the rainforest area. Along the entire East African coast the highly regular seasonal switch in wind direction has been used for centuries as an aid to sea travel between Africa and Asia.

At the other climatic extreme is the desert, represented in Africa by the vast Sahara (stretching across the continent in the north) and the Namib (along the coast of southwestern Africa). Ringing both are transitional zones of subdesert steppe, which in the north extend into the coastal areas of the Horn of Africa. The Kalahari, usually called a desert, is the equivalent steppe extension into the interior of southern Africa.

By far the most widespread ecological type for most of Africa is the grassland savanna, variably mixed with woodland, the latter being more extensive along the edge of the rainforest and in scattered patches of more moist conditions throughout the continent. Africa is certainly not a land of jungles; even within the true rainforest there exist large areas of lighter tropical forest and savanna. The predominant African environment is the wooded savanna, a mosaic of forest and grassland with scattered trees.

The African savanna is basically a seasonalized combination of the conditions which produce both the desert and rainforest types. Summer rainy seasons, often worthy of the dense tropical rainforest, alternate with the parching aridity of the desertlike dry seasons. Moreover, the timing and amount of annual rainfall are frustratingly variable. Because there are no major mountain barriers to "regularize" the movements of the ITCZ, years of severe drought are often followed by years of excessive rainfall.

Another ecological zone, termed Mediterranean, refers to the Mediterranean climate and vegetation of the northern and southern tips of Africa. This zone is similar to the savanna except that the winters rather than the summers are rainy, due to the extension of the middle-latitude circulation system toward the equator. Temperatures are also cooler here since these areas extend into more temperate latitudes (although the thermometer rarely dips much below 50 degrees except in a few highland areas).

Temperature varies only slightly during the year relative to the great seasonal contrasts in rainfall throughout most of Africa. In the rainforest, with its relatively even annual rainfall distribution, and in many coastal and highland areas there is usually less than 10 degrees' difference between the warmest and coldest months, and frequently the difference is even smaller (temperatures in the Congo Basin, for example, are consistently in the range of 75 to 80 degrees). The highest average daily temperatures in Africa (over 90 degrees) are found during the summer months in the Sahara and in much of the savanna region;

in most of Africa temperatures seldom reach the extremes encountered over the central United States during the summer months.

In the higher elevations of eastern Africa, the average annual temperature is about 20 degrees less than that of the adjacent seacoast; the altitude produces what may be one of the most comfortable climates on earth. In the highest portions of Ethiopia, Lesotho, and several scattered mountain peaks, temperatures are cool enough to distinguish a distinctive highland type of climate.

POPULATION PATTERNS AND DISTRIBUTION

Africa has a population of more than 300 million in an area of 11.5 million square miles. The latest United Nations estimates by country are shown in Table 1 (slightly earlier estimates and figures for estimated gross national product per capita for 1965 are given in the essay by Rivkin in this volume). A detailed map of population distribution is presented following p. 20.

From this information, some very general conclusions can be drawn. As a continent Africa is second only to Asia in areal size, but it is far less densely populated. More important, population is unevenly distributed, with pockets of very high density standing in marked contrast to vast areas with no more than ten to fifteen people per square mile.

Several major population concentrations are evident from the population distribution map. The most obvious, perhaps, is the Nile Valley, where nearly 30 million people of the United Arab Republic are clustered. The coastal region of northwest Africa contains another major concentration of close to 25 million. West Africa, however, has by far the largest proportion of the total African population. Nigeria alone, with about 60 million people, contains one out of every five Africans on the continent and ranks among the ten most populated countries in the world.

The pattern of population in West Africa is dominated by two broad bands of high population density. The first coincides with the Sudanic belt, stretching from Senegal eastward through northern Nigeria, where the heaviest concentrations are found, and into the Republic of the Sudan, joining up with the important Middle Nile cluster around Khartoum. The second zone of high density extends along the Guinea Coast and again reaches a peak in Nigeria. In between lies a less densely populated area, often called the "Middle Belt," which has acted as an environmental and cultural transition zone between the Sudan savanna, site of many historic African states and empires, and the coastal forests, which were also sites of early African state formation as well as being areas of early European contact and trade.

The size of some of the ethnic groups in West Africa is often surprising to the

TABLE 1
POPULATION OF AFRICAN STATES AND TERRITORIES: 1967 ESTIMATES

State or Territory	Population Estimates (in thousands)
1. Algeria	12,540
2. Angola	5,293
3. Botswana	593
4. Burundi	3,340
5. Cameroon	5,470
6. Cape Verde Island	232
7. Central African Republic	1,459
8. Chad	3,410
9. Comoro Islands	250
10. Congo (Republic of)[Brazzaville]	860
11. Congo (Democratic Republic of)[Kinshasa]	16,353
12. Dahomey	2,505
13. Equatorial Guinea	277
14. Ethiopia	23,457
15. French Territory of the Afars and Issas	— —
16. Gabon	473
17. Gambia	343
18. Ghana	8,143
19. Guinea	3,702
20. Ifni	53
21. Ivory Coast	4,010
22. Kenya	9,948
23. Lesotho	885
24. Liberia	1,110
25. Libya	1,738
26. Madagascar	6,350
27. Malawi	4,130
28. Mali	4,745
29. Mauritania	1,100
30. Mauritius (excluding dependencies)	774
31. Morocco	14,140
32. Mozambique	7,124
33. Niger	3,546
34. Nigeria	61,450
35. Portuguese Guinea	528
36. Réunion	418
37. Rwanda	3,306
38. St. Helena (excluding dependencies)	5
39. São Tomé and Princípe	60
40. Senegal	3,670
41. Seychelles	48
42. Sierra Leone	2,439
43. Somalia	2,660
44. South Africa	18,733
45. Southern Rhodesia	4,530
46. South-West Africa	594
47. Spanish North Africa	161
48. Spanish Sahara	48
49. Sudan	14,355
50. Swaziland	385
51. Togo	1,724
52. Tunisia	4,560
53. Uganda	7,934
54. United Arab Republic	30,907
55. United Republic of Tanzania	12,173
56. Upper Volta	5,054
57. Zambia	3,947

Source: *U.N. Demographic Yearbook, 1967* (New York: United Nations, 1968), pp. 124–25.

non-specialist. The Yoruba (primarily in southwestern Nigeria), for example, number over 12 million, about the population of Norway and Sweden combined. The Hausa-speaking peoples (concentrated in northern Nigeria but scattered throughout West Africa as tradesmen) number over 15 million. Other large ethnic groups include the Ibo (about 8 million), the Akan people (including the Ashanti) of southern Ghana (3.6 million), and the Fulani (6 million or more throughout West Africa).

In the remainder of Africa, population distribution is more irregular. Ethiopia has a population of over 23 million, Congo-Kinshasa over 16 million, and the Sudan over 14 million, but these are territorially large countries (the Sudan is close to one million square miles), and population densities, except in small pockets, are not very high. There is a large area of heavy population concentration in what is called the Great Lakes region, particularly along the northern shores of Lake Victoria and in the highlands of Rwanda and Burundi (which are the most densely populated independent states in Africa). Elsewhere, small areas of high density are found in the highlands of Kenya, portions of the East African coast, southern Malawi, the Witwatersrand and Natal areas of South Africa, Lesotho, and parts of the Kasai region of Congo-Kinshasa.

Is overpopulation, then, a problem in contemporary Africa? From the overall density, it would appear that it is not. Large sections of Africa, particularly in the Ethiopian Highlands and portions of the Congo Basin, could undoubtedly support many more people than occupy these areas today. But one must consider not only existing densities of population but also availability of resources and environmental potential. Examined from this view, there are indeed many areas in which population pressure is already a major problem and will become increasingly so in the future if no steps are taken to curb population growth. In a recent study it was estimated that about 142 million people in Africa inhabit areas which are experiencing some population pressure.[1] Of this total, 57 per cent occupy urban or high-density rural areas (that is, the Nile Valley, Rwanda, Burundi, and most of the other pockets of high density previously mentioned). But the remainder occupy areas of moderate to low density, including most of the drier desert and savanna regions, where the capacity of the land to support its population, given present technology, is low.

Although population pressure in Africa is certainly not as great as it is in portions of India and China, it is probably more serious and widespread than is generally thought. Rapid rates of urbanization (as discussed in the essay in this volume by Mabogunje), extensive soil erosion, rainfall variability from year to year, and a very high rate of population growth all contribute to the problem, which, although not immediately acute for most of the continent, must be considered a factor of great importance to the future economic growth of Africa.

1. William A. Hance, "The Race Between Population and Resources," *Africa Report*, XIII (January 1968), 6–12. See, in particular, the map on p. 10.

RACE AND SKIN COLOR

Contemporary archaeological evidence strongly suggests that the ancestors of modern man first evolved in East Africa around two million years ago, and from this early nucleus (and perhaps from other, later "cradlelands") he moved out to occupy the land surface of the earth. During this long period of migration a great variety of physical environments were encountered, and man adapted, or became specialized, physically and technologically in accommodation to them. Evolution and this interrelationship between man and his environment produced the great physical-racial variety in mankind.

Before examining the racial characteristics particular to Africa, however, it must be emphasized that no substantial scientific evidence has ever been presented to show that racial and cultural evolution in man are related. There are no inherent racial differences in human mental and behavioral qualities or in human capacity to develop and maintain culture. Very generalized "racial" differences of gesture, speech, and other traits may exist, but it is clear that these characteristics have emerged primarily from the social and cultural matrix and are not genetically determined.

Race is a *biological* concept which refers to the prevalence among human groups of distinctive gene frequencies that produce definable features. The predominance of these features will vary, however, according to the amount of mixing or pooling of genes that has occurred among groups. Since the history of man on the earth has been one of increasing contact and intermixture, there are probably no large populations remaining which can be considered to have "pure" gene pools. Indeed, many specialists feel that there may never have been. Consequently, one can discuss only particular physical characteristics, or groups of characteristics, which tend to be more prevalent statistically among some broadly defined populations than among others.

The population of Africa reflects a complex admixture of many racial groups, but several physical characteristics tend to prevail throughout most of the continent. Many of these characteristics seem to be particularly suited to tropical conditions. The most obvious physical adaptation is dark skin color, which raises the surface temperature of the skin to encourage sweating (cooling) and acts as a screen to prevent excessive synthesis of vitamin D, popularly termed the "sunshine vitamin," which if received in very large amounts can lead to fatal bodily disorders. In the African rainforest, populations tended to develop broad nasal features and lip eversion, perhaps as an adaptation to the high local humidity. Many of these characteristics have spread throughout Africa and beyond to combine with other gene pools more suitable to environments outside the rainforest.

As previously stated, most of Africa consists not of rainforest but of savanna mixed with woodland. Similarly, the predominant physical type of Africa is not the rainforest person but a tall, slim, narrow-featured individual adapted to the dry heat of the desert and savanna. Skin color is generally dark, but varies greatly from place to place, ranging from very dark among certain peoples of the southern Sudan to light in parts of the Horn of Africa. The northern African has an even lighter skin, due largely to the infusion of genes from outside the continent. Between the extremes of the rainforest and the savanna groups, but nevertheless representing a wide range of physical type and skin color, are the Bantu-speaking peoples who today occupy most of Africa south of the equator. The Bantu appear to be a complex mixture of rainforest and savanna types, plus other racial strands, including the specialized hunting populations (probably similar to present-day Bushmen) who occupied much of the continent prior to the Bantu migrations into eastern and southern Africa.

Because of the history of racial mixture, it becomes very difficult to apply to Africa the conventional racial categories of Negroid, Caucasoid, and Mongoloid, even if these were to be defined entirely by skin color. In fact, most geneticists today consider these rigid categories virtually meaningless as a racial classification and much too generalized as a basis for understanding racial differentiation. A brief examination of skin color alone will illustrate the basis for this judgment.

The rainforest people of the West African Guinea Coast and the Congo Basin probably conforms most closely to the Western stereotyped image of the Negro. Just as the Western image of the Chinese is shaped largely by familiarity with the short, stocky, southern Chinese population who formed the major group of migrants outside China, the African tends to be associated almost entirely with the rainforest Negro, who supplied the majority of the black-skinned slave population imported into the New World.[2] Outside the rainforest, however, rainforest type genes have mixed with those of many other groups to produce a great variety of physical types. Since dark skin color is suitable to the consistently high temperatures of Africa, whether wet or dry, one may speak with accuracy of Black Africa as including nearly all of the continent. But a precise boundary line between the population of Black Africa and the lighter skinned population of northern Africa would be difficult to draw because of the considerable genetic intermixture. Many peoples of Ethiopia and Somalia are as dark-skinned as the rainforest or savanna Negro but are commonly classified

2. Although, as W. E. B. Dubois points out, most "racial" types of Africa were represented in the Americas. Thus, he writes, "in origin the slaves represented everything African, although most of them originated on or near the West Coast. Yet among them appeared the great Bantu tribes from Sierra Leone to South Africa; the Sudanese, straight across the center of the continent, from the Atlantic to the Valley of the Nile; the Nilotic Negroes and the black and brown Hamites, allied with Egypt; the tribes of the great lakes; the Pygmies and the Hottentots; and in addition to these, distinct traces of both Berber and Arab blood. There is no doubt of the presence of all these various elements in the mass of 10,000,000 or more Negroes transported from Africa to the various Americas, from the fifteenth to the nineteenth centuries" (*Black Reconstruction in America* [1934; reprint ed., London: Frank Cass, 1966], pp. 3–4).

as Caucasoid, as are many Arabs in East Africa who are also dark-skinned.

Two small, isolated, dark-skinned groups—the Bushmen and the Pygmies—deserve consideration in any discussion of race in Africa. The Bushmen, who are hunters and gatherers, are of small stature with light, yellowish-brown skin, distinctively tufted "peppercorn" hair, and several other physical characteristics which distinguish them as a separate racial group. Today they number about 20,000 and occupy the dry, isolated heart of the Kalahari Desert in southern Africa. Their ancestors, however, probably were the earliest inhabitants of the savanna grasslands of eastern and southern Africa and were subsequently driven into the Kalahari by the expansion of other groups, particularly the Bantu-speaking peoples. Remnants of this early "Bushmanoid" population remain as tiny enclaves in northern Tanzania, while other groups probably have been absorbed into the existing savanna population.

The Hottentots are a group clearly related to the Bushmen and together with them are called the Khoisan peoples. The Hottentots, however, appear to have experienced much greater mixture with other racial groups. Today, there may be no true Hottentots remaining, nearly all having been absorbed into what some call a "hybrid" local race, the South African Cape Coloured (a mixture of Bushmen-Hottentot, Bantu, European, Malaysian, and Indian).

The Pygmies, located primarily in the Congo rainforest but also stretching into such areas as Rwanda and Burundi, are an extremely difficult group to relate to broader genetic mixtures. Specifically, it is not clear whether they are related to the rainforest Negroes or whether they are a completely separate racial group. Although much intermarriage takes place with surrounding peoples, the African Pygmies of areas such as the Ituri Forest of Congo-Kinshasa are today one of the most "pure" breeding populations in the world.

In addition to the very small number of Orientals who have migrated to Africa in modern times, Mongoloid peoples are represented in Africa by much of the population of the island of Madagascar. Although obviously infused with Negroid genes, the Merina of the Malagasy Republic, for example, still display ample physical evidence of the migration of Southeast Asian or Malaysian peoples to their island and today closely resemble such people as the Dayak of Borneo.

In summary, the population of Africa is primarily dark-skinned, due for the most part to the adaptive advantages of this characteristic to the African environment and to the diffusion of dark-skinned genetic characteristics throughout Africa. These dark-skinned peoples vary enormously in physique, ranging from the tiny Pygmy to the very tall Dinka and Nuer of the Middle Nile Valley (perhaps, on the average, the tallest people in the world), and from the relatively stocky forest dweller, with everted lips and pronounced prognathic jaw, to the very slender, long-limbed, narrow-featured occupant of the savanna. In northern Africa, lighter skins are more prevalent, as among Arab and Berber peoples, but there is great variation even within this area.

Whatever categories one wishes to distinguish on the racial map of Africa will not provide causal explanations for African culture history beyond the likelihood that the environment has been a significant factor in shaping both the biological and cultural inheritance of the contemporary African population. Race becomes relevant to the African experience primarily in its role as generator of culturally perceived myths which, despite the total lack of evidence linking race with human behavior and achievement, are nonetheless important to our understanding of certain interpretations of the history of the continent and its peoples. Within the continent itself, racial features may reinforce other characteristics, such as language, religion, culture, or ethnicity, as criteria for social grouping. Racism is a situation in which physical features are the primary determinants of intergroup relations. One of the most notable situations of racism in Africa is the case of South Africa, described in the essays in this volume by Mbata, Mazrui, and Carter.

AFRICAN REGIONS AND REGIONAL GROUPINGS

A region is an arbitrarily defined area which is homogeneous with respect to a particular set of criteria. Ecological and population density criteria, for example, have been used to regionalize Africa earlier in this chapter. Rules of descent (Cohen), language (Berry), patterns of communication and transport (Soja), and religion (Abu-Lughod) are also used to define regions in subsequent essays in this volume. Regionalization is essentially a process of classification and generalization similar to the division of time into historical periods or eras. Since the criteria used for regional classification are virtually limitless, so too is the variety of regions one can identify in Africa.

Nevertheless, there are certain types of regions which have been widely accepted as convenient frameworks for identifying important patterns of variation in Africa and others which are useful simply as a practical grouping of areas for descriptive purposes. An example of the former is the broad distinction between Africa north and south of the Sahara. This division is generally used to distinguish between Black Africa (*L'Afrique Noire*), supposedly characterized by darker-skinned peoples, and North Africa, characterized by lighter-skinned, predominantly Islamic peoples. There is, of course, no single boundary which clearly differentiates two Africas based on these variables. Black Africa extends well beyond the southern limits of the Sahara, and Islam has penetrated into the Guinea Coast, along the eastern African coast, and into the interior. Some of the many problems involved in the use of the Sahara as a significant boundary zone are discussed in greater detail in the essay by Abu-Lughod. There is, however, some justification in differentiating northern Africa from the rest of the continent when discussing certain patterns and processes.

Although no precise boundary is assumed, the division is made primarily as a descriptive convenience—hence the use of the terms Black Africa, Africa south of the Sahara, and sub-Saharan Africa. It should be further noted that South Africa is often excluded from general considerations about Africa because of its unique racial and economic situation.

Simple location (north, south, east, and west) probably provides the most widely used basis for describing Africa. Although the precise outlines will vary slightly, the essays in this volume have adopted the following broad regional subdivisions.

West Africa is the area stretching from north of the mouth of the Senegal River to Lake Chad. It includes southern Mauritania, Senegal, Gambia, Guinea, Portuguese Guinea, Sierra Leone, Liberia, Ivory Coast, Ghana, Togo, Dahomey, Nigeria, and Cameroon along the West African coast, and, in the interior, Mali, Niger, and Upper Volta. The northern part of this region is in the Sudanic belt, which is often divided into western, central, and eastern portions, although at least part of the Central Sudan and all of the Eastern Sudan extend beyond West Africa as defined.

North Africa includes the northern coastal states from the Atlantic to the Red Sea (Morocco, Algeria, Tunisia, Libya, and the United Arab Republic), and frequently the northern parts of Mauritania and the Republic of the Sudan as well. Also included are the tiny Spanish enclave of Ifni (soon to be incorporated into Morocco) and Spanish Sahara along the Atlantic coast. Northwest Africa (Morocco, Algeria, and Tunisia) is often distinguished as the Maghrib (that is, the major western extension of the Islamic world). Crosscutting the eastern portion of North Africa is the Nile Basin, primarily involving the United Arab Republic and the Republic of the Sudan. Ethiopia, containing the source of the Blue Nile, is sometimes included in this grouping of Nile Basin states.

East Africa consists of Kenya, Uganda, and Tanzania (including the island of Zanzibar). Also considered as part of this region today are Rwanda and Burundi, which together with most of Uganda and those portions of Tanzania and Kenya near Lake Victoria are grouped as the Great Lakes, or interlacustrine, region. The East African coast, however, because of its important historical linkages, is considered to extend beyond Kenya and Tanzania to include portions of Somalia and Mozambique.

The Horn of Africa is the northeasternmost extension of the continent and includes Somalia, the French Territory of the Afars and Issas (former French Somaliland), and the Empire of Ethiopia. As previously mentioned, portions of this area are often included in the surrounding regions.

Central Africa is a somewhat more variably defined region which usually includes the equatorial zone between the Sudanic belt and southern Africa. The area involved covers the four states of former French Equatorial Africa (Chad, Central African Republic, Gabon, and Congo-Brazzaville), the ex-Spanish state of Equatorial Guinea (comprising Fernando Po and Río Muni), the Portuguese islands of São Tomé and Príncipe, and the former Belgian Congo, now Congo-Kinshasa. Occasionally Cameroon will be included, as will the former Belgian territories of Rwanda and Burundi (which before the First World War formed part of German East Africa, that is, Tanganyika).

A southern tier of states forms a broad buffer zone between independent Black Africa and white-dominated southern Africa. It is extremely difficult to place this group of states — Portuguese Angola and Mozambique, and the former British-controlled Central African Federation, now broken up into Zambia (formerly Northern Rhodesia), Malawi (formerly Nyasaland), and Rhodesia (formerly Southern Rhodesia) — into either central or southern Africa. Despite the increasing orientation of Zambia to the north and east, the essays in this volume will consider all of these states as part of a broadly defined southern Africa.

Southern Africa includes, in addition to the above-mentioned states of the buffer zone, the Republic of South Africa, South-West Africa (the former German territory which continues to be administered as part of South Africa despite United Nations–supported demands for independence as the state of Namibia), and the three former British High Commission Territories of Lesotho (formerly Basutoland), Botswana (formerly Bechuanaland), and Swaziland. In all of this region there has been considerable domination or influence by white settler communities (see the essays in this volume by Mbata and Carter).

Separate from these regions, although tied to the continent in a variety of ways (for example, through international organizations), are the Indian Ocean Islands, which include the large island of Madagascar (the Malagasy Republic) and such smaller islands as Réunion and the Comoro Islands (both French).

The colonial period established certain groupings of areas within which administration was coordinated and common types of institutions were established. There has been a tendency in the independence period for such colonial zones to continue influencing the patterns of interstate cooperation. One of the most important factors here is language. French, English, and Portuguese were the major languages of colonialism, and French or English has continued to be an official language in most independent states. Combining the language factor with other colonial imprints, one can identify eight major zones of colonial organization: British West Africa, French West Africa, Belgian Central Africa, French Equatorial Africa, British Central Africa, British East Africa, Portuguese Africa, and French North Africa.

The actual degree of coordination within these zones varied. In French West and Equatorial Africa there was an integrated administrative structure focused on Dakar (Senegal) and Brazzaville (Congo), respectively. In British West Africa, there was only coordination of certain monetary and educational structures. In British East Africa, on the other hand, a common services organization was established which centralized control of railways, telephone and postal services, and other economic facilities. But like the French zones, and in contrast to

British West Africa, British East Africa consisted of contiguous states which could more easily be governed under a common framework.

The grouping of independent African states into regions for purposes of political or economic cooperation, with some concern for possible federation or confederation in the future, is a subject explored in the essay in this volume by Paden. Many of the economic unions which have emerged are between states which shared a common colonial language: these include the Organisation Commune Africaine et Malgache, the Central African Economic Union, and the East African Economic Community and Common Market. During the period 1960–63, however, African states were divided into two politically oriented groups which cut across the usual French-speaking and English-speaking language zones: a "conservative" group of states (which met in Monrovia, Liberia) and a "radical" group of states (which met in Casablanca, Morocco). With the formation of the Organization of African Unity in 1963, these earlier distinctions have largely disappeared, although a variety of ideological perspectives still exists in Africa.

In short, therefore, the continent of Africa, with its surrounding islands, consists of at least 57 territorial entities, 42 of which were independent states as of late 1969. These political territories may be viewed as clustering into a number of distinct regions, which are most commonly based on location, colonial legacy and language, and post-colonial patterns of cooperation. In addition, there is a variety of criteria which may be used for social (as distinct from political) groupings in Africa. Thus, regional patterns may reflect ecology, race, population distribution, local language families, religion, and ethnicity. Such diversity presents some notion of the great complexity of Africa and the enormous challenge involved in understanding the African experience.

I

African Society
and Culture

3

Traditional Society in Africa

RONALD COHEN

THE CONTINENT OF AFRICA is a stage upon which the drama of human development and cultural differentiation has been acted since the beginning of history. Yet the continent is so large and the people so diverse that even to approach an understanding of this complexity in any comprehensive way is an overwhelming task. By identifying a number of themes or topics, each of which probes only a limited set of African experiences, the editors of this volume hope to make the complexity more understandable. It should be remembered, however, that given the enormous volume of material now available on Africa—and it is constantly expanding—each of these topics could in its turn be further broken down for even more intense examination.

In this essay we will consider in general terms the study of traditional societies of Africa. Let us examine first, therefore, the two basic concepts being used, "tradition" and "society," to see whether as categories they adequately represent the material upon which our accumulated knowledge is based.

Within anthropology, and now increasingly in other disciplines, the concept of "traditional" has proved to be useful. In Africa, what is called the traditional period refers fundamentally to that quality of African social life in which contact with the Western world was not a significant part of the lives of the majority of the population. There has, of course, been contact with the outside world, especially trade relations at the edges of Africa, for a very long time. In some places, such as along the West African coast, this contact has stimulated significant changes in the historical development of society over the past several hundred years. However, these changes were not in the direction of a Western model of society. Following this distinction, our conception of traditional thus refers to social life in which the direction of change and development in society is primarily determined by indigenous events and patterns of behavior. For the majority of African peoples, such changes generally have taken place slowly in response to local problems and to neighboring African peoples.

Similarly, the traditional aspect of African social life refers to a quality in which neither the leaders of the people nor the masses were (or are) dedicated to the goal of changing the nature of their society. In modern Africa such rapid and planned change is a primary focus of national ideology and is promoted actively by the state. The whole idea of "underdeveloped" or "developing" implies a gap that must be filled and produces what could be called a "catch-up" ideology; that is, it is thought that the gap is undesirable and must be closed. To close the gap, a number of processes are initiated, especially those aiming at industrialization. This in turn implies an increase in urbanization and wage-labor and a radical change in the basic social organization of African society. The relative absence of this "catch-up" ideology, and of the stresses and changes induced by it, is an important characteristic of traditionalism.

Finally, and combining the previous facets, traditionalism reflects a genuinely indigenous quality in each society and culture, such that most of a society's social and cultural institutions are rooted in its own adaptations to its own patterns of growth. This is somewhat difficult to define in clear-cut operational terms but is, I believe, a real and ultimately even a measurable facet of sociocultural existence. There is a difference in adapting or creating a local pottery style based on new experience as opposed to giving up pottery entirely due to the greater utility and attractiveness of imported steel enamelware. Similarly, there is a difference in creating a mutual-aid society based on aspects of traditional social organization as opposed to taking out an insurance policy from a newly founded corporate business enterprise devoted to selling insurance to the public.

I am not suggesting that either of these modes, the traditional or the modern, is necessarily more valuable. Each has its own value in its own context. The Africans themselves and the conditions of their lives will ultimately decide what mix of traditional and modern elements is to go into the development of their new states. My objective here is merely to point out that there are clusters of characteristics that can usually be thought of as traditional for purposes of identification and analysis.

The concept of traditional is not without its detractors. There are those who feel that a dichotomy between traditional and modern creates an artificial division which obscures the facts of change in times past. Given the merits of such criticism, there is still the problem of magnitude of change. It is assumed in this essay that the kinds of changes involved in contemporary modernization in Africa are so widespread and profound that they provide a watershed in the history of the entire continent.

Thus, we may isolate in theoretical terms a set of practices called traditional which may be applied to any society in which a radical change has affected the entire way of life of the people concerned. The notion of traditional then refers to the set of conditions that existed before radical change took place.

Our second major concept, "society," is, like "traditional," an abstract and relative idea. Basically it refers to a group of people whose boundaries are defined by whatever criteria seem appropriate to the problem being examined. Thus a family, a small group, or a village can be thought of as a society, as can the people of a city, province, region, country, group of countries, or even the entire world population. The term is applicable as long as there are identifiable criteria for putting people into a category which involves some form of interaction.

These interactions usually increase in frequency in inverse proportion to the scale of the unit. There also tend to be significant modifications in the nature of these interactions as the scale is changed from one level to another. Thus the number of interactions among all members changes significantly when we go from family to village to province. By scale is meant quality that can be shown to increase and decrease, and scale as we are using it refers to two aspects of society: that of the space involved and that of the numbers of actors occupying this space. Human actors are the basic units, while space and number are variables that determine what scale of society we will be referring to within traditional Africa.

THE INDIVIDUAL ACTOR IN
TRADITIONAL AFRICAN SOCIETY

Within the scope of this essay I wish to examine the individual African only from the point of view of the social systems within which he or she operates. It is now widely accepted that actors in differing cultures may not have the same set of personality features, and furthermore that there appear to be clusters of personality traits that are characteristically "African." These psychological features crosscut local variations in social life and reflect the similarities in African society rather than the differences. The prevailing common feature can be summarized briefly as an emphasis on social relations as a primary value, regardless of the particular form of organization in the society itself. This strong bias in traditional cultural values and personal attitudes to life implies a lack of individual alienation in traditional society.

In discussing this point with a young Tanzanian I was surprised by the intensity of his feeling. After deriding North American attitudes toward social relations (referring to his own experiences in the West), he rushed into a description of the greetings that would be extended to any stranger who came to Tanzania. He assured me that if I were to visit him, there would be a large crowd at the airport to greet me and I would be shown the entire city, because "that is the way we do things." He promised that in his country I would never be alone, as he had been in mine.

Experience teaches people that group membership is necessary for marriage, for political membership in a community, and for obtaining a livelihood. In most of Africa, marriages, especially first marriages, concern the family groups uniting through the spouses more than they do the bride and groom, and without kin support, marriage is often extremely difficult.

In northern Nigeria, if a man is accused of a crime or moral offense of some kind against his neighbors he is called to court. Everyone knows this means he must appear in court with his brothers, his father, and perhaps his father's brothers and his father's father. If he receives a fine, then all people related to him through the male line, both men and women, contribute to its payment. Corporate kin responsibility is widespread throughout Africa, and the social security of kin membership has often been noted.

Many migrant laborers such as the Mossi of Upper Volta[1] and the Mambwe of Zambia[2] return periodically from their wage labor in Ghana and the Copperbelt respectively. They are reported to feel that life cannot be tolerated without their kin membership, symbolized in land ownership, and the status they receive from being members of the traditional political structures of their people.

Furthermore, social advance usually means obtaining and maintaining an increasing number of social relationships. Greater income or wealth means more dependents, which results in more prestige and feelings of achievement for the individual concerned. While increased wealth may be spent on new consumer goods in modern Africa, income rise must also be seen against the traditional background, which requires a concurrent increase in number of dependents.

Gainful employment is also a question of group membership. In northern Nigeria most people acquire the requisite skills for their occupation within the family. Alternatively, the head-of-family pays a non-kin member to take the trainee as an apprentice. In this case the boy is taken into the household of the master, where he must show loyal obedience at all times in return for his training. This is true not only for such traditional crafts as barbering, candymaking, and trading but also for newer skills such as truck-driving and sometimes even for skills associated with the lower levels of the civil service.

Within the sphere of traditional values, moral prescriptions are clearly focused on interpersonal relations.[3] In northern Nigeria parents admonish their children constantly about behavior norms to be learned concerning interaction with people. These are not abstract standards, such as "Honesty is the best policy," or "An apple a day keeps the doctor away." The Kanuri of Bornu, Nigeria, say to their children, "You must treat so-and-so in such-and-such a way," or "Remember to take your shoes off when you pass in front of the chief's house,"

1. Elliott P. Skinner, "Labour Migration and Its Relationship to Socio-cultural Change in Mossi Society," *Africa*, XXX (1960), 375–401.
2. William Watson, *Tribal Cohesion in a Money Economy* (Manchester: Manchester University Press, 1958).
3. See Margaret Read, *Children and Their Fathers: Growing Up among the Ngoni of Nyasaland* (London: Methuen, 1959); and Ronald Cohen, *The Kanuri of Bornu* (New York: Holt, Rinehart & Winston, 1967).

or "Your religious teacher surpasses your father [in fatherly qualities]." Literally dozens of specific prescriptions about interpersonal behavior are drilled into children at a very early age.

The cultural contrast between traditional African values and those of the Western world has been dramatized by African writers and novelists. William Conton, in his novel *The African,* has his hero rage out against "the European's exaggerated individualism, his constant exalting of the single human being, at the polls, in the classroom, and in the sight of God." When Peter Abrahams, in his autobiography *Tell Freedom,* asks a man who is running away from an industrial job about his people, the man answers, "I am my people." This view may be extended to include political implications, as in Nkrumah's book *Ghana: The Autobiography of Kwame Nkrumah.*[4]

Although little is known as yet about the relation of personality to society in Africa, it would seem that the cultural emphasis on social relations can be associated with certain personality characteristics.[5] If a person is continually made to feel that his obligations to other people are the most important part of his life, then his anxieties, his personal goals, and his security must derive primarily from these relationships. In our society it is possible for a career-oriented bachelor novelist to find satisfaction and even to achieve status in his individualistic relationship to his work. In traditional African society an individual would not be likely to seek such isolation from institutionalized personal relationships, and certainly the approval and support of the society would be withheld from any member who did wish to pursue a solitary or individualistic occupation. Jahoda, in a systematic study of attitudes in Ghana, suggests that Africans consider their way of life to be superior to that of Western society in that Africans attach greater value to social relationships.[6]

Evidence of this point comes from other parts of Africa as well. Marwick has pointed out that in central Africa anxiety over the breakup of traditional social relationships in new urban centers is likely to lead to more, rather than fewer, accusations of witchcraft during the modernization period.[7] In other words, fear of malevolence and increased attribution of evil-doing to others as expressed by accusations of witchcraft increase when people feel their important bases of security, that is, their stable social relationships with others, to be breaking up. Dr. Field has made a similar observation in Ghana.[8]

To suggest that Western life is antithetical to African life in its manner of

4. S. L. Fisher, "Africa: Mother and Muse," *Antioch Review,* XXI (1961), 305–18.
5. See Robert A. LeVine, "Personality and Change," in this volume, for a discussion of psychological aspects of African peoples.
6. Gustav Jahoda, *White Man: A Study of the Attitude of Africans to Europeans in Ghana during Independence* (London: Oxford University Press, 1961), p. 40.
7. Max Marwick, "The Continuance of Witchcraft Beliefs," in *Africa in Transition,* ed. Prudence Smith (London: M. Reinhardt, 1958).
8. M. J. Field, *Search for Security: An Ethno-Psychiatric Study of Rural Ghana* (Evanston, Ill.: Northwestern University Press, 1960).

social relationships would, of course, be quite misleading. However, the tradition in Western culture that leads us to admire individuals who sacrifice social relations for ideals when necessary is in sharp contrast to African culture in which social relations are always at the center and are considered to be the most important ideals.

In contemporary Western society we admire the lone hero who acts in accordance with ideal standards of values rather than submitting to social pressures. On our TV screens the cowboy combats evil in society, and then rides off alone into the sunset. The viewer is made to feel that the moral purity and the Samson-like strength of the hero is revitalized in his solitary communion. Popular entertainment thus dramatizes an ideal of individualism which in the life of the more average man is eroded and corrupted by the social and economic necessities of his daily existence.

Africans, conversely, feel that only through social life can the highest ideals of morality be realized. Among the Kanuri of Nigeria the man who lives alone is called *ngudi*, or unfortunate, and he is not to be trusted because his lack of social ties indicates that he may not be bound by the moral precepts of his own society. Africans as individual actors in their traditional society are strongly oriented to their fellow actors, not to some abstract notion of conscience or superego—certainly not to one in which the man-god relation pervades or intervenes among the man-man relationships. African morality stresses the man-man relationship, and individual matters of conscience stem from this fact. As a generalization, it can be said that to compare the Westerner to the African is to go from high levels of narcissism to very low ones respectively.[9]

KINSHIP IN TRADITIONAL AFRICA

Like individuals everywhere, every individual born into a traditional African society is a member of a local residence group and kinship system. In some cases these are the only organizations in the society; in other cases these are the smallest scale social units and are embedded in larger organizations. In all cases, however, kinship involves three categories of interpersonal relations: genealogy, descent, and affinity.

Genealogy and Descent

Genealogy refers to the relationships between an individual (called "ego" in kinship terminology) and those persons who are related to him through a network of biologically traceable links. As a category, genealogy is less important than descent or affinity. This is due to the fact that the fundamental determi-

9. Robert A. LeVine, in conversation with the author.

nants of genealogy are biological; given bisexual reproduction and the incest prohibition, most human genealogies are very similar. They do vary somewhat in depth (number of generations) and range (number of persons per generation), but since these variables refer for the most part to cultural norms, this aspect is in many respects a function of descent and affinal relations.

Descent as an aspect of kinship refers to the way in which a set of loyalties, obligations, rights, and duties is passed on to succeeding generations. From the actor's (ego's) point of view, it refers to the patterns and precedents by which are determined the rights and obligations of new members born into a family with respect to other members of the family. Genealogical links join the actors to a set of relatives, but descent has a variable capacity to create groups that may act corporately. Thus, for example, descent groups can hold property in common, and can act as a political unit, a marriage unit, and even an economic unit. The degree of corporateness is generally low or absent when descent groups are bilateral (usually referred to as cognatic). In a bilateral, or cognatic, group, ego reckons descent through both parents and all four grandparents. On the other hand, when descent groups are unilineal (or reckoned through only one parent), corporate activity is easy and is very often practiced. In Africa there are three types of unilineal descent: patrilineal, which means reckoned through males only (also referred to as agnatic); matrilineal, which means reckoned through the female line (also referred to as uterine); and duolineal (sometimes called double unilineal or bilineal). Duolineal descent describes a situation in which ego is a member of two unilineal descent groups. Often, as with the Yakö (Nigeria), this means a patrilineal and a matrilineal group. The difference between bilateral and duolineal is that in a bilateral descent group ego is related to four grandparents, and in a duolineal descent group he is related to only two grandparents.

The types of descent groups in Africa fall into the following classification: Given the relative accuracy of our present statistics, 85 per cent of African descent is unilineal, and only 15 per cent is cognatic; of the unilineal descent groups, three-quarters of the different ethnic groups are traditionally patrilineal, and most of the remaining one-quarter are matrilineal; a small number of groups (almost all in West Africa) have duolineal systems. Africa, then, is a continent in which unilineal descent is the dominant form, and among the unilineal descent groups the patrilineal descent form is by far the most frequent.[10]

Why these regularities should exist on a continent so large and so diverse is an important question—but one for which there is as yet no clear-cut answer. Unilineal descent is associated with corporate activities by descent groups, and Africa is dominantly unilineal. Unilineal descent groups in Africa are in fact

10. The quantitative data for the generalizations in this paper have been obtained through the facilities of the African Data Bank, Council for Intersocietal Studies, Northwestern University. The sample sizes range from 55 to 92, with all areas of the continent represented. The author wishes to express gratitude to this program for permission to use these materials.

widely used for organizing social life. Their adaptability is enormous; they can serve multiple functions across a wide spectrum of activities, and the means for their continuity are simple and universal—namely, marriage and birth. Although exact data are lacking, it would seem that the elaboration of such groups into "nesting" or segmentary units of increasing scale is a function of the degree of population mobility within a geographical context. In other words, the less an African group has remained in settled, stable villages, using the locality itself as a basis for social organization, the greater the tendency for individuals in the group to unite on the basis of actual or putative descent (clanship). This tendency can increase to such an extent that in a mobile population like the northern Somali several million people can be linked into one overarching patrilineal descent system.

Unilineal descent is dominant in Africa partly because it is used as a means for organizing corporate group life. But this function does not account for the prevalence of patrilineal systems rather than matrilineal or duolineal systems. This becomes an even more intriguing question when we consider the conclusion of a leading anthropologist, G. P. Murdock, that in sub-Saharan Africa "matrilineal descent prevailed generally in the not too distant past."[11] Why or how such a monumental continent-wide change from matrilineal to patrilineal descent systems occurred is not at all clear. Has there been some great ecological change, or demographic change, or technological change—or has patrilineal descent spread southward from North Africa for reasons we do not yet understand?

It may be, however, that the problematic change from predominantly matrilineal to patrilineal descent systems did not occur. In other words, perhaps Africa has always been dominantly patrilineal. My reasons for supporting this view are as follows. Matrilineal descent is essentially an unstable descent system, depending upon two factors: high divorce rates, which prevent fathers from having long periods of association with their own children, and an ecology in which simple hoe agriculture is the dominant form of food-getting activity. Any tendencies away from such features seem to provoke tendencies away from matrilineal descent. The so-called matrilineal belt of Tropical Africa (illustrated by the map on page 45) is an area where these conditions obtain.[12] On the other hand, most of Africa is open, dry, savanna country where cattle-keeping or at least mixed farming has been practiced for a very long time. The correlation between nomadic pastoralism and patrilineal descent is one of the oldest and best established in anthropology.[13] This results from the fact that men care for herds of animals, and herds can be most easily and efficiently maintained as a corporate holding among a group of agnates (that is, a group of persons related

11. George P. Murdock, *Africa: Its Peoples and Their Culture History* (New York: McGraw-Hill, 1959).
12. *Ibid.*, p. 28.
13. L.T. Hobhouse, G. C. Wheeler, and M. Ginsberg, *The Material Culture and Social Institutions of the Simpler Peoples* (London: Chapman and Hall, 1915), pp. 150–54.

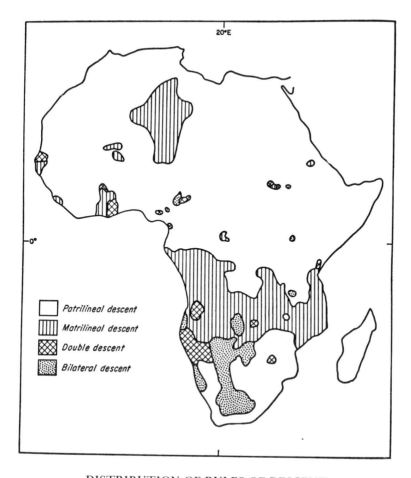

DISTRIBUTION OF RULES OF DESCENT
From *Africa: Its Peoples and Their Culture History* by George Peter Murdock. Copyright 1959 by the McGraw-Hill Book Company. Used with permission of McGraw-Hill Book Company.

through the male line) who then live off the proceeds of the herd. Surplus animals may be used to pay the costs of marriages, thereby making possible the recruitment of women who carry on the group by contributing their childbearing properties to it. Although it is possible to obtain a stable group of men related by descent through the use of either bilateral or matrilineal principles, each of these systems has a difficult problem with corporateness. Either the group is not the same for every member (bilateral) or the men tend to be dispersed rather than together (matrilineal).[14]

14. This does not mean to imply that corporate groups never obtain among people with bilateral or matrilineal descent—they do, as the Kanuri (Nigeria) and Suku (Congo) material will illustrate. However, to do so requires either patrilocal residence (Kanuri) or "home" territory (Suku).

Marriage

Another aspect of kinship, after genealogy and descent, is that of affinity, that is, relationship by marriage. Although there is a bewildering number of different marriage forms in Africa, some clear-cut patterns do predominate. Marriage inception almost always entails some form of consideration or value provided by the groom and/or his group of kin, friends, and supporters to the girl and her group. This pattern pertains in almost 90 per cent of African societies; 80 per cent are in the form of bridewealth payments, and 10 per cent are bride-service arrangements. Only 1 per cent of the sample material used indicates that marriage inception is accompanied by a dowry to the girl instead of bridewealth payment or bride service. Women are traditionally considered to be of value to the prospective spouse and his group, and to obtain such value some compensation must be made to the group giving up the girl. Her value lies partly in her fecundity as a childbearer and partly in her contributions to the work force of the group she joins through marriage.

Marriage inception patterns in Africa must also be seen as divided into primary and secondary marriages. Primary marriages are first marriages for one or both partners; secondary marriages are subsequent unions. In general there is an age gap in Africa so that women marry earlier, sometimes before puberty, while men contract their primary unions later. The later the age of primary marriage, the less stringent are the rules of premarital chastity. Secondary marriages are less formal, less expensive, and each party to the marriage, depending on age and social status, has more freedom to contract the union on his own.

Both single-spouse marriages (monogamy) and plural marriages (polygamy) are found in Africa. Within the sphere of plural marriages, Murdock notes that 88 per cent of all traditional African societies allow for some form of polygyny, in which a man may have more than one wife.[15] The practice of polyandry, where a woman may have more than one husband, is relatively rare. This should not be taken to mean that all polygynous societies in Africa practice the custom uniformly; in some, only a minority of the people actually live in polygynous families, while in others well over half of all marriages are polygynous at any given time.

The dominance of polygyny as an African institution has led to an interesting theoretical problem about the supply of women. If most African societies prefer polygyny, but sex ratios approach a 1:1 relationship, where do the extra women come from? One hypothesis is that only a few successful men are able to gain extra wives. Research has shown, however, that in a number of cases where we have data the ratio of married women to married men is 1.5:1, while overall sex ratios remain at approximately 1:1. Another hypothesis is that age disparity at first marriage produces significantly more marriage years for women than for men, thereby creating an artificially or culturally induced surplus of women.

15. Murdock, *Africa*, p. 25.

This hypothesis requires that there be an age disparity at first marriage when there is a high rate of polygyny—and commonly there is. But in many of these same societies women leave marriage to become single as they grow older, while men go on being married until they die. This corrects for the imbalance at marriage inception but still leaves the sex-ratio problem unanswered. (It also creates an age-class of old, unmarried women who are taken care of by their kin group.) It has recently been suggested that the problem can be solved by looking at interethnic relations and hypothesizing that politically dominant groups import a surplus of women from less powerful neighboring groups and that the polygyny rate is thus a correlate of political dominance in a region.[16] But like many other problems in our understanding of African society, or in social science in general, final solutions escape us.

Family Life

Family life in Africa, in general, can be classified into two types. First, there are families that include one married generation with their children, that is, nuclear families (56 per cent in our sample of African societies). Second, there are variant forms of extended, often polygynous, families (44 per cent in our sample) in which marriage units from two or more adjacent generations, linked by descent ties, live together as a family.

The stability of relationships of any particular set of actors within the family is governed by two analytically distinct sets of factors: (a) those resulting from the structural and functional features of kinship, and (b) those resulting from the nature of local residence groupings. Marital unions have been found to be more or less stable depending upon descent type, rural-urban distinctions, socio-economic status of the husband, fertility of the wife, and the degree of wife absorption into her husband's group. In general, patrilineal descent is associated with more stable family life than is matrilineal descent, while bilateral descent is associated with both high and low stability of marital unions. Rural marriages are more stable than urban marriages, low status makes for more stability than does high status, fertile marriages are more stable than infertile marriages, and higher absorption creates more stability than does lower absorption. Given these factors, in general I would estimate that traditional African unions are highly unstable, even though there are celebrated cases, such as the Nuer of the Sudan and the Zulu of South Africa, where divorce is rare or nonexistent.[17]

For family life in general this implies several distinct qualities. In those societies with high divorce rates, children lose household contact with their mothers.

---

16. Ronald Cohen and John Middleton, eds., *From Tribe to Nation in Africa* (San Francisco: Chandler, 1970).

17. This statement implies comparison with countries like the U.S., where divorce rates reach 25 per cent; that is, 25 per cent of all marriages end in divorce. I consider such a rate low, while rates of 60 per cent or more are high.

This follows from the fact that 78 per cent of traditional African societies require the wife to live at her husband's family residence, or at least at her husband's own residence. That is, the great majority of marriages are patrilocal (where the wife may live with her husband's family) or virilocal (where the wife lives with her husband, but not necessarily with the group of her husband's agnates). At divorce, mothers leave the house, generally taking only unweaned children who may have to be returned to their father's house when they are weaned. Children must therefore adjust to their mother's former co-wives, or to subsequent wives of their father who become senior females in the household.

Sibling relationships in African families, therefore, are complicated by polygyny and high divorce rates. The concept of full sibling and half sibling is widespread, and in many cases the sibling bond is extended to cousins. These may be parallel cousins (children of parents' siblings of the same sex), especially where unilineal descent is emphasized, or, as in the cases of the Hausa, the Tuareg, and the Kanuri, these may be both parallel and cross cousins (children of parents' siblings of the opposite sex). This makes for a three-point scale, at least, of social proximity among siblings—full, half, and cousin. In segmentary societies where agnatic ideology can produce extremely wide and inclusive use of sibling terms, there may be even more categories of sibling relationship. At the level of the nuclear family, however, the distinction between full and half siblings is important at the death of a father; full siblings still share a mother, while half siblings each have a different surviving parent. The tendency, then, for siblings to break up at this point and go their own way is a function of the genealogical difference between them.

The relationship of co-wives is, as implied above, a difficult and tenuous one at best. Given widespread polygyny, the possibility that a traditional marriage may involve co-wives is fairly high. In all cases that I am familiar with, co-wife relations—especially their relations to the common husband—are defined by rules which protect what might be called a right of equal treatment, or as nearly equal as possible. Obviously, the inequality of man to women ratio in such a marriage creates scarcity (access to the husband) and competition among the wives. But such tensions are carefully controlled by rules. Thus, among the Kanuri of Nigeria a man must take nightly turns with each wife in his sleeping hut or room whether he has sexual relations with her or not. To avoid such a responsibility is tantamount to open conflict. A very widespread variant of the equal treatment rule is the situation of the senior wife (the first one married by the husband). Often she has special privileges and is regarded as the senior female authority in the household of her husband. Usually such authority continues down the marriage order, so that marriage order itself is a status hierarchy among the women. Sexual attractiveness, domestic skills, fertility, the importance of a particular wife's own descent group, and other qualities, however, tend to vary the ideal ordering and to create jealousies and tension among the women.

Father-child and husband-wife relations in Africa are generally defined culturally in terms of respect, obedience, and loyalty. These terms refer to the hierarchical qualities surrounding the role of husband-father in his relations to the other family members. In practice there is much variation, but the essential concept of adult male dominance over family life is extremely widespread and is considered to be a morally superior role expectation.

WIDER SCALED SOCIAL ORGANIZATION

The Household

Turning from role network aspects of the family to the spatial criteria for organization, the most widespread local unit for social organization is the household or domestic group. Such units overlap with kinship systems but are not identical to them. Because of the life cycle of individuals, domestic groups generally are organizationally dynamic; as pointed out by Fortes, domestic cycles have three phases.[18] First, there is an expansionist period that covers the marriage union until the birth of the last child. This, then, is limited by the duration of the last wife's fertility. Second, there is a fission phase in which children reach adulthood and marry. The children's marriages then lead to the real or potential breakup of the original unit. Finally, there is a replacement phase in which the children take over the roles of the previous generation and the concomitant power and authority such roles involve with respect to the resources of the original domestic unit.

What factors affect the nature of the domestic group and determine widespread characteristics of domestic groups in Africa? First there is the life cycle of the individual members. Growing up in an African household means belonging to a larger group of people than simply the nuclear family. The child must learn to interact appropriately and gracefully with various people and to treat each one according to a traditionally defined role. As already noted, combinations and permutations of such interpersonal relations are infinitely more complex in a typical African household than in its Western counterpart. Thus the child must sort out the subtleties of full, half, and cousin sibling differences and similarities, wife and co-wife distinctions, seniority among male and female household members, as well as the idiosyncrasies of the individuals actually filling such roles.

For example, in most African societies differences are not limited to the age,

18. Meyer Fortes, *The Development Cycle in Domestic Groups*, Cambridge Papers in Social Anthropology, No. 1, ed. Meyer Fortes, J. R. Goody, and E. R. Leach (Cambridge: At the University Press, 1958).

sex, or seniority of one's relatives as is the case among Westerners. With some relatives there are strict avoidance relations which must be learned to prevent disruption of local social life. Usually such customs involve not eating with the person, not looking at him directly, and often, if the avoidance is a male-female one, not even being in the same group together. Such relations must be handled gracefully and with the proper etiquette. Because any individual will have many prescribed relationships and because these vary in quality, social learning is complex for an African child.

After childhood, the rules and preferences of residence guide the practices concerning who will move at the time of first marriage. As noted above, in the majority of African societies it is the woman who relocates, though in general she does not move very far. Nonetheless, households lose their own women at marriage and gain stranger-women through marriage. Similarly, birth and death create shifts and changes which require adjustment. The intricate web of household relations must be altered to fit new members into the group. Conversely, the death of a member means that a link in the role network has been lost. Should all the role obligations held by the deceased be carried on? In many African societies there is a tendency to answer in the affirmative, especially with respect to marriage. This means that there are institutional means for continuing a marriage through the custom of marrying a surviving spouse to a brother, or sister, of the deceased partner. This is known as the levirate and sororate. Thus spouses are assured that their relations to a descent group will be maintained even after the death of a marriage partner. In the levirate, a woman is often married to a dead spouse's younger brother, while in the sororate the dead wife's younger sister replaces her with little or no recompense to the girl's kin group.

Ecological factors are important in determining the size and annual changes in composition of the domestic group. Thus semi-nomadism, which is widespread over many parts of Africa, produces a breakup of the group on an annual basis, with the herders leaving home to return later. Land shortage or poor soil fertility may cause domestic groups to break up because individual members want new or more farm plots. Also, housing size limitations and possibilities for expansion are factors. In most of Africa the usual household plan is that of the compound. This includes one or more huts inside an enclosure. In rural areas, then, the group may accommodate more members simply by building more huts and enlarging the enclosure. In areas of climatic extremes, such as the Sahara and Kalahari deserts, environmental conditions are more likely to control the size of dwellings and therefore the size of domestic units.

Economic factors also affect the size and nature of the domestic group. Thus access to greater economic resources is correlated with larger household size in terms of wives, clients, and the successful operation of patrilocal marriage preferences. Conversely, economic indigence is correlated with smaller household size and, as in parts of West Africa, with the institution of "pawning."

Pawning involves the seconding of a member from the debtor's household to that of the creditor. The pawn thus transferred works off the debt incurred by his or her household head. Underlying this correlation is the attractiveness to younger members of economic opportunity outside their natal households either in other domestic groups or in other regions of the country altogether.

The practice of "fostering" is widespread in Africa as a means of adding to household size. Often children are raised in a number of households or are given to a particular relative, often a childless woman, to be raised. Fostering is not the same as adoption, for the children are kept aware of their natal kinship relations even though they are raised in households other than that of their natural parents. Sometimes fostering is an aspect of clientage. This occurs when a man gives a child to a powerful person to be raised in the latter's household. The hope is that the child will develop a profitable relationship with the household head that will bear fruit as the child grows older.

Many African households are also expanded by taking in adult servants, followers, or apprentices. Formerly, the practice of domestic slavery (male and female) was used to expand household size. Patterns of slavery in traditional Africa, however, varied significantly depending upon the sociopolitical structure of the societies concerned. In general, acephalous, or non-centralized, societies absorbed slaves into descent groups within a stipulated number of generations so that slave ancestry was gradually discounted over time. In a few cases, as in the Sahara, slaves became a special caste of settled oases people who maintained a subservient position to their former masters, the desert nomads. In the more complex centralized societies slaves were a more permanent group, although various manumission procedures were practiced. It should be noted that many of the most important offices in the West African emirates and kingdoms were reserved for slaves. Slavery can be described more accurately as a legal status than as a social status. In many cases persons became slaves when captured in warfare, and often such persons retained or acquired considerable status in the host society.

From the point of view of the wider society, it is important to note that the cycle of household organization could to some extent be controlled by using such institutions as fostering, clientage, and slavery. If the relationships between a household head and his household members were not based on kinship alone, then he could maintain the organization or expand it as he became capable of doing so. Such an organization could become a powerful political force in the local community, or it could serve as a nucleus for the development of a new community or a ward organization within an already well-established community. Such control over household expansion is associated with the more complex chiefdoms and centralized state societies rather than with the acephalous ones. In cases where large-scale expansion of a household unit occurred within the simpler societies, as in Bonny, Nigeria, the household became a focal point around which more complex social and political organizations developed.

Community Patterns

Community patterning refers to the forms of organizations in which localized groups of people, in households and kin groups, interact with one another. The bases of such units vary from specific, fixed geographic areas to larger, and sometimes shifting, systems of alliances based on marriage and/or descent. These circumstances may occur concurrently, as in the case of the Kung Bushman bands, who are (a) basically patrilocal (with temporary uxorilocality, that is, residence with the wife's relatives, based on bride service), and (b) isolated spatially for most of the year from other bands. In such cases community boundaries are clear-cut and precise. Similarly, among the settled villages of West Africa, even though marriage and descent lines may not correspond, geographic boundaries between villages are clear-cut, although they may change over time due to ecological, political, or economic conditions of the specific locality in which the villages are found. On the other hand, Colson tells us that among the Tonga of Zambia community boundaries are defined as (a) neighborhoods, or localized areas in which people have rights to land use, and (b) vicinages, or wider groupings that take in several neighborhoods and are defined as areas in which intermarriage between groups takes place.[19] Outside of the vicinage all people are considered "aliens," and among aliens non-Tonga speakers are "foreigners." Because vicinage is defined by affinal ties, it is basically a shifting set of alliances rather than a fixed one. Therefore community boundaries in such cases cannot be said to be fixed and clear-cut. They are stable at any one point in time, but they vary with the interaction (marriage) patterns of the community members.

The degree to which community life in Africa is associated with marriages is striking. The occurrence of endogamous demes, that is, communities revealing a marked tendency toward local intracommunity marriage, is characteristic of 67 per cent of our African societies sample. The opposite pattern is that of local exogamy, that is, a localized descent group in which individuals must marry outside of the group. Local exogamy characterizes 26 per cent of the societies sampled. The remaining 7 per cent is made up of several variant patterns, running from agamous communities with no rules or tendencies at all to exogamous communities in which there are no descent links governing the marriage practices. Thus, African communities are predominantly in-marrying localized groups, although in a significant minority of cases there is a tendency toward localized community exogamy.

Another criterion for characterizing community organization in Africa is the mobility-stability continuum. Murdock has developed a series of eight categories along a continuum. At the one end of the scale are fully migratory or nomadic bands (10 per cent). Next are semi-nomadic communities whose mem-

19. Elizabeth Colson, "Incorporation in Tonga," in Cohen and Middleton, *From Tribe to Nation.*

bers wander in small bands for at least half the year but occupy a fixed settlement at other times (8 per cent). At the next point on the scale are communities that shift as a whole from one fixed settlement to another, as in cases of flood-plain living, or from which a substantial population is nomadic during part of the year, while a remnant group is left behind to occupy the settlement (4 per cent). Next are communities that have compact but impermanent settlements whose locations shift every few years, usually because of soil depletion (2 per cent). Increased physical stability is found in communities made up of dispersed neighborhoods, family homesteads, or households (27 per cent). Next are communities made up of separate small families in which several of the separated units are conceived of locally as a single community (9 per cent). The next most stable communities are those made up of compact and relatively permanent settlements, not much different in structure and functions from one another (36 per cent). Finally, there are complex communities in which a local village, town, or even city is surrounded by satellite outgrowths, hamlets, and households (4 per cent).

Summarizing these data, we can say that in 76 per cent of the traditional African societies community life takes place in locationally stable communities, while in 24 per cent of the societies people live a fully or partially mobile existence. These figures, however, do not account for the forced relocation in new territory of formerly stable groups subjected to the expansionist pressures of neighboring peoples. This produces another form of mobility, characterizing such groups as the Tiv (Nigeria) and the Nuer (Sudan), which is not considered in the Murdock data. If we consider these relocated peoples along with the traditionally impermanent groups, in all likelihood the proportion of mobile African societies would be well over 25 per cent.

In population size, traditional African communities appear to cluster around two characteristic levels. The upper limit of the first group would be about 1,000 persons, with a median in the range of 100–200 persons per settlement. Almost 75 per cent of the communities falling into this category have between 50 and 400 persons per settlement. In the second group, which includes settlements of over 1,000 persons, two-thirds of the communities have one or more indigenous towns with populations greater than 5,000, but none has more than 50,000. For the remainder (only seventeen societies in all), the distinguishing feature is the existence of one or more indigenous cities of 50,000 or more inhabitants. Within the entire sample, two-thirds of all African societies have no communities larger than 1,000 persons, while the rest are characterized by having towns of at least 5,000 people. This division of societies into small- and relatively large-scale categories reflects in general the contrast between the more widely dispersed populations of eastern and southern Africa and the larger population clusters in West Africa. There are, of course, some notable exceptions to this generalization, such as the denser and more urbanized populations of the Ethiopian Highlands and the East African coast.

POLITICAL ORGANIZATION IN TRADITIONAL AFRICA

Non-centralized Societies

The ways in which African communities are organized politically reflect ecological, historical, and political factors in the society at large. The idea of a separate political sector in traditional society, however, is not always present. There is widespread lack of differentiation among functions in a majority of traditional African societies. Constituted authority not only serves strictly political functions but is often responsible for a wide variety of economic, social, and religious activities as well. This broad, and often diffuse, political structure provides one of the most comprehensive ways of describing community patterning and intercommunity relations in traditional African societies.[20]

The boundaries of African political systems are defined by the limits of the jural community.[21] The set of persons within this legal zone is called a polity. The basic feature of the polity is the ability of its members to settle disputes among themselves through institutions utilized for conflict resolution. Outside the polity there are no such institutions, and, therefore, conflicts at the inter-polity level may result in war, an indication that the issues of a conflict cannot be adjudicated. In many African societies violence within the polity and between polities has a totally different character: violence increases significantly in quality and intensity outside the polity unit. It is important to note that the polity does not necessarily correlate with ethnic groups, language, or religion. In some African societies there are many polities, while in other societies the entire group is part of a multiethnic polity which encompasses differing cultural entities.

At the least complex level of polity are hunting and gathering bands which may include twenty to fifty people each. Heads of constituent household units confer on decisions and resolve conflicts among themselves within the band. Unresolved conflicts can lead to band fission, although such an outcome is generally considered to be injurious to all concerned because the resource base must then be divided. There may or may not be a headman; if there is, his power is limited. Women gather food in the area near the camp while men hunt farther afield. Cooperative activities such as communal hunts are possible when ecological conditions are able to sustain such activities. The basic unit is a domestic one, generally made up of a monogamous or polygynous family with the possible

20. Ronald Cohen, "Political Anthropology: The Future of a Pioneer," *Anthropological Quarterly*, XXXVIII (1965), 117–31; Ronald Cohen and John Middleton, eds., *Comparative Political Systems: Studies in the Politics of Pre-Industrial Societies* (New York: Doubleday, Natural History Press, 1967).

21. John Middleton and David Tait, eds., *Tribes without Rulers: Studies in African Segmentary Systems* (London: Routledge & Kegan Paul, 1958); Cohen and Middleton, *Comparative Political Systems*.

additions, temporary or permanent, of affines in the form of sons-in-law or the unmarried kin of either spouse. Relations between bands are based primarily on marriage, which is generally patrilocal with the possibility of extended bride service. Among the Congo Pygmies there are also economic relations between band headmen and local Bantu villagers in which forest products are exchanged for those of agriculture. It is important to remember that in a continent of several hundred million people there are at most half a million living in hunting and gathering bands. This is approximately one-fourth of one per cent of the total African population, and their numbers are dwindling steadily.

When agricultural techniques of production are utilized, as they are for the bulk of Africa's people, then the degree of physical mobility of the population becomes an important determinant of the political structure. Mobility is a function of several phenomena: population expansion, the proportion of pastoralism to horticulturalism in the subsistent state, soil fertility, and intergroup relations between ethnic units. Given the dominance of an agricultural technology in Africa, traditional polities can be divided into two types: the non-state, or acephalous variety, and the centralized state. Although there are varieties of political systems that seem to hover between these two basic types, the distinction is nonetheless useful and applies to a large majority of African authority systems.

For the acephalous, agriculturally based polities the problems of continuity of membership, rights over property, and prerogatives of office increase enormously over those of the hunting band. In addition, basic resources for subsistence and continuity of the group, such as land, cattle, and storable surpluses, tend to be alienated from the individual or his domestic unit. A widespread institution for handling such problems in an acephalous polity is that of unilineal descent groups. Such groups increase in scale and in the numbers of activities which they tend to govern in proportion to their degree of population mobility. In the more mobile cases, clans are common as means of linking lineage segments to one another in a set of ever widening relations. The polity here is often quite large and may cover great amounts of territory, since new groups have split off from parent groups to find pasturage or for other reasons. Yet in this process of segmentation the new groups remain in contact with, and maintain the memory of, their relations to the parent group. In warfare these contacts can be reactivated, and several related communities can be united against a common foe.

As groups settle down into more or less permanent villages, however, the locality itself, rather than lineage, may serve as an organizing principle for community relations. It is common for the more sedentary of the acephalous societies to subdivide and use village groups as jural communities (or polities); once formed, these tend to be autonomous with regard to one another.

Religious congregations in acephalous societies tend to be associated with the mobility factor. The more mobile segmentary societies may link up religious activities with their nesting sets of lineages and clan organizations so that religious offices and functions become part of the overall lineage and clan structure. The individual actor obtains his religious duties and obligations from his lineage role. In more sedentary populations, on the other hand, cult membership may reside in one or more closely related sets of lineages, and such membership is often based on local residence whether or not ego is a member of the founding or original lineage of the village.

With regard to lineage relations, there are variations in the degree to which ideal and normative behavior correspond. Recently it has been suggested that the nomadic Bedouins of North Africa, who seem to guide their interpersonal and intergroup relations by the principles of a classic segmentary lineage system, do not in fact practice such norms. Instead, they link up to groups that are genealogically very distant, leaping over genealogically closer segments to form alliances for reasons of self-interest.[22]

The way in which descent groups can form the core around which communities develop is indicated over and over again in the anthropological literature on Africa. If, for example, patrilineal descent and patrilocal residence practices come together, as they often do in Africa, then a core settlement starts to grow. This group is related by descent through the male line. Each adult man may head his own household, but he feels closely allied to his agnates in surrounding houses. The senior male heads the organization and represents it, either to other settlements or to neighboring wards of a village or town. In-marrying women provide or represent affinal links to other lineage groups nearby, and out-marrying females of the descent group perform these same functions with respect to the core groups. If, as is often the case, the men practice the same occupation or set of occupations, then any occupational specialization in the society at large places all groups in a position of economic interdependency and specialization. Non-core members are either clients or brothers-in-law who use affinal connections as recruitment channels into residential groupings other than those of their own lineage.

Crosscutting such lineage links, especially in eastern and southern Africa, are age-set organizations. These organizations generally unite all the members of the community within specified age brackets. Such age-groupings may provide specific services to the community. Invariably the young men assume military roles, which in some cases also involves enforced bachelorhood. In one extreme case, that of the Nyakyusa, a new village site is created for the age-set members as each new group of boys reaches puberty. In general, older age-groups provide leadership and decision-making skills for the wider community.

Explanations of age-set organizations vary. Wilson attempts to explain the

---

22. E. L. Peters, "Some Structural Aspects of the Feud among the Camel-Herding Bedouin of Cyrenaica," *Africa*, XXXVII (1967), 260–82.

phenomenon by using Freudian ideas concerning the fear of parent-child sexual knowledge and possible relations. Thus age-set organizations, by separating parents and children, create institutional buffers to the psychic strain imposed on such relations through the Oedipal conflict.[23] The Nyakyusa themselves explain their society in this way. I would support another type of explanation. Almost all of the societies with age-set patterns have strong orientations toward cattle, intergroup hostility, and the need to protect herds. Herds are tended by young boys who develop strong social links across lineages; they also become warriors together. These needs and interaction patterns are then institutionalized and expressed in the customs surrounding the elaboration of age-set organizations.

A somewhat different crosscutting function is served by the widespread use of initiation rites and secret-society memberships. Such initiations, among the acephalous sedentary peoples of Africa, link up the young boys within a community and often across several neighboring communities. The boys are removed from their families and tutored in the sacred lore of the adult male societies; then they are "reborn" into their communities as beginning adults. Such age-graded organization has been interpreted in several ways. Some authors emphasize the idea that these rituals dramatize the entrance into manhood of the new members of the society and provide a basis for solidarity and cooperation among the group, which will eventually become the dominant decision-making body for each community. Others suggest that the elaborate ritual and rites represent a cultural recognition and dramatization of the fact that the child must be taken away from his natal family, especially his mother, and become to some extent an independent member of the wider community. Both of these ideas, that of separation from a natal group and that of solidarity with a new group, seem to be important in formulating an explanation of such initiation rites.

Centralized State Systems

At the level of chieftaincy and centralized state systems, community patterning is basically similar to that already discussed with reference to acephalous societies. However, there are important differences. Recruitment to office is through traditional lineage or widespread clan organizations, and the jural community is enlarged in scale beyond that of the local settlement or clan group. Disputes can be settled at points along an authoritative hierarchy going from local household heads to village heads to the chiefly office beyond the village. The chief very often fulfills functions in addition to that of conflict resolution. Generally he is a religious leader, and as a military commander he unites his

23. Godfrey Wilson, "The Nyakyusa of South-Western Tanganyika," in *Seven Tribes of British Central Africa*, ed. Elizabeth Colson and Max Gluckman (Manchester: Manchester University Press, 1959), pp. 253–91.

people against others outside his domain. Elsewhere I have suggested that African chieftaincy is often attractive to peoples surrounding centralized chieftaincies but not having this institution themselves,[24] and that the evolutionary path from non-chieftaincy to chieftaincy lies through differential ranking of kin groups (often clans) in mobile societies and the differentiation of groups based on wealth in the more sedentary groups.[25]

African states vary in the degree to which they can maintain centralized control over their constituent parts.[26] They are generally multiethnic polities, and there is always some form of central bureaucratic organization surrounding a monarchy that has dynastic qualities. The basic problems lie in the relations between the central government and its constituent local settlements, between the kingdom and surrounding peoples, and in the methods used to recruit personnel into the political system. The latter problem is crucial since it is the major determinant of centralized power. It varies with the hereditary rights to office of the subordinates in the state. When these rights are not clearly hereditary, or when slaves and/or eunuchs can be used in positions of authority, the state is more centralized in the monarch and his councilors. When power positions and rights are more stringently hereditary, the authority of the monarch decentralizes and the kingdom is weakened.

Centralized political authority solves certain problems of organization and resource adaptation that arise from situations in which local groups have to coordinate control of their external relations with surrounding groups. Some of these problems can be isolated. First, there are difficulties brought about by increasing cultural heterogeneity within a polity as it absorbs groups from outside and the associated or at least similar problems of social stratification with the differentiation of various elements within the society. Second, there are problems arising from the movement of a group into a new territory in which leaders decide to control the local population as subordinates; in this case the leaders may found a dynasty. Third, there are problems facing groups that surround a centralized state and are stimulated to emulate it for reasons of power and prestige and for defense. Fourth, there is the pattern of acephalous groups attaching themselves to apparently superior ritual leaders in order to share in the blessings of supernatural powers. Fifth, there are states that result either from vassal or tributary states becoming independent or from integral parts of older states breaking away under the leadership of dissident factions, royal usurpers, or rebellious nobles.

24. Cohen and Middleton, *From Tribe to Nation*.

25. Ronald Cohen and Alice Schiegel, "The Tribe as a Socio-Political Unit: A Cross-Cultural Examination," in *Essays on the Problem of Tribe*, American Ethnological Society Proceedings (Seattle: University of Washington Press, 1968).

26. Jan Vansina, "A Comparison of African Kingdoms," *Africa*, XXXII (1962), 324–35; Ronald Cohen, "Political Anthropology," in *West African Kingdoms in the Nineteenth Century*, ed. Daryll Forde and Phyllis M. Kaberry (London: Oxford University Press, 1967).

Traditional African kings were usually held to be sacred or divine. At the very least they were felt to embody some supernatural attributes. The rulers were rarely despots; their kingdoms involved a chain of authority running from the monarch down to the local residential groups, in which the intermediaries represented those below and those above to each other. This dependence was typically expressed in tribute, in the form of taxes, labor, or more symbolic objects. As there is always some concept of representativeness or accountability of superiors in the hierarchical chain to those over whom they have authority, pressure groups, factionalism, and political patronage were constant features of the African centralized state.[27]

THE CONCEPTS OF TRIBE AND ETHNIC SOCIETY

A final aspect of traditional African society which is of great importance, but which is extremely difficult to capture in any definitive term, is the concept of a whole society. This concept has been spoken of in the past as the "tribe." This reference has given birth to contemporary ideas of "tribalism" and, in more complex thinking, to such notions as "detribalization"—usually meaning urbanization and the loss of identity in the modern situation. Yet, as we have noted, the patterns of African polity do not necessarily correspond to cultural or ethnic groupings. In Africa, and very likely elsewhere as well, ethnic identity has been forming, reforming, and disappearing for literally thousands of years.

The problem is made even more complex by a number of other non-congruences. Race and language are not clearly bounded within so-called ethnic entities. Vast numbers of Africans, perhaps most Africans, are multilingual, so language differences are not necessarily a barrier between groups. Descent groups, language groups, residential units such as towns, cities, local regions, and subregions, religion, and even occupation (especially with respect to pariah activities such as blacksmithing) serve to give identity and ethniclike qualities to segments of population that subdivide so-called tribes and may even cut across several widely recognized ethnic groups.

What, then, is an African "tribe"? The simple answer often used by former colonial officials, journalists, or political parties in contemporary Africa is that it refers to groups which are politically significant subdivisions in a nation, and which possess some widespread consciousness of common identity and cultural distinctiveness. Yet it often goes unnoticed that so-called tribes may have great variations within their own group, even possessing named subgroups. Moreover, people can define their own group, even though it may, and indeed does,

27. See Jeffrey Holden, "Empires and State Formation," in this volume, for a further elaboration of the characteristics of African state systems.

change through time.[28] The reasons for this are complex and have been discussed elsewhere.[29] The important point, not often mentioned by the non-specialist, is that a "tribe" is *never* an immutable entity. On the contrary, it is exactly the opposite, and to be understood at all it must be seen as an adaptive identity that changes in relation to outside forces as well as to a number of important internal forces. Once this point is clear, it becomes nonsense to speak of "reverting to tribalism" or of "ancient tribal rivalries." Instead, we must ask questions about the traditional ethnic identities in an area and the relationship of these to the traditional and modern political structures, and then ask what has produced the contemporary ethnic identities and solidarities (or lack of them). Partly to emphasize the non-static nature of the "tribe," and partly to allow greater flexibility of conceptualization and description, the term "ethnic society" is being used increasingly by social scientists in place of the term "tribe."

To name something is not to know it. There are in Africa clusters or categories of peoples who have had some traditional similarity to one another. But whether these clusters represented any real social units in the past is a matter for research, not speculation. Nevertheless, within and sometimes across these units there were, and are today, real working societies. The forms of social organization they developed stemmed from fundamental human needs that are shared by all men everywhere. All men want a good life for themselves, their families, and their communities. In Africa the potentialities of the environment and the traditional technology used to exploit them have produced genuine ongoing societies and cultures. As already noted, such societies are ones that are capable of adapting and changing in response to their indigenous needs. This is the essential and fundamentally important quality of traditional African society, for it allows us an insight into the nature of human potentialities. Man's problems are often very similar, but as stimuli or challenges they have produced many different solutions. Traditional Africa is not just an exotic jigsaw puzzle of tribal groupings, but represents a wide range of experiences in attempting to solve the problems of human existence.

28. M. H. Fried, "On the Concepts of 'Tribe' and 'Tribal Society,'" *Essays on the Problem of Tribe*.
29. Cohen and Middleton, *From Tribe to Nation*.

4

Traditional Economic Systems

GEORGE DALTON

TRADITIONAL AFRICAN ECONOMIES used to be a subject of interest only to a few anthropologists and agricultural economists. Since the middle 1950s, interest has deepened and widened for several reasons. The end of colonialism was followed by an explicit drive to "modernize" the newly independent states of Africa, particularly to develop them economically: to commercialize and diversify production, to create new economic institutions such as modern banking and taxation and extend them nationally, and to incorporate modern technology in production lines. Intelligent development policy required not only an understanding of the present structure and performance of African economies but a knowledge of their economic history as well.[1] Those concerned with changing Africa's future must understand its economic past and present. African governments, aid-giving governments of Europe and America, United Nations agencies, and philanthropic foundations, such as Ford and Rockefeller, all sponsor research designed to improve our understanding both of traditional economies and of the changing economies of Africa today.

The colonial revolution in Africa (and Asia), and the subsequent need for intelligent analysis and policy for the purposes of economic development and modernization, has profoundly affected university subjects, particularly teaching and research in the social sciences. Anthropology, economics, sociology, psychology, and political science now contain subfields of specialization concerned with traditional and modernizing Africa. An entire university establishment of lecture courses, seminars, doctoral degree programs, field research

1. See George Dalton, "Traditional Production in Primitive African Economies," *Quarterly Journal of Economics*, LXXVI (1962), 360–78; reprinted in *Tribal and Peasant Economies: Readings in Economic Anthropology*, ed. George Dalton (New York: Doubleday, Natural History Press, 1967).

projects, and new journals, all concerned with African studies, has come into being.

Economic anthropology has attracted considerable interest since the 1950s. It studies the structure and performance of village-level economies under traditional and modernizing conditions. To the older literature of ethnographic description are being added analytical writings which delineate principles of socioeconomic organization, measure levels of performance, and make systematic comparisons between primitive and peasant economies, as well as between these economies and their modern and developed counterparts.[2]

Economic anthropologists, however, have been confronted with problems in the creation of a theoretical framework. Among the most acute of these problems is that of the unavailability of sufficient quantitative data to measure economic performance effectively. There is a base of factual knowledge of industrialized capitalist and communist countries stated in quantitative terms that has no counterpart in traditional African economies. The structure and performance of large industrialized economies in which money and pricing are pervasive are capable of quantification at all levels. The composition and growth of total national output are measured by national income accounting, and the production activities of individual business firms are measured by cost and profit accounting. Indeed, that branch of statistical analysis called interindustry economics, associated with the name of Wassily Leontief, creates a set of accounts for an entire national economy, showing the relation of each sector supplying resources and acquiring products to every other sector in quantitative terms.

Quantitative information about the structure and performance of traditional African economies is rare. There are very few village-level economies for which the following kind of information is known: How much equipment, buildings, and foodstuffs of all kinds is produced per year? What are the fluctuations in output experienced from year to year? How equal or unequal is the distribution of ordinary consumption goods, compared to prestige and "treasure" items? What proportion of produce is self-consumed, and what is given away, sold locally, or involved in external trade transactions?[3]

The absence of quantitative information is due in part to the difficulties in measuring and collecting such data in the field; there are also difficulties in

---

2. See George Dalton, "Theoretical Issues in Economic Anthropology," *Current Anthropology*, X (1969), 63–102.

3. Some representative examples of the kinds of quantitative data that exist for traditional African economies may be cited here. William Allan, *The African Husbandman* (London: Oliver and Boyd, 1965), brings together information on population density and amounts of land cultivated per capita. Audrey Richards, *Land, Labour and Diet in Northern Rhodesia* (London: Oxford University Press, 1939), estimated food consumption for an African group. Phyllis Deane, *Colonial Social Accounting* (Cambridge: At the University Press, 1953), measured village output and discusses problems and techniques of measurement in rural Africa; see also *African Studies in Income and Wealth*, ed. L. H. Samuels (Chicago: Quadrangle Books, 1963).

acquiring quantitative information in economies that do not use money and prices. Where social scientists have been able to make quantitative measurements in the field, their analyses of structure and performance have been markedly improved.[4]

Another difficulty, which will be discussed in greater detail later in this essay, relates to the separating out of a distinctly "economic" sector from society as a whole. Culture and society, economy and technology, polity and religion mutually influence one another both in modern industrialized societies and in traditional African societies.[5] In traditional society, however, this integral connection is a central feature. An earlier generation of anthropologists talked of "patterns" or "configurations" of culture. They were impressed by the congruence or mutual fit of the different sectors of a given culture. More recent writers have shown us how economic, technological, social, and cultural features mutually affect one another not only in the traditional but in the modernizing societies as well.[6]

SCALE AND DIVERSITY OF TRADITIONAL AFRICAN ECONOMIES

To understand the distinctive features of traditional African economies, one must first understand what they share with all other economies. The economies of the United States, the Soviet Union, and the Tiv[7] of central Nigeria may be regarded as systematic arrangements to provide societies with material goods and specialist services. The need to structure such provisioning, that is, to have an "economic system," stems from the recurrent physiological needs of persons for food, clothing, and shelter, and the recurrent social needs of communities for services such as defense, religion, and dispute settlement. Societies consist of people who, as individuals, require continual material sustenance and who, as members of a culture, polity, and neighborhood, have shared needs for community services. Both private and public life require continual provisioning.

4. Scarlett T. Epstein, *Economic Development and Social Change in South India* (Manchester: Manchester University Press, 1962).

5. See Mary Douglas, "Lele Economy Compared with the Bushong: A Study of Economic Backwardness," in *Markets in Africa*, ed. Paul Bohannan and George Dalton (Evanston, Ill.: Northwestern University Press, 1962).

6. Gunnar Myrdal, *Rich Lands and Poor* (New York: Harper & Row, 1957), Chaps. 1–3; Everett E. Hagen, *On the Theory of Social Change* (Homewood, Ill.: Dorsey Press, 1962); Irma Adelman and Cynthia Taft Morris, *Society, Politics, and Economic Development* (Baltimore: Johns Hopkins Press, 1967).

7. See Paul Bohannan and Laura Bohannan, *Tiv Economy* (Evanston, Ill.: Northwestern University Press, 1968).

The means of provisioning any society are basically the same. The Americans, the Russians, and the Tiv make use of (1) natural resources, such as land, minerals, forests, and waterways; (2) human resources, such as skilled and un-skilled labor; (3) tools and technical knowledge; and (4) organizational pro-cedures, practices, devices, and activities that we call institutions, such as divi-sion of labor, rules of land tenure, foreign trade, forms of money, and market places. (There are others, such as trade unions, that are used only in certain types of economies or certain kinds of economic activity.) The economies of the U.S., Soviet Russia, and the Tiv differ with regard to the quantity, quality, and diversity of the natural resources and human labor at their disposal; the quantity and quality of the tools and technical knowledge they have; and the kinds of structured arrangements or institutions they make use of.

With reference to traditional Africa, it has been noted that "it is this smallness of scale, so hard for a modern European to grasp imaginatively, which is the fundamental characteristic of primitive life."[8] Traditional Africa comprised thousands of small economies. If we examined them separately, without com-paring them to the familiar economies of present-day Europe and America, we would be struck by their diversity. They differed with regard to the quantity and quality of natural resources at their disposal, and therefore the principal foodstuffs they relied upon. Some were hunters, gatherers, or fishermen pre-cariously depending on natural environment for livelihood; others were herders living off their herds and flocks; more were agriculturalists. Most combined several of these subsistence activities. Many of the hunters, gatherers, and herd-ers moved with the seasons, and some of the shifting agriculturalists moved every few years. Others were permanently settled.[9]

We would be struck too by the diversity in their tools and technical knowledge. Although most of the peoples of traditional Africa display ingenuity in their knowledge of local plant and animal life, some had few tools beyond digging sticks, containers, and spears,[10] while others could make poison to kill fish, and could construct pipelines for irrigation and traps to ensnare large animals.

When we examined their organizational arrangements for growing crops or hunting, we would again be impressed by diversity. The customs governing land tenure, the ways of organizing work, the rules for allocating produce, and the procedures for conducting external trade varied within and among economies.

If we looked at the measurable performance of traditional African economies we would similarly be struck by diversity in the amount of goods produced or acquired, variations in the amounts from year to year, the frequency with which

8. Godfrey Wilson, "An Essay on the Economics of Detribalization in Northern Rhodesia," Rhodes-Livingstone Papers, No. 5 (1941), p. 10.

9. See Allan, *African Husbandman.*

10. Elizabeth Marshall Thomas, *The Harmless People* (New York: Knopf, 1959).

hunger or famine threatened, the extent of material inequality among households (or among stratified groups) within each economy, the range of material items and services produced or acquired, and the intensity of work life.[11]

The same is true for the social and cultural characteristics of community life. Aside from diversity in natural resources, tools, economic institutions, and measurable economic performance, we would find diversity in religion, language, and political organization.

But if we compared traditional African societies with the industrialized national societies of present-day Western Europe and North America, we would see that even though they differed among themselves, as a group they differed more sharply and systematically from, for instance, the U.S. or France. The most important differences are in size and effective integration (the extent and forms of mutual dependence and shared culture). Here, language betrays us. "Economy," "polity," "culture," and "society" have no size dimension attached to them. They are elastic words which we stretch as needed. We speak of the "economy" of a hunting and gathering band consisting of twenty persons in the Kalahari Desert, but we use the same word to speak of the "economy" of the United States comprising two hundred million people. So too with the words "culture," "society," and "polity."

African societies, with important exceptions in the Islamic areas, did not have that set of mutually reinforcing, large-scale, integrative institutions which characterize modern Europe and America—institutions through which are expressed socioeconomic interaction, cultural identity, and common awareness by millions of persons.

African polities were neither organized along the lines of modern nation-states, nor did they provide the range of common public services that modern governments do. To be sure, lineage heads, chieftains, and kings existed, but their political jurisdictions and their activities to promote community cohesion extended only to hundreds, thousands, or, exceptionally, a few hundred thousand persons.[12] In contrast, the modern nation-state creates a focus of common allegiance of much greater scope. Millions of citizens are made subject to common laws; all sectors of the nation pay common taxes and receive common educational services, roads, and other social services.[13] In parliamentary democracies, the millions of citizens identify themselves with common political parties and participate in nation-wide electoral processes.

Traditional Africa spoke hundreds of languages. To be sure, a few were

11. See Deane, *Colonial Social Accounting*; and Samuels, *Income and Wealth*.

12. See Meyer Fortes and E. E. Evans-Pritchard, *African Political Systems* (London: Oxford University Press, 1940); and John Middleton and David Tait, eds., *Tribes without Rulers: Studies in African Segmentary Systems* (London: Routledge & Kegan Paul, 1958).

13. See Gunnar Myrdal, *Beyond the Welfare State* (New Haven: Yale University Press, 1960).

spoken by millions of persons, others were mutually intelligible, and many Africans spoke more than one language. But most languages were entirely local. These were, moreover, non-literate cultures, or cultures in which only a tiny fraction of the population was literate. It is not too much to say that literacy is to culture what machine technology is to economy. The absence of written language and literature limits wider cultural expression, awareness of external events and people, and knowledge of alternatives, just as the absence of machine technology limits wide economic interaction. Clearly, two of the important reasons for the small scale of traditional African economy and society were the absence of literacy and of widely shared language.

THE ABSENCE OF MACHINE TECHNOLOGY
AND APPLIED SCIENCE

The absence of machine technology and applied science in traditional Africa is a matter of great importance. The major consequences are obvious: industrialized economies produce a quantity of output per person roughly fifteen to twenty times as great as do traditional African economies; moreover, there is continual growth in output in industrialized economies—an average factory worker in the U.S. sees his real income at least doubled over his working life. The range of material items and services produced and imported by developed industrialized economies is enormous; hundreds of thousands of items are bought by households, business firms, and governments. The automobile, modern surgery, the paperback book—all the results of applied science and machine technology—create a diversity and quality of material life which vastly affect culture, society, and polity, as well as economy.

The principal lines of production in traditional Africa were agriculture and herding. The absence of pesticides, chemical fertilizers, disease-resistant seeds, irrigation facilities, veterinary medicine, and the other technical knowledge and equipment available to American and European farmers and herders meant an unusual and direct dependence on physical environment; that is, there was a high degree of ecological dependence. The absence of machine technology also meant low productivity and uncontrollable fluctuations in output. In agriculture and herding, applied science is a substitute for and a controller of physical environment; irrigation equipment creates its own rainy season. Similarly, agricultural synthetics (for example, dacron for cotton), as well as the specialized equipment and technical knowledge applied to U.S. agriculture, may be regarded as man-made devices to reduce ecological dependence, to increase material abundance, and to decrease the incidence of drought, flood, and disease to plant and animal life. Traditional African economies could not significantly control or compensate for the vagaries of physical environment. Their under-developed technology also meant that they could not make effective use of all the natural resources, such as minerals, in their physical environment.

The absence of machine technology in Africa also meant the absence of a most characteristic feature of modern life: the factory system within massive cities.[14] In modern industrialized economies of both the capitalist and communist sorts, the use of machine technology makes special forms of large-scale, econ-omy-wide economic organization necessary (resource and product market integration in the U.S. and the "command economy" of central planning in the U.S.S.R.). Special forms of local organization are also necessary. Engineering efficiency requires a factory system because machines must be operated in a special sequence, and the use of machines requires extreme specialization of labor; that is, workers of the machines do one task, or a few tasks, repetitively. Machine technology also requires a labor force that has special skills and is disciplined to a special set of work habits — for instance, punctuality and the eight-hour workday. Wherever industrialization has taken place a laboring force "committed" to sustained factory employment has been created, typically from a first generation of factory workers who had to unlearn agricultural work habits.[15]

Aside from the engineering constraints — the fact that efficient use of machines requires factory organization and that workers acquire a special set of work habits — there are also economic constraints created by machine technology. Machines are expensive; economic efficiency (that is, low costs) requires that machines be used within a large economy organized so as to assure the certain supply of labor and material resources to work the machines and the certain dis-position of the machine-made products.[16] Under capitalist institutions national and international market organization (including the price system and what we shall call general purpose or commercial money) allocates the inputs and dis-poses of the outputs of the factory system. Industrial communism employs a

14. Larger towns and cities in traditional Africa, as in pre-industrial Europe, were either the locations of kingly government or "ports of trade," that is, locations for foreign trade. See Rosemary Arnold, "A Port of Trade: Whydah on the Guinea Coast," in *Trade and Market in the Early Empires*, ed. Karl Polanyi, C. M. Arensberg, and H. W. Pearson (New York: Macmillan, The Free Press, 1957); Karl Polanyi, "Ports of Trade in Early Societies," *Journal of Economic History*, XXIII (1963), 30–45, reprinted in *Primitive, Ar-chaic, and Modern Economies: Essays of Karl Polanyi*, ed. George Dalton (New York: Double-day, Anchor Books, 1968); and Gideon Sjoberg, "The Preindustrial City," *American Journal of Sociology*, LX (1955), 438–45.

15. See Reinhard Bendix, *Work and Authority in Industry* (New York: Harper & Row, 1956). Labor "commitment" means a disciplined labor force which shows up on time, does not change jobs frequently, and does not stay away from work unnecessarily. Com-mitment does not necessarily mean that the workers enjoy factory work.

16. See Karl Polanyi, *The Great Transformation* (New York: Farrar & Rinehart, 1944; reprint ed., Boston: Beacon Press, 1957).

functionally equivalent set of institutions (sometimes called a "command economy") to service the requirements of machine technology.[17]

THE ABSENCE OF MARKET ORGANIZATION

Traditional Africa lacked not only machines and applied science but also large-scale integrated resource and product markets with their accompanying monetary systems, which were created in response to the Industrial Revolution in Europe and America.[18] That traditional Africa lacked machine technology and the factory system is obvious; machines are visible. That it lacked resource and product market integration (the institutional network of capitalism) is less obvious, partly because Africa had some petty markets (which were different in scope and function from integrative national markets) and partly because only a portion of market institutions takes tangible form (for example, banks and business firms); the rest consists of transactional rules and rules of law which are less visible.

In an economy integrated by market-exchange institutions all the natural resource and labor ingredients of production are organized for purchase and sale at money prices: land and minerals; tools, equipment, and buildings; unskilled, skilled and professional labor; power, transport, and communication services—all are sold to producing firms. The seller's return is a money income in the form of wage, salary, fee, rent, interest, or profit. The seller then uses his income to make purchases from the enormous range of consumption goods and services produced by business firms, to pay taxes, and to save in one form or another. All persons depend on market sale of their labor or property for livelihood. Purchase and sale at money price is the dominant transactional mode in our economic system. Millions of households and hundreds of thousands of business firms are integrated, that is, made mutually dependent, by purchase and sale transactions. The monetary and pricing arrangements integrate the nation-wide system and also govern the network of international market transactions such as imports, exports, lending, borrowing, and investing.

In a national market economy, households, villages, and towns—the local

17. See Gregory Grossman, "Notes for a Theory of the Command Economy," *Soviet Studies*, Vol. XV (October 1963).
18. See Polanyi, *Great Transformation*, Chap. 4; George Dalton, "Economic Theory and Primitive Society," *American Anthropologist*, LXIII (1961), 1–25; Bohannan and Dalton, *Markets in Africa*; Montague Yudelman, "Some Aspects of African Agricultural Development," in *Conference on Economic Development for Africa South of the Sahara*, ed. E. A. G. Robinson (London: Macmillan, 1964), pp. 554–87; and Adelman and Morris, *Society, Politics, and Economic Development*, Chap. 5.

community counterparts of African villages—depend for livelihood on customers and suppliers external to their local communities. Just as machine technology and applied science reduce reliance on the vagaries of nature and climate, large-scale market organization reduces the economic dependence of persons on their friends, neighbors, and relatives within the local community.

THE SOCIAL CONTEXT OF TRADITIONAL ECONOMIES

Traditional African economies differed from the economies of industrialized Europe and America in the several ways discussed. More particularly, their small size and undeveloped technology meant low productivity and extreme dependence on physical environment. The absence of market integration and commercial money created local social dependence (that is, the need for household, lineage, or tribal cooperation and mutuality) in production processes:

> There is a domestic technology which does not change from one generation to another and which supports a subsistence economy of each household, domestic group, or band. The whole society consists of a number of such domestic groups or local bands linked together by cross-cutting ties of kinship and affinity. . . . This network of kinship ties provides almost the sole framework of social action, within which a variety of activities are performed. Everyone of the same age-group and sex participates in the total range of activities. . . . In such societies the level of technology sets narrow limits to the choice of means adopted to the attainment of certain goals; but within these limits rational action is "hemmed in" by the social prescription of means and ends; economic rationality is severely limited. The norms of economic conduct are embedded in a total set of norms; there is relatively little autonomy for economic criteria of evaluation.[19]

This description of a typical simple society is meant to point up those socio-economic characteristics of traditional societies which differ sharply from the social context of industrialized national societies:

> In the most complex form of society there is a reversal of most of these characteristics. There is a machine technology which is continuously changing, partly as a result of the organization of science and partly as a result of pressures within the economy itself. The division of labor, a necessary concomitant of this technology, cuts across domestic groupings and, indeed, most other ties in the society. Each individual is involved in many networks of interpersonal and impersonal relationships, which are governed by different and specific norms and interests.

19. Percy Cohen, "Economic Analysis and Economic Man: Some Comments on a Controversy," in *Themes in Economic Anthropology*, ed. Raymond Firth (London: Tavistock, 1967), pp. 111–12.

> No one participates in all or even most social activities . . . different individuals, groups, or categories of people internalize different norms and different sets of norms. . . . Unity and order . . . are maintained largely by economic interdependence, by the efforts of central administration, and by acceptance of certain diffuse values and identification with common symbols. . . . Rationality is less "hampered" by the immediacy of social relationships, and economic rationality, in particular, is allowed considerable scope for expression.[20]

Traditional African societies were not only small but also semi-isolated—culturally separated from one another by language, religion, and polity. Inherited animosities constituted another factor of separation. The risks of travel and poor facilities of transport and communications contributed to physical isolation. In these locally contained communities in which the people all know one another and in which the same persons share many activities and relationships, custom is tenacious. Children grow up to lead much the same lives as their parents led. Traditional practices and values are transmitted intact. Cultural and physical isolation means the absence of knowledge of real alternatives; whether in child-rearing practices or techniques for growing crops, the traditional African community did not have much knowledge of different, alternative ways. Choice was severely limited by the knowledge and techniques within the experience of the local people.

To deviate from traditional practice, moreover, was risky. To experiment with new crops or new techniques of production was to risk hunger if the innovation failed. To introduce non-edible cash crops successfully, such as was done with cocoa in Ghana and cotton in Uganda, there had to be food markets locally or the growers had to be able to grow the new crops and sufficient foodstuffs simultaneously.[21] Where social rank was sharply defined, for the lowly farmer to be too ambitious or too successful was to risk punishment by social superiors for attempting to rise above his station and thereby to threaten more highly placed persons.

But even where social rank was not sharply stratified and the boundaries of permissible activities not clearly circumscribed, sanctions for doing the traditional were strong. Mutual dependence meant mutual obligation. To fail to appear at a work party to clear your cousin's land, to fail to pay first-fruits to your chief, to fail to contribute to your younger brother's bridewealth—such actions would invite retaliation by cousin, chief, and brother, people upon whom you depended to reciprocate when you needed them. European colonialism in Africa eroded these attributes of traditional society, and in so doing induced socioeconomic change. Cultural and physical isolation were lessened, and Africans thereby gained knowledge of new alternatives. Cash-earning by sale of

20. *Ibid.*, pp. 112–13.
21. See Allan, *African Husbandman*, p. 351; and Yudelman, "Agricultural Development," p. 573.

crops and labor outside the community lessened mutual dependence within the local community.[22]

Anthropologists analyze religion, polity, and the rules and roles of kinship (marriage, descent reckoning, lineage) in detail because these permeate all activities, including economic activities. One cannot understand the organization of traditional African economies without understanding their cultures and societies.

Several terms and summary expressions are conventionally used to point up this interpenetration of economy and society in traditional life. Traditional societies are referred to as "organic" (rather than "mechanical"), *Gemeinschaft* (rather than *Gesellschaft*), "status" societies (rather than "contract" societies), "subsistence-based" (rather than "commercial-based"). These terms all convey the point that underlying social relationships provide the rules and channels for the allocation of land and labor, for work organization, and for the disposition of produce. From the viewpoint of individual persons, it is the roles of husband, father, brother, lineage member, elder, chief, neighbor, and friend that determine how and where one works, and how much of what range of material goods one has command over.[23] There is a sense in which it is true, therefore, that one consequence of organic social organization in traditional African economies is that a minimum level of material sustenance is guaranteed to all persons. In the absence of market organization, land and labor are acquired as a matter of social right, and in emergencies such as illness or accident persons draw on their social relationships to receive gifts and food.

PRODUCTION PROCESSES IN TRADITIONAL AFRICA

Production of any sort—farming, herding, manufacturing—in any kind of economy may be regarded as comprising three component processes: (1) the acquisition of natural resources, labor, and tools; (2) the organization of work tasks; and (3) the disposition of produce. If we contrast the organization of agricultural production in a traditional African subsistence farm and an American commercial farm, we can point up some distinctive features of African economy.

In the typical case, the African acquired farm land, at no cost to himself, as a right of membership in a social group, that is, because of his lineage or tribal affiliation.[24] This right to land was inalienable as long as he was a member in

22. There were exceptions. For an example of how wage labor outside the local community served to strengthen traditional structures within, see William Watson, *Tribal Cohesion in a Money Economy* (Manchester: Manchester University Press, 1958).

23. See Marshall D. Sahlins, *Tribesmen* (Englewood Cliffs, N.J.: Prentice-Hall, 1968).

24. See Paul Bohannan, "Africa's Land," *Centennial Review*, 1960, No. 4, pp. 439–49, reprinted in Dalton, *Tribal and Peasant Economies*; and Isaac Schapera, *The Bantu-Speaking Tribes of South Africa* (London: Routledge & Kegan Paul, 1937).

good standing. The African had a right to use the land but usually not to dispose of it in any way he pleased or to leave it unused.

> Almost invariably the land is not regarded as the private property of individuals, but rather as vested in social groups, whether these be tribes, clans, lineages, or extended families. Always individuals have the right to cultivate and to enjoy the produce of the land they till, but their rights in a particular piece of land are conditional. They depend, usually, on the community's acceptance of them, also on actual residence and cultivation. If a cultivator leaves an area which he has been living on and cultivating, after a time his rights in this area of land lapse. . . . Very often the allocation of cultivation rights is the responsibility of a lineage or clan head, or of a village headman. But the person who exercises this authority is not thought of as "owning" the land; rather he administers it on behalf and in the interest of the community he represents.[25]

By contrast, in American agriculture rights of acquisition or use of so .ieone else's land are acquired by money purchase or rental, and no previously existing social relationship between buyer and seller, or landlord and renter, is necessary.

So too with tools and farm labor. The African typically made his own digging stick or hoe, and he and his wife (or wives) and children supplied the ordinary farm labor. For tasks requiring an unusual amount or intensity of labor, such as clearing land or harvesting, the African drew on his social relationships — neighbors, friends, age-mates, clients, kin — whom he thanked by feeding them and sometimes by hosting a beer party at the end of the workday, or he reciprocated by helping clear their land and harvest their crops. In contrast, the Iowa wheat farmer purchases his tools and equipment and hires most of his labor at a money wage. Unlike the African, who depends on local social relationships, the American farmer depends on a variety of impersonal markets for the resources and labor needed in farming.

The African farmer's own household consumed most of what he produced. Some portions of produce could be given as gifts, paid as tribute to chiefs, or sold. The American farmer sells almost all he produces. As with an American manufacturing firm, the farmer's money-proceeds recover the money-costs of production (tools, seeds, pesticides, labor, transport, interest on loans) with the residual being profit, out of which he pays money-taxes.

In traditional society, the African farmer's activities were an integral part of his local community only. He relied on no person or agency external to his community for livelihood. The Iowa farmer is utterly dependent on strangers outside the local community: on chemical firms in Pittsburgh to provide him with pesticides; on factories in Detroit to provide him with tractors and other farm machinery; on banks in Iowa City to lend him money; and, ultimately, on

25. J. H. M. Beattie, *Other Cultures* (New York: Macmillan, The Free Press, 1964), p. 192.

households in several states to buy the bread made of the wheat he produces. Forde and Douglas summarize traditional economies as being characterized by

preoccupation with the daily and seasonal food supply, limitation of transport, difficulties of storage, overdependence on one or two major resources. These restrictions derive mainly from a low level of technical knowledge, which severely limits productive capacity. . . . The economic unit is small and, save for occasionally bartered specialities, does not transcend the population of a small village. Social relations are of the personal, face-to-face kind. Everyone has known everyone else from childhood, everyone is related to everyone else. The sick and unfortunate are able to depend on the kindliness of immediate neighbors. The sharing of tools and of supplies to meet individual shortages are matters of moral obligation between kinsfolk and neighbors. Impersonal commercial relations hardly exist. The group which lives and works together has strong feelings of solidarity, partly because they are isolated from other groups by poor communications.

The small size of the social group within which production is organized and exchange effected also reduces the opportunity for specialization. Such skills as are practiced are known to everyone of the appropriate age and sex . . . in the community. Certain kinds of work are traditionally assigned to men, others to women, but full-time specialists are very rare. The work of the potter, boatbuilder, smith, or magician is a voluntary spare-time task.

In such a setting economic relations have not been separated out from other social relations. There is no question of one man working for another whom he knows only as an employer. Men work together because they are related to each other, or have other social obligations to one another. Important economic processes are thus embedded in wider social needs, and are inextricably mixed with politics, ceremonial, and general festivity. . . . In an economy for which these general conditions hold true, economic exchange is necessarily limited. Markets remain undeveloped because the advantages of internal exchange are slight. The household provides for its daily needs from its own production. Surpluses cannot speedily be sent to areas of scarcity because of the difficulties of transport. . . . if the surplus is to be used at all, it must somehow be distributed at once, because of the technical difficulty of storage. As everyone produces much the same range of articles as everyone else, there will be little demand locally for any excess production. Often the only way an individual can dispose of a surplus is by holding a lavish feast or simply by giving it to kinsmen and neighbors who will feel bound to repay one day.[26]

ANALYTICAL CONCEPTS FOR NON-MARKET ECONOMIES

Thus far, we have described traditional African economies in non-technical terms. In the last ten years, anthropologists and a few economists have created

26. Daryll Forde and Mary Douglas, "Primitive Economics," in *Man, Culture and Society,* ed. Harry Shapiro (New York: Oxford University Press, 1956), reprinted in Dalton, *Tribal and Peasant Economies.*

special concepts to analyze the preindustrial economies of Africa and else-where.[27] Just as the special conceptual vocabulary devised by economists—oligopoly, marginal productivity, elasticity of demand—allows for a more precise and systematic analysis of market economy, so too with the use of special ana-lytical concepts in the analysis of non-market economies.

It is useful to regard all economies as being composed of sectors or segments—domestic as compared to foreign trade sectors, agricultural as compared to industrial sectors, the public as compared to the private sector, and so on. Econ-omies are never of one piece; they are mixed in several senses. Even in our economy, in which market purchase and sale and the price mechanism so per-meate and integrate the system, a portion of goods and services is transacted differently: gift-giving on ceremonial occasions (Christmas, birthdays, wed-dings), obligatory military service (the draft), the free provision of elementary education (regardless of the taxes, if any, one pays) are obvious examples. We could summarize the mixture of modes of transaction in the U.S. economy by saying that market exchange is the dominant and integrative, but not the only, mode of transaction. It is dominant because the greater portion of the economy's total output is disposed of by market sale. It is integrative because the basic resource ingredients of labor, land, minerals, and technical equipment are channeled to production processes through market sale. In the U.S. economy, the gift-giving transactions that we shall call "reciprocity" are much smaller in amount. We may define them formally as two-way transfers (gifts and counter-gifts) of goods, money, and services induced by a social relationship between the gift partners. Fathers and sons exchange gifts at Christmas because of their kinship tie. The proper ratio of exchange, that is, an adequate return gift,[28] is determined by social criteria such as the closeness between the two, their age, and their status. A rich father who gave his six-year-old son a Christmas present costing fifty dollars is not enraged by receiving in return a two-dollar gift. The closeness of their kinship and their utterly different status sanction the unequal exchange. If the son were a prosperous man of forty and the father an impecu-nious man of eighty, the socially sanctioned ratio of exchange would be reversed. We shall call reciprocity a socioeconomic transactional mode because of its double dimension: material transfers induced by social relationships. And just as there are many variations of the general transactional mode we call market exchange, such as pure competition, oligopoly, and monopoly, so too there are varieties of reciprocal transactions.[29]

27. See Polanyi, Arensberg, and Pearson, *Trade and Market*; Marshall D. Sahlins, "The Sociology of Primitive Exchange," in *The Relevance of Models for Social Anthropology*, ed. M. Banton (London: Tavistock, 1965); Sahlins, *Tribesmen*; Bohannan and Dalton, *Markets in Africa*; Dalton, "Economic Theory and Primitive Society"; Dalton, "Tradi-tional Production"; and Dalton, *Primitive, Archaic, and Modern Economies*.
28. One indicator of adequacy of the return gift is that the social relationship (which induces the gift-giving) remains unimpaired.
29. See Sahlins, "Sociology of Primitive Exchange"; and Sahlins, *Tribesmen*.

Just as market exchange transactions occur in all phases of capitalist production, reciprocal transactions may occur in all phases of traditional African production. There are economies in which reciprocity is the dominant and integrative mode of transaction. This is especially so in societies lacking formal political organization.

"Redistribution" refers to upward and downward transactions between the political center and its village-level constituencies.[30] In chiefdoms and kingdoms, rank-and-file persons pay tribute, in the form of goods, labor, or military service, upward to the central political authority, which uses the receipts for its own maintenance and to provide public services, such as defense and religious ceremonies. Schapera has written with respect to southern Africa that,

> . . . by virtue of his official status as head of the tribe, he [a Bantu chief] also played an important part in the economic organization. . . . He received tribute from his people, both in kind and in labor. He was given a portion of every animal slaughtered or killed in the chase; the *lobola* [bridewealth] for his chief wife was paid by the members of the tribe; he had the right to call upon his subjects to perform certain tasks for him, such as building his huts or clearing the land for his wives' gardens; above all, he received fees for hearing cases and fines for misdemeanors, . . . all this accumulation of wealth by the chief was really made on behalf of the tribe. One quality which was always required of the chief was that he should be generous. He had to provide for the members of his tribe in times of necessity. If a man's crops failed he would look to the chief for assistance; the chief gave out his cattle to the poorer members of his tribe to herd for him, and allowed them to use the milk; he rewarded the services of his warriors by gifts of cattle; his subjects frequently visited him in his kraal and during their stay he fed and entertained them.[31]

In traditional Africa, the intimate connections between economy and social organization are also expressed in what anthropologists call "prestige economy" or, more accurately, prestige sectors or spheres of economy. These refer to a special set of valuables or "treasure items" (for example, cattle or blocks of camwood) which are highly prized and paid out in a special set of transactions (for example, bridewealth or bloodwealth) involving honorable fulfillment of obligations, social status, prerogatives, and rank. These treasure items and the social situations in which they serve as necessary means of reciprocal payment are charged with emotion and moral fervor. They are symbols in the sense that in our culture wedding rings, sports trophies, military medals, family heirlooms, and crown jewels are symbols. They play socioeconomic roles, however, that have no close counterparts in Western societies. They are, indeed, a kind of "social money" for a circumscribed set of reciprocal transactions in the prestige

30. Polanyi, Arensberg, and Pearson, *Trade and Market,* Chap. 13.
31. Isaac Schapera, "Economic Changes in South African Native Life," *Africa,* I (1928), 175, reprinted in Dalton, *Tribal and Peasant Economies.*

sector.[32] The conditions under which an individual acquires and pays out treasure items — the permissible transactional situations — are carefully prescribed in non-market economies. They form a superior sector or sphere of exchange when contrasted with ordinary subsistence goods and the permissible modes of acquiring and exchanging them.

EUROPEAN INFLUENCE ON AFRICAN DEVELOPMENT

Each period of African history is marked by different sorts of social change. Current social-science research, however, has concentrated more on the kinds of change presently under way in the brief period since political independence than on the events of pre-colonial and colonial Africa.

In pre-colonial Africa, the important changes experienced were principally of the sorts experienced in preindustrial Europe. Ravages of nature, such as epidemic disease, decimated peoples or the plant and animal life upon which they depended. People moved in Africa, as they did in Europe, in response to physical decimation. So too with man-made ravages, such as slave-trading, wars, and their consequent military and political subjugations. Kingdoms rose and fell in Africa as they did in Europe.[33] And, as in Europe, portions of Africa were also converted to new religions, and foreign traders brought new goods and foodstuffs from other continents. For Europeans to have regarded pre-colonial Africa as dark, stagnant, or static was merely an indication of ignorance of African archaeology and history.

With the period of European colonization, some different kinds of change came about. Where enclaves of ordinary Englishmen, Dutchmen, and Portuguese were planted, as they were in eastern and southern Africa, bits of European economy, polity, and culture were transferred. Black Africans in these areas were employed on the periphery of European life and culture as agricultural, commercial, and industrial workers and as household servants.[34] In most of Africa, however, the Europeans were present not as enclaves of private farmers or merchants, but in much smaller numbers as colonial administrators, missionaries, and teachers, and as individual, and frequently isolated, managers

---

32. George Dalton, "Primitive Money," *American Anthropologist*, LXVII (1965), 44–65; see also Mary Douglas, "Raffia Cloth Distribution in the Lele Economy," *Africa*, XXVIII (1958), 109–22, reprinted in Dalton, *Tribal and Peasant Economies;* and Mary Douglas, "Primitive Rationing: A Study in Controlled Exchange," in Firth, *Themes in Economic Anthropology.*

33. See Jan Vansina, *Kingdoms of the Savanna* (Madison: University of Wisconsin Press, 1966).

34. Schapera, "Economic Changes in South African Native Life."

and technicians of plantations and mines in an otherwise all-black setting.[35] For most of colonially administered Africa without permanently settled European enclaves, the changes induced were slow and piecemeal.[36]

A frequent pattern of sequential change during the colonial period might be called "cash income growth without development."[37] Many forces worked in the same direction to propel Africans into earning cash income by selling wage-labor and cash crops. Colonial regimes put an end to tribal warfare and provided public health services, thereby reducing death rates; population growth created land shortages where traditional agricultural technology remained unchanged. One response to the land shortages was to grow cash crops and sell wage-labor.[38] The need to pay colonial taxes in cash and the attraction to Western merchandise and services such as education (which required a cash outlay) similarly propelled Africans into cash-earning activities. In retrospect, these were the beginnings of that massive set of long-run changes required for economic development and modernization.[39]

THE STUDY OF ECONOMIC CHANGE
AND DEVELOPMENT AT THE VILLAGE LEVEL

Politically independent Africa is barely fifteen years old, but it has generated intense awareness of Africa and great interest in its past, present, and future. Increasing numbers of economists, sociologists, political scientists, psychologists, geographers, and historians have joined the anthropologists in doing field work and other research on traditional and modernizing Africa.

Just as several of the social sciences have converging interests in the processes and problems of transforming the newly independent national economies and societies of Africa—what the economists call macro-development and the political scientists call modernization—so too there are now converging interests in what we shall call micro-development, that is, processes and problems of socio-economic change at the local community level in present-day Africa.

The literature of micro-development is of two sorts: case studies of specific village-level communities based on field-work experience, and attempts at theoretical insights and generalizations relating to many small communities.

35. See Margery Perham, *Colonial Reckoning* (London: Fontana Books, 1963).
36. See George Dalton, "The Development of Subsistence and Peasant Economies in Africa," *International Social Science Journal*, XVI (1964), 378–89, reprinted in Dalton, *Tribal and Peasant Economies.*
37. See Dalton, "Theoretical Issues in Economic Anthropology."
38. See P. H. Gulliver, "The Evolution of Arusha Trade," in Bohannan and Dalton, *Markets in Africa.*
39. See Adelman and Morris, *Society, Politics, and Economic Development.*

The best of the specific case studies answer questions of theoretical interest and also provide insights of use to those who make policies for community development: What in traditional economy and society makes for receptivity or resistance to economic and technological innovations?[40] Under what impetus and in what sequence have African communities experienced economic and social change?[41] Once Africans have moved into new cash-earning activities, how have traditional social organization and culture changed?[42] Under what conditions has successful transition to cash-earning activities taken place?[43] Under what conditions has recent social and economic change induced novel sorts of conflict and malaise within communities?[44]

The theoretical literature is not based on any particular field-work experience but on many such published empirical studies. Gunnar Myrdal, applying an idea he found useful in his famous work on the American Negro, *An American Dilemma,* shows how the condition of underdevelopment (traditional societies) consists of an interlocking set of economic, technological, and sociocultural forces which he calls "cumulative causation."[45] Adelman and Morris show how these many forces can be measured, and which modernizing innovations are the most important in the different stages of transforming traditional economies.[46] In a quite remarkable application of psychonalytical theory, Everett Hagen shows how personality formation in traditional societies affects entrepreneurial initiative.[47] Neil Smelser shows that the new activities and institutions that comprise development and modernization generate similar processes of structural transformation and require new forms of social and economic integration.[48]

Ethnographic case studies of individual villages and tribal groups provide us with many good descriptive accounts of specific African economies. These first-hand accounts by anthropological fieldworkers frequently include descriptions of historical and recent change as well.[49] There are also some good descriptive

40. Douglas, "Lele Economy."
41. Schapera, "Economic Changes in South African Native Life"; and Robert Manners, "Land Use, Trade, and the Growth of Market Economy in Kipsigis Country," in Bohannan and Dalton, *Markets in Africa.*
42. Watson, *Tribal Cohesion*; and David Brokensha, *Social Change at Larteh, Ghana* (London: Oxford University Press, 1966).
43. Polly Hill, *Migrant Cocoa Farmers of Southern Ghana* (Cambridge: At the University Press, 1963); and John De Wilde, *Agricultural Development in Tropical Africa,* 2 vols. (Baltimore: Johns Hopkins Press, 1967).
44. M. A. Jaspen, "A Sociological Case Study: Communal Hostility to Imposed Social Change in South Africa," in *Approaches to Community Development,* ed. Phillips Roupp (The Hague: W. van Hoeve, 1953); and Gulliver, "Evolution of Arusha Trade."
45. *Rich Lands,* Chaps. 1–3.
46. *Society, Politics, and Economic Development.*
47. *On the Theory of Social Change.*
48. "Mechanisms of Change and Adjustment to Change," in *Industrialization and Society,* ed. B. F. Hoselitz and W. E. Moore (Paris: UNESCO, 1963), reprinted in Dalton, *Tribal and Peasant Economies.*
49. See Bohannan and Bohannan, *Tiv Economy*; Gulliver, "Evolution of Arusha Trade"; Watson, *Tribal Cohesion*; and Richards, *Land, Labour and Diet.*

summaries of the salient characteristics of traditional economy.[50] To these are being added analytical accounts which compare the organization and performance of traditional African economies with traditional economies elsewhere, and with developed industrial economies.[51]

We are only just beginning to analyze the organization and performance of preindustrial economies and the processes of their transformation in a comparative framework. Africa is particularly important for such comparative studies. For the Inca of Peru before the Spanish conquest, Aristotle's Greece, or a thirteenth-century English village, there are only the fragmentary accounts derived from historical documents. For Africa, there is a rich literature recording the firsthand field-work observations of trained social scientists. Compared to Asia and Latin America, Africa presently is at an earlier stage of transformation from traditional society, so that a great deal of information about early sequences of modernization is still attainable through field work. The size and diversity of Africa, moreover, mean that information on a great many specific matters relating to traditional as well as to modernizing economies can be provided by African studies. Old theoretical problems can be investigated, such as the conditions under which feudal institutions appear and disappear,[52] and new practical policies formulated, such as how to increase agricultural productivity.[53]

50. See Forde and Douglas, "Primitive Economics"; Beattie, *Other Cultures*; and Sahlins, *Tribesmen*.

51. See Polanyi, Arensberg, and Pearson, *Trade and Market*; Dalton, "Traditional Production"; and Dalton, "Theoretical Issues in Economic Anthropology."

52. See Jacques Maquet, *The Premise of Inequality in Ruanda* (London: Oxford University Press, 1961).

53. See De Wilde, *Agricultural Development*.

5

Language Systems and Literature

JACK BERRY

MULTILINGUALISM IN AFRICA

THE SINGLE MOST IMPRESSIVE LINGUISTIC FACT about Africa is surely its multi-lingualism, not only in the sense that the number of languages spoken is large but that in almost every community, certainly in every urban center, two or more languages exist in a kind of symbiosis, each bearing part of the communicative burden. Most urban Africans find it necessary to use more than one language regularly. The Federal Republic of Cameroon is an example, albeit an extreme one, of the linguistic complexity of the new African nations. In this relatively small state at least one hundred African vernaculars are spoken. The vehicular languages include two pidgins (one English-based, the other indigenous): pidgin English and Ewondo *populaire;* and five major indigenous lingua francas: Douala, Bulu-Yaounde, Mbum, Fulani, and Hausa. And there are two "official" or "national" languages: English and French.

We are still counting the languages spoken in Africa, but the figure usually given is eight hundred. This is certainly on the low side; one thousand might even be too conservative an estimate. This would represent at least one-fifth of the languages of the world. Very few of these African languages are major languages in the sense that they can claim even a million or more speakers. Most of them are unwritten, only superficially studied, if at all, and certainly not susceptible as yet to being catalogued with any precision.

Why Africa should be the most multilingual area in the world is a challenging question which can only be answered by conjecture. In the known historical cases of language imposition or change, multilingualism in an area often seems to have favored the extension of a single language over that area, usually in a period of administrative and economic domination following military conquest. Acceptance of an imposed language usually starts with its use by an elite who function as intermediaries between the subject people and their conquerors. The new language then gradually filters down through the mass of the population.

This type of language spread is characteristic of Africa during the colonial period. But lingua francas existed in Africa in the pre-colonial period, and they too spread in very much the same way. The large Muslim empires were always ruled by an elite from a particular ethnolinguistic group. The expansion of internal and external trade tended to favor traders of the dominant group, and it thus became expedient for others to learn their language in order to carry on trade. The widespread use of Malinke and Hausa over an extensive area of West Africa today is no doubt due to the linguistic dominance of the former in Mali and of the latter in Sokoto and Gwandu.[1]

The "opening-up" of Africa in colonial times created even more favorable conditions for the spread of lingua francas, but also introduced the European languages as competitors. Certainly the expansion of Hausa in West Africa and Swahili in East Africa during the last century owes something to the suppression of interethnic warfare and the establishment of rail and road communications in the colonial and post-colonial periods. But these languages might well have extended themselves further and faster had they not been confronted by the spread of European languages in addition to the changed political pattern brought about by the colonial powers.

Lingua francas are by definition second languages, and despite the proliferation of these languages and their rapid and extensive spread in Africa under the impact of Westernization, there are very few instances of a people giving up their mother tongue in favor of a lingua franca, however insignificant their own language may be and however useful the lingua franca. Stable bilingualism is a characteristic condition in Africa, and in places it is known to have endured for centuries. Language attitudes (about which all too little is known either in Africa or generally) are undoubtedly important factors in the perpetuation of multilingualism. The ethnic language is connected with a sense of group identity and loyalty to traditional ways and ancestors; the lingua franca, which is more widely understood, is useful and is often the linguistic avenue to material success. Language loyalties remain strong in Africa, and concern for the mother tongue and what it represents appears to outweigh the inconveniences of multilingualism.

Planners who see linguistic unity as essential for the economic advancement of newly emergent states in Africa, and politicians who would encourage it in the interest of nationhood, are basically unrealistic if they believe that linguistic unity can be achieved in anything like the foreseeable future. On the existing evidence, few of Africa's hundreds of languages are in any real danger of

---

1. Joseph H. Greenberg, "Urbanism, Migration, and Language," in *Urbanization and Migration in West Africa*, ed. Hilda Kuper (Berkeley and Los Angeles: University of California Press, 1965), pp. 50–59.

extinction. Where there is failure to impose a single language in a community, diglossia (a special type of bilingualism) usually results and is often institution-alized, as in the Islamized empires of the Western Sudan.[2] In the Mali Empire of the thirteenth to sixteenth centuries, for example, it seems that the subjected peoples continued to use their own languages for intragroup communication, but used Malinke, the language of an elite, for communication with their rulers. Arabic, the sacred language of the state, was the language of external affairs.

In communities where more than one language is spoken, not all languages have the same range of uses. Different social relations are expressed in different languages, and certain social functions may call for the use of particular lan-guages. Some languages are rarely written and speakers of these languages must therefore use another language for their correspondence. Topics may determine a language preference. In these sorts of multilingual communi-ties, speakers change languages much as monolingual speakers change styles, using the one that is considered most appropriate in a given situation. In Ghana, for example, a middle-class Ghanaian whose mother tongue is, say, Gā, will certainly use that language with Gā-speaking intimates and within his family circle. He is likely, however, to address inferiors, such as watchmen and ser-vants, especially if they are from northern Ghana, in Twi, however badly he or they may speak that language. In other contexts which are interpreted as "mod-ern," or if the servants to whom he is speaking come from outside Ghana, es-pecially from Nigeria, he may use "Kru" (or pidgin) English. Certainly on most formal occasions he will judge standard English to be the appropriate language in which to address mixed groups. Most of his correspondence, too, however intimate, will be in English, though he will have learned to read and write Gā in school.

LANGUAGE CLASSIFICATION IN AFRICA

Confronted with the extreme linguistic diversity of Africa, it is understand-able that language classification has occupied an important position within the field of African linguistics. Furthermore, African linguistic classifications have attracted great attention from other disciplines, particularly history and anthro-pology, because of the insights they provide into patterns of ethnic interaction, population migration, and culture contact.

Since Bantu languages cover a greater proportion of sub-Saharan Africa than any other group of similarly related languages, it is not surprising that Bantu

2. Charles A. Ferguson, "Diglossia," *Word*, XV (1959), 325–40.

has been a primary focus of African linguistic research. The essential unity of the Bantu languages was recognized at an early date. It is generally thought to have been noted first by Lichtenstein in 1808 in a paper which suggested a division of the languages of southern Africa into two groups: Kaffir (i.e., Bantu) languages and Hottentot. Subsequent classifications of African languages added three more families to the Bantu: the Sudanic, Hamito-Semitic (of which the Hottentot languages were thought to be part), and Bushman.[3] This fourfold classification of the languages of sub-Saharan Africa was generally accepted until the late 1940s.

In 1949 and 1950, Joseph H. Greenberg published a series of articles with the general title of "Studies in African Linguistic Classification."[4] In these articles Greenberg presented what purported to be a new and comprehensive "genetic classification" of all African languages. That is, this classification not only grouped languages, but also sought to trace their historical origins and development. In fact, he addressed himself primarily to two major problems.

The first problem was the theory of the Hamitic group of languages which Carl Meinhof had put forward in 1912 in his *Die Sprachen der Hamiten*. Meinhof's theory, in fact, had very few adherents by the time Greenberg published his attack; the theory had already been subjected to severe and basically sound criticism by Drexel in the early 1920s. Meinhof's views, briefly, were that the Hamitic languages in present-day Africa were represented in their "purest" and oldest form by the Fulani language, and further that the Bantu languages had descended from an admixture of a language such as Fulani with a Western Sudanic one. Hottentot, which some authorities had grouped with Bushman because of its "clicks," and which others thought to be Hamito-Semitic because of the presence of a masculine-feminine distinction in its nouns and pronouns, was, for Meinhof, a Hamitic language strongly influenced by Bushman. Similarly, Masai was typologically Hamitic, heavily influenced by Eastern Sudanic languages.

Greenberg rejected entirely Meinhof's notion of Hamitic. He brought Semitic, Egyptian, Berber, Cushitic, and Chadic together into a single higher-level grouping which he called Afro-Asiatic. In the Greenberg analysis (see map on page 84) Fulani was shown conclusively to be related to Wolof, Serer, and Biafada (as Mlle Homburger had suggested years earlier), and it was therefore

3. The most influential of these language classifications are those of Carl Meinhof and Diedrich Westermann. Alice Werner provided a popular and readable account of Meinhof's and Westermann's theories in *The Language Families of Africa*, 2d ed. (London: Kegan Paul, Trench, Trübner, 1925). For earlier views about African languages, R. N. Cust, *A Sketch of the Modern Languages of Africa*, 2 vols. (London: Trübner, 1883) should be consulted.

4. *Southwest Journal of Anthropology*, V (1949), 79–100, 190–98, 309–17; *ibid.*, VI (1950), 47–63, 143–60, 223–37, 388–98; *ibid.*, X (1954), 405–15; reprinted as *Studies in African Linguistic Classification* (New York: Viking Press, Compass Books, 1955).

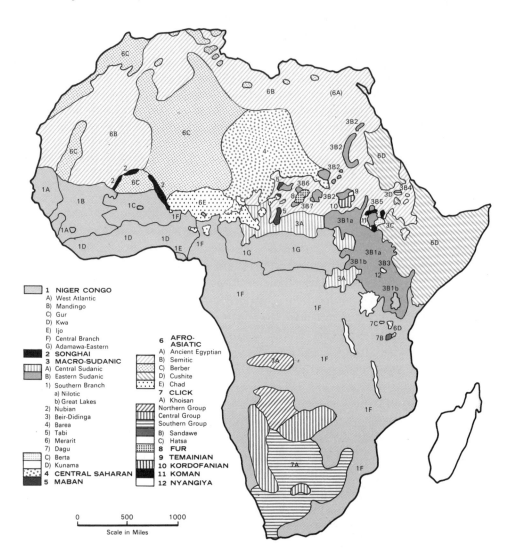

CLASSIFICATION OF AFRICAN LANGUAGES: GREENBERG, 1955
After Joseph H. Greenberg in *Studies in Linguistic Classification*, 1955.

as much a Western Sudanic language as the others. Masai was returned to Eastern Sudanic and Hottentot was put back with Bushman and a few other languages in groupings first labeled "click" and later "Khoisan."

Greenberg secondly, and more importantly, addressed himself to a problem propounded by Diedrich Westermann, who in his studies of what he called the Western Sudanic languages had suggested that these languages were related, albeit distantly, to the Bantu group. Greenberg accepted the proposed linkage but restated it as a much more recent and closer relationship. The Bantu languages were now seen as an offshoot of a subgroup within Western Sudanic itself. This was undoubtedly one of the most controversial parts of Greenberg's otherwise fairly conservative classification. Two other controversial points were his Khoisan grouping and his subsumption of the so-called Nilo-Hamitic and Nilotic languages under a single family.

Greenberg's articles occasioned a considerable amount of controversy when they first appeared. In retrospect it seems that in Europe at least, where the articles were not at first well received, the adverse reaction was due as much to the somewhat intemperate language in which Greenberg made his case and to the uncritical accceptance with which American scholars in other fields heralded his work as it was to. any serious misgivings about his hypotheses. Greenberg's recent reduction of the number of postulated independent language families from sixteen to four (see map on page 86) is a more radical and consequently more controversial formulation.[5]

There is, however, a basic difference of opinion about language classification involved in the lessened but continuing debates over his work. In traditional comparative linguistic practice, the only acceptable proof of cognation (genetic relationship) is the establishment of precise sound correspondences. Greenberg, however, has used the techniques of "mass comparison"; that is, he has long lists of putative cognates (words thought to have a common root) among languages for which he claims an interrelationship, but nowhere does he advance the types of regular phonological transformation rules that would satisfy some critics. Until such time as these processes of transformation are fully elucidated, Greenberg's claims will continue to be regarded by some linguists as merely speculative hypotheses.

In an area of language comparison where the traditional methods are especially productive, Greenberg's neglect of them has seemed all the more reprehensible to his critics. The chief critic, and the only one to offer a serious alternative to Greenberg's hypothesis concerning the relationship which obtains between the Bantu languages and those of West Africa, is the Bantuist, Malcolm Guthrie. In a well-known article, Guthrie asks whether the features that appear to be common to West African languages and Bantu languages display the same regularity of correspondence as that found within the Bantu language family itself.[6] He finds that they do not and concludes, therefore, that the Bantuisms in West African languages are due to the incorporation of Bantu features into languages of quite distinct origin.

Greenberg's cognate lists (similar forms with much the same meaning) are impressive, but it is doubtful whether it will be possible to establish correspondences between items in the Niger-Congo group with the regularity that is such a feature of the Bantu languages. Certainly a great deal more work will be needed. Meanwhile, for those linguists who take an "operational" view of

5. Joseph H. Greenberg, *The Languages of Africa* (Bloomington, Ind.: Indiana University Press, 1963).

6. Malcolm Guthrie, "Bantu Origins: A Tentative New Hypothesis," *Journal of African Languages*, I (1962), 9–21.

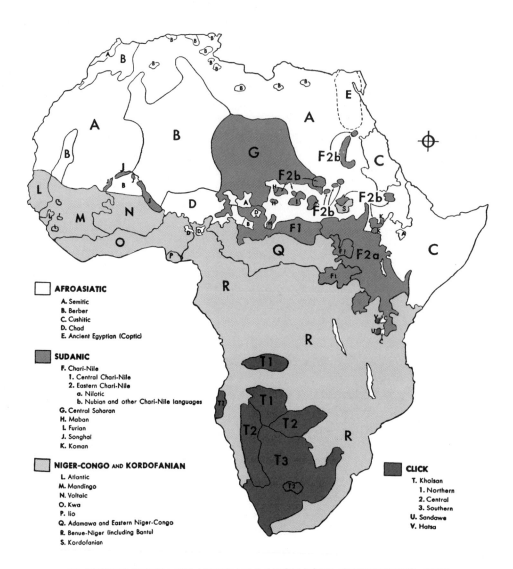

CLASSIFICATION OF AFRICAN LANGUAGES: GREENBERG, 1963
From *Collier's Encyclopedia*, Vol. 1, 1966. Used with permission of Crowell-Collier Educational Corporation.

language comparison,[7] explanations of structural resemblance in terms of "borrowing" or "common descent" or quite simply "chance" are all equally irrelevant. It is to historians and students of social change that Greenberg's classification is most likely to appeal, since it is the first and as yet the only complete genetic

7. An explanation of "operational" may be found in Jack Berry, "Structural Affinities of the Volta River Languages and Their Importance for Linguistic Classification" (University of London, 1952).

classification of African languages and one which can seemingly offer corroborative linguistic evidence in support of non-linguistic hypotheses regarding population origins, migrations, and interactions.

THE CHARACTERISTICS OF AFRICAN LANGUAGES

The question of strict genetic relationship aside, it is true that the languages of Africa show many striking resemblances in structure and idiom. In moving from one language to another which need not be related in any conventional sense of the term, the linguist frequently experiences the most lively feeling of *déjà vu*. There are, for example, some sounds which are common in African languages but not elsewhere. The "clicks" of southern Africa and parts of eastern Africa are only found there, and the labiovelars (that is, sounds produced through combined use of the lips and the soft palate, as in the sounds *gb* or *kp*), so widely spread throughout the languages of the Western Sudan, have not been reported from outside Africa except in one insignificant instance.

The structure of words in African languages is such that they frequently end in a vowel or a nasal consonant and often begin with a nasal or combination of nasal consonants. Almost every one of the languages spoken south of the Sahara is tonal, using pitch distinctions to differentiate words in much the same way as most European languages use stress.

Certain grammatical constructions are typically African (though not exclusively so). True adjective constructions are rarer than in European languages; constructions with so-called adjectival verbs or with abstract nouns are used to express the same concepts as the European adjective. Thus, for "I am hungry," the equivalent expression in many African languages would be something like "hunger holds me." In West African pidgin or creole English the phrase is, in fact, exactly that: "hungry catch me." Similarly, phrases corresponding to "it is black or red or tall or short" would be verbal predicates in many African languages, as if we were to say in English "it blacks, reds, talls, or shorts."

Comparison is nearly everywhere expressed by means of the verb "to surpass," so that the word-for-word translation of an African equivalent for "I am bigger than he is" would read "I am big surpass him" or perhaps "I surpass him as to size."

Though reduplication is by no means exclusively an African feature, it is so very common in African languages that it perhaps deserves some mention here. It is used to form plurals of nouns and verbs and in the formation of adverbial and other constructions. For instance, to say "come immediately!" in Hausa, one would say, literally, "come now-now!" Reduplication is especially a feature of the characteristically African "ideophone," or *lautbild* as the German scholars called it (that is, a sound which suggests the meaning of the word, as in "squish").

In the Bantu languages, an elaborate system of noun classes functions in much the way that gender does in European languages. Thus in Swahili the noun for "shoe" belongs to a class which is marked by the prefix *vi-* in the plural, and so in accordance with a system of agreements which functions throughout the phrase "all my shoes are red," the words dependent grammatically on "shoe" also take the *vi-* prefix: *viatu vyote vyangu viko vye vikundu.* Similarly, the same root noun is modified in meaning by prefixes associated with different noun classes. For example, the Baganda (singular: Muganda) are a people who occupy the area north and west of Lake Victoria in East Africa, an area which they call Buganda in their language, Luganda. The name of the modern state in which the Baganda are located is Uganda, the Swahili form for Buganda.

Resemblances in idiom are less easy to state precisely, but the use of words for body parts to denote spatial relationships is very common, as is the use of a locative verb with the meaning "to have" and the use of "child" to indicate a diminutive. The range of different meanings associated with single words parallel each other in many languages, so that "eat," "win," and "conquer" are expressed by the same verb, and "to hear" may also mean "to understand," "to feel," and "to perceive."

Linguists differ in the importance they attach to these similarities, and as to whether they require explanation and, if so, in what terms. Unrelated languages that have a good many characteristics, words, and idioms in common elsewhere in the world are sometimes said to form a linguistic union (*sprachbund*). The half-dozen languages spoken in the Balkan Peninsula are interesting in this respect, and the Balkanist linguists have done much to develop *sprachbund* theory.[8] Linguistic unions, they hold, are as real as language families, but are due to causes other than common descent: to the same substratum, for example, or to reciprocal influences, or to a common civilization and religion. In the case of Africa, as Westermann suggests, wholesale borrowing over an extended period of time has been a significant factor.

WRITTEN LANGUAGES IN AFRICA

Relatively few of Africa's many languages can be said to have a written tradition. Those languages that have a well-established writing system in daily use by the community, or at least the literate sections of it, are likely for the most part to have acquired it only in the quite recent past, and the system itself is most probably based on the Roman alphabet or on some adaptation of it such as the Africa script recommended by the International African Institute.

8. Greenberg has examined Africa in terms of *sprachbund* theory in "Africa as a Linguistic Area," in *Continuity and Change in African Cultures,* ed. W. R. Bascom and M. J. Herskovits (Chicago: University of Chicago Press, 1958), pp. 15–27.

There are exceptions to these statements. There are a few languages with a long tradition of writing and which employ scripts other than the Roman. The Arabic script has been applied to a number of African languages, sometimes in special versions like the *ajami* script of the Western Sudan. (Technically, *ajami* refers to any language other than Arabic which is written in Arabic script.) Swahili, Hausa, Kanuri, and Bambara-Malinke, for example, have all been written at one time or another in Arabic script. In nearly every case, however, the Arabic has now been replaced or supplemented by the more adaptable Roman alphabet. The Ethiopic, a Semitic script of respectable antiquity, is still used to write Geᶜez, Amharic, and Tigrinya, and the Greek alphabet in modified form was used for Coptic and Old Nubian.

Over and above all these "imported" scripts, Africa has a few indigenous examples of written languages. Somali is unofficially, but widely, written in the so-called Osmania script invented by Ismadu Yusuf Keradid. The Vai script, a syllabary (that is, a set of characters, each of which denotes a syllable rather than a single sound) devised by Momadu Bukele in the 1830s, is still very popular in Liberia and is used by Vais, generally in informal correspondence. At least four neighboring West African languages, Mende, Loma, Kpelle, and Bassa, have recently acquired similar scripts which undoubtedly owe something to the Vai inspiration.[9] These latter are syllabaries, but in 1936 a true alphabetic script was discovered by Adams among the Efik in southeastern Nigeria where it was used in writing the secret language of a religious sect.[10] Better known, perhaps, and better studied is the Bamum script invented by King Njoya of southern Cameroon. Originally conceived as a logographic system (that is, with symbols representing words or groups of words), it was gradually changed by successive royal decrees first to a syllabary and later to a true alphabet.[11]

TRADITIONAL AFRICAN LITERATURE:
ORAL AND WRITTEN

To say that most African languages are still unwritten is not at all to say that there is no African literature. On the contrary, all African peoples have within the basic corpus of their oral traditions some which deserve to be considered literature or verbal art, if only because they show a concern for forms of expression beyond that of the casual language of everyday communication. These

9. See David Dalby, "A Survey of Indigenous Scripts of Liberia and Sierra Leone: Vai, Mende, Loma, Kpelle and Bassa," *African Language Studies*, VIII (1967), 1–51.
10. See R. F. G. Adams, "Oberi Ɔkaimɛ: A New African Language and Script," *Africa*, VII (1947), 24–34.
11. See, for example, Idelette Dugast and M. D. W. Jeffreys, *L'Ecriture des Bamum* (Dakar: L'Institut Français d'Afrique Noire, 1950).

forms of expression are recognized indigenously as "art" and are characteristically designated as such by formal stylistic devices as well as by other indications
of design.[12]

Poetry in verse is, for the most part, restricted to the Islamized peoples of
Africa: the Fulani and Hausa in the West, the Swahili in the East, and the
Nubians and Berbers in the North. Among some of these peoples there exists
a learned poetry which employs verse patterned after classical Arabic forms.
This exists side by side with popular poetry, composed and recited in the traditional African style. In much of Africa the poetic traditions of its peoples are
contained in song, but not all song-texts constitute literature in any sense of
the term. The songs, for example, which intersperse prose narrative (cant-fable
is everywhere used as an effective means to enliven the performance of racon-
teurs) are largely composed of nonsense-words and have interest only for their
rhythmic or prosodic content. On the other hand, much of what is sung in Africa
can be called, without violence to traditional terminology, lyric, or melic, poetry.

Sometimes sung; sometimes recited, and found everywhere in Africa are
praise-poems. These are of such importance in the poetry of African peoples
that they are usually treated as a separate genre. Praise-poems are composed
not only about kings, chiefs, headmen, famous warriors, and other prominent
individuals, but also about ordinary people. There are praise-poems about
ethnic groups and their subdivisions; about animals, both wild and domestic;
about plants, trees, crops, rivers, hills, and other natural features; about clothing; and even about railways and bicycles!

In some societies the composition of praise-poems was originally a task imposed on all boys going through the initiation rites preceding the creation of
an age-set, and every well-brought-up adult was able to compose and recite
a respectable eulogy on appropriate occasions. The composition of praise-poems
is also in some societies the business of professional bards who not only recite
their own compositions but declaim the traditional poems which have come
down from earlier times.

Prose-narratives, both fictional and non-fictional, are part of the cultural
tradition of all African peoples. The latter category includes historical tales
(that is, official traditions aimed at recording the history of ethnic groups,
lineages, clans, and families) and myths which have an essentially religious or
didactic character. Folktales, on the other hand, are fiction. Their main purpose
is to amuse the listener, though rather frequently they contain a moralizing or
didactic element which may be summarized for the audience in the form of a
concluding proverb.

By far the best documented of African prose-narratives are the animal trick-

12. For an introduction to African oral literature, see Jack Berry, *Spoken Art in West
Africa* (London: Oxford University Press, 1961); and W. R. Bascom, "Folklore and
Literature," in *The African World: A Survey of Social Research*, ed. R. A. Lystad (New York:
Praeger, 1965), pp. 469–90.

ster tales, but in some areas human tricksters like Yo, and trickster deities like Legba of the Dahomey cycle recorded by Herskovits, are almost as important. Not all tales have tricksters. There are tales of ogres, witches, and werewolves; of children, especially of twins and orphans; and of children-who-are-born-to-die. Some tales are told simply to pose a problem to the audience and end unfinished with a question.

Intimately connected with narrative forms, often as integral parts of them, are the two other major genres of African oral literature: the proverb and the riddle. The importance of the proverb in Africa cannot be exaggerated. As is well known, proverbs enter into almost every form of interaction. They are also used as literary devices for thematic statement in poetry and in heightened or elegant prose. Riddles are equally widespread, but they have not received the attention of scholars to the same extent as proverbs. Their primary purpose is of course to amuse, but this apart, they serve almost as many and varied functions in African societies as do proverbs. They are often used in greetings and nicknames, in informal education to train the memory of children and to sharpen their wits, and as a form of indirect abuse. They are even used in some societies as a kind of alarm; a feature of riddles among the Chagga (Tanzania) is that they may be sung to warn others of imminent danger.

Of the written literature of Africa, not all is of recent origin or of European derivation. The literature of Ethiopia, for example, consists of writing in Ge'ez, which is classical Ethiopic, and in Amharic, the vernacular that replaced Ge'ez and is now the official language of Ethiopia. The earliest known manuscripts in Ge'ez date from the fourteenth century, though the oldest compositions are certainly of a much earlier period. Amharic has been used for serious literary purposes for over four hundred years and today possesses a flourishing literature which includes plays, verse-dramas, history, biography, and a recent popular genre, the allegorical novel composed partly in prose and partly in verse.

In Nubian, documents of a religious nature, largely translations from Greek, date from the eighth century to the beginning of the fourteenth century and are of great interest because they are the only true evidence of an early language still spoken by Negroes in Africa.

The Swahili literary tradition goes back for more than three hundred years, and in this respect is without parallel among the Bantu-speaking peoples of East Africa. Its origins are in the Arabic writings that the Sayyid families brought with them when they settled in East Africa, especially the didactic and homiletic, that is, moralistic, verse and the popular tales of Islam. These compositions were later paraphrased into Swahili, often with an interlinear Arabic version in the text. The earliest Swahili manuscript known to scholars is the poem "Ntendi wa Tambuka," written in Pate (now in Kenya) for the Sultan Laiti Nabhani in A.D. 1728.

Elsewhere in sub-Saharan Africa, Islam produced at a relatively early date a literate elite which for the most part preferred Arabic as the medium of communication. The *Tarikh-es-Soudan* of Es-Sa'di, who was born in Timbuktu in A.D. 1596, is perhaps the best-known example of an early indigenous work of any considerable literary merit in Arabic. It is only one of many such works from the Western Sudan.

THE EUROPEAN INFLUENCE
ON AFRICAN LITERATURE

Such instances of earlier literatures apart, widespread writing by Africans cannot be said to have begun on any scale much before the middle of the last century. The assumption of responsibility for education, first by European missionary enterprises and later by the colonial governments, marked the beginnings of literacy in most of Africa. The different policies of the colonial powers toward African languages had differing effects on the literary output of Africans. The official British and Belgian educational policies assigned a place to African languages, both as a medium and as a subject of instruction. In sharp contrast, the French prescribed the exclusive use of French. As a result, French West Africa in the pre-independence period produced a whole new literature of its own in French. In British Africa, on the other hand, in the same period a meager output in English reflected all too often the neo-Victorian tastes of uninspired schoolmasters. Africans under the British were encouraged to participate in the reduction of their languages to writing and to translate European classics and describe their local customs and traditions in their own languages. This "literature of tutelage," as it has been called, contains few authors of stature. It belongs properly to the years before World War II and no longer exists, except in the Republic of South Africa.

In the former British territories of West Africa, the literary efforts of Africans since the 1950s have tended to be channeled into English forms, but in East and central Africa, the vernacular pamphlet still constitutes the bulk of published work. Swahili is the language most widely used, and, in addition to verse, some Swahili prose of real merit has appeared. Shaaban Robert of Tanga (Tanzania), for example, has written a biography, an autobiography, and several volumes of essays in Swahili—all of which have been well received.

The present situation in Africa, then, is one in which two literatures exist side by side: a written and an oral. Of the many questions such a situation poses, some can be answered with greater or less assurance now. Others at best must remain the subject of individual conjecture and hypothesis for many years to come. It seems reasonably certain, for example, that written literature will ultimately supersede the oral tradition, which may then be preserved as true folk literature.

What is less certain is whether English and French will continue to replace the vernacular languages as the media of creative writing. Faced with a choice of a vernacular or a world language in which to write, Africans over the past two decades have opted for the language which offered them the wider audience and perhaps the easier apprenticeship. But others before them have had the same decision to make, and not all have been willing to forego communication with the majority of their countrymen. Much may depend on the success which attends attempts like those of the Nigerian writers to "Africanize" their English (French attitudes being what they are, it is difficult to imagine anything of the kind happening in French).

But how much will the new writing in whatever language be influenced by the coexisting older oral styles? The traditions which seem so far to have most influenced younger African writers are often adopted in the literary language of their choice. There have been some fairly obvious attempts to use the devices of oral literature with differing degrees of success. The early South African writers, Mafolo and Plaatje especially, interspersed the prose of their novels with the songs and moralizing sentiments that are such a feature of the African storyteller's art; and Rabearivelo and Renaivo of Madagascar, even when writing in French, struggled to free themselves of French influence and patterned much of their poetry on the poetic dialogues long popular in their native land. Other African writers in French have occasionally cast their material in the traditional form of the folk tale, Dadie, Birago Diop, and Jean Malonga among them.

But the more subtle influences—perhaps the more important in the long run—are less easily identified. A disproportionate amount of scholarly attention is still being given to the new writing in Africa, but there are encouraging signs of a reawakening of interest in the oral composition.

LINGUISTICS AND THE STUDY OF AFRICA

The history of African linguistics is by no means a long one. The serious study of African languages goes back little more than a hundred years. And for a good part of that time, much of the work was done by foreign scholars, such as missionaries, administrators, and others not primarily interested in linguistic study for its own sake, but forced into offering some account of the languages with which they lived and worked. There are a few notable exceptions, but for the most part these accounts are, by today's standards, amateurish and inadequate.

It was not until the twentieth century that African languages claimed the attention of professional linguists in any significant numbers. These scholars brought a much needed technical expertise in such matters as tonal analysis and accurate phonetic description. In the years immediately following World

War II interest in African languages increased, first in London with the massive expansion of faculty at the School of Oriental and African Studies (as a direct result of the recommendations of the Earl of Scarborough's commission) and later, as independence for most of Africa became a real and immediate possibility, almost everywhere else. The United States under the National Defense Education Act and through government agencies like the Peace Corps has had a late, but enormous, influence on these studies. Before World War II the great names in African linguistics were for the most part German; now the field is truly international. There are larger and smaller centers of African linguistics in most capitals of Europe, in several universities in America, and, more importantly perhaps, in several of the newly independent African countries themselves. There are some impressive examples of recent international cooperation, as in journals, such as the *Journal of African Languages,* and in actual field surveys. The first such survey was the Linguistic Survey of the Northern Bantu Borderland, conducted under the auspices of the International African Institute in 1949. This was followed in 1956 by the West African Language Survey. Another, the Survey of Language Use and Language Teaching in East Africa, is still in progress. A cause for satisfaction in all these developments is the growing number of professional African linguists working on their own languages. There are areas of language description that ultimately only the native-speaker can hope to handle adequately, and it is usually in his own language that the linguist does his best work.

With the growing numbers of linguists professionally engaged in these studies it is reasonable to expect the development and application of theoretical linguistic insights from the African language field. Equally promising are the beginnings of interdisciplinary research in which linguists have begun to take a proper role alongside their colleagues in history, sociology, and other related disciplines.

One such area is the collection and study of African oral data. The historian working in pre-colonial African history must handle, even collect, his own oral data. The relevance of linguistics for such research is obvious. The historian Vansina, in *Oral Tradition,* has written:

> When one comes to study a testimony composed in the language of a people without writing, it often happens that no description of the language exists, or that, if there are any, they are not to be relied upon. In that case the research worker's first task will be to study the structure of the language before he can even begin to collect testimonies. This amounts to saying that a historian must either have had a fairly thorough linguistic training, or must work only among peoples whose language has been studied by a competent linguist. In any case, the historian must always indicate the linguistic studies on which the interpretation of his documents is based.[13]

13. Jan Vansina, *Oral Tradition: A Study in Historical Methodology,* trans. H. M. Wright (Chicago: Aldine, 1965), pp. 65–66.

Going on immediately to discuss "a second problem, that of knowing the exact meaning of words used in a testimony," Vansina seems to refer briefly (though not explicitly) to *situationstheorie* and to recommend the textual methodology first developed by the anthropologist Malinowski. In his *Coral Gardens and Their Magic*, Malinowski treats native words in perhaps the fullest cultural context of ethnographic description in English. These problems of definition and statement of meaning by translation are not, of course, peculiar to historical studies; they are crucial problems in most of the social sciences.

In addition to the contributions of linguistics in an applied or ancillary role, there are some historical questions of interest which linguists are uniquely equipped to handle. These include problems of dating. The much debated techniques of "glottochronology" have tried to provide answers to a whole range of problems in the historico-comparative field, from the establishment of specific languages no longer distinct, such as proto-Bantu, to a detailed consideration of the distribution and form of sets of terms (for example, those for food crops, crafts, domestic animals, and for politically significant terms like "chief").

The techniques of glottochronology are derived from two basic assumptions: (1) that there are certain situations and things for which all languages have a "basic vocabulary" of words; and (2) that the rate of change in this "basic vocabulary" is constant over long periods of time. Consequently it should be possible to compute the interval of separation between two documented but undated stages of a language by comparing the proportions of unchanged basic vocabulary or to compute the approximate date of a common ancestor by comparing the basic vocabularies of two or more related contemporary languages in order to estimate the most recent date at which they could have been identical.

The results of M. Swadesh's recent work on a number of West African languages are still to be published. Meanwhile there are two papers which apply glottochronology on a limited scale to Bantu problems.[14] This is, however, a controversial area, and there are many who would agree with the view of glottochronology recently expressed by Robert Hall:

> We are therefore justified in being cautious with regard to the degrees of relationship and the time perspectives which glottochronology may seem to indicate. There are too many possible variables entering into the situation; the structure of human speech as a whole (and especially that of lexicon, which is one of its most easily changeable parts) is too flexible to be as rigid in its rate of change as, say, an individual radioactive element. To arrive at even an approximately valid measurement of any aspect of linguistic change, we would have to have far more extensive and accurate data for a number of related languages, and over many more centuries, than there is any hope of our ever having. In all probability, any

14. See A. E. Meeussen, "Lexicostatick van Het Bantoe," *Kongo Overzee*, XII (1965), 86–89; and A. Couper, "Application de la Lexicostatique au Congo et au Ruande," *Aequatoria*, XIX (1956), 65–75.

hope of being able to apply valid statistical techniques to the measurement of linguistic change is illusory, and had best be abandoned; our best approach to language history is still through comparative reconstruction, which does not depend on arithmetical or mathematical measurement of any kind.[15]

Place and clan names are also matters for linguistic investigation. The author has examined some putative principles of onomastic (place name) investigation in languages with little or no recorded history,[16] and there are papers by Stevens and Tait along similar lines. As Professor Kuper has recently pointed out, "A historian who uses language as evidence of diffusion or borrowing requires the assistance of both the formal linguist and the sociolinguist."[17]

The body of oral traditions belonging to an African people is important to the historian who sees these traditions as unwritten history. Yet, as mentioned above, much of what the historian collects for his own purposes will be regarded by others as unwritten literature or spoken art. J. H. Nketia has shown very clearly in *The Funeral Dirges of the Akan People* what can be expected when the texts of traditional verbal art are subjected to a stylistic analysis which uses the established techniques of linguistic description.[18] As yet few scholars have followed Nketia's example, but a number of recent papers promise exciting insights into the non-casual language of various African peoples.[19]

It requires little effort to extend almost indefinitely the range of topics on which the African linguist could potentially contribute. Linguistic considerations enter into the description and analysis not only of individual and folk styles in unwritten literature but of the differences between the prose and non-prose forms of a language, the use of a language in song, especially in respect to the relation between musical and lingual pitch patterns (where the language is tonal), and in a variety of other ways. As yet only small beginnings have been made to implement these potentialities.[20]

The areas of interdisciplinary effort so far mentioned have involved "pure" linguistics. Equally exciting, and interdisciplinary in nature, is the study of

15. R. A. Hall, Jr., *Introductory Linguistics* (Philadelphia: Chilton Book Co., 1964), p. 392.

16. Jack Berry, *Place Names of Ghana* (London: School of Oriental and African Languages, 1960); and Jack Berry, "Some Preliminary Notes on Ada Personal Nomenclature," *African Language Studies*, I (1960), 177–84.

17. Kuper, *Urbanization and Migration in West Africa*, p. 7.

18. (Legon: Achimota, University Bookshop, 1955).

19. See, for example, C. L. Laloum and Gilbert Rouget, "La Musique de deux chants liturgiques Yoruba," *Journal de la Société des Africanistes*, XXXV–XXXVI (1965–66), 109–39; and Rouget, "Notes et documents pour service à l'étude de la musique Yoruba," *ibid.*, 67–107.

20. See, for example, Berry, *Spoken Art in West Africa*; and Jack Berry, ed., "Transactions of a Conference on the Teaching of African Languages and Literatures," mimeographed (Evanston: Northwestern University, 1966).

sociolinguistics. Joseph Greenberg has indicated the scope of this field and its relevance to African studies in general in his contribution to Robert A. Lystad's *The African World:* the relation of language differences to social class, the differential social roles of languages coexisting in the same society, the development and spread of lingua francas as auxiliary languages in multilingual situations, the factors involved in the differential prestige ratings of languages, the role of languages as a sign of ethnic identification, language in relation to nationalism, and problems of language policy, for example, in education.[21] There is also a more specific and detailed statement by Berry and Greenberg in a recent issue of the *African Studies Bulletin.*[22]

The relevance of sociolinguistic inquiry to the many practical problems confronting the emerging African states is immediate and obvious. In general, the linguistic communication system is an overall factor in economic development, and in the area of political action the often distressing discrepancy between stated official policy and national behavior may have its origins in language and translation. In modern African societies, ideologies have replaced myths as the means by which institutions and political actions are sanctioned, but the ideologies are framed largely in English or French. They are thus intelligible to only a limited elite.

There is growing acceptance in Africa that simple solutions to language problems are at best unrealistic. Multilingualism is a fact with which the majority of Africans are willing to learn to live, even in their newly Westernized world. In this world, both in school and in later life, the vernacular languages have a place. Indeed, from the viewpoint of national mobilization and development, the vernaculars are dismissed only at considerable cost. Thus, Karl Deutsch has said:

> Disclaiming native languages as mere "vernaculars" is fraught with many costs. These costs include some educational retardation; forcing all children through a language barrier for their access to education; making linguistic and verbal aptitude a crucial test in the selection of scientists and engineers, and thereby sacrificing a substantial part of the nation's potential technical and scientific talent; reducing appreciably the reading speeds and comprehension scores of at least a part of the personnel forced to work in a language which is not native to them; and the less readily calculable but not negligible damage done to the self-image, self-esteem and sense of identity of at least some part of the population.[23]

21. Joseph H. Greenberg, "Linguistics," in Lystad, *The African World,* pp. 416–41.
22. Jack Berry and Joseph H. Greenberg, "Sociolinguistic Research in Africa," *African Studies Bulletin,* IX (September, 1966), 1–9.
23. Karl Deutsch, "Conditions for the Spread of Interregional Languages: The Experience of Medieval Europe," in *Language Problems of Developing Nations,* ed. Joshua A. Fishman, Charles A. Ferguson, and Jyotirindra Da Gupta (New York: Social Science Research Council, 1968).

Once there is acceptance of the fact that the vernacular languages have a proper and important role in the life of a nation, the problems of standardization and modernization assume a new dimension. In all these problems of language engineering, cooperation between linguists and other social scientists is clearly required.[24]

24. An early account of problems connected with the use of African languages in education and their standardization and modernization is Jack Berry, "Problems in the Use of African Languages and Dialects in Education," in *African Languages and English in Education* (Paris: UNESCO, Educational Clearing House, 1953). Two conferences on multilingualism in Africa have published their proceedings and provide useful, if somewhat technical, introductions to the subject: Papers of the Leverhulme Conference on Universities and the Language Problems of Tropical Africa, published as *Language in Africa*, ed. John Spencer (Cambridge: At the University Press, 1963); and *Symposium on Multilingualism* (Brazzaville: Committee for Technical Cooperation in Africa South of the Sahara, 1963).

6

Conceptual Systems
in Africa

ETHEL M. ALBERT

IN THE MIDST OF RAPID CHANGE in politics and economics, conceptual systems are not likely to be a central concern. Anthropological field-work conditions are hardly favorable for lengthy philosophical discussions. Governments are preoccupied with more practical matters. Looking back over the past ten years of African research we find a diminution, at least proportionally, of studies of conceptual systems. The idiom employed in most descriptions of African conceptual systems or their component parts, moreover, is far from flattering. A precondition of demonstrating the utility, theoretical and practical, of studies of conceptual systems in Africa and elsewhere is a thoroughgoing review of objectives and theories.

A *conceptual system* is a pattern of beliefs and values that defines a way of life and the world in which men act, judge, decide, and solve problems. Equivalent terms include world view, philosophy, and beliefs and values. It is assumed here that in each culture—as distinct from each nation or society—reality is distinctively conceptualized in implicit and explicit premises and derivative generalizations and that a conceptual system is as distinctive of a culture as its language, its institutions, and its customs—and as subject to change.

When we speak of African conceptual systems, we refer perforce to a large and varied assemblage. Not enough is known to permit anything but vague generalizations about the continent as a whole. Literary necessity justifies employing the general word "African" for a particular ethnic group whose concepts we wish to describe when that group is not widely known by name. However, we ought not to be misled by this device into speaking of "African thought," and certainly not in the manner of earlier works that purported to reveal what lay "back of the black man's mind." If there is any progress to be reported for the past decade, it is in the recognition of the great variability and complexity of African conceptual systems and of the need to refine our instruments of inquiry. We shall be concerned here with the literature of anthropology and linguistics, partly out of professional pride and interest but chiefly because these are the disciplines that make conceptual systems their central, explicit business.

Materials relevant to the construction of conceptual systems are abundant. Between the lines of almost all descriptions of a culture, or a society, or a kinship system, or an economic or political system, we can read elements of the conceptual system. For conceptualization is intrinsic to human behavior and institutions. In chapters of anthropological studies and in specialized monographs, we find accounts of religion, myth, and ritual; witchcraft, sorcery, and magic; the arts, language, and oral literature; and cosmology, ethics, and law. In his work on the traditional kingdom of Ruanda, Jacques Maquet provides a terminal chapter elaborating the significant "premise of inequality," a fortunate philosophical term that serves as the title of the English translation of the work in question.[1] Explicitly addressed to presenting world views, or systems of thought, is the useful collection edited by Daryll Forde and a more recent symposium edited by Meyer Fortes and Germaine Dieterlen.[2] In both volumes, however, conceptual systems are interpreted as equivalent to religion, art, myth, and other categories mentioned above.

There has not in the past decade been work on the order of Marcel Griaule's *Dieu d'eau.*[3] This presentation of the complex symbolism of one of nature's philosophers, Ogotemmeli, has raised many questions. It is far from clear whether we have an account of an unrepresentative, individual mystic's interpretation of the world, or an approximation to a West African culture pattern, or some mixture of these with the outside observer's invention. Whatever the situation, there is an instructive contrast between the complexity and systematic quality of Griaule's description of the world view of the Dogon and the bits-and-pieces approach of most literature on African systems of thought. The more elaborate construction enjoys greater a priori credibility, for there is a correct proportion between the complexity of the description and what we should expect to find in a cultural conceptual system. Only very few papers on African cultures utilize the model established by Clyde Kluckhohn in his paper, "The Philosophy of the Navaho Indians";[4] examples are Robin Horton's "The Kalabari World View," and my paper, "Une étude de valeurs en Urundi."[5]

1. *Le Systeme des relations sociales dans le Runda ancien* (Tervuren: Annales du Musée Royale du Congo-Belge, 1954); *Premise of Inequality in Ruanda* (London: Oxford University Press, 1961).
2. *African Worlds* (London: Oxford University Press, 1954); *African Systems of Thought* (London: Oxford University Press, 1965).
3. (Paris: Editions du Chêne, 1948).
4. In *Ideological Differences and World Order*, ed. F. S. C. Northrop (New Haven: Yale University Press, 1949), pp. 356–84.
5. Horton in *Africa*, XXXII (1962), 197–219; and Albert in *Cahiers d'études africaines*, No. 2 (1960), 148–60.

Such papers call attention to the interrelations of the component parts of world views, to the *systematic* rather than the atomistic view.

Only rarely do we find serious consideration given to the question of what is thought by the people whose world view we are trying to understand. The meaning, structure, and internal logic of a conceptual system are accessible to observation but are rarely found on the surface level represented by descriptions of rituals or the texts of myths. Victor Turner, in his recent work, *The Forest of Symbols,*[6] takes into account and interrelates in an interesting and significant synthesis both what he has noted as an observer and what his informants say they mean by the symbols they employ.

It is proper and necessary to describe religion, law, folklore, magic, and the other perhaps too familiar categories of the ethnographic literature. These are useful as data, but of dubious value as categories and clearly unfortunate in their connotations. Conspicuously absent from the literature are papers on logic, epistemology, technology, and other obviously intellectual facets of world views. The omissions reflect a point of view about non-Western, non-scientific conceptual systems that is incompatible with good research and that has the added disadvantage of alienating the educated members of African and other non-Western cultures. "Culture-bound distortion" is a cardinal sin, not to be excused on the ground of ignorance of one's own underlying ethnocentric attitudes. There has been continuing dispute in the anthropological literature about the use of the term "primitive" for any characteristic of any presently existing society and about the utility or correct usage of such terms as magic, sorcery, and witchcraft. In the long run, quarrels about vocabulary are futile. Bad public relations apart, continued use of the traditional vocabulary has entailed explicit or implicit invidious comparisons between our own supposedly scientific, rational conceptual system and its meaningless, miscellaneous alternative, that is, so-called "non-Western cultures."

Suspicion of defects in the vocabulary in general use for describing conceptual systems tends to be confirmed by the peculiar circumstance that African religions, magic, witchcraft, myth, and ritual too strongly resemble religion, magic, witchcraft, myth, and ritual in Oceania, Asia, or New World Indian cultures. The resemblances seem less to reflect the unity of mankind than a systematic error introduced by the terminology itself. The influence of our own tradition on studies of the conceptual systems of other peoples is becoming increasingly a matter of concern and the object of research. To insist upon our categories to describe other systems is to do as the fabled tourist does when he tries to get his message through to the "natives" by repeating his statement several times, each time more loudly and emphatically than the last.

The effect of the familiar vocabulary is negative because it distorts data and permits omissions of significant, relevant data. It therefore places obstacles in

6. (Ithaca, N. Y.: Cornell University Press, 1967).

the way of constructing adequate theoretic models. Justly or unjustly, the impression given by most descriptions of African conceptual systems is that the observers have serious doubts as to whether Africans think, or, alternatively, as to whether Africans think the way "we" do, that is, rationally, logically, scientifically. In brief, the shadow of the myth of "primitive mentality" continues to hinder inquiry. Demonstration of the fact that even in the heart of our "scientific" culture there are powerful currents of ritual—that science itself is entangled in Western myths—does not really help. The tone of generalized wonderings about "mentalities," ours or theirs, is determined by questions that have no proper place in an endeavor to represent adequately and objectively the nature and contents of cultural conceptual systems.

The systematic, objective study of conceptual systems is, then, an underdeveloped area. The situation is neither better nor worse for Africa than for other parts of the world. Sensitivity to and remedies for the deficiencies in our techniques, methods, and theories are, fortunately, very much in evidence in the anthropological and linguistic literature of the past decade.

Although in different ways, both E. E. Evans-Pritchard and Claude Lévi-Strauss are reshaping the issues inherited from the past.[7] Addressing the theoretic issues directly is but one way to go about reshaping the foundations of our inquiry. Increasingly, and largely due to the influence of linguistics, questions are being asked about the reliability and adequacy of the data employed to construct cultural conceptual systems. Attention is being given the question of how we can represent a set of beliefs or institutions in our language and idiom that will nevertheless be a faithful account of the system we are trying to describe. This is not a problem of translation. Primarily it involves methods and techniques of procuring information that will be reliable and representative. Studying religion, law, myth, and literature is not enough. Everyday discourse, everyday behavior, and the ordinary technology of a culture are immediately relevant data and indispensable to discovering system and pattern. Ultimately every observer of a culture must consult with the people he is studying, but it is not enough for the observer to ask about what interests him. On the contrary, we begin our research with our questions only because we cannot know in advance what is significant in the culture we are studying. If we want to find out what people think and how they think, we must pay attention to what they say and to what they think they think. To be sure, it is not feasible, even if our informant is highly educated and verbal, to ask simply, "Tell me please, what is your conceptual system?" Detailed questions must be asked, but we do not know which are likely to be productive unless we get our cues from the people we are studying.

7. See Evans-Pritchard, *Theories of Primitive Religion* (Oxford: Clarendon Press, 1965); and Lévi-Strauss, *La Pensée sauvage* (Paris: Librairie Plon, 1962).

The term *ethnoscience* refers to a variety of techniques and theories of linguistic anthropology intended to produce a representation of the conceptual system of a culture determined primarily by that system.[8] In this, as in so many ventures, the initial steps are small. The immediate results appear very humble by contrast with the grand generalizations of theories, old and new. For example, there has been a spate of studies of color terminologies. To us, the spectrum seems a natural source of color terms. While virtually all human groups know what a rainbow looks like, only very few of them have chosen it as the basis for naming colors. Thus, for Navaho Indians, there is no word for orange; one word serves for both blue and green; but there are two words for black, and two kinds of black to correspond. In Burundi, color terminology is oriented largely to the colors of the hides of cattle. In an Oceanian agricultural community, color terms depend chiefly on color changes in vegetation. The size and detail of this category tax the linguistic resouces of the anthropologist.

Studies of disease terminologies and of ways of naming the parts of the body are also of little apparent significance or utility outside the small sphere of specialists in semantic field analysis. But they establish a direction for inquiry that we should be most eager to follow. For it is a virtual certainty that if the afflictions of the body and its very constitution, as well as the operation of the senses, are conceived in such radically different ways in different cultures, then less biologically linked phenomena will surely present novelties well worth documenting.

More instructive than studies of words for colors are some of the results of ethnoscience taken in its earlier sense as the study of cultural technologies. In the practice of agriculture, as many outside specialists have discovered, local interpretations of what to plant and where to plant it have often proved scientifically sound. A sloppy looking garden, with tobacco and peas, sweet potatoes and millet, squash and beans, planted in no observable geometric pattern, offends our aesthetic sensibilities. Without our sophisticated jargon, the common African farmer nonetheless knows that his combinations are right, that plants have different appetites for the nutrients in the ground, that some plants produce what others need. Translated into more familiar terms, the intellectual processes and practical results meet the criteria laid down in Western technological culture for explaining and justifying procedures.

Even more striking, hence even more instructive, are recent developments in ethnobotany and ethnopharmacology. It has been difficult or impossible for

8. See, for example, B. N. Colby, "Ethnographic Semantics," *Current Anthropology,* VII (1966), 3–32; A. K. Romney and R. G. D'Andrade, eds., *Transcultural Studies in Cognition,* special issue of *American Anthropologist,* LXVI (June 1964); E. A. Hammell, ed., *Formal Semantic Analysis,* special issue of *American Anthropologist,* LXVII (October 1965); and J. J. Gumperz and D. H. Hymes, eds., *The Ethnography of Communication,* special issue of *American Anthropologist,* LXVI (October 1964); see also the encyclopedic collection, *Language in Culture and Society,* ed. Dell H. Hymes (New York: Harper & Row, 1964), especially Parts 1, 4–8.

anthropologists to procure detailed information from local curers. Professional American botanists—speaking as one expert to another—have enjoyed a great success. Knowing what questions to ask and understanding what their informants tell them, they have obtained detailed data on medicinal recipes. What to the untrained eye is some rigmarole involving mashing up dried leaves or wandering about at odd times of day or night to collect ingredients is in fact often translatable by knowledgeable individuals into serious, effective, empirical science. The results of ethnobotanical research for pharmaceutical firms are a medically and financially rich harvest. It is understood that the curer's lore is not our kind of science. There are probably non-empirical components in their procedures. The important lesson for us here is to leave judgments of what is rational or efficacious to qualified experts, not amateurs.

It is precisely in the realm of technology that we stand in greatest danger of being misled by our own vocabulary. If we choose to call something ritual or witchcraft or magic, we choose at the same time to assume that it cannot really work, or that if it works at all it is only by the power of suggestion. We are by no means rejecting science as establishing the criteria appropriate for our research. On the contrary, it is precisely the demands of scientific method that are being extended to the study of cultural conceptual systems when we reject the preconceptions inherent in our usual vocabulary in favor of laboratory tests. It does not seem odd, when we stop to think of it, that we have much to learn, even in science, from the accumulated experience of other peoples.

Another facet of the influence of linguistics on anthropology and its studies of conceptual systems is represented by sociolinguistics. In Africa and elsewhere research has been directed toward detailed information about social variations in language use that are a needed safeguard against the dangers of oversimplification and overgeneralization. Differences in the way that language is used are highly reliable indices of social differences within a culture. To the awareness that there is no single African culture or African language or African conceptual system, we must add the active realization that within even the simplest society there are significant internal variations. These have both theoretical and practical importance, especially in a period of planned change.

In their recent summary statement on sociolinguistic research in Africa, Jack Berry and Joseph Greenberg categorized the studies in process as (1) description of habitual language usage, (2) behavior toward language, and (3) dynamic study of psychological and social variables.[9] Their recommendations for the extension of the study of language behavior take cognizance of the great complexity of the linguistic situation in Africa and of the changes occurring in African languages and cultures.

The nature of the relationship between language and thought is not easily

9. "Sociolinguistic Research in Africa," *African Studies Bulletin,* IX (September 1966), 1–9.

stated. A great deal has been said, chiefly in a speculative way, about the determinative power of language over the content and order of thought. Perhaps the most influential but least verifiable theory was the so-called Sapir-Whorf hypothesis. Whorf, an amateur linguist interested in American Indians, was supported by the distinguished linguist, Edward Sapir, in his efforts to demonstrate the determinative power of linguistic as well as lexical forms over the content of thought. As a theory relating to conceptual systems, the notion of complete or nearly complete linguistic determinism may be considered a fad that failed. It was, however, a stimulus to those concerned with the problems of verifying the role of language in thought. Current research, in the form of specific and detailed inquiry, is helping to correct the exaggerations of linguistic determinists. More than this, it is redirecting research on language toward a concern with its biological foundations and psychological characteristics.

These universals provide a useful general matrix for understanding the complex processes of human physiology and the psychology of language and cognition in the human species. So far, however, no theory has been developed to link these general phenomena to the well-documented cultural differences of language and thought. The specific contents of a cultural conceptual system can be ascertained only by direct empirical study. Understandably, the importance of language in such studies is great. Knowledge of the language spoken is in some degree and form a necessary instrument of inquiry. We gain access to a cultural conceptual system chiefly, perhaps exclusively, by means of its language. The heuristic value of language study is, in our present situation, also critical. For as we attend to the special characteristics of the language spoken by those whose conceptual system interests us, we are almost automatically redirected from the categories implicit in our own language and thought to those suggested by the thought patterns of those we are studying. The requirement of reporting our findings in terms comprehensible to our fellow-professionals can in principle be reconciled with assigning descriptive priorities to the object of study. Presumably, if we pay adequate attention to our informants we can discover not only the specific, distinctive contents of their conceptual systems but also their specific distinctive ways of relating concepts.

The study of cultural logics and epistemologies is very new and hence uncertain of its techniques and goals. To assert that there are different cultural logics—different ways of putting ideas together—is essentially like asserting that the actual contents of beliefs are culturally variable. A distinction is necessary between what is logical in the strictly formal sense and what is logical in a particular culture because the ideas are familiar in content and relations, as a result of long associations that have the psychological force of compelling interdependence. It is all too easy, even within our culture, to designate as "inconsistent" or "illogical" what, on careful examination, is simply unexpected or different. Also it is too easy, even for a trained observer, to confuse a difference in the content of beliefs with an error in formal logic.

Risk of misinterpretation of a cultural logic is in part related to Western evaluation of the logical. The risk is intensified by the difficulty of assembling a complete set of premises when working in some other culture. Missing pieces of a cultural conceptual system can easily have the effect of making it appear that there is inconsistency. Since premises and other fundamental propositions in a cultural system are only rarely spontaneously produced, the researcher has the task of digging beneath the surface of discourse. The safest procedural assumption, when a system appears inconsistent, is that there is a gap in the observer's information. There is time enough after exhaustive inquiry has been made to label residual inconsistencies.

One of the likeliest candidates for misunderstanding, given our Western world view, is fatalism in any form. Widespread in Africa and in other continents, fatalism has a stereotyped definition that militates against its correct interpretation. Generally, we conceive of fatalism in negative terms. Fatalists, it is assumed, believe that man is helpless, in contrast to the dominant Western orientation that represents man as able to predict and control by means of knowledge and effort, and thus to determine, large ranges of the course of events. In Western terms it appears odd that men should resign themselves to fate, and even somewhat distasteful if not outright immoral. Examination of the details of fatalism presented by individuals who espouse the doctrine in any one of its many forms produces a different impression. The stereotype generally held in the West is only about half true.

Fatalism is indeed a world view in which it is believed that men do not have the power to cause events, nor are their intellects such as to make it possible for them to understand, let alone to predict, the future with confidence. But the assertion that man is casually impotent is the natural complement and logical consequence of a belief in the omnipotence or greatly superior casual power of one or more superhuman forces, divine or spiritual or impersonal. The belief that man's intellect is too feeble an instrument to understand all that happens or to foresee what will come in the future is the natural complement of a belief in the omniscience or near-omniscience of fateful powers and of the belief that a god of destiny or other forms of fate enjoy great or even perfect freedom of will. It is logical that God's free will should be man's necessity. It is also logical that man's actions and their moral significance should be eclipsed by the greater force and dignity of fateful powers. Like any world view, fatalism is in some measure a self-fulfilling prophecy, so that accidents and failures may be more numerous than in a "doing-oriented" society. It is also a self-correcting mechanism. Far from teaching men to sit back and do nothing, fatalism teaches dignity in the face of adversity and humility in the event of prosperity. Intellectual resources are not expended on the natural world but are reserved for the serious business of navigating the individual's destiny in a world characterized by risk and uncertainty. Regularities—the stock in trade of science—are not interesting. Ingenuity is needed to devise ways to appeal to the causers of events, and appeals are phrased in ways to please or to move the higher powers.

Logic is used, but it is not greatly valued; knowledge of nature exists, but it is not significant. The strength of the emotions is acknowledged and acted upon, both among men and between men and the higher powers. Goodness is necessarily in large part aesthetic, quite unlike the "Protestant ethic," where whatever we find attractive is sinful, or fattening, or otherwise forbidden. For fatalists as for others, men can and indeed must act, but the view is steadfastly maintained and daily verified that no matter how conscientiously a man may perform his duties, he may fail or suffer, whereas some men who are worthless or evil may prosper. By and large, fatalism is a self-consistent, faithful reflection of actual human existence, with its unpredicted ups and downs and its often outrageous injustices and undeserved strokes of luck. We can only envy those Europeanized Africans who can use a scientific world view when they want to know *how* things happen and who have in reserve the rich resources of fatalism to help them understand *why* things happen and to guide their moral attitudes through the vicissitudes of human life.

Apart from its intrinsic interest as a widespread and convincing world view, fatalism is worth our attention in relation to the changes being made in economic and political systems. There is nothing new in the realization that many of those involved in modernization programs have lived their lives with a minimum of confidence in the power of the intellect, in active awareness of the uncertainties of human effort and planning, and hence in a state of hopeful, prayerful pessimism. There is at best an uneasy peace between the bustling optimism of innovations from European culture and the older and sadder outlook, not infrequently confirmed by failures of the new ways. In no case is the process of modernization confronted merely with an ill-assorted collection of superstitions or quaint notions, easily overturned because they are without foundation. Any fatalist worth his salt can collect an imposing body of fact to defend his view as truer to life than others. Fact as well as custom makes him stubborn.

Even so inadequate a sketch of a system of ideas different from our own may vindicate the continuing study of conceptual systems around the world. In African studies, it will fill out our information about that continent's cultural resources and at the same time add several fascinating chapters to the culture history of ideas. In ethnophilosophy, better acquaintance with African conceptual systems should enable us to continue to refine our methods and our theoretic models. Further, the more we study other cultures, the better able we are to understand our own, including the part of our world view from which we look at others. Where changes in behavior patterns require changes in concepts or patterns of inference, reliable information about conceptual systems is relevant. That there are risks entailed is obvious, but we might do worse than include in our studies of conceptual systems provision for factual data that may shed light on safe and sane ways to bring about changes of thought called for by changes in life conditions.

7

Visual Art
in Africa

FRANK WILLETT

APPROACHES TO THE STUDY OF AFRICAN ART

WHEN WE SPEAK OF AFRICAN ART, people usually think first of sculpture, especially in wood, as most of the collected material is in this form; there is also sculpture in stone, mud, pottery, bronze, and even iron. Painting also exists as an art form in Africa; in fact, the oldest art we know in Africa consists of paintings on the walls of caves and rock shelters.[1] Painting today, however, is usually restricted to the decoration of sculpture and of house walls. Neither is commonly seen in the West; painting on sculpture has often been removed by the collector, and decorations painted on walls are almost impossible to collect as originals and so are known generally only from photographs in the literature.

The scope of African art also includes music and dancing, which are not only important art forms in their own right but are far more widespread than sculpture and painting. In this essay, however, we shall confine ourselves to the visual arts—sculpture and painting—though, as we shall see, these cannot be studied profitably in isolation from other forms of expression. Take for example a carved wooden mask. In museums we usually see these exhibited for our admiration of their sculptural form; yet as Kenneth Murray has shown,

> [they] are intended to be seen in movement in a dance; frequently one which is inferior when held in the hand looks more effective than a finer carving when worn with its costume. It is, morever, essential to see masks in use before judging what

---

1. A useful introduction to African rock painting and engraving is in H.-G. Bandi et al., *The Art of the Stone Age*, trans. Ann E. Keep (London: Methuen, 1961). On the Tassili paintings, see J. D. Lajoux, *The Rock Paintings of Tassili*, trans. G. D. Liversage (Cleveland: World Publishing Co., 1963); and Henri Lhote, *The Search for the Tassili Frescoes*, trans. A. H. Broderick (New York: E. P. Dutton, 1959).

they express, for it is easy to read into an isolated mask what was never meant to be there.[2]

A mask, then, is only part of a whole complex of a costume worn in a dance and accompanied by music. Unfortunately, the overwhelming proportion of the masks in our museum collections have been torn from this context without any record being made of these related arts.

Although it has often been claimed that African art was "discovered" at the beginning of this century, this is not strictly true. African sculptures in the Ulm Museum in Germany were collected in the seventeenth century.[3] Although these were regarded as curiosities at the time of their collection, by the late nineteenth century there were large numbers of art objects in museums, and serious study of them began in an atmosphere permeated with the idea of evolution. The Pitt-Rivers Collection, now at Oxford, was established with the specific intention of demonstrating evolution in all human artifacts. The earliest studies of art were directed at producing theories of the origin and development of art. Unfortunately there was no dated ancient material available, so contemporary material was studied. Such study led to the "degeneration theory," which asserted that slavish copying of an original led to purely geometric forms; the supposedly archaic features in the contemporary material were called "survivals." It is perfectly clear today that art had multiple origins, although it is usually an unprofitable task to seek them. We content ourselves instead with recording the historically documented materials and studying the relations between them.

The old method, which we may call the ethnological approach, was pursued more intensively on American and Oceanic material than on African. One of the most influential workers in the field was Franz Boas, who worked entirely on American Indian material, most of which is symbolic and two-dimensional. His most important contribution was to demonstrate that identical forms could convey different meanings in different societies, and thus to demonstrate that form and content cannot be studied separately. Boas himself, however, did not seem to have realized the importance of this, nor have many of his pupils. From this demonstration of the link between form and content the basic principle of the ethnological approach to African sculpture has been developed; that is, a knowledge of the content and context of a work of art is essential to its understanding and even to the full appreciation of its aesthetic qualities.

In contrast to the ethnological approach is the aesthetic approach, adopted chiefly by practicing artists, which considers that knowledge of the content and

2. "The Artist in Nigerian Tribal Society," in *The Artist in Tribal Society*, ed. M. W. Smith (London: Routledge & Kegan Paul, 1957), p. 95.

3. For illustrations see W. B. Fagg and Margaret Plass, *African Sculpture: An Anthology* (London and New York: Studio Vista, 1964), pp. 112, 114.

of the function of the work of art is unnecessary to its appreciation. In the extreme form of this approach such knowledge was held to interfere with aesthetic enjoyment.[4]

These two schools of thought have gradually converged. Anthropologists pay increasing attention to aesthetics, while art critics give consideration to the cultural background—for what is form but a means of conveying content? Yet the bulk of the general literature on African art as a whole has adopted the essentially subjective attitude—the approach which asks "What does this sculpture mean to me?" This is understandable when the authors are practicing artists, but it does detract from the value of their books.[5]

Vatter, however, tried to set the artist in his social and cultural background, pointing out that the artist's role is not, as in Europe, to express his own personality, but rather to serve the community.[6] From this he goes on to argue that the artist is anonymous, an error which has often been repeated. In most cases the artist is not anonymous; rather, the collector simply had never bothered to ask his name. Indeed, the better the artist, the better his name is known over an extensive area.[7]

A number of important studies of continuing value were prepared between 1930 and 1950, based mainly on material which was available in museum collections.[8] Gradually, however, it became apparent that study in Africa was necessary to resolve many problems and to provide reliable documentation. Melville Herskovits, a pupil of Boas, undertook a study of African art in the field (in Dahomey as part of a wider piece of research).[9] Herskovits' pupils, William

4. Carl Einstein, *Negerplastik* ("Negro Sculpture") (Munich: K. Wolf, 1920).

5. See, for example, Leon Underwood, *Figures in Wood of West Africa* (London: Tiranti, 1947); Underwood, *Masks of West Africa* (London: Tiranti, 1948); and Margaret Trowell, *Classical African Sculpture* (London: Faber & Faber, 1954).

6. Ernst Vatter, *Religiose Plastik der Naturvolker* ("Religious Sculpture of Primitive Societies") (Frankfurt: Verlags-Austalt, 1926).

7. See, for example, W. B. Fagg, "Perspective on Africa," in *Symposium on the Artist in Tribal Society,* ed. M. W. Smith (London: Routledge & Kegan Paul, 1962), pl. 15 and pp. 119–20.

8. See Eckart von Sydow, *Handbuch der Afrikanischen Plastik* ("Handbook of African Sculpture"), ed. Gerdt Kutscher (Berlin: D. Reimer, 1930); *Afrikanische Plastik* ("African Sculpture") (Berlin: Mann, 1954); C. Kjersmeier, *Centres de style de la sculpture nègre africaine,* 4 vols. ("Stylistic Centers of African Negro Sculpture") (Paris: A. Morance, 1935; Copenhagen: Illums Bogafelding, 1938; New York: Hacker Art Books, 1967); F. M. Olbrechts, *Plastiek van Kongo* ("Congolese Sculpture") (Antwerp: Standard-Boekhandel, 1946), translated as *Les Arts plastiques du Congo belge* (Brussels: Editions Erasme, 1959); F. H. Lem, *Sculptures soudanaises* ("Sudanic Sculptures") (Paris: Arts et Métiers Graphiques, 1948); P. S. Wingert, *The Sculpture of Negro Africa* (New York: Columbia University Press, 1950).

9. M. J. Herskovits, *Dahomey: An Ancient West African Kingdom,* (1938; reprint ed., Evanston, Ill.; Northwestern University Press, 1967); M. J. Herskovits and F. S. Herskovits, "The Art of Dahomey," *American Magazine of Art,* XXVII (February 1934), 67–76, 124–31.

Bascom, Justine Cordwell, and James Fernandez followed this example. Similarly, several students of the Belgian scholar Olbrechts worked in the field; Maesen, Vandenhoute, and Biebuyk are the best known. And from France, Marcel Griaule worked among the Dogon with his students Denise Paulme, Germaine Dieterlen, and J.-P. Lebeuf. Most of these workers have concentrated in their writings on the areas in which they did their field work.

One of the most influential writers on African art, William Fagg, began his work with studies of the collections in the British Museum, and only later undertook field work. Much of his research has been centered around exhibitions of African sculpture which he has organized in many parts of Europe and America. As a result, his main contribution has been in the improvement of documentation of African, and especially Nigerian, art. His study of the sculpture of Benin and his work in distinguishing the Owo style has brought order to these researches; he has identified also the individual styles of a large number of artists whose works he has illustrated.[10]

THE DATA AVAILABLE FOR STUDY

There are essentially three main sources of information available for the study of African art. We have first the museum collections, both public and private; but the value of museum collections as sources is limited by the quality of the documentation of individual pieces. The studies based on them are similarly limited, as Kjersmeier pointed out in explaining why he could give only a general idea of the sculpture of the Ibo, Ibibio, Ijo, and Efik of Nigeria.[11]

As a second source, we have the literature based on observations in Africa. Early travelers made passing references to art. Ibn-Battuta observed masked dancers in the Sudan as early as A.D. 1352; Dapper described the bronze plaques decorating the palace in Benin (Nigeria) in 1668 (yet by 1702 when Nyendael described the palace in great detail, mentioning the bronze heads supporting carved tusks, the plaques apparently had been taken down). These references afford valuable dating evidence, but in general such early references do not describe the art in detail nor illustrate it accurately. Anthropologists' accounts are generally of greater value, even though in many cases the art object is viewed simply as a social fact, rather than as something of interest in itself. Their studies do at least help us to understand the setting of the art.

The most valuable sources of information, however, are studies of African art

10. See, for example, Fagg and Plass, *African Sculpture;* and W. B. Fagg, *Nigerian Images* (London: Lund Humphries, 1963). This section of the essay has relied heavily on the very valuable study by A. A. Gerbrands, *Art as an Element of Culture: Especially in Negro Africa* (Leiden: E. J. Brill, 1957).

11. Kjersmeier, *Centres de style*, II, 28.

and artists done in the field. Unfortunately for the student of art, as African societies adopt more Western modes of life many of the institutions which required the traditional art objects are being abandoned. Traditional art in most of Africa is thus either dying out or being substantially modified. The need for intensive field studies of African art, both by anthropologists (who are in any case very much preoccupied at present with the phenomena of social change) and by art historians, is most urgent. Increasingly, we are becoming aware of gaps in our information which can be filled only by investigations in the field. We must see that these investigations are carried out as a matter of the greatest urgency, partly as a means of better understanding those materials which are already stored in museums, secure at least from the termite and the weather if not from greater threats.

INTERPRETING THE DATA

African sculpture is an expression of the world view, or the philosophy, of the society which produced it. Since nearly every ethnic group has its own view of life—its own ethical and religious system—it is difficult, indeed dangerous, to attempt to generalize about African art. We can make some statements about the conditions in which art is found, but generalizations about the art itself are likely to be wrong.

We can assert, for example, that since African hunting societies migrate to follow their quarry, their homes are likely to be simple and their possessions few. Their homes are not likely to be decorated, and their domestic utensils will probably have only the simplest ornament; incised ostrich-eggshell containers are used among the Bushmen, for example. Nevertheless, hunting communities do express their artistic impulses, usually on natural features, producing engravings on exposed rocks and paintings in cave shelters. Very probably these are made on occasions when the small bands of hunters gather together to form larger groups for religious or ceremonial purposes. Similar considerations apply to pastoralists, who, although they travel with their herds, were able to produce a large number of the finest paintings of the Tassili in the Sahara. Major achievements in art seem to depend on the regular return to particular centers or else on the permanent occupation of a village or town, which is usually possible only for agricultural communities.

The area in which wood sculpture is found in Africa probably corresponds roughly to the area of forest and woodland, not as these exist today but as they extended in the past. The forested and wooded areas of Africa have been reduced in size by increasing desiccation of the climate over the last 4,000 years and also by the hand of man in clearing the forest for his farms. Movements of people have further obscured any correspondence there may have been in the past, but wood sculpture is not likely to have arisen in an area where trees did not once grow.

Attempts have been made to contrast the arts of the rainforests and the dry savannas. It has been claimed, for example, that the peoples of the forest do not form large social groups—that they live in isolated communities in fear of the forest and each other and that the continuous fight to keep their clearings from being encroached upon by the forest absorbs all their energy and depresses their spirits. In contrast, the peoples of the savanna built up empires (Ghana, Songhai, the Sokoto Empire) with state organizations, large and specialized administrative machinery, governing classes to patronize the artist, and public feasts and ceremonies to use his products.[12]

This is a very imaginative picture, based not on observed facts but rather on how a European might expect an African to react to his environment. The Pygmies of the Ituri Forest (Congo-Kinshasa), whose life is quite arduous, are some of the most happily disposed people in the world and look upon the forest as a friendly provider of food.[13] Moreover, some of the most important of the city-states arose in the forests: Benin, Ijebu, and Ife, in Nigeria, for example. In any case, the savanna states of the Sudanic zone were not as centralized as many European scholars have imagined. The power of the savanna state authorities was over people as sources of labor rather than over land. Administration usually operated through family and village heads, whose authority derived from their role in the ancestor cult and their connection with the land. In addition, and of major importance, was the fact that many of these empires were based on Islam and thus discouraged or even prohibited representational art, though in many areas this survived as a means of serving the ancestors, not the court.

On the other hand Griaule points out that

> the Bambara, the Kurumba, and the Baga . . . have certainly not founded states. But they have created certain institutions, like that of initiation which can develop . . . an accumulation of material; in the life of art they play the role of a state by establishing rules which extend beyond narrow horizons and remain applicable, with some variations, to the larger districts.[14]

This concept of institutions as patrons of art is a valuable one. We think at once of the Poro Society, best documented from Liberia[15] but also influential in Sierra Leone, Guinea, and Ivory Coast.

---

12. Paraphrased from Marcel Griaule, *Folk Art of Black Africa* (New York: Tudor Publishing Co., 1950), pp. 31–33.

13. C. M. Turnbull, *The Forest People* (New York: Simon & Schuster, 1961).

14. *Folk Art*, p. 38.

15. G. W. Harley, *Notes on the Poro in Liberia*, Papers of the Peabody Museum, Vol. XIX, No. 2 (Cambridge: Harvard University, Peabody Museum of Archaeology and Ethnology, 1941); and Harley, *Masks as Agents of Social Control in North East Liberia*, Papers of the Peabody Museum, Vol. XXXII, No. 2 (Cambridge: Harvard University, Peabody Museum of Archaeology and Ethnology, 1950).

Margaret Trowell has made generalizations about African art which are quite different in scope.[16] She distinguishes three types of art which she calls "spirit-regarding," "man-regarding," and "the art of ritual display." This classificatory device has the great merit of emphasizing the function of the art in the society which produced it, though any one society may produce sculpture which belongs in more than one category. The sculptures of the Dogon (Mali),[17] both ancestor figures and masks, are clearly directed toward influencing the world of the spirits, whether of the ancestors or of the animals and trees around them; similarly, the sculpture of the Kalabari Ijo (Nigeria)[18] pays attention to the spirits rather than to man. Yet the Yoruba (Nigeria) have masked dances, the *egungun,* which are directed both at ensuring that the ancestors will rest in peace and at entertaining the living. On the other hand, their house posts and sculptured doors on houses and in palaces are intended for the glorification of the house-owners, while similar carvings in shrines are for the honor of the spirits worshiped there.

Clearly then, we need to have detailed studies in the field before we can understand the sculpture of any one society. Such studies have frequently disproved many of the generalizations formulated by scholars working only in museums, and in so doing have often produced positive interpretations of an innovative character. It has been found, for example, that, although sculpture in Africa is very commonly painted, the paint is often applied without any attention to the sculptural form. In the case of Kalabari masks, Horton has discovered that the painting is not simply an embellishment of the sculpture, but is the means of effectively bringing the spirit to occupy the mask.[19]

A feature of African sculpture which intrigued scholars from the first is the fact that the head is almost invariably shown as disproportionately large. For a long time this was thought to be a childlike characteristic due to the carver paying more attention to the details than to the overall proportion. Field studies from many parts of Africa, however, have shown that sculptors begin by dividing up the block of wood very carefully into separate parts which will eventually be the head, body, and legs. In this way the proportions are deliberately established at the outset of the work and are not due to a lack of skill. One of the first to observe this technique was a French doctor, Robert Hottot, traveling among the Teke on the lower Congo as early as 1906; unfortunately his most valuable observations were not published until after his death.[20]

There is a danger, in studying African art, of generalizing from data observed among one people as if they were typical of Africa as a whole. Scholars, however

16. *African Sculpture,* pp. 25–40.
17. Conveniently described in Griaule, *Folk Art.*
18. Robin Horton, *Kalabari Sculpture* (Lagos: Department of Antiquities, 1965).
19. *Ibid.,* p. 21.
20. R. Hottot, "Teke Fetishes," *Journal of the Royal Anthropological Institute,* LXXXVI (1956), 25–36.

objective they may attempt to be, remain human beings, and their individual personalities will lead them to investigate different phenomena. Consequently, we do not have a homogeneous collection of data covering the various peoples of the continent. One worker may have recorded certain artistic phenomena among one group of people, and similar observations elsewhere might demonstrate that the phenomena were widespread; but only too often the requisite substantiating observations have never been made. In consequence, books on African art as a whole may tend to generalize from observations made among a single group of people as if these were typical of the entire continent.

The present need, and it is most urgent, is to fill such gaps in our knowledge, and in some cases these gaps are very wide indeed. Before we can make general statements about African art, we need far more information. A brief survey of some of the problems which have been studied will help to clarify our ideas of what still needs to be done.

SOME STUDIES IN AFRICAN ART:
THE FUNCTION OF ART

It has commonly been asserted that there is no "art for art's sake" in Africa and that all African art is religious. In Western society when art critics speak of "art for art's sake," they mean that the artist produces an object which is valued for itself, which does not attempt to instruct or edify; it is a product in which the artist is concerned exclusively with the solution of artistic problems of composition, color, or form. The content of the work of art is secondary to these considerations. The final product, however, does have an acquired social function—it may be used to decorate a room, for example, and it may also be a status symbol.

This restricted attitude to art appears to be of recent origin. At one time all European art had a social purpose—whether to instruct the faithful, to edify the devout, or to commemorate the noble. Traditional African art similarly has its social purposes, but there are some products whose purpose is less clearly defined. The Fon of Dahomey, for example, make brass castings of animals and of people at work or in processions which have no religious or didactic intent. They are made as objects of beauty by the brass-smith and in this respect are to be considered as examples of "art for art's sake." Yet they do have a social function which is entirely independent of the subject represented; since brass is regarded as a semiprecious metal, these castings are objects of prestige. Only the wealthy can afford to buy them, and they are displayed in the home both as objects of beauty and as status symbols.[21]

Similarly, it is not true that all African art is religious. Adrian Gerbrands has

21. Herskovits, *Dahomey*, pp. 354–61.

demonstrated this very clearly,[22] using the documented pot lids collected by the Fathers Vissers among the Woyo of Cabinda, just north of the mouth of the Congo River. It is the custom among these people for the husband to eat separately from his wife. When the wife has a disagreement with her husband she covers his food with a wooden lid sculptured with figures which convey, through the proverbial expressions they represent, the substance of her dissatisfaction. (The wife chooses an occasion when her husband is entertaining his friends, so that they, representing the community at large, can arbitrate.) She usually receives a number of these lids from her mother and mother-in-law when she marries, but if she does not possess a lid appropriate to her problem she has one made.

The lids vary in complexity. One shows a round pot supported on three stones. With fewer than three stones, the pot would fall over; hence, it signifies the proverb "All good things come in threes" (that is, a husband must give his wife clothes; a wife must cook for her husband; there must be children). This lid, therefore, is a general indication that there is something lacking in the marriage. The husband himself will know what.

In some cases the lid is decorated with a large number of objects including audiovisual puns; such as the conus shell, called *nsosse*, a word which suggests a sucked-in sound of annoyance and means, "I am angry and am going to tell you why"; or another shell called *zinga*, a word which also means "life," hence family life and harmony, and so conveys the exhortation to "live in harmony with your family." Clearly this is purely secular art.

Nevertheless, although there are other examples of secular art, it is true that a great deal of African art has a religious purpose. At the same time, however, even within the field of religious sculpture, there are a great variety of practices. It is usual for the act of carving itself to be hedged around with rituals, since the tree which provides the wood is generally regarded as the home of a spirit which needs to be placated. In the case of sculptures which are to provide a home for a spirit, such as the masks and ancestor figures of the Dogon, it is easy to see that a conflict between the two spirits inhabiting the wood must be avoided. But where no later spirit occupation is involved, as in Yoruba drums, and even in the case of secular objects such as stools, the spirit of the tree nonetheless has to be propitiated.

It sometimes comes as a surprise to find that, despite the investment of religious meanings, old carvings are commonly neglected. This is especially true of masks which are thought to be occupied by the spirit only during the ceremonies; but it also applies to fetish figures in which the "medicine," or magical substance, houses the spirit power and where by removing this medicine the figure can be deconsecrated.

22. *Art as an Element of Culture*, pp. 111–21.

ART IN CONTEXT: STUDIES AMONG
THE KALABARI AND THE DAN

There is a serious disproportion between the small number of field studies of African art and the large amount of African sculpture in collections. Few people interested in African sculpture see it in use and therefore must form their impressions from museum displays. A museum will usually possess only the wooden part of a mask, and this may be displayed under a spotlight which projects a single interpretation onto the sculpture. To appreciate the carving as it was conceived by the artist, we need to see it in movement, possibly above eye level, and perhaps illuminated by the intermittent light of torches. Moreover, to isolate the mask is to take it from its meaningful context. Often the mask itself is only part of a costume, and it does not come to life until the costume is worn — with the music and dancing the mask becomes inhabited by the spirit. Indeed, there are many ceremonies in which costumes are worn which hide the face but which do not employ sculptured masks at all (as in some Yoruba *egungun* ceremonies), and others in which the dancer's face is painted but no mask is worn (as among the Kissi of Guinea and Sierra Leone); yet the total effect is similar to that of the masked dances.

It is surprising, too, to find that many African masks are not seen at all when they are in use. Robin Horton, describing the sculpture of the Kalabari, has shown that many of their masks (such as the Otobo masks, which represent a water spirit with human and hippopotamus features) are worn on top of the dancer's head so that the main features of the sculpture are facing the sky and the mask as a whole is hidden from the eyes of the spectators by a ruff.[23] The whole masquerade is directed toward the spirit, not toward the spectator — an excellent example of Margaret Trowell's class of "spirit-regarding art."

Horton's study has exploded a number of myths about African art. Because we look upon sculptures as objects of beauty, we imagine that the works are regarded as beautiful by their makers and users. Yet the Kalabari view their sculptures with apathy or distaste; even when the spirit is being invoked, the mask itself does not attract admiration. The sculpture in fact may evoke revulsion; a man's ugliness will be compared to a spirit sculpture, or even to "the sculpture of a god by one who does not know how to carve." Moreover, pregnant women are advised not to look at sculptures "lest their children acquire its big eyes and long nose, and so turn out ugly." The Kalabari, in fact, often keep sculptures of spirits in dark shrines which people may not enter and cannot see into. In one case, even the priest does not see the sculpture, which is hidden behind a screen of skulls.[24]

23. *Kalabari Sculpture*, p. 15.
24. *Ibid.*, pp. 12–13.

In contrast, however, the Kalabari ancestor memorial screens are intended to be seen. These screens are of interest, too, in that they constitute another exception to the generally accepted idea that African sculpture is subtractive (carved out of a single block of wood), for these are constructions (that is, carved in sections and fitted together).[25] This carpentry may reflect European influence resulting from the slave and palm oil trade in the Niger Delta. The screens seem to have originated as a form in the eighteenth century, and perhaps were modeled on the rectangular bronze plaques at Benin, which in turn seem to have been originally inspired by European woodcuts in books.

Not all Kalabari masks are hidden from view. The central character of the Ngbula play, for example, is a native doctor whose ugliness, which is emphasized in the headpiece, helps him to drive away evil spirits.[26] Horton points out, however, that the Kalabari do not possess any masks which represent beauty—in contrast to the Ibo, who have pairs of masks representing ugliness (the elephant spirit) and beauty (the maiden spirit).[27]

Examples of African sculpture exhibited in museums are commonly considered representative of the style of the people from whom they were collected. This is an oversimplification; for, whereas it is true that many sculptural styles have a distribution which limits them to one small area, some styles are distributed far more widely. Sometimes a mask is acquired by trade from another area—Ibibio masks carved at Ikot Ekpene in southeastern Nigeria are commonly used by unrelated peoples on the west side of the Niger River. At other times, a single group of people will use different styles of sculpture for different purposes, as when a mask-using cult has been introduced from an adjacent area or where there are localized cults with markedly different styles, as among the Bembe of the eastern Congo.[28] The same religious society may use a variety of styles of masks in different areas, as in the Poro Society mentioned above, an example of an institution which encourages the production of art for ceremonial purposes. Among the Dan of Ivory Coast, the Poro Society uses the traditional masks of the ancestor cult which are very smooth and sleek in form; whereas, in contrast, among the neighboring Ngere, Poro masks are highly cubistic in style and usually only roughly finished. Moreover, it has been shown that both these styles may be carved by the same artist.[29]

In use the Dan masks vary in ranking and function, but this differentiation is not related to their appearance. For the Dan, the mask is a channel of communication between men and the high god, Zlan, but the real intermediaries are the spirits of the ancestors who are invoked and controlled through the

25. *Ibid.*, p. 14.
26. *Ibid.*
27. Illustrated, for example, in Fagg, *Nigerian Images*, pls. 118, 119.
28. Daniel Biebuyck, *Tradition and Creativity in Tribal Art* (Berkeley and Los Angeles: University of California Press, 1969).
29. Reported and illustrated in Gerbrands, *Art as an Element of Culture*, pp. 89–90.

mask. The power of the mask reflects the social prestige of the owner. A man can reach prominence only with the help of the ancestors; his very success, then, demonstrates that the ancestors favor him. An inherited mask retains its power over the ancestors; the more prestigious the owner was in life, the more powerful he will be as an ancestor. Similarly, old masks which span several generations are considered especially powerful. The prestige of a mask is thus an acquired characteristic which cannot be deduced from its appearance; to understand and interpret an individual mask, the appropriate history must be collected in the field.

Again, masks of identical appearance may have quite different functions, and these too are classified into categories of higher and lower rank. The use of the mask among the Dan is regulated by the *go*-master, the priest of *go*, the highest imaginable power. In his hut is the powerful fetish which is the source of his power, as well as the actual presence of the ancestors, for prominent people are buried in the hut and their masks are kept there. These masks are of the highest rank, followed by sacrificial masks on which heads of families make sacrifices to their ancestors. Next come avenging masks, which act as police and judiciary combined; these sometimes act independently of the *go*-master, thus forcing him to employ one of his highest-ranking masks in order to maintain his authority. Other high-ranking masks include those used in initiation, not only to teach the initiates but also to entertain those who have remained behind in the village. On the edges of the forest and savanna are the *sagbwe* masks, which have their own hierarchy; their task is to protect the village, especially from fire—a major hazard. The lower-status categories of masks are described as dancing, singing, begging, and palaver, and are mainly intended to entertain. They often teach as well, and frequently fear of the supernatural can be detected in the audiences.

Masks can move up in these hierarchies—usually on the death of their owner if he has achieved eminence in his lifetime. Thus, there is no correlation between the rank or function and the form of a mask. Masks may also be demoted if they are damaged, for they have to be beautiful in order to please the ancestors. Formerly, damaged masks were thrown away, but now they are often retrieved and sold to Europeans; this is why so many of the specimens in European museums are inadequately documented.[30]

AFRICAN AESTHETICS

A number of important studies of African art have been based on the Dan and related groups,[31] the most recent being that of Fischer, who worked closely with

30. These observations, based on Vandenhoute's work among the Dan, are derived from Gerbrands, *Art as an Element of Culture*. Note that more recent work by Himmelheber suggests that Vandenhoute's picture is no longer true.
31. Harley, *Notes on the Poro* and *Masks as Agents*; Hans Himmelheber, *Negerkunst und*

four sculptors, Tame, Si, Tompieme, and Sõn, studying their individual development.[32] He has shown, for example, that although they use similar tools
they use them in different ways, and that these techniques change with time
even for the individual artist, just as his style changes. Several observers have
remarked that the Dan carver will often work voluntarily, inspired, for example,
by a beautiful face; but he does not attempt to represent faithfully what he has
seen. Si expressed the attitude well in criticizing a spoon carved by Tompieme
to represent his daughter's face: "That isn't carved, it's a photograph," he said;
"some abstraction from reality is necessary in a work of art."

Such observations have rarely been recorded. It has usually been assumed that
there was no vocabulary in African languages to permit aesthetics to be studied.
The first aesthetic studies were experiments in ranking groups of sculptures.[33]
More recently Robert F. Thompson solicited criticisms of a number of sculptures
from Yoruba informants. He recorded their comments fully and then analyzed
the frequency with which reference was made to various criteria. He found that
moderate resemblance is of primary importance—that is, the sculpture should
look like a man, woman, animal, or whatever—but that the degree of resemblance has to be somewhere in the middle between exact portrayal and abstraction. Balanced visibility is also sought—an evenness of sculptural emphasis so
that no one part of the sculpture stands out more than another. The surface of
the sculpture is expected to be smoothly finished. Symmetry is also expected,
though a slight degree of asymmetry, as in the turn of a baby's head in a mother
and child figure, is acceptable. Human beings are also expected to be portrayed
in their prime. Facial expression is expected to be one of composure ("coolness"
is the Yoruba word).[34]

These criteria were established by informal discussions of works of art, not
by direct questioning; they appear to be valid criteria. It is interesting to compare

Negerkunstler ("Negro Art and Artists") (Stuttgart: Strecker und Schröder, 1933); P. J. L.
Vandenhoute, *Classification stylistique du masque Dan et Guéré de la Côte d'Ivoire* ("Stylistic
Classification of the Dan and Guéré Masks of the Ivory Coast"), Vol. IV (Leiden: Mede-
lingen van het Rijksmuseum voor Volkenkunde, 1948); and Vandenhoute, *Masks of the
Dan: Ivory Coast,* Art in Its Context Series: Studies in Ethno-Esthetics (The Hague: Mou-
ton, 1963).

32. E. Fischer, "Kunstler der Dan: die Bildhauer Tame, Si, Tompieme, und Sõn—
Ihr Wesen und Ihr Werk" ("Artists of the Dan: The Sculptors Tame, Si, Tompieme, and
Sõn—Their Life and Work"), *Baessler-Archiv,* n.s. X (1963), 161–263. Some of Fischer's
data and photographs appear in Hans Himmelheber, "Personality and Technique of
African Sculptors," *Technique and Personality,* Lecture Series, No. 3 (New York: Museum
of Primitive Art, 1963), pp. 80–110.

33. Gerbrands reports the experiments of Himmelheber and Vandenhoute, in *Art
as an Element of Culture,* pp. 67–93.

34. R. F. Thompson, "Esthetics in Traditional Africa," *Art News,* LXVI (January
1968), 44–45, 63–66; and more fully in Warren d'Azevedo, ed., *The Traditional Artist
in African Society* (forthcoming).

them with any good description of Yoruba sculpture and to note that some have been remarked upon by sensitive Western observers: the moderate naturalism has always been pointed out; the careful finish has been observed but not always mentioned; symmetry of pose is generally regarded as a basic African characteristic, as is the portrayal of human beings in their prime. Balanced visibility and composure of expression seem not to have been expressly remarked upon, yet these characteristics are obviously there to be seen in all good Yoruba sculpture. The judgment of sympathetic American or European observers, such as curators of collections of African art, of what is good and bad in Yoruba sculpture would probably agree with the judgment of the Yoruba themselves, even without knowing the criteria which Thompson has demonstrated. Yet without the demonstration of these criteria by field research, we would not have been justified in inferring them. In later field work Thompson has been able to show that the concept of "coolness" is admired in the other arts as well and is a reflection of a moral ideal. Armed with these criteria, the Western critic is able to check his own intuitive judgments of Yoruba sculpture by reference to the qualities the artist was seeking.

Thompson's analysis should not mislead us into thinking that Western sensitivity will produce judgments of all works of African art which will coincide with the aesthetic standards of their makers. Among the Lega (eastern Congo-Kinshasa), for example, Biebuyck found that all the traditional sculptures used by the Bwami Society in their rituals were judged to be "good," by which was meant that they fulfilled their functions. "Criticism of their appearance is inconceivable." As a result, celluloid dolls obtained by trade and used in the ritual enjoy equal regard with the traditional sculptures in ivory and wood.[35] This is surprising because the traditional objects served to demonstrate membership in the prestigious association and only initiated members could possess them; moreover, each traditional carving used in the ritual is associated with a proverb which expresses the ideal of moral beauty to which initiates aspire. It seems strange that objects which are presumably inexpensive and easily obtained should be accepted for use in this relatively exclusive society. Biebuyck observed that the possession of large numbers of the traditional objects reflected great prestige for the owner, for in order to acquire them he must have taken part in many rituals, and he must have served as head of the funerary ceremonies of other high-grade members since the objects are acquired chiefly by inheritance.[36] It is this very fact, however, which explains the acceptance of the foreign artifact, for the numbers alone are what matter; the quality and age of the pieces are of no importance.

35. Biebuyck, *Tradition and Creativity.*
36. Daniel Biebuyck, in *The Arts of Leadership,* ed. Douglas Fraser and Herbert Cole (forthcoming).

ARTISTIC INDIVIDUALITY AND ART HISTORY

One of the most interesting aspects of the study of African art in recent years has been the demonstration that the African artist is an individual. Most of this work has been done in Nigeria, where Kenneth Murray's pioneering work is recorded in the files of the Department of Antiquities. William Fagg's work among the Yoruba has already been mentioned, and Sieber's work in northern Nigeria is also noteworthy.[37] One of the first individual artists to be recognized, however, was the master of Buli, a Luba district in the southern Congo, whose work was identified by Olbrechts.[38] A recent study by Willett and Picton has attempted to establish the criteria by which the work of individual sculptors may be identified in a society in which the apprentice works with the master on major works.[39] This is a problem familiar to the historians of European medieval art, and it demonstrates again that African art is art and can be studied in just the same way as any other art. The serious study of African art is still young, but despite this, rapid progress has been made in some aspects of the work. In 1950, Griaule was able to write:

> It is hardly possible . . . to envisage the evolution of this art. Our knowledge is too fragmentary: that is to say that we shall not speak of historical art, where the data are non-existent.[40]

Less than two decades later, there is a substantial and growing literature dealing with the history of sculpture, especially in West Africa; and, thanks to the techniques of archaeology and of radiocarbon dating, we can already sketch the outline of the succession of artistic styles even though the precise details of connections remain obscure.[41]

On sites at Taruga and Nok (northern Nigeria) we have radiocarbon dates of 440 B.C. $\pm$ 140 (I-2960), 300 B.C. $\pm$ 100 (I-3400), and 280 B.C. $\pm$ 120 (I-1457) (Taruga), and A.D. 207 $\pm$ 50 (Y-474) (Nok)[42] from deposits which contain the

37. Roy Sieber, *Sculpture of Northern Nigeria* (New York: Museum of Primitive Art, 1961).

38. Olbrechts, *Plastiek van Kongo.* Since then, more pieces by the same hand have been discovered; see, for example, Olbrechts, "La Statuaire du Congo Belge," *Les Arts plastiques* (Brussels: Editions Erasme, 1951), fig. 3.

39. Frank Willett and John Picton, "On the Identification of Individual Carvers: A Study of Ancestor Shrine Carvings from Owo, Nigeria," *Man,* n.s. II (1967), 62–70.

40. *Folk Art,* p. 24.

41. Frank Willett, *Ife in the History of West African Sculpture* (London: Thames & Hudson; New York: McGraw-Hill, 1967).

42. Radiocarbon dates are expressed with a standard deviation which shows not the absolute range of possible dates but the limits within which there is a two-to-one chance that the true date lies. Doubling the standard deviation increases the probability to nineteen to one, while trebling it makes the chance 997 to 3 — almost certainty. The number quoted in parentheses is the laboratory reference number which serves to identify the

oldest known sculptures from Africa south of the Sahara. These Nok figures are highly sophisticated in style and are worked in terracotta. They are now commonly thought to be ancestral in some way to the naturalistic sculptures of Ife, which are found in brass as well as in terracotta. Ife sculptures in brass have not yet been recovered by archaeological excavation, but terracotta sculptures excavated in 1963 were found to have been already broken and collapsed in buildings which were occupied about A.D. 1060 ± 130 (B.M.-262) and A.D. 1150 ± 200 (M-2119). Stylistic studies in Ife have shown the development of this art into the modern Yoruba style. Oral traditions as well as stylistic studies have demonstrated that the Benin bronzes also derive from the Ife tradition; their evolution has been well demonstrated by William Fagg.

Another remarkable style of bronze casting is represented by finds made at Igbo Ukwu in southeastern Nigeria. Radiocarbon dates from different parts of this site are A.D. 840 ± 145 (I-1784), A.D. 840 ± 110 (Hv-1515), A.D. 850 ± 120 (I-2008), and A.D. 875 ± 130 (Hv-1514), much earlier than had been considered possible.[43] The mound at Daima in the extreme northeast of Nigeria has furnished evidence of the evolution of culture from a late stone age through to recent times. In these deposits there are simple sculptures in terracotta whose evolution is currently being studied and dated by radiocarbon.[44] The results of the study should throw light on the evolution of "Sao" terra cottas found in Chad by Lebeuf,[45] for which only two radiocarbon dates have so far been published: A.D. 1700 ± 90 (Gsy-92) and A.D. 1785 ± 100 (Gsy-93). The sculptures at Daima begin earlier than a level dated A.D. 450 ± 670 (I-2371) and A.D. 480 ± 270 (I-2370) and continue much later.[46]

A much neglected field in art history is the study of architectural history. The archaeologist will have an increasingly important role to play in recovering plans of buildings and evidence for dating. At present, the study of the Zimbabwe complex (Southern Rhodesia) is the outstanding example of a published study of this type,[47] though clearly there will be others. That the data need not be

particular sample which furnished the date. For an account of the technique involved, see W. F. Libby, *Radiocarbon Dating* (Chicago: University of Chicago Press, 1955). A shorter account, especially helpful to the non-specialist, is Harold Barker, "Radio Carbon Dating: Its Scope and Limitations," *Antiquity*, XXXII (December 1958), 253–63.

43. Thurstan Shaw, "Radiocarbon Dates from Nigeria," *Journal of the Historical Society of Nigeria*, III (1967), 743–57.

44. G. E. Connah, " 'Classic' Excavation in North-East Nigeria," *Illustrated London News*, Archaeological Section 2276, October 14, 1967, pp. 42–44.

45. J.-P. Lebeuf and A. Masson-Detourbet, *La Civilisation du Tchad* ("The Chad Culture") (Paris: Editions Payot, 1950); Lebeuf, *L'Art ancien du Tchad, bronzes et céramiques* ("Ancient Art of Chad, in Bronze and Pottery") (Paris: Grand Palais, 1962).

46. Shaw, "Radiocarbon Dates from Nigeria," pp. 741–42.

47. K. R. Robinson, R. Summers, and A. Whitty, *Zimbabwe Excavations 1958*, Occasional Papers, III (Salisbury: National Museum of Southern Rhodesia, 1961).

restricted to stone buildings has been demonstrated by the excavation of mud walls at Benin.[48]

Other points of growth for the future study of African art will clearly center on studies of individual artists, their training, and the development of their style. The uses and meanings of art in the society also need much more explanation. Horton's work on the Kalabari has recorded a great deal of their iconology, as has Bastin's work on Chokwe art.[49] At the moment such works are quite exceptional. And of course we need to know more about the standards of assessment of art in different societies. That these problems be studied in the field is a most urgent need as the traditional arts are being eroded by changes in the societies which produce them.

ART AND SOCIAL CHANGE

Traditional African art is subject to change owing to a number of influences originating outside the continent. One of the oldest of these influences is Islam. Islamic religion and cultural patterns have been so firmly established in North Africa, the northern parts of West Africa, the Horn, and along the east coast that they can be regarded almost as a traditional way of life in these areas. At the same time, in many respects these areas belong with the Islamic world as a whole. This is especially true of their art, for Islam discourages the representation of nature and encourages instead elaborate ornamental designs. As early as the eleventh century the area from the Senegal River northwards and into Spain fell within the Almoravid Empire, and although this rule collapsed in the following century we find no representational art in this area. This conversion to Islam, however, was not always total. The conversion of the Nupe (Nigeria), for example, probably began some centuries ago and was considered complete by the early nineteenth century, yet some pre-Islamic cults are still practiced among the Nupe. A number of their masks were collected in Mokwa in 1911,[50] and others are reported to be still in use today. In general, however, most Nupe art of the present day consists of strictly non-representational ornament—for example, the decoration on sculptured doors and stools and on embossed and *repoussé* brass and silver work.[51]

48. G. E. Connah, "Archaeological Research in Benin City, 1961–1964," *Journal of the Historical Society of Nigeria*, II (1964), 465–77.

49. M.-L. Bastin, *L'Art décoratif Tchokwe* ("Chokwe Decorative Art") (Lisbon: Companhia de Diamantes de Angola, 1961).

50. For illustrations see W. B. Fagg, *African Tribal Sculptures I: The Niger Basin Tribes* (New York: Tudor, 1966), pl. 17; and Fagg, *Nigerian Images*, pl. 140.

51. See, for example, Phillips Stevens, "Nupe Wood Carving," *Nigeria Magazine*, No. 88 (1966), pp. 21–35.

Christianity, too, has long been an influence in Africa. Coptic Christianity in Egypt and Ethiopia goes back almost to the time of Christ. Nubia was Christian from the sixth century until the early seventeenth century, when it was finally converted to Islam. What ideas and artistic motifs may have been transmitted to the peoples of West Africa we do not yet know. Sporadic attempts at proselytization were made by European missionaries on the west coast of Africa from the fifteenth century onwards, the most substantial result of which was the establishment of the Portuguese-speaking Christian kingdom of Kongo. This kingdom reached its height in the first half of the sixteenth century (a Bakongo bishop was consecrated as early as 1521). However, there was a war with Portugal in 1665, after which Christianity was rejected by the Kongo people. The Christian period is commemorated in a crude series of cave paintings at Mbafu (Congo-Kinshasa),[52] and the emphatic naturalism of sculpture in the lower Congo area may well be due to European influence.

Christian missionaries in general, even up to the present day, have been culpably ignorant of indigenous African religions. In attempting to undermine these religions, they have attacked the sculptures which gave expression to spiritual ideas in the often mistaken belief that these were idols and the object of worship. There have also been iconoclastic movements of a non-Christian type—the Atinga cult, for example, in 1951 was responsible for the destruction of sculptures on a massive scale throughout southwestern Yorubaland in its attempt to root out witchcraft and sorcery.[53] Fortunately ecumenism is overtaking these parochial attitudes. A pioneering effort was made by a group of Society of African Missions (S.M.A.) fathers in Nigeria, who established at Oye Ekiti a center for craftsmen who employed traditional forms of sculpture, weaving, embroidery, leatherwork, and beadwork to help in the worship of the Christian God. The scheme was closed down after a few experimental years, but Father Kevin Carroll was able to continue privately to encourage a number of sculptors, who, although not necessarily Christian themselves, were told stories from the Bible and then carved them on doors, screens, and sedilia for a number of churches. The visual representation of these stories corresponds to the sculptures, paintings, and stained glass in the European churches of the Middle Ages, which served both to inspire Christian sentiments in the worshipers and to instruct those members of the congregation who could not read. Father Carroll has described this work himself.[54] The plates in his book show that the traditional

---

52. G. Mortelmans and R. Monteyne, "La Grotte peinte de Mbafu, témoignage iconographique de la première évangelisation du Bas-Congo" ("The Painted Cave of Mbafu, Pictorial Evidence of the First Evangelization of the Lower Congo"), *Actes du 4ᵉ Congrès Panafricain de Préhistoire* (Tervuren: Musée Royal de l'Afrique Centrale, 1962), pp. 457–86.

53. Peter Morton-Williams, "The Atinga Cult among the South-Western Yoruba," *Bulletin de l'Institut Français d'Afrique Noire,* XVIII (1956), 315–34.

54. *Yoruba Religious Carving: Pagan and Christian Sculpture in Nigeria and Dahomey* (New York: Praeger, 1967).

sculptural forms are well able to convey the ideas of the new religion. Yet there is a close association between traditional forms of sculpture and traditional religions; and as Christianity or secular humanism replaces traditional beliefs, this sculpture tends to decline and die out. Father Carroll's work affords a real hope of replacing the religious basis for art and resuscitating the traditional art before it dies completely.

There are other influences undermining the traditional bases of sculpture in African societies. The migration of young men to the towns takes away many of the candidates for initiation, and thus reduces the demand for ritual art. The increasing interest in African art throughout Europe and America has resulted in certain able and well-known artists being overworked, to the detriment of their art. Easier transportation has also led to the development of a souvenir trade, the products of which are sometimes known as "airport art." The carvings, often in ebony (which seems never to have been carved in Africa before the death of Queen Victoria's consort, Prince Albert, gave a fillip in England to all things black), bear slight resemblance to traditional forms and are carved with European tools to fulfill the European's stereotypes of African art. Identical pieces can be bought at any international airport in Africa. If the term "art" implies an individual creation by the artist, then airport art is non-art.

The European demand for African sculpture has not always been so debasing in its effects. The Afro-Portuguese ivories, made in the sixteenth century to suit European taste without doing too much violence to traditional form, are of high artistic quality. Most of them seem to have been made at Sherbro off the coast of Sierra Leone though some were made in Benin.[55]

Western education is also influencing the work of African artists. Since the colonial period, artistically talented people have been drawn into the European educational system; if they have cultivated their gifts it has been along European lines. "Modern" (as opposed to "traditional") African artists have been trained as Western artists; many of them see the traditional art of their own society from outside rather than from within. They no longer subscribe to the religious beliefs which gave meaning to the art of their ancestors, and so see the external forms of the traditional sculptures but may not be any closer to grasping the inner meaning than were Derain, Vlaminck, or Picasso, who saw African art simply as new interpretations of natural forms.

The wheel has come full circle. Modern art was liberated from nineteenth-century naturalism by the example of African and other non-European art forms—now African artists are being absorbed into the cosmopolitan world of modern art, which seems, as a result of the modern media of communication,

55. W. B. Fagg, *Afro-Portuguese Ivories* (London: Batchworth Press, 1959); A. F. C. Ryder, "A Note on the Afro-Portuguese Ivories," *Journal of African History,* V (1964), 363–65.

to have lost regional distinctions. This offers a new hope for mutual understanding; but, perhaps equally important, the study of traditional African art may provide the newly independent states with their best hope of acceptance and understanding by the world at large—a world which already recognizes African art as part of the heritage of the whole of mankind.

8

Ethnomusicology in Africa

KLAUS WACHSMANN

> What then *is* time? If no one asks me,
> I know; if I want to explain it to a
> questioner, I do not know.
> —Augustinus [Africanus], *Confessiones.*

THE MOST RECENT BIBLIOGRAPHY on music in Africa lists some 3,000 references, essays, and books.[1] This is a formidable accumulation of sources on a subject which not so long ago seemed unimportant. Students whose main interest is the role of music in society may now find it possible to obtain a fairly accurate and balanced picture of African music from the literature alone. Others whose concern is with musical sound will have to turn in addition to the many collections on disc and tape that are now listed in discographies.[2]

To listen to recordings is not as simple as to read a book. What sort of experience is the listener of African music supposed to be after? In the "Scènes de la vie des Dogon," a famous disc from Mali, an example of funeral music is included.[3] Does the student who plays the disc within the four walls of his study, adjusting the volume and the quality of the sound to suit his own taste, listen to a funeral or does he listen to music? Much depends on when and where the listening takes place and who the listener is. Obviously, the experience of a Dogon musician in a real performance among the Dogon is different from that of the foreign student at home in his study.

1. L. J. P. Gaskin, comp., *A Select Bibliography of Music in Africa* (London: International African Institute, 1965).
2. Alan P. Merriam, *African Music on LP: An Annotated Discography* (Evanston, Ill.: Northwestern University Press, forthcoming).
3. Geneviève Calame-Griaule and Blaise Calame, collectors, "Scènes de la vie des Dogon (Soudan Français)," Les Tresors de l'art musical populaire, No. 9 (Paris: Resonances, 1958).

It would not be surprising, then, if students felt that there should be two different disciplines to match the two kinds of inquiry: one concerned with music per se, and the other with music as human behavior.[4] In this way—so the argument might go—justice would be done to the world's music, and the main needs of Western scholars of this decade would be met. Yet, in the music of Africa, in practice and on philosophical grounds, such a twofold approach appears to be selective rather than comprehensive, leading in the end to a limited understanding of African musical experience. There is a harshness in the dichotomy of the approach that needs softening; after all, the approach has its effects on feeling and thinking, and considerations of this kind should provide the guiding principles of the discourse.

Musical experience is complex wherever it occurs, and it cannot be reduced to simple formulas without distorting it. The word "music" itself is used as if everyone knew what it was and as if the concept existed everywhere in identical form. This may be an illusion engendered by the kind of terminology that writers on music use when they compare their own music with that of other peoples. Usually, the terminology is the vocabulary of Western music communication and education, and with the terminology goes the Western habit of analyzing and categorizing.

In musical experience in general, and in African music in particular, analysis is a double-edged weapon. Teilhard de Chardin spoke of analysis as

> that marvellous instrument of scientific research to which we owe all our advances but which, breaking down synthesis after synthesis, allows one soul after another to escape leaving us confronted with a pile of dismantled machinery, and evanescent particles.[5]

Teilhard de Chardin is brought into this discourse because the foremost African poet and philosopher of our time, Léopold Sédar Senghor, shares his sentiments.[6] Senghor sets himself against the Western habit of analysis and strives to protect the African arts from its influence. Although research that analyzes (that is, that differentiates individual traits) will remain with us—unless our concepts change radically—the scene is set for the search for the wholeness

4. This issue is thoroughly discussed by Mantle Hood in "Music, the Unknown," in *Musicology*, by Frank L. Harrison, Mantle Hood, and Claude V. Palisca (Englewood Cliffs, N.J.: Prentice-Hall, 1963), pp. 215–326; Alan P. Merriam, *The Anthropology of Music* (Evanston, Ill.: Northwestern University Press, 1964); Harold S. Powers, review of *The Anthropology of Music* by Alan P. Merriam, in *Perspectives of New Music* (Spring-Summer 1966), pp. 161–71; Charles Seeger, "On the Tasks of Musicology," *Ethnomusicology*, VII (1963), 214–15.

5. Pierre Teilhard de Chardin, *The Phenomenon of Man* (New York: Harper & Row, 1955), p. 257.

6. Léopold Sédar Senghor, *Pierre Teilhard de Chardin et la politique africaine*, Cahiers Pierre Teilhard de Chardin, Vol. III (Paris: Editions du Seuil, 1962).

of vision in African music. And thus it is probable that a search for synthesis rather than analysis will inspire students in African music in the coming years. The desire in many universities and schools in Africa and in America to set up performance laboratories and workshops might conceivably be a part of this trend toward synthesis. But the quest for the wholeness of musical vision is a challenge, not only for performers but also for musicologists, linguists, social anthropologists, and, of course, philosophers.

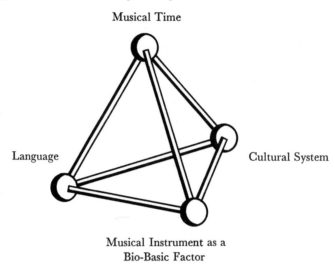

Musical Time

Language   Cultural System

Musical Instrument as a
Bio-Basic Factor

A drawing of a three-dimensional model of the entity "music" conceived as a system of four interacting factors.

Because of the complexity of the experience, one would wish that musicians could do what according to Medawar is done by scientists, namely, "build explanatory structures, *telling stories* which are scrupulously tested to see if they are about real life."[7] One would wish, for instance, that there were in music a way of thinking that was analogous to the use of molecular models that has been so important for the understanding of the physical universe. Like music cultures, molecules have their individual identity which differs in accordance with the kind of atoms of which they are composed and the kind of arrangement in which the atoms hold together. While this excursion into science must seem farfetched, nevertheless the fact remains that scientists can make models of invisible, intricate interrelations and find such models useful in research and teaching. Here may be a fresh approach to analogous problems in African musicology, where scholars similarly conceive of an entity as a complex arrangement of basic units that are said to combine in some definable fashion. The diagram above is in-

7. P. B. Medawar, *The Art of the Soluble* (London: Methuen, 1967), p. 152. See also p. 127, note 2: "A 'story' is more than a hypothesis: it is a theory, a hypothesis together with what follows from it and goes with it, and it has the clear connotation of completeness within its own limits."

tended to illustrate this analogy between the procedures of the physicist and those of the musicologist.

The diagram, in a manner of speaking, represents a model of a conceptual "molecule," that is, of music-in-general. The four corners are the musical "atoms": cultural system; musical instrument as an extension of the body of the performer, that is, as a bio-basic precultural factor; musical time; and language. The figure is a regular tetrahedron and thus emphasizes the viewpoint that the four aspects are of equal significance in music—the distances between them, that is, the six "rods" that bind the four aspects together, are of equal length, and the angles at which these bonds meet are identical; none can be said to dominate. What the figure is intended to convey, then, is that, ideally, music-in-general (and music-in-particular, as in the African context) *is* an integrated whole and that, in discussing it, none of the four aspects and none of the six bonds that interrelate them can be disregarded without weakening the concept of the integrity of the whole. In the present discussion we are concerned with "African music," and in this sense the figure also represents Senghor's philosophy, the only explicit philosophy of music as an entity that has so far come out of Africa.

At the same time the diagram serves as a plan of procedure for this discourse. The discourse falls into two parts: the first part discusses the four aspects or universals of music, and the second part is devoted to a discussion of the interactions among the four aspects.

THE FOUR ASPECTS IN AFRICAN MUSIC

Any attempt to define the four aspects separately brings with it a weakness in that it diverts attention from African music as an entity and creates an illusion that the aspects are isolated and do not merge into one another. At this stage of African musicology it would be helpful to the student to become aware of the merging of these aspects rather than to proceed heuristically *as though* one could isolate them. Concern over the definitions of these factors in the past has led to a fragmented view. It is precisely this fragmentation that African philosophers like Senghor have found distorting and reprehensible, and that, ultimately, can be said to separate Occidental from Oriental aesthetics. However, a discussion of definitions does not have to result in simple formulas; it will have served its purpose if it provides opportunities to discuss the demands that the definitions will have to meet.

Cultural System

Musicians have always talked about their affairs, their masters, their public, their pupils, their status, and their attitudes. In African musical studies, emphasis is often placed on social behavior, but this emphasis is also strong in Western music. A glance at the rows of biographies and histories on the shelves of the music libraries shows how deeply musicologists have been concerned with the human, as opposed to the purely sonal, dimension of music.

To approach the music-making of another people through the life histories of its musicians is most useful, as has been demonstrated by the studies and seminars that were undertaken by J. H. Nketia's program of African musicology at the University of Ghana.[8] In these biographical pursuits the musician's role stands out in relief against his environment, regardless of whether his reaction to the environment is active or passive.

Rightly or wrongly, culture is commonly understood to refer to the secondary environment that man has created for himself. The very term "African music" has the connotation that for an African musician this environment is different from that of a non-African. While the statement is obviously true, it reveals a bias in method because it focuses on differences rather than on similarities.[9] However, this bias may be losing its hold: witness Nettl's thesis that the music of Europe and Africa were sufficiently alike to be set off against the music of the rest of the world,[10] and Horton's reminder that the search for common concepts that social anthropology had neglected in the past ought to be pursued systematically in the future.[11]

Within the corpus of African music Western musicologists generally place more emphasis on similarities over vast distances than on the features that distinguish the music of one community from that of its neighbors. Musicologists, like linguists and ethnographers, are accustomed to thinking of their data in regional terms. An excellent example is Norma McLeod's recent survey of musical stylistic criteria in Madagascar.[12] What makes this survey especially commendable is the fact that here the musical cultures of Madagascar are mapped out not merely by reference to a few selected parameters but on the basis of a comprehensive picture.

If influences from outside Africa have added to the variety of culture in the

8. See, for example, Nicholas Z. Nayo, "Akpalu and His Sons" (M.A. thesis, University of Ghana, 1964). Professor Nketia and I conducted a joint seminar at the University of Ghana in 1965 on Music in African Society in which biography took a prominent place.

9. Studies with regard to generalities and universals in music, that is, a world-wide approach, have been made from time to time. See, for example, Curt Sachs, *Geist und der Werden der Musikinstrumente* (Berlin: Dietrich Reimer, 1928); André Schaeffner, *Origine des instruments de musique* (Paris: Editions Payot, 1936); Heinrich Husmann, *Grundlagen der Antiken und Orientalischen Musikkultur* (Berlin: de Gruyter, 1961); Marius Schneider, *Geschichte der Mehrstimmigkeit, Part I: Die Naturvölker* (Berlin: Julius Bard Verlag, 1934).

10. Bruno Nettl, *Folk and Traditional Music of the Western Continents* (Englewood Cliffs, N.J.: Prentice-Hall, 1965).

11. Robin Horton, "African Traditional Thought and Western Science," *Africa*, XXXVII (1967), 50–71.

12. "The Stylistic Characteristics of the Music of Madagascar" (Paper read at the African Studies Association meeting, Los Angeles, October 1968).

continent, music is hardly likely to have remained unaffected. Apart from the European contacts in recent centuries, one can speculate about Arab traits, Islamic as well as pre-Islamic, and about the impact of Mediterranean antiquity and of Persia, India, Indonesia, and China. The place of the civilization of ancient Egypt in relation to the rest of ancient Africa has a fascination of its own. One would like to write the history of music in Africa in terms of these influences, but too many pieces in the puzzle are missing.

Musicologists find it difficult to distinguish between various kinds of foreign influence, for instance, between simple borrowing that does not affect the musical system as such — like the occurrence of English or Arabic loanwords in African languages — and wholesale exchange of one musical system for another; similarly, it is difficult to decide where common traits can be accounted for by derivation from a common stock. The scarcity of reliable data, either in sound or in notation, is responsible for many of the problems in African ethnomusicology. No recordings are available from before 1900, and in any case the first decade of this century did not yield a rich harvest.[13] One often wishes that travelers throughout the centuries had been more observant in musical matters; if they could not record music they could at least have noted the musical values of the peoples they visited in Africa. However, even this approach is not without difficulties; those travelers who did report on musical values were guided by their own value systems. Even a skillful scholar like Ludolf remained a prisoner of his cultural bias: on being told by his Ethiopian informants in Rome that Ethiopian priests danced in the church before the Ark of the Covenant, Ludolf was disgusted.[14] Such a response to another culture is not uncommon, although today students of African music are sometimes known to go to the other extreme in being ready to accept any music, as long as it smacks of Africa. The theories and methods of social anthropology in their dealings with other cultures can teach musicians a great deal.

Musical Instrument

It must be stated from the outset that the use of the term "musical instrument" in this essay embraces the bio-basic factor found in the movement required in playing and thus goes well beyond the narrow meaning which it has in Western music.[15] In Africa neither "musical" nor "instrument" can be taken for granted, and thus it is advisable to begin an investigation of the term from the broadest possible base. The statement that a musical instrument is a sound-making object

---

13. K. P. Wachsmann, "Music" (Paper read at the Oral Data Conference of the African Studies Association meeting, Los Angeles, October 1968), to be published in *Journal of the Folklore Institute,* Indiana University.

14. J. Ludolf, *A New History of Ethiopia,* trans. J. P. Gent (London, 1682).

15. Edward T. Hall, *The Silent Language* (Garden City, N.Y.: Doubleday, 1959), p. 60: "There is an unbroken continuity between the far past and the present, for culture is bio-basic — rooted in biological activities."

would provide such a base: any object will do as long as its manipulation has the desired effect. Yet the term "object" is not as simple as it appears at first glance. In Africa the definition is extended well beyond the limited usage of the Western instrumentalist who, quite unreasonably, separates in his thinking (but of course not in his action) the manner of performance from the object on which he performs.

Yet, object and bio-basic factor can hardly be separated. If a musical instrument were to be separated from usage, it would be difficult to tell whether a drum was a stool or a table or a container or a parrying weapon or a garden roller. "Usage" implies here the dependence of the object on the human body in a most intimate manner. In a trumpet it is obvious that the player's lips, the essential mechanism, are not a part of the object, if "object" is the thing by itself. This generally is the Western view, where one thinks of the human physique as something apart from the object, so much so that "singing" is differentiated from "musical instrument" because there is no visible object involved. In African music there is hardly a performance that is purely instrumental or purely vocal either in concept or in execution, and thus in this essay musical instrument embraces voice.

It is desirable therefore to shift the emphasis from "object" to "manipulation," removing the inquiry from the sphere of the inanimate to that of the living. Such a step would make exacting demands on a museum's curator. It would mean that his card index—for instance, in the case of a drum—would describe the object not only in terms of itself but also in relation to the manner in which it is played in terms of the drummer's physiology. If an instrument is to be regarded from the point of view of the sound that it is meant to produce, the object itself can yield only superficial insight. The word "inanimate," however, should not be applied too rigidly where African attitudes are under review. Among the Gola of Liberia, loss of or damage to an instrument provokes the same response of distress as would the loss of a beloved person,[16] and in the interlacustrine kingdoms of East Africa a drum may be treated as if it were a person and not an inanimate object.

If musical instruments belong to the corporeal equipment of the player, if they are extensions of the body, as it were, and if *any* object is acceptable as an instrument because of its potential as a sound-maker, then the student finds himself involved with human *movement* in a much more general sense—not only the movement of performers seated in the orchestra but also of performers who, as in many African contexts, move around and dance while they play. In the final account it may even be logical to include dance in the study of musical instruments. Many students of the arts in Africa believe that they must free

16. Warren d'Azevedo, "The Artist Archetype in Gola Culture" (Paper read at the Conference on the Traditional Artist in African Society, Lake Tahoe, 1965).

themselves from the Western preconception that music is one thing and dance is another, or that when music and dance occur in conjunction one must be subordinated to the other. Western musicians tend to speak of accompaniment rather than of collaboration, although it is difficult to determine on what grounds they decide which mode "accompanies" and which leads.

In short, in African musical studies the instrument must be regarded essentially as "an extrapolation of basic motor activity."[17] It will also be seen later that although an instrument is a sound-maker it has other roles in which sound is of only secondary significance. (But it might be remembered that what is secondary and what is primary is not so much a matter of fact as a matter of viewpoint, and it is viewpoints that a discussion of African music must take into account.)

Language

Enough has been said elsewhere in this volume to make special reference to language seem redundant here.[18] However, a musician sees speech in several special ways.

First of all, language enables him to communicate about "musical time"; everyday words provide him with the vocabulary that he needs for the specific references that must be made about music. The very fact that the study of music in Africa requires an informant or teacher who "informs" not only by demonstration but also by verbal emphasis and explanation makes this point.

Second, since music and language have in common pitch, timbre, loudness, duration, and also social reference and the potential of message content, speech is bound to print through on music. In Africa a useful working hypothesis is that there is little music that does not have some affinity with words.

Third, in Africa, as elsewhere, the word is said to have force of a kind that cannot be separated from music. Senghor will be quoted on this in the section below on language and musical time. One almost begins to suspect that Africa does not express a concept of music qua music because, as in ancient Greece, concepts about speech embrace music so intimately.

Fourth, there are elements in language that have special significance for musicians, for instance, that commonplace "speech notation," the alphabet. To the musician, the letters of the alphabet look like a timbre notation. In a word like *Rumpelstiltskin,* or even a simple phrase like *go home,* the letters would indicate a rapid transition from one timbre to another, and, in consequence, the words themselves would not only be names or have "literal" meaning but could be interpreted as the "orchestration" of the human voice. A logical end to this line of thought is the use of "word sounds," for instance in the music of Berio.

17. Lewis Mumford, "Technics and the Nature of Man," *Technology and Culture,* VII (1966), 303–17.
18. See Jack Berry, "Language Systems and Literature," in this volume.

(In Western composition it is the technique of orchestration that deals with timbre; in Africa one might usefully surrender to the impact of this kaleidoscopic timbre usage.)

Fifth, music everywhere uses verbal formulas to give continuity to musical form. The frequent responses on sounds like *eh eh eh* may or may not be speech, but the harpist's sung formulas certainly are; a few examples might be *wulira* (listen), *nkwebaza* (I thank you), and *nkola ntya* (what shall I do) in the Luganda language, or *jobano* (you there) in Ateso.[19] The voice is both an organ of speech and a musical instrument of non-speech. Bushman music, for instance, although it may be vocal, does not have to have words,[20] and the voice in collaboration with certain apparatus, for example, the kazoo and flutes proper, ceases to articulate words.[21] The vocal organ is also most noticeably in evidence in the ὀλολυγή (the exultant shout of the women uttered at the extreme upper range of the voice, often around high C), which is so important and whose special significance is acknowledged in several African languages by naming it differently from ululation proper.

Sixth, it is often the language in which a song is sung that decides for the ordinary man the attitude he adopts toward it. In Buganda (Uganda), for instance, it was found that a Bach chorale with Luganda words was first of all identified as *kiganda*, that is, a thing in Ganda fashion; thus it was altogether difficult to speak of the setting of the music in isolation from the text.

Finally, it is not always fruitful in Africa to break down the entity "verbal art" into the dichotomy of narration versus song. The *chante fable*, a mixed form, is widespread, but musicologists and artists have not taken much notice of it. In the *chante fable*, sections that are relatively more like narration alternate with sections that are relatively more like sung poetry (and in Africa most poetry is sung).

Musical Time

African music is readily identified with the word "rhythm," but the sense in which this term is understood with relation to Africa is comparatively narrow. (There is already among the ranks of African musicians some reluctance to accept for their music the role of "red-hot drum rhythm and wild tunes" into which the West has cast music in all of Africa.[22])

19. K. P. Wachsmann, collector, LP disc and commentary on music and Uganda (Los Angeles: Institute of Ethnomusicology, University of California at Los Angeles, forthcoming).

20. Nicholas M. England, "Bushman Counterpoint," *Journal of the International Folk Music Council*, XIX (1967), 59.

21. Simkha Aron and Geneviève Taurelle, collectors, "The Music of the Ba-Benzélé Pygmies," LP disc in UNESCO collection: *An Anthology of African Music*, ed. Paul Collaer (Kassel: Bärenreiter-Musicaphon).

22. For example, Fela Sowande, " 'Oyigiyigi,' Introduction, Theme and Variations on a Yoruba Folk Theme, for Organ" (New York: Ricordi, 1958).

"Rhythm" in this sense appears to refer exclusively to the bare bones of durational patterns marked off by percussive sounds, but it is hoped that the origins of this selective approach will sooner or later become a subject for the student of the history of ideas. It is well to remember that the word "rhythm" could be used in a broader sense as a kind of time, as in clock time, or biological time, or social time, and with regard to music as musical time. A listener creates musical time by a very complex scheme: there are accents of different loudness and pitch, changes of timbre and sequences of pitches (that is, melody) apart from accent. Timbre includes the phenomena of attack, duration, and decay of "individual" sounds. Since these manifold phenomena change either relatively slowly or relatively rapidly — without change the notion of music would vanish — it can be said that music experience is just another word for the experience of motion; H. W. Fowler has a point when he says that "Rhythm is Flow."[23]

The complexity of musical time in this sense is inaccessible to differentiation of all its components simultaneously, but if they are approached one by one these components may yield some of their obscurity.[24] Different interpretations have been put, for instance, to rhythm in the narrow sense by different musicologists. Merriam's account is a useful summary of these interpretations:

> Ward notes one drum playing a basically unvarying beat; Hornbostel sees the organization [of rhythm] in terms of motor behavior which is the opposite of the Western concept; Waterman postulates the concept of the metronome sense; and Jones makes the point of lack of coincidence of the main beats.[25]

An aspect that has been brought to the attention of performers, especially Western performers of drum music from the Guinea Coast, is the matter of pulse. Mantle Hood believed that these polyrhythmic structures presupposed a flair for pulse. Nicholas England went further by suggesting that Bushmen musicians whom he knew intimately were capable of a subconscious attention to a far more rapid pulse than was possible for Western musicians.[26]

Complementary to the narrow view of African rhythm is the opinion that in African music pitch is of secondary importance. It is on points such as these that current musical thinking fails us. Rightly or wrongly, in the West concepts of pitch require a reference to notions like scale and frequencies and intervals expressed in frequency ratios, with the implication that they must be rigidly and narrowly standardized, preferably by physical, measurable norms. This is what

23. See the discussion in Curt Sachs, *Rhythm and Tempo* (New York: W. W. Norton, 1953), p. 13.

24. On this point, see Anton Ehrenzweig, *The Hidden Order of Art: A Study in the Psychology of Artistic Imagination* (Berkeley and Los Angeles: University of California Press, 1967).

25. Alan P. Merriam, "African Music," *Continuity and Change in African Cultures*, ed. W. R. Bascom and M. J. Herskovits (Chicago: University of Chicago Press, 1958), pp. 49–86.

26. Personal communication.

the textbooks suggest. While these views may have justification in some respects, they certainly are misleading in others.

Enough material is available to alert the student not to shortchange pitch and timbre aspects of African music. The data on tuning procedures,[27] on microtonal interval structures,[28] and on timbre contrast may well persuade him to postpone judgment on the relative value of percussive rhythm and the rhythm that the elements of tone supply. Musical time depends on both. It may be useful to give an example of how, on a very simple level, even in the context of drumming, an African musician may react to a disregard of pitch. The incident took place recently in Uganda when a recording made several years ago was played back to an expert drummer on an inferior machine. The drummer angrily rejected the sounds because he could not hear clearly enough the pitches in which the four drums of the ensemble stood. This led to lively conversation, in the course of which the expert burst forth into vocal demonstration of the pitches which the drum quartet should have sounded had the machine reproduced them properly.

One incident does not establish a rule for the whole continent; however, it may serve to put the student on his guard that rhythm, that is, the "flow" of music, is not solely a matter of counting the time values between percussive sounds, be it literally or metaphorically.

In the second part of this essay, an attempt is made to give an outline of the bonds that in Africa tie together the universal aspects of music—cultural system, musical instrument and bio-basic factors, language, and musical time—as they have been presented in the above paragraphs.

INTERACTION AMONG THE FOUR UNIVERSALS

Cultural System and Musical Time

Music and society are for many people the two sides of one and the same coin, but different cultures speak and think differently about them. In the overtly materialistic ways of life of the West, music would not rank high on the list of needs that a person would want to satisfy. But it would probably be a different matter in Africa—at least this is what one would conclude from the depth of involvement of music in all African social activities. It does not matter under

27. See, for example, Hugh Tracey, *Chopi Musicians: Their Music, Poetry and Instruments* (London: Oxford University Press, 1948); K. P. Wachsmann, "An Equal-Stepped Tuning in a Ganda Harp," *Nature*, CLXV (1950), 40; K. P. Wachsmann, "Pen-equidistance and Accurate Pitch: A Problem from the Source of the Nile," in *Festschrift für Walter Wiora*, ed. Ludwig Finscher and Christoph-Hellmut Mahling (Kassel: Bärenreiter, 1967), pp. 583–92.
28. Gilbert Rouget, "Un chromatisme africain," *L'Homme, revue française d'anthropologie* (September–December 1961).

what headings these activities of a community are grouped; each will have its own musical expression. Take, for instance, the following seven headings, as they might occur to a curator of an ethnological museum: primary food production, including husbandry and hunting; industry; mental and physical health; clothing and adornment; settlement and housing; transport and communication; and status and authority. Beliefs and practices like spirit possession would bear on all the social activities under these headings and therefore need not be treated under a heading of their own.

Okot p'Bitek feels that if the bond between music and society were weakened, music would altogether cease to have meaning.[29] Lomax finds that parameters of music that at first sight are intrinsically musical have correlations with levels of subsistence complexity.[30] Fieldworkers in search of music in African communities find that a calendar of events, seasonal or other, is one of the keys that lead to the musical repertoire of a society.[31] Specific musical forms such as the leader-chorus form and the hocket texture of certain flute or trumpet practices (a rapid interlocking of small simple parts until they make a satisfactory whole) have been explained in terms of social attitudes: the responsorial pattern as a reflection of an attitude to leadership, and the hocket as an expression of a particular kind of community feeling in which a member sees himself as part of a group.[32]

Dance is often the visual realization of musical time and can be a medium for acting out any facet of the seven spheres of social activity mentioned above, including the individual's reaction to them. Music takes its place in the learning of those processes that the seven kinds of activities require.

Musical time can be an important outlet through which tension between tradition and innovation is channeled. Societies do not necessarily verbalize about innovation; in the West, for example, the student attempting to deal with innovation must fall back on the concepts of his own culture, such as invention, improvisation, and variation. Among the Baganda, however, the use of the term *ekisoko* (loosely, an addition to or variation of theme) resolves the issue. One learns, for instance, from Kasirye's book on the history of the kingdom of Buganda how public opinion and reaction to events were reflected in *ebisoko* of well-known old songs.[33] An interesting analogy to *ebisoko* accessible to Western

29. G. W. Kakoma, Gerald Moore, and Okot p'Bitek, eds., *First Conference on African Traditional Music* (Kampala: Makerere University, December 15–19, 1963).

30. Alan Lomax, *Folk Song Style and Culture: A Staff Report on Cantometrics* (Washington, D.C.: American Association for the Advancement of Science, 1968).

31. Wachsmann, "Music."

32. See K. P. Wachsmann, *Folk Musicians in Uganda* (Kampala: Uganda Argus [1956]), p. 8; and Wachsmann, "African Ethnomusicology: The Interrelation of Institutions, Musical Forms and Tribal Systems" (Paper read at the conference of the American Association for the Advancement of Science, Dallas, December 1968), p. 12.

33. Joseph S. Kasirye, *Abateregga ku Nnamulondo ya Buganda* ("The Princes in the Line of Succession to the Throne of Buganda")(London: Macmillan, East African Literature Bureau, 1959).

students is the topical texts that the children of London put to traditional games and nursery rhymes.[34]

Stylistic features are like flags that identify the group to which a people belong, and consequently differences in style make for xenophobia. Middleton reported from the Lugbara (Uganda) that new dances, fashionable with the young, were resented by the older people on the grounds that the dances were bad, naturally, since they had been imported from their non-Lugbara neighbors.[35]

Specific stylistic features may also lend themselves to specific activities, witness Neher's theory that dissociation takes place when drum pulses beat at the same rate as the alpha rhythm of the brain, and that these drum pulses are used deliberately in order to bring about a state of dissociation.[36]

Attitudes to rates of pulse and to changes in that rate may vary from group to group. Apparently, with regard to Africa, this was noticed rather late in the history of ethnomusicology. In 1948 Muller found that on the Somali coast "rhythm was slow at the beginning but accelerated towards the end of the dance."[37] In 1957 Calame-Griaule observed a similar practice among the Dogon; she interpreted the acceleration as generating spiritual force to promote the growth of the crops.[38] Since then, other instances of tempo and pulse-rate changes have been found in Africa. Dogon symbolism also expresses the differences in status and role between the sexes by demanding that songs with specifically female connotations be sung in binary meter, while those that are male be sung in ternary meter.

To observe matters of this sort requires sensitivity and training, and it is no accident that one of the most perceptive studies on tempo variation should have been published by an African student, Ben Aning from Ghana, on music of his own culture, as a result of an ethnomusicology seminar.[39] Aning showed that in religious performance tempo changes were closely correlated to the action of the religious drama. But, of course, Aning's data also bear upon the interaction between cultural system and language.

Language and Musical Time

It was inevitable that some observations on the bond between these two universals were anticipated when I tried to show on how broad a front the musician

34. Iona Opie and Peter Opie, *The Lore and Language of School Children* (Oxford: Clarendon Press, 1959).

35. John Middleton, *The Lugbara of Uganda* (New York: Holt, Rinehart & Winston, 1965).

36. Andrew Neher, "A Physiological Explanation of Unusual Behavior in Ceremonies Involving Drums," *Human Biology*, XXXIV (1962), 151–60.

37. Robert Muller, "Les Populations de la côte française des Somalis," *Mer rouge Afrique orientale*, Coll. fondées par Robert Montagne en 1948 Cahiers de l'Afrique et l'Asie (Paris, 1949), pp. 45–102.

38. Calame-Griaule and Calame, "Scènes de la vie."

39. "Tempo-Change: Dance-Music Interactions in Some Ghanaian Traditions" (Paper

in Africa is concerned with language. To pinpoint the interaction in specifically African terms, one could do no better than turn to Senghor himself.[40]

In speaking of language, Senghor concludes that all arts are only special forms of the verbal art. But "music in Black Africa is not in the first case a concert, a feast for the ears. Rather it is intended to accompany poetry or dance, which is nothing but dynamic sculpture." He then goes on to speak of a dance for the spirit of the sun and ram which he saw in Ivory Coast and to report that the steps of the dancers and the orchestral setting expressed the same thing: the sacred madness of the ram. He noted that words do not have to be abstract but rather should suggest an image, an experience at once and directly, to the recipient. But—and this is the crucial point—the image and the experience conjured up by the word remain without effect if they lack rhythm.

> Rhythm is consubstantial with the image. It completes it by unifying into a single whole sign and sense, flesh and spirit. To separate the two elements, as for the sake of clarity in exposition as I have done, is artificial. In the music accompanying the poem or dance, the rhythm forms the image as much as the melody.

When Senghor uses the term rhythm, the narrow meaning of the word does not seem to match his intentions. On the one hand, "the word takes precedence"; on the other hand, "rhythm arises not from the alternation of long and short syllables but entirely from the alternation of stressed and unstressed syllables, strong beats and weak beats." This is one kind of rhythm, one that attends to relative loudness and to accent—but what is the meaning of "accent"? Senghor, without discussing it in any further detail, compares it to movement in dancing, and thus it can be assumed that "accent" refers to "prominence given to a syllable, whether by higher musical pitch or by stress." It would be interesting to hear the views of the linguists on the meaning of "accent" in relation to those African languages that Senghor had in mind. However, Senghor acknowledges the overwhelming importance of *expression* in African poetry and music, and he defines expression as "rhythm, the sharp falls, the inflexions and *vibrati*," and thus places rhythm in the context of language in a wide sense.

Senghor clearly distinguishes yet another kind of rhythm, namely, "not that of speech but of percussion instruments that . . . mark the basic rhythm." However, this kind of rhythm is the subject of the section on instrument and musical time.

---

delivered to the Symposium on Ethnomusicology, Institute of Ethnomusicology, University of California at Los Angeles, May 1966).

40. Quotations in the following four paragraphs are taken from Léopold Sédar Senghor, "L'Esprit de la civilisation ou les lois de la culture Negro-africaine," *Présence Africaine*, Special Nos. 8, 9, 10 (June–November 1956); translations appear in *Prose and Poetry*, ed. John Reed and Clive Wake (London: Oxford University Press, 1965). Also see extracts from Léopold Sédar Senghor in "Der Geist der Negro Afrikanischen Kultur," in *Schwarze Ballade*, ed. Janheinz Jahn (Frankfurt: S. Fischer Verlag, 1965), pp. 203–27.

Although verbal description and essays on music cannot substitute for musical time itself, they can nevertheless be a worthwhile experience, as long as they are understood to be an experience essentially different from that of musical time. There are many passages in African writing that use language to convey musical experience. One example will be given here; it is taken from Henry Owuor's essay on Luo (Kenya) songs, the *oigo*. Here are Owuor's words:

> The style of oigo singing is extremely distinctive. The singer trills in a bird-like voice and conveys an impression of being possessed by a stream of song within her, breathless and helpless. The emotions expressed are often sorrowful and almost hysterical, yet the singer exults in her ability to sing endlessly like a bird.[41]

And then he goes on to say that "singing appears to be the natural outpouring of the life force itself."

Special syllables are used in teaching a tune both with regard to time in the narrow sense and with regard to tone. One need only read aloud the syllables *to tɛ to to tɛ to*, for a percussion pattern for instance, or *to lɛ ro lɛ ro, to lo lɛ ro li* for flute music, to feel the shape of the melody. The Burden texts help in teaching and memorizing music, for instance among the Akan.[42] Clans in Buganda use whole sentences as slogans to proclaim the identity of the clan, but the sentences do not have to be articulated orally; it is sufficient to give a tonal profile of the phrase on a drum.[43]

Speech phrases and musical phrases do not have to coincide. A striking example is the manner of performance of the praise recitations of the Bahima of Uganda.[44] Speech duration and music duration must pose problems where speech is as important as Senghor claims. Songs that at first sight seem free and comparatively capable of absorbing different texts and tonal variations may nevertheless be found to be highly consistent in their regard for durations. In one of the "Freedom Songs" of the Somali Republic, of five different strophes it was found that each strophe took 44 to 45 seconds.[45] Little is known as yet about the interaction between text and music with regard to duration.

The use of proverbs is of course a purely verbal phenomenon, and yet the manner in which proverbs are quoted in conversation is in line with the ubiquitous leader-response form of African music. If a Muganda wanted to quote the proverb *asugumbira okulaba ensolo . . . gw'erya* ("He who burns to see the beast . . . is the

41. "Luo Songs," *Black Orpheus*, X [1962?], 51–56.

42. J. H. Nketia, *Drumming in Akan Communities of Ghana* (Edinburgh: Thomas Nelson, 1963).

43. M. B. Nsimbi, *Amannya amaganda n'ennono zaago* ("Ganda Names and Their Meaning") (Kampala: East African Literature Bureau, 1956).

44. Henry F. Morris, *The Heroic Recitations of the Bahima of Ankole* (London: Oxford University Press, 1964).

45. Chet Williams, Hassan Hussein, and Mussa Gallal, "The Freedom Songs of the Somali Republic," Ethnic Folkways Library FD 5443; and review of this recording by K. P. Wachsmann in *Ethnomusicology*, X (1966), 239–42.

one the beast devours"), he would quote the first three words and leave it to his partner to complete the phrase by saying *gw'erya* or by giving an understanding smile.[46] This custom of quoting proverbs also reflects the difference between the one who takes the initiative and the other who knows his place and responds.

Cultural System and Language

At first glance it is difficult to see what concern it is of a musician to inquire into this particular bond. However, one need only recall that the repertoire of an African musician in some way or another is based on a verbal phrase. Even in performances in which song seldom occurs, as in the xylophone music of Buganda, the pattern of three themes is named by the opening lines of a traditional poem. The poem texts refer to the affairs of the society and historical events; that is, they are statements that are not *musical* in the Western sense of the word. When an Acholi chief listened to a lament on the death of a close friend, he walked away in grief and hanged himself. It is easier to argue that the words of the lament affected the chief's mind than to claim that the tune per se led to his death. Other instances presenting similar problems could be quoted. The Western musician who wishes to converse with his African colleagues about the mood of a certain music—an aspect which Westerners are apt to believe is invested in the music itself—may find that the key to the mood is in the text. Little is known as yet of the correlation between the mood content of the word and the sound pattern of the song.

Texts are often a direct reflection on events, and the creation of topicality seems to be mainly invested in the words. Merriam could distinguish seven major classes when he classified the song texts of the Bashi of Ruanda.[47] The role of topical texts is not difficult to trace. In praise songs it is clearly in the maintenance of the natural and supernatural orders that their main function lies.[48]

Although the word and the text are such strong sources of inspiration for performers, they may nevertheless become limiting factors. In Africa it is conceivable that composers may speak of the "tyranny" of the word in the same way in which Béla Bartók could speak of the "tyranny" of the traditional major-minor system. Rycroft tells us that the famous guitar player Jean Bosco changed at times from his mother tongue, Sanga, to the lingua franca, Kingwana (or a local lingua franca, "Congo Swahili"), or even to French, and to other words 'not yet identified" to escape the tyranny of Sanga. In these "foreign" languages the rule of word accent and duration did not have to be observed closely.[49]

The medium of language explains how and where music stands in the cultural

46. P. Le Veux, *Manuel de langue Luganda* (Algiers: Maison-Carrée, 1914).
47. Alan P. Merriam, "Song Texts of the Bashi," *Zaire*, I (January 1954), 27–43.
48. David Ames, "A Sociocultural View of Hausa Musical Activity" (Paper read at the Conference on the Traditional Artist in African Society, Lake Tahoe, 1965).
49. David Rycroft, "The Guitar Improvisations of Mwenda Jean Bosco," *African Music*, II, No. 4 (1961), 81.

system. In this way music is accounted for in cosmologies and stories of genesis. At the same time the creation of the world is said to have been effected through the Word, the Logos. The Bambara (Mali) show the relationship between dance and song and the word in the following manner as related by Zahan:

> Le *n'guma* [crested crane] est un oiseau particulièrement beau, remarquable aussi par son double cri. Parmi tous les animaux connus des Bambara, il est le seul à "enfléchir" la voix, en produisant une sorte de son de trompe. En outre, le *n'guma* exécute, à l'époque du rut, des danses qui offrent un spectacle inoubliable. Ces trois qualités remarquables: la parure, le cri, la danse, ont fait de la grue couronnée l'oiseau de la parole car, dans l'esprit bambara, ces trois notions sont corrélatives. Le vêtement est une "parole" à l'état statique, la danse (ou le rythme) est le "déroulement" du verbe. Toute la littérature concernant le *n'guma* fait allusion à ces trois caractères.[50]

Words are set to bird cries to teach children rules of behavior and wisdom. It is unknown how widespread this practice is in Africa; few students have been interested in data of this kind in the past. Zahan is one exception; another is E. Y. Egblewogbe, a student of J. H. Nketia's in Ghana, whose thesis dealt with the uses of music in enculturation and socialization; the ties between music and teaching words formed an important aspect of the work.[51]

The use of special language, sometimes referred to as secret language, is common in music. For instance, among the Gurage of Ethiopia, the low-caste Fuga know the secret songs and language for the rituals of the high-caste Gurage girls. At these rites "novices are taught the ritual language *Fedwät* which only Gurage women and Fuga are said to speak, and which is kept carefully guarded from Gurage men. . . ."[52] But even without the complication of caste system and secret language, African songs are, more often than not, oblique in reference and obscure in meaning, not only for strangers but even for fellow members of the musician's tribe fully versed in most facets of their culture. Words are powerful, and they have multiple meanings so that it is not always possible to decide which is the right interpretation.

Cultural System and Musical Instrument

Many aspects of the cultural ensemble center on musical instruments. An extreme example would be one in which the non-musical connotation was so strong that it left no room for the recognition of a specifically acoustic element. Such an example came to the notice of a student of Baule (Ivory Coast) music.

---

50. Dominique Zahan, *La Dialectique du verbe chez les Bambara* (Paris: Mouton, 1963), p. 58.

51. E. Y. Egblewogbe, "Games and Songs as an Aspect of Socialization of Children in Eweland" (M.A. thesis, University of Ghana, 1967).

52. William A. Shack, "Notes on Occupational Castes among the Gurage of South West Ethiopia," *Man*, LXIV (1964), 50–52.

Baule girls shake rattles of unusual design during circumcision rituals. On being shown a picture of a girl with attributes of the ritual including the rattle, Baule informants easily identified the subject as "a girl to be circumcised" but could not be brought to recognize the rattle as such.[53] Similar but perhaps less extreme circumstances show how deeply musical instruments are integrated in the cultural ensemble in any sphere of social activity. The role most easily recognized is that of status. Two examples will illustrate this point: in the one, the instrument is intimately linked with the status of a person on the basis of his sex, in this case female, and in the other, the instrument is part of a chief's regalia. The first example refers to the female status of gourd instruments in western Nigeria described by the Timi of Ede:

> During the inter-tribal wars the Ikotun people migrated to other parts of the country for protection. Those of them who came to Ede, finding that they were safe and secure in Ede, forgot the worship of Eleyiko, and for this reason their wives became barren. They consulted the Ifa oracle and it was revealed that their wives were barren because they had neglected the worship of a certain ebora (deity) whose music was made up of rhythms supplied by beating a gourd. They were told to make certain sacrifices and beat the gourd as was their family custom. They did as they were told and their wives became fruitful. Since then they have continued to celebrate Eleyiko festival every year when the Suku [a gourd instrument] is used for music. Marriage ceremony of any female member of the family is incomplete without Suku music.[54]

Gourd instruments belong to a context of this sort in many African communities.

The second illustration refers to regalia instruments at the court of the former kabakas of Buganda as contained in the oral traditions recorded and published in the Luganda language by Sir Apolo Kagwa.[55] Kagwa mentions regalia instruments on numerous occasions which have several features in common. First, the name of the kabaka who created a particular drum is remembered, and the fact is mentioned in the recitation of the history of the kabakas like a formula; one could recite the generations of rulers by listing the names of the drums established by each of them. The kabaka and the regalia drums are closely identified with one another, so much so that the phrase *balina nannyini ng'oma* (literally "They have the owner of the drum") meant "they have captured the

53. René Ménard, "Contribution à l'étude de quelques instruments de musique Baoule—région de Beoumi," *Jahrbuch für musikalische Volks und Völkerkinde*, I, ed. Fritz Bose (Berlin: de Gruyter, 1963), 48–99.

54. Oba Adetoyese Laoye I, "Music of Western Nigeria: Origin and Use," *Composer*, XIX (Spring 1966), 34–41.

55. *Ekitabo kya Basekabaka be Buganda* ("The Book of the Kings of Buganda") (1901; reprint ed., London: Sheldon Press, 1927); *Ekitabo kye Bika bya Baganda* ("The Book of the Clans of Buganda") (1908?; reprint ed., Kampala: Uganda Bookshop and Uganda Society, 1949); *Ekitabo kye Mpisa za Baganda* ("The Book of the Customs of Buganda") (1905; reprint ed., London: Sheldon Press, 1934).

kabaka."[56] Second, it was a matter of course that the king and also certain important chiefs included instrumentalists in their households. Third, the clans jealously guarded the memory of their association with events in the lives of the rulers and the musical hereditary offices that derived from these events.

In West Africa this last point is made dramatically in the epic of Sundjata of the Mandingo in which a national crisis is solved by the hero's sister with the help of a royal musician, a *griot*; the acceptance of the xylophone into Mandingo culture is part of the story.[57]

There is an even chance that musicians have memories and traditions regarding the origins of the musical instrument. Distribution maps of instruments pose many problems, but they also corroborate at times the theories of historians and ethnologists. They can illustrate the migrations of a people, help to identify culture clusters, show the workings of acculturation processes, and in a few rare cases they can throw light on ancient history. As an example of the latter, the discovery of a hoard of ancient Greek *auloi*, instruments of an oboe type, in a burial site south of Khartoum dating from between 200 B.C. and A.D. 200 contributes to the scanty knowledge of the extent of the reach into Africa of ancient Mediterranean influences.[58]

The bond between musical instruments and cultural systems is indeed significant on several levels. There is a danger that the study of this bond might become an end in itself and upset the student's sense of perspective with regard to the functions and uses to which musical instruments are put. Once more it will serve a useful purpose to consult Senghor:

> Toute parole *sociale,* toute parole solenelle est rythmée en Afrique noire, et toute parole rythmée devient musique, *s'accompagne souvent d'un instrument de musique* [italics added].[59]

Musical Instrument and Language

The Nigerian composer Akin Euba once said during a lecture (unpublished) that a "talking instrument" was present in almost any Yoruba ensemble. The Ghanaian musicologist Nketia described the bond between instrument and language in the following terms:

> Because oral literature is based on the spoken word or sung word, it can also be conveyed through musical instruments capable of imitating speech: instruments

56. Le Veux, *Manuel de langue Luganda.*
57. Djibril Tamsir Niane, *Soundjata ou l'épopée Mandique,* 2d ed. (Paris: Présence Africaine, 1960).
58. D. M. Dixon and K. P. Wachsmann, "A Sandstone Statue of an Auletes from Meroë," *Kush,* XII (1964), 119–25.
59. "Le langage intégral des Negro-Africains," preface to "Anthologie de la vie africaine Congo-Gabon," by Herbert Pepper (Paris: Ducretet-Thomson, 1958), p. 4.

such as drums, bells or gongs, horns or trumpets, and flutes. In some places such as North West Ghana, the xylophone may be used for a similar purpose.[60]

From the transformation of oral literature into instrumental sound one could move to less obvious bonds like the Burden texts used in the teaching of drumming, the teaching syllables *to* *tɛ*, etc., of the Baganda already mentioned, and the philosophy of Senghor summed up at the end of the previous section.

The imitation of speech also extends to timbre. Anyone who has heard African bowed lutes (fiddles), like the *masinko* of Ethiopia, the *endingidi* of Uganda, or the *godjie* of the Niger Valley, could not have failed to notice how similar the timbres of voice and instrument are. It also holds true of the conical oboes, *gaita*, that alternate with the shouted eulogies of the praise-singer—for instance, among the Hausa of northern Nigeria. The question as to who accompanies and who leads cannot be decided on the basis of aesthetic response or by an evaluation of stylistic criteria alone. Viewpoints as general as those held by Senghor or local opinion ought to have the last word on these issues, regardless of Western ideas about "accompaniment" in music. Besides, this kind of evaluation may change from generation to generation, not only in Africa but elsewhere.

Instrumentalists also use language for naming their "tools" and the components of these tools. The Iteso (Uganda) use a terminology for naming the strings of the harp (*adeudeu*) that would have been familiar to the ancient Greeks. At times there are telling associations between a technical musical meaning and human status, as in the case of the harp of the Kotoko (Chad), who name the five strings of the instrument from low to high as follows: (1) the trumpeting of an elephant, something very strong, i.e., a married man; (2) a worthless thing, i.e., a bachelor; (3) the thing in the middle, a dispenser of justice, i.e., a married woman; (4) a bird, i.e., a prostitute; (5) something sweeter, for instance, a female voice in relation to a male voice, i.e., a young girl.[61]

The use of language for naming mannerisms and phases of play in an instrument deserves close attention. Following are two brief illustrations, both from Buganda. The repertoire of xylophone (*amadinda*) music as transcribed by Kyagambiddwa shows the time signature 3/8 in 53 out of 62 pieces included in the collection.[62] Kyagambiddwa accounts for the nine exceptions—which are almost all in duple time—partly because they deal with heroic subjects and partly because they have spiritual connotations. Of these duple rhythms, he says that they are called *biggu*. Literally, *biggu* are "sorcerer's rattles." In using this instrumental term to name heroic music, he relied on an idiomatic expression, *njasa-*

60. J. H. Nketia, "The Techniques of African Oral Literature," *Proceedings of the Ghana Academy*, II (1964), 11.

61. Monique Brandily, "Un exorcisme musical chez les Kotoko," in *La Musique dans la vie*, I (Paris: Office de Coopération Radiophonique, 1967), 31–75.

62. Joseph Kyagambiddwa, *African Music from the Source of the Nile* (New York: Praeger, 1955).

biggu, a daredevil, which is immediately intelligible to a Luganda speaker.[63] The second example refers to the naming of a style of motion in playing a xylophone, that is, to a particular manner in which the player strikes the keys. One of these motions is named *ensetule,* a term with many different applications that have one thing in common, namely, the element of diminishing effort, like letting something slide to the ground or dragging one's feet.[64] *Ensetule* effectively expresses a rather intangible aspect of xylophone-playing.

The ability of African musicians to endow ordinary, everyday terminology with specific musical meaning can be observed in many contexts, and one may feel tempted to argue that talking about music is in itself an art.

Instrument and Musical Time

As a result of exposure to music in Uganda for many years, an impression began to form in the mind of this writer that he might recognize certain concepts that inspire the music of Uganda. Other peoples' concepts are usually elusive, especially if the other people do not verbalize about those notions that interest the observer. Certainly, some notions can be consciously expressed, but others cannot be put into words; this is presumably true of all music.

One of these never-spoken-of concepts of Uganda is the manner in which the musical roles of an ensemble of instruments relate to one another. A few examples will make the point. When Mr. A. Oduka wrote the scores for the traditional tunes to be played by the magnificent police band of which he was the musical director, he did not define the drum parts but left their execution to the discretion of the drummers.[65] Similarly, Kyagambiddwa in his "Uganda Martyrs African Oratorio" wrote out the vocal parts and their texts, but prescribed for drumming only by a few words of reference to certain well-known dance styles.[66] Of course, Oduka and Kyagambiddwa are composers in the Western sense of the word. But what about the other obviously older practices of music that are transmitted by purely non-literate means? Take, for instance, the clapping of hands—an instrumental device—that may be obligatory in some performances or music cultures but may be ad lib in others. A more sophisticated example, again from Buganda, is that of the kabaka's flute ensemble, the *ekibiina ky'abalere,* that consists of a "sextet" of flutes plus a "quartet" of drums. Both examples have in common that their music seems to be conceived on two levels, or in two currents representing not a quality, but a synthesis of disparate elements. No technical term is available for this phenomenon, but in a discussion of these matters with a young British avant-garde composer, he referred to these

63. R. A. Snoxall, *Luganda-English Dictionary* (Oxford: Clarendon Press, 1967).
64. P. Le Veux, *Premier essai de vocabulaire Luganda-Français* (Algiers: Maison-Carrée, 1917).
65. Personal communication.
66. (Rome: Casimiri-Capra, 1964).

levels of participation as the "double phenomenon," a term which is as good as any other for such a general musical trait.

In the case of the flute ensemble, the flutists played highly melismatic and flowing phrases that had close affinities to the text lines of a well-known song; their performance seemed to be the very opposite of the idea of percussion. The drums to be effective also required tonal distinctiveness (as has been stated above); they were not melismatic, although rapid changes of timbre in drumming do have the characteristics of melisma. However, the emphasis here is on percussiveness, and in comparison to the fluid runs on the flutes, the drum sounds adhered to rigid meters.

Percussion is a vague term and a relative matter, and this weakens the notion of the "double phenomenon," especially if the notion is held by a foreign musician about music that is not in his mother tongue. Yet, when all is said and done, these observations and impressions of music in East Africa seem to find some confirmation in West African philosophy, namely, in the writings of Senghor.

We have seen in the discussion above of cultural system and language what Senghor's views are with regard to the word in music. When he speaks of the rhythm of poetry he adds,

> But its essential rhythm is not that of speech but of the percussion instruments that accompany the human voice, or rather those instruments that mark the basic rhythm. We have here a polyrhythm, a kind of counterpoint.[67]

The paragraph from which these lines are quoted finishes by saying that "the poem thus appears as an architecture, a mathematical formula based on *unity in diversity*." The notion of the double phenomenon has become verbalized here in terms that are familiar to students of Senghor. It may apply to Western music too, but there is a significant difference in emphasis, not only in terms of philosophy but also in terms of stylistic criticism.

The bond between musical instrument and musical time is strong in subtle matters like motion patterns and motion quality; the problem of the interaction between "touch" and tone, so familiar to pianists, is posed in Africa in many different ways. One example must suffice: In Ashanti drum instruction the teacher may tap out, with his hands on the pupil's bare shoulders, a counter rhythm to that being played by the learner. According to Mr. Attah Mensah, this procedure did not merely teach meter and duration patterns but let the pupil experience through physical contact the kind of touch that was required.[68]

The tonal range of an instrument obviously influences music structure, and so do tuning procedures. A question frequently asked is whether there is an African scale, and the answer often given is that its tunings are diatonic rather

67. In Reed and Wake, *Prose and Poetry*, p. 88.
68. Personal communication.

than chromatic. But this classification has an air of unreality; instrumental tunings may be very different from either "scale." In many places musicians claim that they tune, first of all, to a mode that would set the mood of the piece they are going to play. For instance, M. S. Eno Belinga made this point emphatically with regard to music in Cameroon.[69] However, little is known about the standards that are adopted in these procedures.

The intimate relation between the motion of instrumental playing and the effect it produces in terms of music need not be elaborated upon. This relation has, however, led to a theory that received a prominent place in the first issue of *Africa*, the journal of the International African Institute, in 1928 and that has been revived from time to time.[70] According to Hornbostel,

> What really matters is the act of beating; and only from this point can African rhythms be understood. Each single beating movement is again two-fold: the muscles are strained and released, the hand is lifted and dropped. Only the second phase is stressed acoustically; but the first inaudible one has the motor accent, as it were, which consists in the straining of the muscles. This implies an essential contrast between our rhythmic conception and the Africans'; we proceed from hearing, they from motion.[71]

A distinguished Ghanaian drummer, well known in American jazz circles, noticed that an antithesis of this kind existed, but he expressed it in opposite terms.[72] This writer went through a personal experience—and remarked upon it in his notebook—that also contributes to the discussion of Hornbostel's theory. In watching a film with sound track of fiddle-playing from West Africa, an interesting dimension in string-playing and bowing was noticed:

> While I listened I became disconcerted by the direction of the bowing that I saw on the screen. When my own expectation desired a down-stroke in the context of the music, the fiddler in the picture played an up-stroke, and vice versa. The

69. In discussion at the 18th meeting of the International Folk Music Council at the University of Ghana, 1966.

70. See, for example, John Blacking, "Some Notes on a Theory of African Rhythm Advanced by Erich Von Hornbostel," *African Music*, I, No. 2 (1955), 12–20; and David Rycroft, "Stylistic Evidence in Nguni Song" (unpublished paper). It is interesting to note that Hornbostel put forward this theory as early as 1910, when little was known of African music, and that he linked the phenomenon that he thought could be observed to aspects of tempo. See Carl Stumpf and Erich Von Hornbostel, "Über die Bedeutung ethnologischer Untersuchungen für die Psychologie und Ästhetik der Tonkunst," in *Bericht über den 4. Kongress für experimentelle Psychologie*, ed. F. Schumann (Innsbruck, 1910), esp. p. 267.

71. Erich Von Hornbostel, "African Negro Music," *Africa*, I (1928), 30–62.

72. He refers to "a 'down' beat, you see, which is the African thing. So most of my tunes are written with this beat in mind, and, of course, when it comes out, it's stronger, because now you have the natural beat. This beat is not easily understood by people in the West. They can't think in terms of 'down-down.' They think in terms of 'up-up.' So I guess that's where we lost contact with Africa" (Guy Warren, *I Have a Story to Tell* . . . [Accra: Guinea Press, 1963?], p. 172).

technique that I witnessed forced me to correct my Euro-centric approach to musical agogic elements which was especially strong because I am a violinist myself.

CONCLUSION

Most of the instances used in this essay to illustrate general concepts about African music came from Uganda, because this is the area in which the writer did most of his field work. Generalizations regarding Africa are, like all generalities, suspect, but as we have seen, it is part of human experience in music to think in general terms. Wherever possible, African musicians were consulted and their opinions quoted. Yet this kind of musical dialogue inevitably remains imperfect: "People from different cultures inhabit different sensory worlds. They not only structure [musical time] differently, but experience it differently, because the sensorium is differently 'programmed.'"[73] If this is true of differences in culture, it is also true of differences in social stratum and generation that have become so noticeable and so painful in Western music. It is possible that in a few decades no one will talk about African music in the manner in which it has been done in this essay. Music is adopting radically new concepts and is evolving a new vocabulary. As the concepts of twentieth-century *society* change, so will the concepts of *musicians* change about their craft. Though one may not exchange one's own musical condition for that of an African colleague's simply by adopting his fashions, the dialogue with him adds new dimensions and new insight to one's own musical equipment, and this relationship works both ways.

73. Edward T. Hall, "Proxemics," *Current Anthropology*, IX (April–June 1968), 84.

II

Perspectives
on the Past

9

Major Themes in African History

JOHN A. ROWE

THE STUDY OF AFRICAN HISTORY is a new phenomenon in the American academic scene.[1] Its development and expansion in the last ten or twelve years has been remarkable. No courses or seminars on African history were offered at any major American university prior to 1957.[2] In that year Boston University introduced a seminar, and the following spring semester saw the first lecture course at Wisconsin. Today African history has become recognized as a respectable course of instruction in colleges and universities across the United States and is being introduced increasingly into the curricula of high schools as an important part of world-history courses.

It seems hardly a coincidence that 1957 saw both the independence of Ghana — the first African colonial territory to achieve sovereignty — and the introduction of African history into American classrooms. In an era of dramatic news from the African continent, the appearance of new figures at the United Nations representing new states, the increasing American diplomatic involvement in

1. A special debt is owed to the following works: Basil Davidson, *East and Central Africa to the Late 19th Century* (London: Longmans, Green, 1967); John Fage, "History," in *The African World: A Survey of Social Research*, ed. R. A. Lystad (New York: Praeger, 1965), pp. 40–56; Mushin Mahdi, *Ibn Khaldun's Philosophy of History* (London: Allen & Unwin, 1957); Daniel F. McCall, *Africa in Time Perspective* (Boston: Boston University Press, 1964); Nassif Nassar, *La Pensée réaliste d'Ibn Khaldun* (Paris: Presses Universitaires de France, 1967); Merrick Posnansky, ed., *Prelude to East African History* (London: Oxford University Press, 1966). Terence Ranger, ed., *Emerging Themes in African History* (Nairobi: East African Publishing House, 1968); Robert I. Rotberg, *A Political History of Tropical Africa* (New York: Harcourt, Brace & World, 1965); John Sutton, "Olduvai: Discoveries and Publications," *Tanzania Notes and Records*, LXV (March 1966), 95–96; Leonard Thompson, "African History in the United States," *African Studies Bulletin*, X (April 1967), 51–56.

2. At Howard University the late Leo Hansberry lectured on African history before 1957, following a lifelong interest in Africa as the origin of American Negroes, but he was not given a position of tenure and ultimately severed his connection with Howard.

154

Africa, and the increasing importance of the policy of "non-alignment" in a world previously dominated by cold war politics, American interest, however belated, in the background to these events was understandable. So too was interest by black Americans in the history of Africa before the colonial era. No longer was it deemed satisfactory in world-history courses to pass over the "dark continent" with a few generalizations referring to the achievements of sturdy missionaries and explorers like Livingstone and Stanley, or summing up the "scramble for Africa" as a reflection of European power diplomacy, or character-izing the European colonial impact in terms of the policies of "direct" or "in-direct rule." No longer, in short, was it possible to view Africa simply as a scene of European activity determining the destiny of natives, passive or truculent as the case may be. The very term "native," associated by force of habit with superstitious, primitive, and unpredictable behavior ("the natives are restless tonight") was as manifestly out of date as the racist stereotypes which it reflected.

Stereotypes, of course, are indicators of ignorance as well as of raw prejudice. Knowledge helps to dispel stereotypes, and as centers of knowledge university history departments would be expected to introduce courses in the area of African history. This they have done, but only tardily and after a great show of reluctance. The reasons for that reluctance are threefold: (1) the natural mental inertia which characterizes academics at least as much as other human beings (some would say more so) and makes it hard to break out of established patterns of thought and behavior; (2) the customary approach, transformed into a principle, whereby history is concerned entirely with written documents; and (3) stemming from that principle, genuine doubts about the validity of methods being proposed for utilizing "oral data" to recover the history of nonliterate societies.

The first type of objection was perhaps typified by an eminent Oxford profes-sor who pronounced African history as nonexistent; history is the record of human change and achievement, but Africa, he asserted, presented the monoto-nous spectacle of arrested development where the only discernible movement was the pointless gyrations of generations of savages. The second type of objec-tion was voiced by those historians who agreed with Lord Raglan in his view that human memory is so fallible that only written sources are worth considering. Raglan defended his view with the assertion that, two generations after Na-poleon, French peasants could be found who did not know the emperor's name. The third objection was held by historians who were convinced by the great cultural anthropologist Malinowski that in African states such traditions as were remembered served the immediate functional purpose of legitimizing whoever was in power. The traditions provided a historical "charter," and in the process history was so twisted or selectively presented as to be useless as a source.

These were formidable objections which could only be met effectively by prac-tical demonstrations of their inaccuracy or exaggeration. Research beginning in the 1950s at newly founded African university colleges began to demonstrate that, though cut off from centers of diffused knowledge in the Mediterranean and Near East, southern and central Africa nevertheless experienced development in iron and copper technologies, in political and military organization, and in techniques of social control. Northern and western Africa, of course, were geographically better situated to gain advantage from the exchange of ideas, most notably the spread of Islam and Islamic culture.

Throughout Africa researchers used a variety of sources and methods to assemble bits and pieces of history into more meaningful patterns for interpretation. In the process, they demonstrated the necessity of an interdisciplinary approach. From the work of ethnographers came knowledge of African cultures; from linguists came information about language diffusion and the spread of "loanwords" useful for tracing paths of migration, contact, or trade. Historians also took account of material remains exposed and evaluated by archaeologists, and wherever possible added eyewitness reports from literate travelers (for example, in Arabic or Portuguese documents). A rigorous method for analyzing and utilizing oral traditions was outlined by Jan Vansina in a book published in 1961, *De la tradition orale.*[3] His basic assertions were (1) that oral traditions were not comparable to the fallible memories of French peasants concerning Napoleon, but were usually preserved by skilled and trained specialists, frequently making use of "memory devices" to ensure accurate retention of details; and (2) that while any single tradition might be biased or "doctored," other oral accounts could be found among the clans, occupational castes, or rival lineages of a "royal family." By means of comparison and critical analysis the most plausible version might be obtained, just as with conflicting written documents in European historical practice.

By these methods, and through increasing cooperation in research among specialists in archaeology, linguistics, botany, ethnology, economics, religion, and political science, the African past ceased to be terra incognita and began to yield much new knowledge and many new questions for further research. Since the beginning of the 1960s, books, articles, doctoral dissertations, and even new scholarly journals have begun to deluge the African history specialist to the point where he can now legitimately join his colleagues in European and American history in complaining of his inability to keep up with the published literature. Where only a few years ago worried historians of Africa were calling for a crash program to locate and preserve historical sources, both those on paper and those in the minds of old men, scholars now are increasingly concerned with the practical problems of utilizing the masses of material they have uncovered. Some may even yearn secretly for the "pioneer days" of comparative freedom and speculation before the onerous weight of source material had fully descended upon them.

3. *Oral Tradition: A Study in Historical Methodology*, trans. H. M. Wright (Chicago: Aldine, 1965).

Thus in a very short time the newly generated interest in African history has yielded visible results. Where once the Ford, Carnegie, and Rockefeller foundations felt the need to stimulate an almost nonexistent American scholarly interest in Africa, African studies now have established a continuing momentum. Research and publication largely centered in African studies programs have attracted increasing numbers of graduate students. They in turn have gone into the field to carry out their own researches and have returned to take up teaching and consultative positions, thus adding to our understanding of Africa and helping to spread that understanding beyond the narrow circle of specialists.

AFRICAN HISTORIOGRAPHY
BEFORE THE TWENTIETH CENTURY

What is new to America is not necessarily new to Africa. Of course it is true that scholarly interest in Africa on the present scale, in terms of sophisticated techniques, money for research, publication of findings, and sheer numbers of scholars in the field, has never been seen before. But long before Americans began to wonder if Africa had a history, indeed long before America was known to exist, historians were investigating the African past.

Among the earliest scholars concerned to learn more about Africa were those whose world was centered on the Mediterranean basin and who viewed the African land mass close at hand as it stretched away from the southern shoreline into the unknown. Herodotus sought information about the history and social life of peoples living to the south of Egypt, just as he did for the barbarians of northern Europe. It is from his writings, for example, that the report comes of a three-year Phoenician voyage around Africa (*ca.* 595 B.C.), though Herodotus recorded the account with some skepticism. Strabo and Polybius, Greek historians in the Roman era, traveled the known world gathering information, much of it now lost, but some of it about Africa. Polybius witnessed the Roman sack of Carthage and recovered there an account of a Carthaginian voyage (*ca.* 470 B.C.) down the West African coast as far as Senegal, and perhaps beyond. Whatever works Carthaginian scholars may have produced seem not to have survived the Roman destruction. Roman historians, such as Pliny, were interested in Africa, but, like a later generation of imperalists, they were concerned for the most part with recording the deeds of Romans within and beyond the bounds of their African empire. In the second century A.D., in Egypt, Ptolemy collected the records of travelers and traders along the East African seaboard to draw up his famous map showing the Nile River rising in two large central African lakes bordered by the snow-capped "Mountains of the Moon." His map was far from accurate, but the basic facts were correct, as the explorer Speke discovered 1,500 years later. Today you may stay in the Mountains of the Moon Hotel near the shores of Lake Albert, which feeds the Nile, with the snow-capped Ruwenzori Mountains in the distance.

But certainly the greatest of early African historians and one of the great scholars of all time was ibn-Khaldun. Born in Tunis in A.D. 1332, ibn-Khaldun witnessed the decline of Islamic civilization and sought an explanation in history for the conditions he found. At first he set out to record and analyze the history of the Maghrib (the western fringe of North Africa), a territory which from long residence and frequent travel he knew intimately. His purpose was similar in part to that of earlier historians — to draw wisdom from the past experience of men — but there was a difference. Concerned as he was with the spectacle of Islamic civilization in decay, particularly in North Africa where political disorganization and petty feuding left visible scars on the once prosperous countryside, ibn-Khaldun wished first of all to analyze political history to discover the most enlightened system of government. An academic activist of his time, he hoped (by unscrupulous means if necessary) to put the lessons of history to work by placing himself in a position to influence those in power. Like some other academic activists, his early efforts led to disillusionment, and he concluded, wisely, that he still had much to learn. Retreating from the political arena, he took refuge in scholarship, searching the accumulated writings of the Islamic world for deeper insight. His critical mind soon discerned that perhaps the greatest weakness of historiography was the lack of a "scientific" method of analysis. Historians of the Islamic world, like Herodotus and Strabo before them, simply set down what their informants reported, sometimes with critical comment, but often without. There was no effort to create an analytical framework within which to place the acquired information. Ibn-Khaldun set out to create such a framework, and the results of his efforts have led him to be characterized as "the father of modern social science."

Recent scholarship has led to some revision of ibn-Khaldun's place in intellectual history. He did not invent his new "science of culture" in a complete break with previous accepted thought, for among many Islamic scholars there was a strong secular stream of thinking leading in this direction. But ibn-Khaldun did take that stream further than anyone had before and he culminated the achievement with his great work of history, completed shortly before his death in 1406. The work was composed of an introduction and three "books." The Introduction (*Muqaddima*) set forth the problem of historiography as ibn-Khaldun saw it. Book One dealt with his new analytical method for treating history in terms of human organization and culture rather than as a simple stream of events. Book Two related a "universal history" (that is, of the Islamic world in which he lived). Finally, Book Three contained his originally planned history of the Maghrib. Within these three books was to be found the sum of his political experience, firsthand knowledge from extensive travels (he even interviewed Tamerlane during the siege of Damascus), and results of years of study in the libraries of Damascus, Cairo, Mecca, Tunis, Fez, and Granada. It is difficult to do justice to such a seminal work, but one example—his analysis of the nomad-sedentary conflict—may suggest the richness of ibn-Khaldun's contribution to history.

In his investigations of different types of human culture, ibn-Khaldun observed that the life of pastoral nomadic cultures is basically similar, whether Arab, Berber, Turk, or Mongol. Their economic mode of life, following flocks to and from areas of intermittent rainfall, requires a simple political system, usually one based on kinship loyalty. At the same time the tent life, with its lack of material possessions and permanent defenses, leads to a hardy and occasionally predatory way of life. The migrations of the nomads bring them periodically to marginal pasture land on the fringes of sedentary agriculture settlements. Conflict over these lands, which are usable either as pasturage or for expanded agriculture, ensues. The sedentary culture, controlling larger populations through a more complex political organization, must defend itself against the incursions of the highly mobile nomadic pastoralists. A measure of the health of any sedentary state is its ability to do so. But organized states controlling population and wealth appear subject to cycles of growth and decay—their economic prosperity leads to luxury, comfort, and an eventual unwillingness to stand up to a challenge, whether internal or external. One of these challenges is the ever present nomadic threat on the fringes of settlement, and in the course of history the time comes when a weak sedentary state is unable to withstand the nomadic pressure and collapses. But in such a case, observed ibn-Khaldun, the nomads who capture the state are unable for long to impose their own rule upon the society, because their transitory culture and unsophisticated political institutions render them incapable of coping with the complex problems of state politics or of identifying with its best interests. More often the nomadic invaders loot and sack, and then withdraw.[4]

The world of ibn-Khaldun, that is, the world of Islam in the fourteenth century stretching from North Africa to the Middle East and beyond, was preeminently a land of contact and conflict between agriculturalists and nomads. The sedentary dwellers of the Mediterranean fringe, the Nile Delta, and the Fertile Crescent were frequently locked in struggle with the pastoralists of the Sahara, the Arabian Peninsula, and the Iranian Plateau. Ibn-Khaldun was thus describing and attempting to understand a central theme in Islamic history.

Just as ibn-Khaldun was the historian of his own society, drawing inspiration from its past achievements and directing his efforts toward a comprehensive understanding of its needs and potentialities, so in African states farther south professional classes of historians were using their understanding of the past to serve the needs of their own societies. But there was a difference. The historians

---

4. A recent example of the difficulties of nomadic conquerors in constructing a working urban government was the experience of T. E. Lawrence at the capture of Damascus in 1918. The situation was vividly, if not entirely accurately, depicted in the film *Lawrence of Arabia.*

of tropical African states, the keepers of oral tradition, knew the value of history as a means of binding people together in shared loyalties; but they were without a written language. Thus, they were concerned above all to preserve rather than to analyze, annotate, or revise. Within this limitation, they did evolve a variety of effective techniques for achieving their purposes. Individuals, lineages, and clans were highly conscious that their status and identity were to a great extent dependent on the reputations and accomplishments of their forebears. For example, in the detailed clan histories (which go back some four hundred years) of the Buganda kingdom in East Africa, the early migrations, order of arrival, and original settlement areas of the clans are regarded as especially important. So too are carefully preserved biographical sketches of members who brought prestige to the clan by deeds of valor or attainment of high office. As recently as the 1950s, any candidate for political office in Buganda was required to publicly recite his own lengthy genealogy to prove himself worthy of the position.

In states where a ruling clan or lineage existed, the importance of preserving an account of the significant events of each ruler's reign was clearly recognized, for history not only adds prestige to a royal lineage but provides the "charter" (as Malinowski recognized) legally justifying its right to office. No effort is spared to ensure the careful retention of such histories, which have been found to extend back as far as four or five centuries in the Great Lakes Region of East-Central Africa. In Rwanda, where Professor Vansina carried out extensive research, songs and epic poems were among the devices used to transmit accounts memorized word for word from one generation to the next. Other states used the memory device of buried or stored pots within which pebbles or objects were placed signifying specific facts. The kingdom of Dahomey, in West Africa, used this technique to maintain a population count and record the economic wealth and military strength of the state. In the Empire of Bono-Mansu (Ghana) each buried pot represented a single ruler's reign and gold nuggets within the pot signified his years in office. Rwanda and the Akan states of Ghana preserved objects associated with particular historical events.

By these methods, Africans were able to record and retain such facts of history as they desired; and, like the Gibbons and Macaulays of a later era, they were not above imposing their will upon history. Jeffrey Holden in this volume quotes a professional historian (called a *griot*) from the West African Sudanic state of Mali who takes pride in revealing his power "to teach what is to be taught and to conceal what is to be concealed."[5] He was not the only one. In a splendid piece of historical detective work, Ivor Wilks and Margaret Priestley demonstrated that the official history of Ashanti concealed the very existence of one of their kings (Osei?, 1712–17), who brought disgrace to the state not only by losing a war with a rival power but by losing his head to the victors as well. Unable to display the bedecked royal skull with the rest of those of his dynasty in the state "museum,"

5. See the essay by Jeffrey Holden, "Empires and State Formation," in this volume.

Ashanti authorities decided to suppress the whole episode.[6] It is a measure of their ritual-political power and organization that this drastic step succeeded until the mid-twentieth century. Not many African states, however, could command this degree of loyal and fearful obedience. In most cases it seems safe to say that where one set of traditions may present an "official history," other traditions kept by political rivals, uninvolved clans, or disinterested occupation groups (such as blacksmiths, herbalists, or mercenary soldiers) may reveal a different version of the past.

All these historians—from Herodotus to ibn-Khaldun, from the official historians of Ashanti to the *griots* of Mali—demonstrated the tendency to impose their own views on history. Some may simply have been influenced by an established frame of reference, such as the unquestioned superiority of Greek civilization, or the distressing decline of Islam—God's ordained path to civilization and virtue—or the implicit importance of genealogical identity and status. Others exercised more deliberate influence over the history they recounted, principally by sins of omission, as in the case of Ashanti. And all of them reflected a primary concern with their own society or culture and the place of history within it. Later European historians were to show themselves no different in this respect.

TWENTIETH-CENTURY HISTORIOGRAPHY

European historical writings (as opposed to earlier travelers' accounts) began to be concerned with Africa only as Africa fell within European imperial orbits. And then, predictably, the historians' concern was with European activity in Africa. The actors were English, French, German, or Portuguese, playing their roles against an indistinct African background with a supporting cast of nameless thousands. Certainly there was much in this drama to stimulate the imaginations of desk-bound scholars. They wrote of pioneer explorers and missionaries who followed (or were driven by) their ambitions and ideals, braving disease, savage beasts, and beastly savages to "open up" Africa to the outside world. And then came the drama of the empire-builders: determined captains like Lugard and de Brazza, who raced each other into the interior armed with Maxim guns and treaty pads; and equally determined power magnates, who played the "great game" of land-grabbing from a distance—men like King Leopold of Belgium, who claimed all of Equatorial Africa from the Atlantic to the Indian Ocean, or Cecil Rhodes, who wanted to "paint the map red" from the Cape to Cairo.

Local histories written on a less grand scale, and with much less melodrama,

6. "The Ashanti Kings in the Eighteenth Century: A Revised Chronology," *Journal of African History*, XXV (1960), 83–96.

followed. These histories of individual colonies and studies of colonial adminis-trative practice were often undertaken by resident civil servants with time on their hands. Claridge's monumental *History of the Gold Coast* (1915) falls into this category, though it was largely concerned with Ashanti-British relations in the decades leading up to British annexation. Delgado's *Historia de Angola*, Geary's *Nigeria under British Rule*, and Roberts' *History of French Colonial Policy* are fur-ther examples among many.

The Role of Africans in the Study of African History

Some colonial officials, however, turned their inquiring minds and formidable talents toward the study of the peoples they were governing. This was particu-larly noticeable in Islamic areas, where the fascination was intense and such administrator-scholars as Marty (French West Africa), Delafosse (Senegal, Mali, Niger), and Palmer (Nigeria) made their mark. The administrator-scholar was also common, though to a lesser degree, in non-Muslim areas; Sir John Gray is an outstanding example. In the course of a long and distinguished colonial career, Sir John (who had taken a history degree at Cambridge) wrote important monographs on Uganda, Tanganyika, Zanzibar, Portuguese East Africa, and the Gambia. His researches and those of like-minded administrators formed the opening wedge of a new scholarly concern for the neglected role of Africans in African history. While academic historians continued to pursue their European-oriented studies of Africa, or ignored Africa entirely, Sir John was busily ques-tioning elderly Africans in their own language about personalities and events before the coming of Europeans. In the Buganda kingdom in Uganda, he found that the preexisting African state had left a rich legacy of remembered and recorded history. Utilizing these sources, in 1934 Sir John wrote an account of the reign of Mutesa (ruler of Buganda from 1856 to 1884) which remained the definitive statement until the 1960s.

Sir John Gray's research in Uganda was made comparatively easy by the exist-ence of a number of historical works written in the vernacular by Africans. Hav-ing achieved literacy in their own language through missionary instruction (so that they might read the Gospels), a number of Africans in Buganda set out to record their own oral traditions, that is, the histories of their rulers and their clans. Some of these they printed on the mission press and circulated in editions of a dozen or so copies. As early as 1893, one leading Christian convert named Apolo Kagwa was writing a history of recent events and keeping a personal diary. He subsequently published five books of recorded history, custom, and folklore. Other Christian chiefs were recording the traditions of their clans as well. The largest of these, entitled *Makula* (meaning "treasure"), was compiled over a twenty-year period and exists in six immense handwritten volumes of some 2,400 pages. Interest in Buganda history was not confined to those few scholars who produced books. In the first two decades of the twentieth century, vernacular journals published at the missions had a wide circulation, and in their pages points of historical interpretation (largely issues of questioned veracity) were argued between correspondents.

Elsewhere in Africa during the same period, men with scholarly aspirations who had been educated by Christian missions were writing the histories of their peoples. In 1895 the Reverend Carl Reindorf, an African convert of the Basle Missionary Society, published *History of the Gold Coast*. Two years later in Nigeria, the Reverend Samuel Johnson completed the manuscript *History of the Yorubas* (eventually published by the Church Missionary Society in 1921). In southern Africa in the 1920s J. H. Soga was writing his two books, *The Southeastern Bantu* and *Ama-Xosa Life and Customs*, both issued from the press of Lovedale mission.

These African Christian writers were expressing newly acquired but strongly held beliefs in their histories. They saw the purpose of history as essentially threefold: (1) a means of retaining identity in a period of social-political flux and changing values; (2) a source of pride in past achievements at a time when Europeans were assuming arrogant attitudes and denying educated Africans entry into European society; and (3) a medium of moral instruction with which to reinforce the lessons of their personal creed, which emphasized the wickedness of the pagan past as against the future promise of Christianity, literacy, and material progress.

Yet it is important to qualify the above observations by pointing out that the literate Christian historians were still essentially chroniclers, faithfully setting down oral traditions and eyewitness accounts for the most part as received and reserving their comments and moral admonitions for the preface, conclusion, and occasional asides. As chroniclers they were maintaining and continuing the traditional African historiography of the keepers of oral history. They were also closely paralleling the experience of literate Muslim *griots* of West Africa who had written (and continued to write) Arabic and Hausa chronicles of their own states which they seasoned strongly with Islamic doctrine and moral exhortation. For both sets of scholars, God was manifesting himself in history, and men were called upon to behave accordingly.

If modern academic historians have been reluctant to discover theological purpose in history (with the notable exception of Arnold Toynbee), they have nevertheless demonstrated a moral fervor in some of their writings on Africa. This has been evident in some of the overenthusiastic pro-African writing in recent years; it is also visible in the more traditional European-oriented accounts. Where once historians of the colonial era ignored non-Europeans entirely, the rise of nationalism intruded on academic consciousness and a spate of books ensued which recognized African political and educational attainments. But even these books still concentrated on the colonial devolution of power, which was often alleged to be planned, smoothly carried out, and a triumph for enlightened European leadership. Equally awakened by nationalism in Africa were Soviet and East European historians, who hastened to apply Marxist analysis to yet another set of proletarian revolutions. Their interpretations raised new questions unexplored by other Western scholars, but the theoretical framework provided by Marx and Lenin was awkward and ill-fitted to the African experience. In both cases, preconceived ideas almost untouched by detailed research into African history were being applied.

It is hoped that the detailed research now being carried out will provide a more solid basis on which to erect theoretical structures. But much of the groundwork still remains to be done. Meanwhile the directions taken by research seem to be influenced by two considerations: (1) research distinctly varies according to the changing political and social conditions in modern Africa; (2) it changes, too, as the development of new research techniques both suggest and permit new paths of historical inquiry.

THE EFFECT OF CHANGING
ENVIRONMENT ON RESEARCH

Considering first the African political environment, it is obvious that change (as from a condition of colonial subjection to a strident and forceful nationalist movement) will affect the questions asked by academics concerned with Africa, including historians. And as the political situation rapidly evolves, so do the attitudes and expectations of scholars. For example, in the early 1960s the wave of nationalism crested as many new states attained their goal of independence. The atmosphere was expansive; it was a moment of success and congratulation. The opponents of African self-determination, whether reactionary settler groups in Africa or racists in America preaching the dogma of black inferiority, were confounded. Under skillful leadership, nationalist movements had overcome severe difficulties of organization, communication, divided ethnic loyalties, and colonial delaying tactics to win an impressive success. Political scientists hurried to analyze political parties, sociologists became absorbed with the process by which new loyalties were forged, and social scientists directed an increasing interest toward the new elites.

Historians, as usual, trailed the pack several steps behind the last of the social scientists. But they too became absorbed in investigating the origins of nationalism, for one of the self-imposed tasks of the historian is to discover and explain how things came to be the way they are. This "acorn approach," which seeks to ferret out the seeds from which today's mighty oaks took root, ensured that the spectacle of flourishing nationalism would eventually attract its historical researchers.[7] Meanwhile, conditions in Africa were changing; the expansive mood

7. Students of English history are familiar with the "acorn approach" which focused much attention on a minuscule group of political eccentrics and malcontents in the 1880s and 1890s whose words and deeds quite properly went unnoticed at the time. Yet, they are studied as the seeds from which the Welfare State in the 1950s was to grow.

quickly passed, new and critical problems arose, and academic attitudes and interests were profoundly affected. This was evidenced in a recent conference where historians wished to invite interdisciplinary comment from political scientists on particular problems in studying nationalism. It was found that the political scientists (invited because of their previous studies of nationalist movements) were no longer interested. Newer questions involving national unity, military coups, and social cleavage in the independent African states now beckoned them.

But the fact that historians are influenced, however belatedly, by modern events indicates that Malinowski's "charter" may be a relevant criticism of history today—if not in the sense that history is deliberately distorted, at least in the sense that historians recognize current interests and concerns and to a certain extent serve those interests and reflect those concerns. This represents a potential danger, lest history permit its necessary freedom of interpretation to become eroded in the course of performing some service, such as providing the historical basis for teaching national unity or strengthening national sentiment by glorifying the African past. So far, however, such attempts are remarkable by their absence. There have been a few myth-makers, but not among the ranks of trained scholars, African or European.[8] Occasionally in scholarly discourse the suggestion arises that Africa is qualitatively different and that research undertaken by African scholars will provide a new element beyond mere language skill and cultural background—a mystical quality of African understanding or analysis beyond the powers of any non-African. This prophecy is yet to be fulfilled.

On the other hand, as African studies have progressed the early defensive attitude displayed in some scholarly writings has tended to disappear. The setbacks experienced by some independent African states in maintaining political stability have not resulted in a return to defensive writing despite renewed attacks from right-wing groups in the West. Instead of the unrealistic platitudes of the 1950s or the uncritical enthusiasm for newly independent nations and charismatic leaders of the 1960s, a more balanced attitude prevails.

MODERN RESEARCH TECHNIQUES

The questions historians ask determine in part the answers they will get. And just as current events in Africa and in the academic world affect the questions asked, so do developments in research techniques. As long as written documents were deemed the only respectable source for historians to utilize, the field for

---

8. Manufacturing myths has been the monopoly of popularizers, as in American experience with its instructive patriotic literature composed for the benefit of youth (for instance, the story of Washington and the cherry tree by Parson Weems).

historical research and the questions that could be posed and answered seemed very circumscribed. Some researchers who ventured into the area of oral sources found them to be complex, full of symbolism, and difficult to assess and interpret. How could one be sure that he was getting an accurate rendition of a genuine tradition; and how much of the original tradition was useful evidence as opposed to myth? Opinions differed, and many old hands in Africa could gleefully point to one or another researcher who had been "sold a bill of goods."

Professor Ivor Wilks at the Institute of African Studies in Ghana reports a typical incident. He asked an elderly informant what he knew about the foundation of the neighboring settlements of Fort James and Fort Usher, two long-established slave-trading posts on the coast of Ghana. Hardly pausing for breath, the old man started off with "There were two brothers, James and Usher, and they quarreled. . . ." Now, Wilks knew from easily accessible documents that Fort James was named after the English king and Fort Usher after a former British governor, unlikely siblings in any case, the more so since they lived two centuries apart. In fact, as Professor Wilks was well aware, the story of the two brothers quarreling and then founding neighboring settlements is a commonplace formula in Ghana as a logical after-the-fact explanation when the actual history is unknown. Here was another fable to be added to the collection of myths and inventions that appeared to litter the field of oral history.

Oral Tradition

It was to deal with this and related problems that the Belgian historian-anthropologist Jan Vansina directed his efforts in the 1950s. The results of his investigation and analysis appeared as a published doctoral dissertation in 1961, *De la tradition orale*, which was subsequently translated into English and republished in 1965 with the title *Oral Tradition*. Vansina recognized the problem he was up against. Indeed, its immensity was self-evident. He also recognized that the climate of academic opinion on the topic ranged from purely skeptical to avowedly hostile. Hence his published approach was extremely rigorous, closely defined, and laid out with almost mathematical precision. A younger generation of historians were to march off to Africa clutching this book to their bosoms, as nineteenth-century missionaries had their Bibles, convinced alike of the validity of the Vansina method and of their own inability to meet its exacting standards.

Vansina defined oral tradition as any testimony about the past which is received secondhand (as opposed to eyewitness accounts). These testimonies, which he called "oral documents," could either be in "fixed text," in which every word was memorized like a poem, or "free text," that is, a general account of events. Vansina then proceeded as follows:

(1) First he set out all types of oral testimony in their richness and variety: "official" traditions of ruling groups; clan histories; traditions belonging to

special castes or artisan groups; testimony given by individuals (as opposed to groups); testimony given in verse, epic, or song; testimony given only on ritual occasions; testimony "owned" as the private property of individuals or groups; stereotyped fables (such as the quarreling brothers); symbolic forms in which traditions may be related; and so on.

(2) For each of these categories he described strengths and weaknesses in terms of accessibility and reliability.

(3) All sources then had to be approached by the researcher with every critical faculty alert to the possible distortion, symbolism, and ritual importance in each particular type of testimony.

(4) All versions of a tradition had to be recorded and handled alike, for there is no single "true" version; and every tradition, even a manufactured one, tells something about a society.

No wonder researchers were daunted, for it was implicit in Vansina's method that in order to deal profitably with oral traditions a researcher needed to have an intimate understanding of the society he was investigating. Vansina, however, went on to demonstrate that for the trained, observant, and patient fieldworker the rewards of properly assimilated oral history could be immense. In the last fifteen years he has written a history of the Bakuba kingdom in central Congo, investigated the remembered history of the Tyo or Teke in Congo-Brazzaville, and organized the collection of hundreds of traditions in Rwanda which will form the basis of a historical account of that state. In addition, he combined a study of oral traditions and early Portuguese and Dutch documents to write an outline history of state-building in the central African Luba/Lunda area, one of the seminal books of modern African historiography.[9]

Since Vansina's vindication of oral traditions as a historical source, many more researchers have applied the technique with varying degrees of rigor and varying degrees of success. Few seriously question the potential value of oral evidence any more, though many scholars look critically upon one another's efforts in this field. But even when best utilized, oral traditions have serious limitations as historical sources. First, they may not contain a chronological component, and the further back in time one goes, the more likely that even relative chronology will prove faulty (as, for example, when the name of one king is given to represent four or five individuals, or even a dynasty, a procedure referred to as "telescoping"). Second, Vansina's models for oral tradition were obtained from well-organized states or chieftaincies which had existed over long periods of time. It is far more difficult to recover traditions from non-centralized societies, or from states which were conquered, or have vanished in recent times. Third, there is the problem of "feedback" which sorely afflicts some areas in Africa.

9. Jan Vansina, *Kingdoms of the Savanna* (Madison: University of Wisconsin Press, 1968).

This typically occurs when the researcher enters an area already researched or written up by someone else and the answers he gets are those of the new historical version, sometimes right out of the pages of some other scholar's (or in one notable case, his own) book.

Survey and Interview Techniques

In spite of these difficulties, oral evidence is being sought all across Africa, not in many cases the transmitted traditions investigated by Vansina, but firsthand accounts by eyewitnesses. These are being used by historians and other scholars interested in African reactions to the well-publicized government policies of the colonial era, and, where informants are still living, African reactions to the colonial conquest. Similarly, oral evidence is sought by historians interested in grass-roots reactions of the African peoples. In this connection, the relatively new techniques of social survey employing questionnaires and mass interviews are now being experimented with to see whether large-scale collation of information can be achieved without serious loss of reliability. This kind of "development history" using mass data and computer processing has both a useful potential and an obvious drawback. It is clear that the data emerging from a computer is only as good as that fed in, and the problems of framing an adequate questionnaire and administering it in the right circumstances with properly trained assistants are indeed formidable. It is not to be doubted, however, that attempts will increasingly be made by historians to obtain reliable survey data; the kinds of questions that are being asked now in economic and social history can hardly be answered otherwise.

The Chronology Problem

Turning to the more distant past, one of the most difficult problems facing researchers is that of establishing a firm chronology. Oral testimony supplies only a very tentative and relative chronology for the events related. The sequence is usually known, and events such as battles, famines, and political crises are located in the reign of a particular ruler whose predecessor and successor can be named but not dated. In the kingdom of Buganda, the ruler periodically moved his capital; and events, at least for the nineteenth century, can be chronologically located not only within a particular reign, but within a much shorter period when the capital was on a particular site, such as Banda Hill, Mulago, or Rubaga. But unless one of these capital sites can be connected to some firmly dated event (for instance, the visit of the explorer J. H. Speke to the capital site at Banda in 1862), the historian cannot relate his information to changes taking place elsewhere in Africa or the world.

In attempting to solve this problem of chronology, scholars have exercised considerable imagination and ingenuity, largely in vain. For a while many historians were sanguine about the possibility of establishing a number of fixed dates by solar eclipses. Oral histories often relate incidents such as when darkness came at noon in a particular king's reign and the ruler called on his ritual experts for an interpretation of the omen. Since astronomers have enough information to plot eclipses, both future and past, it was hoped that by systematically charting the dates and paths of eclipses in the last few centuries oral testimony could be strategically pinpointed for a few fixed dates. Unfortunately historians were unaware of the frequency of this celestial phenomenon; it was found that there were so many eclipses and partial eclipses crisscrossing Africa in each century that one was left with several equally plausible dates for each recorded incident. Work continues along these lines with an occasional success, but with much less optimism. In African research, as elsewhere, the old formula holds true: "The more we know, the less we know for certain."

Other attempts to approach the chronological problem have been somewhat less imaginative, but perhaps equally frustrating. Using king-lists, some historians have attempted to work out a theoretical average length of reign for a particular political system, and then to count backwards from the earliest known date. By this method, if an average reign is reckoned at twenty years and the fourteenth ruler is known to have attained office in 1880, one would count backwards (20 years, times 13 rulers, equals 260 years) and reach 1620 as the roughly approximate date when the ruling lineage began and, by inference, the state was founded. One need not be an expert in either history or mathematics to find fault with this line of reasoning. How can one determine an "average length of reign"? Some rulers live long, while others are poisoned by their brothers on the way home from the coronation ceremonies. Aware of this, historians then search the traditions for indications of how each ruler met his end and who succeeded him. The succession system, of course, is of crucial importance: if son succeeds father, reigns *may* be relatively long, but if brothers succeed each other, then an elderly ruler will very likely be followed in fairly quick order by a number of equally elderly surviving brothers. It is important then to have precise information about the succession system throughout the period in question and to know the genealogical position of each ruler. Even so, the margin of error becomes unpleasantly large as one goes further back in time.

Genealogically charted king-lists, large-scale sampling, and oral interviews are just three among many new techniques being applied by historians in their attempts to recover the African past. The formidable obstacles presented by research in Africa have stimulated an attitude of problem solving and experimentation which contrasts sharply with the routine practices of an earlier generation. Where once historians plotted their unswerving course to determine the shortest distance between two archives, the modern historians of Africa are setting out in new directions, occasionally getting lost and having to retrace their steps, but experiencing the satisfaction of intellectual as well as factual discovery along the way.

SOME CURRENT THEMES
IN AFRICAN HISTORIOGRAPHY

The emphasis placed by historians on certain aspects of the history they recover is expressed in terms of themes. These vary, as demonstrated above,
according to the cultural background, environment, and world view of the
particular historian, the problems of his time, and his view of the role of history
in society. What constitute major themes in the writings of Herodotus, ibn-
Khaldun, the Reverend Carl Reindorf, or Sir John Gray may no longer seem
important to historians of the 1960s. Some of the themes one finds expressed
in modern texts appear self-evident; for example, the slave trade, which had
such a far-reaching impact on African and world history. Other themes arise only
because of new research techniques and concerns: bureaucracy and state formation in pre-colonial Africa, or religious protest movements as mechanisms for
mobilizing pan-ethnic loyalties. As new techniques are evolved, new research
undertaken, and present studies completed, the themes of African history will
change. Here, then, are some aspects of the history of Africa that historians now
view as particularly significant.

The Origins of Man, the Neolithic Revolution in Africa, and the Introduction of Metallurgy

The work of Louis and Mary Leakey at Olduvai Gorge in East Africa has
revealed the earliest direct ancestor to man, *Homo habilis* (nicknamed "Handy
Man"), who lived from two to three million years ago. In addition, the unique
siting of this ravine, cutting down through some three hundred feet of ancient
lake sediment, has split open the earth to reveal a history of stone-tool development in which the progressive levels can be read like pages of a book.

Early man in Africa learned to walk on his hind feet, to speak words, to make
stone tools, and later shaft them with spear handles and arrows. About fifty
thousand years ago fire began to be used. At one stage, Africa may have exported its stone hand-ax culture to Europe. Then about 8000 B.C. peoples in
the Near East domesticated plants and animals. From there, these food-pro-
ducing techniques seem to have spread into Africa. But the process of domesti-
cating plants may have been evolving independently in Africa as well; claims in
particular have been made for the domestication of millet in Western Sudan,
where the Niger River forms a vast flood plain similar to the Tigris-Euphrates
and the Nile Delta. The desiccation of the once fertile Sahara region, during the
last 2,000 years B.C., created a formidable but not entirely impassable barrier to
the diffusion of new discoveries and is often cited as a cause for the technological backwardness of Africa vis-à-vis Europe in later centuries. Nevertheless, the
technique of iron-working, originally developed by the Assyrians, probably
crossed the Sahara from Carthage and reached the Nok area in central Nigeria
at about the same time (*ca.* 300 B.C.) as it reached Merowe in the upper Nile

from Egypt. Its subsequent spread across all of Africa is related to the next major theme in African history.

The Bantu Migration

Linguists working in Africa early in the twentieth century were struck by the remarkable similarity of African languages spoken across vast areas of equatorial and southern Africa. Later, linguistic classification confirmed this observation and linked the Bantu language family, as it was called, to West Africa. The degree of similarity could only reasonably be accounted for if the far-flung present-day Bantu speakers had originally and relatively recently migrated outward from some core area. (The time factor is a matter of dispute, but educated guesses often range around 2,000 years ago, or at the beginning of the Christian era.) Here is a fascinating puzzle for Africanist scholars to wrestle with. Where was this core area (or areas)? And why did the Bantu migrate? Because of increased population due to the introduction of new crops? Because of increased population due to the introduction of iron blades for hoes, scythes, adzes, and axes? Or because of military superiority owing to iron spear blades and arrowheads? These suggestions have all been put forward. At present most scholars hold that the Bantu expansion was relatively slow, not a sudden wave of conquest; hence agricultural development seems indicated. One thing does seem certain on the basis of the present evidence: in central and southern Africa the introduction of iron was usually associated with the migration of newcomers, presumed to be Bantu speaking.

The point of origin for this dramatic migration of peoples is also disputed. Historians following the linguistic analysis of Joseph Greenberg have argued that the Bantu expanded from the Nok region of Nigeria, an attractive theory in view of the known presence of iron-working and agricultural techniques associated with domestic crops such as yam, millet, and sorghum. However, the proposed migratory path had to cross the Congo forest zone, seen by some scholars as a major obstacle. Historians following the linguistic analysis of the British scholar, Malcolm Guthrie, have argued for an expansion outward from a core area in the savanna region of the southern Congo. This theory is strengthened by the probable introduction of important Southeast Asian food crops (bananas, yams, coconuts) from Madagascar into continental Africa. Compromise efforts to combine the two theories of origin have so far appeared contrived, and much regarding this question will hinge on future research. It should be pointed out, however, that the question of the distribution of food crops, indigenous and introduced, remains a crucial one, and might easily be considered a separate theme in its own right. Certainly in a later era, when American crops such as cassava, sweet potatoes, maize, and peanuts were introduced, beginning in the sixteenth century via the slave trade, the effect on African subsistence efforts, population growth, and resulting political activity was evident.

Trade

An obvious major theme for almost any period of African history is trade. In the Horn of Africa it helped to account for the rise of Axum and the eclipse of Merowe in the first centuries of the Christian era. In later centuries, Red Sea trade stimulated the rise of the Muslim states of Ifat and Adal, which posed a threat to Christian Abyssinia and motivated Portuguese aid to the embattled Christians. On the East African seaboard, the regularity of the monsoon winds brought a contact with the Near East and India that was recorded as early as Roman times. City-states rose, competed for dominating shares in the gold and ivory exports, and later fought the Portuguese interlopers in the sixteenth century. In central Africa, long-range trade routes radiated outward from the Katanga copper-mining area, whose wealth has lost none of its attractiveness in more recent times. And in West Africa, trade was all-important; gold and forest products, such as kola nuts, were exchanged for Saharan salt and manufactured goods from North Africa. The importance of trade was politically recognized as states, large and small, were organized partly so that the inhabitants could better control commerce and enjoy its profits. And along the paths of commercial exchange moved literacy, Islam, and cultural exchange. In all these areas, historians are concerned both with charting the patterns of trade over time and with relating its economic stimulus to evolving social and political structures.

State-Building

Closely involved with trade in some, but by no means all, cases is the rise of centralized political rule, which created new techniques for controlling larger and often more heterogeneous populations. In investigating any of the countless examples of state formation in Africa, historians are concerned with assessing, where it exists, the degree and type of external stimulus. Were political techniques "borrowed"? If so, from whom and with what local adaptations? Was there an external challenge in the form of military aggression or natural disaster? What was the effect of local environment? Two examples of the latter are (1) the Lozi Kingdom of the Zambezi Flood Plain, with its dry, elevated settlements forming political subunits and its organized mass agricultural efforts as the flood waters receded; and (2) the Kilimanjaro mountain slopes where generous rainfall and fertile volcanic soils supported a dense population, which shared similar culture traits but was politically separated into feuding petty states by the deep ravines running up the mountainside.

What techniques were invented or adapted to create new loyalties and ensure obedience? For instance, in the Pare Highlands of Tanzania, efforts were made to transform ritual authority over rainmaking into political authority by the deliberate creation of new "national" religious ceremonies. And long before Moise Tshombe appeared on the scene, mercenary soldiers were employed in many parts of Africa to provide a centralizing ruler with reliable coercive power. Studies in military organization and technology have branched off from state-building analysis to become an important subtheme in recent African research. Similarly, the role of literacy and the creation of a state bureaucracy (though not necessarily related to one another) have been the subjects of modern historical investigation, particularly in West Africa. For the pre-colonial Ashanti state, Professor Wilks carried out an intensive study of the process of bureaucratization, beginning with the creation of appointive offices with chains of command and responsibility, continuing through the division of administration into departments according to function, and finally resulting in a specialized civil service with an identity and special interests of its own.[10] Undoubtedly similar research into the bureaucratic structure of African states will be undertaken wherever surviving sources, human or institutional, still exist.

Another subtheme of state formation concentrates on the development of partially Westernized African states in the nineteenth century, sometimes termed "secondary empires." These states owed their existence to a newly acquired local superiority in European arms, administrative techniques, or some other borrowed advantage (hence the term "secondary"). Some even acquired the assistance of European missionaries as diplomatic agents in dealing with gradually encroaching European powers, as in Basutoland in South Africa, Buganda in East Africa, and Abeokuta in West Africa. Most of the budding "secondary empires" were prematurely terminated by the colonial conquest.

The Slave Trade

The slave trade has always fascinated historians and it continues to do so. It cost so many lives, forcibly transplanted so many people, lasted so long, and had such enduring aftereffects. Yet for all the scholarly research hours expended and books published on this theme, in many respects the surface has hardly been scratched. Many books on the slave trade seem to travel the same ground over and over again without adding significantly to our knowledge. The same well-known sources are quoted to re-evoke the suffering and horror, reawaken the pangs of guilt, and restate the most bloated of estimates for the numbers of lives expended and bodies transported. On the other hand, there has been a tendency for colonial apologists to diminish the degree of European responsibility for the presumed ravages of the slave trade by recalling pre-European customs of slavery indigenous to some African societies. In fairness, however, it must be recognized that the sources that would permit deeper studies are widely scattered and difficult to collate. That, however, also holds true for other themes in African history.

10. Ivor Wilks, "Ashanti Government," in *West African Kingdoms in the Nineteenth Century*, ed. Daryll Forde and P. M. Kaberry (London: Oxford University Press, 1967), pp. 206–38.

New efforts are being made, notably by Philip Curtin and Jan Vansina at Wisconsin, to systematically plot the numbers of slaves shipped and the areas from which they came during each decade of the eighteenth and nineteenth centuries. It appears from their initial efforts that the figures for the nineteenth-century trade have been greatly exaggerated. For modern writers to continue to use these early estimates, which issued largely from abolitionist propaganda, suggests that the emotional issue and the need to pronounce guilt is strong even today.

Africanists presently viewing the slave trade are approaching it with new questions and from new directions. There is much to be learned about the trade within Africa before the European slaver's ships were ever sighted. Other questions concern the effect of the trade in state formation and destruction, the economic effect of depopulation in some raided areas and regroupment in other resistant areas, and the way in which previously isolated cultures reacted to the exchange of information, ideas, and material goods in the process of furthering the trade in human beings. The later Karl Polanyi compiled an economic study of the slave-trading state of Dahomey which showed, among other things, that a significant proportion of captured slaves were used as plantation labor by the Dahomeans for the production of palm oil. Dahomey further demonstrated how an external trade created an internal market economy and market-mindedness facilitated by circulating currency in the place of customary barter.

If the larger issue of the African Diaspora is considered with the slave-trade theme, one can include the returnees from Brazil and the West Indies, some of whom became agents of the trade, others of whom settled in Sierra Leone and in Yoruba areas to become agents of social change.

Islamization

Studies in West Africa which are concerned in part with earlier themes of trade and state-building have revealed a rich Arabic and Hausa literature closely related to Islamic issues in history. Indeed, in this area the "data explosion" of source material is particularly noticeable. The Institute of African Studies in Ghana estimates that there are at least 20,000 extant manuscripts useful to the study of Ghanaian history, of which only 500 have thus far been catalogued. The Fulani Jihad of the early nineteenth century in northern Nigeria produced a large body of contemporary documents, of which at least 300 are currently available to scholars. This wealth of source material permits research into many questions of a social and political nature about the process of Islamic growth in West Africa, and about its characteristics and effects. The field is a new one and the manuscript source discoveries are recent. Unfortunately those perhaps best qualified to study Islam, the specialist-scholars of Near Eastern studies, have hitherto regarded West Africa (in fact, all of Africa outside of Egypt) as a backwater area on the fringe of true Islamic culture and therefore not a rewarding field for study.

Within the overall theme of Islamization, attention seems presently concentrated on the reform movements of the nineteenth century, probably because these were dramatic, significant in terms of wider issues, and above all well documented. As movements intended to purify Islam, their impact was felt in all aspects of society; H. F. C. Smith, at Ahmadu Bello University in Nigeria, credits them with sparking a nineteenth-century "literary renaissance" in the Central Sudan.

Social and Cultural History

If a major theme of Islamization is expressed in terms of social and cultural change, it is representative of the growing interest by African historians in similar questions for all periods. Religious conversion, literacy, changes in life and values are being investigated in the sixteenth-century Kongo kingdom as well as in twentieth-century Kenya. Conversion by Christian missionaries, by Muslim *dyula* traders and scholars, and by modern messianic movements equally invite attention. So does the adoption of Masai culture traits and military weaponry by the neighboring Kikuyu and Nandi of Kenya, or the supposed spread of *Ntemi* ritual chieftaincies into northern Tanzania. Far from being "stagnant," Africa was experiencing continuing social change in the pre-European period. Rapid Westernization in recent decades is, of course, well known. But even here current research is qualifying earlier generalizations by demonstrating the selective nature of the Westernizing process.

Field work within social and cultural history ranges from biographies charting the changes of belief and way of life of a single individual at one end of the spectrum to studies of institutional change at the other. "Development histories," such as the work done by James Graham in Tanzania[11] on migrant labor, cash-cropping, and receptivity to, or rejection of, colonial agricultural schemes, easily fall at the institutional end of the spectrum. So would the "urban history" projects now under way in a number of African countries. Research in social and cultural history will undoubtedly continue to grow in coming decades, for this is where new interest and research skills are being mobilized.

Resistance, Rebellion, and the Politics of Survival

It was to be expected that the spectacle of independence movements in mid-twentieth-century Africa would stimulate studies of earlier struggles to defend African sovereignty against the colonial onslaught. Similarly, the origins of modern nationalism were sought in earlier rebellions and political protest

---

11. "Changing Patterns of Wage Labor in Tanzania: A History of the Relations between African Labor and European Capitalism in Njombe District, 1931–1961" (Ph.D. diss., Northwestern University, 1968).

movements. Once initiated, these studies have proved fascinating in their own right, revealing a new interplay of forces, motivations, and aspirations.

It is now recognized that last-ditch resistance to European conquest and large-scale rebellions in the period of European rule were more than just *reactions* to European initiative, more than blind resorts to violence in the face of hopeless odds. Colonial administrators, ironically, were the first to recognize that Africans might be fighting *for* something, as well as against certain impositions. But the official view customarily confined such motivations to the purely selfish ambitions of a few backward-looking chiefs and witch doctors, or, in later periods, unscrupulous political agitators. Modern studies, such as those of Terence Ranger on the 1897 revolt in Rhodesia, and John Iliffe on the 1905 Maji-Maji rebellion in German East Africa, have gone far to penetrate the rhetoric of repression and reveal the internal anatomy of rebellion in all its complexity. There were mixed motives involved and internal rivalries in existence long before the colonial era. In both of the above cases, the leaders of rebellion were religious authorities who had little political power but whose spiritual status could transcend local political and ethnic divisions. Appeal was made to supernatural forces to aid in driving out the Europeans, but quite understandably the rebels then looked forward to inheriting European possessions and wealth. These were not, therefore, attempts to deny the present and return to the past. Yet the past was important, for it provided a priestly leadership unstained by the shame of earlier political and military defeat. When the pressure of new economic demands by colonial regimes was painfully experienced by the mass of peasant agriculturalists (hitherto relatively unaffected by the loss of sovereignty at the top), the result was a mass uprising with a religious leadership to give it direction.

Research into some well-known, and some relatively unknown, rebellions is just now gathering momentum. Studies of the other side of the coin — deliberate collaboration by African authorities with their colonial overlords — have hardly begun. There are many cases where a responsible African leadership saw more advantage for their people in cooperation, often in instances where long-time rival groups were seen to be in opposition. Of course, personal ambitions were important too, and substitutes could always be found for a deposed chief. But no chief could govern long without the support of his people, and to gain that support he had to be visibly serving their immediate or long-range interests. In the era of alien domination, what has been called "the politics of survival" could thus take on many different patterns and shapes.

These, then, are some of the themes which emerge from current research into African history. The technical and financial resources necessary to systematic study have only recently become available, and Africa today is yielding a historical experience which may compel new directions in research, new themes, and new understanding.

10

Empires and
State Formation

JEFFREY HOLDEN

THE STUDY OF AFRICAN STATES

IT IS STILL DIFFICULT to make meaningful generalizations about the political history of Tropical Africa before the European conquest of less than a hundred years ago. Efforts have been made by scholars to place African societies and political systems within analytical categories and to isolate certain characteristics of these peoples and states. The two main groups of scholars to have made this attempt are the Marxist historians and the non-Marxist Western scholars. Marxists, with some differences over the appropriateness of terminology, see African societies as having followed a universal sequence of development from primitive communalism to tribalism to feudalism, with corresponding developments in their modes of production. This establishes the distinction between states and prestates, depending on whether the social structure is class or preclass. The "state" only comes into existence when property inequality has produced antagonistic classes. Rigorous attempts have recently been made to fit those historical African societies which were preclass, and therefore prestate, into a Marxist category known as "Oriental despotism," which is the political system associated with the Marxist "Asiatic mode of production." More will be said of this later. Inadequate data leaves the success of this attempt in question, and deductions made on the basis of this classification, where data is lacking, are hazardous. The discussion has been fruitful, however, and the analytical technique involved is none the worse for being over a century old.

Non-Marxist scholars usually have been asking rather different questions and, on the basis of case studies in African political anthropology, have attempted to construct typologies of political systems which would cover the complexity of the African examples. From these attempts certain trends can be observed, such

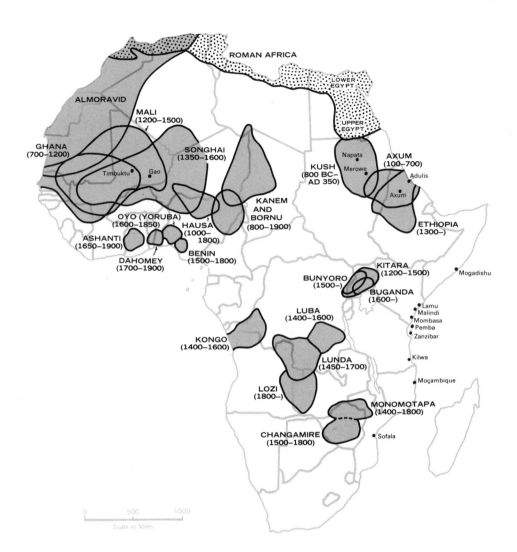

MAJOR PRE-COLONIAL STATES AND EMPIRES

as the transition from "segmentary" to "unitary" political structures. Correlations can be established between types of political authority, such as that based on kinship, and the corresponding political systems, such as the segmentary state, the pyramidal state, and the hierarchical state. Predictions based on observation have been made, not always wisely, such as that a segmentary state based on kinship loyalty is likely to be less stable than a unitary state in which political authority is based on such factors as wealth, coercive power, and religion. The complexity and diversity of Tropical African states make the erection of such typologies very unsatisfactory.

For purposes of this essay we will not attempt a survey of the full range of

African states. Such a survey would produce only a patchwork of names, dates, and places, each with a brief inventory of cultural, political, social, and economic achievements. It will be our purpose to describe and analyze the political continuum which existed within a more limited geographical area, the states of the Western Sudan: that is, the area of West Africa south of the Sahara and north of the equatorial forest, from the Atlantic to Lake Chad, in the period from about the third to the seventeenth century A.D. This vast area, with very large populations, does exhibit a considerable degree of continuity in political innovation and state-formation processes, but before we examine this area more fully, we should indicate the extent at least of state formation in other areas (see map on page 178).

STATE FORMATION IN EAST AND CENTRAL AFRICA

One of the earliest states in Africa was Kush, located along the Nile in what is today northern Sudan. Kush existed as an independent political entity (though not continuously so) from the eighteenth century B.C., and became a significant power in the eighth century B.C. It was characterized by a diversity of agricultural and manufactured products and became a commercial and political power of international significance by the late seventh century B.C. We know that one Kush dynasty ruled for one thousand years, that its inhabitants used a literary language which had developed a cursive script probably by the third century B.C., and that a vast iron industry at Merowe was at its height in the sixth century B.C. But we can only guess at how the state came into existence and, more important, to what extent its political ideas and techniques spread elsewhere.

Axum, in modern Eritrea and Ethiopia, was founded in the fifth century B.C., only 400 miles from the later Kushite capital of Merowe. It reached its territorial and administrative peak in the fourth century A.D. We know of its codified property law, its advanced social and religious organization, its complex urban architecture, and its trade links with Greece and Rome. But although Kush was conquered and for a while administered by Axum, it is not realistic to regard the latter as a successor state to the former in the same way that medieval Songhai can be said to have inherited the political, economic, and cultural role of Mali. We do know that the rulers of Axum from the early fourth century A.D. were of the Monophysite Coptic denomination, and that Christianity probably played an important role in the solidification of the state. We can say that in some ways modern Ethiopia has evolved from Axum.

After the eighth century A.D., when the people of Axum had withdrawn into the Ethiopian Highlands, there is a dearth of significant information on eastern Africa until the beginning of the sixteenth century. We do have accounts of Arab and Indian settlement along the East African coast during the period from the seventh to the eleventh centuries. Kilwa (in modern Tanzania) became the leading commercial town of East Africa during the twelfth and thirteenth centuries, a commercial prominence which lasted until the mid-fourteenth century. Its rhymed coinage almost certainly predated that of India and Persia, and its control of the raw materials of the interior (gold and copper in particular) made it a formidable economic as well as commercial power. The development of Kilwa and of other coastal city-states (for example, Mogadishu, Lamu, Mombasa) shared many common features which together contituted a fairly coherent series of related characteristics. But despite the Arab, Indian, and, later, Portuguese immigration, which strongly influenced the political nature of these coastal states, there is a dearth of helpful documentary sources on the East African coast until the fourteenth century.

Zimbabwe (in modern Rhodesia), where there are extensive and complex archaeological remains, is thought to have been in continuous use from at least the twelfth century to the beginning of the nineteenth century A.D. The city of Zimbabwe was the capital of the Karanga empire, which stretched from the Zambezi to the Limpopo and encompassed an area of rich gold workings. Although complex stone architecture and other archaeological discoveries are not in themselves adequate indications of advanced social, economic, and political organization, the collection of oral histories and the firsthand descriptions of early Portuguese visitors to the area virtually confirm the existence of a centralized political system. Nevertheless, many significant questions about the nature and extent of this system remain unanswered and await further historical research.

Mention must also be made of the central African states of Kongo and Ngola (modern Angola). These were territorially large states which were later to be powerfully influenced by contact with Portuguese Christianity. Throughout most of the southern Congo Basin this contact led to the disintegration of existing African states, although disintegration was in some cases delayed by an initial period of increased prosperity based upon expanded trade. Like Monomotapa, these states have become better understood in recent years through the techniques of oral history.

CRITERIA FOR STATE SELECTION

Emerging from this brief summary are certain fairly obvious criteria which will be used to determine the overall significance of the states to be discussed. The size of the population and territorial area affected and the time span covering the initiation, development, and continuous application of political techniques are significant. Other major bases for our choice of the medieval Western Sudanic states are the degree to which one state can be said to be the successor of another and the nature of this inherited role; the extent to which the political forms under discussion can be described as "indigenous"; and the availability and weight of reliable data, both documentary and oral, and the manner in which they can corroborate each other.

We might, bravely, add another. This would concern the influence of these political systems upon the attitudes of the people within their control. We will try to examine, for example, the success of the ruling groups involved in creating among their subjects and citizens a degree of identification with the state, or, in some cases, with the nation. This may shed light on such contemporary questions as whether the "identity" of Mande (Mali) some four hundred years after its disappearance as a large-scale political system still has a functional evocation among the Mande-speakers scattered throughout West Africa. Clearly it does have an influence, although the technique of isolating and evaluating this influence is difficult and must await future research.

This set of criteria for state selection would suggest that were more space available our study of the Western Sudan would be continued into the later period characterized by the sequence of Islamic state formations in the late eighteenth and throughout the nineteenth century. These very closely related political movements took place over the area from Senegal to Bornu and began some 150 years after the economic, cultural, and, to a degree, political unity of the area had been destroyed by the Moroccan conquest of Songhai. Here there is a great wealth and accessibility of contemporaneous, indigenous, documentary data to assist an analysis.

Unlike the equally interesting cases of, say, late eighteenth-century Ashanti (in modern Ghana) or nineteenth-century Buganda (in modern Uganda), many of the nineteenth-century Western Sudanic state-builders using the Arabic script can be allowed to speak for themselves. For example, the main founders of the Sokoto caliphate (centered in what is now northern Nigeria), ʿUthman b. Fudi (Usman dan Fodio), together with his son Muhammad Bello and his brother ʿAbdallah, left almost 300 known books and articles, many dealing directly with the reasons for, and the difficulties faced in, their attempts to create a new state. This literary profusion was continued by their followers and descendants. As evidence of the existence of a sense of common destiny and nationality—a crucial, if sophisticated, aim of statecraft—such writings are not conclusive; but without articulation of purposes and goals, which in essence is what these writings constitute, the question cannot even be broached. When these primary sources are combined with the stock of past and present-day local, oral accounts and the European eyewitness and archival sources (which, of course, are also rich for Ashanti and Buganda), the states to be researched enter a different category of historical analysis.

Despite the existence of these sources, a current bibliography of African political history would in no way reflect the predominant position of the Western

Sudan in African history. This neglect may, in part, be attributed to the under-standable but unfortunate reluctance of academics, both African and non-African, to research into themes which are not connected with the European contact. Whatever the reason, this neglect has caused a serious distortion in our view of African history and has produced a vastly inadequate appreciation of significant historical determinants of the modern African state systems. This essay, in dealing with an area where European influence was almost nonexistent until eighty years ago, is a minor attempt at a corrective focus.

The framework of the simplest political grouping includes (a) a ruler, who can be one or several; (b) his subjects; (c) a set of motivations for each with some overlap; and (d) a mechanism to ensure that the aims of the ruler are achieved without so frustrating the aims of the subjects that they withdraw their acquies-cence, enforced or otherwise, in the exercise of his authority. This latter mecha-nism constitutes the political system; it consists of a set of functions which are more or less common to any political grouping and a set of structures, which vary greatly from time to time and from place to place, to perform these func-tions.

It will be our purpose to examine these elements in the political systems of the Western Sudan, covering a period of over a thousand years and using historical sources which are unique in Tropical Africa for their breadth, depth, and de-tail. Emphasis will be placed on the continuity and evolution of the political structures under examination as they respond to changes in the economic, social, and cultural environment. Our primary focus, however, will be on the establish-ment, legitimation, and maintenance of authority.

THE WESTERN SUDAN IN PERSPECTIVE

The term *Sudan* (Arabic for "black") refers to the 3,000-mile-wide region stretching eastward from the Atlantic to the Ethiopian Highlands and lying between the Sahara to the north and the rainforest to the south. Lake Chad is generally considered as the dividing line between the eastern and western sec-tors, although occasionally a "central" Sudan is distinguished which includes the areas on either side of the lake. The Western Sudan, in the latter case, would then extend roughly from coastal Senegal to the northern borders of Nigeria, with its major focal centers in the Senegal and upper and middle Niger River basins. It is this delimitation of the Western Sudanic region which will be used here, although occasional reference will be made to some areas in the Central Sudan as well.

Several factors may be briefly noted which would qualify the Western Sudan, thus defined, as one of the cradles of world civilization, rivaling the valleys of the Nile, Yangtze, and Tigris-Euphrates in its influence upon the history of man.

From neolithic times basically the same groups of people have inhabited the Western Sudan, producing a relative cultural homogeneity and a deep sense of continuous and shared history. The desiccation of the fertile land of the Sahara, which occurred roughly between 2000 and 500 B.C., resulted in the desert as we know it today and appears to have produced a chain of migrations and interactions between nomads and sedentary people, between pastoralists and cultivators, which was still in progress during the period from the third to the seventeenth century A.D. Certainly the ecological changes in this area and the resultant population movements must have been factors affecting the formation of the relatively large-scale political units which came to exist.

The antiquity of the civilization which developed in the Western Sudan is illustrated by the presence of iron tools and weapons, smelted locally, dating back to the fourth century B.C. Agricultural innovations and favorable natural conditions made the area a leading producer of cereal, while the abundance of gold and the scarcity of salt had inspired a large-scale trade network by the early years of the Christian era. By the time of our first reliable historical references, in the eighth century A.D., the Western Sudan was already the scene of well-developed urban life, a center of advanced agriculture of which the surplus product was able to sustain the towns, and an integral part of a large-scale, intercontinental trading network. Over the next thousand years these advances were to continue and would produce in Ghana, Mali, and Songhai the highest levels of social and political development in pre-colonial sub-Saharan Africa.

THE ESTABLISHMENT OF AUTHORITY
IN THE WESTERN SUDAN

Space permits only a brief speculation about the origins of these Western Sudanic states and the establishment of their ruling groups, although the methods by which the dynastic and territorial foundations are remembered are interesting and instructive. These methods mainly concern oral traditions, which are memorized by specialist groups who act as official historians and who often perform a crucial ideological function insofar as they are officially required to "edit" history as well as remember it. As one such royal *griot* has written:

> Without us the names of kings would vanish into oblivion, we are the memory of mankind. . . . I teach kings the history of their ancestors so that the lives of the ancients might serve them as an example, for the world is old, but the future springs from the past. . . . I learnt the origins of Mali and the art of speaking. Everywhere I was able to see and understand what my masters were teaching me. But between their hands I took an oath to teach only what is to be taught and to conceal what is to be concealed.

Oral traditions tend to telescope and conceptualize events which probably took place over long periods of time and involved several people instead of the single hero in whom is usually vested the credit for the collective achievements of the period. The settlement of immigrant groups in an uninhabited place, or their seizing or accepting authority over the original occupants, or the gradual transition of nomadic pastoralists into sedentary cultivators is usually told as an event in the life of a single founder-hero. Early documentary references in Arabic to the foundation of Ghana's ruling dynasty only repeat these oral traditions, so even in written documents we are sometimes left with a very impressionistic outline.

THE STATE OF GHANA

Traditions have Ghana's "origin" going back to the fourth century A.D., and possibly as early as the third century B.C. But however the starting point is calculated, it is of importance if the people concerned chose to remember a particular person or event as beginning their political system. The *Ta'rikh al-Sudan,* or "History of the Western Sudan," an invaluable locally written seventeenth-century manuscript, states that Ghana's first ruling dynasty was "white." We know, however, that by the tenth century the rulers of Ghana were black. We can perhaps conclude from this change of dynasty that some continuity in political structure was maintained. Some degree of structural formulation at an early period could thus be assumed. An alternative explanation is that the "white" rulers became black through intermarriage over six or seven centuries; this explanation would indicate a contact of different political traditions and perhaps techniques.

By the mid-eleventh century, when our accounts became fuller, the ruler of Ghana was firmly established as head of his own lineage, as direct ruler over large groups of Soninke cultivators, and as the recipient of tribute from a large number of minor, neighboring monarchs. The farming peoples of this area had long been familiar with the idea of membership in a large-scale political unit; contact with the representatives of the ruling head of that unit, and the demands made by them, may have been slight — however, we have no evidence on this point. The leaders of other political formations, from Tekrur on the Atlantic to Gao on the middle Niger, had similarly become accustomed to the fact that tribute should be paid to any ruler with enough long-distance power at his disposal to enforce his demands and enough military strength to protect the tributary state and to secure trade.

Inevitably, these peripheral tributaries ended their relationship with the center when the rulers of Ghana were weakened by the Almoravid invasion and by the capture of their chief city in A.D. 1076. This incursion of Berber Muslims was short-lived. Ghana as a ruling dynasty and as a political system did not come to an end when the local Susu conquered its towns early in the thirteenth century and attempted to take over its sphere of authority. It survived, in shadow, paying tribute to emergent Mali, at least until the mid-fourteenth century.

THE STATE OF MALI

Within about fifty years of the Susu invasion, the political unity of what had been the empire of Ghana was restored and enlarged, with the addition of many more tributaries, by a dynasty of another Mande-speaking group. The establishment of the authority of Sundjata, revered as the founder of Mali, was by military means, but the point remains that to some extent he had inherited, through his own efforts, a political system. The defeat of an enemy in battle did not entail the dismemberment of his territory or the radical alteration of his political-economic-cultural complex. It meant the assumption of the political rights and obligations, as well as the material wealth, of the defeated predecessor. It might also mean the elimination of his family to prevent rivalry for the throne.

The state structure of Mali did not seem to have been much shaken by succession disputes which deposed three rulers in about twenty years and which temporarily put a freed slave, Sakura, on the throne. A nine-month civil war and several other succession disputes may well have weakened the loyalty to the man in power, but the centralized structural framework of the empire, strengthened by Islamic bureaucratic techniques, remained solid.

THE STATE OF SONGHAI

In 1464, Sunni Ali assumed office as head of the Songhai people (often spelled Songhay), which were centered around the ancient town of Gao. According to the *Ta'rikh al-Fattach*, another important Western Sudanese history written in the sixteenth century, he was the fifteenth head of a dynasty founded by a Mande, or possibly a Soninke, adventurer. The power base of this dynasty in Gao was already well established when Sunni Ali set out to reconstruct the declining Mali empire from the east. His conquest was relatively easy, and the vast and complex system of the Mali empire seemed to be waiting for a ruler with adequate coercive force and the disposable wealth assured by it. With these resources, the new ruler was to restore the relationships and loyalties which by then were centuries old. The administrative achievements of Sunni Ali were often undertaken without utilization of his Muslim subjects in the urban areas. Later, Askia Muhammad usurped the throne with a change of dynasty, consolidated Sunni Ali's conquests through his well-equipped and experienced cavalry and river navy, and deliberately used Islam as a device to bind these enormous areas together.

As late as 1583, at the end of the long reign of Askia Dawud, the highly complex empire was apparently functioning more or less without strain. Trade was secure, and the perennial external threats from the Tuaregs (nomadic Berbers of the Sahara) were being controlled. Yet, within ten years, a tiny Moroccan army, using firearms for the first time in the Western Sudanic area, had not only defeated the Songhai armies but were in the process of systematically exploiting the wealth of the system in a way which had not been attempted before.

The Moroccans were operating under a different set of conditions than had previously governed military campaigns, conquests, and tributary relations in the Western Sudan. They took out resources and put nothing back, except an administration whose sole purpose was exploitation. Furthermore, they apparently had no interest in, or resources for, administering an area wider than the middle Niger, and there was not an indigenous dynasty able to do so. The end result was a destruction of the political unity of the Western Sudan. Trade became insecure and shifted eastwards (where Hausaland and Bornu reaped the benefits). Towns declined and Islam stagnated. A clear watershed is provided, therefore, to end our survey of the manner in which central political authority was established over the territorially vast empires of the Western Sudan.

LEGITIMATION OF AUTHORITY IN THE WESTERN SUDAN

We will now examine the means by which authority was legitimized in the Western Sudan. At this point, the institution of kingship assumes a crucial role. With few exceptions, centralized political systems in Africa have taken a monarchical form, and the Western Sudanic states have followed this pattern. Some Islamic states in the Western Sudan in the eighteenth and nineteenth centuries could best be categorized as democratic republics (for example, Futa Toro), but these Islamic theories, which stressed the sovereignty of the group as a whole, were not a major determinant of political authority in the medieval empires.

Separating, for the moment, the office of king from his powers, we find the office already hallowed by tradition in our early descriptions of Ghana. The court ceremonial described by Al-Bakri in A.D. 1065 and the distinction between what the king wears and what his nobles wear are surely pointers to the way in which the monarch had gradually set himself above not only his subjects but the members of his own lineage. By the time of ibn Battuta's visit to Mali in the 1350s, the king, or "Mansa Mali," wore trousers which were exclusive to this office. This was part of a process of elevating the office, if not always the office-holder, above the normal authority of lineage status, even if the lineage had become "royal."

RITUAL REINFORCEMENT OF AUTHORITY

Theories of divine kingship, or at least of a ritual leadership, were often employed to enhance the mystique or magic of the ruler's office. To look to North Africa or Egypt for the source of the diffusion of these concepts of divine kingship seems hardly necessary and probably misdirected. Religion was invariably harnessed to the ideology of the ruling groups, at times in very obvious ways. In Ghana, for instance, gold nuggets which were mined were handed over to the king—in part, because it was regarded as bad luck to discover one, but the ruler had sufficient religious power to overcome whatever evil influence might be attached to the gold. As ritual ruler, the king became more than just the contact between his lineage members and their ancestors; he attempted to become the living representative of all the ancesotrs of all the lineages included within the political unit, which, through administrative and ideological means, was being shaped into a kingdom or empire.

Apart from some extreme examples in Bornu, the function of "ritual" leadership common among the Western Sudanese monarchs was generally blended with other functions and corroborated them. The king was head of the government, the judiciary, and the army, as well as being the chief lawmaker. These were the functions of kingship, combined in the person of the officeholder, and these were the rights and obligations, privileges and duties which despite war and conquest were handed over intact to each successor to royal power. The ritual function should not be underestimated; it is most clearly important in matters related to the succession to leadership.

Some information about the ritual aspects of kingship can perhaps be gleaned from linguistic evidence concerning the various titles of the Ghana ruler. "Ghana," when used as the king's title, appears to have meant chief of war; he was also called Kaya-Maghan, or chief of the gold. Throughout the Western Sudan spoken words have special powers, and the name given to a king in a myth of origin can be very enlightening. Such names are generally connected with attributes such as health, wealth, and fertility, and they emphasize the ritual role of the king as protector of the land and the families on it. Assumption of the throne, therefore, buttressed by the ritual sanctions which surrounded it, was the most common and most efficacious means of legitimation.

The adherence to Islam of many rulers may not have been intended to enhance their legitimacy, but it clearly could have had this effect. In the first place, Islamic law, which was codified and taught in the schools, laid down quite clearly the various aspects of the ruler's role and the basis on which he held his authority. In Islamic theory, this was because God willed it and also because the ruler was chosen or accepted by the Muslim community. Withdrawal of one's allegiance to the temporal ruler was a grave sin. The return of Askia Muhammad from Mecca to Songhai after his appointment as caliph for the Western Sudan presumably added another unifying, legitimizing factor to the political system.

The detailed nature of Islamic law, with its regulations for taxation and administration, could also be expected to provide a theoretical legitimacy for the core of the royal administration, as well as for the royal power itself. There is, of course, no historical answer to the question of whether Islam did help to legitimize these states; this would require knowledge regarding the attitudes of the subjects to the claims of the ruler.

The Islamic factor worked in reverse, however, and a non-Muslim ruler could never be sure in times of religious upheaval, or during wars or crises in general, of the loyalty of devout Muslims. The Western Sudan has been famous not only for its accommodation of Islamic and traditional beliefs and practices but also for its periods of fanatical proselytization and intolerance. Sunni Ali was very severe on the Muslims of Timbuktu for what he considered their lukewarm support of him against the Muslim Tuaregs. It seems that their chief judge, however, viewed himself as an independent ruler of a Muslim city within the largely non-Muslim state of Songhai. Later, the Askia's secretary and adviser is supposed to have betrayed him when confronting the Moroccans because of his coolness toward Islam and his encouragement of pagan practices. Strictly interpreted, Islamic doctrine did not permit a Muslim to live in a pagan state; and in times of religious upheaval, withdrawal of allegiance from the pagan ruler, followed by emigration, followed in turn by holy war, was a common pattern.

Clearly a ruler embracing Islam faced possible gains and losses. He gained a broader base for his legitimacy, if not among all his subjects, at least among the Muslim traders, many of them foreigners, staying in his realm. The vast and ancient trade network had brought many non-Sudanese trading families into permanent residence in the towns of the area. A separate residential area for "white" Muslim traders within the urban complex of the Ghana capital was noted by Al-Bakri. The Susu invasion of Ghana soon produced an emigration of the Muslims to Walata, away from the rule of a non-Muslim king. The same emigration occurred when the pagan Denianke dynasty was established in the Futa Toro region (in Senegal), with such cities as Tekrur, Silla, and Berissa rapidly declining in consequence. Dia Kossi of Songhai became Muslim, we are told by the *Ta'rikh al-Sudan*, to please the traders upon whom he relied for caravan trade. Different peoples needed different spurs to their loyalty, and the effort to secure overall legitimacy was always a matter of walking a tightrope.

The Muslim ruler stood to lose the loyalty of those of his subjects who were non-Muslims and who were most concerned with the survival of the old beliefs and rituals. Presumably this is one of the major reasons why pre-Islamic customs and rituals were allowed and maintained in the courts of the Muslim rulers. This was noted of all the rulers of whom we have descriptions. Dia Kossi made no attempt to force his new religion upon his subjects, and even such a thorough-going Muslim as Askia Muhammad was careful to retain traditional observances.

THE MAINTENANCE OF AUTHORITY IN THE WESTERN SUDAN

We now turn to the maintenance of political authority which has been "established" and "legitimized." It is here that we can deal with the practical side of Sudanic government and observe the clearest lines of development. Two major issues are involved: first, the maintenance and extension of the ruler's authority over both the core and the periphery of the empire, and, second, his authority over other members of the ruling elite. The essence of the political relationship between ruler and ruled is the monopoly of coercive force held by the ruler. The fact that in most traditional African political systems there were institutionalized channels by which the subjects could make their voices heard and could exercise sanctions against misrule does not invalidate this relational principle.

Administrative Structures

The head of a mere lineage, meeting traditional problems with traditional resources, would outwardly differ little from his peers. He would not need many officers to assist him. When the area and nature of his political authority is enlarged, however, the development of an administration becomes necessary and, indeed, provides a valuable indicator as to the scale of this enlargement. The "Oriental" system, referred to earlier, administered its vast domains with only three departments of state: those concerned with finance, war, and public works—or as Engels put it: plunder at home, plunder abroad, and reproduction of self. In the Sudanic region, ʿUthman b. Fudi taught and wrote that oppression exists only because government exists and that the number of public officers should be kept at a minimum. Governments, however, seem to develop a momentum of their own which inevitably makes for enlarged and more complex administrations. In this way, a lineage head could become an emperor.

By the time of our first full accounts of Ghana in 1065, the ruler had with him at court his counselors, the town governor, and the sons of princes. Already, therefore, there are indications of a palace administration and a government. Possibly the princes' sons, and not their fathers, were there because the latter were concerned with provincial administration. To keep the families of provincial administrators at court as hostages for the loyalty of their fathers is a practice well known to this area. At the Mali court in 1352, there was both an inner circle of officials and an outer circle of cavalry commanders, executioners, heralds, and so on. Sunni Ali (1464–92), after dividing the empire into provinces, ensured that his local governors had administrations of their own; and Askia Muhammad (1495–1528) took over this bureaucratic framework, enlarged it, and made it more detailed and complex than ever before. Aside from the military administration, there were separate civil officials in charge of justice, finance, royal buying and selling, farming, forestry, wages, property questions, court arrangements, food supplies, and other functions. From at least the eleventh century, when Al-Bakri tells us that the Ghana ruler's major ministers were Muslims, the royal administration can be assumed to have had a literate bureaucracy supporting it. The effect of this factor in strengthening and standardizing the administration and in spreading awareness of the law and decrees of the central government must have been great. A literate bureaucracy is also more open to the diffusion of new administrative techniques, which in turn can help buttress its own power.

Finance and Taxation

The ever increasing size of administration meant growing problems of finance. These were generally handled through gifts to the officials by the ruler or by the granting of what amounted to privileges-of-exploitation on their own behalf. Though greatly enlarged in size and detail, this disbursement was still only a continuation of the process whereby the ruler expropriated from society a disposable surplus with which he then secured the loyalty of his followers. The titleholder was usually an administrator in the Western Sudan, and the collection and retention of part of the royal revenue was a routine way to reward the elite.

A steady increase in oppressive exploitation was a burden upon those who paid the "taxes," namely, the traders and craftsmen of the towns, the tributary monarchs, and the farmers of the countryside. Askia Muhammad, for example, was apparently able to exact one-third of Kano's revenue as tribute. In Kanem-Bornu under the rigorous rule of Mai Idris Alooma (1570–1602), the spiral effect of enlarged administration, necessitating increased taxation which in turn necessitated and facilitated further extension of the administration, was seen at its clearest.

With the growth of administrations the numerous administrators began to constitute a barrier between the ruler and his subjects, thus further attenuating the links of lineage and traditional loyalty. Access to the royal ear must have been more and more limited to the chosen few. Another important development to be noted at this stage lies in the extension of the concept of "public affairs" which the expansion of the administration indicates. More and more activities and problems which had formerly been conducted and settled by traditional, local, or kinship institutions were now becoming the concern of the central government. The scope of "public affairs" increased step by step with the enlargement of the public power.

Communications are clearly crucial for the maintenance of centralized authority, so that the imperial existence can be observed and made familiar, and so that its decisions can be received and obeyed. This necessitates large-scale public works, and it is the provision of surplus wealth and availability of labor to accomplish these which has led some scholars to observe similarities between the "Oriental despotism" system and that obtaining in, say, early sixteenth-century Songhai.

The Extension of the Bases of Authority

Let us now turn to the ruler's maintenance and extension of authority vis-à-vis the ruling elite—the normal source of a potential rival. We have seen that the earliest basis for the ruler's authority lay in his position as lineage head and as repository of vital ritual functions. Within this framework, traditional institutions were in operation to control and balance his exercise of authority. At the same time it would seem that the ruler could enlarge his authority both within the limits allowed him by tradition and outside those limits, in opposition to the customary restraints imposed upon him.

In the former case, within the traditional limits, he might, for example, build up a basis of acquired wealth by operating as a trader in a personal capacity. This would not necessarily preclude his use of the state machine to serve this enterprise, and the distinction between his personal and official power and wealth would be blurred. Another basis for the ruler's wealth was possession of force adequate to collect protection money. Thus, the Ghana ruler's import, export, and productivity taxes on trade and gold mining had the effect of building up a surplus of wealth which was at his disposal and presumably without traditional restraints on its disbursement. One of many examples of the ruler intervening in trade is given by Leo Africanus, who tells us that in Kanem-Bornu in the early years of the sixteenth century only royal agents were allowed to trade slaves for horses. The colossal fortunes amassed by the Mali and Songhai rulers can be regarded in this light, though by this period extension of the political authority of the ruler had long broken out of the strictly traditional limits set to it.

This accumulation of mobile wealth by the ruler (gold, agricultural products, livestock) was paralleled by his acquisition of a servile labor force, still presumably within the customary limits of his authority. The *Ta'rikh al-Fattach* tells us of the twenty-four servile castes of specialist workers which the Songhai ruler in some way had inherited from the days of the hegemony of Mali. If these castes can be regarded as a kind of domain of the office of Mansa Mali and thus of the Askia of Songhai, this is a vivid example of the institutionalized continuity between Mali and Songhai. These castes had specific obligations to perform for the ruler, such as the provision of a hundred spears and a hundred arrows yearly from each family among the groups of metal workers. The sailors and fishermen had to provide dried fish, canoes, and crews. Other castes provided bodyguards and palace servants. Still others cut grass for thatching and as fodder for the cavalry.

These castes seem to have been of great antiquity, but there is no indication that the disposal of the wealth they produced was limited by anything other than the ruler's inclination and exigencies of state. Some of them, in fact, were eventually disposed of by sale, though this seems to have been a breach of tradition. The demand for compulsory labor from freemen was also probably against ancient custom, though in late fifteenth-century Kano we find Muhammad Rumfa demanding labor of his free subjects.

To this fund of acquired wealth (gold, goods, and labor), we might, with qualifications, add land. The statement that the ruler was owner of the land is best regarded as a juridical fiction, probably stemming from his ancient ritual function of allocating land to fellow lineage members. Land, however, was allocated to officials for the support of their office and was also available to the ruler, and others, for the settlement of slave plantations. This later development was probably more common in Hausaland and Kanem-Bornu than farther west. In 1450, the ruler of Kano, at that time a tributary of Kanem-Bornu, sent out expeditions specifically for the acquisition of slaves and is said to have established twenty-one settlements, each one containing a thousand royal slaves. In Kanem-Bornu at the time of Mai Idris Alooma, slavery was becoming institutionalized in new and wider forms, side by side with, and probably due to the demands of, the growing weight of the administration.

The ruler thus established a secure basis in wealth to support his attempt to shake off the restraints on his authority and power set up by the traditional lineage systems. This wealth would also support him against his rivals within the elite. However, as other members of the royal lineage became administrators, they also could move toward the establishment of a non-traditional power base.

The traditional opponents to a ruler's enlarged power were usually to be found in such institutions as his council, whose membership would originally be representative and perhaps hereditary. Whoever controlled the investiture ceremony would also be expected to be a force for the preservation of customary, limited authority, with potent sanctions at his disposal. In sixteenth-century Hausaland we find examples of traditional councils in conscious counterpoise to the court officials, the former seemingly retaining some of their ancient representative quality. This process can perhaps be seen as part of a gradual transition from a "segmentary" to a "pyramidal" to a centralized political system. Yet the defense of law and custom and the attempt to limit the centralized power of the ruler can perhaps be seen behind many of the depositions of the rulers of Mali and Songhai. Oral traditions on the whole support this interpretation, but evidence is still inadequate.

There was here, as everywhere, a difference between the formal law or "constitution" and actual procedures. It is not clear whether the introduction of a codified law, as in Islamic states, made for more or less flexibility on the part of the government. In the medieval period the newness of Islam was generally accommodated to traditional practices and beliefs and seems to have produced a greater adaptability to change. This is part of what has been described as the "open predicament," where the availability of alternative modes of thought and behavior is held to produce the possibility of a leap beyond the traditional belief systems. Thus, breaches made in the traditional structure of law and beliefs may have made possible the extension of royal power in other areas.

In general, the ruler attempts to increase his power by such techniques as controlling the succession process, appointing his kinsmen to administer the provinces, and making ritual additions to the office of kingship. At a later stage, however, he begins to recruit to the administration personnel whose loyalty to him is personal and not due to traditional lineage ties. His wealth and control of the army enable him to secure this loyalty.

The new basis for recruitment to the elite is therefore central to this extension of authority: power and privilege being accorded to the king's men on the basis of achieved status rather than ascriptive right—that is, recognized merit (or expected loyalty) rather than hereditary position. From the evidence, it is quite likely that in early Ghana tribute was collected by servile officials who had their own administrative staffs for particular regions. Slave officials were common and often influential in administrations, such officials being unable, of course, to have an independent hereditary power base from which to contest the authority of their master. A servile royal bodyguard to strengthen the palace against traditional threats was a common feature of this period and area. Slaves, however, were known to successfully challenge their royal masters, as when the slave Sakura usurped power in Mali. Under Mai Idris Alooma in Kanem-Bornu this process was well advanced, and although the old customs were preserved, the ruler depended very much on officials whom he had appointed personally, such as the palace eunuchs, whose most important attribute was that they would not be in a position to build up a dynastic challenge to the ruler. Other candidates for office under a ruler protecting himself from the perpetual rivalry of members of the royal lineage would tend to be affinal and/or maternal relatives or loyal supporters from non-royal groups within the ruling class. The creation of new chieftaincies, or offices, is usually a sign that the ruler is centralizing power in his own hands by creating chiefs who will be unlikely to have natural bonds of loyalty with the older traditional chiefs. The extension of the administration by Sunni Ali and Askia Muhammad must surely be seen in this light. A point to note is that this tendency to promote officials from outside the traditional circles of recruitment produced, at the top, a considerable degree of two-way social mobility which may well have affected relations with non-ruling segments of the community.

In summary, then, the ruler built up a solid basis of wealth and force; his administration grew in order to cope with new conquests and peaceful expansion of control. The administration was maintained by this wealth and in turn created more wealth. At this level the state can be said to be centralized—central authority was exercised over outlying provinces, and public power intruded more and more into the life of the village, the family, and the individual. At a different level, the state became centralized when the ruler asserted his control over various hereditary officeholders, using his wealth and power to secure the services of officials who had no basis of power other than through him. By these means the centralized political authority of the rulers of the Western Sudan was maintained over a vast area for a thousand years.

11

West Africa and the Afro-Americans

PETER B. HAMMOND

THE BLACK ANCESTORS of many Americans began arriving in the New World from West Africa in the early 1500s, nearly five centuries ago, long before the migration of most Americans' European and Asian ancestors. The importation of these old-stock, black inhabitants to the New World profoundly affected the historical and cultural development of almost every American nation—from Chile to Colombia in South America, all of Central America, the islands of the Caribbean, and most of North America from Mexico to Canada.

During the more than four centuries that the slave trade was in operation, between four and five million West Africans were captured, sold into slavery, and brought forcibly to the New World. Today their descendants number close to one hundred million, not counting the several million Indian and white Americans whose partial African ancestry is no longer apparent from their appearance.

But despite the many nations and the enormous numbers of peoples involved, the consequences of the centuries-long, intensive, forced migration of West Africans to the New World are still poorly understood. This is partly because a number of misleading myths have been kept alive—such as the idea that black Americans had come from so many parts of Africa and were possessed of such differing cultures and languages that their traditions were necessarily lost in the confusion, or the idea that the blacks abandoned their own "inferior" customs once they had a chance to adopt the "obviously superior" culture of the whites—and partly because much about the African aspect of the black Americans' origins still remains to be learned.

From what is known so far, there appear to be three principal dimensions to the problem of accurately assessing the effects upon New World cultures and upon individual Americans of the centuries of intensive contact with West Africa. First, the part of West Africa from which the ancestors of most black

Americans were taken and sold into slavery needs to be identified. Second, the institution of Negro slavery and its relation to the plantation economy need to be examined. Finally, the post-emancipation phase of Afro-American cultural history requires attention.

To attempt such an assessment in a short essay, it is necessary to generalize about West Africa, about slavery and the plantation, and about the more recent historical past of the Afro-Americans. This is not so difficult. While the parts of West Africa from which slaves were taken vary in specifics of environment and culture, just as did the interrelated institutions of slavery and the plantation, and while there have been important local differences in the post-emancipation history of Negro Americans in various parts of the New World, a generally accurate overall picture can nevertheless be drawn.

WEST AFRICAN ORIGINS

Most Africans captured and sold into slavery in the New World were taken from an area along the west coast of the continent which stretches from what are now Senegal and Gambia in the north, south through Guinea, Liberia, Sierra Leone, Ivory Coast, Ghana, Togo, Dahomey, and Nigeria, and across the coastal region of Cameroon through the Congo and into Angola.

Slaves were subsequently brought to the Americas from other regions of Africa, after the first arrivals from the West African coast had established a pattern of life and an accommodation to slavery to which later Africans could adjust relatively easily. Most non–West African captives were taken from Portuguese Mozambique in East Africa. Smaller numbers came from Tanzania and Kenya, farther north on the East African coast. A negligible number were brought from Ethiopia and from the huge interior of the continent, and practically none from the countries of North Africa.

Although the peoples of West Africa from whom so many Americans are descended possess distinctive cultures and speak many languages—several hundred dialects in Nigeria alone—the cultural and linguistic differences which separate them are less significant for an understanding of Afro-American cultural history than are the underlying similarities which unite the peoples of this region.

Most of the coastal area of West Africa is heavily forested, temperature and humidity are high, and rainfall is heavy. From earliest times to the present the peoples of the forest region have made their living in one of two principal ways: as farmers working garden plots cut out of the thick rainforest and as fishermen in the coastal waters of the Atlantic or in the larger rivers. Inland and to the north where rainfall is lighter and vegetation is more sparse, farmers cultivate cereals, mostly millet and sorghum, during the few short months of summer when there is adequate rain. Herding is also an important activity in this drier zone. Most cattle, sheep, and goats are tended by pastoral nomadic groups, principally the Fulani.

Farmwork, the herdsmen's tasks, and fishing are all organized on the basis of strong family ties. Kinsmen may share ownership of the land, or of the animals they tend collectively. Family organization complemented by cooperative relationships between neighbors also provides the organizational basis for the distribution of almost all food, housing and household materials, clothing, and other consumption goods. Traditionally markets have functioned primarily as an adjustive mechanism for the reallocation of surpluses.

Kinship is equally important in the organization of traditional West African social life. The extended family—a man and his wife or wives, his dependent children, his married sons and their wives and children—often inhabit a single compound residence, usually located near the similarly organized households of other closely related family groups. Most kinsmen trace descent through the paternal line. However, a number of West African peoples, especially in the forest zone, are matrilineal, reckoning descent through the mother's line. But whatever the specific family organization, the authority of the male family head has always been strong in West Africa, both in the regulation of activities within the kin group and in the social life of the local community.

Because most West Africans live close to the level of subsistence, producing relatively small surpluses in excess of their basic material needs, and, more important perhaps, because of the strong traditional emphasis on sharing both within the kin group and with others in the local community, there has been little material basis or need for the private accumulation of wealth necessary for the development of social classes. Beyond the family, age-grade, and other ascriptive ties are the principal alternative bases of community organization. The development of systems of social stratification based on significant differences in the relative wealth of various groups within the population is largely to be explained as a consequence of the growing influence of a market-oriented economy which resulted from colonial and pre-colonial contact with Europe and the Americas. Otherwise the social differences which separate groups within the traditionally organized West African community are based principally on differences in ethnic, political, or ritual status, not on differences in economic power.

The political systems of most West African coastal peoples also appear to have developed out of systems of status and authority based on family organization. Among centralized societies, the right to hold political office as a village or provincial chief, or as king, is usually passed on from father to son within a descent group regarded as the founding family of the local population sector, village, province, or kingdom. In the many West African communities which lack any tradition of centralized authority, the relations outside the kin group are regulated and conflict is controlled by religious leaders or other ritual intermediaries with limited power.

Religion in West Africa is also significantly influenced by family organization. Ancestor worship, that is, the veneration of the protective spirits of deceased members of the kin group, is an important aspect of the belief systems of nearly all the peoples of the rainforest region. Living members of the family endeavor to maintain a benevolent relationship to their ancestral protectors by means of periodic sacrificial offerings and by conducting their affairs in accordance with the ancestors' rules.

Worship of the powerful beings believed to vitalize the natural environment is another characteristic aspect of West African religion. These deities are also propitiated with sacrificial offerings and through the observances of other rituals, especially taboos and prohibitions relating to land use, hunting, fishing, and the gathering of wild foods. Typically these various supernatural beings are propitiated within the context of elaborate rituals which utilize almost all aspects of traditional West African aesthetic forms—sculpture and painting, dance, costume, music, poetry, and mythology.

Other gods and a rich variety of major and minor spirits are also venerated, providing the West African believer with a diffuse field of sources of supernatural support. If one god fails him, there is almost always another to turn to. The result is a perception of the supernatural which mirrors, in a sense, the West African's perception of his society. So long as he lives by the rules and meets his diffuse obligations to his fellow men and to the varied sources of his supernatural support, he can be reasonably certain that they—one or another among them, at least—will meet their responsibilities to him. Worship of the supernatural often takes the form of dancing, to the accompaniment of rhythmic drumming, singing, and hand clapping, intended to induce possession by various spirits and deities.

While music and the dance are highly developed as aesthetic forms, most music is related to religion. Specifics of musical style vary considerably from region to region, but the similarities between the musical traditions of particular peoples are greater than the differences—the use of overlapping call and response patterns, the stress upon rhythm, percussive sounds, multiple meter, and off-beat phrasing are used throughout West Africa. Sculpture, wood carving, brass casting, and iron work are also widespread and popular aesthetic forms. Finally, myths, proverbs, and fables, most of them transmitted orally, often by professional poets and storytellers, serve as an important aesthetic mode for the expression of values, and often as a repository of historical traditions—lessons from the past which serve as useful guides for action in the present.

Although the many languages and dialects of West Africa are often mutually unintelligible, most of those within the forested coastal belt are structurally quite similar; they are as closely related, for example, as the Romance languages of Western Europe. Furthermore, most West Africans are bilingual and probably speak, in addition to their own language, one of the several widely understood trade languages, such as Hausa, Bambara, or Dioula.

BEGINNINGS OF THE SLAVE TRADE

Although slavery existed in West Africa before the Europeans appeared there, it was generally a more benign institution than that developed by the colonists in the Americas. In West Africa, there was no technological or economic basis for the profitable employment of a large slave labor force. Most farmers held the right only to the amount of land they needed and could work themselves. According to the rules of the economic and social systems which still prevail throughout most of West Africa, men are expected to redistribute among needy kinsmen any land they hold in excess of their own subsistence requirements.

Where slaves, usually captives taken in war, were held, their masters typically worked in the fields beside them. Often they lived as members of their owners' households, and frequently they married into, or were formally adopted by, the slaveowners' families. Only a few despotic rulers—often West African kings whose traditionally limited wealth and power had been greatly expanded by the profits they took as intermediaries in the European-sponsored slave trade— made use of slave labor on a scale and under conditions of oppressiveness comparable to those which prevailed in the Americas.

The Portuguese and Spanish explorers, forerunners among the European slave traders, had originally made contact with the coastal peoples of West Africa in order to establish provisioning stations for ships sailing south around the African continent en route to the rich trading centers of the East Indies and mainland Asia. Later, missionaries were sent out; diplomats followed. Several West African rulers reciprocated, sending their representatives to Lisbon, Madrid, and the Vatican Court in Rome.

During the late fifteenth and very early sixteenth centuries, slavery was a familiar institution in parts of the Mediterranean world. The Turks and the Moors held Europeans in bondage, and in Spain and Portugal both captive Arabs and smaller numbers of European and African slaves were held. However, it was only with the discovery of the Americas in the late 1400s that slavery became important as an economically profitable institution.

The fertile tropical and subtropical lands bordering the Caribbean and the islands of the West Indies were rich both in minerals and in agricultural potential. But workers were needed to exploit the new territories. The small, widely scattered Indian populations of the Caribbean region were inadequate to meet European needs. Lacking the centralized political systems which might have made conquest of the Indians possible by establishing domination over their leaders, the whites often had to kill most of the inhabitants of an area in order to control it. In any case there were not enough Indians to fill the labor needs resulting from the expanding European-controlled mining operations and the spreading plantation system.

And so West Africa took on new interest for Europeans who until the discovery of the New World had been interested in the region primarily as a stopping place for ships in the East Indies trade. Initially, efforts had been made to maintain friendly relations with the blacks in order to safeguard trade routes, to protect the provisioning stations, and—somewhat incidentally—to save souls. These motives gave way to an economically and politically more compelling interest: the need for laborers to work the rich new lands across the Atlantic. The missionaries' original purpose was reinterpreted to justify their converts' enslavement. The traffic in West African bodies was rationalized and justified both on the basis of providing the blacks with an opportunity to benefit from contact with the "superior" culture of the Europeans and, by conversion, to increase their chances for salvation.

By the seventeenth century the provisioning stations and missionary settlements along the West Coast of Africa had been transformed into slave-trading forts. The Europeans, as before, remained in these fortified settlements, most of which were located either on easily defensible coastal promontories or on offshore islands. From there the already well-organized network of trading relationships with nearby ethnic groups was expanded and transformed. From the exchange of guns, ammunition, rum, and other manufactured goods for food supplies and small quantities of gold and other minerals, the European traders turned to the exchange of weapons, spirits, and other goods for human captives.

The neighboring West African groups among whom slave raiding was encouraged often had long-standing traditions of mild hostility toward one another; or, more exactly, they shared no common interests and were often in conflict over territory at their frontiers. This indifference of ethnic groups to the welfare of neighboring peoples who shared no recognition of common cultural identity or interests facilitated the white traders' efforts to incite open hostilities. By promoting warfare the traders justified the capture of prisoners who were then sold to the European slavers and shipped off to the Americas.

Most of the West African states among which warfare was induced were small in both population and territory. Since slave-raiding forays were generally made against neighboring groups, most captives were taken quite near the coast, rarely from more than a few hundred miles inland. Consequently, although blacks taken from different parts of West Africa were distinct from one another in many aspects of appearance, custom, and language, they nonetheless shared essentially similar geographical and cultural origins.

The trade routes between Europe, West Africa, and the New World formed a triangle. From European ports manufactured goods were shipped south to the West African slave-trading forts. There other ships specially fitted out as slavers (designed to accommodate the maximum number of persons in the minimum space and with only the most primitive facilities for keeping the human cargo alive) set out for the Americas. Over the four centuries of active slave trade millions of West Africans died in passage from disease or injuries resulting from overcrowding and mistreatment. But the profits from slave trading were high enough to allow for such losses. Those who survived the trip were unloaded at slave markets initially established on the islands of the Caribbean.

Spain and Portugal were soon joined in the trade by British, French, Dutch, and Scandinavian slavers. Most of these European powers soon set about developing colonial empires on the American mainland as well, at first in the coastal region of northeastern South America from what later became Brazil through the Guianas, Venezuela, and Colombia, then into Central America from Panama and around the Gulf of Mexico and into the southern part of what was to be the United States.

The third side of the trade triangle was formed by ships sailing out from New World ports for the burgeoning markets and factories of Europe, carrying the goods produced by captured West African laborers—sugar, coffee, tobacco, cotton, gold, and silver.

It was from the island slave-trading centers of the Caribbean that the first blacks were dispersed to the mainland and inland throughout tropical and subtropical America—wherever minerals were available or conditions were right for the development of plantations. Later, especially in the eighteenth and nineteenth centuries, slave cargoes were taken directly to ports on the mainland.

With time, of course, the numbers of the original West African slave populations were augmented by natural increase, and thus new generations of Americans were born to slavery. It was into these already well-established slave populations of the Americas that later captives from West Africa were introduced. The cultural traditions which developed in these early black communities were strongly influenced by the customs of the first arrivals. Slaves from Dahomey predominated among the earliest black cargoes landed in Haiti, for example, and specifically Dahomean cultural usages persist even today among the Haitian peasantry. Where the Yoruba were settled early and in large numbers, as in Cuba and northeastern Brazil, Yoruba cultural usages were particularly strong. The smaller numbers of slaves coming later, from other parts of West Africa, directly or by way of the West Indies, found it easy to adjust their customs to the prevailing Afro-American culture patterns already established.

THE INSTITUTION OF SLAVERY
AND PLANTATION ECONOMY

Just as the specific West African cultural and geographical origins of the slave populations differed from one New World region to another, so did the institution of slavery itself. In colonial areas under Catholic control, for example, recognition of the slave as a man with a soul, and thus a human being with rights which his owner and the political system were formally required to respect, affected the legal definition of the slave's status, his conditions of work, the circumstances under which he might be emancipated, and his position in society once he was free. Over time there was a tendency in all parts of the New World to equate racial identity with social status; but in the Latin areas of the New World this association was never as immutable as in the territories under Anglo-Saxon control. In the Latin American regions there persisted as part of the legacy of slavery in Spain and Portugal the tradition that the status of slave was simply one of several possible positions a man might have—an admittedly disadvantageous position, but one which might be altered in several ways. A slave might work to purchase his freedom. He might petition his master or the government for his emancipation. Or he might be freed at his owner's death. That a slave might wish to be free was regarded as natural. Assisting him to obtain his freedom was defined as a religiously and ethically commendable act.

In contrast, in most of the New World territories under British, French, and American control, slavery was a new institution, specifically developed as a legal means of defining the economic, social, and political position of the captive black workers in such a way as to provide for the most profitable exploitation of their labor and to assure perpetuation of the institution of slavery itself. To provide for the continuity of the system, it was necessary to justify enslavement of the children of slaves and to assure the continued servitude of those few blacks who were able, despite the obstacles placed in their way, to acquire proficiency in the culture of the dominant whites. Enslavement of the West Africans had originally been justified on the basis of their cultural "inferiority" and "heathenism." To perpetuate the system it was necessary to make the fact of being black, or of African descent, reason enough for enslavement. This rationale gained needed support from development of the useful concept of the blacks' innate, racially determined inferiority. At worst the blacks were animals; at best, children. Enslavement of people who were by nature presumed to be unfit for freedom was clearly and conveniently justified. The fact of being black and the fact of being a slave were thus almost irrevocably linked.

Most of the earliest plantations were established in the lowland areas immediately inland from the coast of the Caribbean, the Gulf of Mexico, and the South Atlantic where it touches the southern United States. The most profitable plantation operations involved the large-scale, intensive cultivation of cash crops of coffee, sugar, and cotton, using large gangs of slave workers. As in West Africa, most field work on the plantations was done with the hand-held hoe. There was little irrigation, and fertilizers and draft animals were not usually employed. In many ways the technology to which the slaves were forced to adjust was similar to that they had known in West Africa.

In striking contrast to the familiarity of the technology and the tasks the slaves were required to perform on the plantations was the radical transformation of the black workers' economic and social position. This was especially true for male slaves. In West Africa, they and their kinsmen owned the farmland they worked, the tools they used, and the goods they produced. And, of course, they owned themselves and the right to their own labor. They were in control of their family-based work organization, and together with the other local family heads they also controlled the community-wide economic system. All this was totally changed under slavery. Black laborers did not own the land they worked, the tools they used, the goods they produced, or even themselves. They were property — part of their master's capital goods — to be utilized in production or sold on the market in accordance with the slaveowner's economic interest.

The economic powerlessness of the slaves affected nearly every other aspect of their lives and strongly influenced the distinctive patterns of the Afro-American subculture which was emerging throughout the New World. Such powerlessness limited the black man's ability to control his own destiny and that of his family and community. In West Africa an important aspect of a man's authority has been and still is today derived from his control over the allocation of almost all goods — land, tools, and what is produced by them — which his dependents required to meet their material needs. As a chattel in the New World, the black man found that his economic powerlessness made this tradition difficult to maintain, and the black father's authority was seriously undermined, both within his family and within the slave community. In dealing with white-dominated society his powerlessness was even more complete and was further reinforced by a variety of laws limiting his right to hold property, to engage in certain occupations, or to sell his own labor.

In the Americas under slavery, the strong, male-oriented family of West Africa could rarely exist. The slave family in the New World was generally centered around the mother. The role of the black father was often little more than biological, especially in areas such as Maryland and Virginia, where slaves were bred for sale farther south. The existence of strong family ties within the black community was a threat to the slaveowner's most profitable use of property and to the perpetuation of the slave system itself. Where strong family ties persisted in the slave community they were a testament to the black captives' resistance to relentless external pressure for their dissolution.

In West Africa the male-dominated household was typically an integral part of a closely organized system of extended kinship relations, complemented by associational ties of various sorts, such as bond-friend relationships, joking alliances, secret societies, and voluntary associations. But in the Americas the matrifocal slave family often became the only stable social unit within the otherwise purposefully nucleated and inevitably unstable slave society.

However, New World slave society was not entirely without internal structure. The superior social and economic position of house servants and slaves who worked as artisans was accompanied by differences in behavior, speech, manners, consumption patterns, and other aspects of life style. House servants had both a better opportunity to model their behavior upon that of their masters and greater material means for emulating aspects of their owners' living habits.

Despite the various restrictions usually placed on the status of free Negroes—on their right to hold property, to exercise the franchise, to live in particular areas, even to dress in particular ways—all of which were enforced with the intent of inhibiting their social mobility and preventing them from competing with whites, these "free people of color" usually occupied a somewhat more elevated social position than did the blacks, field hands and house servants alike, who were still enslaved. A few ex-slaves themselves owned slaves. With time, further differences in social class developed within the free black population based on differences in economic status and frequently also on degree of "white admixture." These distinctions were for the most part a reflection of the social class divisions of the dominant white society.

Under slavery, changes in traditional West African patterns of political activity were as drastic as those which marked the alteration of economic and social relationships. Slaves were almost universally excluded from authority positions, except within the servant hierarchy. They could neither vote nor hold office. While they were subject to punishment under the law, they were permitted no part in lawmaking or in its enforcement. Even their access to the courts was limited largely to litigation involving other blacks, and most such conflicts were settled outside the formal judicial system. Most of these same limitations on participation in the political system were extended to free blacks as well.

THE DEVELOPING BLACK-AMERICAN SUBCULTURE

The sphere of cultural expression least affected by slavery was religion. Religion is a profoundly important aspect of all West African cultures. To the extent that religion provided a means of channeling black frustration and hostility in a manner not threatening to the dominant social order, the blacks' observance of many aspects of their traditional African religious practices was often actually encouraged. The degree of retention of West African religious observances was largely a function of the cultural isolation of the various New World black groups. Among the Bush Negroes of Dutch and French Guiana, for example, many aspects of West African religion were retained in almost pure form; these included the West African names of the deities, specific beliefs concerning their powers, and the observances involved in their worship. Elsewhere, among other Afro-American groups in closer contact with European culture, as in Haiti and Brazil, aspects of African religious belief and practice were more often syncretized with elements of Roman Catholicism. Thus, St. Patrick, alleged to have driven the snakes out of Ireland, was identified with the Dahomean snake deity, "Dambala Wedo," by voodoo practitioners in Haiti; and in Brazil, "Yemenjá," the Yoruba goddess of the waters and of purity, was fused with the Catholic image of the Virgin Mary.

In those parts of the Americas where the black population was less culturally isolated and as a consequence became more highly acculturated, elements of West African religious practice were often reinterpreted. This can be seen in the United States, among fundamentalist sects in the rural South and in the store-front churches of the northern ghettos, in the use of repetitive, rhythmic body movements made to a syncopated musical accompaniment, intended to induce possession, no longer by an African deity or a being from the voodoo pantheon, but by the Holy Ghost himself.

The greater tolerance by white society of traditional black religious observances—because this was the one aspect of the blacks' cultural tradition which did not interfere with their status as slaves and because of the tenaciousness of this part of their heritage—provided also for development of one channel for status achievement and authority within the black community—the role of religious leader. Access to positions of religious leadership was facilitated by the importance given to criteria such as strength of personality and evidence of contact with supernatural power, as opposed to formal education and wealth. Thus during the centuries of New World slavery, almost the only leaders in the black communities of the Americas were religious leaders, and almost the only organizations permitted the blacks were religious organizations.

Partly as a result of the close relation between art and religion, many of the West African forms of aesthetic expression brought to the Americas by the enslaved blacks were retained. Music and dance, as well as a variety of plastic and graphic art forms, are an integral aspect of most indigenous forms of worship in West Africa. Vocal and instrumental music, dancing, and the symbolic representation of supernatural beings in the form of sculptured figures and masks have been for centuries essential aspects of observances in West Africa in which worshipers attempt to achieve some control over the supernatural powers which they believe affect their destinies.

As with religious beliefs and practices, the degree to which traditional West African aesthetic forms have been retained in the New World, syncretized with aspects of European or Indian art, or reinterpreted has been largely determined by the relative cultural isolation of particular black populations. For example, in parts of the forest regions of the Guianas, where escaped slaves from the Dutch- and French-owned plantations fled into the interior and reestablished an essentially West African pattern of life, West African oral literary traditions were retained in almost pure form. Characteristic West African tales such as the one concerning the Spider Trickster, "Anansi," continue to be told with most elements of their original narrative style and plot intact.

Elsewhere, where contact between the captive blacks, their descendants, and the whites has been more intensive, the proverbs, folktales, and riddles which are the most characteristic forms of West African oral literature have been more extensively reinterpreted or syncretized. "Anansi" has become "Miss Nancy" among blacks in Jamaica, for example. In the American South another stock West African character, the Hare, has become Br'er Rabbit.

Although most of the languages brought to the Americas by the West Africans were related in their essential linguistic elements—underlying morphology, grammar, and syntax—they were usually sufficiently dissimilar on the level of vocabulary to be mutually unintelligible. Consequently, in nearly all areas of the New World new languages developed as a means of communication among the captive blacks themselves, with whites, and with the Indians. Out of the merging of the distinctive linguistic traditions of these three groups—West Africans, Europeans, and American Indians—creole languages developed which took different forms in the different areas where slave populations were settled. In Haiti, for example, and in other of the Caribbean islands intermittently under French and Spanish control, a creole language developed in which essentially West African speech patterns were overlaid with a vocabulary derived from French, Spanish, and several West African sources. Elsewhere, the principal European linguistic element added to the mixture was Dutch. In the islands of the West Indies which ultimately passed from Spanish to Dutch control, a distinctive creole, called Papiemiento, developed, which incorporated aspects of Carib Indian speech as well; and in the more remote areas of Dutch and French Guiana, a derivative language called Taki-Taki was spoken. In the Sea Islands off the coast of South Carolina and Georgia a language called Gullah emerged; this is still spoken by much of the coastal black population of the southeastern United States and has influenced the speech of blacks and whites throughout all of the South and much of the North.

The factors of greatest significance in explaining the persistence or disappearance of the distinctive subculture which developed under slavery among most Afro-Americans, therefore, have been the relative geographical and cultural isolation of particular New World black groups and the relative technological and economic stagnation of the areas in which they are found. The relationship between the degree of technological and economic stagnation and relative pace of culture change is particularly striking. Where the single-crop-oriented plantation system established under slavery has persisted, as in most of Haiti, in northeastern Brazil, in the Guianas, in coastal Venezuela and Colombia, and in parts of the American South, the rate of change in other aspects of culture has also been slow. Consequently, elements of West African culture and of the distinctive subculture developed by Afro-Americans have been most persistent in these areas. Centuries-old patterns of life have continued because there was little reason or opportunity to change them.

SOCIOECONOMIC AND CULTURAL FORMS
IN THE POST-EMANCIPATION PERIOD

In the more isolated regions of the Americas, the economic arrangements developed under slavery have also persisted. Even today most of the land is still in the hands of the dominant white minority, who also own most of the tools used in the processing, transport, and marketing of whatever is produced. Most black workers in such areas still live on the periphery of the market economy, producing most of their food in small gardens and sharply limited by their meager income from participating—except as credit purchasers or petty entrepreneurs—in the money-oriented, white-controlled market. Many, working as sharecroppers, tenant farmers, or migrant workers, are so chronically in debt to the landowners and the stores which advance them food and clothing against future wages or the value of their share in the harvest that their money income is spent before they receive it.

The chronic precariousness of their economic position is exacerbated by the absence of available alternative forms of production or means of marketing either their goods or their labor. Where a single-crop economy is still in operation, as it is in much of the Caribbean and circum-Caribbean area, the farmers must sell their cash crops at world-market prices which they cannot control; and in most instances they lack both the skills and the capital necessary to develop other means of making a living. If they are in debt they frequently cannot leave the land to seek work elsewhere; if they have paid their debts often there is no money left for such travel. Where technological innovations are occurring, where mechanized farming is being introduced or crop lands are being converted to livestock range, unskilled labor is no longer needed. Thus, the blacks frequently lose even their marginal position in the economy and are pushed out entirely into idleness and onto welfare, or are forced to emigrate.

The consequences of the technological and economic impasse which is so often a paramount characteristic of the black American subculture are reflected in nearly every aspect of their way of life—in social organization, in relationship to the political system, in religion, in forms of aesthetic expression, and even in language.

A prominent social consequence of the stagnant technologies and economies of many areas in which Afro-Americans are found, and/or of their exclusion from new forms of technological and economic activity, has been the persistence of the matrifocal family and the characteristically unstable role of the male as a source of economic, social, and emotional support within the family. Another consequence is the fact that most blacks throughout the Americas continue to belong to the lowest social class—if they are not, in fact, relegated to a separate, pariah-like caste.

In turn, economic instability and insecurity and inferior social status are manifested in the peripheral and precarious relation of the black to the political system. In a few areas the tradition, developed under slavery, of excluding Afro-Americans entirely from participation in government still persists. Blacks are discouraged, intimidated, or actually refused the right to vote, to seek political office, to testify in the courts against whites, and to enjoy equal protection of their property and civil rights. In most instances, Afro-American participation in government is "lopsided," limited largely to punitive experience with the police, the courts, and the prison system; they continue to be excluded from the positions of power which would give them a greater part in making the political decisions which affect them.

An important aspect of black American subculture is religion, in which the retention, syncretism, and reinterpretation of Africanisms is particularly high. As with economic and political deprivation, this phenomenon is explained by the continued, and general, cultural and social isolation of black Americans. Today, as they have for almost five centuries, black religious leaders and their black churches continue to serve as a principal source of cohesion and group action within Afro-American communities. Only within the last decade have secular leaders begun to emerge widely within black communities; the resistance they encounter from whites is related to a centuries-old tradition designed to preserve white domination and black subordination. Aesthetic forms distinctive to Afro-American subculture still relate to religious behavior and, as with secular forms, persist most strongly among black Americans who are most isolated culturally.

The languages distinctive to black communities in the New World also tend to be perpetuated in those regions where black cultural isolation is greatest and where the technology and economy have been slowest to change. Creole is still the language of the majority in Haiti, and related creole languages are predominant on most other islands of the Caribbean. The majority of the bush blacks of Dutch and French Guiana continue to speak Taki-Taki. On the Sea Islands off Georgia and South Carolina and along the coast of the southeastern United States Gullah still prevails among many blacks, and "de-Gullahfied" dialects of English are spoken by the majority of blacks and by many whites throughout the rest of the South.

AFRO-AMERICAN CULTURE CONTACTS

Thus far, contact between West Africa and Afro-Americans has been one way. From time to time small numbers of blacks have "returned" to Africa—ex-slaves were sent back to Liberia from America in the nineteenth century, and some Afro-Brazilian families have maintained intermittent contact with their kinsmen among the Yoruba of Nigeria for centuries. But most Americans, black and white, have had neither occasion nor opportunity to visit West Africa or to acquire an objective understanding of its culture. For a long time black scholars and intellectuals, especially in the United States, shared the whites' negative bias toward African culture and frequently denied its relevance as an aspect of their cultural past. As for the unpleasant subject of slavery, it was apologized for, piously condemned, or ignored—rarely, until quite recently, has it been analyzed objectively.

In the last decade attention given to the newly won independence of many of the former West African colonies has precipitated a growing awareness among Americans of the richness of West African culture and of the vitality and value of many of the cultural traditions distinctive to the black American community. The result has been a degree of reconciliation, especially among black intellectuals, with the West African aspect of American racial and ethnic identity, as well as a growing appreciation of the full dimensions of nearly five centuries of Afro-American culture contact.

In this reconsideration of the Americas' cultural ties to West Africa, the interesting but occasionally somewhat esoteric search for "Africanisms"— retentions in forms of religion, dance, and music, fascinating though they may be—is beginning to give way to an appreciation of the need for scholarly attention to equally or more important questions, such as the effect of slavery upon the quality and content of American life and culture and upon the development of the Americas' most critical internal problems, racism and poverty.

The ancestors of present-day Afro-Americans contributed more to the New World than jazz, spirituals, chicken gumbo, and Br'er Rabbit. For four centuries they contributed without pay their labor, and often their lives, to the economic development of nearly every American nation—not only to development of the plantation economies of the tropics and subtropics and to the shipping fortunes of New England, but to the accumulation of capital derived from the profits of slave labor that significantly helped finance the industrialization of much of Western Europe and all of North America.

Today the most compelling issue related to the study of Afro-American culture contacts does not concern the academically interesting identification and analysis of Africanisms in New World culture, but rather the attainment of a proper understanding of the historical and cultural causes of a centuries-old black-white conflict, a conflict first violently manifested in slave revolts, later in race riots, and now in near revolution.

12

Race and Resistance
in South Africa

J. CONGRESS MBATA

THE AFRIKANER NATIONALISTS in South Africa have often asserted that theirs is the "South African way of life." If one views the tangled web of black-white relations over a span of centuries, then one must concede that this assertion is not without a measure of accuracy, for the threads of racism and suppression have remained remarkably continuous in South Africa. The terms *apartheid* and *separate development* may belong to the post-World War II glossary, but the ideas they connote are much older. They were not born in 1910 with the founding of the Union of South Africa, nor did the concepts originate in 1948 with the ascendancy to power of the Afrikaner nationalists. The ideas are as old as the first black-white confrontation in the Cape Colony.

EARLY SETTLEMENT

On April 6, 1652, three ships of the Dutch East India Company anchored at Table Bay in Capetown. The following day, Jan van Riebeeck, the commander of the expedition, set foot on South African soil to establish a provisioning station for Dutch ships plying between Holland and the East. They were welcomed ashore by a party of about fifty Hottentots,[1] of whom it is reported that their chief, Autshumao, "had spent some time on board an English ship, in which he had visited Bantam, and had acquired a smattering of the language of those among whom he had lived."[2]

1. "The Hottentots termed themselves Khoikhoi, men of men" (George M. Theal, *History and Ethnography of Africa South of the Zambesi* [London: S. Sonnenschein, 1910], I, 36).
2. George M. Theal, *History of South Africa before 1795* (Capetown: C. Struik, 1964), II, 42.

210

The Hottentots, who occupied most of the Cape area, were cattle-breeders and thus proved a useful source of supply to the provisioning station that was being established. The main interest of the Dutch East India Company was trade, and instructions were therefore issued to van Riebeeck to maintain friendly relations with the Hottentots. According to entries he made in a journal kept from 1651 to 1662, however, van Riebeeck would have liked to seize the cattle belonging to the Hottentots and to capture the owners and sell them as slaves. He wrote:

> If their cattle cannot be obtained in a friendly way, why then suffer their thefts without making reprisals which would only be required once, for with 150 men, 10,000 to 12,000 cattle could be secured, and without danger, as many of these savages could be caught without a blow for transmission as slaves to India, as they always come to us unarmed.[3]

The company vetoed the suggestion, and van Riebeeck continued to maintain relations with the Hottentots. He did not, however, abandon the idea of overwhelming them and depriving them of their cattle and land — a dream which was shared by others.

Within six weeks of his arrival in South Africa in 1652, Jan van Riebeeck made a request to the company for slaves.[4] The handful of people who had come with him were not able to cope with the amount of work involved. The company replied that it could not spare any slaves.

In 1657 nine men of Dutch and German origin, together with their wives, were released from the service of the company, to minimize the expenses of the station and so that they might eventually become suppliers of meat, grain, and wine for the station. The nine men set free by the company became known as free burghers and were settled in what was called the Liesbeeck Valley on small farms, which were tax-free for twelve years. Problems of labor soon arose. The free burghers could not handle the job by themselves, but white labor would be too expensive, and the Hottentots, who regarded the settlers as intruders, could not be easily reduced to a servile state. The process of undermining their social organization and forcing them to a level at which they would be completely at the disposal of the whites was not yet under way.

Van Riebeeck, as a means of solving the labor difficulties of the farmers, in 1657 once again appealed to the company for slaves, and the first group of them arrived from Java and Madagascar in that same year.

Evidence of ill-treatment of slaves began to accumulate almost from the beginning. Van Riebeeck issued a statement that, despite warnings, the farmers were continuing to treat their slaves in a cruel and tyrannical manner, resulting

3. Alex Hepple, *South Africa: A Political and Economic History* (London: Pall Mall Press, 1966), p. 42.
4. Victor de Kock, *Those in Bondage* (Capetown: Howard Timmins, 1950), p. 16.

in many escapes which caused trouble for the company. The farmers were in-structed to bring offenders before the public prosecutor, who would deal with them under the Laws of the Indies.[5] In spite of this, the inhumane practices associated with slavery in the New World became prevalent in the Cape. Slaves were chained and whipped, and punishments such as cutting off an ear were administered for even petty offenses. Conditions in the Cape were perhaps less severe than those in the West Indies, but, as W. M. Macmillan has pointed out, "that it was no worse, does not make it better."[6]

In 1658 a fruitless attempt was made to establish a school. In 1663 another attempt was made, and an integrated school was opened with seventeen pupils—twelve were white, four were slaves, and one was Hottentot. In this early period, the emphasis on the "cultural incapacity" of nonwhite people was not strong. The fundamental division was between Christian and non-Christian, and con-version and baptism were the means by which a non-white might enter the Chris-tian community and achieve equality. The shortest route to this goal was via the school, and it was not long before the slaves, particularly the women, discovered this. Goske, who was governor between 1672 and 1676, accelerated the process by decreeing that all slave children should attend school. With the growth of the settlement, the number of slaves increased. They were imported from Angola and Guinea on the West African coast, as well as from Mozambique, Madagas-car, and Southeast Asia. Many of those who came from West Africa escaped, and slave imports from that region were discouraged. A number of slaves, however, managed to gain their freedom through education and conversion. Others were able to buy their own freedom, and some were freed by their owners in ap-preciation of faithful service.

Another factor affecting the status of slaves was the shortage of white women in the settlement. The Hottentots (who at this stage were still economically and politically a free people) kept their women beyond the range of the Europeans. Thus, of the five marriages solemnized in the first four years of the settlement, only one was between black and white. In 1657, when the first group of slaves arrived from Java and Madagascar, eight females were among them. These eight were to become the ancestors of the Cape Coloureds. A slave woman had only to profess Christianity and be baptized to become free and eligible for marriage with a white man. Frequently, therefore, emancipated slave women either mar-ried or cohabited with white men. The school played a significant role here. The records of the eighteenth century show many mixed marriages and many bap-tisms of children of such marriages. Girls of mixed parentage also married white men, "and the husbands they obtained were sometimes men in established posi-

---

5. M. Whiting Spilhaus, *The First South Africans and the Laws Which Governed Them* (Capetown and Johannesburg: Juta, 1949), p. 126.
6. *The Cape Colour Question: A Historical Survey* (London: Faber & Gwyer, 1927), p. 75.

tions in the community or men who later attained eminence."[7] The white men were also attracted to these girls because of their ability to run homes without the aid of servants.

Mixed marriages, however, tended to undermine the economic foundations upon which the Cape society was being established. It was important not only that the non-white people be inferior but also that their status remain perpetually depressed. They had to be kept in a position in which they could be readily manipulated for economic reasons, and the problem that presented itself to the settlers was how to circumvent "the assimilative effects of conversion to Christianity." In an effort to counter Goske's decree demanding compulsory school attendance by all slave children, a separate non-white school was established in 1678. It was contended that integrated schooling as well as the tendency of whites to associate publicly with slave women were factors "destructive of that respect for the European which should be the best safeguard of order in general."[8]

In 1682 Visiting Commissioner Ryklof van Goens abolished the practice of freeing unconverted slaves unless a strong case of good conduct could be made out. He also made the position reversible by decreeing that the free but unconverted, if deemed idle and dissolute, might lose their freedom. This was an early manifestation of a tendency that has persisted in South African legislative and administrative practice, namely, the establishment of machinery to enable an administrator to alter the status of nonwhite persons. Another tendency which became evident at this time was the practice of converting rights enjoyed by non-white people into privileges, thus vesting the administration with the power to withdraw these at will. Van Goens decreed that the right of baptized slaves to be freed should cease and that freedom under such circumstances would be conferred as a favor.

From the earliest days, those who have sought to consolidate white power in South Africa have not hesitated to use the people's inclination toward religion as a weapon against them. In spite of the fact that Christian principles are incompatible with racist doctrines, the established churches in South Africa have shown an alarming degree of accommodation. In particular, the Afrikaans churches have assumed a vanguard role in the religious reaction to a progressive policy of race equality. They established themselves quite early as champions and leaders of the "white purpose" in South Africa and have consistently tried to supply philosophical justification in terms of biblical doctrines for the denial of equality to the black man. It is not surprising therefore that in 1792 the church council in Capetown decided that there was no scriptural incompatibility

7. "The Origin and Incidence of Miscegenation at the Cape during the Dutch East India Company's Regime, 1652–1795," *Race Relations Journal*, XX, No. 2 (1953), 25.
8. Spilhaus, *The First South Africans*, p. 130.

in keeping baptized persons in a state of continued slavery. Thus the church re-assured the slave-owning farmers in their anxiety over the drainage of slave labor. Yet the same church and the secular authorities, realizing the problems created by the disproportionate number of white men to white women, wel-comed and encouraged mixed marriages, "recognizing them as desirable, if not essential, to the welfare of the settlement."[9]

SUBJUGATION AND SERVITUDE

"The welfare of the settlement" is the theme that runs consistently through all black-white politics in South Africa. The settlement is white, and its "welfare" rests upon an assumption that consigns the black man to a position in which he is no more than a factor of production. To achieve this, a process of subjugation and of dispossession was begun in the early days of the Cape settlement. Eric Walker, the South African historian, writes that "all the economic and social problems which exercise South Africa today had begun to take place before van Riebeeck's eyes."[10] In 1657, Visiting Commissioner Ryklof van Goens, recog-nizing the tension that was developing between the settlement and the Hotten-tots, proposed South Africa's first partition scheme. His suggestion was that a canal be built to separate the white-occupied peninsula (the Cape) from the rest of Africa. A report dealing with this period states that "the colony was growing and the clansmen dwelt long upon our taking every day . . . more of the land which had belonged to them from all ages."[11] Van Riebeeck, perhaps contem-plating the prospect of seizing land and cattle and enslaving the Hottentots, objected. His objections prevailed with the company, which then disallowed the canal scheme. A much modified version of the idea has found official support today. This "homelands" program is suitably manipulated so that the area re-served for African use constitutes only 12 per cent of the land comprising South Africa.

Hottentot tribal organization involved recognition of rights to land, and they were not willing to give up this land nor would they give up their independ-ence and supply labor to the farmers. They felt that their rights were being violated, and they became increasingly restless over what they considered an injustice. War broke out in 1658 when Jan van Riebeeck arrested one of their leaders, Herry die Strandloper, and kept some of his men as hostages to be exchanged for runaway slaves and for the people who killed the company's herdsman in 1653. The struggle was indecisive, and in 1660 it was agreed to hold peace talks. The Hottentots, in no uncertain terms, accused van Riebeeck and the

9. "The Origin and Incidence of Miscegenation," p. 26.
10. *A History of Southern Africa*, 3rd ed. (London: Longmans, Green, 1962), p. 42.
11. H. B. Thom, *Journal of van Riebeeck, Vol. III: 1659–1662* (Capetown: A. A. Balkema, 1958), p. 195; Walker, *History of Southern Africa*, p. 40.

settlers of waging war on them with the sole purpose of depriving them of their land. Van Riebeeck made no effort to refute the allegation but instead rather arrogantly proclaimed that the Hottentots "had now lost the land in war and therefore could only expect to be henceforth entirely deprived of it." He stated: "Their country had thus fallen to our lot, being justly won in defensive warfare and . . . it was our intention to retain it."[12]

The first step in the process of systematic subjugation and dispossession of the aborigines had begun. By van Riebeeck's admission the land belonged to the Hottentots. It was they, therefore, and not the Dutch who were fighting a defensive war. It is clear that the land and cattle of the Hottentots aroused the greed of the white settlers. It was this greed, coupled with the urge to make the "Kaffir," that is, the black man, "furnish as large and as cheap a supply of labour as possible,"[13] which was to structure future Dutch relations with the Africans and set the pattern for black-white politics in South Africa.

In 1662, Jan van Riebeeck left the Cape for an appointment in the East. He left behind him the free burghers of Dutch and German origin who formed the nucleus of what was to become white South Africa. But, faced with the intractable Hottentots and frustrated by the company's orders that friendly relations be maintained with them, these early settlers continued to suffer the tensions caused by inadequate labor supplies. The economy of the settlement was showing signs of strain, and the directors in Holland began to ask questions in an effort to find the reasons for the decline. In 1717 the captain of the garrison at the Cape, Dominique de Chavonnes, made proposals which would have eliminated slavery and at the same time increased the white population. His plea was for free, rather than slave, labor. He contended that slavery was uneconomical, as it only encouraged the plantation system at the expense of intensive cultivation of the soil. His proposals were voted down by the company, which stated that white labor was lazy, incompetent, uncontrollable, given to drunkenness, and expensive. The importation of slaves was stepped up, and their numbers remained higher than the population of the settlers until abolition of the slave trade in 1807.

The situation of slavery established a class structure based on color in which the lower socioeconomic groups were nonwhite and those at the top of the pyramid were white. The eventual abolition of slavery did not affect either this socioeconomic structure or the attitudes that were associated with it. Indeed, as late as 1948 the South African Social and Economic Planning Council stated that there was a "basic caste structure of South African society, which must be accepted as a datum for any realistic short term racial policy in the Union."[14]

---

12. Thom, *Journal of van Riebeeck*, p. 196.

13. Sir George Grey, quoted in E. D. Morel, *The Black Man's Burden* (New York: B. W. Huebach, 1920), p. 30.

14. Social and Economic Planning Council, *The Economic and Social Conditions of the Racial Groups in South Africa*, Report No. 13 (Pretoria: Government Printers, 1948).

Basic to this structure has been the idea of white supremacy; as long as white supremacy was maintained through white socioeconomic dominance, whites could allow slavery in a technical sense to be abolished. The whites, by birth, remained a community "to be served rather than to serve."[15] They did not work with their hands, since this was considered degrading and was therefore something to be done by "Kaffirs." The black people might not be called slaves, but they nonetheless remained an exploitable commodity. The relation of master and servant was fixed in South African society from an early date.

Britain had occupied the Cape from 1795 until 1803. When the Cape was taken over by Britain for the second time in 1806, abolitionist pressure began to be felt. With abolition of the slave trade in 1807 slaves became an irreplacable commodity, and the settlers turned their gaze more steadily upon what they considered to be the natural and proper successors to the slaves. Eric Walker has stated that "the slave and the Hottentot problems were intimately connected, for the Hottentots were the alternative labour supply to the slaves."[16]

The device used to tap this alternative source was to introduce control measures for the Hottentots. Until this time they had technically remained outside the jurisdiction of white administration. But in 1809 a proclamation was issued abolishing their tribal system and placing them under colonial rule. The missionaries who had established mission reserves for the Hottentots were accused by officials and settlers of draining off labor at a time when the labor supply was threatened by the stopping of the slave trade. In November, 1809, Governor Lord Caledon issued a proclamation which marked the beginning of the pass system which has plagued the black man in South Africa to this day. The intention behind the proclamation is reflected in the pious exhortation that accompanied it:

> They [the Hottentots] should find encouragement for preferring entering the service of the Inhabitants to leading an indolent life, by which they are rendered useless both for themselves and the community at large.[17]

What was meant by "leading an indolent life" became clear in a proposal made in 1834 to amend the Vagrancy Law. The proposal stated that

> the searching for and the digging for roots, or fruits, the natural produce of the earth, or wild honey, or the searching for, taking and killing any game, or any other wild animal of what kind soever, on any ground not being the property of the person so doing, not previously having obtained permission, shall not be

---

15. Baron van Imhof, quoted in Jan H. Hofmeyr, *South Africa* (London: Ernest Benn, 1932), p. 34.
16. *History of Southern Africa*, p. 169.
17. G. W. Eybers, *Select Constitutional Documents Illustrating South African History, 1795–1910* (New York: E. P. Dutton, 1918), p. 17.

deemed to be lawful employment by which any person can honestly earn the means of subsistence.[18]

This proposal was passed but was never signed by the governor. Nonetheless, it illustrates how the Hottentots, having been dispossessed of their land, were to be forbidden their traditional methods of food gathering on land "not being the property of the person so doing." In this way they could be coerced into supplying the labor formerly provided by the slaves. The purchase of land by Hottentots was out of the question. The threat of arrest under the pass laws completely immobilized them, restricting them to specific areas where they could be readily tapped to meet demands for labor. In 1812 Governor Cradock had decreed that Hottentot children born while their parents were in the service of a farmer could be apprenticed until they reached the age of eighteen. In 1819 Governor Somerset empowered the magistrates (*landrosts*) to register orphaned Hottentot children as apprentices, thus reducing them "to the level of serfs at the disposal of the local officials."[19] With increasing economic and political subjugation, Hottentot social organization began to disintegrate. More children of Hottentot-white parentage were born, and over time the Hottentot people tended to merge with the growing population of Cape Coloureds.

In 1894 the Glen Grey Act was passed. The Africans rightly saw it as a measure prejudicing their rights and property. By the terms of the act they were required not only to surrender their rights to their land but also to pay a labor tax.

In 1906 the administration of the colony of Natal imposed a poll tax on the African people. The measure was being adopted in all the colonies of South Africa as a means of inducing the Africans to leave their homes and to work for white employers, particularly in the mines. The Zulus refused to pay the tax. Martial law was declared. Several incidents took place in which whites were killed. Government troops were ordered in, and Bambata, the leader, and 500 of his men were killed. The Zulu rebellion was thus put down, but the resistance of the Zulus to the encroachment of that insidious "qualified slavery" of which the Cape Africans had spoken a few years before did mark the African's reaction to domination by white power.

There have been interludes, albeit of short duration, in which the otherwise continuous suppression of blacks was relieved. In 1828 the Cape administration passed Ordinance No. 50, the effect of which was to grant legal and civil rights to "Hottentots and other free persons of colour." The ordinance lifted restrictions which had been operative against these people and allowed them freedom of movement, including the right to be unemployed provided they could prove by due process, if so required, that they were not vagrants. But such acts have

18. Quoted in Macmillan, *The Cape Colour Question*, p. 235.
19. Walker, *History of Southern Africa*, p. 149.

been only sporadic in a policy whose continuity has remained essentially unbroken. (Today there exists Government Notice No. 851, of June, 1967, requiring all persons in the so-called Bantu homelands to register as work-seekers, in spite of the much-vaunted freedom promised the African in the "homelands.")

In 1807 the British had abolished the slave trade to South Africa, and in 1833 the British Emancipation Act was passed requiring that all persons still held as slaves be granted their freedom. The act fixed the allocations to be made to the various colonies as compensation for the loss of slave labor. The Cape farmers received only £1.25 million as against the £3 million they had estimated. This was afterward quoted as one of the causes of the Great Trek of 1836 in which at least one fourth of the Cape Colony's Afrikaner population migrated north, taking their slaves with them, in reaction against British policy in the Cape. The liberalizing policy of the metropolitan government threatened, they felt, the "natural" balance of superordination and subordination. Piet Retief, one of the leaders of the Great Trek, prepared a manifesto which set out the reasons for the trek. One of these was what he termed "the turbulent and dishonest conduct of [Hottentot] vagrants"; another was the "vexatious laws" connected with the emancipation of slaves. His daughter, Anna Steenkamp, however, is quoted as saying, "It is not so much their freedom that drove us to such lengths, as their being placed on an equal footing with Christians."[20] In another part of his manifesto Piet Retief confirms this attitude. He writes:

> We are resolved wherever we go that we shall uphold the just principles of liberty; but whilst we shall take care that no one shall be held in a state of slavery, it is our determination to maintain such regulations as may suppress crime and preserve proper relations between master and servant.[21]

The maintenance of master-servant relations between white and black has lain at the core of South African politics since 1652. Slavery set the pattern. The Hottentots then lost their freedom and in effect became serfs. The attitudes established in the period of slavery became inseparable from the life of the settlers in the colony. Walker describes the position as follows:

> Living in patriarchal isolation, the Boers developed a lively sense of self-reliance and independence. They held as of faith that a man might do what he would with his own, including the slaves and Hottentots the good Lord had provided for the service of the Christian. . . .
>
> The pastoralists desired to live the "*lekker lewe.*" Life fell far short of that ideal for many, but even an approximation to it demanded at least three things: unlimited land for nothing or next to nothing, a sufficiency of the cheapest con-

20. Quoted in J. A. I. Agar-Hamilton, *The Native Policy of the Voortrekkers* (Capetown: Maskew Miller, 1928), p. 88.
21. George M. Theal, *History of South Africa from 1795 to 1872* (London: George Allen & Unwin, 1926), II, 267.

ceivable kind of labour, and security wherein each man might live in quietness on his own place far from his nearest neighbour.[22]

The Dutch were not unique in this respect. British liberalism in the Cape, which had been ushered in by Ordinance No. 50 of 1828, took a different turn in 1841 when the Masters and Servants Law was proclaimed, replacing the earlier ordinance. It could not be said that there was discrimination on the grounds of "race" — the law made no reference to race — but the slaves and the Hottentots had come to be called "servants," and economic circumstances had been sufficiently manipulated to ensure that they would remain servants for all time. With economic dependence of the nonwhites assured, the whites could afford to talk of the new spirit of "liberalism" which had banished the mention of race from legislation (while retaining all the advantages to the whites of a race- and class-structured political, economic, and social system).

THE STRUGGLE FOR TERRITORY

With the continuous expansion of white settlement throughout the eighteenth century, frontier struggles between the settlers and the indigenous African people became increasingly common. The African groups (collectively known as the Bantu-speaking peoples) which the settlers encountered in the Cape were the Tembu, the Xhosa, and the Fingo. In Natal they met the Zulu, and in the north, the Basuto and others. The frontier struggles of the eighteenth century reached a peak in the nineteenth century in a series of armed conflicts which have been called the Kaffir Wars. African resistance to white expansion culminated in the Zulu uprising of 1907.

The first serious encounter between the settlers and the Africans came in 1700 when an expedition of free burghers set out beyond the fifty-mile limit of the Cape settlement. They were away for seven months, in the course of which they raided Hottentot kraals, seized their cattle and other stock, and even killed women and children.[23] The governor, Adriaan van der Stel, ordered an inquiry into the whole misadventure, but the results of the inquiry were never made known.

In 1736 a white hunting party clashed with a band of Xhosa about 350 miles east of Table Bay. In 1770 a boundary commission reported that some farmers had moved beyond the Fish River and were trading with the Xhosa. In 1778 Governor van Plettenburg visited the eastern frontier and erected a beacon at Colesburg to mark the northern boundary of the settlement. He followed this

22. Eric A. Walker, *The Great Trek* (London: A. & C. Black, 1943), pp. 63, 67.
23. Hepple, *South Africa*, p. 51.

with an arrangement with some petty chiefs about recognizing the Fish River as the eastern boundary. In terms of African law and custom this arrangement was not, of course, valid. Similar "treaties" were to be concluded in the years to come, and much of the trouble on the frontier stemmed from a misinterpretation of the nature of these agreements.

Following further plundering by the whites, the Xhosa carried out reprisal raids to recover their cattle. Soon the farmers were complaining that the Xhosa were "stealing" cattle. Skirmishes became frequent. The Council of Policy in Capetown stepped in, in an attempt to enforce the van Plettenburg "treaty." As a result, what became known as the First Kaffir War began in 1779. The attempt of the settler administration to enforce the "treaty" was an attempt to consolidate land gains which the Africans did not recognize. As Walker put it, "Land and water and not cattle have been the keys of the problem of the frontiers from that day to this."[24]

In 1789 two officials of the Dutch East India Company, H. C. Maynier and J. J. Wagener, were sent to the frontier to seek a new understanding with the Xhosa. They examined the situation and carefully sifted the available information. The conclusion they reached was that the white farmers were responsible for the trouble on the frontier. They reported highhanded action on the part of the farmers, who tried to get cattle from the Africans. They found that many were "guilty of violent conduct in their dealings with the Xhosa . . . many were engaged in gun running . . . and farmers were cruel to their farm hands."[25]

The white farmers became impatient with a policy that did not seek to crush the black man. They organized unofficial commandos and resumed their raids on the Xhosa. Thus, the Second Kaffir War was begun. The Xhosa were pushed back as far as the Buffalo River; the whites then sought peace, the terms being that each side retain the territory it held at the cessation of hostilities. The white man had won the first two rounds in what was to be a series of wars which has extended into this century. To the whites this war was a historic occasion. To the black man it was an early phase of a long struggle to retain possession of what was his. It was the struggle of black and white for possession of South Africa, a struggle whose end is not yet in sight.

Seven other wars with the Xhosa followed, the general pattern remaining the same: white provocation, retaliation by the Africans, war, the triumph of superior technology, and peace, with the annexation of more territory by whites. C. W. de Kiewiet has summarized the position as follows:

> As the Europeans advanced they did not succeed in driving the Kaffirs back into their hinterland. The Kaffirs were crowded into areas which steadily grew less able to maintain them, or lived as squatters and labourers upon the land that had fallen

24. Walker, *History of Southern Africa*, p. 115.
25. Hepple, *South Africa*, p. 52.

to the Europeans. This was the pattern of every subsequent frontier of contact between Europeans and natives.[26]

The protagonists of apartheid today try to suggest that these crowded areas were the total of the land occupied by Africans when they first made contact with whites.

A curious feature of those early wars was the alliance formed between the whites and certain sections of the blacks, notably the Fingo, against the Xhosa. Without these alliances the results of the wars might have been different. It is significant, however, that the whites regarded these as alliances of convenience; they never envisaged collaboration among equals. Alex Hepple has stated this as follows:

> Whites of the age, no less than those of succeeding generations, were not averse to linking arms with non-whites where there was promise of material gain. The relationship, however, was never one of comrades-in-arms but of master and servant temporarily elevated to higher status, under the paternalistic guidance of the master, to suit the master's purpose.[27]

The establishment of the Native Reserves, the small pockets of land into which the whites pushed the Africans in their process of dispossession and subjugation, might also be interpreted in these terms. The present government, in its more stringent application of segregation and also in its efforts to give the impression that separate African states are being set up in South Africa in the only areas ever occupied by Africans, calls these reserves Bantu "homelands." (The term *Bantustan* arose from the concept of separate African states and is now widely used in nongovernmental circles.)

THE DRIFT FROM LIBERALISM

By 1850 South Africa was divided into two camps, the British colonies of the Cape and Natal and the Afrikaner republics of the South African Republic (Transvaal) and the Orange Free State. After the Anglo-Boer War of 1899–1902 the two Dutch republics also became British colonies. These four colonies became the four provinces of the Union of South Africa in 1910.

In the mid-nineteenth century, Britain was concerned with the processes of establishing representative government in the Cape and Natal. In 1852 the Cape

26. *A History of South Africa: Social and Economic* (London: Oxford University Press, 1964), p. 49.
27. *South Africa*, p. 52.

of Good Hope Constitution Ordinance, by which the first parliament and legislative council were established, granted representative government to the Cape. Article 8 of the ordinance stated the conditions under which a person might be disqualified from becoming a voter and from participating in the elections of members to the Legislative Council or to the House of Assembly. The disqualification clause made no mention of race or color. The granting of responsible government to the colony in 1872, by which a prime minister and cabinet assumed the administrative functions of the governor, made no change in the voting rights of the black people, but other events were destined to affect them.

Natal had received its charter in 1856, under which the vote, although restricted by economic qualifications, was open to all adult males. A law passed in 1865, however, deprived the Africans of the franchise, except those who were exempt from Native Law. At the same time the conditions under which registration could be achieved were such as to make the vote virtually unattainable by Africans.

In 1877, the last pocket of Xhosa resistance fell, and the need for Fingo and other black allies disappeared. Intrigued by Lord Carnarvon's idea of a united South Africa under the British flag, the governor and those who worked with him took care to demonstrate to the settlers that their "native policy" could be firm and purposeful. The "Peace Preservation Act," No. 13 of 1878, ordered private persons to hand in all guns and ammunition in their possession. These were to be returned by the authorities to the "proper persons." Those who did not qualify as "proper persons" would receive compensation. The effect of the law was to disarm all Africans, including the Tembu and the Fingo, whose guns had recently helped to crush the armies of the Xhosa. A feature of the act was the concealment of its true purpose. (Modern examples of similarly misnamed laws include the Extension of University Education Act, the Abolition of Passes and Co-ordination of Documents Act, and the Suppression of Communism Act.)

In 1868 the Basuto had asked to be placed under British protection. The government of the Cape inherited this responsibility, and thus the gun registration affected Basutoland (now called Lesotho) as well. To Africans in all the territories guns had become something priceless. There was, therefore, strong resentment of the disarmament law, but the fragmented tribes of the Cape could do nothing about it. The position was different in Basutoland. The Basuto defied the law, and what became known as the Gun War followed in 1880. Africans from neighboring tribes rallied to the support of Basutoland, thus turning the episode into the first national campaign of resistance against oppressive legislation. The white force which had been sent to discipline the Basuto retreated without accomplishing its mission, thus conceding to the Africans a political victory of broad significance.

In the republics which the Trekkers had established in the north the principle that the black man was inherently inferior and should be denied equality was entrenched. The South African Republic (Transvaal) stated in its constitution of 1858 that "the people desire to permit no equality between Coloured people and the white inhabitants, either in Church or State."[28]

By the middle of the nineteenth century, the Cape had found it necessary to differentiate, for purposes of the pass system, between the Fingo and the other Africans from beyond the boundaries of the colony. Certificates of citizenship were issued to the Fingo, but bureaucratic indifference rendered these certificates worthless.

Harassment under the pass system and the realization that such privileges as had existed were being taken away led to an increasing recognition by Africans of the need for unity. There arose a consciousness that all Africans had a common political destiny. The foundations of African nationalism were forming. The magistrate at Kingwilliamstown described the position in these terms in a letter written in July, 1881, to the undersecretary for native affairs:

> There is very bitter feeling on the part of both Kafirs and Fingoes against the Government. There is now a warm sympathy between them which never existed before. . . . The Fingoes and loyal Kafirs say that for their loyalty they have simply been punished and made the laughing stock of those who fought and rebelled . . . and that their attachment to the government is now a thing of the past. . . . They have at present no faith in our honesty, truth or justice and they openly state that they have been driven to this by our harsh treatment of them.[29]

Industrialization was a factor in the regrouping of various tribes and the consequent development of a sense of solidarity among workers. The men who assembled in the diamond fields of Kimberley and in the gold mines of the Witwatersrand began to think of themselves not only as Basuto, Xhosa, or Zulu, but also as Africans. From about 1870, when the first diamond mines were worked, a nucleus of urban Africans developed which eventually populated the "native locations" of the new towns. Today a third or more of the total African population of the country live in urban areas. It is important to note that some of the people which the present South African government seeks to uproot are the grandchildren of the industrial pioneers and that they and their fathers before them have known no home other than the town or city. Nonetheless, the Afrikaner nationalist postulates that if a man is black he cannot be of the city, even though he may have been born there.

The British tendency to regard the black man as expendable — a tendency that was manifest in the treatment of the Fingo and Tembu after the final defeat of the Xhosa — was again made evident in the formulation of the peace terms that ended the Anglo-Boer War of 1899–1902. On March 7, 1901, the British government stipulated as follows:

28. Quoted in Agar-Hamilton, *Native Policy of the Voortrekkers*, p. 88.
29. Quoted in Lionel Forman, "Birth of African Nationalism," *Africa South in Exile*, II (January–March 1961), 54.

As regards the extension of the franchise to Kaffirs in the Transvaal and Orange River Colonies, it is not the intention of H. M. Government to give such franchise before representative Government is granted to those Colonies, and if then given, it will be so limited as to secure the just predominance of the white race. The legal position of coloured persons will, however, be similar to that which they hold in the Cape Colony.[30]

The Boer republics had asked that the question of the African franchise be left for settlement until after the granting of representative government. Britain was willing to accept this limitation provided that the position of the Coloured people could be guaranteed. However, when the final draft of the treaty appeared in May, 1902, it simply stated that "the question of granting the franchise to natives will not be decided until after the introduction of self-government." Britain had yielded. The matter of the African franchise was deferred as "a question to be determined by South Africans in South Africa."[31] The term "South Africans" referred, of course, to whites.

In 1906 Britain granted responsible government to the Transvaal, limiting the franchise to white adult males and thereby excluding women and non-Europeans.

African reaction to Britain's retreat from liberalism may be judged from the resolution passed in 1906 by the South African Native Congress (not to be confused with the African National Congress, which was founded in 1912). The resolution read:

The Native Congress feels called upon to record its deep regret at the apparent decline of British views in the treatment of the native question. . . . Congress feels that the attitude of the late Imperial Government in relaxing those bonds which bind the native and coloured races to the Imperial Government has contributed materially towards the regrettable conditions in which native affairs are placed at the present time in the several South African colonies . . . they view with extreme gravity any relaxation on the part of the British Government of this all-vital principle.[32]

LEGISLATING SEPARATION AND EXCLUSION

When the all-white convention which drafted the constitution of the Union emerged from its 1908–9 sessions, the worst fears of the nonwhites were confirmed. Not only were the northern colonies to retain their system of excluding

---

30. Quoted in L. M. Thompson, *The Unification of South Africa, 1902–1910* (Oxford: Clarendon Press, 1960), p. 11.
31. Hofmeyr, *South Africa*, p. 156.
32. Quoted in *The Aborigines' Friend* (London: Aborigines Protection Society, 1906).

Africans from all political rights, but no nonwhite would be allowed to sit in the Union Parliament. The Cape African vote was retained, but a clause prescribing how it might be removed was included. This clause was regarded by some as an entrenching clause because of its requirement for special procedures. The clause, however, proved to be no barrier to the eventual limitation of the Cape African vote.

In 1905 the South African Native Affairs Commission, appointed in 1903 to make recommendations for a uniform native policy for the four colonies (Transvaal, Cape Colony, Orange Free State, and Natal), had argued against the provision of equal opportunities for land ownership for white and black, contending that the effect would be to make difficult the preservation of "the absolutely necessary political and social distinctions."[33] In 1913, after the establishment of the Union, the Natives Land Act was passed, with the effect of enforcing territorial separation while retaining white political domination.

Solomon T. Plaatje, foundation secretary of the African National Congress and a member of the two deputations (the first in 1914 and the second in 1919) which were sent by the ANC to petition the British government, wrote a book which gave graphic descriptions of the effects of the Natives Land Act on Africans. He wrote of the shock it produced: "Awakening on Friday morning, June 20, 1913, the South African Native found himself, not actually a slave, but a pariah in the land of his birth."[34]

Since 1913 the world has seen an unprecedented volume of discriminatory legislation placed on the statute book of South Africa. The Natives Land Act removed any rights possessed by African sharecroppers and limited the acquisition of land by Africans to specific areas, generally known as reserves. In 1936 the Native Trust and Land Act made provision for the addition of further land to be known as "released areas" which could be purchased for African settlement. The minister of native affairs, P. G. Crobbler, admitted that, even with the additional areas, the total land available for African occupation was only 12 per cent of South Africa's area, but he contended that the land assigned the Africans had good rainfall.

The prime minister, J. B. M. Hertzog, had been campaigning since Union for complete segregation. The Native Trust and Land Bill was the second of twin bills which became known as the Hertzog bills. The first was the Representation of Natives Act, No. 12 of 1936, which effectively narrowed the scope of African participation in government. The act specified that no more African names were to be added to the voters' roll in the Cape. Those Africans who already had the franchise would keep it, but would be able to exercise it only on a separate roll to select three whites—known as native representatives—to sit in a House of Assembly of 156 members. For the rest of the country, a communal voting

33. *Report of the South African Native Affairs Commission 1903–5* (Capetown: Government Printer, 1905), p. 35.
34. *Native Life in South Africa*, 4th ed. (New York: The Crisis, 1920), p. 17.

system was instituted for the election of four senators to represent the African people. At the time the act was passed there were 11,000 African voters in the Cape. A separate voters' roll having been established, two seats were reserved in the Cape Provincial Council for whites to represent Africans. The act also set up a Natives Representative Council for the whole country, to consist of twenty-two persons, of whom six were official members, including the secretary for native affairs as chairman and five white native commissioners. The governor-general was empowered to nominate four members, and the remaining twelve members of the council were elected under a block voting system.

In August, 1946, ten years after its establishment, the Natives Representative Council ground to a halt. The end was the result of the cumulative frustration experienced by the members. The immediate cause was the failure of the government to extend to the council the courtesy of an explanation or a comment following police action against striking African mine workers, some of whom lost their lives in the shooting. After voting for a motion blaming the government for the strike because of its refusal to recognize African trade unions and calling for the establishment of a board of arbitration, the council went on to give unanimous approval to the following resolution:

> This Council having since its inception brought to the notice of the Government the reactionary character of Union Native Policy of segregation in all its ramifications deprecates the Government's post-war continuation of a policy of Fascism which is the antithesis and negation of the letter and the spirit of the Atlantic Charter and the United Nations Charter.
>
> The Council therefore in protest against this breach of faith towards the African people in particular and the cause of world freedom in general resolves to adjourn this session, and calls upon the Government forthwith to abolish all discriminatory legislation affecting non-Europeans in this country.[35]

In 1948 the Afrikaner National Party, committed to the policy of total segregation and white dominance, was brought to power in the general election. Since African representation of any kind would run counter to this policy, the Natives Representative Council was never revived. It was finally erased from the statute book by what was called the Promotion of Bantu Self-Government Act of 1959. Indeed, this act repealed the entire Representation of Natives Act of 1936, thus completely excluding Africans from the political processes of the country.

Satisfied that the foundations for territorial separation had been firmly laid, and assured of the virtual exclusion of Africans from the sphere of government, South Africa's white rulers proceeded to build up a body of legislation to reinforce white control.

Social segregation was enforced by such laws as the Population Registration

35. "Verbatim Report of the Proceedings of the Natives Representative Council" (Adjourned Meeting of the Ninth Session), August 14–15, 1946, p. 10.

Act, No. 30 of 1950, which defines racial categories and catalogues individuals. Factors taken into account are appearance, general acceptance, and reputation. The 1967 amendment of the act introduces descent as an important factor in race classification. The Prohibition of Mixed Marriages Act, No. 55 of 1949, is another social control. An amendment passed in 1968 stamps as null and void mixed marriages contracted in other countries by South African citizens. The Immorality Amendment Act, No. 21 of 1950, extends to all nonwhite persons the laws prohibiting sexual intercourse with whites.

Under the Natives (Urban Areas Consolidation) Act, No. 25 of 1945, as amended, the legal wife of an African is not entitled to live with her husband if she comes from a town different from that in which her husband was born and has lived continuously.

Laws which effectively prevented African participation in a common governmental structure included the Bantu Authorities Act of 1951, the Promotion of Bantu Self-Government Act of 1959, the Urban Bantu Councils Act of 1961, and the Transkei Constitution Act of 1963. The basic policy behind all these acts is the revival of traditional institutions under white direction. An example of attempts to make access to law courts difficult for Africans is the Natives (Prohibition of Interdicts) Act of 1956, under which an African must comply with a removal order before he can seek the protection of the courts.

The pass system, first introduced in 1809, was consolidated by what is called the Natives (Abolition of Passes and Co-ordination of Documents) Act of 1952. Its effect was to consolidate the various control documents into five types bound together in what is called a reference book. Attempts have been made to create the impression that the reference book for the African and the identity card for the other groups have the same function, but in fact the only portion of the reference book that constitutes an identity card is the reverse side of the front cover. The operation of the pass system is a chronicle of injustice. The reference book must be produced on demand; failure to do so is a criminal offense. No such requirement applies in the case of identity cards. The Industrial Conciliation Act excludes all persons bearing a reference book from its provisions. (Similarly, African trade unions are not recognized, and it is illegal for Africans to strike.) Persons carrying reference books (that is, all Africans) are subject to curfew regulations and other restrictions on their movements. They are restricted in other ways, for instance, in their choice of employment.

AFRICAN REACTION TO IMMOBILIZATION AND CONTROL

The black man in South Africa has never accepted his subjugation as ultimate and has used every available opportunity to voice his protest. With the passage of time Africans have had to adjust their tactics, but they have maintained the same resolute goal—freedom and full rights for all in South Africa.

It is paradoxical that although the Christian missions were a stimulus to national consciousness among Africans in South Africa, as indeed in many other parts of Africa, one of the most significant expressions of African national striving for self-determination has been the revolt against white-controlled churches. The early missionary movement was associated with white colonialist expansion. Often the missionary was an explorer, and in his wake followed the colonizer. The missionary and the colonizer belonged to the same color and culture group. They claimed, in effect, that the ways of the West were Christian, and the African accepted this association.

African nationalists in South Africa challenged the white church as early as the nineteenth century. In 1884 Nehemiah Tile, an ordained minister of Tembu origin, left the Wesleyan Methodist Church and set up the Tembu National Church in the Transkei, with the Tembu paramount chief as head. He proclaimed that his church would accept all, without distinction, as members.

In 1892 the Reverend Mangena Mokone also seceded from the Wesleyan Methodist Church in protest against color discrimination in the church. He formed an African-directed separatist movement called the Ethiopian Church. Reverend James Dwane, another Wesleyan Methodist minister, joined the movement in 1898. These two men envisaged a church that was national in scope and character, a church that would provide opportunities for self-fulfillment for the African. The Ethiopian movement snowballed. It adopted the motto "Africa for the Africans," and the church banner bore the inscription "Ethiopia shall stretch forth her hands to God." The two ministers then sought, and obtained, affiliation with the African Methodist Episcopal Church in the United States. The movement, one of the largest nonwhite churches in South Africa, now bears that name. Some of the members of the original Ethiopian Church, however, felt that affiliation with the church in America was collaboration with foreigners and would defeat the idea of self-determination. They refused to join the new alliance, and thus a segment of the Ethiopian Church still remains.

In addition to those African churches whose motive is to rid the church of white domination, there are numerous small groups whose distinguishing feature is Zionism. While these groups are not expressly nationalistic in orientation, they have found that they can support many of the traditional African beliefs while following practices from the Old Testament. They take the injunctions of the Old Testament seriously and literally, and they look with contempt upon the orthodox Christian churches. The commentaries of theologians have no place in their scheme of things. The inconsistencies between what the Bible teaches and what is practiced by the Christian West have further destroyed any respect which these people might otherwise have for the morals and culture of the white man. In this they are in agreement with those breakaway churches which regard the missionaries in Africa as agents of imperialism.

By the late nineteenth century a sense of African unity was beginning to crystallize, and in 1882 the cry went up for the formation of *Imbumba yama Afrika*

("Union of Africans"), a unity organization within which Africans could speak with one voice. The divisive influence of denominationalism was decried, and political unity was urged. The next two decades were to see increasing articulation of African grievances, largely through the medium of the earliest established African paper, *Imvo Zabantsundu* ("Native Opinion"), which was first published in 1884.

The founding of the African National Congress in 1912 was another significant step. The ANC was the embodiment, in sharper form and bolder relief, of the idea of African unity which had first been given public expression in 1882. The subsequent history of African reaction to conquest has been in the main the history of the ANC, buttressed at intervals by thrusts from other, younger, and from time to time more vigorous, organizations. Spearheaded by the ANC, the African people had petitioned the British Parliament and had waged a bitter but fruitless battle against the Natives Land Act of 1913.

The pass system, used since 1809 as an instrument for immobilizing and controlling the non-white people, provoked the first campaign of resistance after Union. In 1913 African women in the Orange Free State withstood attempts to extend the system to them. Refusing to carry passes, they filled the jails. Their struggle was still in progress when the second decade of Union began. The men took up the cause in 1919. In the Transvaal region the ANC launched a passive resistance campaign during March and April of that year. On the Witwatersrand hundreds of sacks were filled with surrendered passes and taken to the pass office where they were dumped. Large numbers of Africans were arrested, but the demonstrations continued until they were broken up by mounted police which charged the crowds. White civilians joined in, assaulting the Africans and in some cases using firearms. The campaign was lost, and the pass system continued.

On the labor front, the Africans had also begun to make demands for improvements in their conditions. In 1918 sanitation workers in Johannesburg went on strike, and were arrested and sentenced. There were unsuccessful strikes by mine workers in 1918 and 1920. A strike by Coloured and African dock workers in Capetown in 1919 failed because of lack of support from the white dock workers. Earlier in that year, the Industrial and Commercial Union had been established in Capetown. Merging with other nonwhite trade unions in 1920, it became the Industrial and Commercial Workers Union of Africa (ICU). For more than a decade the ICU dominated the African industrial and political scene.

The late 1920s and the early 1930s saw the continued growth, albeit at reduced tempo, of African political consciousness. In 1935 General Hertzog published his "Native Bills." The threat to the Cape African franchise brought together various organizations, resulting in the formation of the All African Convention. Using the old technique of resolutions and deputations, the AAC fought the bills but was unsuccessful. In the decade that followed there were calls for Africans to close their ranks. This was also the period of the Representation of Natives Act of 1936. It was not long before the fundamental differences of ideology, outlook, and approach between the government and the African members of the Natives Representative Council became evident. The council became critical of the government's tardy implementation of the Land Act. The pass laws came in for severe criticism. The language of the councilors became stronger: "It is the Government itself which is inciting our people to violence," said Councilor R. V. Selope Thema at one meeting, "and all these strikes which you see are the result of the disabilities imposed on my people. It is these things which are inciting them to violence. . . . The time is coming when we shall have to preach 'Africa for the Africans.' "[36] In 1946 the council adjourned indefinitely. Councilor Paul Mosaka called the experiment a failure. He said:

> We have been fooled. We have been asked to cooperate with a toy telephone. We have been speaking into an apparatus which cannot transmit sound and at the end of which there is nobody to receive the message. Like children we have taken pleasure at the echo of our own voices.[37]

The year 1944 had seen the birth of the African National Congress Youth League, a group of militant young men, many of whom were to play significant roles in the subsequent history of the ANC. The League's manifesto stated that "the Congress Youth League must be the brains, trust and power station of the spirit of African nationalism; the spirit of African self-determination." In 1949 the African National Congress, at its annual meeting, adopted a program of action which envisaged, among other things, the use of civil disobedience and non-cooperation through the boycott and the strike.

In 1952 the ANC and the South African Indian Congress called for protest meetings "as a first stage in the struggle for the Defiance of Unjust Laws." The "Defiance Campaign" began on June 26, 1952. The response was great, and thousands courted arrest by defying segregation laws. The government responded by passing the Criminal Law Amendment Act in 1953, making civil disobedience as a means of protest an offense punishable by very severe penalties. The measures taken by the government broke the campaign.

In March, 1954, the African National Congress, the South African Indian Congress, the South African Coloured People's Organization, and the white Congress of Democrats joined in an effort to canvass opinion on a new South African constitution. The new alliance put many months of work into the preparation of the draft constitution, and on June 26, 1955, the "Congress of the People" met in Kliptown near Johannesburg and adopted what became known as the Freedom Charter. An aftermath of the Congress of the People was to be the ar-

36. "Verbatim Report of the Proceedings of the Natives Representative Council" (Adjourned Meeting of the Ninth Session), November 7–14, 1945, pp. 129–30.
37. *Ibid.*, August 14–15, 1946, pp. 36–41.

rest on December 5, 1956, of 156 people of all races on charges of treason. The trial dragged on until March, 1961, when the court delivered a judgment of not guilty.

One year before the treason trial judgment, the Pan-Africanist Congress (PAC), which had broken away from the ANC in 1958, launched a campaign which it called "Positive Action Against the Pass Laws." All men were to leave their passes at home on March 21, 1960, and were to proceed to police stations and submit themselves for arrest. The slogan was to be "No bail, no defense, no fine." Sharpeville, an African township on the southern boundary of the Transvaal some thirty miles from Johannesburg, responded enthusiastically to the call. About 10,000 people went to the police station. The police panicked and opened fire, killing 67 persons and injuring 186. In Capetown there was more shooting by police. Here 2 Africans died, and 49 were injured. The stay-at-home work boycott at nearby Langa was broken by force. On March 30 the government declared a state of emergency and proceeded to make mass arrests. Shooting continued, and the death toll mounted. On April 8 the ANC and the PAC were declared "unlawful organizations." The two main African political organizations were thus forced underground.

On December 16, 1961, handbills appeared in the streets of Johannesburg urging violence against state property and announcing the formation of *Umkhonto We Sizwe* ("Spear of the Nation"). They stated:

> Units of Umkhonto We Sizwe today carried out planned attacks against Government installations, particularly those connected with the policy of apartheid and race discrimination. . . . It is . . . well known that the main national liberation organizations in this country have consistently followed a policy of non-violence. . . . The time comes in the life of any nation when there remain only two choices: submit or fight. That time has now come to South Africa. We shall not submit and we have no choice but to hit back by all means within our power in defence of our people, our future and our freedom.[38]

From the 1880s Africans had protested Western exclusivism, hoping that their experiences were only the result of some error and that the racist policies would change. They pleaded, they prayed, they respectfully submitted. "What has the native done to have such treatment meted out to him?" asked Jabavu in 1887.[39] "We are your Majesty's most loyal and dutiful subjects," pleaded the inhabitants of a small Cape African township in the same year.[40] "However desirable the unity of the white races may be . . . any conception of unity which is founded on the political extinction of the native element . . . would, to

38. Cited in the *Times* (London), December 28, 1961.
39. Editorial, *Imvo Zabantsundu*, March 23, 1887.
40. "Petition of the Native Inhabitants of the Location of Oxkraal in the District of Queenstown," July 1887.

our mind, be unwise and in the highest degree unstatesmanlike," remarked the South African Native Congress in 1903.[41] On the eve of Union, the *Imvo* exhorted:

> Let us have faith in the God who rules over all, and in the justice of our case, and let us be patient in the well doing, and be willing like the Syro-Phoenician woman to accept thankfully even the crumbs of justice which fall to our lot from the Constitution, while manfully and constitutionally claiming our heritage.[42]

And so the story continued—with the Africans praying, pleading, protesting, and hoping. Later, sterner voices were heard, until in the 1950s and 1960s the Africans openly challenged the system in a series of defiance and passive resistance campaigns. White exclusivism remained inflexible, and the balance sheet reveals increasing use of violence on the part of the government. The utterances of government spokesmen and others make it clear that the whites in South Africa have no intention of allowing the black man to participate as an equal in the running of the country. The laws are designed to maintain the relationship of superordinate and subordinate. Power rests in white hands, and in the words of former Prime Minister Strydom, "The White man must therefore remain the master."[43]

On the other hand, the mood of the politically conscious among Africans has changed. A new phase in black-white relations has been ushered in. The future may hold the longest and bitterest of the African's struggles for repossession of South Africa.

41. "Questions Affecting the Natives and Coloured People Resident in British South Africa," issued from the office of *Izwi Labantu* ("Voice of the People"), 1903.

42. Editorial, *Imvo Zabantsundu*, August 31, 1909.

43. Union of South Africa, *House of Assembly Debates* (April 20, 1955), cols. 4198, 4200.

13

The Impact
of Colonialism

MICHAEL CROWDER

To ATTEMPT AN EVALUATION of colonialism in Africa when few of its countries
have been independent for more than a decade and while some are still under
colonial rule is clearly premature. What follows therefore is not so much an
evaluation of colonialism as an exploration of the criteria by which it is likely to
be judged in the future. This exploration is made with particular reference
to France and Britain in West Africa. Colonialism in Africa presents so many
aspects that to encompass the whole of the continent in the framework of this
short chapter would be impossible except in a superficial way.

A major obstacle in evaluating colonialism arises from the great variations in
its impact. There were seven European powers in Africa during the colonial
period: Britain, France, Spain, Italy, Portugal, Belgium, and Germany. And in
South Africa people of European stock, although they have long since gained
their own independence from Britain, maintain a colonial relationship with
the majority of African inhabitants of the country. The policies of the various
colonial powers in Africa can easily be distinguished from one another, though
each power did not apply its policies in a uniform fashion. Britain pursued a
very different policy in West Africa from that in East Africa. The French, more
inclined than the British to uniform solutions to colonial problems, treated
Algeria as a *département* of France and Morocco as a protectorate in which she
recognized the sultan as sovereign; in Senegal she pursued a policy of political
assimilation in one part of the country and of paternalistic direct rule in the
other. With the exception of the politically assimilated *Quatre Communes* of Senegal, France's administration was uniform for West and Equatorial Africa. But
where there were European concessions, as in French Equatorial Africa, Ivory
Coast, and Guinea, her policy was modified considerably. Within the framework of such differences, however, each colonial power succeeded in imposing
its own personality on the territories it administered. The most striking testimony to this is the way in which Togo and Cameroon differ from the rest of

French-speaking Tropical Africa as a result of their short period under German rule. Even today the German imprint is striking to the most casual visitor.

Moreover, Africa was not a *tabula rasa* on which the colonial powers freely drew the pictures they wished. The variation in patterns of colonial rule in Africa was very much a response on the part of Europeans to the varied structures of African society. Different policies had to be adopted for the centralized Muslim state from those for the acephalous society. Where a colonial power like France determined to establish a uniform administration for West Africa (outside the *Quatre Communes* of Senegal) she had to contend with the reduction in powers of the traditional rulers of centralized states and with the amalgamation of peoples who had known no political entity above the village into manageable administrative units. Even when she succeeded in breaking up the pre-colonial states in the Senegalese hinterland she had to contend with the emergence of a type of political leader which did not fit into her administrative framework: the caliphs, or *marabouts*, of the great Muslim brotherhoods like the Tijaniyya and the Mouridiyya. The variety of traditional political organization in Africa is not indicated even by the vast number of ethnic groups inhabiting the continent. Within some ethnic groups political organization differed considerably from area to area. Perhaps the most notable example of this are the Yoruba of western Nigeria.

The greatest obstacle to an assessment of the achievements and failures of colonialism in Africa, however, is the difficulty of viewing this recent period of history objectively. The history of colonial rule in Africa is unevenly documented, and much of the available literature is in the nature of an apologia or a polemic. Few people can take a neutral stand on the question of colonialism. One is either for or against, even if one has had no colonial experience either as ruler or as subject. This comes out very clearly in debates on colonial issues at the United Nations. The majority of writers who are nationals of one of the former colonial powers tend either to seek justification for colonial rule or to be more critical of it than Africans themselves. The majority of African scholars have a bias against colonial rule which leads to ready condemnation of that which was bad and sparing praise of that which was good. It will be a very long time, judging by the American experience, before the colonial period of African history can be judged as dispassionately as Roman rule in Britain is today.

THE BRITISH AND FRENCH IN WEST AFRICA

Though an evaluation of colonialism in Africa may not be possible at this stage of history, we can establish some of the criteria by which future generations, less emotionally involved in the many issues raised by colonialism, will attempt their evaluation. To do this, we will refer to the experience of French and British rule in West Africa.

West Africa as an area has several advantages for such a task. With the exception of Portuguese Guinea, all its territories have been independent for at least eight years—some for ten years. The multiplicity of problems experienced by the thirteen countries of West Africa since independence has tended to focus attention on the evils of the present rather than on those of the past. This, coupled with the fact that they have had their independence for a comparatively long time, and, with the obvious exception of Guinea, have achieved it in comparatively harmonious relationship with the outgoing colonial powers, has meant that colonial rule is viewed less bitterly than elsewhere on the continent.

This area has another advantage in that it had no white settlers. Though there were large European populations in Senegal and Ivory Coast, settlement was never on the same scale as in Kenya or Algeria. Even in Ivory Coast, where land was "sold" to Europeans, the Europeans never thought of the colony as the home in which they would retire and in which their children would live. As far as the administrators of France and Britain were concerned the European presence was incidental to the governing of Africans.

In discussing colonial rule in West Africa, and in Africa generally, one of the first problems is to decide whether "colonial rule" is the appropriate term to describe the European occupation and administration of Africans. "Foreign rule" may well be the term future generations of Africans will choose to describe an administration which their forefathers did not want and which for the most part was imposed by force or threat of force. We shall use the term "colonial rule" because it is for the present the generally accepted one, and also because the European occupation of Africa is a special instance of the occupation of one people by another.

Technologically, the occupying powers were overwhelmingly superior to those they had occupied. Before the Industrial Revolution of the nineteenth century, the disparity between African and European technology had never been so great as to allow the latter to contemplate occupation of the interior. But at the end of the nineteenth century the African had no answer to the recoil-operated Maxim gun. The European considered his technological superiority as one more proof of the racial superiority he assumed over the African. Social and "scientific" theory in the nineteenth century asserted the inferiority of the nonwhite races and established a hierarchy, at the bottom of which was the black.

The European therefore never felt that there was anything wrong in occupying the African's land, even if this had to be done by force. Indeed he considered his occupation positively beneficial in that Africans would thereby be brought into the orbit of his superior civilization. Since he believed he had a right to occupy these lands, he never considered himself a foreigner in them. Thus it was possible for the French to talk in terms of "Overseas France" and Portugal in terms of her "Overseas Provinces" when referring to their African possessions.

Finally, there was another distinction between the colonial empires of the twentieth century and those that preceded them: telecommunications and the steamship kept the colony in constant touch with the metropolis. The expatriated European therefore did not feel alienated from his motherland.

A major difficulty in discussing colonial rule in West Africa is in deciding exactly what period of time we are concerned with. Both France and Britain had been installed as colonial powers in West Africa since the beginning of the nineteenth century, but they possessed only minute enclaves on the coastline — France in Saint Louis (Senegal); Britain in Sierra Leone, the Gambia, and the Gold Coast forts. Not until the end of the nineteenth century did France and Britain extend their coastal colonies into the interior. By 1900 much of West Africa was not yet under colonial rule; and much of that which was, was not effectively "pacified." But by 1910 France and Britain can be said to have been firmly in the saddle in West Africa.[1]

The usual terminal date given for colonial rule is the date when each territory gained its independence; but in assessing colonialism in West Africa, there is a strong case for taking 1945 as the terminal date. Prior to 1945 the colonial powers, France and Britain, were the sole arbiters of the fate of their subjects. What international criticism of their policies there was — and this was remarkably little — had a negligible effect on the decisions they made. With the outbreak of the Second World War, West Africa, from being the private preserve of France and Britain, became of concern to America and Russia because of its value to the Allied war effort. West Africa not only supplied men and materials for the war but was also of immense strategic importance to the defense of the South Atlantic and as a staging post for the Allied campaigns in North Africa and the Middle East. Both Russia and America were resolutely anti-colonial, and both openly criticized the colonial policies of Britain and France. The Americans forced on Britain and France that clause in the Atlantic Charter which recognized the right of all peoples to self-determination. At the end of the war the United Nations, with its own trusteeship territories, became a forum for criticism of colonialism. Both France and Britain accepted the need to liberalize their colonial regimes and to allow their colonial subjects increased participation in their own administration. This liberalization was such that colonial policy could no longer be made without consulting Africans.

There is, then, a major difference between prewar and postwar colonialism. After the war the colonial powers in West Africa were not only subject to, but

1. Parts of Ivory Coast were not pacified until 1914; much of Upper Volta and modern Mali were in open revolt against the French in the First World War, protesting the recruitment of soldiers for the European front; the British sent their last "punitive expeditions" against the Ibo as late as 1918.

responded to, international and African pressure in determining their policies. In discussing colonial rule in West Africa, therefore, we will be primarily concerned with the period *ca.* 1910–45.

THE COLONIAL RATIONALE

The European powers justified their occupation of Africa on the grounds that they were bringing order and civilization to a chaotic and barbarous continent. They were bringing light into the "heart of darkness." This was very much an ex post facto justification. The "scramble for Africa," from about 1885 until the beginning of World War I, was not of course the result of a rush on the part of European powers to secure territory in Africa in which they could carry out charitable works for the African; rather, it was the result of deep economic and political fears about one another's intentions in Africa. All would have preferred to have kept out of Africa administratively, or at least to have reduced their administrative obligations to a minimum. But fears that one of them might secure so large an area in Africa that it would upset the balance of power in Europe, or that areas in which they had trading interests might be occupied by a rival intent on establishing a monopoly of trade, led them to preemptive action. Furthermore, the disturbed state of many parts of the continent at the time led traders, anxious to secure their sources of supply, to put pressure on their governments to occupy the areas in which they were interested. Where railways were seen as the best method of opening up the interior to European commercial exploitation, the argument in favor of occupation was even stronger. European capitalists and governments were not inclined to risk the enormous sums of money involved in building railways unless they had control over the lands through which they passed.

To disguise their fundamental economic interests in occupying Africa, the Europeans salved their consciences by introducing arguments about their own inherent moral and racial superiority to the Africans. They drew a picture of Africa as a continent without any meaningful culture or history, where peoples indulged in slavery, cannibalism, and human sacrifice, and were constantly at war with one another. Only outside intervention by the European could save Africans from themselves and bring them into the orbit of the modern world.

The African was depicted as indolent, incapable of innovation, reversionary in character—in sum, a grown child in need of a stern father to guide him. Thus he could be taxed without his consent or without representation, because if he wished to be regarded as civilized he "must share the common burden of civilization."[2] He could also be forced to work, for late-nineteenth-century Europe

2. Sir Fredrick Lugard, *Revision of Instructions to Political Officers on Subjects Chiefly Political and Administrative* [known as the *Political Memoranda*] (Lagos, 1906; London: HMSO, 1919), Memo No. 5, Par. 6.

conceived of work as a moral duty. Thus the French and British compelled the African to work on roads and railways designed to facilitate the export of crops needed in Europe. The French, in order to meet their domestic demands for African crops, forced the African to cultivate those crops, and justified this form of naked exploitation on the grounds that they were curing the African of the "idleness [that] keeps him in a state of absolute economic inferiority" and argued that

> [it was] therefore necessary to use the institutions by which he [was] ruled, in this case slavery, to improve his circumstances and afterwards gently lead him into an apprenticeship of freedom. Scorning work, the black is not aware that, for us, work ennobles a man's character.[3]

Such interpretations took little or no account of the debilitating diseases from which the African suffered, which drastically lowered his physical endurance. Nor did they consider the extremes of climate that made sustained work much more difficult than in the temperate zones. The context of the African's apparent "laziness" was conveniently ignored to justify colonial occupation. Also ignored were the achievements of the African past. The empires of Ghana, Mali, Songhai, Benin, and Oyo found no place in the European history book. Great cultural achievements, admired today, were dismissed as barbarous. Where, as with the Ife heads, such achievements could not be disregarded, they were attributed to white initiative. Fantastic theories of wandering Romans were thought up to "explain" the achievements of the Ife sculptors. So, too, where African political achievements in the construction of states and empires could not be ignored, the genius for them was attributed to a mysterious, light-skinned, non-Negroid race of Hamites.

The original goal of occupation by the European powers—economic exploitation—was superseded by a moralistic goal of trusteeship where the European powers would act as guardians for "irresponsible" Africans. If colonial rule were to be judged in terms of its original economic aims, it would be judged remarkably successful. The colonies cost the colonial powers almost nothing and they were able to secure the products they wanted largely on their own terms. If, however, colonial rule is judged in terms of the lofty aims of the "civilizing mission" we shall see it is found wanting. As "trustees" the colonial powers were very much like the parent who sends his child to school only so long as is necessary to prepare him to go out into the world and earn his own living. They were not prepared to make the sacrifices necessary to send him to high school and university.

3. Aspe Florimond, Report to the Minister of Commerce on "L'Organisation économique de la côte occidentale française: réglémentation" (Paris, 1901), cited in Eugéne Lestideau, *La Question de la main d'oeuvre dans les colonies françaises et spécialement dans celles de l'Afrique occidentale francaise* (Rennes: Guillemin et Voisin, 1907), p. 80.

COLONIAL CONQUEST AND AFRICAN RESISTANCE

A commonly accepted thesis during the colonial period was that the Africans readily accepted European conquest and occupation. Since they were so easily conquered, it was assumed that they welcomed colonial rule. That some did cannot be denied. The Yoruba historian Samuel Johnson wrote of the conquest of Ijebu-Ode by the British:

> To the vast majority of the common people it was like the opening of a prison door; and no-one who witnessed the patient, long-suffering and toiling mass of humanity that week by week streamed to and from the coast with their produce, could refrain from heaving a sigh of gratification on the magnitude of the beneficial results of the short sharp conflict.[4]

The colonial powers frequently described what was often the bloody conquest of Africa as the establishment of peace. A well-known book on former French West Africa describes the French conquest as "La Paix Française."[5] While many Africans did accept colonial occupation passively, and at times with relief, the majority resisted. The penalty for resistance was often savage. In Sierra Leone the British in their ten-month war against Bai Bureh resorted to systematic burning of the towns and villages that supported him. In the Western Sudan large towns were razed to the ground by French columns, and prisoners were given as slaves (*captifs*) to the African soldiers. In contrast to their aims of imposing "civilization" on the Africans, the Europeans frequently resorted to standards of warfare that would not have been tolerated in Europe.

For the most part African resistance was weak. Few states had standing armies. Their weapons were inferior to those of the Europeans; the Maxim gun quickly dispelled the conventional African cavalry charge or the massed head-on attack of infantrymen, usually equipped at best with dane guns. Some African leaders like Bai Bureh or Lat Dior (Senegal) were able to adapt fighting techniques to deal with European superiority of weapons. They appreciated that guerrilla warfare was the only way in which the army of a small state could deal with the European forces. Samory Touré alone among the rulers of the major states of the nineteenth-century Western Sudan was able to adapt his military strategy in such a way that a large army could contain the French. By a series of strategic withdrawals, a scorched earth policy, and the brilliant use of military intelligence he kept the French at bay. Often the hardest battles fought by the Europeans were against the stateless societies like the Ibo, and against the tiny chiefdoms of Ivory Coast. There, "pacification," the euphemism so frequently used by the European to describe his military occupation, was achieved village by village.

4. *History of the Yorubas* (Lagos: C.M.S. Bookshops, 1937; reprint ed., London: Routledge & Kegan Paul, 1966), p. 623.
5. Jacques Richard-Molard, *Afrique occidentale française*, 2nd ed. (Paris: Berger-Levrault, 1952).

African states rarely combined with their neighbors in common defense against the European invader.

In at least two-thirds of West Africa the European gained his right to rule not by treaty but by conquest. Colonial occupation was accepted where it was seen as the means of ending otherwise interminable wars with neighbors, of avoiding occupation by a rival state, or of gaining access to European trade. It is, nevertheless, essential to an understanding of the colonial period in West Africa to appreciate that the majority of people were reluctant to sacrifice their sovereignty to the European.

THE IMPACT OF COLONIALISM ON AFRICAN LIFE

For the vast majority of West Africans life was not radically changed by the imposition of colonial rule. Many Africans live today in much the same way as they did before the conquest. Comparatively few were affected economically by colonial rule. Only a tiny percentage of the population became wage-earners in the urban centers. Earnings from cash crops like cocoa and coffee brought wealth to farmers in Gold Coast, Ivory Coast, and western Nigeria. But the other main cash crops — groundnuts, palm oil, cotton — earned the peasant farmer little more than enough to pay his taxes. The reality of colonial rule for most Africans was not an economic revolution in their lives, but the presence of the European administrator, who symbolized the new order of things. If the European colonial powers brought nothing else to West Africa, they brought peace. The European administrator represented in his presence the end of wars and slave raids and the guarantee of freedom of movement for everyone. He was an agent for stability rather than for change. Stability in itself of course represented change, but once peace had been established the European district officer saw himself for the most part as a conservator rather than an innovator.

This was particularly true of British West Africa where policy was to rule the people "indirectly" through their own institutions, which were designated "native authorities." The British attempted to develop such institutions as the basis for local self-government. Such institutions had, of course, evolved to deal with situations utterly different from the Western world into which the colonial powers insisted they were initiating the African; and, as in the obvious case of the northern Nigerian emirates, they tended to act as breakwaters to Western innovation. It is significant that it has been independent Africans, Western educated, who have dismantled the British system of native authorities and tried to replace it with a Western-oriented system.

In French West Africa the chiefs did not run their own native authorities. French rule was much more direct than British, and the chief was essentially a functionary of the French administration without any powers of his own. He merely carried out the orders of the French administrator. Unlike his British-administered counterpart he had no courts, no police, no prisons of his own. He did not have the right to any of the taxes he collected, as did the British chief. Often the chief was not even the one who traditionally had the right to rule but was appointed because he had shown loyalty to France as a soldier or as a clerk in the administration. Chieftaincies were streamlined, being either increased or decreased in size, to establish uniformity in the size of administrative units in West Africa. While the French concept of the role of the chief was more innovative than that of the British, it did not change society radically, for it allowed no initative to the African, whether chief or subject. However, in the long term, by whittling away the traditional power of the chiefs, who were representatives of the conservative forces in West Africa, it did prepare the way for their removal from the political scene. By contrast all the British West African colonies at independence had constitutions in which the chiefs continued to play a political role.

The systems of administration in both French West Africa and British West Africa did not do much to initiate change. Innovations, such as regular taxation, did little to improve the lot of the peasant. The bulk of the money raised was spent on supporting the administration, or on providing an infrastructure of roads, railways, and ports which passed through only those areas that were of economic interest to the colonial powers. The vast majority of Africans, in some cases as much as 90 per cent of a territory's population, as Suret-Canale has shown,[6] was unaffected by these developments. Where taxation forced Africans to cultivate cash crops for the first time, the result was of little benefit to them. Over and above the labor used for their subsistence crops, they could usually afford to cultivate only enough cash crops to pay their taxes and buy a few yards of imported cloth. They rarely had sufficient resources to grow a surplus so that they could purchase anything more. Even today many farmers in cocoa-rich western Nigeria can earn only enough from their crops to pay their taxes. In areas where no cash crops could be grown, men were forced to migrate to earn money. But by the time they returned home they had only enough to pay their taxes and buy a small selection of imported goods.

Though European administrators undertook a wide variety of tasks, including in the case of the French administrator the enforcement of obligatory cultivation of crops, their primary role was that of keepers of the peace. Significantly both French and British administrators had judicial powers, those of the French being much greater than those of the British. The French administrator had judicial authority in all criminal cases, since the native chiefs were deprived of all their judicial powers in criminal matters. Also the *indigénat*, or summary administrative justice, to which all Africans with the exception of a tiny minority of assimilated citizens were subject, gave the administrator the

6. Jean Suret-Canale, *Afrique noire: L'Ere coloniale 1900–1945* (Paris: Editions Sociales, 1958), p. 19.

power of imposing fines and imprisoning without trial for up to fourteen days. The *indigénat*, to which even chiefs were subject, was bitterly hated by the African and resulted in the French administrator being more disliked by the people than was his British counterpart, who because of the native authority system was more aloof from them.

THE IMPACT OF COLONIALISM ON ECONOMIC DEVELOPMENT

Many writers on colonial rule in Africa have seen it as the prelude to an economic revolution. Yet, as we have already intimated, the standard of living for the average peasant did not improve substantially under colonial rule. From an economic point of view, then, in what way can colonial rule be seen as a revolutionary influence?

The cash-crop revolution in Africa—the change-over from the subsistence economy geared primarily to providing food and goods for immediate local consumption to one geared to producing crops for export overseas in exchange for cash or for bartered imported goods—is invariably attributed to colonial rule. But in fact this change-over had been undertaken autonomously by Africans in the nineteenth century; groundnuts, cotton, and palm oil were being produced for export in sizable quantities outside the spheres of European administration. The imposition of alien administration, then, was not a prerequisite of cash-crop production. What colonial rule did was to intensify and extend the area of that production through the imposition of taxes and by building railways and roads that made it possible for peasants to export crops economically to the coast.

New crops, notably coffee and cocoa, were introduced under colonial rule; and because of their high price on the world market these crops produced real change in the economic status of the cultivator. But before 1945 coffee was produced on a very small scale by Africans, and then only in Ivory Coast. Only cocoa in the Gold Coast, in western Nigeria, and to a lesser degree in Ivory Coast (where European planters were installed) involved a large number of peasants. In the Gold Coast the massive increase in the production of cocoa was due largely to the peasant farmer himself. Most of the feeder roads and bridges necessary to link the cocoa areas with the government railway or road were built by him. He modified his system of land tenure and arranged for the import of tenant farmers to cope with the rising overseas demand for cocoa. The phenomenal increase in cocoa production in the Gold Coast from 12 tons in 1892 to over 118,000 tons in 1917 was primarily to the credit of the cocoa farmer himself. As Sir Hugh Clifford, governor of the Gold Coast, and later of Nigeria, declared:

> This man, reputed to be lazy by the superficial globe-trotter or the exponent of the damned nigger school, has carved from the virgin forest an enormous clear-

ing, which he has covered with flourishing cocoa farms. Armed with nothing better than an imported axe and matchet, and a native-made hoe, he has cut down the forest giant, cleared the tropical undergrowth, and kept it cleared. With no means of animal transport, no railways and few roads, he has conveyed his produce to to the sea, rolling it down in casks for miles and carrying it on his own sturdy cranium. Here is a result to make us pause in our estimate of the negro race.[7]

Before 1945 the colonial powers did little to improve the agriculture of the African. This was partly because of their lack of knowledge about Tropical African agriculture, and partly because of the minimal amounts they devoted to agriculture in their annual budgets and capital schemes. This was despite the fact that the bulk of colonial revenue was derived directly or indirectly from agriculture. The research stations and experimental plantations they established and the work of their small corps of agricultural officers brought some results, but to a later generation.

With the exception of the Germans in Togo, the colonial powers in West Africa were concerned exclusively with the improvement of export crops. Subsistence crops like cassava, yams, and maize were of no interest to them, though during the 1914–18 war a hard-pressed France did import these products. Agricultural research was characterized by an almost total lack of interest in the crops on which the mass of Africans depended for sustenance.

Similarly, the roads and railways of the colonial powers were not designed to develop internal trade but to facilitate the evacuation of the cash crops required by Europe. Only incidentally did internal trade develop as a result of the new roads and railways. This transportation network and the allied telegraph lines nevertheless constituted a revolution in communications. But it was only in the years immediately preceding independence that the second stage of this revolution was embarked on: the development of a system of roads to facilitate internal trade.

The introduction of a portable currency was not as great an innovation as some suppose. Africans in many areas had developed their own forms of currency, although, as in the case of the *manilla* and the cowrie shell, these were very cumbersome. Colonial coin was only slightly less so, for the produce buyer traveling upcountry had to load donkeys with sacks of it, since paper money was not accepted until late in the colonial period and payments were usually of a small order necessitating the use of the lower value coins. Much trade continued to be conducted by barter, as it still is today in the more economically backward areas of West Africa.[8]

The most dramatic change brought about by colonial rule was in the structure of the economy itself. In the nineteenth century Africans not only had

7. *Times* (London), June 2, 1925.
8. Nigerian research workers undertaking a social and economic survey of the peoples whose land is being flooded by the Niger (Kainji) Dam found barter a common means of trade in the area.

produced the crops required by the Europeans but also had acted as the middle-men responsible for collecting and delivering them to the European exporters on the coast. Some Africans had been exporters in their own right. Toward the end of the nineteenth century the Europeans started encroaching on the Africans' role of middlemen. They were followed by the Lebanese and Syrians, who had begun immigrating to West Africa in the late nineteenth century from their bitterly poor homeland and were able—through great business acumen, a willingness to live in conditions intolerable to their African and European coun-terparts, and an acceptance of marginal profits—to cut both Africans and Eu-ropeans out of the middleman trade. The Europeans facilitated this by showing themselves more willing to give credit to the Lebanese than to the Africans, whether such credit was given through their banks or in the form of an advance of goods from their import-export houses. By the 1920s, therefore, the Africans had been edged out as agents in all but the smallest transactions.

Similarly, the few African importers and exporters who had established them-selves were cut out of business by the large European commercial firms. They did not have the capital resources available to these firms, they lacked the con-tacts these firms had in Europe, and they did not have the same access to bank credit. The European firms had priority of space in, and cheaper rates on, cargo boats through the notorious West African Shipping Conference. Also some of the factories in Europe supplying these European firms with textiles and other stock-in-trade goods for the African market were owned by the same parent companies. As if this were not enough, the slump that followed the 1920 boom killed off all but a handful of African import-export businesses. They were caught with too large a stock on credit and insufficient capital reserves to tide them over the difficult two years that followed the slump.

By the outbreak of World War II, the West African economy was dominated by a handful of expatriate trading companies, which exercised a quasi mono-poly over the market. Even where two firms were ostensibly in competition, by mutual agreement they paid the same prices for labor and for crops. The most notorious example of combination by European firms was the Gold Coast "co-coa-pool" of 1937–38, when nine expatriate companies agreed to pay a fixed price for cocoa much lower than that which prevailed on the world market. The laissez faire colonial governments usually turned a blind eye to such ex-ploitation, though they were forced to do something about the cocoa-pool be-cause of the severe reaction of the Africans (a coordinated hold-up of sales).

The companies did not plow back their profits into West Africa, and they rarely established secondary industries to process crops in West Africa before shipping them to Europe. Thus palm oil was exported to Europe for conver-sion into soap and then re-exported to Africa. The only major industries to develop under colonial rule were the extractive industries: tin in Nigeria, gold in the Gold Coast, iron in Sierra Leone. There was no mining of consequence in French West Africa.

The colonial economic regime was a primitive one designed essentially to provide Europe with the raw materials she needed from Africa. Benefits to Africans were secondary and incidental.

THE IMPACT OF COLONIALISM ON EDUCATION

If there was any aspect of colonial rule that was revolutionary, it was the spread of Western education. For the African, Western education represented the key to the understanding of the technological superiority which had enabled the white man to occupy and rule Africa so easily. Western education with its emphasis on individual achievement attacked the very basis of traditional life with its ideas of corporate identity and mutual responsibility.

Though assimilation represented an important strand in French policy, the pursuit of a successful assimilationist policy could be carried out only through education, and the French provided much less education for the African than did the British. The French realized this, but were anxious to control the size of their elite so that only enough educated Africans were produced to fill the jobs the French were prepared to make available to them. The British government did not spend significantly more per capita on African education, but because they gave Christian missions much wider scope for establishing schools, there were many more educated Africans at all levels in British West Africa than in French West Africa. In French West Africa the great majority of children went to government schools; in British West Africa the great majority attended mission schools. The notable exception to this was in northern Nigeria, where government policy prohibited missionaries from operating in the Muslim emirates without the consent of the emirs.

In either case the numbers educated before 1945 were small. In 1944 only 76,000 children were at school in French West Africa, out of a population of about fifteen million. Only a handful of these were at a *lycée*, or secondary school. In British West African conditions varied from territory to territory. In 1939 northern Nigeria, with a population larger than that of French West Africa, had only 25,067 children at school. But the year before, the Gold Coast (Ghana) had 76,000 children at school, as many as did all French West Africa in 1944, and of these a substantial number went to secondary school.

Though the number of children going to school in relation to the population was small, the impact of education was enormous. The child was initiated into the world of his colonial master, and found that it was a possibility, although remote, for him to become a doctor, lawyer, or engineer. At secondary school he learned about the political ideals of the metropolitan powers: "democracy," "one man–one vote," "no taxation without representation," "liberty, equality, and fraternity," "all men are equal in the sight of the law," "habeas corpus."

Increasingly, he began to wonder why these ideals and principles were not applied to him. Thus in educating the African the colonial rulers were engendering the end of colonial rule.

Not all those educated became lawyers and doctors or even clerks and minor civil servants. The vast majority gained only a basic knowledge of the three Rs, enough to make them so discontented with rural life that they migrated to the towns to secure jobs as shop assistants, messengers, drivers, mechanics, storekeepers, stewards, and even laborers. The migration of the youth to the towns was one of the most dramatic results of colonial rule. The new administrative and commercial centers acted as magnets to the partly educated youth, desperate to escape the monotony of agricultural work, the authority of their elders, and the restrictions of traditional society. The towns became the melting pots of different ethnic groups, of new ideas, and of new aspirations. The towns were the hunting ground of those with political ambitions in the years that followed the Second World War. Though a young man working as a clerk or a laborer could earn as much in a month as his family at home did in a year, Western education by stimulating his ambition had sown discontent in him. The successful politicians of the postwar years were the ones who harnessed this discontent. The city did not, however, prove the disruptive or dislocating force it has become in the Western world. The newly arrived immigrant sought out his kinsman or townsman and lodged with him till he found a job. People of the same ethnic group or town formed credit unions or voluntary associations where they discussed their common problems and helped one another. Religion, too, provided an anchor for the immigrant. Ethnic religions could rarely be exported to the towns, since the priests stayed at home and shrines could not be moved; immigrants therefore became Muslims or Christians, thus attaching themselves to a new community. In some cases, notably in Freetown, churches and mosques were organized on an ethnic basis.

It was in the towns that Christianity and Islam made their most spectacular progress under colonial rule. While Islam tended to be a conservative force, Christianity, with its emphasis on individual accountability and its insistence on the equality of all men, added fuel to the discontent that educated Africans felt with a regime which insisted on the superiority of the colonial master over his subject. Only now are Western education and Christianity in Africa being studied in depth as the revolutionary forces they were during the colonial period.

THE IMPACT OF COLONIALISM ON GOVERNMENT

Before 1945 Africans had negligible influence on the way they were governed. Major policy decisions regarding administration, agriculture, and economic development were made by the colonial governments without consulting those most affected. The French at one time described their policy in Tropical Africa as one of "association," but this was very much the association of horse and rider. The horse did not decide where it wanted to go. In both British and French West Africa the rider, or administration, was almost exclusively European. Africans in British West Africa were specifically excluded from the administration proper until the Second World War; and where they were employed as doctors they were on a separate and junior scale from their British counterparts, however high their qualifications and however long their experience. In French West Africa it was *possible* for Africans to serve in the administration on equal terms with the French, but the number so employed was insignificant.

In French West Africa the outlets for African opinion were minimal. Under the *indigénat*, African *sujets* who criticized government actions could be imprisoned without trial for fourteen days, and there was little to stop an administrator from putting the offending person back in prison for a further fourteen days when he came out. There was no free press. Denied legitimate expression of grievances and aspirations, some Africans resorted to the alternative of violence. Large numbers of Africans broke into open revolt against France's policy of recruiting Africans for service on the European front during World War I, and workers staged illegal strikes.

Only in Senegal was there any possibility of political expression. In the *Quatre Communes* (Dakar, Saint-Louis, Rufisque, and Gorée) Africans had the rights of citizens, and elected their deputy to the French National Assembly. They also elected their own *conseil-général* and municipal councils. Their press was as free as any press in Tropical Africa. The two African deputies of the interwar period, Blaise Daigne and Galandou Diouf, supported the policies of metropolitan France. The former even became Undersecretary of State for Colonies and in 1930 at Geneva defended France's policy of forced labor in the colonies.

In British West Africa the legislative councils to which a few African members were elected, and others nominated, provided some outlet for grievances and hopes. But those elected came from the sophisiticated coastal towns only, and the vast hinterlands were represented, if at all, by nominees of the administration who could be relied on not to oppose government policy. Where members or nominees did oppose government policy, they were faced by an overwhelming official majority committed to supporting the policy of the governor in whose hands lay their prospects of promotion.

As in French West Africa, the most significant form of protest was of the extraconstitutional kind: illegal strikes such as the Sierra Leone railway strikes of 1919 and 1926; the Cocoa Strike in the Gold Coast in 1937–38; the Aba Women's Riots in Nigeria in 1929. By such methods Africans were able to bring their grievances to the attention of the administration and force it to action. The Gold Coast Cocoa hold-up resulted in a Commission of Enquiry that strongly condemned the European companies and eventually led to government marketing of cocoa with profits used for the benfit of the producer. The Aba Women's Riots led to a Commission of Enquiry that recommended the dismantling of the unpopular warrant-chief system of administration in eastern Nigeria.

Though the political institutions of the interwar years were relatively impotent, when the colonial powers in West Africa decided to liberalize their regimes to allow greater African participation in government, these institutions served as the basis of the liberalization. The French introduced *conseils-généraux* like that of Senegal for all the other colonies of West Africa, which could now send deputies to the French National Assembly. The British extended the competence of their legislative councils to cover the whole of the territory, rather than just the coastal colony. They increased the number of elected members and gave a majority to the unofficial members.

The people who took advantage of this liberalization were of course the educated elite, supported by the urban educated. The postwar years were characterized by a change-over from the old formula, that the Europeans were trustees for the African and sole arbiters of what was "good" for him, to one of partnership in which the African had an increasing say in his destiny.

CONCLUSION: AN EVALUATION OF COLONIALISM

The colonial period is still considered the most important in Africa's history by many Africans. Yet, when future generations come to view it in a deeper perspective than is possible for us today, the changes that took place as a result of colonial rule will appear less dramatic than they do now. The apparent break that colonial rule represents will seem to be less important than the underlying continuities of African history.

Future generations will probably see as the most significant result of colonial rule the amalgamation of diverse states and ethnic groups into new political units, which formed the basis of the newly independent states of Africa. Yet the continuity of African history is unhappily demonstrated in the attempt of the Ibo of eastern Nigeria to break away from the Federation of Nigeria and form a state based on their pre-colonial identity as Ibos rather than as Nigerians. Almost every state in Africa has had this problem of the competing nationalisms of pre-colonial and post-colonial Africa, the former often being described as "tribalism." While the colonial powers were responsible for the creation of these new colony-states, they did little to foster among their subject-inhabitants a sense of identity with the new political unit within which they were forced to live. The colonial powers, on the other hand, did provide these colony-states with a vital tool for their survival as independent countries: a lingua franca—the French and English languages in the case of West Africa.

Perhaps the most devastating effect of colonial rule was to sap the confidence of Africans in themselves, by its insistence on the absolute superiority of the white man's world. African religions and culture were damned and those of the white man held up as the only valid ones. Thus was produced what President Sékou Touré has called "the colonial mentality." The Yoruba even to this day say *"Aiye d'aiye Oyinbo"* ("The world has become a white man's world").

Perhaps the most urgent task of independent African nations is to cast off this colonial mentality so that they can not only assert but also believe in their equality with those who ruled them for sixty years.[9]

9. For a detailed study of the colonial period in West African history, see Michael Crowder, *West Africa under Colonial Rule* (Evanston, Ill.: Northwestern University Press, 1968).

III

Processes of Change

Major Themes in Social Change

PIERRE L. van den BERGHE

SOCIAL CHANGE IN THE PRE-COLONIAL ERA

A COMMON MISCONCEPTION concerning social change in Africa is that prior to the colonial era the pace of change had been slow. "Traditional" or "tribal" societies were viewed as isolated from one another and as evolving only gradually until they were suddenly "opened up" by contact with Europe. The rapidly accumulating body of historical facts about Africa clearly contradicts any notion of static traditional societies.

The "neolithic revolution" (that is, the development of a polished-stone, agricultural, and sedentary civilization) took place along the Nile and Niger rivers between 6,000 and 7,000 years ago, only slightly later than in the Middle East, roughly at the same time as in eastern and southern Asia. Contacts with Europe and Asia across the Mediterranean Sea, the Red Sea, and the Indian Ocean, and regular trans-Saharan trade have a history of 3,000 to 4,000 years. Greeks, Romans, Phoenicians, Arabs, Indonesians, and Persians have had extensive contacts with Africa since the dawn of recorded history, and they settled in North and East Africa and in Madagascar. Christianity penetrated Ethiopia long before it reached most of Europe, and Islam swept over North Africa within a century of its inception.

By the early eleventh century Islam had crossed the Sahara, and in the following centuries most of the black population of the Sudanic belt, from Senegal to Somalia, became Muslim. Great kingdoms such as Ghana, Mali, Songhai, Morocco, Bornu, Kanem, Dahomey, Ashanti, Kongo, Luba, Lunda, Oyo, Benin, Kush, and Axum, to name but a few of the larger ones, rose and fell. Vast armies swept over the savannas. Entire societies migrated in successive waves. Agriculturists displaced hunters like the Pygmies and Bushmen. Pastoralists conquered agriculturists. Muslims from East and West Africa made the pilgrimage to Mecca. Trade caravans established regular circuits and markets, and merchants traveled thousands of miles. African gold, ivory, and other luxury goods reached Europe and Asia centuries before Prince Henry the Navigator sent his sailors off to "discover" the coast of West Africa and well before the voyages of Columbus.

Clearly, political turmoil and economic interaction were accompanied by profound cultural changes. New food plants from Asia, and later from the Americas, revolutionized agriculture. Metallurgy spread from the lower Nile to the entire continent. Techniques of warfare, animal husbandry, and artisan production spread with migration, trade, and conquest. Language groups expanded with great rapidity. The implantation of Islam in the Sudan transformed a wide range of social institutions such as kinship and political structures. Politically acephalous or uncentralized societies became states. Social classes developed in hitherto egalitarian cultures. Games, folktales, musical instruments, and sculpture styles traveled with people. Cities sprang up in North Africa, the Sudan, Yorubaland, and across southern Africa.

When one considers the cultural heterogeneity of Africa today, one gets a glimpse of the extreme complexity of social change during the last several millennia. Almost all of this history, except that of the last four to five hundred years, is lost to us. But broad outlines of African cultural history are now being brought back to life, largely due to the efforts of a new generation of scholars who patiently collate oral traditions, date potsherds, compare vocabulary lists, and analyze genetic distributions.

During the more recent past, the period of the slave trade was characterized by a quickening of the pace of change in the areas where slaving was most intensive: the coast of West Africa from Senegal to Cameroon, the Angola region, and the coast of East Africa from Mozambique to Kenya. The trade in human chattels took different forms and had different effects in various parts of the continent. It was most complex in West Africa, especially in Nigeria, Ivory Coast, Dahomey, and Ghana; and this is where its effects were most profound. The main direction of long-distance commerce gradually shifted from the trans-Saharan routes of the north to the sea routes of the south. Thus, Sudanic cities like Timbuktu and Gao declined, while coastal cities such as Accra and Lagos boomed. Some groups of coastal peoples gained a new found power through the acquisition of firearms. Warfare between West African nations intensified and became chronic. Traditional political systems with intricate checks and balances in the exercise of power became transformed into slave-raiding war machines such as those of the Dahomean kings of the eighteenth century.

In East Africa, the Portuguese sacked most of the flourishing coastal cities and disrupted the long-standing trade with Arabia, Persia, India, and Southeast Asia, until the Persians and Arabs reestablished their control over the East African coast from the seventeenth to the middle of the nineteenth century. At the Cape of Good Hope, permanent European settlement began in the mid-seventeenth century and expanded, much like the North American frontier, to give rise to the white-dominated Union (now Republic) of South Africa with its large urban, mining, and industrial complexes.

Next to the Dutch settlement at the Cape, the French conquest of Algeria in 1830 marked the most important extension of direct European control in Africa. After a few more decades of European trading, military, and missionary activities, the "scramble for Africa" was unleashed in the 1880s, and by the turn of the twentieth century all of Africa except for Liberia, Ethiopia, and the remaining Turkish possessions of North Africa had been partitioned among Britain, France, Germany, Portugal, Belgium, Spain, and Italy.

Although the colonial era lasted only for some seventy-five years, and although the European regimes were firmly established only for the short quarter century between the two world wars, the changes which took place under colonialism did much to shape contemporary African states. But any understanding of modern Africa calls for an analysis of the complex interrelations between pre-colonial societies, the colonial system, and the anti-colonial reaction.

THE COLONIAL IDEOLOGY OF CHANGE

Although traditional African societies were dynamic even before coming into contact with the West, Europe did bring a new element into the situation. For the first time, an encompassing *ideology of change* was imported. Contrary to most political ideologies and social philosophies, which tend to rationalize the status quo and to favor inertia, colonialism imported ideologies which stressed the desirability of change. Imbued with a self-confident feeling of superiority, most European administrators and missionaries shared the belief that Africans must be made to renounce their "idolatry" and their "barbarous" and "immoral" practices. Polygyny, bridewealth payments, witchcraft, and clitoridectomy had to be stamped out. "Indolent" and "ignorant" peasants had to be shown how to "rationalize" their agriculture, how to improve their livestock, and how to work steadily for wages and pay taxes. In short, the "natives" needed to be shown the way to progress through the guiding hand of benevolent white teachers.

Paternalism, common to all colonial regimes, was politically conservative; but it was, nevertheless, an ideology of change. There were, of course, some white settlers who believed that Africans were genetically inferior, and, hence, that attempts to change them were doomed to failure. Some Europeans were able to foresee that the very changes introduced by the West, especially in the educational sphere, would undermine white domination, and therefore many advocated a policy of leaving Africans as they were. (The Afrikaners in South Africa were probably most consistent in this approach, but even they were quite unsuccessful in preventing the changes they opposed. Ironically, even apartheid is an ideology of change, though of reactionary change. The South African government is engaged in a losing race back to the nineteenth century.) The dominant ideological theme of colonialism, however, and its most basic rationalization, was the notion of the "civilizing mission" of the West.

Other proselytizing movements before colonialism, notably Islam, had tried to change Africans. In its early phases, Islam, like Christianity, was a fairly revolutionary doctrine, but by the time it reached sub-Saharan Africa, it was largely content with a simple profession of monotheism and adherence to a few religious practices. Muslim missionaries, unlike so many of their Christian counterparts, did not generally lash out in anger and moral indignation against the entire indigenous way of life. They accommodated themselves to it to a greater extent than did most Christians, especially most Protestants, and as a consequence the Islamic religion soon came to be regarded as indigenous to Africa south, as well as north, of the Sahara. With the exception of a few waves of puritanical reformism such as the Jihad of Usman dan Fodio in the early nineteenth century, Islam in Black Africa was not an ideology of change.

Today paternalism in its colonial form seems outdated, yet numerous programs of economic development, technical aid, military assistance, overseas volunteers, and revolutionary agitation which foreign countries try to export to Africa and other "developing" areas are still based on an assumption of Western (or Eastern) superiority. The "developed" countries, East or West, are the teachers; the Third World is expected to play the part of the grateful recipient.

The emerging ruling classes of the newly independent states have also eagerly adopted a pervasive ideology of change. Everybody is in favor of change, especially of economic development. The conservative Western powers see in economic development an instrument of influence and an antidote to social revolution and political instability. The Communist countries view economic aid as an entree to ideological infiltration and as a ferment for more profound changes. The ruling elites of the Third World favor development largely because it is fashionable, prestigious, and frequently lucrative to themselves. Thus, an ideology of change has become a common universe of discourse between the world's bureaucratic and technocratic elites, however different their aims may be. Only peasants seem, by and large, to be reasonably satisfied to stay as they are; but then, unlike the experts, they do not know what is good for them.

Ideologies of change introduced during the colonial era took several forms, and their effects were varied. Intricate though the relationship is between attitudes toward change and actual change, few people would deny that ideology has a bearing on the rate and direction of change. Often, of course, the changes are not the ones anticipated by the "changers." Ideologies frequently contain internal contradictions and call forth their antitheses. Thus the discrepancy between Western and Christian ideals of democracy, brotherhood, and equality and the tyranny of colonial rule was seized upon by African intellectuals in calling for independence. In South Africa, the official ideology of racial separation and inequality has led to the development of a counter-ideology of African nationalism, egalitarianism, and non-racialism. The French and Portuguese ideology of assimilation of a small elite of "black Europeans" in their colonies led to the rejection of Western culture by some intellectuals and to the development of the concepts of negritude and *africanite*.

Many of the changes introduced during the colonial period were ideologically motivated, at least in part, and these changes in turn initiated a long chain of further changes beyond the intentions of the initial promoters. For example, the introduction of Western education in Africa was linked with missionary efforts at religious conversion. However, many graduates of mission schools, instead of becoming devout Christians, used their skills for political ends and became leaders of liberation movements.

WESTERNIZATION AND THE COLONIAL LEGACY

Change in contemporary Africa (and in other non-Western countries) is all too often equated with Westernization. It is frequently assumed that as predominantly rural societies become urbanized, industrialized, and modernized they will increasingly resemble the industrial nations of Europe and North America. To some extent, of course, this is true. Modernization and development impose certain constraints, raise certain problems, and bring about other changes which do in fact lead to a structural convergence and homogeneity between industrial countries. For example, urbanization and industrialization almost invariably result in higher living standards, more centralized government, lower fertility, greater longevity, replacement of human labor by machines, and so on.

Given a certain level of technology, the range of workable solutions to the satisfaction of human needs is relatively limited. This means that in broad structural characteristics all industrial societies are somewhat alike. Striking similarities, for instance, were found in the distribution of income and in the prestige ranking of occupations in countries as diverse as the Soviet Union, Japan, Sweden, Great Britain, France, and the United States. (This order of similarity can also be found between cultures at comparable levels of pre-industrial technology. The complex pre-industrial societies of medieval Europe, North and West Africa, China, and pre-Meiji Japan were also alike in important respects. So are the hunting and gathering societies of North America, southern Africa, and Australia.)

Having noted that broad similarities exist between industrial countries, it does not follow that agrarian societies in the process of development are becoming

Westernized. Indeed, the evolution of countries such as Japan has shown that "advanced" non-Western countries remain culturally quite different from the Western countries which they once appeared to have emulated. No society which is exposed to external change reacts simply by taking over an alien culture in its entirety. Adoption is always quite selective, technology being the most readily "borrowed" aspect of a culture. When new elements of a foreign culture are taken over, they are usually adapted and reinterpreted in terms of the borrowing society. The latter in turn modifies and adjusts itself to external change through a series of new changes in terms of its own internal dynamics. Thus when the spread of urbanization in Africa made traditional forms of social security obsolete, there developed various forms of voluntary mutual-aid associations that were not in any sense "imitations" of Europe. Frequently, though not always, based on ethnicity, these associations were original, creative, and specifically African responses to changed conditions.

In spite of considerable change in recent decades, the cultural impact of Europe in Africa as a whole has been relatively limited. African societies have shown remarkable resilience in the face of foreign constraints. This is striking when one compares Africa to the Western Hemisphere. Except in the Andes and the Maya area, the pre-Columbian societies of America have been shattered to pieces. Nothing like the extensive Europeanization of the Americas took place in Africa, except for the Western Cape region of South Africa.

To discuss reasons for these differences in degree of Westernization would take us too far afield. We would have to compare the colonial regimes, to examine the impact of conquest and slavery, to analyze the independence movements and the class structure of the two continents, and to take into account climate, demography, and many other factors. We will limit ourselves here to the general observation that European cultural penetration remained shallow in most of Africa. It usually did not extend beyond the coastal zones and the urban centers, and it modified in depth the way of life of perhaps no more than 5 to 10 per cent of the indigenous population. And only in South Africa is the trend toward continued Westernization clear. Elsewhere, European cultural influence, which was never very strong to begin with, probably has tended to recede somewhat since independence. Traditional religions frequently remain viable in spite of the spread of Islam and Christianity. Most African languages hold their ground quite well against French and English, and some, like Swahili, Lingala, Hausa, and Wolof, continue to spread. African family structures, although rapidly changing, remain notably un-European, even in the cities. African states are increasingly turning away from the political institutions modeled on European forms with which they entered their independence. In short, there is very little prospect of Angola ever becoming a second Brazil, or Gabon a second Quebec, or Nigeria another United States. Few Africans show any inclination to become black Europeans. Moreover, there is every indication that most African cultures (with the possible exception of the few remaining hunters such as the Bushmen and the Pygmies) are fully viable under modern urban conditions. Far from having shown themselves unadaptable, African cultures have shown remarkable vitality, flexibility, and capacity to adjust creatively to new conditions.

At a first glance, the downtown sections of Nairobi, Dakar, or Kinshasa (formerly Léopoldville) look very European or American. The life style of African professionals, managers, civil servants, and intellectuals seems, and indeed is, quite Westernized. But the urban elite represents only a small (though powerful) minority of the population. Most African states have a thinly spread and fragile superstructure of alien institutions inherited from colonialism at the top and a broad indigenous substratum at the bottom. Thus, subsistence economy exists side by side with the money sector; a Western, bureaucratic type of central government coexists with traditional local authorities; modern schools and Koranic schools function in parallel fashion.

The political institutions and the administration of African states are probably least well adapted to local conditions. Politically, the newly independent states are successor states to the colonial territories, a fact which contributes both to the stability and to the instability of African states. Their boundaries, administrative machinery, civil service, armed forces, constitutions, parliaments, and judicial systems are still heavily European in character and function. The new bureaucratic ruling class of university-educated civil servants has inherited the high salaries and perquisites of their colonial predecessors. In the political as well as in the economic sphere, then, the continuities between colonialism and independence continue to overshadow the discontinuities, at least in a number of states like Senegal, Ivory Coast, Kenya, and Malawi.

This lingering foreign legacy is in most cases what holds African states together in their present form. Were it not for the administrative structure inherited from colonialism, it is likely that the heterogeneous and artificial territories created during the "scramble for Africa" would disintegrate and reconstitute themselves on different lines. This threat of disintegration and separatism makes it essential for African governments to hold to the inviolability of their artificial frontiers and to create the illusion of unity in their arbitrary association of nationalities or ethnic groups.

Europe has, in effect, imposed its political institutions on Africa and prevented the development of a viable alternative. In a number of states, independence and "Africanization" have meant little more than a change in the pigmentation of the ruling class. In some cases, the new ruling class has even adopted the European outlook to the extent of openly expressing its concern for maintaining "European standards" and for proving its worth by emulating the behavior of its former masters.

There is another side, however, to the political and economic legacy of colonialism. To the extent that the central polity is alien to African societies, it is often ill-adapted to local conditions and lacks legitimacy and effectiveness. Sometimes a strong charismatic leader and a political party which have gained legit-imacy during the independence struggle may provide a certain measure of democracy and rule by consent; but, more commonly, African governments are either too weak and too poor to effectively penetrate down to the grass roots or they have to govern by force in much the same way as did the old colonial re-gimes. The Westminster model is no more suitable to Africa than, for example, the Chinese mandarin system would be to the United States. Pressures toward more democratic, representative, and indigenous forms of government contrib-ute to the instability of many African regimes today. In the economic sphere, the persisting foreign control of banking, commerce, and industry, the con-tinuing privileged position of Asian and European minorities, and the highly unequal distribution of income between the Western-educated African minority and the mass of peasants and workers also constitute ferments for social change.

In the Americas, a century or more elapsed between political emancipation and social revolution. In many countries, the social revolution has yet to come. In Africa, on the other hand, the political and social revolutions are being com-pressed into a shorter time span. The pace of change is much faster. Nkrumah, Nyerere, and Sékou Touré combine the historical roles of Bolivar and Castro. Some African countries, such as Algeria, Guinea, Mali, Ghana, and Tanzania, launched into social revolution at the same time as they achieved political eman-cipation. Others, such as Rwanda and Zanzibar, did so within a few weeks or months of independence.

The southern third of the African continent still remains under white settler or colonial control. Some nominally independent states, such as Lesotho, Botswana, and Malawi, are in fact reduced to the status of economic clients of the Republic of South Africa. And, farther north, such countries as Morocco, Liberia, and Ethiopia are still ruled by traditional elites with modernized trap-pings. However, these conservative regimes do not seem to have much of a future in their present form. Africa is on the verge of a period of acute, indeed revolutionary, change. The very continuities between the colonial and the inde-pendence periods help create the ferment of change.

Having tried to indicate some of the general parameters of change in Africa, let us turn to some important trends, problems, and dilemmas of change in more specific aspects of social life.

DEMOGRAPHIC CHANGES

Population censuses during the colonial period were generally taken in con-nection with poll-tax collection, using inexpensive, makeshift, and unreliable methods. In most cases, the population was underestimated by margins of 10 to 20 per cent. For many countries, no decent census was taken until the 1960s, and thus we lack good longitudinal data (that is, data taken over time). What we do know, however, indicates that African demography has many characteristics in common with other developing countries. Africa is clearly in the second phase of the demographic cycle — that is, its population is increasing at a rate of 2.5 to 3.0 per cent a year. Probably until the first two decades of this century, Africa was still in the first phase of the cycle: the birth rate was high, but so was the death rate; and growth was fairly slow, perhaps around 1 per cent per annum. Now the death rate, while still about twice that of developed countries, has declined to around twenty per thousand; the birth rate is somewhere in the upper forties, or close to twice that of Western Europe, Australia, Japan, or North America.

With increasing urbanization and other social factors, the birth rate may soon begin to decline in Africa in much the same way as it has elsewhere. However, due to the fact that the population is still 80 to 90 per cent rural, this decline is as yet barely perceptible. The immediate future cannot be regarded with optimism. The total population of the continent, which is now close to 300 million, will almost certainly exceed half a billion by the turn of the century. In the long run, the rate of population growth probably will decline, but so slowly as to give little respite in the present population explosion. At best, the demographic gallop will slow down to a canter. The relatively low population density of Africa, as compared to Asia or Europe, does not relieve the problem. In terms of existing natural resources and technology, much of Africa is already overpopulated, overgrazed, eroded, and incapable of providing its existing population with an adequate diet. Without radical technological change, increasing food scarcity can be expected to occur in the foreseeable future. Population control should thus be an essential ingredient of any development program if population growth is not to outstrip, or even wipe out, economic growth.

Other demographic changes are evident in African countries. As hygiene improves, life expectancy increases, and the population becomes older. The urban population becomes more stable (that is, people reside in cities longer than before), its age pyramid becomes more normal, and its sex ratio becomes more equal. In short, the urban population tends to more closely resemble the rural population in terms of age and sex composition. The city becomes less a temporary place of employment (and unemployment) for adult males of working age, and more a permanent place of residence for family units.

In its basic demography, therefore, Africa behaves much like other parts of the world with similar ecological, technological, and economic characteristics. Being less urbanized and less developed than Latin America or Asia, however, Africa may be expected to lag demographically one or two decades behind the rest of the Third World. The *rate* of urbanization itself, however, is faster in Africa, because the baseline is so low. Also, a rapid rate of urbanization is characteristic of early phases of industrial development.

RELIGIOUS CHANGE

By far the most important religion of Africa is Islam. Probably around 40 per cent of the continent's population is Muslim, and something like one-third of the world's Muslims live in Africa. Nor is African Islam confined to the north; there are about as many black African Muslims in the Sudan belt as there are Arab and Berber Muslims north of the Sahara. Christianity, which was the religion of the colonial powers, except in Ethiopia, comes in a poor second, with probably about half as many adherents as Islam. Finally, perhaps some 40 per cent of Africans, the so-called pagans, practice indigenous ethnic religions. Both Islam and Christianity continue to gain converts at the expense of the traditionalists, but Islam seems to be gaining ground considerably faster than Christianity in the areas where the two world religions are in direct competition. The southward thrust of Islam appears as strong as ever.

These crude facts tell us practically nothing about the extremely complex processes of change which have taken place in the religious sphere. The interplay between Islam, Christianity, and the various indigenous faiths has been one of the principal and most interesting aspects of social change in Africa. Indigenous religions vary enormously in beliefs and rituals, though a great many share certain elements such as sacrificial rites, a cult of ancestors, and the concept of a supreme creator ruling over a hierarchy of lesser gods and of humans. African religions range from pantheism to polytheism, and some are as monotheistic as, for example, Catholicism. Many are still thriving concerns, notably the traditional beliefs of some of the larger ethnic groups such as the Yoruba (Nigeria). Quite a few African religions probably surpass both Islam and Christianity in theological, philosophical, and cosmological sophistication. There is no relationship between the complexity of a people's religion and the level of technological development. This helps explain why material culture may readily be accepted from the outside while traditional religion frequently remains vital or may be only superficially affected.

Political power is, of course, related to the spread of religions and has been an important factor in the diffusion of both Islam and Christianity. Even when conversion was not imposed by force, the material advantages and social prestige accruing to those who adopted the religion of the dominant group were powerful incentives for at least nominal conversion. By and large, Islam has had several tactical advantages over Christianity. In the Sudanic belt and North Africa it is now regarded as an indigenous religion, a status which Christianity has attained only in Ethiopia.

During the colonial regime, the basic egalitarian ideology of Islam was translated into practice to a greater extent than was the case with Christianity. With few exceptions, Christian missionaries were an integral part of the colonial system and practiced racial discrimination much as did lay settlers. While

Christianity frequently attracted misfits, deviants, malcontents, and low-status persons, Islam generally endeavored, frequently successfully, to convert populations from the top down, beginning with the king and the nobility. Furthermore, in traditional monarchies, Islam provided a powerful legitimizing force for the existing political order, whereas Christian missionaries had long abandoned the theory of divine right of kings and tended, in fact, to undermine the status quo. Christian doctrines were thus regarded by many ruling classes as subversive, while Islam easily became the official religion of traditional kingdoms.

Finally, and perhaps most important, Islam made few attempts at reforming the entire way of life of its converts and tolerated or even favored widespread pre-Islamic African customs, such as polygyny and bridewealth payments, which Christianity sought to eradicate. In short, Islam was often more tolerant and less presumptuous than Christianity.

Much of whatever acceptance Christianity achieved is attributable to the fact that the European missions preserved a virtual monopoly of Western education for Africans until independence. Colonial governments provided few state schools for Africans, and lay private schools were even scarcer. As soon as Africans realized the value of Western education, the demand for it increased rapidly. Conversion to Christianity was typically the price to be paid for a modern type of schooling leading to wage employment. Eventually the missions contributed to the demise of colonialism through the spread of Western education, in that almost all leaders of African independence are products of mission schools. Though a great many rebelled against the colonial form of Christianity, the fact remains that Christianity, more than Islam, was one of the main agencies of political and educational change in sub-Saharan Africa. Christianity was both an adjunct of colonialism and one of the principal agents of its undoing.

There is much more to religious change in Africa than the spread of Islam and Christianity. As a consequence of contact with the West there developed in various parts of Africa a great number of syncretistic and messianic movements, which adopted some elements of Christianity and combined them more or less liberally with indigenous beliefs and rituals. Some sects remained fairly orthodox and simply sought to substitute African for European leadership in the church. Others were quite unorthodox and seized on prophetic and messianic ideas from the Scriptures to herald the arrival of an African savior who would overthrow white rule. Most of the movements were clearly the political as well as the religious expression of frustrated and oppressed peoples in search of a better life. Some of these sects became quite subversive against the colonial regimes and were the precursors of later independence movements. In the post-independence era the political significance of messianism has continued. As late as 1964, for example, the Lumpa sect of Zambia under prophetess Alice Lenshina created a serious threat to the newly independent government. Sociologically, these syncretistic movements offer fascinating examples of dramatic responses to rapid social change.

EDUCATIONAL CHANGE

In the broad sense of the socialization of youth for adult roles, education, of course, has always existed in traditional and Islamized African societies. In many cases, long before the colonial era, educational functions were assumed by specialized, extrafamilial agencies. Koranic schools in Islamic areas and initiation schools in many non-Islamic societies functioned as formal educational institutions quite distinct from informal family socialization. The same was true of the long apprenticeships served prior to acceptance into skilled craft occupations such as those of musician or blacksmith.

Africans quickly realized, however, that a Western type of education, including literacy in a European tongue, was essential for success in the modernizing sectors of the economies which were beginning to take shape during colonialism. With the rapid Africanization of technical and administrative personnel since independence, the premium on Western education is even greater today than it was during the colonial period when the Europeans imposed rigid ceilings on the occupational mobility of Africans. Modern educational skills are a prerequisite to modern technical societies. Increasingly, even such relatively unskilled tasks as driving an automobile or working on an assembly line require literacy. Most African governments therefore invest relatively high proportions of their budgets (as much as half) in the development of human resources.

Literacy rates are now climbing to between 25 and 50 per cent of the school-age population in some areas like southern Nigeria, southern Ghana, Algeria, Tunisia, and the Republic of South Africa; but rates of 5 to 20 per cent are still typical of most of the continent. It is probably still true that in most African countries at least half of the children never go to school at all; over 90 per cent never complete primary school; well under 1 per cent complete high school; and less than one child in a thousand graduates from a university or technical college. Throughout Africa the better post-primary education is heavily concentrated in a few urban centers and is often beyond the reach of the rural masses.

Such a highly pyramidal system of education, combined with a low degree of economic development, produces a vicious circle of stagnation. A low level of modern skills makes for low labor productivity, high birth rates, administrative inefficiency, and other ills associated with the countries which, in nearly all cases, can only euphemistically be called "developing." Most underdeveloped agricultural economies cannot absorb and effectively utilize large numbers of highly educated persons. Thus some countries, such as India, are beginning to experience the tragic paradox of having both a very low educational average and a growing class of "unemployable" university graduates who emigrate to the greener pastures of Europe and America. Few African countries have enough university graduates to fill top positions; but some, like Nigeria, Ghana, Senegal, and Ivory Coast, are already starting to experience a "brain drain" and a loss of trained talent.

The pyramidal education system has other consequences. One of the most obvious is that it contributes to the rise of an increasingly elitist ruling class of technicians, professionals, and civil servants who come to form a kind of mandarinate, or what has been aptly called a "meritocracy." These problems of elitism are compounded by the fact that African school curricula at all levels are still heavily foreign in character in spite of superficial attempts at "Africanization." The French and English languages hold a complete, or nearly complete, monopoly as media of instruction in universities and secondary schools in the former Belgian, French, and British colonies. In some countries the importance of European languages in primary schools has increased rather than decreased since independence. Likewise, the subject matter taught in the schools almost entirely reflects the needs and traditions of European rather than African countries.

The educational tasks faced by African governments are formidable. Nothing short of a profound revolution in both the quantity and the type of education will accomplish the progressive aims of some governments. The curricula must be thoroughly revised in line with policy objectives, and rapid expansion of facilities must take place simultaneously at all levels of education. A crash program of university expansion can be effective only if the lower schools that feed into the universities are also expanded; the opposite approach, a gradual upgrading and broadening of the school system from the bottom up, implies a steady expansion in the number of qualified teachers, and it would take some twenty years before it would produce top-level scientists and technicians. To succeed, African states must try to do everything at once with extremely limited financial resources. Without education there can be no development, and without development there is little money for education. Short of foreign aid on a much more massive scale than is currently available, escape from the vicious circle can only be painfully slow.

FAMILY, MARRIAGE, AND KINSHIP

Most traditional African kinship systems share certain characteristics which sharply differentiate them from Western systems. Almost all African societies have extended, polygynous, virilocal family groups, in contrast to the European family, which tends to be nuclear, monogamous, and neolocal. Traditionally and ideally, the large family group sharing common residence consists of a man, his wife or wives, his unmarried daughters and granddaughters, his sons and grandsons and their wives, and his brothers with their wives, sons, and unmarried daughters. Upon marriage, a girl goes to live with her husband's kin. In practice, even in rural districts, there are a great many departures from this ideal residence group; but the local family sharing a house or compound is almost invariably much larger than a nuclear family of a man, his wife, and his unmarried children. Polygyny is at once the rule in theory and the exception in practice. For demographic and economic reasons, there are seldom more than 20 per cent of the men in any society who have more than one wife at any given time.

Another nearly universal feature of traditional African marriage is that it involves the payment of bridewealth (often in livestock) by the groom's family to the bride's family. Sometimes misconstrued as a "purchase" of women, the bridewealth has, in fact, a number of functions, most of which are not economic in character. The bridewealth usually constitutes a legal guarantee for the validity and stability of the marriage, a warranty for the good behavior and good faith of the parties, and a jural claim by the husband not only on the wife herself but also on her offspring.

In Western types of kinship systems, all lines of descent are of equal (though often minimal) sociological significance. Except for the patrilineal inheritance of surnames, Westerners do not distinguish between categories of cousins, grandparents, and uncles and aunts. This is known as a bilateral system of descent, one of the consequences of which is that Western societies cannot be neatly divided into mutually exclusive kinship groups. Almost all African societies, by contrast, have unilineal descent; that is, an individual has only one relevant line of descent. In the vast majority of cases the patrilineal line is the significant one, but some societies of West Africa, the Congo, and Zambia are matrilineal, and a few have double descent systems, that is, both patrilineages and matrilineages.

This, then, is the broad matrix of traditional African systems of kinship and marriage. Until recently, many sociologists assumed that the Western type of family was the only one suited to urbanized and industrialized societies, and, hence, that non-Western kinship systems would break down and come to resemble Western systems. In fact, the changes that took place in Africa, Japan, India, and other non-Western countries are much more complex than this simple model would suggest.

In the urban areas polygyny is indeed declining, if only for economic reasons. Polygyny, which is an asset in agricultural societies where women do a great deal of the productive work, becomes a liability in a urban environment where the productive process is male-oriented. But polygyny is not replaced by the missionary ideal of monogamy. The urban poor, often unable to pay the bridewealth and unable to find a spouse in a city where there are two or more men for every woman, resort to prostitutes or more or less unstable cohabitation. The rich can afford divorce and serial monogamy. Common law unions and illegitimacy, which are not the norm in Europe or in traditional Africa, have become frequent in large African urban centers, especially in the south.

With urbanization, the kinship ties and obligations which are so important in most African societies are beginning to recede to a secondary position. The extended family, however, still remains the ideal norm, and while large traditional families frequently cannot be housed together in town, living groups continue to be typically larger than nuclear families. Large family compounds are not uncommon, especially in the more traditional cities of West Africa, and kinship obligations (such as the extension of hospitality, of mutual aid, of financial help to meet educational costs, and the like) continue in force. Urban life does not generally entail the breakup of family ties, even of the extended family. In fact, studies in urban Europe and North America have shown that in the working class, in some immigrant communities, and in many upper-class circles extended family ties have been of great importance. The real situation is radically different from the expectations of some sociologists, who seem to have generalized the behavior of the highly mobile middle-class population of American suburbia to all urbanites.

Traditional kin groups, especially patrilineages, show no indication of disappearing, though the range of their social functions may sometimes become more restricted. In any case, urban Africans are not turning to a system of bilateral descent. If anything, under Western influence and urbanization matrilineal systems have tended toward patrilinearity.

Bridewealth, in spite of concerted attacks by a number of missionaries and some of their converts, is so central to indigenous marriage systems that it frequently retains its vitality as a social institution. Here too, rather than disappearing, bridewealth often undergoes changes in form and function. Thus cash is substituted for payments traditionally made in cattle. And instead of being collected from a wide circle of patrilineal kinsmen, it is earned by the groom through wage employment in town, or occasionally even by the prospective bride herself in order to hasten her marriage.

ECONOMIC CHANGE

The central economic fact about Africa is poverty. In terms of such criteria as gross national product, per capita income, percentage of the population who are wage-earners, share of world trade, labor productivity, and percentage of GNP attributable to secondary and tertiary industry, Africa is indeed grossly underdeveloped, more so than most of Latin America and Asia. This is not to say, however, that Africa is the most destitute continent of the Third World in terms of subsistence. There is probably less overpopulation and chronic food scarcity in most of Africa than in such Asian countries as India, China, and Pakistan. In large parts of central and East Africa which have not yet been converted into cash-crop economies, there is still a diversified subsistence agriculture which provides the rural population with a reasonably adequate diet. Paradoxically, the dietary situation is sometimes worse in the more developed economies of

West and southern Africa which are based on cash crops, mining, or manufacturing. For example, the vast inequalities in the distribution of wealth, the high cost of living, the tax structure, and other factors make the relative "prosperity" of the Republic of South Africa illusory for the urban African proletariat. There is probably more malnutrition in Johannesburg, Africa's richest and most developed city, than among the Pygmy hunters of the Congo rainforest.

In the "modern" sense, however, Africa clearly stands out as the most underdeveloped of the continents. In most African countries, less than one-tenth of the adult population is literate, lives in towns, or works for wages. The vast bulk of Africans are either pastoralists or subsistence peasants. In certain more developed regions, mining and cash crops have raised productivity. Such is the case for the Copperbelt of Zambia and the Katanga part of the Congo with copper mining, and for Ghana, Ivory Coast, and parts of Nigeria and Uganda with coffee, cocoa, cotton, groundnuts, and other cash crops. Especially privileged countries like Kenya have a well-diversified agriculture. The only truly developed economy with a broad industrial base in the whole of Africa is that of the Republic of South Africa. But this development has been achieved through the ruthless exploitation of black Africans, not only within the Republic but also in Rhodesia, Zambia, Mozambique, South-West Africa, Malawi, Lesotho, Botswana, and Swaziland. The last four in particular have become utterly dependent reservoirs of cheap labor for South African mines and industries.

The underdevelopment of African economies is only one of the important elements of the situation. The other is the very special and exploitative nature of such development as did take place as a result of contact with Europe. For four centuries, significant portions of Africa were literally bled of their human resources. After the slaving period was over, Africa was transformed by the European colonial powers into a source of cheap raw materials for the economies of Europe, and, secondarily, into a market for manufactured products. In a certain sense, the colonial powers did develop Africa: they opened roads and railways, introduced currencies, built cities and mines, and planted cash crops. (More precisely, they supervised the African labor which actually accomplished these tasks.) This, of course, was development in the economic sense of increasing GNP and capital formation, but it was also exploitation of the most systematic and ruthless sort.

All colonial economies, by means of taxation and land alienation, compelled the local population to work for low wages in order to produce cheap raw materials. These materials, in turn, were to be traded, on terms dictated in part by monopolistic boards and cartels, directly and solely with the mother country. The alleged "free-trade" capitalism of Europe was transformed in Africa into a protectionistic and monopolistic form of mercantilism almost entirely for the benefit of the colonial powers. Colonial economies reduced African countries to a state of helpless and unilateral dependence on the exploiting countries. All trade and all labor contracts were on terms unfavorable to Africans. The whole continent was carved up into zones of economic exploitation by individual whites or, on a much larger scale, by monopolistic trading, mining, and transport companies which received charters from their respective European governments. Subsistence farmers were often transformed into a floating mass of urban subproletarians and rural serfs.

This process of "development" was most advanced in South Africa, Algeria, Rhodesia, the Belgian Congo, and Kenya, and least advanced in countries like Chad, Niger, Somalia, Upper Volta, and Gabon, which had little in the way of exploitable resources to offer. The Congo was exceptional in that it was initially, by treaty, a "free-trade" area. As the price for recognizing King Leopold's annexation of the Congo, the other European powers in the late nineteenth century made the Congo into an open field for exploitation. A few countries like Uganda and Ghana, where cash crops were cultivated in small holdings by indigenous farmers, did benefit somewhat from this kind of development, but these are the exceptional cases.

The irony of colonial "development" is that even Europe did not really benefit from this plundering of a continent. A few individual settlers and private concerns profited enormously, of course, but the African booty had but a slight effect on the colonial powers at large. Portugal, itself an underdeveloped country, remained poor in spite of its vast empire (which turned out to be an albatross around its neck). The postwar growth of French, Dutch, and Belgian prosperity continued unabated after the liquidation of their empires. Even Britain's economic sluggishness is largely unrelated to the loss of colonies. For European governments most African colonies were liabilities rather than assets. Being poor, Africa had little to offer except a few scarce minerals and some luxury tropical foods. As a market for manufactured products Africa was, and still is, relatively insignificant. Since the 1930s Africa's share in world trade has been no more than 5 per cent; and, if anything, that percentage has tended to decline recently. Industrial nations find synthetic substitutes for tropical products such as cotton and sisal and even manage to produce food more cheaply than "developing" countries.

The great paradox of economic change in Africa during the colonial era is that, on balance, colonial development has meant widespread impoverishment of the indigenous population. This process, which in many ways still continues, has been referred to by many authors, including Dalton and Rivkin in this volume, as "growth without development." This signifies the simple expansion of investments, GNP, and per capita income without a concurrent spreading of this wealth on the emergence of a wider, efficiently integrated economic system involving and benefiting the masses of the people. One need only survey the eroded Native Reserves of South Africa, or the ramshackle shantytowns and *bidonvilles* of West and central Africa, or the mining compounds of Johannesburg, or the growing dustbowls of North Africa, or the scarred forest of the

Congo Basin and the Guinea belt to realize how much change has taken place.

The economic dilemmas of Africa appear at the moment to be almost insoluble. Many African countries lack significant mineral resources. Agricultural yields can almost always be increased, but not without enormous capital and human investment. Cash crops lead to highly unstable and precarious economies subject to world price fluctuations. Investment in secondary industries is costly and is hampered by the debility of the consumer market, by low labor productivity, and by other factors. Emancipation from expatriate control is essential for long-range, balanced growth; but growth is impossible without capital, and capital comes in large part from conservative Western countries. Modern skills are scarce, and so is money to develop them. Subsistence agriculture is becoming increasingly deficient with unchecked population growth, and in the urban areas the narrow industrial base makes for high unemployment. Fewer and fewer people can live on the land, but many displaced farmers cannot find jobs in towns. Of the main factors of production—capital, land, and labor—Africa has an abundance of labor, but unskilled labor is increasingly redundant and unproductive. In fact, African countries have to import expatriate labor at enormously high prices while the overwhelming majority of the indigenous population contributes little to the gross national product.

In short, much of Africa seems to be in a position where it cannot return to traditional subsistence economies. Irreversible processes of modernization and monetization make such a solution unthinkable. At the same time, it lacks the technical and capital resources to reach the "take-off point" of self-sustaining growth. Behind the rhetoric of African socialism hides the stark reality of continued economic dependence and stagnation.

SOCIAL STRATIFICATION

Proponents of African socialism sometimes state that traditional African societies are egalitarian and that modern African countries do not have social classes or class conflicts. They conclude that the Marxian model is therefore not appropriate to African conditions. It is certainly true that, by and large, property, especially ownership of the means of production, is not the most significant criterion of class in Africa. But to deny the existence of social classes and of class conflicts does violence to the facts. Interestingly, African socialism, the official ideology of the new African ruling classes, has often become the status quo ideology of a bureaucratic mandarinate.

Pre-colonial African ethnic societies varied greatly in the extent to which they were stratified. Some groups, especially hunters and pastoralists (for example, the Bushmen, Pygmies, Nuer, and Masai) but also some agriculturalists (for example, the Ibo), were quite democratic and egalitarian, at least so far as adult men were concerned. Many of these societies were stratified into age-classes or age-sets, but all adult men of a given age group had much the same duties and privileges. Some prestige differences existed, based on individual qualities such as bravery in war; but these societies had no marked differences between identifiable social groups in status, in life style, in wealth, or in power. Age stratification was a way of differentiating functions and obligations according to strength and experience without creating invidious distinctions between social classes.

Aside from age and sex inequalities, at least a couple of hundred traditional African groups can be described as classless in the sense that they have no inheritance of differential power, status, and wealth within well-defined social groups.

At the other end of the spectrum, however, one finds a great many highly stratified pre-colonial ethnic societies. These are usually the largest politically centralized groups. Included in this category would be most of North Africa; the great empires of the Sudan belt; the Hausa-Fulani emirates of Nigeria; the kingdoms of the Guinea belt (Ashanti, Yoruba, Bini, Dahomey); the Amharic empire of Ethiopia; the kingdoms of the Great Lakes region such as Rwanda, Burundi, Buganda, Ankole, and others; and the traditional monarchies of the Bakongo, Bakuba, Baluba, Balunda, and Barotse in the subequatorial savanna. Many of them were states based on conquest, where military expansion probably accelerated the process of stratification.

These societies were generally divided into fairly rigidly defined groups which are best described as *estates* (in the medieval European sense) rather than classes. At the bottom, there were often domestic slaves who were acquired by war or by purchase but who were typically assimilated as free men within one or two generations and who could sometimes rise to high political office. Next in the hierarchy was the mass of commoners—that is, the peasants who paid the taxes and did most of the productive work. Distinct from the peasants, though sometimes of lower status, were smaller groups of specialized artisans, such as blacksmiths, weavers, potters, leather-workers, musicians, praise-singers, and so on, who typically constituted hereditary castes or guilds similar to those of medieval Europe. Priests and scholars also had a distinct and higher status than commoners in Islamized societies. At the top was a nobility, often only partially hereditary, which was itself frequently divided into several specialized segments. One or several of the noble families constituted the royal clan within which the king was chosen according to a wide variety of methods, strict primogeniture being the exception rather than the rule.

These societies had many characteristics in common with the *anciens régimes* of medieval and Renaissance Europe. Between the two extremes of estate societies and egalitarian ones were a number of groups which were in the process of becoming more stratified but had not yet reached the level of complexity of the great kingdoms. The Swazi, Zulu, and Ndebele of southern Africa, for example, developed the notion of a royal clan and, hence, an aristocracy; but no sharply distinct life styles emerged between nobles and commoners.

Traditional status distinctions began to break down during the colonial era. The colonial powers outlawed slavery (though it frequently lingered on through the institution of clientage), they unwittingly undermined the authority of the traditional aristocracies through which they tried to rule, and they deposed sovereigns and hence frequently destroyed the legitimacy of the kingship, which was often religious as well as political.

The colonial powers did much more than disrupt traditional status systems. They also created a new one, namely, the colonial system itself—an extremely rigid hierarchy based on "race" and culture. Whites, Africans, and, in eastern and southern Africa, Asians came to constitute racial castes with distinct duties and privileges, separate juridical status, widely different living standards and styles, and either customary or legal segregation in residential areas, schools, means of transport, hospitals, hotels, and churches. The French and Portuguese were less racist than the British, Belgians, and Germans; but in practice there was little difference among colonial powers in regard to the relative status of Africans and Europeans. All colonial societies were in fact rigid caste or quasi-caste systems, considerably more stratified and ascriptive than any of the traditional systems or, for that matter, than contemporary European societies.

Within the African population, the colonial powers sowed the seeds of a new status system based largely on the acquisition of modern skills through the school system. Thus the Europeans not only undermined the old societies and imposed themselves as a new ruling class but also initiated a new process of status differentiation within the African population itself. In short, they created the embryo of the stratification systems of independent states. As many of the mission-educated children were of commoner status, the new educated elite showed little overlap with the traditional elite where such an elite existed. The new elite tended to develop antitraditional attitudes and claimed high status by virtue of such skills as literacy and formal education in French, Portuguese, or English.

The dynamics of class formation since independence, though extremely complex, are reducible to the following basic elements: an acceleration of the breakdown of traditional elites, the elimination of the racial structure imposed by the colonial regime, and a restructuring of African societies into a new system of social classes which cut across ethnic groups.

Some traditional systems were overthrown by violent revolution soon after the colonial powers withdrew. The two bloodiest examples were the anti-Watutsi revolution in Rwanda and the anti-Arab revolution in Zanzibar. In Uganda, the kabaka of Buganda was overthrown by force, and the other monarchies were abolished; in Nigeria, the sardauna of Sokoto was assassinated. In most cases, however, the displacement of traditional elites by the Western-educated elite was somewhat more gradual. Chiefs were often kept as figureheads and as ritual functionaries; they were even "kicked upstairs" into Houses of Chiefs patterned after the House of Lords, but they were generally stripped of all effective power, a process which had started under colonialism. With the recent demise of the mwami of Burundi, there are no ruling monarchs left in central Africa. The one remaining significant region in Africa where traditional aristocracies still play a leading political role is Ethiopia.

The second aspect of change in status systems, the overthrow of the colonially structured racial castes, is still far from complete. The Republic of South Africa and Rhodesia maintain a rigid color bar in every aspect of social life, but both countries are facing revolutionary change. Portugal still retains its Overseas Provinces, but it is fighting a losing guerrilla war against African freedom fighters in Guinea, Angola, and Mozambique. The nominally independent Americo-Liberian settler regime of Liberia still maintains its minority domination. Even in some countries under African majority rule the remnants of the colonial caste structure are still very strong. In Kenya, for example, the Europeans, Asians, and Africans still constitute mutually exclusive social groups with only token formal interaction at the top. The distribution of power in Kenya has been altered in favor of the Africans, but Asians and Europeans still retain strongly privileged positions in the economic and occupational spheres, and, aside from some land redistribution, the bulk of the country's wealth is as much in alien hands as during the colonial era.

Expatriate Europeans in Africa still enjoy a highly privileged economic status and are able to maintain much of their exclusive social position through economic barriers. The rigid pattern of racial segregation in public or semipublic facilities, which was typical at least of Belgian, British, and German colonialism, has been largely eliminated in the independent countries, and some African governments are attempting to gradually abolish the economic privileges of their expatriate minorities. The most serious current problems are faced by East African countries that have a sizable Asian as well as European population; the future problems of the reconstruction of Rhodesia and South Africa along non-racial lines will also be quite formidable.

What is happening to the class structure of the indigenous African population? Because of their pre-colonial and their colonial experience, African societies are very unlike those of Europe, America, or Asia in respect to their stratification systems. Certain social classes which played prominent roles elsewhere are conspicuous by their absence or insignificance in Africa, or at least in Tropical Africa.

Apart from the areas of extensive white settlement (South Africa, Algeria, Rhodesia, and Kenya), a sizable class of large landowners did not develop in Africa. Even the traditional aristocracies were not for the most part made up of landowners. The reason for this lies in the nature of African land-tenure systems. The European notions of individual freehold tenure and of land as a freely marketable and alienable commodity do not exist in most traditional

African systems. In almost all African societies land was neither bought nor sold; occupation of land conferred certain users' rights, but not ownership in the Western sense. Furthermore, claims over land were often vested in groups such as lineages, or even in an entire ethnic group through the nominal "owner-ship" of the king. Periodic land redistribution according to need sometimes took place.

Agrarian conflicts—which are typical of countries with plantation labor, debt peonage, sharecropping, and other forms of exploitation of landless peasants—have not been common. The colonial regimes generally preserved systems of communal tenure in the Native Reserves, and even in the few places where cash crops were cultivated by individual African farmers (as was the case in Uganda and Ghana) no large land estates developed. Small owners organized in marketing cooperatives remained the dominant pattern of agricultural pro-duction.

Just as modern Africa has no indigenous landed aristocracy, it also lacks a bourgeoisie, or middle class, in the Marxian sense of industrial entrepreneurs and owners of capital. During the colonial era capital ownership remained al-most exclusively in European (and, secondarily, Asian) hands. In West Africa, there has been a traditional merchant class, and petty entrepreneurship (much of it conducted by women) flourished in Nigeria, Ghana, Ivory Coast, and Senegal. Graft has made some capital accumulation possible in highly corrupt regimes such as the former Nkrumah government in Ghana. In North Africa, the indigenous mercantile bourgeoisie is relatively well established, especially in Egypt and Morocco. Elsewhere, however, indigenous entrepreneurship is largely confined to petty retail trading, and the native bourgeoisie is still em-bryonic and insignificant. In short, then, Africa lacks, to all intents and purposes, indigenous property-holding classes with a stake in the economic status quo. There is a rapidly growing ruling class, but the basis of its status and power is not economic.

Schematically, the emerging stratification system of most African countries is based on two criteria: urban versus rural residence, and formal education. At the bottom of the prestige and economic latter are the masses of rural dwell-ers—the farmers and pastoralists with only traditional skills. They still constitute 80 to 90 per cent of the population of most countries. In contrast to the rural dwellers are the urbanites, who roughly stratify themselves into a still weak but growing proletariat of mine-workers, factory operatives, and domestic servants; a smaller middle class of clerks, salesmen, artisans, small merchants, technicians, and semiprofessionals; and, at the apex, a tiny, educated ruling class consisting mostly of civil servants, army officers, and top-ranking politicians, with an ad-mixture of academics, independent professionals, and managers. How far one has gone in the elitist and alien educational system is the principal determinant of one's position. The proletariat has received little or no formal education; the middle class is typically literate, knows some French or English, and has gone at least through primary and often through some secondary or vocational school-ing; the upper crust has completed at least high school, frequently has a uni-versity degree, and has fluent command of a European language.

Naturally, this analysis could be refined. Where commercial crops are im-portant, for example in Ghana, cash-crop farmers have risen as a class above subsistence peasants, thereby complicating the rural stratification system. Finer distinctions are made within the middle class between, say, an uneducated petty tradesman and a practical nurse. The elite is by no means a monolithic, undif-ferentiated group. Nor is the elite quite the same in all countries. In one state, the ruling group may consist of relatively uncouth and corrupt political par-venus; in another, of idealistic and puritanical young army officers; in a third, of urbane intellectuals who became bureaucrats.

In the present transitional phase, professional success and elite status are still to a large extent the results of individual achievements of persons of above-average abilities who frequently are only one or at most two generations away from rural illiteracy. During the last ten or fifteen years, when this new bureau-cratic mandarinate was being educated, access to the elite was wide open to talented, ambitious, and aggressive persons who had the luck to be within reach of good mission schools. At present, there is still little relationship between family membership and modern social status, except in the coastal regions of West Africa. Wide status differences between members of the same family are still quite common. However, there are many indications that the ruling class is rapidly becoming closed and self-perpetuating through the monopoly of European language and culture and through the inheritance of privileged access to elite secondary schools and universities. Increasingly, the roster of senior civil servants in some states consists of the "old boys" from African Etons and Oxfords. This is, of course, more true of such conservative states as Senegal, Ivory Coast, or Kenya than of more radical states like Tanzania or Guinea.

In Africa, however, perhaps even more than in Europe, revolutionary and socialist ideologies and rhetoric have often gone together with the arrogance and elitism which characterize the rising class of technocratic intellectuals. Modern mandarins of the Third World have taken to quoting Castro, Mao Tse-tung, or Nkrumah instead of Confucius. Nevertheless, they are a funda-mentally conservative class, enjoying salaries of at least fifty times the per capita averages in their countries. They are, notwithstanding their rhetoric, the suc-cessor elite to the colonial administrators. And in the present state of economic stagnation of Africa they are virtually the sole beneficiaries of independence. They are isolated from the masses not only by their salaried affluence but also by their foreign education, their use of French or English as a lingua franca, their acquired Europeanized tastes, and their participation in the international jet set of diplomacy, U.N. agencies, and globetrotting experts. It does not take much acumen to see the potential internal conflicts in such a situation — conflicts which may have been responsible for many of the recent military takeovers in Africa.

This sweeping survey of social change in Africa has, of necessity, been sketchy. It is no easy task to generalize about the nearly forty independent states, a handful of dependent territories, and hundreds of traditional cultures which, except for their colonial past and contemporary underdevelopment, have little more in common than do Eskimos and Greeks. It is hoped, however, that the broad scope of the essay will serve not only to emphasize the continuity of social change in Africa by attempting to draw on the more detailed material of preceding essays in this volume, but also to introduce some of the central themes which will be elaborated in the contributions to follow. Some of the generalizations presented here may be contested by scholars who have had experience in different parts of the continent. We all become, more or less, prisoners of where we have done our field work. The note of controversy and involvement in this essay, however, is deliberate. I hope that some of my pessimistic conclusions and predictions will be invalidated. I also hope that my opinions will raise some controversy, because discussion is the salt of intellectual life.

15

Personality and Change

ROBERT A. LeVINE

THE IDEA OF AN AFRICAN PERSONALITY

Is there an African personality? Can the population of an entire continent like Africa be said to have a personality? Not with any accuracy, given the size of Africa and its ethnic and ecological diversity.[1] How is it, then, that Western and African writers alike persistently speak of "the African personality" and "the African mind"? The assumption that Africans are psychologically homogeneous is due in part to conditions surrounding the social perception of Africans by outsiders and indigenous intellectuals. One of these conditions is ignorance. African history and cultural diversity are less well documented and understood than the histories and cultures of Europe and Asia, and ignorance favors the presumption of homogeneity. One who knows Europe but not Africa would consider a "European personality" which lumped together Sicilians and Swedes, Poles and Portuguese an absurdity, but the same observer might readily accept the idea of a distinctive "African personality." Another condition is racial visibility: the distinctive skin color, hair form, and facial features of Africans are their most immediately recognizable characteristics. Homogeneity on visible attributes favors the presumption of behavioral homogeneity. The naïve observer who might be skeptical about an "Asian personality," because he has heard of India and China and knows that there are brown people in one and yellow people in the other and that they dress and live differently, would more

1. The population of Africa consists of more than a quarter of a billion persons divided along linguistic and cultural lines into at least a thousand ethnic societies spread over the second largest land mass in the world, with ways of life ranging from those of isolated pastoral nomads and hunters of the deserts to those of villagers and urbanites in the complex kingdom states of West and central Africa.

easily accept that all Africans, being "black," have a single personality. A third condition is the known history of colonialism: Africans all over the continent were subordinated to European rulers, a situation which produced a superficially common framework within which Africans may perceive themselves, and be perceived by others, as essentially similar. Thus from the popular European or American viewpoint, Africans are black colonials, from a continent south of Europe, whom one cannot distinguish from one another on any known historical, cultural, or behavioral basis; why not believe they are psychologically homogeneous?

But the concept of an African personality has persisted not simply because of ignorance and the intellectual laziness involved in judging people on the most superficial aspects of race and history but because there have been those who had a stake in perpetuating the idea. There were and are those white writers who, seeking to justify European domination in Africa or slavery and the racial caste system in the Americas, have found it convenient to posit an "African mind" or some similar concept to which they could attribute various kinds of mental inferiority. Then there are the journalists, film-makers, pornographers, and even some serious novelists who have found profit and popularity in using the undifferentiated African as a fantasy figure of uncontrolled hedonism, malevolent savagery and superstition, and orgiastic sexuality in order to provide entertainment for the bearers of a puritanical culture. This stereotype has a long history in Europe; it is probably as old as the familiar anti-Semitic stereotype, perhaps even older, but has suffered less debunking by intellectuals and so remains current even in literate segments of society.

There are also those African political leaders and writers who, in their urgent drive to construct an ideology for opposing European domination and promoting Pan-African unity, have accepted the psychological homogeneity of Africans while insisting on equality with, or superiority to, Europeans. In some cases they have even accepted the content of European stereotypes but have reversed the values from negative to positive; in other cases they generalize their own local cultural background to the whole continent or even to all blacks everywhere. At the same time, however, the term "African Personality" as popularized by Kwame Nkrumah is used by African intellectuals more in the sense of "spirit," "tradition," or "philosophy" than in reference to the mental characteristics of persons, and more as a call for a unified defense of African distinctiveness than as a statement of what actually exists. Hence "African mind" or "personality," as most frequently encountered in print, tends to be a stereotyped image designed either to derogate and dehumanize or to defend Africans, rather than an attempt at understanding them.

So pervasive is the influence of partisan stereotype on discussions of the psychology of Africans that it is perpetuated by some academic treatises which purport to be scientific or scholarly. The most notorious of these in the racist tradition is *The African Mind in Health and Disease* by J. M. Carothers, a British psychiatrist.[2] Another example is *The Personality of the Urban African in South Africa* by J. C. de Ridder, a South African psychologist.[3] This book reports biased impressions disguised as objective data; these "data" happen to confirm the popular white stereotypes of Africans as immature, violent, and undisciplined. The defensive literature has its representative in *The Mind of Africa* by W. E. Abraham, a Ghanaian professor of philosophy and Fellow of All Souls College, Oxford.[4] Although not distorted by pseudoscientific methodology like the volumes of Carothers and de Ridder, this book does little more to shed light on the subject of its title: "African culture" is vaguely characterized as "essentialist," "rationalist," and "communalist," labels apparently intended to provide a philosophical basis for a rambling and unscholarly review of African history and current problems. The works cited illustrate that in publications on this controversial topic the academic credentials of the author are no guarantee of an objectivity which reflects the expected standards of science or scholarship.

There have, however, been some systematic works on the psychology of Africans which are objective and scientific. Attempts have been made in review articles to sort the wheat from the chaff and to give emphasis to the more meritorious studies in this new and slowly developing field.[5] But any of these studies that have general significance for understanding Africans, no matter how objectively conducted and reported, are highly susceptible to misinterpretation, to being viewed as efforts to support one or another kind of stereotyped image of Africans. And they are indeed used by ideological partisans outside behavioral science circles to support their own political positions and prejudices. There is no easy way to eliminate this misinterpretation and abuse in an area where issues like racism and interethnic relations are involved, apart from a growing recognition of the scientific study of man as a legitimate and socially constructive activity. We are now beginning to see how the study of culture and personality in places like Japan, Latin America, the United States, and Scandinavia can contribute to a deeper understanding of individual adaptation and maladaptation to changing social and cultural environments; Africa has much to contribute to, and gain from, this kind of international enterprise. One benefit will be a more complex and realistic view of African populations and their similarities and differences in the psychological dimensions underlying contemporary social behavior.

2. J. M. Carothers, *The African Mind in Health and Disease* (Geneva: World Health Organization, 1953). For a review of this and other publications by Carothers, see Robert A. LeVine, "Africa," in *Psychological Anthropology: Approaches to Culture and Personality*, ed. Francis L. K. Hsu (Homewood, Ill.: Dorsey Press, 1961).

3. J. C. de Ridder, *The Personality of the Urban African in South Africa* (London: Routledge & Kegan Paul, 1961). For a review of this publication, see Robert A. LeVine, "Beclouded African Ids," *Contemporary Psychology*, VIII (1963), 147–48.

4. W. E. Abraham, *The Mind of Africa* (Chicago: University of Chicago Press, 1962).

5. See Leonard Doob, "Psychology," in *The African World: A Survey of Social Research*, ed. R. A. Lystad (New York: Praeger, 1965); and LeVine, "Africa."

In this paper I shall ask the reader to divert his attention from the possible political implications of our subject and to consider it from the stance of a neutral scientific observer. For purposes of this discussion I shall assume what I know to be untrue: that the question of psychological differences between Africans and others can be explored without inhibition and in some depth and still be received as an honest attempt at objective description reflecting no hidden desire to defame or defend.

ENVIRONMENT, PERSONALITY, AND PERSONALITY PROFILES

In psychology, the term "personality" refers to consistencies in the behavior of a human individual, consistencies that cannot be attributed to temporary states of his organism or temporary conditions in his environment but which endure over substantial periods of his life, making him to some degree predictable. Psychologists differ as to whether these consistencies are organized into a uni-fied whole for each individual or are simply numerous independent traits. They do agree, however, that in its most fundamental sense personality is charac-teristic of individuals rather than of groups or other collective entities. Per-sonality characteristics vary widely among individuals in a given population, just as do physical characteristics such as height and weight. Like height and weight, personality characteristics (as measured by standard tests) tend to show a normal bell-shaped distribution in which the majority of individuals are clustered toward the middle of the range near its average, with relatively few at both extremes. These distributions are not identical across all human populations; they differ in central tendency and in other ways. Just as the average heights of two popula-tions may differ considerably (although many individuals in one are identical to those in the other), so too may personality. Thus, though personality refers to consistencies of individuals, the individuals of a given population when statis-tically aggregated tend to show some central tendencies among themselves as well as average differences between themselves and some other populations. It is my assumption and that of most personality psychologists that these average differences are caused primarily by differences in the social and cultural en-vironments in which individuals of different populations grow up. According to this theory, if environmental conditions are similar in two populations, the distribution of personality characteristics should also be similar.

From this perspective, the question of an African personality takes us back to two prior questions: (1) Are there environmental differences among African populations of a quality and quantity to lead us to expect average differences in personality distributions? (2) How does environmental variation among African populations compare in magnitude with environmental differences between

Africa and other parts of the world? In other words, are African societies and cultures, regardless of their differences from one another, distinguishable as a group from societies and cultures elsewhere?

The available evidence indicates that African societies and cultures are as a group distinctive.[6] This is not to deny the major variations along lines of economy (hunting and gathering, pastoralism, agriculturalism, presence or absence of markets, degree of occupational specialization), kinship (patrilineal, matrilineal, nonunilineal), social and political stratification, community structure (urban, clustered village, dispersed settlement), religion, and aesthetic tradition. Some of these points of difference among African communities will be considered, as they relate to personality, later in this essay. There are, regardless, strong central tendencies of economy, social structure, and culture among African populations, and these are somewhat distinctive in a comparison of regions of the world.

The relative homogeneity and distinctiveness of African sociocultural environments have been considered elsewhere in an analysis of the cross-cultural data provided by Murdock on 565 ethnographically defined societies, of which 116 are from Africa south of the Sahara.[7] From these data it can be said that, within the economy, agriculture is overwhelmingly dominant over hunting and gathering and animal husbandry, but it is an agriculture in which male members of the community are less frequently involved than in any cultural region of the world. The association of animal husbandry with men, even where it is not a dominant subsistence activity, is strikingly evident, however, and exceeds that of other world regions. In family and kinship institutions, Africa leads the world in the incidence of polygynous societies, and the associated mother-child household is so widespread that Africa has the lowest frequency on two other household variables that are quite common in other regions (extended household and bilateral descent). Patrilineality, patrilocality, and brideprice prevail among African societies as they do almost nowhere else in the world. Indigenous slavery and hereditary succession to local office are considerably more frequent in Africa than in other regions. Although lacking figures, I would nevertheless argue that aspects of indigenous religion such as ancestor cults and witchcraft and sorcery beliefs have similar high frequencies.

6. The findings here have been confirmed independently in a world-wide sample of 863 societies by Herbert Barry ("Regional and Worldwide Variations in Culture," *Ethnology*, VII [1968], 207–17), who states, "Seven dichotomized traits pertaining to marriage and the family are shown in Table 4. Among the six regions, Africa is in the extreme position of having the highest or else the lowest incidence of five of these traits" (p. 211); he concludes, "Africa thus appears to be differentiated from the rest of the world with respect to the prevalence of certain cultural traits" (p. 215).

7. See Jack Sawyer and Robert A. LeVine, "Cultural Dimensions: A Factor Analysis of the World Ethnographic Sample," *American Anthropologist*, LXVIII (1966), 708–31. The data analyzed are found in George P. Murdock, "World Ethnographic Sample," *American Anthropologist*, LIX (1957), 664–87.

Other cultural characteristics could be added, but this sampling of facts indicates that there is substantial homogeneity in socioeconomic institutions in sub-Saharan Africa. Basic characteristics like agriculture, polygyny, and patrilocality are shared by at least four out of five societies in the Murdock sample; others, like patrilineality, brideprice, and hereditary succession to local office, are present in about three out of four societies of the sample. Together with what social anthropologists know less formally about Africa, this suggests a common context of experience for Africans growing up in diverse parts of the continent. The second implication of the data concerns the distinctiveness of these socioeconomic characteristics. None of them is uniquely African, for they are all found elsewhere as well; it is the *particular combinations* of traits that may be distinctively African. There is not simply agriculture, but agriculture in which women supply a large proportion of the labor; not just polygyny, but polygyny in which each wife and her children have a physically separate residential unit; not only patrilineality, but patrilocality as well. The traits in themselves are not uniquely African, but the *profile of traits* appears to be. In other words, it is not the customs that are distinctive but the patterns or constellations of cultural characteristics. This suggests that the common context of experience shared by so many Africans is not widely shared by populations outside of Africa, even though many of the specific customs are. Those inclined to generalization might say that there is something that could be called "the African experience" which, though allowing for many exceptions, derives from a common core of environmental patterns shaping individual development in Africa.

Do these shared and distinctive environmental patterns produce similarly shared and distinctive personality distributions among the populations of Africa? The data to answer this question do not exist and are so far from being obtained that we are limited to discussing what form they might take if we had them. Speculating from a personality-trait perspective, I would argue that there are no distinctively African personality traits, but possibly profiles of traits, like the cultural profiles discussed above, that are *more frequent in Africa than elsewhere.* In other words, even if there are one or more profiles of traits that distinguish African populations from populations elsewhere in the world, these profiles will not characterize all or even a majority of Africans, but just a larger proportion of Africans than non-Africans. In general, we can expect more variation at the level of individuals than at the level of societies. First, there are hundreds of millions of individuals and only hundreds of societies; and second, within the population of each society, there is a great deal of interindividual variation in personality that is due not.to patterns of economy, social structure, and culture but to genetic factors and idiosyncratic developmental events. Thus "the African personality" cannot be more than a matter of statistical tendency and is likely to show less uniformity across African populations than do patterns of culture.

From a different perspective, that of a conception of personality as a structure rather than a cluster of traits, a somewhat different picture would emerge. In this view, personality is a system with interdependent parts, and the focus is less on the parts in themselves than on their organization, their relations to one another, and their contributions toward the functioning of the system. Psychologists espousing this view believe that the trait approach mistakenly isolates discrete traits for measurement without reference to the overall system in which they operate, concentrating on the individual bricks in a house rather than on the design that determines their place and functions. A structural approach would therefore attempt to identify characteristic patterns in which the major aspects of personality were related to one another. In the psychoanalytic view, for example, personality is seen as comprising a drive organization, a reality organization, and an organization of moral constraints; and it is their relative strengths and degrees of development and their characteristic ways of interacting that constitute the individual's enduring patterns of reaction to events in his environment and in his physical organism. If we assume that environmental adaptation is a major goal for a functioning personality structure, and that environmental forces help create a structure that will be adaptive, then it seems likely that a population having faced common adaptive problems for many generations would tend to share structural solutions to them. Thus, environmental similarities at the level of a population or a continent would tend to produce similarities in personality structure, just as they would tend to produce similarities in profiles of personality traits.

But here is where a psychoanalytic view of personality structure diverges more radically from the trait approach, for in the former view not all parts of the functioning personality are equally affected by the environment and its pressures. The personality is thought of as having a surface, in close contact with the social and cultural environment, which consists of stabilized compromises between the individual's drives and the environmental demands (that is, the demands of reality and the moral order); these compromises make up his character structure. Those parts of personality that are deeper (that is, less accessible to consciousness and thus further from the surface at which social interaction takes place) have been less affected by environmental demands and therefore do not reflect the society and culture to the degree that the character structure does. In these terms, the question of whether there is a distinctively African personality can be answered only in terms of a particular level of personality structure: at the bottom, there are similar forces and structures in all functioning human adults, and at the top, or social surface, each individual has his own peculiar character structure that sets him off from his fellows; it is in the intermediate levels that we can observe the effects of social experience in homogenizing individual adaptations to a more or less common environment.

In these intermediate levels of personality structure, the degree to which we see population-wide or continent-wide commonalities depends to a certain extent on the level of abstraction of our concepts rather than on what is really there. It is possible, for example, to conceptualize the fear of witches in its concrete cultural context so that it is seen as specific to a single cultural group. Or it may be considered as an instance of a general category of witch-fear so that it is seen as characteristic of many African and non-African societies. Or it can be viewed in terms of projection of hostility so that it is applicable to all populations in some measure but in varying degrees and varying contexts. This arbitrariness cannot be dispelled until comparable data not only on behavior but on its functions for the individual are available on enough populations in Africa and elsewhere so that scientific agreement can develop on structural similarities and differences. Until then, characterizations of personality at the level of population, region, or continent must reflect the observer's range of experience and knowledge, the level of abstraction at which he chooses to operate, his ability to detect (accurately or mistakenly) psychological similarities in diverse contexts, and his guesses as to whether behavioral similarities represent similarities in personality structure and function.

UNIFORMITIES IN AFRICAN BEHAVIOR

Despite the skepticism of the foregoing section, I shall attempt here to describe patterns of personality in Africa in terms of those characteristics that I see as broadly shared across the continent and those that distinguish one African population from another. Description of the uniformities will be based on my personal experience and observations in East and West Africa and on my reading of the ethnographic literature; the variations among groups will include those that have been demonstrated in systematic psychological comparisons.

Several qualifications are necessary concerning my outline of widespread African personality patterns. First, it is limited in scope to the agricultural societies of sub-Saharan Africa and does not apply to primarily pastoral or hunting groups, to the modernized elites of the cities, or to North Africa and the East Horn. Second, it is limited to the more observable, social personality characteristics; it is description at the level of the social surface of personality structure rather than in the underlying dynamics. The dynamics may show through, particularly toward the end of the outlines, but I do not attempt depth interpretations. In fact, some of the tendencies dealt with are social expectations and might seem better described as properties of roles than of persons. I concede this to the point of using the term "behavior" rather than "personality," but I would contend that in order for large numbers of persons to internalize these role demands and social expectations their personality structures must already be compatible. The reader may reach his own decision on this issue. I make no effort to portray personality as a functioning system of coordinated structures because this would be even more speculative than such portraits usually are; thus my account appears to be that of trait psychology, with the door left open to future structural analyses. Finally, it must be emphasized that this is a personal account in which I have allowed myself to generalize rather freely while hoping to remain objective. The point of view is that of the Western culture shared by this writer and his intended readership, and contrasts between Western and African behavior and attitudes are explicit or implicit throughout. The discussion below is organized around seven characteristics which I believe to be widespread among the populations of sub-Saharan Africa.

Social Distance Between Persons Differing in Age and Sex

African social life involves institutionalized restrictions on social contact between age and sex groups. The arrangements of social activities in space and time tend to separate males from females and older from younger generations. Interaction between the sexes and generations tends to be highly prescribed by custom and, from a Western view, seems to be relatively formal and unspontaneous. What to a Western observer is most striking about these social-distance patterns is that they apply to interpersonal relations within the family, which we are used to thinking of as a unit of relaxed informality. Relations between husbands and wives, parents and their children (especially adult children), and junior siblings and co-wives are regulated in accordance with institutionalized restrictions, segregation patterns, and customary prescriptions. The evidence for this is vast and can be discussed in terms of avoidance, segregated activities, and formality of interaction.

The most institutionalized avoidance patterns have been documented by anthropologists. The in-law avoidances of East Africa, for example, may mean that a man and his mother-in-law must never meet or see one another or (as among the Zulu) that a young wife must carefully avoid mention of potentially sexual or aggressive topics in the presence of her senior in-laws. In western Kenya and other parts of East Africa there is generational avoidance, in which young men and those whom they call "fathers" must avoid a wider range of interpersonal situations, from physical contact to discussing sexual topics or even jointly hearing them discussed. Relations between these generations tend to be stiff and restrained, with the younger people especially inhibited in the presence of their elders. In the Western Sudan avoidance of the eldest son is especially common and takes a variety of institutionalized forms. Sometimes the eldest son must be raised apart from his father and must make efforts to avoid being seen by him; in other groups avoidance between father and eldest son becomes a social necessity only when the son reaches maturity. Among the Hausa the eldest child (of either sex) of each wife must be raised apart and must avoid social contact with both parents; the avoidance is sometimes applied to the second child as well.

These customs, and others like them, have meanings in their respective local contexts which anthropologists have taken pains to elucidate in terms of a potential for conflict that would be disruptive to the social structure if not regulated by avoidance. What is significant here, however, is that the members of these African societies are reported to experience the avoidance patterns as being concordant with their own desires and fears and that these institutionalized avoidances are but the dramatic aspects of a much more general tendency.

The tendency for persons and groups distinguished by sex and age (or generation) to avoid one another is often concealed by segregated residential and other social arrangements that provide external barriers to their contact so that little individual initiative or exertion is necessary to maintain social distance. Houses and settlements and the explicit customs concerning their use constitute structural arrangements for eating, sleeping, sexual activity, work, and recreation in which contact between the sexes and certain age groups is effectively minimized. Different age-sex categories are assigned their particular spaces for carrying out their activities, and they develop different activity schedules that limit interaction across social-distance boundaries. The most massive forms of age segregation, for example, the age-villages of the Nyakyusa (Tanzania) and the young warriors' settlements (*manyatta*) of the Masai (Kenya and Tanzania), have perhaps received the most attention; but more subtle forms of age and sex segregation are pervasive in African societies. For example, houses are often laid out to provide husbands with space where they can eat and sleep separately from their wives and children; sexual contact between husband and wife is often confined to a brief segment of the night. Married women usually have their own distinctive routines and activity spaces that tend to unite groups of them and to separate them from other adults in the domestic group and neighborhood. The following description by an Acholi (Uganda) woman of life in her home community is typical:

> At meal time all the children eat with the mother, sitting on the kitchen floor, while the father eats alone. It is common in the villages to find a group of two or three families eating together, each woman having cooked two separate dishes, one for the men and one for the women and children. If there are a large number of children, one separate dish can be served to the children only. The two or three men, heads of the different families, will sit together near a fire outside or inside a house[8]

It is impossible in this brief summary to do justice to the rich variation in arrangements of this sort described by ethnographers of Africa. Suffice it to

8. Anna Apoko, "The Feeding and Care of Children," in *East African Childhood: Three Versions*, ed. L. K. Fox (London: Oxford University Press, 1967), p. 53.

say that such arrangements share the characteristic of creating barriers to interaction between categories of persons whom Westerners feel belong together, particularly when they are members of the same family, and that Africans find this a satisfactory and desirable order of things. In fact, when men and women and young and old do participate jointly in a public event, they are likely to go and return separately and to cluster by age-sex groups at the event, thus spontaneously maintaining social distance (even between husbands and wives, parents and adult children) when the customary barriers are temporarily lowered.

Despite the limits set by avoidance and segregation customs, the sexes and generations do come into contact in African families and communities. When they do, their interaction is often highly institutionalized. There are explicitly prescribed greetings, conversational topics, role obligations, and safeguards against intrusions on privacy. Deviation from these prescribed norms is regarded as punishable if publicly revealed. To a Western observer, behavior among family members and other kinsmen appears formalized, allowing little leeway for voluntary idiosyncratic variation or what sociologists call "renegotiation of role contracts." There is a degree of social prescription and proscription in African families and other primary groups that we are accustomed to only in organizational or bureaucratic settings. Furthermore, the adherence to institutionalized norms of behavior acts as a barrier to what Westerners regard as *intimacy*, that is, the sharing of innermost thoughts and feelings, the giving and taking of emotional support, the private regression to childish means of expressing affection, the experience of temporary union (loss of ego boundaries) with another person. It seems that intimacy in this sense, and the individualized relationships that accompany it, are of less importance to Africans than other goals of interpersonal relations described below. So the relative formality of behavior, like the customs of avoidance and segregation, maintains social and emotional distance between persons.

Some Westerners would see this prescriptive aspect of interpersonal behavior as meaning that Africans are "slaves of custom," but this overlooks the fact that Africans regard their greater formality as perfectly "natural" and "normal"; they do not experience their social boundaries as uncomfortable, isolating, or destructive to their individuality. It is because they do experience these types of role demands as natural and comfortable that the maintenance of social distance in African societies must be regarded as a *psychological* characteristic of the participating populations as well as a *structural* characteristic of their social systems.

Age and Sex Hierarchy

Turning to the content of prescribed interpersonal behavior among Africans differentiated by age and sex, no aspect is more in evidence than the giving and receiving of deference, respect, and precedence. Variations in rank, status, and power at every level tend to be given public emphasis, and each society has its distinctive hierarchy of social positions. Taken as a whole, African status hierarchies vary widely in differentiation, depth, distribution of decision-making functions, and in ritual elaboration. But for all of these societies, in most aspects of social life men are ranked higher than women, married persons are ranked higher than those who are socially immature, and men with adult children are ranked higher than their juniors. A great deal of social interaction is accounted for by the deference and respect paid to men by women, to adults by children, and to elders by youths. The display of deference does not always signify the dominance of one person over another—indeed, sometimes the person deferring is quite autonomous—but it is nonetheless regarded as an indispensable feature of proper behavior. Deference is expressed in such forms as respectful terms of address, appropriate greetings and blessings, submissive gestures like bowing or prostration, and receiving a gift with two hands instead of one. The elaborate deference displayed daily in an ordinary Yoruba (Nigeria) compound might find its nearest Western counterpart in a European royal court. While the Yoruba are extreme among Africans in the flamboyance of the gestures used, they are not extreme in other aspects of their deference. Respect entails not only deferential behavior but also various kinds of restraint and avoidance. Perhaps the most widespread form of restraint is refraining from disagreeing with a status-superior to his face. Thus one rarely sees open arguments across the most important age and sex boundaries, and when they occur they are regarded as serious if not downright scandalous.

It is in the distribution of leisure and other conspicuous advantages that the African age-sex hierarchies contrast most sharply with Western values. This can be seen clearly in a contemporary African home that has Western-type chairs but not enough to go around. An honored guest is always given precedence in seating, but immediately thereafter come the senior men of the house or neighborhood. Women and children are regarded as marginal to a gathering of men and would yield a place of honor to someone higher in the age-sex hierarchy. A similar situation obtains for the distribution of meat, which is a rare delicacy for most Africans. The senior men are served first, women are allowed to have what is left over, and children may receive none. The frequent exclusion of children from meat-eating occurs even among relatively affluent urban families, and in western Nigeria we found that one of the most typical childhood memories of punishment reported by adolescent pupils was being beaten for sneaking meat out of the cooking pot. From the other side of the continent comes this recollection by a man from the Idakho area of the Luhya people (Kenya):

> I once helped myself to *shihango*, the roasted meat that is kept for emergency cases, without the permission of my mother. When she came home and discovered that the hidden treasure had been removed and eaten, she did not wait to report

me to my father. She gave me a thorough beating then and there, threatening to
cut off my hands, these being the limbs I had used for stealing![9]

The basic principle is that in any public or semipublic situation those of higher
rank must be served or relieved of burdens by those lower in the hierarchy, and
the former must be granted precedence in the use or consumption of any valued
good. Thus wives must carry heavy loads for the husband while he walks unencumbered, and children are constantly sent to fetch and carry and convey messages around the home and community. The same principle holds among senior
and junior siblings and co-wives and other kin, and has been applied to bureaucratic relationships such as those between schoolteacher and pupil and high- and
low-ranking civil servant. Thus the allocation of work, especially menial, burdensome, or servile tasks, reflects the distribution of status: the higher one's status,
the less work visibly performed and the greater the tendency to delegate tasks to
inferiors. Giving orders and discussing whether or not they have been carried
out, like deference and respect behavior, account for much of the content of
social interactions between unequal persons in African societies.

Emphasis on Material Transaction in Interpersonal Relations

In considering the content of socially prescribed interpersonal behavior we
have seen that much of African behavior is hierarchically ordered, and that this
order involves the giving and receiving of deference, respect, commands, and
tribute between persons occupying unequal social positions. There is another
dimension of content, however, that Africans emphasize when describing
relationships of equality or inequality, namely, obligations to give material
goods—food, gifts, financial help, property, and babies. Relationships are
frequently characterized by Africans primarily in terms of the type of material
transaction involved: who gives what to whom and under what conditions. Even
premarital sexual liaisons and courtship are discussed in these terms.

In contrast with the Western attitude (genuine or hypocritical) that the emotional component in interpersonal relations is more important than any transfer
of material goods involved (the latter being thought of as something incidental),
Africans are frankly and directly concerned with the material transfer itself as
indicative of the quality of the relationship. This is best illustrated with respect to
food and feeding. Volumes could be written on the social and cultural meanings
of food and feeding in African societies. Family relationships are often described in terms of feeding or providing food. Visitors are accepted, honored,
or rejected in terms of the food and drink provided for them, and they in turn
show their friendliness and trust by accepting food and drink. Husbands reject
their wives and neighbors and express suspicious hostility by refusing food when
offered, behavior which invariably creates alarm and tension. The sharing of

9. Joseph Lijembe, "Moral Training," in Fox, *East African Childhood*, p. 17.

food at an ordinary meal or at a sacrifice to the spirits creates important bonds between persons. As Audrey Richards pointed out many years ago, African chiefs feed their followers in times of famine, thus serving as a reserve food supply for the group, and local political leaders build their following through providing food for them.[10]

Beyond the realistic realm, food and feeding are prominent features of belief and imagination. When interpersonal suspicion mounts within the family or neighborhood, people fear that their enemies will poison their food. Ancestor spirits are often viewed as hungry or greedy, wanting to be fed through sacrifice. In many domains of behavior that do not involve actual feeding (for example, economics, sexuality, political succession) linguistic idioms, metaphors, and imagery derived from eating are widely used. It sometimes seems to an outside observer that the processes of eating and being fed are central to the symbolic interpretation of social reality in African populations.

Food is just one (although a basic) example of the concern for material transfer in interpersonal relations. Among kinsmen, land, cattle, and (increasingly) money are importantly involved, and in more transient relationships small gifts play a significant role. Something of the flavor of the material emphasis that can affect brother-sister relations is conveyed by the Acholi woman quoted above:

> If a boy sees his sister misbehaving in any way, he is authorized by his parents to give her a good beating. The sisters are very important to the brothers, whose future can largely depend on them. A brother whose sister has good manners and is married is sure to have a wife himself. The money paid to his father as his sister's brideprice is the money he will use for his own marriage. Since he cannot marry until his sister is married, it is his real concern to see that she is well-behaved enough to be married early.[11]

In considering the part these material goods play in African social life, several points should be emphasized: (1) A certain amount of material giving is obligatory in a relationship, particularly in a kin relationship, and is not dependent on how the individual feels about, or even how well he knows, the other person. (2) Persons are evaluated partly in terms of how much and how freely they give to others; those who give more than the obligatory minimum may be better liked as generous persons or may become special friends or leaders of others. (3) Failure to meet the material obligations of role relationships cannot be compensated by a friendly attitude or emotional warmth and support; since the relationships are conceptualized in terms of material transactions, attitudes and feelings are concomitants but not substitutes. (4) Relationships that have goals of obtaining valued resources generate competition, particularly when the resources are limited, the scope of obligations wide, and the rules for allocating resources somewhat ambiguous. Potential recipients or heirs are naturally competitive with

10. *Hunger and Work in a Savage Tribe* (London: G. Routledge & Sons, 1932).
11. Apoko, "Feeding and Care of Children," p. 67.

one another, and Africans grow up in an interpersonal climate in which such competition is ubiquitous, although held in check by a variety of social controls. In novel institutional settings Africans are sensitive to the material rewards offered and are ready not only to demand their promised share but also to compete with one another for preferment. Thus the obligatory giving and taking of resources as a major theme in social interaction has as its concomitant the non-obligatory, but inevitable, competitive striving for resources.

In the husband-wife relationship, babies are thought of as material goals for both spouses: a husband "gives his wife children" and she bears children "for him." It would be hard to exaggerate the personal importance of fertility to individuals of both sexes or the fear they have of being sterile. Giving and bearing children are absolutely obligatory no matter what the emotional quality of the husband-wife relationship. Children are often thought of as being like wealth, although non-economic. If the wife is barren, the husband takes another wife, and the first woman may eventually run away to try her luck with someone else. If the husband proves sterile or neglects her sexually, the wife most frequently leaves him for another man, although sometimes, if he allows her to be impregnated secretly, she may stay. Africans generally like to have as many children as possible, so long as there is enough time between births to allow each child to thrive. Continued childbearing to menopause is regarded as a *sine qua non* of the marriage, and no amount of conjugal love and understanding can make up for its absence. Occasionally, a couple will stay together without children, but their attachment, however strong, is subjected to the constant stress of personal frustration and anxiety about not having children, and they lose the esteem of others. After the wife who has borne children reaches menopause the spouses may have little to do with each other, as she is preoccupied with her grown and growing children, he with his younger wives. Finally, if co-wives differ in their fertility, competition quickly turns into jealousy and suspicion; there is no resource more valued among women than children.

Functional Diffuseness of Authority Relations

Sociologists have described traditional societies as having "functionally diffuse" role relationships. By this they mean that whereas in a specialized and bureaucratic society like ours social behavior between persons becomes limited to the specific function that brings them together (buyer-seller, employer-employee), in the traditional societies relationships are less narrowly defined by a single functional context. We have legislators, judges, and administrators in our government, but Africans have chiefs whose roles often include all three functions and are not even limited to "government" in our narrow sense of the term. This functional diffuseness may indeed be common to a wide variety of societies, but I want to call attention here to its characteristically African forms and the expectations that Africans bring to authority relationships. (I do not use the word "traditional," because it seems to me that diffuse authority is at least as common in introduced as in indigenous institutional settings in Africa.)

In Africa, when someone is in a position of authority there are characteristic demands and expectations he makes of others and has made upon him. He expects that his followers will obey his commands, not only concerning the function that may have originally brought them together but for any other purpose he deems significant. They must, for example, help maintain and enhance his social status by providing him with the conspicuous leisure appropriate to someone of high rank. In other words, they must perform menial tasks for him and serve him so that he can appear unencumbered in public and can offer a degree of hospitality that is beyond his private means. The school can serve as a striking example here, although parallel illustrations could be drawn from other institutional spheres. In schools all over English-speaking Africa, primary and secondary school pupils are pressed into service by the teachers as domestic servants in their houses and seasonal laborers in their fields and gardens. This may strike a Westerner as exploitation, but African parents do not complain except when the practice extends to using the female students sexually; then there is a public outcry and the teacher is dismissed. African parents who have had little schooling themselves often send their children to an educated kinsman, usually a schoolteacher, knowing that the boy or girl will be used as a house servant or in any other way the teacher wants, but with the hope that the teacher will help the child with his schooling.

The situation in the schools is an extreme one because children are in no position to press their own demands upon the teacher, but when adults are the subordinates their willingness to serve in menial capacities is based on great hopes and expectations which they make known to those they follow. From the Western observer's point of view, the very willingness to become a lackey to a leader and do his bidding might seem demeaning to an adult man, but Africans do not see it that way. When a young African becomes the employee, assistant, supervisee, political or religious supporter, or even student (in higher education) of someone in a relatively high position, he often does so with hopes and expectations that are of great personal significance to him. First, he tends to exaggerate the power, wealth, and skill of his leader, in extreme cases believing him to have boundless power including magical means of escaping death. Second, he tends to have conscious fantasies that this great leader will use his power to raise his devoted follower from obscurity and make him into a great man too. He may actually propose this to the leader, while asking for help to support his self-improvement efforts in education or business. Third, and more realistically, he expects the leader to be generous with food and drink when his followers spontaneously visit and to give them financial aid to meet urgent family obligations and pay debts. Every African of relatively great wealth is besieged by potential

devoted followers seeking financial assistance and hospitality; a man with political aspirations must satisfy as many as he possibly can, straining his resources to
the utmost. Finally, the subordinate will go to his leader for advice, guidance,
and the use of influence, prevailing upon the leader to settle family quarrels,
provide contacts and letters of recommendation, and give counsel on a variety
of personal matters. In the hope that his relationship with someone of eminence
will eventually lead him to prosperity and even greatness, the young man is eager
to prove himself the dedicated servant, obediently carrying out his master's commands even when they involve menial and burdensome tasks. In his personal
contacts with the leader he will temporarily fall into an attitude of exaggerated
respect and admiration, naïve hopefulness, and dependence upon the leader
for advice, support, and protection. Hence the leader's diffuse and apparently
limitless control over the labor of his subordinates has as its counterpart their
diffuse and grandiose expectations of him as their patron. Rarely can he gratify
their most ambitious expectations, but he can keep their hope alive through
generosity and hospitality; if he did not do so, his followers might disappear in
search of a more rewarding patron.

The Tendency to Blame and Fear Others When under Stress

Despite the placid and cheerful surface of interpersonal relations in most
African communities, there are strong disruptive forces that must be held in
check and socially regulated to maintain an orderly existence. These disruptive
forces have their visible starting points in the personal disasters and interpersonal friction of African life or, more correctly, in the typical reactions of
Africans to such difficulties. When disaster befalls an African family (for example,
the death of its patriarch, sterility, insanity, a series of infant deaths, a crop
failure) the most common reaction of the persons involved is to see it as resulting from the malevolent design of an enemy, often someone who is a competitor
in a struggle for inherited property, job advancement, or educational achievement. Having decided that the misfortune is caused by someone else, through
poisoning or a variety of magical practices, the afflicted family takes steps to
protect itself from the enemy's continued malevolence and possibly to strike back
through public or private means.

From a psychological point of view, there are two particularly notable characteristics of this reaction to personal difficulty or disaster: (1) the suspension of
empirical criteria for interpreting natural events in favor of the attribution to
unseen forces acting at a distance, and (2) the choice of other humans in the
immediate interpersonal environment as the causal agents rather than the self
(as in a guilt reaction), malevolent gods or spirits (which do exist in some African
belief systems but are less frequently blamed), or impersonal natural or cosmological forces. However one interprets this pattern psychologically, these distinctive features must be accounted for. Rather than attempt such an analysis

here, I want to point out the implications of this stress reaction for social relationships as we have discussed them so far.

The emphasis on material transactions in social relations has been described, and the competition generated by it has been mentioned. There are many primary group relationships in African societies that engender competition for scarce resources: co-wives competing for the favor of their husband and the property he can allocate to them and their children, brothers and cousins struggling for the patrimonial inheritance (especially land), neighbors quarreling over boundaries and damage to crops caused by one another's children or animals, peers in a variety of bureaucratic settings striving to become the favorite of their superiors. Intense feelings of jealousy and hatred accompany these forms of competition. It is the task of those in authority to settle competitive disputes in a legitimate way that is recognized as just, so that the jealously and hatred do not give rise to violence and conspiracy. To this end Africans spend a vast amount of time in mediation, adjudication, and litigation, not only in the courts but in judicial proceedings organized within extended families, lineages, compounds, and villages. However, personal grudges do not necessarily end when the case is publicly settled, even when disputants accept the impartial judgment of the elders or the court. The stress of a sudden misfortune induces a regression from that mature acceptance to the deep-seated motives aroused by the competitive situation in the first place. When this regression takes place the individual feels personally threatened by the hostility he attributes to his competitor. One sees this at funerals and public trials where suspicions of witchcraft and sorcery are publicly voiced in the emotional atmosphere of the occasion.

The beliefs concerning witchcraft and sorcery so prevalent in African societies offer the threatened individual a definitive interpretation of his stressful situation that is compatible with his own personal motives. And these beliefs offer as well the feeling that there is something he can do about it—through a public witch trial, retaliatory sorcery, or emigration and subsequent avoidance of the designated enemy. In the past these recourses to action appear to have functioned to keep interpersonal hostility within well-defined bounds, but in contemporary Africa witchcraft and sorcery are increasingly associated with disruptions of community life. What I want to emphasize here is that the personal reaction to stress involved in utilization of the witchcraft-sorcery complex is one that is widely characteristic of African populations, is generated in the context of interpersonal competition for resources, is precipitated by serious or sudden misfortune, and takes both normal and pathological forms. Only the normal form has been described. In its pathological varieties, common to many parts of Africa, the reaction involves delusions of persecution (sometimes accompanied by hallucinations) and violence directed at persons in the immediate environment, sometimes with homicidal result. Although this is clearly a psychotic reaction, not to be confused with the typical reaction to stress described above, it shares with the latter the tendency to attribute malevolence to other persons and to move from fear to retaliation.

The Relative Absence of Separation Anxiety and Related Affects

We now turn from patterns of interpersonal behavior to affects, or emotional states, which are difficult to compare across cultures — especially with objectivity — but which cannot be omitted from an attempt to assess patterns of personality. There are many possible contrasts in affects and their customary expression between Africans and Westerners, but I shall discuss one that I believe to be central for an understanding of social relationships. The Western desire for intimacy in social relationships, and its relative absence among Africans, has already been mentioned. Another aspect concerns separation and the anxiety that Westerners have about leaving or losing loved persons in their environment. We are accustomed to making strenuous efforts to avoid separation from our most intimate loved ones, often engaging in tearful departures and reunions and making the assumption that separation in physical residence, as when a child leaves home, has a final quality about it like a death and must be similarly mourned until the original emotional investment is irrevocably withdrawn or attenuated. These tendencies are widespread in Western populations and are exalted in a variety of cultural forms ranging from sentimental literature and films to humanitarian ideologies with their concern about those who are rejected and abandoned.

Some of these cultural forms and practices involve such an exaggerated image of unconditional and everlasting love that they draw attention to their primary function for the individual — the complete denial of hostility within the self and the transformation of the hostility that is surely there into an excessive concern about the well-being of others. It is in the affect of pity that the unconscious hostility shows through most clearly; in fact "pity" has become a bad word in our culture because of this, but pity as an affect remains. Pathological separation anxiety, as Anna Freud describes it for children with school phobias, for example, is due to the child's need to be constantly reassured that his unconscious hostile wishes did not magically kill his mother; the same mechanism operates for neurotic mothers who get up innumerable times during the night to see if their children are all right. Much of our normal and culturally valued affectionate concern for others, particularly the most exaggerated sentimentality in our cultures, is reinforced by this tendency to convert hostility into its opposite. A related phenomenon is seen in relationships of a sadomasochistic nature in which two persons are bound together, so to speak, by the suffering that one inflicts on the other; both seem to need the emotional transaction, cannot give it up, and have come to think of the hostility as a necessary component of their love. Separation anxiety, sentimentality, pity, and sadomasochistic attachments are all ways which our culture, with its idealized concept of love, has of managing the unacceptable hostility necessarily involved in intimate relationships.

Many of these patterns of behavior seem to be absent among Africans. They appear to find physical separation from loved ones emotionally less upsetting, and they do not regard it as being final. Sentimental attachments and their residues in longing, weeping, and nostalgia are not conspicuous in African communities, and the more sentimental outpourings of the Western mass media have little appeal there. The reactions of Africans to the pet-keeping practices of Britons and Americans living in Africa is usually one of astonishment and amusement at the personalized concern and affection for animals. In caring for infants, the aged, and seriously disabled persons, there is a noticeable absence of the anxious concern and pity characteristic of Westerners, and none of the thinly veiled disgust that sometimes accompanies pity. Africans are not immediately drawn into an attentive and solicitously caretaking attitude by the sight of a weak, enfeebled, or helpless person or creature. Their casualness, relative to our attitude, often causes puzzlement and irritation in Westerners, who see this as an incomprehensible lack of humanitarianism.

In public, African mothers rarely lavish on their infants the kind of verbal and physical affection that we think of as "instinctively maternal" behavior; and they are capable not only of carrying on conversations or tasks like trading while nursing their infants but also of inflicting necessary pain on them (in force-feeding and bathing) without hesitation and without concern over their crying. Mary Ainsworth made an intensive observational study of mother-infant interaction among the Ganda of Uganda. She states:

> In our American households the parents, loving relatives, and interested visitors alike bend over the baby as he lies in his crib, presenting him a smiling face, and waggle their heads and talk to the baby in an effort to coax a smile. This kind of face-to-face confrontation was not observed to occur in this Ganda sample. Indeed it was rare for an adult even to hold a baby so that there could be a face-to-face confrontation.[12]

She also notes that "No Ganda infant was observed to hug, kiss, or embrace."[13]

Finally, Africans do not bring to social relationships the need to torment or be tormented that we see in sadomasochistic attachments in our society, and their interpersonal life seems unusually free of these profoundly ambivalent motives. In this connection it might be mentioned that deliberate mortification of the flesh, as in the specialized asceticism of the West and India, is virtually absent in sub-Saharan Africa. Africans usually cannot understand what moral virtue there can be in extreme forms of self-denial and self-punishment.

To explain these differences in affective reactions and relationships between Africans and Westerners would take a great deal of psychological investigation; indeed, even testing the validity of my assertions about manifest behavior would be a big project. But we can try to understand them in relation to earlier observations on patterns of interpersonal behavior. For example, the social distance and

12. *Infancy in Uganda: Infant Care and the Growth of Love* (Baltimore: Johns Hopkins Press, 1967), p. 334.
13. *Ibid.*, p. 332.

formality of primary group relationships helps us understand the relative absence of separation anxiety. Since the relationships are not as intimate as their
Western counterparts in the first place, it is not surprising that they are more
easily given up temporarily, and the greater social distance of daily interaction
makes the loss of contact in actual separations seem less discontinuous, less
final, more tolerable. Furthermore, the material obligations that are emphasized
in role relationships can be fulfilled at a distance, with only occasional reunions,
in a way that is difficult (even in intensive correspondence) if intimate emotional
transactions are the goals. In other words, Africans can more easily keep up
their primary social relationships at a distance than can Westerners, a point to
which we shall return in the concluding section. At this juncture I want to stress
that less separation anxiety must be understood in terms of the goals and means
of interaction among Africans, which differ from those of Westerners.

As for pity, sentimentality, and sadomasochism, we must consider the way
Africans handle their hostility. Social anthropologists have found that Africans
all over the continent have a keen awareness of the hostility generated in social
life and especially in its jealous competition. Unlike Westerners, they do not
deny—at least to themselves—the potential for hatred in even the closest of
relationships, given failure to meet material obligations or the development
of irresolvable competitive dispute. In fact, a number of African belief systems
contain the idea that unexpressed grudges cause disease and social disruption
and that it is healthier to release the hostility than keep it pent up (which does
not mean that the advice is always followed, but it does indicate public recognition of the problem). Without the need to deny and repress hostility toward
others, there is no need to transform it into anxious and excessive concern for
their welfare, as we do in pity and sentimentality, or into the pretense that
hostility is love, as in sadomasochistic attachments. Altogether, it would seem that
for Africans the control of hostility tends to be managed through the institutional structure of their society, whereas for Westerners it is more frequently
(though of course not entirely) managed through the structure of their personalities and particularly through the regulation of consciousness about hostile
impulses in the self.

This is a rather glib formulation, but to go beyond it would take us too far
from the main course of this brief outline. It must suffice to note here that a
more adequate formulation would have to deal with the representation of self
for African individuals, the perceptual boundaries between self and environment, and the mechanisms of social and personal control.

Concreteness of Thought

A variety of pieces of evidence suggests that as a whole Africans in their indigenous cultures are more inclined to think and conceptualize in concrete than
in abstract terms. This does not imply that complex thought processes are not

involved, but rather that concrete objects and actions are used to communicate metaphorically. Anyone who has asked an African elder to explain a difficult proverb has encountered this rich metaphorical wisdom in its full concreteness. Generalities have been captured, but are not discussed in general terms. The foreign inquirer unfamiliar with the concrete local context of behavior is likely to have a difficult time understanding the explanation of a proverb. Likewise, unschooled Africans, particularly children and youths who have not acquired a reservoir of generalizable experience on which to draw, often have a hard time understanding disembodied abstractions and switching over to thinking in abstract terms for solving abstract problems.

The tendency to think in concrete terms is at the root of two characteristics previously discussed. First, the tendency to define relationships in terms of material expectations and material obligations involves primary attention to the objects given and taken and the actions of giving and taking rather than to dispositional qualities of the persons and their mental traits; second, there is little interest in the idiosyncratic patterns of thought and feeling characteristic of oneself and others, patterns for which one needs abstract verbal labels before one can even notice them. In other words, the emphasis on material transactions and the avoidance of introspection in social relationships constitute a reflection, in the domain of interpersonal cognition, of the more general inclination toward concreteness of thought.

The tendency to blame and fear others under stress is another reflection of this general mode of thinking in the sense that it concretizes the causes of misfortune as familiar humans in the immediate environment. Africans are rarely satisfied with believing that disease, death, and disaster strike randomly in a community or are the result of forces beyond human understanding; they do not accept that degree of ambiguity. Instead they insist that agents of disaster be identified with certainty as particular neighbors or kinsmen. Frequently, the neighbor or kinsman turns out to be a competitor in a dispute over material resources of obligatory transactions, another concrete element involved.

VARIATIONS IN AFRICAN BEHAVIOR

Having allowed myself to generalize in these seven points about characteristics I see as common to most Africans, I would emphasize again that Africa's populations are not psychologically homogeneous. My characterization is limited to the agricultural majority of sub-Saharan Africa, exempting the pastoral populations and the modernized urban elite. These groups, however, are significant minorities, and they do manifest personality differences from the others. The psychological differences of the elite, who derive mainly from the agricultural populations, seem to be due largely to the influence of education, which has powerful effects on cognitive development and values.[14] Also, overseas experience and the adoption of a Western middle-class life style have significant effects on the way their children are raised.[15] This group is of course increasing in number, and it plays a leading role in African national societies.

As for the pastoralists, the recent evidence of Edgerton indicates that they too are psychologically different from the agricultural majority.[16] Edgerton's study is important because it includes, in a total sample of more than five hundred persons, members of both agricultural and pastoral segments of four East African ethnic groups (Pokot, Kamba, Hehe, Sebei); therefore the effects of cultural background can be distinguished from those of subsistence economy. Psychological test data available so far indicate that the pastoralists express their hostility more directly than the agriculturalists, are less preoccupied with witchcraft and sorcery, and place a higher value on personal independence. Pending further evidence, it seems reasonable to forecast that the African pastoralists will exhibit a personality profile distinct from that of the settled agricultural populations and related to the particular environmental conditions for individual development created by their distinctive way of life.

The agricultural societies of Africa, similar though they be in many respects, also offer a range of environmental conditions for individual development and can be expected to show a corresponding range of central tendencies in personality distributions. There is some evidence for this type of variation, although relatively little relevant research has been done to date. I have experienced some sharp differences between the two agricultural groups I have worked with: the Gusii of Kenya and the Yoruba of Nigeria. There are many social and cultural differences between the two, but none perhaps as overwhelming as the density of their settlements. The Gusii family lives on its own piece of land, separated from other families and with no community clustering; the Yoruba live in large towns and compact villages. I found urban Yoruba children and adults much more gregarious than Gusii children and adults, and theirs was a deep-seated sociability that expressed itself in many domains of their lives. Perhaps most dramatically, two- and three-year-old Gusii children tended to run away crying when I approached the first time, whereas their Yoruba counterparts, who had no more experience with white foreigners, would cheerfully run up to greet me. I find it hard to believe that this behavioral difference is unrelated to the residential conditions of life in the two groups. In a more sys-

14. See Doob, "Psychology."
15. See Robert A. LeVine, Nancy H. Klein, and Constance R. Owen, "Father-Child Relationships and Changing Life-Styles in Ibadan, Nigeria," in *The City in Modern Africa,* ed. Horace Miner (New York: Praeger, 1967).
16. R. B. Edgerton, "'Cultural' vs. 'Ecological' Factors in the Expression of Values, Attitudes, and Personality Characteristics," *American Anthropologist,* LXVII (1965), 442–47. See also R. B. Edgerton, "An Ecological View of Witchcraft in Four East African Societies" (Paper presented at the Eighth Annual Meeting of the African Studies Association, Philadelphia, October 28, 1965).

tematic comparison of three agricultural societies of Nigeria, the Ibo, Hausa, and Yoruba, I predicted differences in personality distributions on the basis of variations in the pre-colonial status mobility systems.[17] The predicted differences in achievement motivation and obedience and in social compliance values were found in samples of secondary-school students, but it was not possible to conclude with certainty that the pre-colonial status systems caused the psychological differences. We need more studies on this subject, but at the moment I would venture the prediction that strong differences in personality traits like gregariousness or sociability, achievement motivation, authoritarianism, and mistrust of other people will be found among African agricultural societies and that they will correlate with differences in size and density of settlements, social mobility patterns, the democratic or authoritarian nature of decision-making, and other aspects of social structure.

ADAPTATION TO SOCIAL CHANGE

One could relate the foregoing discussion of uniformities and variations in African personality patterns to many aspects of change in Africa, but I shall limit myself to illustrating how a few of the uniformities might be affecting personal response and adjustment to institutional change.

Personal Adjustment to Mobility

As discussed above, the formality of primary-group relationships and the relative absence of separation anxiety make physical separation of husband and wives, parents and children, less painful and disruptive to the individual than in our culture, and the emphasis on material obligation makes it possible to maintain role relationships during prolonged absences. For example, so long as the husband provides his wife with a place to live (a home), a social group to live with (his family), a livelihood (a piece of land or some capital for trading), and a pregnancy every two and a half years, his prolonged absence for economic or educational reasons is regarded as quite tolerable. This kind of relationship has allowed individuals to respond to economic incentives by moving themselves—in labor migration, for overseas education and vocational training, and when transferred to a better job—with a minimum of personal disruption.

African families do not have to be residentially intact in order to remain socially and psychologically real for their members, nor do the obligations of marriage and kinship diminish with prolonged absence. This was demonstrated

17. Robert A. LeVine, with the assistance of Eugene Strangman and Leonard Unterberger, *Dreams and Deeds: Achievement Motivation in Nigeria* (Chicago: University of Chicago Press, 1966).

by Evans-Pritchard in his description of forms of marriage among the Nuer of the southern Sudan.[18] It is true throughout much of contemporary Africa and provides an elasticity in relationships that is highly adaptive under modern economic conditions. Since there is never any pretense that the obligations of kinship are based on emotional intimacy or residential proximity, kinship groups are able not only to remain intact even when their members are dispersed but also to play a central role in the redistribution of economic resources. No matter how far away an individual has moved from his natal home he is obliged to provide regular aid to his wives, children, and aging parents; to contribute, when asked, to the school fees and other important expenses of a number of more distant relatives; and to provide hospitality for an indefinite period for kinsmen who come to visit him or who have migrated to his place. A mature man will also be called upon to return home occasionally for meetings at which major group decisions regarding internal disputes and collective property are reached. In rural homes and in the cities, the unemployed, the disabled, and the elderly are taken in by their kinsmen, whether or not they are well acquainted. These unfortunates may not have a great deal of attention paid to them, but, in societies that have few public welfare facilities, they *are* cared for.

Thus the social distance, formality, and material obligation of African relationships operate at present to help preserve indigenous kinship organization in the face of increased mobility, to redistribute income from participants in the modern economy to their less fortunate kinsmen, and to provide care for the needy. None of these goals could be achieved if Africans made their obligations as contingent on intimacy and proximity as we do or allowed them to atrophy in prolonged separation.

The short-run adaptiveness of these behavioral patterns at the group or societal level is unquestionable, but what of the individuals involved? The advantages to them are obvious. They can count on their kinsmen for care, protection, and emergency relief even in a strange city and even when they have had no prior contact or acquaintance with the available kinsman. As the kin disperse, the spatial range of one's potential relations expands. Africans do take advantage of this potentiality, and it eases their adjustment in urban areas and in new settlements at home and abroad. The dangers of maladjustment and breakdown in personality functioning increase greatly when African individuals move outside the network of kin and ethnic affiliations where care and protection cannot be guaranteed. Such has been the case of some students in America.[19] But there are disadvantages, too, which are experienced primarily by the wealthier and more

18. E. E. Evans-Pritchard, *Kinship and Marriage among the Nuer* (London: Oxford University Press, 1953).

19. Warner Muensterberger and Ira A. Kishner, "Hazards of Culture Clash: A Report on the History and Dynamics of a Psychotic Episode in a West African Exchange Student," in *The Psychoanalytic Study of Society*, IV, ed. Warner Muensterberger and Sidney Axelrad (New York: International Universities Press, 1967), 99–123.

successful Africans who find themselves on the giving rather than the receiving end in the network of kinship obligations. They are constantly called upon to help close and distant relatives, including many they barely know. Those wealthy Africans who are comparatively unschooled and have not lived abroad take their position as donors for granted and even exploit it for political ends, but those who have become Westernized in their conception of social roles tend to resent not only the immense drain on their resources but also the intrusions on their privacy and the limitless demands on their hospitality. These latter individuals sometimes see themselves as victims of an outdated system that coerces their participation and makes it more difficult for them to provide as adequately for their own children and immediate families as can their individualistic Western counterparts.

Response to Economic Incentives

The indigenous emphasis on material transaction in role relations, and the competition stemming from it, provided a psychosocial basis for African response to novel economic incentives introduced from the West. Although early colonial officials found it necessary to establish a compulsory tax to pull Africans into the labor market, such artificial devices have not been necessary in most areas for many years. Since Africans have seen the material advantages resulting from employment and the education which fits one for employment, they have been actively seeking jobs, clamoring for schools, and making sacrifices to obtain higher education. Some of the strength of this response, as compared with "traditional" peoples in other parts of the world, is competitive; men want to do better than one another, and each wants his own children to do better than the others. This competition is sometimes fraught with jealousy, suspicion, and hostile intrigues, but it has promoted among Africans a receptivity to innovations that have a demonstrable economic advantage, and a high degree of readiness to participate in new economic institutions. In my opinion, this deep-seated competitiveness as an aspect of individual personality has some roots in the polygynous family, where the intense striving of the co-wives for equivalent or preferential treatment of themselves and their children provides an early model of jealous competition.

Personal Adjustment to Intergenerational Differences in Acculturation

Another adaptive outcome of the pattern of interpersonal relations described above is the remarkable absence of serious conflicts between conservative and modernizing segments of families and small communities. Americans accustomed to the clash of generations in immigrant families and anthropologists acquainted with the schisms of American Indian communities along conservative and progressive lines cannot help noting the ease with which Africans manage this potentially troublesome problem. To understand this intergenerational accommodation properly we must refer to the competitive materialism just discussed. Since Westernization almost always gives an individual an economic advantage over his less Westernized brethren, it also gains him their respect and dependence, and from this position they are not likely to question his values. More specifically, however, there is the material aspect of role obligations and the relative unimportance of sharing thoughts and feelings. So long as the Westernized individual responds to the customary demands of his kinsmen described above, and provides financial assistance, gifts, and contributions where they are expected, he will be favorably regarded, even if he has forsaken the home community, its way of life, and its beliefs and practices. Neither his parents nor the others in his home village or town will expect him to share their values, opinions, or life styles, and they may not even discuss the differences between them except insofar as they affect material obligations. The greater social distance between the generations in Africa allows culturally differing parents and children to make their peace on the ground of formal obligation without invading one another's cultural domain. Hence we find a cultural relativism among Africans that is impossible where closely related persons expect to be "of the same mind."

Reactions to Increasing Scarcity of Resources

Institutional and demographic change in Africa has not been completely unstressful by any means. Though unevenly spread across the continent, there is overcrowding of land in some rural areas, unemployment and overcrowding in the growing cities, and fierce economic and political competition in urban life. Responses to these stresses have varied, as they would anywhere; but the tendency to blame and fear others has been strongly in evidence, particularly where there is competition for scarce resources—land, jobs, occupational and educational advancement, political office, revenue for community improvement. When the resources are so scarce that an equitable distribution is impossible, or when there is no institutionalized mechanism for distribution, competition has given rise to conflict, which has taken the forms described above, as well as other forms in political behavior. One of the most striking developments has been the apparent increase in witchcraft and sorcery accusations in many parts of the continent, particularly in some of the most overcrowded rural areas of East Africa and in southern African cities. These are areas in which Western education and Christian missions, with their antagonism to magical beliefs, have been most active, but they are also areas of the most stressful competition, in which people have more frequently fallen back on the underlying tendency to see malevolent designs in their neighbors.

This brief discussion of adaptation to change has attempted to convey illustratively the functions in contemporary settings of some of the indigenous behavioral characteristics of Africans. I shall end by warning the reader that adaptation is relative to the time span over which one observes it; thus in a cost-benefit analysis of the behavioral characteristics discussed, those that look highly adaptive now might prove disastrous in the long run, and those that look maladaptive now might prove their worth in time.

16

Education
and Elite Formation

REMI CLIGNET

MANY SCHOLARS ARGUE that African economic growth and political development are slowed down by the absence of a sizable African educated elite. Allegedly, the number of local skilled technicians is limited; supervisory and managerial functions too often remain in the hands of expatriate personnel. At the same time, however, it has been observed that African nations are suffering to some extent from the same "brain drain" which plagues the Middle East and the Far East. Highly trained African individuals are often found in Europe or even in the United States. In 1967, a group of French experts in international assistance published a manifesto to advocate reform in the allocation of the funds devoted to educational development in Africa and to redress the inequities resulting from the presence of more Dahomean doctors in metropolitan France than in Dahomey itself.

Given the low level of international cooperation and aid made available to the Third World in the field of education, it is quite important to assess relationships between educational progress in an African country and the processes of elite formation. The examination of such a relationship should enable us to have more accurate expectations about the returns from educational investments.

Although educational functions have always been provided under the umbrella of traditional society, the growth of modern school systems in Africa has been a by-product of colonial experiences. A step toward a better understanding of the processes of elite formation requires, therefore, an examination of the convergences and divergences in the educational policies of the main colonial powers: France, Great Britain, and Belgium.

THE FRENCH EXPERIENCE

It is frequently argued that the French colonial experience[1] has been consistently assimilationist and that the goals of colonial administrators and educators were to mold African populations into "black Frenchmen" with a system of norms and values identical to those of the metropolitan French people.

The historical reality is somewhat different. Initially, the French colonial administration had few resources, both in men and in material, and was furthermore obliged to fight tooth and nail with a National Assembly in Paris fearful of engaging the country in colonial adventures. The major part of educational expenditures could be derived only from local resources, and such a limitation shaped both the extent and the form of colonial educational enterprises. There were a small number of missionaries and professional schoolteachers, but the majority of the teaching force was provided by Senegalese ex-soldiers who had received a basic training in the army. Communications between territories were sporadic and difficult and each governor was given considerable leeway to define the curriculum that he deemed best to fit the needs of his territory. Insofar as the pursuit of assimilationist objectives and the emergence of a class of "black Frenchmen" required uniformity in programs and curriculums, these conditions were far from fulfilled during the early days of the colonial period.

Even more important than this diversity in the classroom were the divisive theoretical questions argued by laymen and specialists alike; the issues concerned the optimal goals of educational development in the African territories. At one end of the political spectrum certain French leaders held a highly pragmatic view of colonial adventures; for them, the only socially acceptable purpose for establishing an empire was to find additional markets for the industrial products of French manufacturers and to obtain easy and cheap access to raw materials. Those who held this view of French interest in the colonies contended that the spread of formal schooling among Africans should remain as limited as possible, mainly because of its cost, but also because "the more you educate individuals in this situation, the more they hate you."

Leaders at the other end of the political continuum agreed among themselves that colonization implied the diffusion of educational experiences, but they disagreed as to the extent and the form of this diffusion. Certain educators advocated the need to give a basic education to the largest possible number of Africans. Others, recognizing the merits of the particular efforts undertaken by General Faidherbe in Senegal in the 1860s, claimed that education should be

---

1. For a review of this theme, see Remi Clignet and Philip Foster, "French and British Colonial Education in Africa," *Comparative Educational Review*, VIII (1964), 191–98; Clignet and Foster, *The Fortunate Few* (Evanston, Ill.: Northwestern University Press, 1967), Chaps. 1–2; J. B. Bolibaugh and P. R. Hanna, "French Educational Strategies for Sub-Saharan Africa: Their Intent, Derivation, and Development," mimeographed (Palo Alto: Stanford Comparative Education Center, 1964).

a privilege granted exclusively to the children of local chiefs and elites. Thus, the first conception emphasized the merits of a quantitatively massive, but necessarily qualitatively limited, educational development, whereas the second approach stressed the values of an elitist system.

The first conception shaped the majority of educational endeavors undertaken before the Second World War. Local territories increasingly became integrated into two political and administrative frameworks, French West Africa (l'Afrique Occidentale Française) and French Equatorial Africa (l'Afrique Equatoriale Française), with a resulting uniformity in the organization of local school systems. It was decided, however, that school enrollments should be determined by the pace of economic and social development of each colony and in all cases would remain less than that of metropolitan France itself. Accordingly, there were marked contrasts in the size of these enrollments along territorial lines. These contrasts reflect interaction between two distinctive sets of forces.

On one hand, French colonial authorities were eager to promote a certain division of labor among the territorial components of each of the two federations. For example, the economic growth of Ivory Coast was supposed to rest upon the development of large-scale agricultural activities. This particular country, then, needed the services of an unskilled labor force, and local school enrollments consequently were kept at as low a level as possible. At the same time, French authorities were inclined to consider that the inhabitants of other countries, such as Senegal or Dahomey, should constitute the backbone of the semiskilled and skilled administrative labor force needed to run the empire. In addition to the efficiencies of differentiating between the colonies in this way, it was also thought that if Ivory Coast, for instance, were to be partly administered by Dahomeans or Senegalese these territories might be prevented from forming a united front against the demands of French administrators.

On the other hand, Africans were not uniform in the importance they attached to the rewards resulting from formal schooling. In Dahomey, former slaves, returned from Brazil, had been exposed to European organizations and were able to perceive the potential gains derived from academic experiences. In Senegal, too, the individuals who were most intensely subjected to French influences did participate in public services and obtained a preferential treatment from colonial authorities. But in other territories the advantages which accrued to the educated were less apparent, and thus individuals had fewer incentives to acquire academic experiences.

There were limitations not only in the output of African educational systems but also in their curriculums. The major purpose underlying these curriculums was to prepare a limited number of students for the specific occupational "slots" open to them. Rural schools had gardens which were to be cultivated by students and which were to constitute the industrial crops that authorities were eager to introduce on a large scale. Regulations specified both the acreage to be cultivated by each institution and the yields to be obtained. Thus, the idea was to use schools as places for agricultural experimentation and as relays for the spread of modern agricultural techniques. Alternatively, urban students learned specific industrial and clerical skills; they were trained to become railroad engineers, general mechanics, nurses, primary-school teachers, and secretaries or accountants. The largest proportion of the graduates of urban schools were to be recruited by the public administration, and it was assumed that the private sector of the economy had to provide its own workers with on-the-job training programs.

In summary, French colonial administration was eager to maintain a strict balance between educational and economic developments. Variations in the needs of the labor market were supposed to condition variations in school enrollments rather than the reverse. Officials were concerned with avoiding the creation of a mass of "urbanized and educated unemployed individuals" and thus with having to cope with the political unrest that could be provoked by this situation. There were few attempts to build bridges between African and metropolitan educational structures; the assumption was that the function of schools was to mediate an adjustment of local populations to their own environment rather than to the norms and practices of the metropolitan French society. In general, African students were not admitted into French universities, and the diplomas delivered to African students had an exclusively local value. The only exception to this particularistic conception of schooling concerned language— French was taught from the very first year of primary school. The stress placed upon French did not seem, however, to result from the belief that this language was more appropriate than local vernaculars but rather from the observation that vernaculars were too numerous to be taught in an efficient manner.

The Second World War obliged French colonial authorities to change their educational policies. First, they obtained cooperation from African leaders by promising to give a more equalitarian treatment to local populations. Secondly, it became apparent that industrialization of African countries required colonial subjects to be more mobile and more skilled. Thus, political demands were congruent with the requirements of economic change.

African educational institutions became organized on the metropolitan model. *Lycées* — the equivalents of American high schools — were opened in a variety of territories and provided their students with an education analogous to that obtained in metropolitan France. A large number of African students were sent to France in order to accelerate their adjustment to the norms and values of a modern society, and school enrollments were increased in all colonies. Given the formation of political pressure groups in Africa, colonial authorities were most eager to assimilate individuals rather than existing political and social structures. The multiplication of "black Frenchmen" was supposed to counterbalance the effects of centrifugal forces exerted by political agitation. The fear of such forces accounts for the reversals in the educational efforts undertaken in several of the colonies. Up to 1950, Ivory Coast was perceived as the "black sheep" of the colonial territories because it was plagued by political unrest. But an agreement was concluded between the most important local leader, Houphouet-Boigny, and the French Minister for Overseas Affairs that Ivory Coast was to become the showcase of the new colonial approach. Though they had previously lagged far behind those of other territories, school enrollments for that particular country increased rapidly and a large number of scholarships were given to Ivoiriens for studying in metropolitan primary, secondary, and postsecondary schools.

To sum up this period, the increasingly assimilationist tendencies of French policies can be explained by the threatening growth of nationalist movements. Assimilationist measures demanded greater uniformities in the school enrollments observable in France and in Africa and in the organization and the curriculums of African and metropolitan institutions. In short, these policies required the linkages between African schools and societies to be similar to those of metropolitan France.

THE BRITISH EXPERIENCE

Two important factors have contributed to educational developments in the African areas colonized by Great Britain.[2] First, contacts were initiated early and educational developments accordingly have more historical depth than those of the regions under French authority. By 1850 British authorities already had a strong control over large segments of Ghana, Gambia, and Sierra Leone. As a result, schools there started functioning quite early. In 1644 there was an educational institution in Elmina (Ghana), and a second school was opened in 1722 in that area by the Danes. Thus, the number of generations exposed to a European form of schooling tends to be larger in the parts of West Africa initially controlled by Great Britain.

Second, British colonial enterprises have been dominated by private initiative. As a result, religious missions have been quite influential in the expansion and the organization of educational facilities. Initially, the curriculum of the schools was based on the model of institutions serving the poorest segments of European societies: teachers taught reading, writing, a little arithmetic, and there was a heavy emphasis on religious instruction. Rapidly, however, an increase in the number of missions was accompanied by a differentiation both in the type of clientele attending schools and in the type of materials presented to students. On the one hand, Wesleyans were eager to establish institutions in

2. For a review of this theme, see Clignet and Foster, "Colonial Education in Africa"; and Philip Foster, *Education and Social Change in Ghana* (Chicago: University of Chicago Press, 1965).

the cities of the coastal area. They taught in English, stressed the academic aspect of the curriculum, and recruited most of their students from the mulatto segments of the population and from the growing class of merchants. On the other hand, the Basle missions tended to concentrate their efforts in the hinterland. They taught vernaculars and emphasized instruction in agricultural techniques.

Soon enough, British authorities were obliged to face the same kinds of dilemmas experienced by their French counterparts. Their decision to subsidize the efforts undertaken by missionaries made it important to determine guidelines and criteria likely to promote an optimal diffusion of schooling. The first type of dilemma pertained to principles of recruitment. In 1842 the governor of the Gold Coast (Ghana) deemed it advisable to open schools with higher standards for the sons of chiefs, the underlying idea being that the curriculum should vary with the social characteristics of the student population. The second type of dilemma pertained to the objectives of educational development. Should formal schooling accelerate the diffusion of modern norms and values by removing students from their home environment and placing them in boarding schools, or should education facilitate a better adjustment of children to their traditional milieu?

A report published in 1867 by the Education Committee of the Privy Council to the Colonial Office gives some indication of the objectives and the ideal organization of schools as perceived at that time by British authorities. Four types of institutions were to be created. Elementary schools would provide children with basic skills and would lead on to two specialized kinds of institutions: schools for boys would be self-supporting institutions devoted to the teaching of trades, agriculture, and gardening; schools for girls would train their students in the practical skills of housewifery; and the series of normal schools would ensure a proper recruitment of teachers. Thus, the report, which stressed the negative influence exerted by a bookish type of education, insisted upon the significance of the relation between education and economic development. In short, schools were supposed to have a strong vocational orientation and were to lead to the formation of a "settled and thriving" peasantry. African populations, however, did not necessarily respond enthusiastically to such proposals; they were convinced, with some reason, that participation in educational structures implied above all the opportunity to enter the most highly rewarded positions within the exchange sector of the economy.

Implementation of governmental recommendations, however, was made impossible by the very structure of educational institutions. After all, the extension of missionary schools was subordinate to the primary aim of proselytization, and missions were accordingly obliged to provide their students with the kind of training they demanded. The training most desired by these students reflected their perceptions of the existing occupational structure rather than their anticipations of problematic future developments.

Development of educational facilities was relatively rapid. For example, by the late 1860s there were 135 schools in Ghana, the majority of which were operated by Basle missions, with a total number of 12,000 students registered. The expansion of these facilities obliged colonial authorities to adopt more flexible views about the optimal organization of any school system, and the conditions under which individual institutions could be eligible for receiving grants-in-aid were rather loosely defined. The dominant feature of educational developments in the British colonies in the nineteenth century was the large amount of autonomy enjoyed by schools, and hence the large amount of variance in the quality and the content of the teaching that they provided. The Wesleyans, for example, remained in favor of giving their students a highly academic form of training without detaching them from their milieu. The Basel missions, conversely, provided their students with an initial three-year program of instruction in vernaculars, with a strong emphasis on agricultural and industrial techniques. Older students were gathered in boarding schools where they received a more advanced form of training in vocational skills.

The expansion of schools and the corollary growth in the number of graduates led to the formation of a nationalist elite opposed to an "Africanization" of the school system; that is, this elite opposed the introduction of quantitative and qualitative restrictions in educational development. They advocated African institutions organized on British models and the opening of secondary schools to any student. In the Gold Coast (Ghana) the first of these schools began to operate in 1876, was obliged to close its doors in 1889, but finally resumed its activities because of the pressures exerted by highly educated Africans.

These pressures toward both an increase in the number of educational facilities and an improvement of their curriculum became more manifest as the independence period drew closer. Indeed, Africans perceived the development of the labor market and were eager to obtain access to the expanding numbers of clerical positions in the modern sector of the economy. By 1950, there were almost 3,000 schools of all sorts in Ghana, with a total enrollment of about 280,000, the majority of which were students in private institutions.

Yet quarrels about the optimal form of education to be given to African students remained as urgent and divisive in the twentieth century as in the nineteenth. Certain high civil servants were aware of the dangers accompanying a too-rapid expansion of vocational schools and argued that to train artisans without guaranteeing them profitable placement in the occupational hierarchy was politically dangerous. Yet the Phelps-Stokes report published in the early 1920s still stressed the view that educational institutions should aim at facilitating the adaptation of African students to their environment. Thus, the report recommended (1) the use of vernaculars as vehicles for teaching practical subjects; (2) a stress on vocational, agricultural, and technical training at the expense of more traditional subjects; (3) an expansion of the educational facilities offered to girls; and (4) a tighter control by colonial authorities over private in-stitutions. Such proposals were not entirely welcomed by Africans, who con-tinued to think that any Africanization of the curriculum would limit their chances for geographic and social mobility. Local elites therefore resisted any attempt to introduce new vocational techniques into the curriculums of the existing schools and continued to exert pressures in order to obtain a larger number of secondary schools with programs analogous to those of their counter-parts in England.

To sum up, British and French colonial experiences in education present many similarities. The main difference between the policies practiced by these two powers concerns the relative importance accorded to public and private institutions. An increase in the share of private institutions leads the quality of educational facilities to vary within wider limits and the number of such institu-tions to depend more markedly upon the demands and pressures exerted by local populations. It is often tempting to debate the relative merits of the French and the British methods of colonization, but we can see that it is difficult to derive any definitive conclusions.

THE BELGIAN COLONIAL EXPERIENCE

Of the three major colonial powers, the Belgians have been the most prag-matic in their educational policies.[3] Their efforts were directed at the provision of literacy in the vernaculars for a large proportion of the population, combined with a minimal development of postprimary schools except for a few with tech-nical and vocational emphasis.

Like the British, the Belgians placed educational facilities under the authority of private missions, mainly Roman Catholic. In 1951, 515,000 students were attending private schools subsidized by the government. Of these, only 115,000 were enrolled in institutions whose organization and curriculums were con-trolled by government authorities; and government educational facilities ac-counted for only 7,000 students.

Like the French, Belgian authorities opted for linking educational develop-ment with economic growth. In 1951, 30,000 individuals were enrolled in post-primary institutions, from which it was impossible to gain access to universities. It was only a few years prior to independence that Belgian authorities decided to establish bridges between postprimary educational facilities and universities.

3. For a review of this theme, see Foster, *Education and Social Change in Ghana*, pp. 151–52; and N. Zydias, "Le Travail: Conditions, aptitudes, formations, effets sociaux de l'urbanisation a Stanleyville," *Aspects sociaux de l'urbanisation et industrialisation en Afrique au sud du Sahara* (Paris: UNESCO, 1956).

Their inability to perceive the pressing nature of African demands along these lines resulted from their initial decision to open the Congo to a massive white immigration; they preferred to reserve the most rewarding positions of the occupational structure for European expatriates and hence to bar Africans from skilled and managerial professions.

Belgian perceptions of educational development also implied a tight control over both the curriculum and the organization of schools; and this constitutes another similarity to the French colonial system. Yet Belgian authorities differed from their French counterparts in the amount of political control they imposed upon the graduates of their school systems. Immigration to towns was allowed only for these Africans who had been trained for "urban" occupations and were able to prove that they could be employed.

COMPARISON OF THE CONSEQUENCES OF COLONIAL POLICIES

Although French and British colonial authorities at various points in history provided the offspring of African aristocracies with a special education, or at least gave them preferential access into the school system, formal education failed to contribute to the persistence of traditional structures. African chiefs or kings initially perceived Westernization as a threat imposed upon the existing social order. Since individual positions were traditionally defined according to ascriptive criteria (such as familial affiliation, sex, seniority, social background), any move toward the introduction of criteria based on achievement (such as academic success) was thought to minimize the legitimacy of the existing authority structure. Accordingly, the first children who were sent to European schools were the sons of slaves, of junior lineages, and of marginal categories of local societies. It was believed that the exposure of such individuals to new ideas and norms would not influence the functioning of traditional political, social, and economic institutions.

Acceptable in the context of a short-term analysis, this view was wrong in the long term. Europeans were eager not only to export to African societies their own cultural norms and values but also to recruit in Africa the semispecialized labor force that was needed to ensure even a minimal amount of economic, political, and social development. Obviously, the first subgroups to enter educational institutions were also the first to participate in the profits of new economic enterprises. As a consequence, initial steps toward educational development resulted in the emergence of a dual African social hierarchy: traditional chiefs maintained a part of their traditional prestige and wealth, but their position became increasingly threatened by the advantages gained by the minority of educated Africans. Rapidly, larger numbers of individuals began to perceive the rewards associated with formal schooling. They were tempted to abandon agricultural activities and to move toward urban centers where they could escape the formal control of traditional authorities and would have more opportunities to earn stable, high incomes. Educational developments, then, have been uniformly accompanied by a decline in the significance of traditional institutions and an increased mobility toward urban centers.

Educational developments have also been uniformly associated with an increased demand for white-collar occupations. Many observers of the African scene have noted the predilection of Africans for clerical positions and have argued that this reflects a cultural distaste for manual work and a questionable attraction for nonproductive types of employment. On the contrary, occupational aspirations of African students along these lines appear to have been quite realistic. There is no doubt that in a colonial environment the most powerful and economically influential European actor was the district officer. One can easily understand why African students were eager to enter occupations as similar as possible to this model. Indeed, European entrepreneurs themselves were often subjected to the authority of the district officer and could not launch any profitable activity without his approval. Also, in more general terms, it has been demonstrated that attraction toward white-collar jobs is universally greater than toward manual occupations. Opportunities for high income, prestige, and promotion, as well as stability of employment, are perceived to be more characteristic of clerical jobs. Why should Africans be less shrewd observers of the economic scene than Europeans themselves? As long as the economic structure of African countries remains dominated by tertiary activities (that is, activities which provide services rather than produce goods), and more specifically by public employment, administrative jobs will be the most attractive. Regardless of their training and of their actual branch of activity, Africans remain oriented toward public employment, which provides them with a sense of security which is particularly appealing in the context of underdeveloped economies.

In all colonial countries, European powers have come into conflict with local populations on this very issue. Colonial authorities were unwilling to facilitate the access of African students to higher administrative and clerical positions and maintained a truncated educational hierarchy for as long as possible. In addition, they were aware that demands for administrative and clerical occupations were developing more rapidly than the labor market itself and were, accordingly, afraid of the dangers of overurbanization with its growing mass of educated, unemployed males prone to indulge in political agitation. To stress the value of a vocationally specific training in an underdeveloped economy, however, remains a questionable proposition. An underdeveloped economy is characterized by a loose division of labor and by wide variations over time in the needs for manpower in the various sectors of economic activity. It may be wiser, therefore, to provide students with a general basic training that would facilitate their adaptation to a variety of professional situations rather than to limit their education to the acquisition of specific and hence less transferable skills. Further, to think that training agriculturalists or artisans may change the occupational structure of a particular country is to underestimate the influence of economic incentives. As long as agricultural and artisanal activities are less rewarding than white-collar occupations, the most enterprising individuals will do their best to enter the latter type of employment and will not hesitate to abandon the jobs for which they have been trained. In the Africa of today, as in the Africa of yesterday, many planners are too often anxious to see Africans sacrifice their expectations concerning a real and promising present in favor of a problematic future. Yet education cannot significantly change the system of differential rewards attached to various types of economic activities. The demand for education is determined by this system rather than the contrary.

In brief, all educational developments in Africa have been accompanied by a build-up of tensions resulting from the desire of the people to obtain a large number of academic institutions and from the tendency of colonial powers to provide them with a limited number of specific vocational schools.

All colonial educational systems tend to be alike in another way, in the sense that they have duplicated certain crucial aspects of the educational structures of the colonizing power. Thus, French colonial schools presented the same centralized organizations and the resulting rigidity as the metropolitan educational system. Educational philosophy stressed the significance of equality. Norms, examinations, and course sequences were uniform; and after the 1920s French officials in Paris could take some pride in the fact that they knew what African students would learn on a particular hour of a particular day of a given year. Equality also meant that teachers would be subjected to the same kind of training and would present a uniform level of skills. Lastly, equality meant that formal schooling was tuition-free and that students would be recruited on the basis of their merits.

Similarly, it can be argued that Belgian colonial schools have enabled religious missions to play a role in Africa identical to their role in Belgium. In both cases, cognitive and ethical learning have remained undifferentiated.

And, in British territories as in Great Britain, education was perceived as a consumer good to be determined by the conditions of the market. Such a system stressed the significance of individual initiative and of freedom. Education was a privilege to be privately acquired rather than a right guaranteed by the central government. This obliged schools to charge their students tuition. But the British system was also accompanied by greater variations in the quality of the teaching force and of the curriculum, and it limited the quantitative and qualitative control exerted by governmental authorities. Correspondingly, educational developments were more likely to reflect variations in the demand for schooling, and hence variations in the resources of local populations, than variations in ideal models proposed by planners and administrators.

THE POST-INDEPENDENCE PERIOD

Everywhere in Africa nationalist leaders had long protested against the limitations of educational development and against the discrimination exerted against local students in an effort to persuade colonial authorities to change their stands on such issues. Upon assuming office in the newly independent states, these leaders were obliged to maintain their initial platforms. As a result, the present period is uniformly characterized by a dramatic increase both in the number of schools and of enrollments in these schools. This increase has taken place at all levels and includes universities as well as primary institutions.

Recent political developments have been associated with drastic changes both in the organization of school systems and in their curriculums. These changes reflect the dilemmas faced by African governments. On the one hand, the modernization of a country is evaluated according to universalist criteria. This leads to the proposition that elites should receive a universal form of training and should be interchangeable. On the other hand, political development requires a mobilization of the energies of individual citizens and a corresponding emphasis upon the virtues of Africanization (that is, the progressive expansion of specifically African participation in all spheres of modern political, social, and economic life). African leaders are accordingly torn by two conflicting forces. They want their students to be able to enter European or American institutions of higher education but they also have the desire to see these students acquire respect and admiration for African traditions. Indeed, processes of nation-building involve competition with other nations according to a uniform set of rules but also include emergence of particularistic feelings and nationalistic orientations.

Certain African nations have stressed the first alternative. They underscore the necessity of having as many graduates as possible and of assuring that these graduates are as comparable as possible to their European counterparts. Ivory Coast is probably the most typical example of this category, and it tends to adopt the same educational reforms as France does. This tendency is, of course, reinforced by the fact that increases in the output of secondary institutions require the services of a specialized teaching force, which, being mainly derived from former colonial powers, is usually unwilling to innovate, either in terms of curriculum or in terms of teaching method.

At the other end of the continuum, other African countries have realized that variations in levels of school enrollments and of economic development should be associated with variations in the curriculum and the length of each cycle of studies. Accordingly, they are willing to recognize the fact that the profile of African schools should deviate from that of highly industrialized nations. There are differences, however, in the way this policy is implemented. Some countries may argue that educational costs weigh heavily on their gross national product and that the vast bulk of students should enter occupational life as early as possible. Other countries recognize the fact that underdeveloped economies are characterized by erratic shifts in the composition of their labor force. These countries thus tend to believe that students should receive a general training for as long a period as possible and should not be oriented toward specific skills until the very late stages of their academic careers. Furthermore, they are willing to recognize the costs of an early orientation, both to the individual and to the society at large.

THE SELECTIVITY OF SCHOOL POPULATIONS

In our consideration of the development of educated elites, it is not enough to evaluate the number and the relative proportions of individuals processed by school systems. The examination of the recruitment system, or "selectivity," is at least as critical in the sense that it gives us some ideas about the origin of elites, the degree to which they perpetuate themselves, and the ways in which they may prevent the upward mobility of other segments of the population.

Selectivity by Sex

There is no doubt that even today male children constitute a disproportionate share of enrollments. Exposure to European norms and practices has always been selective along sex lines and African populations have seen for themselves that educational achievement tends to be most rewarding for European males. The effects of this perception have been reinforced by the preeminent nature of the status traditionally allocated to African males. Both factors have contributed to minimize the impact of formal schooling on local women. In fact, it is quite clear that female school enrollments do not begin to increase until the percentage of educated males reaches a certain critical threshold. In Ivory Coast primary schools, for example, there is a relatively close association between overall enrollments and sex ratio of student populations. In other words, the higher the school enrollments for a given region, the more even are the proportions of male and female children attending primary institutions. Deviations from this model may reflect the incidence of specific cultural patterns and, for example, variations in the significance of the economic and social roles allocated to women. Bongouanou, for instance, has an unexpectedly higher proportion of females given its level of enrollment, probably because of the high degree of economic and social autonomy of its female population. They may also result from variations in the importance of urbanization. Thus, Abidjan, the capital city of Ivory Coast, fails to fit the general pattern because of the relative importance of economic opportunities that it offers its female residents.

There is a marked contrast not only in the size of male and female educated populations but also in the types of studies that are undertaken by the two groups. In Ivory Coast and in Ghana, girls are likely to have a shorter academic career than their male counterparts, but they are proportionately more numerous both in academic programs and in institutions devoted to the training of skills deemed to be feminine specialties, such as nursing, home economics, and social work.

Selectivity by Age

An initial caveat must be entered before discussing the evidence available on this subject. Within a context of rapid social change, African individuals have a very loose sense of their exact age. Furthermore, they are willing to adopt instrumental views concerning this problem. More specifically, they are aware that age may constitute a legal obstacle on the road of their academic aspirations and they have no hesitation in reporting an inaccurate birth date whenever it helps them to remain enrolled in the school of their choice.[4]

Given the limitations on the amount of evidence available, scholars have come out with conflicting propositions regarding selectivity by age. Using a particular intelligence test (the Cattell test) on Congolese students, N. Zydias has observed that the variance in the results of this test was explained more by the length of the academic experience than by age.[5] In examining a population of students attending the second year of postprimary schooling in Ivory Coast in 1959, I have noted that success both in academic examinations and in psychological tests varies as a negative function of the age of the subjects examined. In other words, the younger students tend to perform better than the older students. These results have been indirectly confirmed by similar observations made in 1963, which indicated that younger students were more likely than older ones to enter, or remain in, the prestigious and rewarding *lycées*.[6] At the same time (but without giving empirical evidence) other scholars have argued that the system of examination practiced by the Ivory Coast school system favors "old-timers" and enables them to acquire the type of rote knowledge demanded in academic examinations.

Regardless of these conflicting observations, it may be that correlation between

4. For a discussion of this problem, see Philip Foster, "Status, Power and Education in a Traditional Community," *School Review*, LXXII (Summer 1964), 158–82. For a discussion of the equivocations attached to age in Africa, see J. C. Caldwell, "Population: General Characteristics," "Population Change," and "Migration and Urbanization," in *A Study of Contemporary Ghana*, Vol. II: *Some Aspects of Social Structure*, ed. Walter Birmingham, I. Neustadt, and E. N. Omaboe (Evanston, Ill.: Northwestern University Press, 1967), 17–144.

5. "Le Travail."

6. See Remi Clignet, "Rapport sur la selection et l'orientation des élèves de la classe de 5ème," mimeographed (Abidjan: Service Psychotechnique, 1959); and Clignet and Foster, *The Fortunate Few*, Chap. 4.

age and academic success primarily reflects variations in the importance of the advantages deemed to accompany precocity. In other words, the measures of age may reflect psychological phenomena rather than an objective chronological quality. Furthermore, the influence of this factor has to be understood in terms of variations in the date at which children begin their educational experience and variations in their ability to pass the differing sorts of examinations imposed upon them. Such variations may reflect distinctions between the types of environment from which such children are derived.

Selectivity by Ethnic Group

Ethnicity is included in two distinctive dimensions of educational selectivity and performance. First, each ethnic culture comprises sets of norms and values which have a varying degree of compatibility with the demands of modernization and of formal schooling. Other things being equal, students derived from ethnic groups emphasizing individual mobility and competition may be expected to have high educational aspirations and to be academically successful. In contrast, for example, it can be argued that in matrilineal societies, where socialization functions are divided between fathers and maternal uncles and where child-rearing techniques are primarily focused upon a lessening of the centrifugal forces exerted on familial groups, there will be a low level of school attendance and great difficulties in stimulating the academic interest of children.

At the same time, however, ethnicity has usually entailed a geographic location for a particular people, which may in turn affect the relative exposure of that people to modernizing forces. A comparison between the representation of various ethnic groups in the secondary schools of Ghana and Ivory Coast shows that the opportunity to enter such institutions declines as one moves away from the coastal areas toward the hinterland and as one gets farther away from the places where Europeans have been concentrated. In Ivory Coast, selectivity ratios vary between 1.6 for southern regions and 0.6 for the north; in Ghana, the corresponding figures are 1.4 and 0.2 (where 1.0 is the "standard" value).

Selectivity by Urban-Rural Origin

Given the above observation, we can expect that the urban populations most exposed to the rewards and norms of a European society will be more likely to enter educational institutions than individuals originating from a rural background. Comparisons between Ghana and Ivory Coast show such expectations to be correct. The intensity of this form of selectivity, however, is lower in Ivory Coast than in Ghana, and such a difference may tentatively be attributed to contrasts in the organization of the urban centers and educational systems of the two countries. Ivory Coast has a primate distribution of urban centers; correspondingly, both urbanized populations and schools are overwhelmingly concentrated in the capital city of Abidjan. Access to such schools depends upon a national examination and urban competitors are swamped by the mass of rural candidates. In contrast, Ghanaian urban populations and schools are more evenly distributed throughout the country. As a result, the size of each educational "market" is more limited and this gives a systematic advantage to urban candidates. In short, we are suggesting here that the importance of urban-rural differentials in the patterns of recruitment to postprimary institutions varies with the number and size of educational markets. A decline in the number of such markets combined with an increase in their size probably favors the most numerous subsegments of the population, and, in the instance of Ivory Coast, candidates of a rural origin. Thus differences in the nature of the colonial model of localization of urban centers and educational institutions are accompanied by differences in the significance of residential forms of selectivity.

Selectivity by Family Occupation

Participation in a cash economy enables individuals to perceive the rewards associated with formal schooling. Increases in the regularity of income and in the amount of cash resources facilitate the payment of educational costs and also limit the consequences of the losses in resources resulting from participation in educational structures. One can expect, therefore, that an individual whose family is still engaged in subsistence activity will have fewer chances to enter a postprimary institution than an individual with both parents engaged in the modern sector of the economy. In Ivory Coast, the sons of professional higher technical and administrative personnel are twenty-five times more numerous in secondary schools than they are in the population at large. In Ghana, the corresponding ratio averages fourteen. At the other end of the continuum, sons of Ivory Coast farmers do not obtain equal educational facilities and those in school represent only 0.8 of their proportion in the entire population. In Ghana, the corresponding percentage is approximately the same, with a value of 0.8. It remains important, however, to differentiate between various types of farmers. In Ivory Coast, the children of cash-crop farmers in postprimary schools are far more numerous than the children of persons still exclusively engaged in subsistence activities.

These observations do not mean that chances to participate in educational structures increase regularly with level of exposure of the parental generation to modernizing forces. In fact, the socio-occupational category most under-represented in the school system is that of semiskilled and unskilled manual workers. This particular class of persons is more exposed to modernizing forces than are farmers and rural populations; yet their participation in the modern sector of the economy is not associated with proportional rewards, and their marginality prevents them from entertaining high aspirations with regard to modernity. Thus, the distribution of enrollments by socioeconomic category tends to indicate that modernization of means and modernization of ends are not necessarily similarly distributed.

Selectivity by Family Educational Characteristics

Of all the forms of selectivity analyzed here, the level of parental education is the most influential. The higher this level, the higher the aspirations that parents have with regard to the academic careers of their children and the tighter the control that they can exert upon the relevant behavior of their off-spring. Obviously, level of maternal education is an even better predictor of whether a person enters a postprimary institution and of how far he will go in this type of study. The number of educated female adults is very limited in Africa, and the presence of a literate woman in a household is therefore an unequivocal index of the level of modernization of this particular group.

Interaction between Forms of Selectivity

At the present time, ethnic affiliations remain important determinants of the position occupied by individuals in the overall structure of the society to which they belong, and there is a relatively limited amount of social differentiation within each ethnic group. It has been observed that socioeconomic differentiation operates most clearly within ethnic groups whose enrollments are minimal. In such cases, students are likely to be drawn from atypical social categories. Conversely, as the level of enrollments of a particular ethnic group increases, parents of the student population have an educational and occupational profile which ceases to differ from that of the bulk of the population.[7]

CHANGES IN THE SIGNIFICANCE OF ELITE SELECTIVITY

The above observations tend to indicate that selectivity in the recruitment patterns of educational institutions reflects two distinctive sets of forces.

First, there are variations in the demand for education. Certain ethnic groups and social categories of the population are not involved enough in the processes of modernization to perceive the importance of education as a mechanism influencing individual placement in the occupational structure. Some of these groups still have a low level of mobility, are still oriented toward traditional gratifications, and prefer their children to remain subjected to the forces underlying traditional networks of interaction. Certain peoples also occupy marginal positions in the political structure of their country and may feel that they will

7. Remi Clignet, "Ethnicity, Social Differentiation, and Secondary Schooling in West Africa," *Cahiers d'études africaines*, VII (1967), 361–78.

remain deprived in all cases of the legitimate rewards accompanying formal schooling.

Second, there are variations in the level of adjustment of various social categories to the demands of an educational system. Given the fact that teaching methods remain influenced by European models, certain subgroups of the entire population are more exposed than others to the cognitive style prevailing among highly industrialized nations. They have an easier access to written material, are exposed to a greater amount of vocabulary and images, and therefore have more chances to give the kinds of answers expected from them in formal examinations.

Forms of interaction between these two forces seem difficult to evaluate. Indeed, students having attended primary institutions in large urban centers have perhaps a higher average level of aspirations than those with a basic training acquired in rural areas. Yet, variance of aspirations is probably greater among rural school populations, and rural students with a high aspirational level are probably in a position to obtain more attention from their teachers than are their urban counterparts. Among students engaged in the second year of postprimary studies in Ivory Coast, it has been noted that those having attended rural schools had better academic results than those whose primary education was acquired in the public schools of Abidjan. Similarly, the former subgroup showed better results in psychological tests.

Such contrasts may account for the fact that students derived from underprivileged ethnic or socioeconomic backgrounds seem to get more than their fair share as one gets closer to the upper rungs of the educational hierarchy.[8] There probably is a closer match between the aspirations and the skills of such students than between those of urban privileged students. Furthermore, the terms of the overall selectivity are probably such that rural students really belong to the cream of the educated population. In other words, given the fact that their exposure to European cognitive style favors urban candidates, rural students who make their way through the system may be particularly talented.

Thus far, our analysis of selectivity has been static, and we must, therefore, turn our attention toward a dynamic examination of this factor. In this context, one can hypothesize that the level at which selectivity operates most severely varies with the overall level of school enrollments of the country investigated and with the age of its school system and its level of economic development. Among countries with a new educational system which is limited in size, it is probable that individuals are differentiated in terms of whether or not they attend school. In other words, selectivity operates at the level of entrance into educational institutions. As schools grow in number and as economic development becomes more manifest, the most crucial cleavage concerns the length and type of studies undertaken. Selectivity enables observers to predict what

8. See Clignet and Foster, *The Fortunate Few*, Chaps. 3–4.

subgroup has the best chances to undertake academic rather than vocational studies, or to follow a long rather than a short cycle of instruction.

In general, levels of selectivity are also affected by cultural factors. For example, I have observed that there are more significant differences between the social and ethnic characteristics of those Ivory Coast academic students who take Latin and those who do not than between the social and ethnic background of these students considered as a whole and that of their counterparts engaged in vocational or agricultural studies. This selectivity takes place in spite of the fact that the distinction between classic and modern academic studies has no implication for the future careers of the individuals involved, whereas the entire populations of the *lycées* have more chances to enter a university than persons undertaking other types of studies.[9] In this case, Ivoiriens seem to have borrowed an obsolescent French model. Although functional until quite recently in metropolitan France, distinctions between modern and classical studies have now ceased to be associated with distinctive rewards. Ivory Coast has nevertheless assumed the old French attitudes toward classical studies, and those Ivory Coast students engaged in such studies tend to represent the educated elite—that is, they are from monogamous Christian families with both parents educated and engaged in the modern sector of the economy.

Comparisons between Ghana and Ivory Coast also suggest that educational development may be associated with a tightening of the various forms of selectivity. Offhand, one would anticipate that a decline in the scarcity of educational facilities should lead to a corresponding decline in the severity of selectivity. Yet a decline in the scarcity of educational institutions may also result from a differential increase in the demand for education. Economic and social development implies accentuated social differentiation—that is, accentuated contrasts in the means and the ends of the distinctive social groups of each country investigated. The problem remains to determine whether these contrasts affect the field of education.

The influence of such contrasts may depend, first, on the nature of social perceptions pertaining to education. Formal schooling may be viewed as a consumer good or as a private or collective investment. Until quite recently, many French-speaking African nations stressed the collective investment aspect of their educational enterprises and gave their students free room and board, clothes, and educational materials. Such a policy naturally limited the severity of selectivity, insofar as student recruitment stressed academic merit. These measures have been progressively abandoned, and it is likely that educational institutions will in the future be recruiting their students from narrower segments of the population. In contrast, many English-speaking countries started with the opposite assumption and considered that formal schooling was a con-

9. See Remi Clignet and Philip Foster, "La Preeminence de l'enseignement classique en Côte d'Ivoire: Un Exemple d'assimilation," *Revue française de sociologie*, VII (1966), 32–47.

sumer good, the distribution of which was to be conditioned by the laws of the market. Such an assumption strengthened the severity of the various forms of selectivity. Yet recently an increasing number of measures have been taken in order to alleviate the financial burdens of African parents. Such measures should lead to a decline in the significance of favored or neglected minorities in the origin of students. In brief, differences between French- and English-speaking countries along these lines should decrease.

Second, the educational consequences of accentuated social differentiation are influenced by the nature of the association between ethnic and occupational affiliations. Persistence of marked inequalities in the level of participation of distinctive ethnic groups in the modern sector of the economy and in political structures may increase differences in the perceived reward system of academic experiences. So far, certain ethnic groups have complained that they are discriminated against in terms of educational opportunities. Governments are not always able to cope properly with this type of complaint. Indeed, the opening of new educational equipment may ultimately produce the greatest profit for peoples with an already high exposure to educational experiences. The introduction of ethnic "quotas" tends to reintroduce particularistic considerations which are at variance with the universalistic nature of educational objectives. The absence of rational solutions in this respect may lead to the creation of a vicious circle and to the strengthening of interethnic antagonisms, with certain peoples being deprived of the "plums" accompanying the processes of modernization.

Third, contrasts are influenced by the tightening of a social class system. So far, socioeconomic selectivity in Africa has remained relatively limited. Given the fact that in both Ivory Coast and Ghana children of farmers do not get their fair share of educational opportunities, they still represent more than 60 per cent of the entire school population, and this suggests that the system is more open than we usually think. This fluidity may very well decline, and African countries may drift toward the kind of situation experienced by European countries where lower classes consider educational activities to be made by, and for, middle and upper classes. In such a situation, participation in educational institutions is determined by the prevailing characteristics of the social structure, but in turn hardly affects such characteristics.

THE FUNCTIONS AND PROCESS OF EDUCATION

In the previous sections, we have analyzed the "inputs" of schools and selectivity patterns in recruitment. We must now turn our attention to the activities of these educational institutions and to their functions as agencies of socialization. Variations in these functions may affect the volume and quality of the elites produced.

The Recruitment of Teachers

For a long time, teaching jobs were considered by Africans to occupy the top of the occupational hierarchy. Opportunities were scarce and teaching enabled talented individuals to enjoy the rewards of a "modern" activity without facing the corresponding costs in terms of personal adjustment. Indeed, subservience of teachers to the colonial system was minimal, and teachers enjoyed a large amount of independence. Educational and economic developments have changed this situation. First, there has been an increase in the number of teachers. Second, with economic development, other rewarding positions have opened up to Africans, and there has been a consistent decline in the prestige attached to the teaching profession. Third, a lessening in the prestige of teachers also resulted from the need for increased manpower in this field and the corresponding decline in the requirements for access to it.

As a result, teachers with the highest seniority tend to leave the profession in order to enter more rewarding positions. A considerable number of political personnel are recruited from this particular category. Senior teachers also tend to be concentrated in the best schools (often the ones closest to the centers of European influence). Differences in the quality of the teaching force among regions or between rural and urban areas could very well serve to maximize differences in the level of academic achievement of the corresponding segments of the population.

The Location of Schools

Changes in the organization of the teaching force have been paralleled by changes in the stereotypes pertaining to the optimal location of educational institutions. As in colonial times, the present policy alternatives are to place schools either near centers where elites are concentrated or in the proximity of the various occupational markets. Now, as before, the second alternative seems to be out of touch with reality. As long as educational experiences facilitate access to white-collar occupations, the creation of schools in the hinterland will not necessarily induce more individuals to undertake agricultural careers.

On the other hand, the location of secondary schools in centers of European influence raises two significant questions. First, it raises the problem of the utility of boarding institutions. In Ivory Coast the academic achievement of boarders tends to be superior to that of day students. It also raises the problem of the consequences attached to the composition of the school population. Thus, the academic achievement of individual Ivory Coast students in the second year of their postprimary studies varies with the ethnic and social composition of their class. The greater the proportion of Europeans in the class, the better the performance of the Africans enrolled. Similarly, the academic performances of the sons of farmers are better when the majority of their classmates are derived from modern environments.

Finally, it should be stressed that changes in the orientations of religious missions have been accompanied by changes in their locations. Initially, many Catholic missions, particularly those in French-speaking Africa, were anxious to participate in the training of potential elites. Thus they tended to concentrate their educational institutions in areas where demand for education was already high. Recently, many missions have become eager to participate more in the spread of education into regions where school enrollment levels are low and where, more specifically, educated women are scarce. In brief, missions have realized the consequences attached to disparities in the educational level of distinctive subsegments of the society.

Africanization of the Curriculum

At an early stage African nationalist leaders opposed the introduction of African materials into the curriculum. During the colonial period few rewards were to be gained from the learning of particularistic skills and values. After independence, however, this view changed. It was argued that to learn African culture and history would heighten individual commitment toward nationalist ideals. There has been, accordingly, an Africanization of the curriculum, and students are increasingly exposed to local materials in the fields of history, geography, natural sciences, and modern languages.

Interestingly enough, however, no effort has been undertaken to promote an Africanization of teaching methods. Yet it is increasingly clear that cognitive styles are culture-bound and that learning processes vary along ethnic lines. For example, I have suggested elsewhere that the role performed by memorization in French and in African schools cannot have the same implications, since African cultures by definition have strong oral mnemonic orientations. Similarly, performances of African subjects on psychological tests involving the use of colors are not alike when words for these colors are present and absent in local vocabularies.[10] At a more general level, it has also been argued that cultural attitudes toward authority and expertise determine the extent to which learning processes involve the use of experimentation.[11] The neglect of strategies likely to maximize intercultural communications and to recognize cultural variations in teacher-student relations cannot but limit the formation of "universalist" elites in Africa.

10. See Remi Clignet, "Réflections sur les problèmes de psychologie en Afrique," *Bulletin de l'Institut National d'Orientation Professionnelle*, Vol. XVIII, No. 2 (1962), 86–94.
11. See *Social Psychological Research in Developing Countries*, Special issue. *Journal of Social Issues*, XXIV (1968), esp. G. Barbichon, "The Diffusion of Scientific and Technical Knowledge," 135–56; see also John Gay and Michael Cole, *The New Mathematics*

Schools as Agencies of Socialization

In Africa, as everywhere else in the world, it is often believed that schools may perform a significant role with regard to the political socialization of the oncoming generation. It is accordingly believed that the influence eventually exerted by educational institutions may be more powerful than that exerted by familial environments. Evidence available so far, however, invites us to remain cautious in this respect. In Ivory Coast, attitudes of students toward occupational opportunities remain as much determined by their ethnic background as by the level of studies undertaken. In fact, interethnic contrasts along those lines remain sizable when one analyzes the vocational aspirations of male individuals who have had ten years of formal schooling.[12] Such evidence, though limited, does not lead us to believe that formal education is associated with the emergence of uniform, modern sets of norms and values. As suggested earlier, views on education may be strictly instrumental, and the student may acquire additional education, hence additional resources, in order to restore culturally specific ends. In brief, under certain circumstances, formal schooling, far from eroding the ethnic particularisms of local elites, reinforces such cleavages.

THE INFLUENCE OF SCHOOLS ON SOCIAL CLASS AND ELITE FORMATION

Thus far we have analyzed recruitment patterns of educational institutions and have considered the processes by which such institutions perform their socialization functions. We must now turn our attention to an examination of the impact of educational developments on existing African social structures.

First, as noted earlier, access to educational facilities remains somewhat fluid. Yet it is quite obvious that education is an increasingly important determinant of the placement of individuals in residential and occupational slots, and that educational achievement constitutes a force pushing toward the formation of social classes and elites. Given this situation, it is not difficult to understand why the demand for education keeps increasing in all areas of Africa.

Second, variations in academic achievement are associated with variations in level and type of vocational aspirations. With the expansion of the occupational structure, most talented students are increasingly attracted toward technical careers, where there are a large number of openings and where rewards are substantial. Conversely, agricultural jobs and professions such as primary-

---

and an Old Culture. A Study of Learning among the Kpelle of Liberia (New York: Holt, Rinehart & Winston, 1967).

12. See Clignet and Foster. *The Fortunate Few.* Chap. 6.

school teaching seem most likely to recruit their new members from groups who have been less successful or have not been able to complete a full cycle of post-primary studies.

An analysis of vocational aspirations of students over time suggests that this particular population is highly sensitive to the fluctuations of the labor market. Thus, as suggested earlier, teaching careers lost their attraction as soon as it became obvious that new opportunities would be open to young Africans. Similarly, the professions of politics and law, so popular in the years immediately preceding independence, ceased to be in high demand when it became obvious that new regimes would minimize the significance of public and private litigations and that the political personnel was young enough to prevent a high amount of turnover. An analysis of vocational expectations yields similar results. When asked what they would do if obliged to enter the labor market without completing their current academic cycle of studies, African individuals are perfectly able to recognize that teaching and clerical jobs are the best opportunities available to them.

Students are uniformly attracted by public employment. The long history of exploitation by private concerns explains this choice, and it is also true that, until recently, the administration was the only employer able to provide its wage-earners with guarantees concerning stability of employment and hence of income. There are certain signs, however, that the situation is changing. The large-scale concerns which still dominate the economic scene of many African countries are particularly anxious to avoid accusations of "neo-colonialism." As a result, they are eager to hire Africans with a high level of skill and to promote their personnel to supervisory positions. Further, they are also reluctant to dismiss personnel without being absolutely sure of winning their case should it come before local courts. Accordingly, the relative stigma attached to participation in the private sector of the economy is slowly disappearing. Though still limited in number, a growing minority of the more advanced students are inclined to consider positions offered by private firms, and some of their predecessors are starting to move from public to private employers. In all parts of Africa, colonial experiences explain why educated elites have been attracted to administrative careers. The problem remains to determine whether such an attraction favors or impedes further economic development. Planners are likely to argue that the growth of European economies resulted from the emergence of a class of private entrepreneurs and that the lack of interest of young African students in entrepreneurial activities necessarily prevents their countries from "taking off" in economic terms. Yet we are not sure about the uniformities of patterns of economic development throughout time. Nor are we sure about the social characteristics of successful and unsuccessful entrepreneurs in European countries of the nineteenth century.

Lastly, and most important, variations in educational achievement are associated with variations in residential choices. The more advanced a student, the more prone he is to live in a large urban center, where the best economic opportunities are concentrated and where his initial exposure to modernizing forces is systematically reinforced. As a result, differences in the social composition of urban and rural populations become more pronounced, and such differences, in turn, are likely to induce contrasts in the relative chances for further development of urban centers and of the hinterland. In short, the gap between urban and rural elites keeps growing, and it may in the long term threaten the economic and political balance of entire African countries.

To sum up this array of observations, African students seem to take advantage of their educational achievement to obtain the best share of the existing economic and social opportunities, rather than to change the economic organization of their country. This is not exceptional. Innovators are rarely recruited from the segments of the population having immediate access to the largest number of most appealing rewards; indeed, innovators are usually derived from strata which are relatively deprived.

Yet, relative deprivation is going to characterize an increasing number of students. There is indeed a growing gap between educational aspirations and the number of educational facilities. There is also an increasing gap between the growth rates of educational institutions and of economic resources. As a result, there is a decline in the payoff of academic achievement. A decade ago, ten years of formal schooling mediated an automatic access to the most rewarding positions of the modern sector of the economy. Today, the rewards derived from ten years of education are far more limited in number and significance. Furthermore, their acquisition is not automatic. There is a marked increase in the number of educated, unemployed individuals. Correspondingly, African governments are faced with the same dilemma as their colonial predecessors. Should they limit educational outputs and adjust them to the growth rate of local economies? Should they limit urban migrations and oblige a certain number of young people to remain engaged in farming activities? If so, what should be the nature of reinforcement used to achieve this goal? Is it better to use negative sanctions and to punish individuals who migrate without permission or to reward persons willing to stay on the land? Lastly, certain experts recommend an acceleration in educational development so that academic achievement may cease to be a decisive factor in the placement of individuals in occupational and social structures.

Relative deprivation resulting from discrepancies between educational and economic developments is likely to affect intergenerational relationships. There have been drastic changes in the amount and form of selectivity underlying access to certain types of studies or certain types of occupations. For example, senior teachers in Africa are necessarily appalled by the conditions underlying the recruitment of their junior colleagues. As the prestige and the economic status of their profession decrease, they are particularly frustrated to see a corresponding decline in the qualities of the incoming teachers. Conversely, certain occupations, the access to which was initially easy, have raised their prerequisites, and present students feel frustrated to see that people who occupy top positions have a lower educational achievement than their own. Such frustrations are likely to be exacerbated by the severity of familial obligations imposed upon upwardly mobile individuals. Indeed, the more successful an individual, the more dependents he must support. To sum up this point, discrepancies in the economic and educational growth are associated with marked variations in the rate of upward mobility experienced by various generations and in the amount of familial obligations to which they must conform.

Discrepancies between educational and economic developments are also likely to affect relationships between sexes. First, orientations of educated males and females toward familial social and economic organizations are highly distinctive. Educated men tend to perceive their female counterparts as threats to the existing social order and, at least temporarily, the life of the educated women is often a lonely one. In addition, any tightening in the labor market tends to limit the employment of women. As a result, there is a growing ambivalence in the attitudes that African individuals adopt toward female education. On the one hand, many people are willing to recognize that disparities between male and female educational levels limit chances for further economic development, since a low level of education does not prepare women for the innovations in child-rearing practices so necessary for modernization. On the other hand, many people keep discriminating against educated women both in occupational and matrimonial terms.

CONCLUSION: EDUCATION AND ELITE FORMATION

One of the most striking characteristics of African educational developments is the continuity of the tensions and strains to which they give birth. The problems of determining whether elites should be universalist or particularist, of deciding whether educational developments should precede economic growth or vice versa, and of controlling the occupational and geographic mobility of educated individuals have been discussed since the very early days of colonization. This continuity is both reassuring and frightening. It suggests that colonial educators were not necessarily "monsters." It also suggests that we have not made a great deal of progress on the road toward economic, educational, and social rationality since the turn of the century.

Thus far, the role played by formal schooling in the processes of elite formation has been positive. It has facilitated a greater mobility among the various segments of African societies and has stimulated a certain reorganization of occupational and social structures. The universalistic values underlying formal schooling have changed the criteria used for defining individual placement in such structures. Achievement becomes more important than ascription in this respect and stimulates individual creativity.

Yet, the role performed by formal education may also introduce dysfunctions. First, we have noted that there is a growing gap in the orientations and the values of rural and urban elites. Second, we have seen that the spread of formal education has tended to favor the emergence of an elite strongly oriented toward positions within the public sector of the economy—a situation which could prevent an indispensable diversity in the economic and political orientations of the leaders. Third, discrepancies in the growth rates of educational and economic institutions lead to tensions between ethnic and age groups, as well as between sexes. Indeed, development always implies social differentiation and hence accentuated tensions between those components of the nation-state most likely to compete for access to the additional commodities brought forth by social change. Lastly, the question remains of determining the conditions under which the circulation of elites may slow down or impede further development.

All these difficulties are not specific to the African scene. They characterize all nations with a fast rate of social change and are visible throughout the Third World. An examination of the processes of elite formation in Africa should be the first step toward a more systematic cross-cultural analysis. It is only after having completed such comparisons that we shall be able to have more realistic expectations about the returns to be expected from educational investments.

17

Urbanization and Change

AKIN L. MABOGUNJE

ALTHOUGH IT IS THE LEAST urbanized continent, Africa is without doubt the area with the fastest rate of urban growth in the world. On the basis of population centers of 100,000 and over, the African continent had an annual rate of growth of 3.9 per cent between 1850 and 1950, compared with 2.6 per cent per annum for the world as a whole.[1] This figure for Africa was almost equaled by the 3.7 per cent for that period in the Americas. But while the rate has decreased in the Americas during the last fifty years, it has continued to rise in Africa.

This phenomenal movement of people from rural to urban areas is perhaps the most important basis of social change on the African continent today. Urbanization is not only a process of population agglomeration but a means whereby skills and aptitudes are constantly being innovated and upgraded and new and more vigorous organizations and institutions evolved to tackle the momentous problems of the age.[2] In considering urban patterns in Africa, therefore, it is this special role of cities as centers of economic, social, and political transformation that will be stressed. Transformation and change also set up strains and stresses in society and some of these will be spotlighted, where a comprehensive treatment cannot be offered.

THE HISTORY OF URBANIZATION IN AFRICA

In spite of the small proportion of African people living in cities today, it is important to remember that the process of urbanization has had a long history in

1. United Nations, European Seminar on Urban Development Policy and Planning, *General Introductory Report* (SEM/URB/POL/WPl), 1962.
2. Rhoads Murphy, "The City as a Center of Change: Western Europe and China," *Annals of the Association of American Geographers*, XLIV (1954), 349–62.

MAJOR PRE-COLONIAL URBAN CENTERS

Africa. Indeed, four major centers of urban development can be identified. Three of these predated the European colonization of the continent: the Nile Valley and the Mediterranean coastland of North Africa, the Sudan and forest belts of West Africa, and the coastline of East Africa (see map on this page.) The fourth area comprises mainly European foundations in the central and southern parts of the continent.

The Nile Valley and the Mediterranean Coast

The flood plain of the lower Nile was one of the major centers for the first urban revolution in the world. About 3500 B.C., the earliest cities in Africa

emerged here as a result of the attempt by the pharaohs to control and centralize the administration of the population of the Nile Valley. The pharaonic hegemony in this area continued unchallenged for nearly 3,000 years. Memphis, then
Thebes and Tell el 'Amarna grew up as the capital cities of the Egyptian kingdom. But there were other cities, subordinate centers of administration, populated by priests, shopkeepers, and craftsmen of the humbler sort. It has been
suggested that these early Egyptian cities lacked a civic tradition, that, unlike
the situation in nearby Mesopotamia, they developed little in the way of municipal organizations to attract the loyalty of their inhabitants or to give them a
personal interest in the running of their own affairs.[3] In short, there was no
responsible middle class to preserve the autonomy and spirit of the city against
the autocracy of the pharaohs. Regardless of the social structure of these cities,
it is nonetheless clear that from this early date the process of urbanization had
begun in Africa.

The period of the ancient Mediterranean world (roughly from 1200 B.C. to
A.D. 500) saw a new flowering of cities in Africa, embracing not only the Nile
Valley but also most of northwest Africa. The development in this latter area
began with the trading and colonizing activities of the Phoenicians and Cartha-
ginians beginning about 1200 B.C. and lasting for some one thousand years. This
area reached its highest level of development during the Roman occupation,
which began with the destruction of Carthage in 146 B.C. and lasted for about
650 years. The Romans brought to these African areas their essentially urban
culture. Although the actual number of Roman colonists in North Africa was
small, their influence on the life and economy of the area was tremendous.
Agricultural production for export was central to the economic activities of Roman Africa, as it was for the colonial economies of modern Africa. Up to the end
of the first century A.D. the emphasis was on the production of wheat for export
to Rome. From then until the termination of the Roman hegemony in this area
in A.D. 430, olive oil and wine were also important export commodities.

The needs of this trade encouraged the development of new urban centers in
North Africa or reinforced and revitalized those deriving from the earlier Carthaginian period. By the end of the Roman period, for example, Carthage was
said to have a population of over 100,000. Most of the other towns were small
(with populations generally between 5,000 and 10,000) and scattered unevenly
throughout the area. Along the southeastern coast of present-day Tunisia, and
in Tripolitania, important port cities served the Roman trading galleys. However, there were few cities in the interior. The undulating countryside which
opens to the sea near Sousse had several large centers such as Thelepte (Feriana)
and Sufetula (Sbeitla). Other areas of major urban concentrations include
the lower Medjerda Valley, the coastal region of Algeria, the region around

3. J. H. Hawkes and L. Wooley, *Prehistory and the Beginnings of Civilization* (New York:
Harper & Row, 1963), pp. 429–33.

Carthage, the Numidian Plateau, and areas along routes to the desert interior.[4]

Details of the characteristics of these Roman cities need not concern us here. Suffice it to say that they were in many respects similar to their prototypes on the European continent. The important point to stress is that these cities, during both the Carthaginian and the Roman periods, had engaged in trade across the Sahara Desert with peoples of the Sudanic belt in West Africa. The barbarian invasions in A.D. 429, which put an end to the Roman control of large parts of the ancient world, seriously disrupted trade relations in Africa and led to a waning of city life everywhere in the former Roman empire. The succeeding four centuries of instability and confusion in Europe are usually referred to as the Dark Ages.

In North Africa, the barbarians (Vandals) were in turn conquered by Byzantium, but in the seventh century the whole coast of North Africa was swept over by the Arabs, expanding from their base on the Arabian Peninsula. The Arabs were essentially a nomadic people, nurtured in the desert of Arabia and totally unused to the settled agricultural and urban economy of the Romans. Moreover, the strong proselytizing nature of the Islamic religion produced a conscious hostility to the survival of the Christian churches, which in Europe at this time were important in preserving the idea of city life until it flowered again with the revival of trade in the medieval period. The nomadic pastoral economy of the Arabs, however, led to the introduction of the camel into North and Saharan Africa between the seventh and eighth centuries.[5] When peaceful conditions began to return to North Africa in the ninth century, this development was to prove very important in linking North Africa commercially with the West African Sudan. In this way the growth of urban centers in both North and West Africa was indirectly stimulated.

The West African Sudan and Forest Belts

Urban development in the West African Sudan was linked both with state formation in the area and with the needs of international commerce. Much of this commerce was with Mediterranean Europe and was conducted through the major ports of North Africa. The most important article of commerce was gold. Mauny suggests, in fact, that the Sudan was one of the principal providers of gold to the European world throughout the Middle Ages, until the discovery of America.[6] Apart from gold, other important items of the trade included slaves, ivory, ebony, horses, hides, and skins—especially the famed "moroccan" leather

4. Eugene Albertini, *L'Afrique romaine* (Algiers: Imprimerie F. Fontana, 1949), pp. 14–19.

5. Rhoads Murphy, "The Decline of North Africa since the Roman Occupation: Climatic or Human?" *Annals of the Association of American Geographers,* XLI (1951), 116–32.

6. Raymond Mauny, *Tableau géographique de l'ouest africain en moyen age* (Dakar: IFAN, 1961); see also Basil Davidson, *Old Africa Rediscovered* (London: Gollancz, 1959), p. 84.

derived from the Sokoto area of northern Nigeria. In exchange came salt from the Sahara desert, a wide range of European manufactured articles (including glass beads from the principal glassmakers of Venice and textiles of various kinds), silver and copper, as well as cowries from the Indian Ocean.

This extensive international trade across the desert encouraged the growth of an equally extensive intraregional trade within the Sudan itself, and between it and the forest areas to the south. The North African explorer Leo Africanus, for instance, writing toward the end of the medieval period, emphasized the trade in textile and leather goods from Hausaland to Timbuktu and Gao.[7] Together, these trading activities encouraged the rise of numerous cities in the area. In general, one can distinguish two broad zones of city development. There was a northern zone at the edge of the desert where the cities served the important functions of terminal markets of trade with North Africa and provisioning stations for caravans about to cross the desert. Such cities included, from west to east, Tekrur, Audagost, Walata, Kumbi, Timbuktu, Lirekka, Gao, Takedda, Tadmekket, Agadès, and Bilma. The southern zone of cities developed in connection with the interregional trade with the forest areas from which most of the gold, slaves, and ivory were derived. They included, again from west to east, such cities as Silla, Bamako, Ségou, Jenne, Ouagadougou, Fada Ngourma, Gaya, Kukia, Kano, Kukawa, Jega, and Katsina.

Farther south during the same period, towns and cities emerged in the kingdoms which were developing in the forest belt (notably Ashanti, Ewe, Yoruba, and Benin). The Yoruba concentration was probably the most important of these city systems and can be used to illustrate their general characteristics. The relation of forest cities with those of the Sudan region is not clear, although the evidence seems to suggest some early contacts between the two areas. Yoruba towns, however, clearly seemed to have evolved as bases for "colonial" expansion by the Yoruba into territory already occupied by societies less organized and practicing a less advanced economy. The Yoruba are regarded as having migrated into their present location from the northeastern parts of the continent some time between the seventh and tenth centuries A.D. According to a Nigerian historian, S. O. Biobaku, this movement occurred in a series of waves.[8] The earliest of these led to the founding of Ile-Ife, which is regarded even today as the cultural hearth of the Yoruba. A later wave led to the founding of Old Oyo, which for a long time exercised political and military dominance over a large part of Yorubaland. From these two centers, minor waves went out to found other cities. Notable among these were Ketu, Owu, Savé, and Illa. Other urban centers emerged later, like Ijebu-Ode, Ondo, Owo, Ede, Oshogbo, Ogbomosho, Shaki, and Iseyin. In the nineteenth century came social upheavals, following

7. *The History and Description of Africa,* trans. Johannes Pory (1600; London: Hakluyt Society, 1896), III, 828.

8. *The Origin of the Yoruba* (Lagos: Federal Information Service, 1955), p. 21.

the active involvement of Yorubaland in the transatlantic slave trade. This was a time of the destruction of numerous small towns and the emergence of large centers such as Ibadan and Abeokuta from the concentrations of the displaced population.

Basically, Yoruba towns were administrative centers, and over the centuries they had evolved an elaborate power structure and a hierarchical system of administration, both at the level of the city and of the kingdom. Nonetheless, they soon exhibited economic patterns significantly different from those of the countryside; trade and craft production became their lifeblood. They maintained extensive trade relations both among themselves and with other areas. Indeed, by the early eighteenth century, John Barbot commented that

> good fine cloths are made and sold by the natives to foreigners, who have a good rent for them at the Gold Coast, especially the Hollanders, who carry thence great quantities, which they turn to good account.[9]

The East African Coast

The early development of cities in West Africa was paralleled on the East African coast. Here, records suggest trading contacts with the Mediterranean dating from the Greek period. The *Periplus* (pilot book) *of the Erythraean Sea*, written by a Greek of Alexandria about A.D. 60, suggests that ships from the Red Sea areas met those from India and together they carried on trade with cities on the East African coast. The number of these cities, however, seemed to have increased with the Arab expansion under Islam in the seventh century A.D. The social upheaval in Arabia led to waves of refugees seeking out the East African coast not simply for trade but, more important, for settlement. The trading cities encountered by the Arabs on the coast were transformed into Islamized communities. Thus, from early times, these cities consisted of highly mixed communities of indigenous Bantu-speaking Africans, Yemenite Arabs, Persians, and even some Malay. Gradually these peoples evolved into the Swahili people of today.

The major cities of the East African coast included Mogadishu, Brava, Lamu, Malindi, Mombasa, Zanzibar, Kilwa, and Sofala. At first, their trade was in ivory, rhinoceros horn, tortoiseshell, and a little palm oil. Later, from the tenth century, iron ore and gold became important. The Arab geographer Edrisi, in A.D. 1154, reported that the inhabitants of this area depended entirely on the iron trade for their livelihood, and that a great number of iron mines were found in the mountains inland from Sofala.[10] He also emphasized that it was from this

9. *A Description of the Coasts of North and South Guinea* (London, 1732; reprint ed., London: Frank Cass, 1969), p. 354.

10. *Géographie d'Edrisi*, trans. P. Amédée Jaubert, 2 vols. (Paris: Imprimerie Nationale, 1836).

iron ore that India produced the famous wootz steel which she sold throughout the medieval world – the steel from which the swordsmiths of Damascus made their much-sought-after blades. The gold-working continued until the Portuguese period. Indeed, mining experts estimated the yield of gold from this area prior to the Portuguese contact at anywhere between fifteen and seventy-five million pounds sterling, which would account in considerable measure for the fabulous wealth of medieval Indian rulers.[11]

Most of the cities of the East African coast developed as independent city-states. There are early references to a certain Ali ibn Hasan, who is said to be the founder of a dynasty which ruled these trading cities until the coming of the Portuguese. Evidence, however, seems to suggest the minimum of administrative centralization. A number of the cities, in fact, developed into strong, autonomous states and enjoyed marked economic prosperity. Kilwa on the Tanzanian coast, for example, founded in A.D. 975, held the distinction of being the only African state south of the Mediterranean to strike its own independent coinage during the medieval period.[12]

Central and Southern Africa

The fourth major area of urban development is central and southern Africa. Urbanization here derives almost exclusively from the European colonization of the area. Beginning with the founding of Capetown by Jan van Riebeeck in 1652, European-type urban centers spread first eastward along the coast and later inland with gold-mining and railway development toward the Zambezi River and beyond. From their very beginning these cities were greatly influenced by economic and social development in Europe. At first, their economic orientation was toward the export of primary products of agriculture, animal husbandry, and mining. But gradually, industrial development, largely for home consumption, came to dominate and transform their economy. In particular, the earlier mining areas matured into major industrial districts. Thus, apart from the coastal ports and cities, the main centers of urbanization in southern Africa are found in the gold-mining areas of Witwatersrand, with Johannesburg as the major city; the Great Dyke region of Rhodesia, with Salisbury and Bulawayo as major cities; and the copper-mining areas of Katanga (in Congo-Kinshasa) and Zambia (the Copperbelt).

In all these urban centers, contrary to the tradition of relatively unrestricted interaction of peoples in other cities of Africa, the European settlers introduced in varying degrees the practice of racial separatism. By denying the local people and others of non-European origin full citizenship and equality before the law, the European minority not only subverted the economic aspirations of the vast

11. G. P. Murdock, *Africa: Its Peoples and Their Culture History* (New York: McGraw-Hill, 1959), p. 211.
12. *Ibid.*, p. 308.

majority of the populace but encouraged the development of shantytowns or *bidonvilles* around all their cities. These ghettos housed the Africans, who were denied most of the benefits of urban life but were required to provide labor to keep the mills of the urban European economic and social life turning.

The European impact on the recent history of urbanization in Africa is, however, not limited to the central and southern parts of the continent. Especially since the nineteenth century, European penetration of the continent has significantly affected the nature and pattern of urban development everywhere. This is most pronounced in the economic aspect of urban life. The economy of traditional African cities was exposed to far-reaching transformations, and this in turn influenced and changed the physical and social conditions in the cities. To assess this impact, it is necessary first to provide a brief summary of the characteristics of the traditional urban economy in Africa, and then to indicate the many ways in which it was transformed in the century of European domination.

PRE-EUROPEAN URBAN ECONOMIES IN AFRICA

Although trade was the lifeblood of the pre-European African cities, craft production was perhaps equally important. The basic unit of craft production was the master craftsman, who was assisted by one or more journeymen and one or more apprentices. In general, most production units were small, seldom comprising more than ten individuals. But there were numerous instances where several production units could be housed under the same roof, giving the appearance of a modern factory. This was particularly true of the weaving, dyeing, and smithing industries.

The master craftsman was someone who had completed a full apprenticeship in the production of a particular commodity or service. Apprenticeship was very often based on ascription, that is, by the fact of being a member of a lineage or family group which had been known in the city to be skilled in the particular craft. The importance of lineage membership in recruitment to apprenticeship varied widely from craft to craft. In general, apprenticeship began as soon as a boy was old enough to help with any stage in the production process. It continued until adult life. When he had mastered the art, there was no formal test or examination indicating that a certain widely accepted standard of competence had been attained. There may have been a ceremony to mark the occasion, but this would very likely have been part of the broader ceremony associated with reaching the age of puberty. For most accomplished apprentices, the immediate prospect was that of becoming a journeyman either to one's own father or to a relative. This period lasted until the youth earned enough to buy the equipment and raw materials necessary to set up on his own as a master craftsman. At that stage, he also had to decide whether to remain in his own town or migrate to another area to seek out new customers and clientele.

The production process was basically manual, though in a few cases it involved the use of animals. There was little dependence on inanimate sources of power such as wind, water, coal, or electricity. This fact, it has been suggested, was a major reason for the small size of the production unit. When, therefore, a basic change occurred involving the use of the imported steam engine as a source of power for production, it ushered in the beginnings of an industrial revolution and subsequently a phenomenal transformation of the character of cities.

Because of their small size, traditional craft industries usually occupied very little space. As a result, traditional African cities showed only moderate differentiation into functional zones.[13] Thus, particular quarters in a city might have been well known for the production of particular goods, or a particular street might have been distinguished by the concentration along its length of numerous craftsmen in the same line of production. Such a street was often called by the name of the dominant craft. Thus, in Fez (Morocco) there is the smith's row, and in Ibadan (Nigeria) there is *agbede adodo*, or the foundry quarter.[14]

The need to regulate the activities and protect the interest of producers in a particular craft industry made the institution of guilds a basic feature of the urban economy of the most traditional African cities. The functions of the guild included not only setting and maintaining an agreed price level, ensuring a certain standard of workmanship, and providing welfare services for its members, but also participating as a corporate unit in the political or religious life of the urban community.[15] The importance attached to guild associations, especially in terms of their corporate role, seemed to vary. Thus, in some cities the guild of wholesale and retail traders was regarded as more important than that of blacksmiths, and the blacksmiths' guild more important than that of weavers and leatherworkers, and so on. Guild associations seldom had connections beyond their particular city. There were instances, however, where in a kingdom the titled heads of guilds in the capital city had responsibility for guilds in other towns of the kingdom. M. G. Smith has noted, for instance, that in the Zaria Emirate (Nigeria) craft heads of the capital city were required to tour the kingdom at the tax season to collect the allotted tax of their particular crafts from the local craft heads.[16] Nadel, reporting on the Nupe area (Nigeria), pointed out that it was to the craft head of the capital city that the ruler of the kingdom gave

---

13. Jennifer Bray, "The Industrial Structure of a Traditional Yoruba Town: The Example of Weaving in Iseyin" (M.A. thesis, University of Ibadan, 1966), pp. 131–32.

14. See Louis Massignon, "Enquête sur les corporations musulmanes d'artisans et de commerçants au Maroc," *Revue du monde musulman*, LVIII (1924), 72–73.

15. Peter Lloyd, "Craft Organization in Yoruba Towns," *Africa*, XXIII (1953), 30–44.

16. *The Economy of the Hausa Communities in Zaria*, Colonial Research Studies, No. 16 (London: H.M.S.O., 1955), p. 15.

bulk orders for craft products such as farm tools, war equipment, metalware, leather goods, and clothing.[17] The craft head, in turn, allocated the orders among the available workers, and sometimes among the towns. In North Africa, there was also the *mohtasseh*, or head of all the guilds in a city, who was usually appointed by the sultan.

Craft goods can be classed into two broad groups: artistic and utility goods. The former were goods produced for the aristocracy and religious cults and included such items as brass, bronze, and silver wares, carvings, fancy leather works, and carpets. The utility goods were intended for use by the general populace. They included agricultural implements, locks and keys, cloth, pottery, shoes, and various wooden utensils. Since the rate of production was necessarily slow, supply factors—in particular the amount of labor available—set a constraint on the level of production. Labor availability, in turn, was conditioned by the low level of productivity in agriculture, in that large numbers of hands were required on the farms to provide the surplus foodstuffs necessary to support the relatively few non-agricultural producers in the cities. In a period of poor transportation development, when movement depended on human porterage, or the use of donkeys or camels, or of dugout canoes, the extent to which the agricultural surplus could be augmented by import from distant areas was greatly restricted.

Thus, it is easy to see why, as a result of a relatively undeveloped production and transportation technology, the number and the size of traditional African cities were kept very low. One of the major consequences of the increased European penetration of the continent during the last century was the introduction of advanced technologies of production and transportation. Their impact was a mixed blessing, but they provided the basis for the tremendous physical, social, and economic transformations going on in most African cities today.

THE IMPACT OF INDUSTRIAL EUROPE ON AFRICAN CITIES

The Industrial Revolution in Europe was characterized by factory-based, mass production of producer and consumer goods, as well as by the invention of means of land transportation which were faster and more capacious than anything the world had known before. These transportation facilities were particularly important in distributing the mass-produced goods from the factories of Europe virtually "to the utmost ends of the world." Indeed, it was only after 1884, when active construction of railways in Africa was initiated, that European penetration had any serious impact on the economy of most African cities. The

17. S. F. Nadel, *A Black Byzantium: The Kingdom of Nupe in Nigeria* (London: Oxford University Press, 1942), pp. 265–68.

railways flooded the cities of Africa with a wide variety of cheap, mass-produced, manufactured goods from Europe, thereby setting in motion far-reaching changes in the nature of the local economy. Of these changes, three deserve further elaboration: the undermining of traditional craft industries; the adaptation of traditional craft organization to modern production processes; and the reappraisal of the locational advantage of individual cities with respect to the new pattern of trade.

Undermining of Traditional Craft Industries

The availability of cheaper manufactured substitutes for local craft products quickly resulted in a fall in the demand for the latter. Especially with respect to utility goods, such as textiles, shoes, and metal wares, the manufactured substitutes had a better finish, greater attractiveness, and could be more easily obtained, usually from stock and in any desired quantity.

More than this, the European impact seriously undermined the social importance and control that attached to craft organization and production. Miner, writing about Timbuktu, pointed out that "the craft organization of pre-French days was supported by supernatural sanctions, physical force, popular consensus, and the right to select apprentices."[18] It was believed, for instance, that if anyone but an apprentice shoemaker tried to sew leather slippers, the needle would turn against him and prick his finger. If a person who was not from a family of masons tried to build a house, he would topple from the wall to his death; besides, no homeowner would have his house repaired by a mason who was not from a builder's family because the owner would not want his house to collapse. Moreover, society permitted the use of physical force against those who infringed upon guild prerogatives.

The liberalizing attitudes of colonial administrations everywhere in Africa weakened the economic cohesiveness of craft organizations. Indeed, in Morocco the French passed a law in 1917 which transferred the powers of the *mohtasseh*, or guild head, to the municipal authorities.[19] The greater social and economic rewards associated with European-type education and employment also impaired recruitment to apprenticeship, even from within the ranks of craft families. The loss of consumers meant that even master craftsmen had to seek new sources of income, either by closing down their workshops and reverting to agricultural pursuits or by converting to more modern production processes, even if on a small scale. During the last one hundred years the picture everywhere was that of a startling decline in the number of traditional, urban craftsmen. Figures are not easy to come by, but the situation in Morocco (Table 2) for

18. Horace Miner, *The Primitive City of Timbuctoo* (Princeton: Princeton University Press, 1953), p. 54.
19. Charles F. Stewart, *The Economy of Morocco: 1912–62* (Cambridge: Harvard University Press, 1964), p. 137.

the eleven-year period from 1947 to 1958 is perhaps typical of the trend in most traditional African cities.

TABLE 2
MOROCCO: NUMBER OF ARTISANS, BY TRADES
1947

Trade	Master Craftsmen	Workmen	Apprentices	Total	Percentage of Total Number of Artisans
		1947			
Textiles	44,341	19,311	5,729	69,381	44.3
Leather	14,724	10,454	5,442	30,620	19.6
Building and Ceramics	17,006	6,982	2,375	26,363	16.9
Metals	5,250	1,814	1,588	8,652	5.6
Wood	4,419	2,810	962	8,191	5.4
Miscellaneous	9,443	2,365	2,044	13,852	8.2
Total	95,183	43,736	18,140	157,059	100.0
		1958–59			
Textiles	20,405	11,223	5,623	37,251	30.0
Leather	10,203	5,988	1,999	18,190	14.8
Building and Ceramics	6,785	4,857	948	12,590	10.2
Metals	4,654	1,882	883	7,419	6.0
Wood	4,449	2,167	1,001	7,617	6.2
Vegetable Products	6,254	769	–	7,023	5.7
Miscellaneous (production)	1,818	4,150	–	5,968	4.9
Miscellaneous (services)	11,655	13,173	2,498	27,326	22.2
Total	66,223	44,209	12,952	123,384	100.0

Source: Data for 1947 are from the Moroccan Ministry of the Economy (Directorate of Handicrafts), "Artisanat, problèmes et perspectives," mimeographed, 1958. Data for 1958–59 are from the report by the production subcommittee (Directorate of Handicrafts) in the Moroccan Five-Year Plan for 1960–64. Both sets of data are reproduced in *Labour Survey of North Africa* (Geneva: International Labour Office, 1960), p. 360.

Although this trend toward a decline in numbers of craftsmen is likely to continue with regard to the utility crafts, the artistic crafts seem to have found a new lease of life, especially with growing tourist demands and a widening employment for as many people as possible. Governments in most African countries today are attempting to rehabilitate the craft industries, not only in cities and towns but also in rural areas. In particular, attempts are being made to organize the craftsmen into cooperatives and to offer them credit facilities for joint purchase of expensive modern equipment. Some countries have, in fact, made elaborate arrangements to stimulate greater craft production. Thus, Morocco as early as 1918 established an Office for Indigenous Industries and Crafts. In 1919, it introduced an official stamp guaranteeing the quality and origin of Moroccan carpets. Since the Second World War, it has also set up a Directorate of Handicrafts with agents to carry out inspections of craft production and to provide occupational training for artisans through special schools and apprenticeship workshops. The result has been a growing increase in the market value of craft products (Table 3) as well as in the amount exported.

TABLE 3
MOROCCO: MARKET VALUE OF HANDICRAFT PRODUCTS, 1957–59
(in millions of francs)

Trade	1957	1958	1959
Leatherwork	606	779	802
Basket-making	78	100	118
Copper goods	86	132	150
Carpets	177	203	223

Source: *Labour Survey of North Africa* (Geneva: International Labour Office, 1960), p.363.

The Adaptation to Modern Production Processes

Urban craftsmen with a more flexible turn of mind, instead of deserting craft production completely, have turned to producing goods of more modern significance. In Ibadan, for instance, Callaway reports cases of blacksmiths' shops which have been transformed into semimodern foundries producing such items as photographers' stands, barber chairs, iron bedsteads, iron chair frames, and a wide variety of farm tools.[20] In some cases, the blacksmith may become a tinsmith, using imported corrugated sheet iron to make such items as cooking utensils, buckets, metal boxes for school books, metal trunks, and sieves.

More commonly, new production processes such as photography, printing, automobile repair, furniture-making, tailoring, baking, sign-making, and shoe-making have taken on some aspects of traditional craft organizations, especially the master-apprentice relation and the guild system. This has involved a number of departures from tradition, however, including the recruitment of apprentices without regard to their lineage or ethnic origin, the precise definition of the period of apprenticeship, and the commutation to a fee of part of the services due from an apprentice to a master, as well as the less direct political involvement sought for the guild. Moreover, some degree of formal education

20. Archibald Callaway, "From Traditional Crafts to Modern Industries," in *The City of Ibadan,* ed. P. C. Lloyd, A. L. Mabogunje, and Bolanle Awe (Cambridge: At the University Press, 1967), p. 157.

is becoming increasingly characteristic of, though not a necessary qualification for, apprenticeship in these small-scale industries.

Governments in African countries are trying to aid these small-scale producers with technical, organizational, and financial assistance. Partly because of their low capital-labor ratio, these small-scale industries are seen as possible means of reducing urban unemployment as well as creating a reservoir of semiskilled industrial labor. It is somewhat doubtful, however, that these small-scale industrial activities have the capacity for development into larger-scale enterprises. But given the need to disseminate technical skills widely and rapidly and to provide, however crudely, much-needed goods and services, the role of craftsmen in both the urban and the national economy has been highly significant.

Locational Advantage and the New Pattern of Trade

The transportation network which colonial administrations in the various African countries established between 1885 and 1930 imposed new patterns of locational importance on traditional African cities. The main elements in the new networks were the railways running inland and their terminal ports, reflecting the export orientation of the colonial economies. Roads were significant at first only as feeders to the railways and did not seriously come into their own as major economic trade routes until after the Second World War. Indeed, until then, the development of roads in competition to the railway was resisted everywhere.

In the structure of this new transportation network little attention was paid to location of cities and towns; rather, areas rich in potential resources for export were sought out. A number of interior cities with limited export potential found themselves poorly integrated into the new economic-spatial order. In contrast, small towns or villages which were located at important nodal points within the new network suddenly blossomed and grew rapidly. The port cities in particular experienced phenomenal growth. In a number of cases, completely new towns were laid out and developed by the colonial administration at strategic points within the network.

These developments strongly affected the economy of traditional African cities. Yet this impact varied significantly between the artisans and the traders, the men and the women, the young and the old. The artisans, for instance, felt the effect more than the traders. Because of the social matrix within which the pre-colonial organization was established, it was not easy for an artisan to move away from his town if its economic health was no longer sound. This was not so with the trader. He was familiar with the vagaries and shifts of trade and was prepared to travel wherever the trade repaid his effort. This willingness to move to new places in response to the opening up of new opportunities was more noticeable in men than in women and more apparent in the young than in the old. The result was a dual picture in most African countries: one of stagnating, formerly important traditional cities, and the other of ebullient, fast-growing, new colonial urban centers.[21]

A TYPOLOGY OF AFRICAN URBAN PATTERNS

From our discussion of urban history and traditional occupations, it is possible to distinguish a fourfold pattern in contemporary African cities based on the type of organization and the character of economic and social life. These four types include (1) the traditional city, (2) the "rejuvenated" traditional city, (3) the colonial city, and (4) the European city.

The traditional city today is one where traditional economic, social, and spatial organization still predominate. It is a city which in general has failed to integrate effectively into the new spatial economy and transportation network. In consequence, its economy is stagnant, and it suffers a high rate of migration of its youthful and more energetic population. This loss weakens the traditional guild organization and denies the cities the aggressive and imaginative leadership which could pull them out of their depression. Social life, although close and intimate and reflecting traditional usages and stratification, shows a certain degree of instability resulting from the general uncertainty of economic fortunes and the awareness that the possibility of emigration either to the rural areas or to other cities is always imminent. The demographic pattern of traditional cities shows a higher proportion of aged people and children, sometimes also of women. Ethnic heterogeneity is not very pronounced. Many houses or rooms in houses are vacant, while others are in various stages of disrepair. Urban utilities are poorly developed and, where they exist, are inadequately utilized. Examples of such cities include Timbuktu, Katsina, Oyo, and Iseyin.

The "rejuvenated" traditional city is usually located on the modern transportation network within a rich agricultural region or close to a mining site. Its population is highly heterogeneous, and it shows a division into three basic areal units: the indigenous town (the *birni* of the Hausa of Nigeria or the *medina* of the Arabs of North Africa), the immigrant quarters, and the European "reservation" area. The reservation was the typical form of European settlement outside, but adjacent to, a traditional African city. In the case of the British particularly, the colonial policy was that of "differentiation"; this emphasized ethnic exclusiveness and found expression in a form of residential segregation. The French too, in spite of a professed policy of "assimilation," strenuously maintained the "reservation area" form of residential segregation. In Morocco,

21. See, for example, A. L. Mabogunje, *Urbanization in Nigeria* (London: University of London Press, 1968); and Hassan Awad, "Morocco's Expanding Towns," *Geographical Journal*, CXXX (1964), 49–64.

for instance, Marshal Lyautey, the French administrator-general, decreed in 1918 that Europeans should live in a quarter of each town separate from that of the indigenes (the *medina*).[22] In recent years, with the attainment of independence in most African countries, the racial exclusiveness of the reservations has been broken down and many Africans in the civil service and in the higher income classes reside here along with Europeans.

The urbanization process within a "rejuvenated" city, such as Kano or Ibadan in Nigeria, shows somewhat contradictory trends. The indigenous town suffers a gradual decline or deurbanization due to a negative selection whereby its more successful members migrate to higher income residential districts, usually in the immigrant parts of the city, and/or migrate away from the city altogether. The immigrant part of the city is itself highly differentiated, physically on the basis of income, and socially on the basis of ethnicity, in a manner discussed more fully below. Thus, while there are residential districts in the indigenous area which are veritable shantytowns, there are also districts of very high-quality housing where members of the professional, business, and administrative classes live. An equally interesting feature of the "rejuvenated" traditional city is the existence of two major commercial centers in the town—one is traditional, comprising a central market or bazaar, and the other is more recent and modern, very reminiscent of the European or American central business district.

The colonial city was essentially a creation of the colonial administration, but intended for a principally African population. It served primarily as a nodal point within the colonial spatial economy which was largely oriented to export. Its population is almost wholly immigrant and the task of generating a civic spirit out of such disparate elements has always been a difficult one. More usually, as an adjustment mechanism to the strangeness and uncertainties of their new urban existence, the immigrants have formed various mutual-aid voluntary associations.[23] The basis of membership of such an association is very often ethnic. Members help one another in securing employment, engaging in various trades, performing social functions, or discharging civic obligations. Because of the importance of these voluntary associations, the colonial town, even though not strikingly differentiated physically, shows a variegated pattern in its social and cultural configuration.

The colonial city in Africa is found mainly within the tropics and is distinguished by the symmetry of its layout. This has occurred because of the need to facilitate both the rental and the registration of land to the immigrant population and to provide urban services such as electricity, water supply, and sewage

22. Stewart, *Economy of Morocco*, p. 141.
23. See, for example, Michael Banton, *West African City: A Study of Tribal Life in Freetown* (London: Oxford University Press, 1957); and Kenneth Little, *West African Urbanization* (Cambridge: At the University Press, 1965).

disposal to individual houses. The city is also remarkable for its wide, straight streets, controlled traffic flow, and clear, functional specialization of areas, usually revealing a central business district in the center of the town and various industrial districts at the periphery. The most developed of the colonial cities are port cities such as Lagos, Port Harcourt, Accra, Abidjan, and Dakar. Where these new cities are also capitals of their respective countries, they have shown the fastest rate of growth of any cities on the continent. Other colonial cities include various mining centers, route junctions, and administrative headquarters.

The European town, like the "rejuvenated" traditional city, is characterized by distinct racial enclaves but gives the appearance of being more European than African, due to the larger number of permanent white settlers. In the center is the European city itself, surrounded by enclaves of Asians and "Coloureds" and by the *bidonvilles* of the African laborers. Usually in such towns emphasis is given to discouraging the Africans from attempting to become permanent urban residents. The provision of accommodation is often such that a man, but not his family, can be housed. At work, the African is legally precluded from acquiring skills beyond a certain level to ensure that occupational mobility does not tempt him to commit himself to an urban existence. In the extreme example represented by the cities of South Africa (Johannesburg, Pretoria, Capetown), even simple physical mobility of Africans within the city requires the carrying of passes. An artificial economic color bar operates which makes a large proportion of the European workers parasites on the economy. Their wages are bolstered up at a level out of proportion to their marginal contribution, and various government subsidies support the generally high standard of living.

POPULATION PATTERNS IN URBAN AFRICA

The last hundred years have witnessed not only a wide variation in the urbanization process but also a remarkable increase in the urban population of Africa. The increase in the urban population may be examined under three headings: (1) growth in the number of cities and towns; (2) growth in the proportion of the total population that lives in urban centers; and (3) growth in the proportion of the urban population that lives in large cities.

A crucial point in the discussion of urban population is the operational definition of an "urban center." For different countries this definition varies with respect to the smallest unit to which the term is applied. Some adopt a population minimum of 2,000; some, 5,000; some, 10,000; and still others, 20,000. In studies of urbanization it is usual to adopt the figure of 20,000. For Africa as a

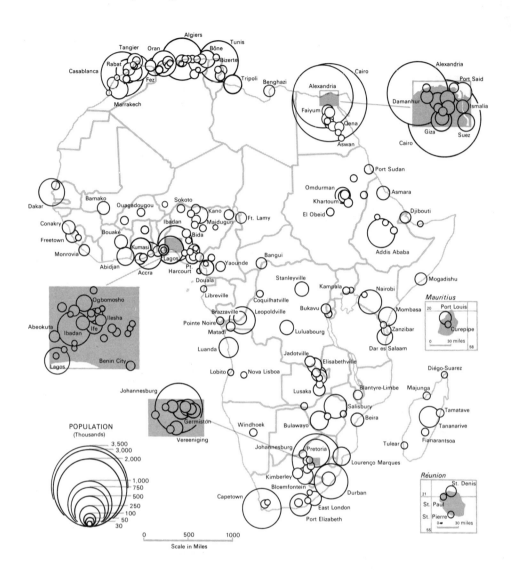

MAJOR CONTEMPORARY URBAN CENTERS
After Map 10 in *The Geography of Modern Africa* by William A. Hance. Copyright 1964
by Columbia University Press. Used with Permission of Columbia University Press.

whole it is not easy to collect statistics on the increase in the number of such centers over time. What is clear, however, is that the number has increased tremen-
dously since 1850. Breese suggests that in 1960 the number stood at 405, of which
62 had 100,000 inhabitants or more (see map on this page).[24]

With regard to the proportion of the total population living in urban centers

24. Gerald Breese, *Urbanization in Newly Developing Countries* (Englewood Cliffs, N.J.:
Prentice-Hall, 1966), p. 32.

(localities with 20,000 people and above), Davis and Hertz pointed out that as of 1950 this represented only 9 per cent of the total population of Africa compared to 13 per cent in Asia, 24 per cent in Latin America, and 42 per cent in North America. Compared to the preceding period of relatively little urban growth, the period since 1950 has been characterized by tremendous increases in the proportion of people in centers of 20,000 and above. It has not been possible to produce a continental estimate, but data from a number of countries typify the general trend. In Ghana, for instance, the proportion of the population living in urban centers rose from 7.2 per cent (1950) to 11.6 per cent (1960); in Congo-Kinshasa from 2.2 (1946) to 9.1 (1959); in Kenya from 3.8 (1948) to 5.9 (1962); and in Zambia from 11.3 (1950) to 16.8 (1960).

The trend toward population concentration in a few very large cities has also been a widespread phenomenon, although again statistical documentation is woefully deficient. A simple measure of this phenomenon is the population living in cities of 100,000 and more inhabitants expressed as a percentage of the total urban population as here defined. The general situation is perhaps typified by Ghana, Congo-Kinshasa, and Kenya. In Ghana, the proportion living in cities of 100,000 or more rose from 46 per cent (1948) to 67 per cent (1960); in Congo-Kinshasa from 48 per cent (1946) to 65 per cent (1959); and in Kenya from 58 per cent (1948) to 88 per cent (1962). If we measure growth of the urban population by reference only to cities of 100,000 or more inhabitants, for the period 1850 to 1950 Africa, as mentioned above, has had the fastest annual rate of growth (3.9 per cent) in the world. Indeed, during the first half of this century (1900–50), cities of 100,000 and more inhabitants have increased three and a half times as fast as has the total population of Africa. At this rate, from the current population increase of seven million per year in Africa, at least one and one-half million persons are being added to the big cities.

An indication of the rapidity of growth of the larger cities is provided in Table 4. As of 1960, according to these data, three cities in Africa—Cairo, Alexandria, and Johannesburg—have passed the one-million mark. Six others each had over half a million inhabitants, and the remaining eleven had over a quarter of a million. What is equally striking is the fact that most of the cities in the list more than tripled their population over the period from 1940 to 1960. Today, there are indications that three other cities on the list—Casablanca, Algiers, and Lagos—have also passed the one-million mark, and most of the remaining cities have grown even more rapidly than before.

Growth in the cities of Africa has been due both to a fairly high rate of natural increase and to immigration. Compared to the rural areas, the birth rates in African cities tend to be lower, but so too is the death rate. Table 5, showing the vital statistics for a few sample countries, well illustrates this point. The fertility rate appears to be higher in rural areas compared to urban areas, though this generalization is not always confirmed by the crude birth rates. This difference in fertility rates is due to the tendency in urban areas toward late marriages and

TABLE 4
GROWTH OF MAJOR AFRICAN CITIES, 1940–60

City	1940	1950	1960
Cairo	1,307,000	2,100,000	3,348,000
Alexandria	682,000	925,000	1,516,000
Johannesburg	286,000	880,000	1,111,000
Casablanca	268,000	551,000	965,300
Algiers	252,000	315,000	883,900
Capetown	187,000	594,000	745,800
Tunis	220,000	365,000	680,000
Durban	115,000	496,000	659,000
Ibadan	387,000	435,000	600,000
Lagos	180,000	230,000	449,500
Addis Ababa	150,000	300,000	444,000
Pretoria	257,000	245,000	422,000
Léopoldville (Kinshasa)	–	208,000	402,500
Oran	195,000	260,000	390,000
Accra	73,000	140,000	388,000
Dakar	165,000	230,000	374,000
Khartoum	190,000	240,000	312,000
Port Elizabeth	125,000	148,000	274,000
Salisbury	51,000	120,000	270,000
Nairobi	100,000	112,000	267,000

Source: *United Nations Demographic Yearbook* (New York: United Nations, 1962), pp. 310–16. Figures refer to the nearest census or population estimate available.

TABLE 5
CRUDE BIRTH AND DEATH RATES FOR URBAN AND RURAL
AREAS OF SELECTED AFRICAN COUNTRIES

Country	Year	Urban rates (per thousand)			Rural rates (per thousand)		
		Birth	Death	Infant mortality	Birth	Death	Infant mortality
Morocco	1962	47	15	–	46	20	–
Congo-Kinshasa	1955–57	52	9	66	41	23	113
Guinea	1955	52	29	189	63	41	218
Mali	1957	52	31	246	54	47	320
Senegal	1960–61	44	10	36	43	19	109
Dahomey	1961	48	12	–	54	27	–
Central African Republic	1959–60	48	26	197	48	26	188

Source: United Nations, *Economic Bulletin for Africa*, V (January 1965), 59.

toward a limitation on the size of family by the wealthier classes. It is, of course, the lower death rates in urban areas that are crucial, and the reasons for this are not difficult to find. High mortality levels in most African countries are due to infectious, parasitic, and respiratory diseases. These causes of death have been greatly reduced by inexpensive medical techniques developed or adopted in recent decades. Moreover, in African countries, public health facilities (such as hospitals, doctors, modern water supply) are much better in urban than in rural areas. There is, of course, no pretense that urban living conditions are always healthy or that they reduce mortality risks; but despite slums and despite malnutrition, it would be very surprising if mortality was higher in the urban areas than in the rural areas. The infant mortality rate, in general, tends to be very high everywhere in Africa, but again it is relatively lower in urban areas.

Migration, however, is more important than natural increase in determining the demographic characteristics of African cities. Especially in the last three decades the volume of migration from rural to urban areas in most countries has been phenomenal. The pattern reveals an unparalleled volume of migration to newer coastal port cities, as well as to mining and industrial centers, and a net loss from old, traditional centers. Everywhere, the major elements of the initial phase of migration flows are males in the age group between fifteen and forty-nine. As the urban economy becomes more mature and diversified and the urban social organization more stabilized, a tendency toward equalization between the sexes becomes more noticeable. For example, the population of Kinshasa (formerly Léopoldville) increased more than tenfold between 1926 and 1955, that is, from 23,000 to 290,000. During this period, the masculinity ratio (the number of males per 100 females for the adult population) decreased from 360 in 1926–29 to 230 in 1930–34, to 190 in 1935–39 and 1940–44, and to 180 in 1945–49, but rose back to 190 in 1950–55.[25]

The age and sex structure of most African cities thus reveals a tendency toward (1) a lower proportion of children of age group zero to fourteen, compared to the position in the rural area, (2) a higher proportion of adults, with more males than females, and (3) a lower proportion of the aged. These characteristics are largely explained by the structure of employment in African cities. As long as a city's growth by immigration continues and available jobs are primarily suitable for men, not only the masculinity ratio but also the proportion of adult male and female to the total population may remain high. Moreover, if it were possible to measure the average length of stay per immigrant and to classify immigrants as "temporary" or "permanent," the masculinity ratios might be very high for the former but perhaps more nearly balanced for the latter. Nonetheless, in a dysfunctional sector, or in the traditional city, the reverse situation is often found, with generally higher proportions of women, children, and the aged in the population.

25. Louis Baeck, "Léopoldville, phénomène urban africain," *Zaïre*, X (1956), 623–25.

THE SOCIOECONOMIC CHARACTERISTICS
OF AFRICAN CITIES

The socioeconomic patterns of contemporary urban populations in Africa illustrate a gradual breakdown of traditional forms of social organization and an emergence of new forms relevant to the modern needs of city-dwellers. The extended family system with its network of kinship relations becomes less important in the city as a reference for social action. Although an acknowledgment of kinship relations persists and remains relevant on specific occasions such as birth and funeral ceremonies, their overall significance is more diffuse and family obligations are less clear-cut. In some cities, the decreasing cohesiveness of the extended family is physically perceptible in the breakup of traditional compound houses and their replacement by smaller structures housing a single nuclear family or multiple of often non-related nuclear families. Thus, in general, the urban residential unit is much smaller than the rural household. A study by the International Labour Office, for example, indicated that while the average urban household consists of four to six persons, the average in the rural areas is nine to twelve.[26] A household is not always equivalent to a family, but it is often a very close approximation.

In place of the extended family, voluntary associations provide the newcomer to the city with a means of adjusting to his new circumstances, of finding employment, and sometimes of protecting his interest at his place of work. Initially, a newcomer may belong to a single voluntary organization comprising people from his village area, clan, or ethnic group. Through this association, he is able to maintain links with his rural origin. In a number of interesting examples, this ethnic association introduces him directly into a craft or trade in which his people already operate a virtual monopoly. Thus, in Morocco, the Ammelu people (from Tafraout in the Anti-Atlas) owned most of the grocery stores in the cities along the coast as far north as Tangier. The management of a store was rotated among the male members of the families, and in this way no individual was away from home for too long and family relationships as well as the traditional social structure were maintained.[27] Similar examples can be multiplied from other parts of the continent. In modern Lagos (Nigeria), for instance, most of the butchers come from the town of Iwo about 120 miles inland.

With longer residence in the city, acquisition of greater skills, and upward social and economic mobility, the city-dweller becomes affiliated with an increasing number of voluntary associations to meet his specific needs or preferences. Thus, he may join occupational associations or trade unions, religious

26. International Labour Office, "Family Living Studies in Africa" (Paper submitted for the E.C.A. Workshop on Urbanization in Africa, Addis Ababa, March 1962).
27. Stewart, *Economy of Morocco*, p. 139; see also J. I. Clarke, "Emigration from Southern Tunisia," *Geography*, XLII (1957), 99–101, for the examples of the Mozabites of southern Algeria and the Djerbians of Tunisia.

associations, literary societies, recreation clubs, or political parties. This widening of interests indicates a greater commitment to urban existence, though not necessarily a complete and permanent break with his rural relations.

In contemporary African cities there are few instances of rigid class or caste differentiation. Virtually everywhere on the continent, with a few significant exceptions in North Africa and southern Africa, the egalitarian or communal basis of traditional land tenure has prevented the rise of a strong class of landed aristocracy. Moreover, the breakdown of the occupational guild system has reduced some of the tenuous social barriers of the past. Although African cities show little evidence of class consciousness, there is increasing evidence of stratification by levels of consumption. However, social mobility is largely unrestricted, and arrival at a certain social stratum may be demonstrated conspicuously by such status symbols as cars, housing, and clothing.

Rapid changes in the economic conditions of cities underlie this pattern of social mobility. In the colonial days the economic organization in most African cities showed an overbearing domination by European interests. The commercial firms that bought the export produce or controlled the mines were, without exception, European-owned. In most cases, the same firms dominated the import trade, and wholesale and/or retail branches were to be found in all major cities of the country. The managers and senior officials of these firms were also European. Africans were normally restricted to the intermediate levels in trade, industry, and administration, and more often were restricted to providing only unskilled labor. In some parts of the continent, notably East Africa, the intermediate levels were, in fact, effectively monopolized by Asians. Except in North and West Africa, entry into the professions, especially law, medicine, and engineering, was seldom open to Africans.

With independence, much of this has changed. Europeans are being almost entirely displaced from administration. In commerce and industry, although European interest is still dominant in terms of capital, there is strong pressure everywhere to Africanize the management. The governments of these new African states have been aiding their nationals through loans, manpower training schemes, or restrictive work laws (against foreigners) to take over an increasing proportion of the economic activities of the country. In many cases, the governments directly participate in economic activities through statutory corporations and development boards. Scholarship schemes of various types have been launched to produce the professional and high-level manpower needed for the rapid development of both the public and private sectors of the economy.

This emphasis on manpower training has meant accelerated educational development at all levels. Some governments have gone so far as to make primary education free and compulsory. Within a decade the younger people have attained a high degree of literacy. The type of education, however, is still largely in the liberal arts, following the humanistic European tradition and paying little or no attention to vocational training in many cases. The result has been a widespread disaffection by youth in the rural areas and a massive influx of young people with an elementary school education to the cities in search of employment opportunities which often do not exist.

Callaway, however, reports that in Nigeria, after an initial phase of disillusionment, a good number of these young immigrants become apprentices, learning either the traditional or modern craft skills. He estimates that in most years some two million elementary school graduates have been so engaged.[28] On completing their apprenticeship some of these are absorbed in the growing manufacturing sector of the urban economy; a good number move out to small urban centers or rural areas to set up on their own; while others remain inadequately employed as journeymen hoping for some fortunate break in the employment market.

In spite of this trend, cities in Africa are increasingly becoming major reservoirs of the unemployed and the unemployables. The rural poor, poorly educated and with few marketable skills, still turn to the city in the hope of survival. It is partly for this reason that African cities are conspicuous areas of income inequality. The contrast in the income of the urban indigent, the recent migrant, or the displaced craftsman and that of the new generation of businessmen and professional people, who have capitalized on risk-taking and on manipulating private property for gains, is unparalleled in most Western countries.

SOCIOPOLITICAL PROBLEMS
OF URBANIZATION IN AFRICA

The major problems of urbanization in Africa stem from two causes: the rapid rate of growth of the urban population and the failure of employment opportunities to keep up with this growth.

The rate of urbanization is, of course, uneven between African countries as well as within countries. As has been emphasized above, urbanization is greatest in large, coastal, port cities and lower in smaller centers or centers poorly situated in relation to the major flow of modern economic activities. With particular regard to the coastal metropolitan areas, four types of problems are highly dependent on the rate of population growth. These are: (1) the provision of adequate housing and removal and/or prevention of slum development; (2) the provision of adequate public utilities to all parts of the metropolis; (3) the organization of an effective and efficient intracity transportation system; and (4) the establishment of a competent and forward-looking urban administration.

Each of these problems has been foreshadowed in previous comments. The

28. Archibald Callaway, "Nigeria's Indigenous Education: The Apprentice System," *Odu*, I (July 1964), 63.

presence of traditional sectors and *bidonvilles* in most African cities emphasizes the serious problems of housing shortage, chronic overcrowding, insubstantial nature of housing structures, and the low level of repair. The situation, in fact, is progressively worsened by the continuing immigration into the city and the overuse of the existing housing supply. It is estimated that to keep pace with the demand for urban housing up to 1975, and assuming a thirty-year period of replacement, African countries would have to produce some 130,000 units of dwellings each year.[29] Part of the problem is in interesting the private sector in providing this much-needed housing for the low-income group. Almost invariably this type of development is left for the governments to undertake. Since governments in the new African states have pressing infrastructural investment obligations to attend to, they have been very niggardly in dealing with the problems of urban housing. Moreover, in spite of the advice of international experts, most African countries have come to realize that there is, in reality, nothing like a low-cost housing scheme for the low-income group of city-dwellers. The rent or mortgage payments on even the cheapest of publicly constructed houses have proved far beyond the means of most African workers. Governmental initiative in this direction has, in fact, lined the pockets of the higher income groups, who buy these government-built houses and then rent them out for fantastic profits.

The provision of adequate public utilities presents a different set of problems since this is squarely a responsibility of the government. The basic issue is the allocation of scarce capital resources between social overhead investments and directly productive activities. Moreover, social overhead investments tend to be of a large, lumpy character and often are technically indivisible. In consequence, except where loans by international bodies such as the World Bank are proffered, most governments at present find such commitments unattractive. As a result, in most cities public utilities such as water supply, central sewage disposal systems, medical services, and electricity are grossly inadequate and suffer from frequent breakdowns or shortages. The undependability of these services tends to discourage foreign investment and helps to perpetuate the phenomenon of urban unemployment. The presence in most cities of a large proportion of people who cannot be taxed heavily enough to produce sufficient revenue for installing and maintaining basic services lies at the root of the problem of inadequate living facilities in these cities.

Intracity transportation also presents special difficulties, partly because of the poverty of the majority of the urban residents and partly because of the ecological pattern of development of most African cities. Especially in the rejuvenated traditional cities in western and northern Africa and in the European cities in eastern, central, and southern Africa, the typical ecological pattern has

29. United Nations, Department of Economic and Social Affairs, *Report of Ad Hoc Group of Experts on Housing and Urban Development* (E/CN.5/367), 1962, p. 61.

the *bidonville* or *medina* of the poorer people displaced at one end of the city, far away from the major centers of work. This is unlike the typical pattern in most European and American cities where the low-income classes are close to the city center and their place of work. The result is that for the low-income classes in most African cities the daily journey to work is a seriously tiring effort. Coordinated urban transport services are poorly developed in most cities, and where they exist they are beyond the means of most workers. A good number of workers thus have to spend many hours each day trekking to and from work. Others find it cheaper to invest in bicycles. The confused and heterogeneous pattern of traffic during rush hours invariably leads to traffic congestion that has to be seen to be believed.

Fundamental to the resolution of all these problems is efficient urban management and administration. For the older African cities, part of the problem lies in the incapacity of traditional governmental institutions to cope with the complex problems of the modern urban center. For the new colonial cities, the problem is to generate an ethos of responsible civic leadership among such a heterogeneous population. In either case, an inadequate financial base and a shortage of qualified and trained personnel tend to thwart even the best of managements. This does not mean that various African governments have not been attempting to modernize urban administrative institutions; the real problem is that so far their efforts have not led to any significant upgrading of the character of urban social and economic life.

Perhaps there is little that can be done in this respect until the second major cause of the problems — the failure of employment opportunities to keep up with the growth of the city population — has been effectively tackled. Until after the Second World War, the urban economy in most African countries, except in areas of relatively dense European settlement, was largely centered on trading, administration, and, in a few notable instances, mining. Since then, the tremendous rush of people to the cities and the independence of most of the countries from colonial status have increasingly turned attention toward manufacturing industries as a means of solving the unemployment situation in the cities. The postwar period, in fact, has seen a remarkable increase in manufacturing employment in the cities, but the impact of this increase on the general unemployment situation has been relatively slight. There are two reasons for this: the locational tendencies in the manufacturing industry and the available choice of technology in most developing countries.

Recent developments in the manufacturing industries have encouraged tendencies favoring concentration in a few locations, notably port cities. Such concentrations are known to result in external economies which enhance the profitability of the individual enterprise, as well as that of the complex. Moreover, in many African countries, even though manufacturing activity is not physically bound to a given location, a number of considerations often severely restrict the range of locational alternatives to a few port cities and regional centers. These include the availability of skilled labor and of basic facilities such as power, transportation, and industrial water; ready access to the procurement of machinery, equipment, spare parts, and intermediate goods, as well as to repair and maintenance services; and the proximity of markets for the manufactured products. The result has been that industrialization in most African countries to date has led to a high concentration of employment opportunities in a few cities while at the same time weakening the capacity of other cities to provide poles of counterattraction.

What makes the situation more serious is the fact that modern manufacturing technology tends on the whole to be more capital-intensive than labor-intensive. This means that the degree to which the overall employment problem can be resolved by even these increases in the number of manufacturing enterprises is greatly limited. Nonetheless, it has been suggested that in the production of certain commodities there may be a number of technological alternatives from which African countries may want to choose. For example, in many areas of engineering activity—building, construction, earth moving—it is possible to substitute in considerable measure labor for machinery. Such substitution is also feasible in certain branches of manufacturing.

Be that as it may, an equally important aspect of the unemployment situation in most urban areas in Africa is that the vast majority of the labor force lacks specialization. This is due both to the low level of development of technical skills and to the high degree of occupational instability. The latter situation is particularly common in those countries of eastern and southern Africa where, until recently, Africans were discouraged from making a permanent commitment to urban existence. The recent emphasis on education in most African countries represents an initial step toward dealing with this problem. But, as has been pointed out, there is a great need for orienting this education to the specific technological needs of the age.

Despite the many problems posed, there is no doubt that urbanization in Africa has been a force for rapid economic and social development. It has been instrumental in introducing many Africans to a money economy and to new consumption patterns. These have served as major influences in motivating increased economic exertions and ever rising aspirations. Urbanization has also been the means of introducing and diffusing new technical skills and expertise as well as new economic and social institutions. It has provided the opportunity for Africans to grapple with novel problems of modern organization and to gain increased confidence in their ability to deal with new and complex situations. Indeed, it is to this organizational ability deriving from the urban situation that most African states owe the early beginnings of the concerted nationalist protest against colonialism and the subsequent vigor with which it was carried through to independence.

It is not surprising that the prospect for Africa is one of a continuing rapid increase in the rate of urbanization. Homer Hoyt estimates that at the current rate of growth the proportion of Africans living in cities of over 100,000 would increase from 8 per cent in 1960 to 16 per cent in 1975 and to 25 per cent in the year 2000.[30] In terms of actual numbers, this would mean an increase of from roughly 20 million people living in these cities in 1960 to 48 million in 1975 and to 129 million in the year 2000. Hoyt's estimates are based on the assumption that world population will increase at the median rate of 2.5 per cent per annum predicted by the United Nations, and that there will be an increasing degree of industrialization throughout the world.

Such a phenomenal increase in the urban population of Africa would compound most of the problems outlined above; these projections underline the urgency with which the urban problems call for solutions. One expedient that has often been suggested is to dam the tide of migration into the cities. Even if this could be undertaken, such a solution would at best serve only as a palliative. For the urban problem is only one side of a coin, with the rural problem on the other side; essentially both problems revolve on the issue of how to modernize traditional economies, agricultural and non-agricultural, rapidly and effectively enough to accelerate increases in per capita productivity and output. Of the two types of locale, urban and rural, the urban offers a greater potential for resolving the problems. Consequently, it can be said that the degree and rapidity with which African countries effectively deal with their urban problems will in large measure determine how soon these countries are able to achieve a sustained rate of economic growth.

30. *World Urbanization: Expanding Population in a Shrinking World*, Technical Bulletin No. 43 (Washington D.C.: Urban Land Institute, 1962), p. 49.

18

Communications and Change

EDWARD W. SOJA

ONE OF THE MOST STRIKING DEVELOPMENTS accompanying social change in traditional societies throughout the world has been an explosion in the breadth, intensity, and impact of communications. In most African societies of one hundred years ago a man's horizons were restricted by the nature of the communications and transport channels available to him. Without written or mechanical means of effectively recording and storing information he was forced to depend upon the memory of his elders to transmit the knowledge of past generations. His physical mobility was usually limited to the distance he could travel by foot. His material possessions and the scope of his technological knowledge reflected the narrow range of his contacts and the great restrictions imposed by distance on the diffusion of innovative ideas and objects. And perhaps most important, his level of expectation, his dreams, and his actions were largely confined to a set of available alternatives which were limited by his experience and shaped by the history and immediate environment of his ethnic community. Sometimes he was able to extend his horizons through participation in trade or political administration or through a "universal" religion such as Islam, but generally he lived his entire life within a small, ethnically defined bubble which bounded an entire existence.

The forces of change which have been operating in Africa in the past century are not entirely new. Ethnic bubbles have been expanded and punctured periodically throughout African history both through the stimulus of external contacts and through indigenously generated innovation. But the introduction of the technologically advanced communications and transport systems of the industrialized West ignited a series of radical adjustments and reevaluations which was unparalleled in its impact on the individual and his society. The automobile and the railway, modern shipping and air transport, the newspaper, the telegraph, the telephone, postal facilities, radio and television—the whole

359

array of media and other channels for the movement of goods, people, and ideas that characterizes modern society—were primary generators of the forces of change which have been shaping Africa for the past hundred years and are still molding the social, economic, political, and psychological makeup of African societies today.

The subject of this essay is the development of circulation systems in Africa and their relevance to contemporary problems of social change and to the creation and consolidation of nation-states. The term *circulation* is used to encompass both communications and transportation systems, that is, any facility or structure which involves the movement of people, goods, or messages from place to place. After a brief examination of the circulation systems in pre-colonial Africa, the essay will turn to a historical and geographic analysis of the phases in the growth of modern circulation systems and their current patterns of development. Finally, an attempt at evaluating the interrelations between circulation, information flow, and nation-building will be offered, not as a final statement on the subject but as a useful preface to some of the most exciting and important processes operating within the modern world.

CIRCULATION SYSTEMS IN TRADITIONAL SOCIETIES

Circulation in traditional African societies was firmly enmeshed in a sociopolitical matrix. Ethnic society, with a number of important exceptions, was characterized by small-scale units, ethnically circumscribed and inwardly focused. Communications were almost entirely immediate and oral. Rarely did there exist distinct circulation organizations or professional communicators, for the flow of information was usually guided by social attributes such as clan membership or position within a social hierarchy.

The environment, especially the existence of physical barriers and the simple friction of distance (the tendency for interaction to be inversely related to distance), restricted both the extent and the intensity of communications so that the effective world view of a particular group was relatively narrow and usually confined to the group itself and its immediate neighbors. In the jargon of modern communications theorists, the "extending media"—those channels which facilitate the spread of information over space and time—were weakly developed. In discussing the question of societal scale and its relation to social change, the Wilsons noted that in traditional African societies

> ancestors are believed to have power over men, but it is the immediate ancestors who are feared. Similarly, logical and conventional pressure are exerted only within a small group. A man is not influenced by the arguments of those living at a

distance or those long dead. He fears the scorn and enjoys the admiration only of neighbors and contemporaries.[1]

But it would be wrong to view ethnic Africa as being composed entirely of an airtight mosaic of tiny cells in virtual isolation from one another. Several forces acted to promote intersocietal linkages and to create larger scale circulation systems. At the most basic level, there was the pattern of societal overlapping whereby large numbers of ethnic groups came to interact in a complex network of both direct and indirect linkages. Group A, for example, might have direct contacts with group B but not with group C. But groups B and C could have direct contacts with one another as well as with several other more distant groups. This pattern was frequently extended, primarily through sociolinguistic and economic ties, to involve large clusters of societies, in much the same way that a "friendship network" of an individual includes not only his immediate friends but his friends' friends and perhaps their friends as well. Thus, although two given societies may not even be aware of one another's existence, both may form part of a chain of interaction which can act as a channel for the diffusion of information, goods, and even people. Much of the widespread similarity in certain cultural features over large sections of Africa (for example, folk tales among Bantu-speaking peoples) is attributable in great part to the intricate web of societal overlapping.

There were other forces which worked to expand the boundaries of community interaction beyond the mosaic of small-scale ethnic compartments and to create distinct channels for information flow between different ethnic groups. Long-distance trade, for example, was perhaps the most important influence in the establishment of routes and focal centers similar in function to those in modern communications and transport networks. It permitted the infusion of external influences while at the same time stimulating the diffusion of information outward from ethnic Africa.

The oldest and probably most important trading system was that which spanned the Sahara to connect North Africa and the Mediterranean with the Western and Central Sudan. Trade in turn extended southward from the Sudan into the forested zone fringing the Guinea Coast. Not only was the historical significance of the Sudanic belt closely associated with this expansion of scale due to trade, but so also was the relative amount of reliable information about West Africa available to areas outside the continent. West Africa was never as "dark" to the Islamic world as it was to Western Europe during the early centuries of contact.

Long-distance trade was also important along the east coast of Africa, which, from at least the beginning of the Christian era, formed part of a vast trading

1. Godfrey Wilson and Monica Wilson, *The Analysis of Social Change: Based on Observations in Central Africa* (Cambridge: At the University Press, 1965), p. 29.

system in the Indian Ocean Basin. Its impact on peoples of the interior is considered to have been rather limited until the last half of the nineteenth century, although a number of non-coastal ethnic groups, such as the Kamba, Nyamwezi, and Yao, actively participated in long-distance trade well before this time. Indeed, further historical and archaeological research may reveal that a more extensive interaction existed between the coast and the interior than has hitherto been known. There were a number of smaller scale trading systems in other sections of Africa, particularly in the Congo and Zambezi basins and in the Great Lakes region of East-Central Africa.

Urbanization was another factor stimulating greater interethnic circulation. The growth of large towns in Africa was related to the elaboration of long-distance trade and to the establishment of centralized political organization, as is clearly seen in Mabogunje's essay in this volume. Although some traditional African cities were "homogeneous" in the sense that their populations consisted almost entirely of the same ethnic group, most did contain representatives from other societies, and some became major centers for contact and interaction among a wide variety of peoples. In the market city of Kano (Nigeria) probably over 20 per cent of the population were non-Hausa-speaking at the beginning of the nineteenth century. Indeed, the Hausa people are themselves a conglomeration of many ethnic communities.

The history of urbanization and African state formation are discussed in greater detail in this volume in the essays by Akin Mabogunje and Jeffrey Holden respectively. The role of Islam in expanding the connectivity and world view of large sections of traditional Africa is analyzed by Ibrahim Abu-Lughod in another essay. What must be stressed here is that well before the colonial era there existed an infrastructure of circulation routes and nodes which did extend communications beyond the ethnic bubbles of traditional Africa. As will be shown in the next section, this infrastructure, as well as more localized patterns of communications, both affected and was affected by the technologically superior and wider reaching systems of circulation superimposed upon it during the colonial period.

THE DEVELOPMENT OF MODERN CIRCULATION SYSTEMS

The growth of modern systems of communications and transport in Africa can conveniently be examined as a series of phases which have affected the continent at varying times and with varying impact. Although the phases to be discussed are derived from the work of geographers dealing generally with the growth of transport networks in underdeveloped countries, each phase is also closely associated with significant developments in the spheres of economic, social, and political organization and behavior.[2] Furthermore, taken together they provide a revealing perspective on the origins and structure of contemporary patterns of communications and transport and on the relevance of these patterns to the problems of nation-building and social change.

First Phase: Growth of Trading Ports

In the growth of modern circulation systems, the first phase reflects the nature of early European contact and pre-European patterns of long-distance trade and urbanization. It is characterized by the existence of a large number of scattered trading centers along the coast which acted as interfaces between Europe and Africa. This phase is most clearly identifiable in West Africa, where between about 1500 and 1900 a string of trading ports was established, each usually consisting of a European trading station and an indigenous settlement. The trade was nearly always carried out by African intermediaries who provided the important link with the interior. The port had a limited immediate hinterland and had only weak connections, via local fishing craft and trading vessels, with other ports along the coast.

These coastal ports served much the same function as the interior trading centers of the Sudanic belt. Timbuktu, Gao, Kano, and Katsina, to name but a few, were themselves "ports," trading goods from the West African forest and savanna for those of North Africa and the Mediterranean. But, to extend the analogy, the ocean-going ship eventually proved more efficient than the "ship of the desert," and trade was re-channeled southward with the intensification of early European contacts. This shift was one of the outstanding geographical changes in West African history. It was stimulated by indigenous developments in the forest zone, was made more compelling to Europe with the growth of the slave trade, and was finally solidified by colonial empire-building. After centuries of leadership, the Sudan became a backwater with respect to the forces of change generated by colonial contact, and the coastal peoples moved into the vanguard.

The older West African coastal ports included St. Louis at the mouth of the Senegal River; Sekondi, Cape Coast, Winneba, Elmina, and Accra along the "Gold Coast"; Whydah in Dahomey; Lagos, Badagry, Bonny, and Calabar in Nigeria; and Luanda and Benguela in Angola.[3] Several of these were to act as the major steppingstones for colonial penetration.

2. E. J. Taaffe, R. L. Morrill, and P. R. Gould, "Transport Expansion in Underdeveloped Countries: A Comparative Analysis," *Geographical Review*, LIII (1963), 503–29. Much of the discussion here is derived from the general model of transport growth outlined in this stimulating article.

3. A reader who is not familiar with these place names and those which follow may wish to refer to a map or atlas. Two good and relatively inexpensive atlases are *Philips' Modern College Atlas for Africa*, 6th ed. (London: George Philip, 1965), and the *Oxford Regional Economic Atlas of Africa*, comp. P. E. Adee (London: Oxford University Press, 1965).

In contrast to the situation in coastal West Africa, the ports of the East African coast had formed part of a complex trading system in the Indian Ocean Basin for over a thousand years before the first Portuguese contacts. Nevertheless, there were some basic similarities: a long string of trading stations dotted the coast from Mogadishu in Somalia on the north, through Lamu, Malindi, and Mombasa in Kenya, and Bagamoyo, Zanzibar, and Kilwa in Tanzania, to Moçambique and Sofala in the south. Each had its own limited hinterland and depended upon African middlemen to tap the ivory, gold, copper, and slaves of the interior. The coastal trade was controlled by Arabs, not Europeans, but as in West Africa nearly every port was an amalgam of indigenous settlement and trading station.

Many ports developed along the coast of southern Africa. At first, these were primarily provisioning and refueling stations for ships sailing around the Cape of Good Hope; only later did they become the bases for the extension of political control and European settlement into the interior. Trade with the local population was never as important as it was in East and West Africa.

Second Phase: Penetration and Port Concentration

Routes were eventually constructed from the coastal ports into the interior. This led to the growth of those ports which succeeded in capturing the largest hinterlands and to the establishment of the channels through which the influences of colonialism spread from the coast. This same pattern of penetration and concentration is identifiable in the early history of the pre-colonial trading systems, but it was dominated in the modern context by the construction of railways during the early decades of the colonial period. Railway lines were often paralleled by telecommunication links and roads; and in some areas, notably in the Congo Basin, the railways were supplemented by river transport as well.

These penetration lines rapidly became the major axes of interaction between traditional Africa and European influences, and their ocean termini developed into many of the great urban political centers of contemporary Africa (see Table 6). It is difficult to overestimate the importance of this phase in the growth of modern circulation systems, for the links and the major nodes along them became strongly entrenched and attracted further attention in the form of financial investment, infrastructural development, the growth of industry and cash-crop agriculture, European and other non-African settlement, and general "visibility" to the rest of the world. New urban centers were created where none existed before (for instance, Nairobi, Port Harcourt, Salisbury, Dakar), while favorably situated older centers grew at the expense of their less fortunate neighbors (for example, Mombasa *vs.* Lamu and Malindi; Lagos *vs.* Badagry; Dar es Salaam *vs.* Bagamoyo and Zanzibar; and Kano, Ibadan, and Kumasi *vs.* most of the interior West African centers). By 1930, a year considered by some scholars to mark the end of the African railway era, the broad framework of modern circulation systems had become firmly established.

TABLE 6
MAJOR PENETRATION LINES

Coastal Terminus	Interior Focus
Dakar	Niger River–Bamako (Mali)
Conakry	Guinea Highlands
Abidjan	Ouagadougou (Upper Volta) and Ivory Coast interior
Accra/Tema	Southern Ghana (Kumasi)
Lagos	Nigerian interior (Ibadan, Kano)
Port Harcourt	Nigerian interior (Enugu coalfields, Jos Plateau)
Matadi-Kinshasa	Congo Basin, especially Katanga
Lobito	Katanga and Copperbelt
Capetown	South Africa (Johannesburg and the Rand)
Durban	The Rand
Lourenço Marques	The Rand and Rhodesia
Beira	Rhodesia and Zambian Copperbelt
Dar es Salaam	Tanzania interior
Mombasa	Nairobi and the Kenya Highlands, Uganda and the Lake Victoria Basin
Djibouti	Addis Ababa and the Ethiopian Highlands
Port Sudan	Gezira and the Sudan interior, including Khartoum

The routes of the early penetration lines were guided at first by military and strategic objectives and later by the desire to reach valuable mineral deposits and productive agricultural areas. Wherever they reached, they introduced revolutionary means of communication and facilitated a wider circulation of goods, people, and ideas than had ever been experienced in traditional Africa. Subsistence farmers and petty traders began to turn to commercial agriculture, industrial employment, and urban life. For many people the world expanded to encompass the London cocoa market and French food; many became involved in two world wars and ultimately in the drive to join the world community of nations on an equal basis. The intensity of these changes was associated in both space and time with the development of communications and transport facilities in the large urban centers, which acted as the primary focal points of social, economic, and political transformation. The more isolated rural areas, in contrast, remained relatively unaffected.

Since each colonial power was concerned with carving out its own distinct set of territorial units, very few of the penetration lines crossed what today are international boundaries. The result was a group of compartmentalized colonies and protectorates, each with its own circulation system and often in closer contact with Europe than with its immediate neighbors. Only since independence has it become possible to telephone between many adjacent French-speaking and English-speaking territories in West Africa without first contacting Paris or London. And even in 1967 the visiting head of state from the Central African Republic flew first to Paris in order to reach Kampala in Uganda (a distance not much greater than that between New York and Chicago), a reflection not only of the difficulty of interstate travel but also of the persistence of ties to the former colonial power.

This fragmentation of Africa into relatively large unconnected compartments had its roots in the competitive struggle for African colonies. It became solidified, however, in the early patterns established in the development of transport and communications systems. The forces of change were contained within different "bubbles"; and the colonial boundaries, so often criticized for their artificiality and ignorance of traditional cultural patterns, assumed a new significance in delimiting areas within which the processes of modernization were directed, coordinated, and interrelated. Ethnic groups were sometimes split by colonial boundaries, and often, despite traditional similarities, the two segments followed different routes with respect to social change. Yoruba in Nigeria and in Dahomey, for example, even those living within a few miles of one another, began to learn different second languages, pay taxes to different authorities, and even supplement their diets with different kinds of food. Moreover, the degree of divergence tended to increase as social change progressed. It is no wonder that the colonial boundaries have come to be considered, at least on the surface, as inviolable by most of the newly independent states. Just as ethnic boundaries in traditional Africa circumscribed distinct circulation systems within which the movement of goods, people, and information was channeled and articulated, so colonial boundaries, both interterritorial and intraterritorial, recompartmentalized Africa with respect to the forces of modernization and change. Except for some minor readjustments and a few changes in function (for example, when an interterritorial border becomes intraterritorial with the federation of two areas, as in Cameroon), not one of the international boundaries established in the colonial period has been modified since independence to reflect traditional ethnic patterns.

Third Phase: Consolidation and Interconnection

The third phase involves the development of feeder lines to, and interconnections between, the major nodes of the urban administrative system and, as with the second phase, is characterized by concentration at key locations within the evolving transport and communications network. Generally, the processes of growth and decline sparked by the initial penetration into preexisting urban and trading patterns become accentuated as certain cities extend their economic, social, and political hinterlands.

This phase involves an areal and societal expansion of modern circulation from the initial axes of penetration. The continuing dominance of the initial penetration axes in Africa, however, is revealed in the weak interconnections between the state-based circulation systems as well as in the poor development of internal networks (still characteristic of circulation in Africa). The common pattern in most African countries is that of a single dominant transport and communications corridor (occasionally two) tapping the most productive parts of the country and functioning primarily to siphon off resources for an external market. Internal connectivity, except for perhaps a skeletal telecommunications and road network, was greatly neglected in comparison. Large areas of the country and probably most of the population, therefore, were only minimally affected by communications and transport growth. Some of the most pressing problems of national unity in Africa today are derived from the circulation patterns established during the colonial period. Whereas the former colonial powers sought maximum security and an assured outflow of raw materials to the world market, the leaders of independent Africa seek instead the expansion of internal markets and the greatest possible interaction and integration between all sectors of the population. It will take many years before the circulation systems inherited at independence are restructured to accommodate the new functions demanded of them by African countries today.

Fourth Phase: Subnetworks of Priority Linkage

Although road transport and the mass media are of great importance in the third phase, they achieve predominance in the movement of goods, people, and messages during the fourth phase. In addition, air transport emerges as an important means of interurban linkage; and certain centers, which are the major nodes in their respective national circulation systems, become even more closely tied together by a range of modern transport and communications media.

This fourth phase is difficult to evaluate in Africa. The developments usually associated with it—developments which are still being elaborated upon in even the most economically advanced countries—are generally based upon an already tightly woven circulation system, something which does not yet exist in any African country except perhaps the Republic of South Africa. Although railways are still being built, it appears unlikely that Africa will ever attain the level of rail density existing in Europe or North America—if only because transportation technology has changed radically since the period of railway expansion in Europe and the United States. And the number of paved roads, telecommunications, and postal and mass-media facilities required to create and maintain integrated circulation systems involving the masses of the population, even on a national basis, is staggering.

Nevertheless, some of the features of this phase are recognizable in contemporary Africa. Probably the most prominent is the growth of high-priority linkages between the dominant urban centers. In Africa, these "main streets" appear more streamlined than elsewhere, in that there are relatively few feeders and connecting links with the rest of the system. This probably reflects the weak development of phase three and the consequent limitation on the areal extent of modern communications and transport networks. High-priority linkages in Africa are associated with wide, heavily traveled highways with adequate lodging and refreshment facilities; major railway lines carrying the primary import and export products of the country in addition to passengers; and the most advanced communications facilities, such as direct-dialing telephone systems (for example, Lagos-Ibadan, Kampala-Jinja, Arusha-Moshi) and radio-television services. In a way, this parallels the process of geographical concentration which occurs in the previous two phases, but instead of ports and interior nodes the emphasis here is on whole corridors of interaction which are the most important circulation routes on the continent.

High-priority linkages in Tropical Africa are still in their early stages of development, but might include the following: Dakar-Thies (Senegal); Tema-Accra-Kumasi (Ghana); Lagos-Ibadan, Port Harcourt–Enugu, Kano-Kaduna (Nigeria); Douala-Yaoundé (Cameroon); Lusaka-Copperbelt (Zambia); Salisbury-Bulawayo (Rhodesia); Nairobi-Nakuru-Kisumu (Kenya); and Kampala-Jinja-Tororo (Uganda). In the future, some of these linkages are likely to become extended or interconnected with further modernization of transport and communications. At the present, however, they are confined to the core areas of their respective countries—a further reflection of the pronounced territorial fragmentation which has characterized the growth of modern circulation systems in Africa.

CONTEMPORARY COMMUNICATIONS AND TRANSPORT SYSTEMS

The growth of modern circulation systems in Africa created a new compartmentalization based upon the framework of colonial boundaries and the geographically uneven development of transport and communications facilities. The traditional ethnic mosaic was not erased, however, but reacted much as it always had to new influences. In some cases, it was completely transformed; in others, it molded the new influences to its own design. This interplay between traditional and modern circulation systems came to shape the nature and pattern of social change.

An accurate evaluation of circulation in contemporary Africa would therefore have to consider both the old and the new. This, however, is an immense task

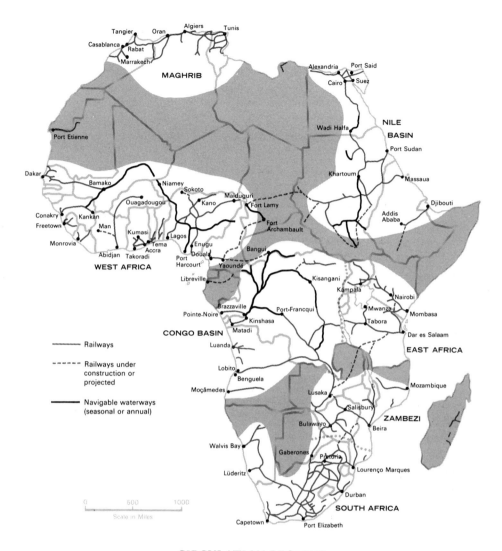

Railways

Railways under
construction or
projected

Navigable waterways
(seasonal or annual)

CIRCULATION REGIONS

unsuited to a general survey of this type. Consequently, only some broad patterns will be identified here, with the overall emphasis on modern forms of
communications and transport.

The map on this page represents the major circulation regions in Africa —
areas in which the growth of modern systems of communications and transport
has displayed some degree of uniformity and articulation.[4] These regions are
the contemporary geographical equivalents of the historical phases discussed
in the previous section. Just as each phase represented a broad uniformity of

4. The broad outlines of these circulation regions are based on a map of transport
regions in Africa included in *Africa: Maps and Statistics* (Pretoria: Africa Institute, 1963),
IV, 55.

events over time, each circulation region is the expression of shared characteristics of circulatory structure, flow, and development through space. Regional boundaries are not simply coincident with political boundaries, but represent major discontinuities in the circulation patterns of Africa. Because of the central role of circulation in human behavior, these regions provide a more meaningful areal division of Africa than the often vague and inconsistent regions described in other types of literature.

South African Region

The South African region has by far the most highly developed and tightly interconnected network of communications and transport in Africa. It encompasses virtually all of the Republic of South Africa (RSA) plus Lesotho, Swaziland, most of South-West Africa, southeastern Botswana, and southern Mozambique. The focal center of the entire region lies in the gold-rich and heavily industrialized Witwatersrand area, centering on the metropolis of Johannesburg. Other important centers include the large ports of Capetown, Durban, and Lourenço Marques (Mozambique). Interurban linkage is high, although significant "holes" in the transport network exist, particularly in the now independent Lesotho and in most of the Bantu "reserves" of RSA. The circulation of people in the form of labor is particularly well developed, with the economy of the entire region heavily dependent upon the manpower supplied by Lesotho, Swaziland, and Botswana, not to mention the African population within the Republic.

Zambezi Region

The Zambezi region also has a relatively well-developed transport network, which is connected to the South African region by rail through Mozambique and Botswana, and to RSA directly by road, air, and a variety of communications media. The major port of this region is Beira (Mozambique), which until recently served as the primary outlet for the productive central spine of Rhodesia, stretching roughly from Salisbury to Bulawayo, and for the rich Zambian Copperbelt. The latter, however, has begun to reorient its traffic to Dar es Salaam (Tanzania) and Lobito (Angola) since the Unilateral Declaration of Independence by Rhodesia, just as Rhodesia in turn has looked increasingly toward the South African region, particularly after the attempts to blockade the port of Beira by Great Britain and other powers. Both of these shifts are symbolized by plans for railway construction, one to connect the Zambian railway system with the central line in Tanzania and another to link the Rhodesian and South African networks directly, thereby cutting across the major transport gaps which hitherto served to define the boundaries of the Zambezi circulation region.

It must be emphasized that the boundaries of all circulation regions are temporary ones, reflecting the structure, direction, and flow of circulation at a given time, and are subject to change with new developments in transportation and communication. The changes mentioned above, for example, seem to signal the disintegration of the Zambezi region, an event touched upon by the *New York Times* in reviewing the economy of Africa in 1966.[5] It observed that, during this year, Zambia was transformed in terms of its regional orientation from the northernmost part of southern Africa to the southernmost part of eastern Africa. But while the Zambezi region is losing its distinctive identity, the re-orientation of Zambia to East Africa is by no means complete. Zambia remains heavily dependent upon trade with the Republic of South Africa.

Congo Basin

The Congo Basin is unique among sub-Saharan African circulation regions in having an extensive system of navigable waterways extending through the heart of the region and providing an inexpensive means of transport. Despite its apparent physical unity, however, the Congo Basin is highly fragmented, not only because of the falls and rapids along the rivers which impede continuous navigability, but more importantly because of the division of the region during the colonial period into separate Belgian, French, and Portuguese administrations. Furthermore, the colonial policies which operated internally, especially in the former Belgian Congo, did not foster effective interaction among the various peoples in the area, thus hampering the growth of communal identity beyond the existing ethnic compartments. In fact, Congo-Kinshasa is today still struggling with powerful centrifugal forces which seem, in terms of circulatory orientation, to be pulling the state in different directions: the northeast toward East Africa, the south toward the Zambezi region, and the west toward former French Equatorial Africa and West Africa as a whole. This diffuse orientation, however, along with the great size and wealth of the Congo, may eventually enable it—despite an extended period of internal instability—to act as a hub for supranational integration in the future. The current activities of Congo-Kinshasa with respect to unification movements in West, Central, and East Africa may signal the start of this process.

The Congo Basin circulation region covers all of Congo-Kinshasa, the areas of Congo-Brazzaville and the Central African Republic served by the Congo River, and nearly all of Angola. Its most productive area is Katanga, with other mining and agricultural areas scattered throughout the basin. Its major ports are Matadi, the main outlet for Congo-Kinshasa, and Lobito (Angola), which also serves Katanga. Interurban linkage is weak, and there is much redundancy in the transport network. Brazzaville and Kinshasa, for example, although facing each other across the Congo River, both have major international airports and

5. *New York Times*, January 27, 1967.

are at terminal points of railways and roads running to separate ports (Pointe-Noire and Matadi) in their respective countries. And despite the shorter distance to Lobito, Katanga copper was forced during the colonial period to follow the "national" route by rail and river to Matadi. Political boundaries, therefore, have often prevented natural features from acting as integrative forces within the Congo Basin.

East Africa

East Africa, comprising all of Uganda and Tanzania and nearly all of Kenya, plus Rwanda and Burundi, forms a compact circulation region with a relatively well-integrated rail and road network serving most of the densely populated and productive areas. With the exception of South Africa, it has achieved a level of economic integration and coordinated communications and transport unsurpassed in any other circulation region. Throughout most of the colonial period, East Africa (except for Rwanda and Burundi) was under British administration and by independence had developed several interterritorial institutions dealing with nearly all forms of circulation in the three territories. The transport network remains rather skeletal and communications are strongly affected by international boundaries, but the region has progressed further toward regional cooperation than any of comparable size in Africa. Building upon this pre-independence unity, East Africa has recently been expanding its sphere of influence in an effort, still in its very early stages, to draw together a "greater" East African area extending from Zambia in the south, to Somalia, Ethiopia, and the Sudan in the north, and westward into Rwanda, Burundi, and possibly Congo-Kinshasa and the Central African Republic, all of which have expressed interest in the newly formed East African Economic Community.

The major port in East Africa is Mombasa, serving the fertile Kenya Highlands (with Nairobi, the focal point of circulation in the region, as its major node) and the rich farming country surrounding Lake Victoria (especially southern Uganda, where Kampala is the major center). Mombasa also serves some areas of Tanzania, but most of Tanzania is oriented toward Dar es Salaam, the capital and main seaport. The only significant international labor migration within the region is between Rwanda/Burundi and Uganda; but communications, transport, and trade between Kenya, Tanzania, and Uganda are greater than those between any other three Tropical African states.

West Africa

When viewed as a whole, West Africa has barely progressed beyond the phase of penetration and port concentration. The largest city in every West African state bordering the sea (taking the total population of Lagos to include its immediate suburbs) is a port at the origin of a major penetration line. Moreover, with one minor exception (Togo-Dahomey), none of these cities is connected with any of the others by rail, and only a few are linked by paved roads. Although it seems contradictory, the only characteristic which unifies this region is its fragmentation. Political fragmentation is greater than in any other region, and the degree of redundancy in the circulation system approaches the absurd. One need only glance at a railway map of West Africa to view the evidence: Togo and Dahomey, thin slivers of territory, have their own north-south railways, which are flanked by but not connected with additional north-south lines in Ghana and Nigeria; Senegal and Guinea have railway lines curving inland to serve areas which could better be served through Gambia and Sierra Leone (or Liberia) respectively. One could almost sketch the political boundaries of West Africa by using the railway map alone.

Only recently have air transport and telecommunications begun to reduce this fragmentation by promoting interaction across international boundaries. But even today it is impossible to speak realistically of a West African network of circulation. At best, there are national circulation networks which occasionally, as between Senegal and Mali or Ivory Coast and Upper Volta, cross territorial boundaries—yet even these are not extensive and are poorly integrated. It would appear from a map that the transport network in Nigeria is relatively dense. It must be remembered, however, that the population of Nigeria alone is greater than the total population of any one of the other circulation regions discussed and that the already weak circulation of people, goods, and information within Nigeria has been further weakened by the civil war which has engulfed the country since May, 1967.

At a very broad, speculative level, one can perhaps identify at least potential subregional circulation networks. The first would radiate from Nigeria and its two major ports, Lagos and Port Harcourt. It would include Nigeria, Dahomey, Niger, Chad, and Cameroon. The second would revolve around Ghana and Ivory Coast, with Upper Volta, Togo, and possibly parts of Mali and other adjacent states at the periphery, overlapping to some extent the other subregions. Its major focal points are Accra-Tema (Ghana) and Abidjan (Ivory Coast). A third subregion would focus on Dakar and would include the states in and around the Senegal River Basin: Senegal, Mauritania, Gambia, Guinea, Mali, probably Sierra Leone, and possibly Liberia. This is the least populated and developed of the three, but it has great mineral wealth and has shown some signs in recent years of increased interterritorial cooperation with the formation of the Organization of Senegal River States (Mauritania, Senegal, Mali, and Guinea).

Although there has been some talk of a West African economic community and some earlier attempts at political federation, it seems quite clear at present that the existing circulation patterns are inadequate even for effective national integration, much less for some form of supranational organization. There are unifying forces: Islam, the Niger River, and, most important, widespread recognition of the great economic disadvantages of fragmentation. The barriers to communications and transport, however, are so great that there is probably less chance of economic or political unity being achieved in West Africa than in any of the other circulation regions on the continent. But it must be remembered that this is a region of ninety to one hundred million people. The achievement of political unity in Nigeria alone would be as significant in terms of population numbers and ethnic diversity as federation in East Africa or the Congo Basin.

Nile Basin and Maghrib

The remaining two circulation regions, one in the Nile Basin and the other in the Maghrib, or northwest Africa, will not be discussed here, although their relevance to sub-Saharan Africa cannot be neglected. In particular, there is some rationale for detaching Ethiopia from the Nile region and including it within East Africa. Ethiopia, however, has perhaps the most inadequate circulation system of any African country, given its large population size (estimated at over twenty million). More likely, it should be included with those large areas which lie outside any major regional circulation system.

COMMUNICATIONS THEORY AND NATIONAL INTEGRATION: A PERSPECTIVE

In this essay, communications and transport have been considered together as the major components of circulation systems. The primary focus has been on the growth of new channels for the movement of goods, people, and ideas, and the general impact of these developments on traditional circulation systems and contemporary patterns of communications and transport at the continental level. We now turn to a more abstract and theoretical examination of circulation in Africa, particularly with respect to the problems of social change and nation-building.

Concepts of Communications Theory

In modern social-science theory the term *circulation* is seldom used, while the term *communications* is broadened in scope to include many of the features of circulation systems. But at the same time the emphasis is shifted from structure to process, from pattern to behavior, and from the movement of goods, people, and ideas to the movement of ideas alone. Within this more behavioral approach, the mass media are distinguished from interpersonal communication: the first is highly organized, professionalized, and objectively oriented; the second is informal and, even in the most developed countries, dependent on personal contact. These two levels interact as part of the overall communications system, and the degree to which there is "feedback" between them—the degree to which the formal institutions of mass media and the informal, society-based processes of interpersonal communications are effectively integrated—is considered a key measure of modernization. Feedback represents, to use an African figure of speech, a "two-way, all-weather road" which promotes interdependence and mutual interests between local village life and the controlling powers of the central government.

Communications, in this sense, has assumed an important role in social-science research. This development has been stimulated by the extension of the mathematically-framed theoretical formulations of such relatively new and closely interrelated fields as cybernetics, information theory, and systems analysis into the social sciences in the desire to provide new and more powerful interdisciplinary perspectives on problems of focal interest. Communications research, in short, has emerged as a common ground for cooperation and exchange of ideas between political scientists, sociologists, geographers, and psychologists, as well as mathematicians, biologists, and representatives from virtually the full spectrum of academic disciplines.

One of the problems which has received increasing attention in recent years from communications theorists within the social sciences has been political development, particularly the growth of integrated political communities. The literature on political development in Africa suggests the great potential of a communications approach to the subject of the consolidation of nation-states. Modern forms of communication are largely responsible for sparking the processes of change associated with modernization, and many have observed that the success of nation-building in Africa today will depend to an equally large extent on the establishment, acceptance, and maintenance of integrated communications systems incorporating these new forms.

Before examining further the relevance of communications research to nation-building in Africa, some mention must be made of the new terminology which has accompanied its application in the social sciences. Some brief observations and definitions are offered to supply only a very basic working vocabulary for the short discussion which follows.[6] Of particular conceptual importance are the terms *transaction* and *information*. A transaction may be defined as an exchange between units which always involves the communication of information and may represent a transfer of peoples, goods, or services. The flow of transactions thus covers much of what is meant by "circulation," although the stress is on the exchange of messages and ideas whether or not this requires, or is associated with, actual physical movements of people or goods. The term *transaction* thus has a more behavioral connotation than does "circulation" as used in this essay. Meier describes a transaction in the network of human relations as

---

6. An elaboration of this discussion and a list of suggested references for further reading can be found in Edward W. Soja, "Communications and Territorial Integration in East Africa: An Introduction to Transaction Flow Analysis," *East Lakes Geographer*, IV (1968), 39–57.

discrete interaction over space, an adjustment to recent events and new opportunities, and a joint experience which accommodates the participants to the changing socio-economic system.[7]

The term *information* likewise is used in communications theory in a highly specialized way. It can be defined as "amount of order" and refers to that which is not random or uncontrollable and which can therefore convey meaning. It is not simply "news" or "data"—an analysis by Huntley and Brinkley carries information, but so does a purposive wink of the eye. Information is also associated with the capacity to select from a set of alternatives, for it involves knowledge of the physical and human environment and thus the potential for controlling or regulating this environment.

The exchange and preservation of information within a community of people, be it a small-scale ethnic group or a modern nation, provide the integrative glue which enables the community to survive as a cohesive, organized unit. In order to more fully comprehend the problems of nation-building in Africa, therefore, it is essential to examine the structure, content, and flow of information through time and space; for it is this dynamic exchange between component parts of a system that creates the bonds of mutual awareness and interdependence which promote integrative behavior.

Communications and National Political Integration

James Coleman has succinctly summarized the relationship between communications and nation-building as follows:

> The problem of integration and the building of consensus in Africa's new territorial political systems is largely a problem of developing patterns of communication which transcend, rather than coincide with, prevailing discontinuities and communal divisions.[8]

Nation-building, as defined by Clifford Geertz and quoted in Zolberg's essay in this volume, becomes in turn

> the aggregation of independently defined, specifically outlined traditional primordial groups into larger, more diffuse units, whose implicit frame of reference is not the local scene but the "nation"—in the sense of the whole society encompassed by the new civil state.

Most African states are attempting to construct cohesive national communi-

7. Richard L. Meier, *A Communications Theory of Urban Growth* (Cambridge: M.I.T. Press, 1962), p. 66.
8. "The Politics of Sub-Saharan Africa," in *The Politics of Developing Areas,* ed. G. A. Almond and J. S. Coleman (Princeton: Princeton University Press, 1960), p. 345.

ties from an amalgam of smaller scale societies found within the territorial boundaries inherited from the colonial period—an interesting reversal of the Western
experience, in which national consolidation defined the boundaries. Many of the
societies are still bound within traditional communications systems which
control the exchange and preservation of information by its adherents and have
only tenuous links with the national transactional network. In other cases, new
patterns of information flow have emerged which have solidified human interaction on a transethnic or regional basis, but not on a scale commensurate with
the accepted view of the nation by the political leaders of the state.

For perhaps the bulk of the population in most African states, old channels of
communication have been radically weakened, but nothing sufficiently binding
has been substituted for them. The people are fully aware of the national idea,
yet they remain ambivalent in the absence of adequately intensive channels
of information flow involving them in the emerging national society. But the
success of nation-building rests largely on the degree to which effective transactional channels, both mass media and interpersonal, can be established to connect the transitional group (located, in status terms, between the more isolated
traditional societies and the educated elites) to the national communications
system.

These observations may seem confusing, as it was asserted earlier in this essay
that the growth of modern circulation systems resulted in a recompartmentaliza-
tion of Africa into what are today national circulation systems based on the
framework of colonial boundaries. The integration of political communities,
however, is a multitiered process in which the salient relationships have a different significance at each level of hierarchy. The generalization about national
circulation systems is relevant to supranational integration. The units involved
here are states which, during their existence as overseas possessions, evolved a
certain degree of identity within their borders but failed to develop sufficient
levels of interconnectivity and interdependence to sustain political federation
after independence. The component parts were—and essentially still are—too
inwardly focused to link together as part of an integrated larger scale organization.

At the national level, however, the next stage down the hierarchy, the pattern
is basically the same although the units involved differ. Referring back to Coleman's observation, the central problem in nation-building is to create and
solidify communications systems which extend beyond subnational communities.
In all cases, the challenge is not to completely destroy the next-lower order of
system, but to develop larger scale systems in which information can be systematically exchanged and preserved, in which the flow of transactions reflects the
requirements and social structure of a modern achievement-oriented society,
and in which efficient feedback is maintained between the higher order mass
media and informal opinion leaders at the local level.

Communications and Modern Ethnicity

The communications problems created at the national level, however, have been made more prominent for two main reasons. First, the nation is still the dominant organizational unit in world politics, the depository of sovereignty, and, by definition, the primary controller of the functions of its internal political system. Second, whereas the barriers between states are largely by-products of modern communications, administration, and political behavior, the pronounced discontinuities within a national state are often further intensified by ethnic identities and loyalties.

Ethnic boundaries continue to present formidable barriers to national integration, not only because of the persistence of traditional communications systems but also because of the way in which traditional ethnicity was transformed during the colonial period. Colonial contact, as previously mentioned, worked effectively to expand the scale of contacts for the African individual. At the local level, he came to interact with a larger population than ever before. This increase in scale, however, was powerfully shaped both by the cultural characteristics of the individual and, particularly in former British colonies where some form of indirect rule was practiced, by the administrative policy of the colonial power.

In cases where ethnicity was reinforced by language similarity, the boundaries of ethnic identity were often redefined to include all people who spoke mutually understandable languages. Where community allegiance was formerly extremely localized — perhaps mainly to the clan or lineage — it soon came to encompass a larger unit, often called the "tribe." People such as the Ewe in West Africa and the Kikuyu in East Africa became effectively consolidated as an ethnic unit primarily during the colonial period. Prior to this time, they rarely acted together as a unit. (For a further discussion of the concept of "tribe," see the introduction to this volume and the essay by Cohen in this volume.)

The phenomenon of changing boundaries of ethnicity was not new to traditional African society. Groups were appearing and disappearing, mixing, blending, and breaking off in response to both internal and external stimuli throughout African history. During the colonial period, just as in the past, African traditional society often readjusted itself in reaction to forces of change. When increased size appeared to be an effective measure of influence within the colonial context, many African societies undertook scale-expanding developments in communications to consolidate into larger ethnic groupings.

The Baluhya of Kenya, for example, are often considered as a single ethnic group of over one million members. But prior to 1900, the people who eventually composed the Baluhya constituted many smaller communities which, although having some cultural and linguistic affinities, were essentially dissimilar in much of their social, economic, and political life. Some were largely pastoral, others almost entirely agricultural. Even physically there were great differences, and intercommunity warfare was not uncommon. Many of these divisions persist today, but there is no doubt that in the period since 1900, and particularly after 1940, a Baluhya identity emerged which had never existed before.

Similar extensions of ethnic identity (within the restrictions of broad cultural similarities) took place throughout Africa. Moreover, many of these changes were stimulated and/or solidified by the superimposed structure of colonial administration, especially when efforts were made to draw internal boundaries which reflected ethnic patterns as perceived by the colonial government. The most immediate effect in these cases was the strengthening of broad ethnic identities without the concurrent context of interethnic communications development. The roots of what is called "tribalism" in Africa today probably lie more in this coincidence between the superimposed boundaries of modern communications and administrative subsystems and those of transformed community identity than in any set of traditional ethnic differences existing before colonialism.

The new patterns of ethnicity are particularly troublesome with respect to the articulation between the nationally organized sector of the communications system and the local opinion leaders who more directly reflect the feelings of the population mass. Ethnic interests in most African countries dominate the flow of political information not only on local issues, where they are perhaps most relevant, but also on issues of national importance and in the national mass media. What feedback does exist between the two levels of the communications system is very often fragmented into frequently antagonistic ethnic subdivisions.

Communications and Urban Concentration

Another factor which has affected the consolidation of nation-states in Africa is the concentration of development within small areas, particularly in the major urban centers. This phenomenon was discussed earlier with respect to the growth of modern circulation systems and can be illustrated further with examples from nearly every African country. The city of Nairobi, for instance, contains only 4 per cent of the total population of Kenya, yet has at least half of its total urban population, postal traffic, radio and television sets, newspaper circulation, and telephones. About 17 per cent of the African labor force is employed in Nairobi, but more significantly it receives almost 30 per cent of all African wages in Kenya. Nairobi is the headquarters for over one-third of the registered political organizations and the origin or destination for a disproportionate share of railway, road, air, and telephone traffic in the country. If just a handful of other urban areas are added to Nairobi, they would together account for nearly all the transactions within the more modernized sector of the national communications system.[9]

9. See Edward W. Soja, *The Geography of Modernization in Kenya* (Syracuse, N. Y.: Syracuse University Press, 1968), Chap. 9.

The situation in most other African countries is not radically different from that in Kenya. There is not only inadequate articulation between the national mass media and local communications from the societal perspective, but there is insufficient interaction between the elite and the masses from the geographical point of view. Although interurban linkages may be relatively well developed, rural-urban interaction is usually very weak, unstructured, and inefficient. This is an extremely important problem, for national political integration must depend on the urban system to act as a transmitter in the flow of communications between all segments of the national society: the elite and the mass, the traditional and the modern, the local and the national. This will not be possible in most African countries until more effective means for disseminating information from these focal centers are established. The continued accretion of development in a few small areas, without the accompaniment of "spread-effects" to the rest of the population, can only work against the long-term aims of nation-building.

CONCLUSION: THE CHALLENGE
OF COMMUNICATIONS RESEARCH

A concern with communications has become a point of convergence for the several disciplines which have an interest in the process of nation-building and social change in Africa. But this communications approach to national consolidation is still in its initial stages. Its great potential, however, is already evident, and there is little doubt that in the near future many of the generalizations suggested in this essay will be supported, or refuted, by more empirical evidence and quantitative data than are currently available.

The following statement by Lucian Pye, one of the leading proponents of communications research, supplies a stimulating challenge to all social scientists interested in the patterns and processes of change which characterize contemporary Africa:

> Communications is the web of human society. The structure of a communication system with its more or less well-defined channels is in a sense the skeleton of the social body which envelops it. The content of communications is of course the very substance of human intercourse. The flow of communications determines the direction and the pace of dynamic social development. Hence it is possible to analyze all social processes in the terms of structure, content, and flow of communications.[10]

10. Lucian W. Pye, ed, *Communications and Political Development* (Princeton: Princeton University Press, 1963), p. 4.

19

Religion and Change

JOHANNES FABIAN

AN EXAMINATION OF THE TERMS *religion* and *change* could involve innumerable permutations with regard to definition, approach, and interpretation. In a short essay such as this, however, there is a need to focus on significant questions which can be examined in a consistent manner, and this requires the introduction of some basic assumptions. These concern the nature and limitations of traditional social anthropology and the current reappraisal of the nature of change in African societies.

Social anthropology has been remarkable for its ability to combine differences in theory with a striking similarity of research interests and findings. Not long ago an important member of the discipline expressed satisfaction with this situation by pointing out that French and British anthropologists were able to collaborate in their investigations of African belief and ritual because "Both groups addressed themselves to social reality; neither began with hypothetical models of systems. . . . They complemented one another"[1]

The fact that social anthropology, concerned as it is with the reduction of complex realities into "social reality," should have achieved the status of an academic discipline within whose confines we are expected to operate does not, in our discussion of religion and change, relieve us of the burden of reflection, but rather leads us to question the orientations of the discipline. It will be an argument of this essay that the orientation of anthropology toward "social reality" has implied acceptance of the facts of colonial partition and that this has had a tendency to blind us to the larger scale processes of ideological change in Africa.[2]

---

1. Victor Turner in *African Systems of Thought*, preface by Meyer Fortes and Germaine Dieterlen (London: Oxford University Press, 1965), p. 9.
2. We use the adjective *ideological* in a non-pejorative sense. *Ideological change* refers to the sum of changes which have occurred in the systems of beliefs and norms held by groups or societies; it includes *religious change* as a more specific aspect.

These processes have transcended colonial boundaries and have gained momentum, purpose, and direction as colonial domination has crumbled.[3]

A second assumption of this presentation may be introduced by the rather blunt proposition that preoccupation with "change" in contemporary studies of Africa may be taken as a sign of our collective bad conscience as well as an indication of our deepened consciousness of the factors involved in change.

Malinowski, one of the pillars of the social anthropology of the colonial era, held that

> In the processes of culture contact and change, impact and interaction takes place as between institutions, i.e., systems of clearly defined activities, carried on by organized groups, associated with some material apparatus, and aiming at the satisfaction of a biological, social, or spiritual need (related activities welded into a permanent system by a charter of laws and customs).[4]

Malinowski's analysis of social change is placed within the context of the 1930s and 1940s. At the root of his views is an acceptance of a state of affairs, that is, of the existence of boundaries between "institutions" created by the exercise of military and technological power. Today we feel that investigations which assume this view of power relationships cannot be meaningful. We now regard power as an abstract force in the social and cultural processes—as something exercised for its own purpose, tending toward self-maintenance and conservation, but which does not explain anything but itself. Power relationships obscure but do not eliminate the real processes of orientation and reorientation of human action.

To put this more concretely, the clash between white institutions and black institutions in Africa is a fact, not a problem. Investigation of "culture contact" and "social change" can begin only when the fact of the clash is questioned, that is, when one becomes morally uneasy about the exercise of power and its consequences for both the colonized and the colonizers. It is this moral and intellectual uneasiness which causes us to revise our image of Africa as consisting of separate, well-administered, and timeless "primitive" societies, and which impels us to make understanding of "change" a foremost occupation.

RELIGION AND CHANGE—A BATTLE OF SYMBOLS

The anthropological study of religion is one of the most confusing fields of an often confusing discipline. Moreover, it is the branch of anthropology which has

---

3. Our argument is diametrically opposed to a conclusion drawn less than a generation ago and repeated recently by Godfrey and Monica Wilson, who think that "our present disequilibrium [in African societies] is due to the outrunning in scale of the religious by the material elements of society" (*The Analysis of Social Change* [Cambridge: At the University Press, 1965], p. 173).

changed the least in the past several decades. Even in recent discussions,[5] the positions taken do not appear to extend beyond those held by Tylor and Durkheim, the intellectual ancestors of contemporary scholars who are still content to define religion by its content, as belief in supernatural beings, and by its function, as symbolization of the moral authority of society. One of the few who have departed from this approach is Clifford Geertz. In his formulation of religion as a cultural system,[6] religious beliefs are not identified simply by their intellectual content and their social function; their definition derives from the problems of understanding they have to solve. Religion is man's way of conquering bafflement, suffering, and moral uncertainty — not by removing any of these problems, but by giving meaning to them. One implication of this view, perhaps not clearly realized by Geertz himself, is that if religion does not remove or conceal the causes of bafflement, suffering, and moral ambiguity, but constantly works on their understanding and solution, then it must be understood as the constantly expanding boundary of human consciousness and conscience. From this we would conclude that, as such, religion must inevitably become a zone in which different cultures in contact will clash. Since religious perceptions and solutions are embodied in specific symbols (verbalized world views, myths, rituals), we may come to see in changing Africa a "battle of symbols" (rather than of "powers" or "institutions").

This view of change illustrates the connection between religion and the study of social change. "Conscience" and "consciousness" are driving forces behind the current reappraisal of change in African societies, and are among the elements which constitute religion. The expanding boundaries of conscience and consciousness may therefore be said to define the nature of religious change and thus to determine the zones of conflict which are influencing all aspects of social change in Africa today.

EARLY PATTERNS OF CONTACT AND ENCOUNTER

The role of religion as a symbolic medium of contact and conflict is striking in the colonial history of Africa. This pattern has survived the changing forms

4. Bronislaw Malinowski, *The Dynamics of Culture Change* (New Haven: Yale University Press, 1945), p. 74.

5. See Raymond Firth, "Problem and Assumption in an Anthropological Study of Religion," *Journal of the Royal Anthropological Institute*, LXXXIX (1959), 129–48; Jack Goody, "Religion and Ritual: The Definition Problem," *British Journal of Sociology*, XII (1961), 142–64; Robin Horton, "A Definition of Religion and Its Uses," *Journal of the Royal Anthropological Institute*, XC (1960), 201–26; and M. E. Spiro, "Religion: Problems of Definition and Explanation," in *Anthropological Approaches to the Study of Religion*, ed. M. P. Banton (London: Tavistock, 1966), pp. 85–126.

6. "Religion as a Cultural System," in Banton, *Anthropological Approaches to the Study of Religion*, pp. 1–46.

of colonial domination, from the barbarous slave trade to the more contemporary tyranny of foreign capital. The patterns and terms in which this battle of symbols has been carried out seem to have been set in the earliest phases of European expansion.

In Asia a handful of Western missionaries challenged, largely unsuccessfully, religious traditions which were reinforced by specialized and impenetrable cultural and social institutions. In Africa, however, missionaries and colonial administrators often found rulers and subjects willing to accept the symbol systems of the white man, even when they were not imposed by force. The European in Africa mistakenly assumed that the flexibility and plasticity of African traditional religion, its ability to incorporate new symbolic expressions without changing its basic premises, was indicative either of childlike simplicity or of cunning dishonesty. In evaluating the history of mission and the impact of Christianity in Africa, however, the impression is that the Christian message for the most part was smothered in the embrace of African religion.

Examples from the history of the Portuguese mission to Africa illustrate the initial situation of contact between Christianity and indigenous religions.[7] It should be noted that the individual missionary acted as the messenger of a complex endeavor. Much of the *élan* of the Portuguese expansion at the beginning of the sixteenth century, for instance, was not only guided by economic motives but driven by a spirit of revenge, a continuation of the religious drive that had liberated Iberia from Islamic domination. In an instruction to Bartolomeu Dias and his fleet (which accompanied Vasco da Gama to the Cape Verde Islands in 1497), King Manuel I said:

> Since, with the help of God, we have chased the Moors from these parts of Europe to Africa, my kingdom has no task more important than to explore India and the empires of the East, not only, I hope, so that, with the grace of God, faith in his Son Jesus Christ will be spread by us in these countries so far away from the Catholic Church — which will earn us the gratitude of the Almighty and fame and honor before men — but also so that we shall conquer the empires, countries, and treasures of the pagans by the force of arms.[8]

A royal instruction to Cabral in 1500 is even more illustrative. The king is reported to have told him:

> Before he fights Moors and pagans with the real and worldly sword he should let priests and religious people use their spiritual sword. That is, they should preach the gospel together with the admonitions and commands of the Catholic Church. They should ask them to give up their idolatry, their diabolic rites and customs, and

7. For information concerning the general historical background to the following considerations, see J. E. Duffy, *Portugal in Africa* (Cambridge: Harvard University Press, 1959).

8. Paul Schebesta, *Portugals Konquistamission in Südost-Afrika* (St. Augustin: Steyler Mission [1966]), p. 10 [my translation].

to convert to the faith in Christ, so that we all may be united and linked together in brotherhood through one savior, Jesus Christ, promised by the Prophets, awaited by the Patriarchs so many thousand years before He came. In that case they should be given all the natural and legal rights, and in doing this [the missionaries] should apply the ceremonies prescribed by canon law. But should they refuse obstinately to accept the law of faith, and should they deny the law of peace which for the survival of mankind must be accepted by men, and should they refuse commerce and traffic, the means apt to found peace and love among people—since commerce is the foundation of human behavior because the partners interact trusting on the law and faith which everyone should have before God— if this should happen, then they should be fought with fire and sword and unconditional war.[9]

We must assume that the earliest missionaries, tied directly to the political powers by the institution of the patronate,[10] were somehow conscious of the complexity and diversity of motives and goals which they were to represent. In the actual situation of encounter with the "pagans," however, these goals seem to have been reduced to symbolic gestures of conversion: sermon and baptism. African potentates such as King Gamba of Tongue, near present-day Quelimane, and the emperor, called the Monomotapa, in what is now Mozambique, to cite only two examples, accepted these simple gestures with equal simplicity, perhaps not entirely without political and commercial ambitions, but sincerely enough so that mass baptisms of hundreds took place during a few days or weeks. Yet time and again both visitors and hosts were disillusioned to realize that the gestures they had exchanged (baptizing and being baptized) did not achieve the peaceful union of the different cultures and societies they symbolized.

Let us take a brief look at such a situation. Around 1560, Portuguese missionaries attempted to penetrate to the interior of the continent from the east coast. Two Jesuits, Gonçalo and Fernandes, arrived from Goa, which was then the center of Portuguese operations in the Indian Ocean. In Sofala (in present-day Mozambique) they made contact with the son of King Gamba and secured his permission to missionize in his kraal at Tongue, southeast of Sofala. After three weeks of instruction in the faith, the king dissolved his harem, and he and his nobles and many other people were baptized. It is highly interesting to read what Gonçalo reported to his confreres:

> It seemed profitable to baptize a larger number at once, because these pagans want to be together like children, and one jumps after the other. Also, with regard to the

9. *Ibid.*
10. The patronate (*padroado*) goes back to a papal edict (Sane Charissimus, 1418) in which Pope Martin V asked all Christian rulers to join Portugal's crusade to fight the infidels and their errors—a document which laid the foundation for the monopoly of Portugal in the political and spiritual conquest of Africa and Asia. In its later development (in which Portugal had to share her privileges with Spain) the patronate implied that the propagation of faith overseas was organized and maintained by the crown. See *ibid.*, pp. 5-8.

impediments of faith, they are like children. Their reason has no objections to faith because here idols and idolatry are unknown. They believe in one god whom they call Umbe; they believe in the existence of a soul, life after death, and receiving punishment and reward, depending on whether the soul had been good or bad. Therefore, our articles of faith and commandments are quite evident to them. Misuses which we observed in the few days I was there are the following: (1) Polygamy: many have only one wife, but the nobles keep many for their prestige, as we keep slaves, and use them in the same way. (2) Superstition, divination, and sorcery: concerning the dead they have some very serious misconceptions; for example, they abandon the house of the deceased. They also carry objects around their necks, calling them "medicines." (3) When they swear, they blow into each other's faces, which is supposed to be an oath. (4) If a man's brother dies without leaving a son, the man takes his brother's wife as his own. (5) The Batonga practice circumcision, which they reportedly took over from influential Moors who arrived there long ago, although they did not accept their religion. Batongas and Mocarangas are inclined toward our faith so that, with the help of God, it seems possible to eliminate the said misuses, which are not rooted in idolatry.[11]

Anyone familiar with Bantu ethnography will recognize that Gonçalo draws a very general picture, but by what we know today very probably a true picture, of the culture he encountered. Gonçalo's conclusions and actions seem incomprehensible, however, unless we return to our assumption that his encounter with Gamba really took place on the religious level, as a battle of symbols, not as a pragmatic action guided by rational ends and rationally chosen means.

The unwillingness of many missionaries to integrate their observations and to understand them as a "system," as we would say today, led many to underestimate the spiritual and political complexity of the states into which they ventured. Having completed his mission to Tongue after seven weeks, Gonçalo set out for the lands of the emperor, the Monomotapa. The sources indicate that this expedition may have had some political and commercial goals (he acted as an envoy for the Portuguese authorities), but when he arrived at the residence of the Monomotapa, he lived inside the kraal and not in the quarters reserved for Swahili and Portuguese traders. He converted his hut into a chapel and immediately began his mission activities. Twenty-five days after the first audience, the Monomotapa was baptized and given the name of Sebastião; the queen mother was called Donna Maria. Many nobles and hundreds of subjects followed their example. Then Gonçalo's mission came to a sudden end. A few weeks after his spectacular "success" he was assassinated, allegedly by jealous Arab traders, but probably by a conspiracy of imperial *nganga* (diviners). Whatever the actual events, it is of interest to note that the missionary was accused (1) of being a spy for the governors of India and Sofala, sent out to explore the conditions for a military expedition with the aim of killing the Monomopata and conquering his

11. *Ibid.,* p. 61.

country; (2) of being an envoy of Chipute (a rival of the Monomotapa) sent to incite the nobles against the Monomotapa; (3) of using the ritual of baptism as sorcery, that is, as a means of gaining power over the people.[12]

These interpretations of Gonçalo's mission illustrate the failure of the exchange of gestures embodied in the baptism ceremonies to prevail over political, social, and economic realities. But the battle of symbols was not always carried out in this simple form. Documents, above all the diplomatic correspondence of the African Christian kings of the kingdom of Kongo in the sixteenth and seventeenth centuries, suggest that African rulers began to play a sophisticated game, using tensions between different European powers and religious orders to their own advantage. Clearly these relationships were highly political in nature, but it is of interest to note that religion remained the medium in which Africa and the West encountered one another, and it provided the symbol language in which they talked.[13]

The mission history in the old kingdom of Kongo in a way prefigured the events of the modern phase (that is, the reintroduction of Christianity into the Kongo in the mid-nineteenth century). After the initial contact, which we interpret as the exchange of "simple gestures," and after a phase of sophisticated but politically motivated symbolic interaction, we have by the end of the seventeenth century a documented case of a true synthesis of Christian and African ideas and values: the prophetic-charismatic movement led by Donna Beatrice, and a number of other prophets. The Capuchin missionary Lorenco de Lucca reported that Donna Beatrice, a member of the Kongo high nobility, claimed to have died and been resurrected as an incarnation of St. Anthony. She based her operations in São Salvador, then the almost deserted capital of the Kongo kingdom. Her immediate disciples she called "angels." The missionary tells us that

> these "angels" were distinguished from other people because they wore on their heads a crown made from the bark of the ensanda tree. This treacherous woman said that this crown was made from the same material as the first dress of the Child Jesus. And she added that the angels who wore this crown would not lack anything, neither gold, nor silver, nor silk gowns, nor whatever they desired.[14]

From other information in the report of the missionary it becomes clear that the movement was concerned with a restoration of the old Kongo kingdom.[15]

---

12. *Ibid.*, pp. 71 ff.

13. See, for example, Louis Jadin, "Le clergé séculier et les capucins du Congo et d'Angola aux XVI*e* et XVII*e* siècles," *Bulletin de l'institut historique belge à Rome*, XXVI (1964), 185–483.

14. J. Cuvelier, *Relations sur le Congo du Père Laurent de Lucques (1700–1717)* (Brussels: Institut Royal Colonial Belge, 1953), p. 226 [my translation].

15. *Ibid.*, p. 159.

But even the short passage quoted above allows us to draw a number of conclusions as to the character of the "heresy." To introduce a distinctive costume was a deliberate effort to mark and promote the identity of the group. It was also a reminder of traditional Kongolese society where the bark of the tree had served as material for clothing. The claim that the first dress of the Child Jesus was made of exactly the same material symbolized the incorporation of Christian ideas into the traditional system. But the terms of this incorporation were defined by the prophetess, not by the missionaries; she composed her own prayers and introduced an important difference in the cult by demanding that the crucifix should not be venerated as the instrument of the Passion of our Lord.[16]

The rise of this movement heralded a new phase in the symbolic encounter between the cultures of Africa and the West, an encounter on an equal basis and at the initiative of the African partner. But at that time the political influence of the missionaries was still strong, and Donna Béatrice was condemned as a heretic. She died at the stake on July 2, 1706.

These accounts of situations from the early history of Christianity in Africa are meant to suggest concrete and at the same time paradigmatic illustrations for our assumption that religion in Africa has been an essential medium of change during the centuries of recorded history. This has been true in more than one sense. Religion has been the boundary at which African and Western cultures have clashed most violently and with the most far-reaching consequences. It is the medium through which members of the different cultures perceive one another most acutely and in which they interact most intimately. It is also a medium through which Africans are entering the mainstream of Western life by achieving a synthesis of African and Western values which they deem an appropriate expression of their own identities. The latter aspect will receive our special attention in a later section of this paper.

RELIGIOUS INSTITUTIONS AND SOCIAL CHANGE

It is important to distinguish between religion as a social-cultural *institution* (in the sense of a membership group) and religion as a social-cultural *process* (that is, as the perception of some reality, and its formulation and deposition in a system of beliefs and standards). We propose to consider religion and social change in Africa from two angles, one focusing on a Malinowskian "impact of institutions," the other on an intellectual process.

In assessing the impact of religious institutions on African society, we should consider to what extent such indigenous institutions have been a factor of change. This is not easily ascertained, mainly because in those ethnographies

16. *Ibid.*, p. 171.

which describe African religion in enough detail to allow valid inferences, emphasis has been on demonstrating that society and religion exist as a system in its ideal state, intact and integrated. Such concern with the "whole" derived from certain theoretical views of society (as expressed, for example, by the British functionalist school of social anthropology). In a time when field study of African culture was at its beginnings, researchers had to concentrate on describing that which they could observe and which appeared to be "stable" ingredients of the systems under consideration. In a later period, when more intensive investigations had revealed tensions and "breaks" in indigenous religion and culture, fascination with the timeless (and directionless) existence of "primitive" societies had become so strong that some anthropologists chose to adopt additional theoretical assumptions to account for these tensions rather than give up the established views. To cite an example, this was the case with Max Gluckman's *Analysis of a Social Situation in Modern Zululand*[17] Drawing on suggestions from A. R. Radcliffe-Brown, he distinguished between "changing" and "repetitive" societies, the latter being characterized by the fact that tensions are ritually resolved (that is, periodically and by standardized means) rather than being resolved by revolution and innovation. "Change" in such societies was seen as a process of reestablishing equilibrium. "Change" then was thought to be directed toward the center of the society itself, toward maintenance of its basic values; it did not lead anywhere.

This approach was adopted recently by Victor Turner in his analysis of ritual among the Ndembu in Zambia.[18] As a model for ritual processes, Turner introduces the concept of the "social drama," which is meant to account for the fact that repetitive societies are not necessarily peaceful societies. Turner states:

> A drama has a kind of circularity of form and intention. There is an intention of restoring an antecedent condition, in this case a condition of dynamic equilibrium between the parts of a society. But any process that involves conflict has its "victims," and any process that reaffirms norms implies condemnation of norm-breakers. It also implies punishment of the innovator as well as the law-breaker, since the introduction of radical novelty would prevent the ultimate closure of the circle.[19]

While we may not share the theoretical assumptions of these authors, it must be stated that on the whole the theoretical conception of African societies as repetitive systems has resulted in excellent descriptions of religious belief and ritual. The idea of constant, if directionless, change allows us, at least, to conceive of the impact of institutionalized religion on society as a dynamic process.

Approaches such as those taken by Gluckman and Turner were probably

---

17. (Manchester: Manchester University Press, 1958).
18. *The Drums of Affliction* (London: Oxford University Press, 1968); see esp. Chap. IX.
19. *Ibid.*, p. 276.

conditioned to a large extent by the fact that both were investigating relatively unmodified traditional situations. Among the numerous studies of religion and change in less ideal conditions (many of them examining the fate of traditional religion in urban and "detribalized" populations), the study by B. A. Pauw, *Religion in a Tswana Chiefdom,* is one of the more important.[20] Pauw collected his data among the Thlaping group of the Tswana cultural cluster of southern Africa. Clearly, the situation in which he worked was characterized by a number of political, social, and economic factors imposed on the group from outside powers. The Thlaping lived on a "reservation," a construct of the colonial administration. Because the outer limits of the society were thus artificially fixed, the Christian missions operating within the reservation seem to have had an exaggerated impact. Pauw indicates the problems of attempting to measure change by institutional affiliation when he points out how difficult it was to establish valid criteria of what makes a true pagan and a true Christian and thus to assess quantitatively the impact of Christianity. Under the heading "Paganism on the Wane," he gives a disconnected picture of the "remnants" of traditional religion. From there he turns his attention to the constitutions, activities, and membership of the "churches" (Catholic, Protestant, and Bantu-Separatist). "Religion" thus is seen as an institution rather than as a process, with the result that change operating on traditional Thlaping religious beliefs can be conceived of only as elimination and replacement of "traits." Certainly there are cases in which religious change seems to have resulted from an externally applied destructive stimulus. Pauw, for example, points out that much of the ritual authority of the chief as the "rainmaker" became obsolete through the introduction of irrigation agriculture.[21] But one should regard this relatively clear-cut case with a certain reserve. Such externally induced change rarely affects religion directly. Symbol systems have their own life and significance and are often maintained even when they have lost their original functions. There is, for example, no doubt that with the increasing depletion of the savanna game population in southern Congo and in northern Zambia hunting is losing its economic importance. But if one reads Turner's account of the hunting ritual among the Ndembu (and his conclusions are probably valid for all societies in the Luba-Lunda sphere) it becomes clear that the symbols employed in the ritual have lost nothing of their importance as the repository of the values of manhood as well as other vital conceptions of Ndembu society.[22]

If attention is fixed on institutionalized forms of religion and on the clash of such institutions, as in Pauw's study, it is difficult to understand religious change

20. (London: Oxford University Press, 1960).
21. *Ibid.,* pp. 4, 27.
22. Victor Turner, "Themes in the Symbolism of Ndembu Hunting Ritual," *Anthropological Quarterly,* XXXV (1962), 37–57.

(and the impact of religion on social change) as a process of orientation or re-orientation. In his conclusions, Pauw summarizes various types of "inter-con-nexions between the old and the new,"[23] a concept which again implies a view of change which is basically directionless, at best descriptive, and clearly oblivious to the power factors of the contact situation.[24]

We must conclude, then, that neither holistic nor atomistic views of traditional African religions and of the processes of change operating on them and through them have successfully represented and interpreted the phenomena of change. Some studies impress us with the fact that traditional religion is a dynamic proc-ess, intimately connected with social life, and not a static, hovering system of disembodied beliefs and ritual. But these efforts do not support our proposition that there is an internal connection between religion and directional change and that the course of history in Africa was thus to a large extent determined by religious forces. The nature of such a proposition prevents it from being con-clusively demonstrated, yet it may serve as a valuable guide to further research and it may help to direct our interests to problems of continental dimensions. There are at least three major themes through which the impact of religion on the growth and change of pre-Western African society might be studied: (1) beliefs and symbols associated with state formation; (2) secret societies; and (3) magico-religious economic groups.

Religious beliefs and symbols have played a prominent role in the processes of state formation in almost all village-organized and kinship-oriented African societies. These processes were brought to a halt by colonial rule, but even in their petrified form, empires such as those of central Africa allow us to speculate on the dynamics of divine-kingship theories. (It is interesting to note that such ideas were resuscitated immediately after independence in Congo-Kinshasa. Kasavubu and Tshombe laid claim to the religious authority of the Congo and Lunda empires, respectively.) We should point out that in the symbolism of divine kingship, sub-Saharan Africa is linked to the intellectual and spiritual centers of Old World civilization in the Near East.[25]

Another phenomenon that has intrigued ethnographers, because it somehow does not fit the image of well-integrated tribal societies, is that of the role played by various kinds of so-called secret societies. While some of these operate within the limits and structures of the village or chieftaincy, others cut across political

23. *Religion in a Tswana Chiefdom*, p. 238.
24. It is consistent with such an approach that Pauw does not really know what to do with the highly interesting figure of the "prophet" Tolonyane, who seems to have been the leader of an early movement of religious response to a changed situation; see *ibid.*, p. 30.
25. The theme of divine kingship has occupied historians of religion for a long time. In the present context two studies are especially important: Percival Hadfield, *Traits of Divine Kingship in Africa* (London: Watts, 1949), and E. L. R. Meyerowitz, *The Divine Kingship in Ghana and Ancient Egypt* (London: Faber & Faber, 1960).

and ethnic boundaries. This illustrates the power of religious beliefs and rituals to organize large numbers of people, who then become a factor for change in the traditional societies.[26]

Other groups worth examining with regard to our problem are trade guilds, such as the hunters and blacksmiths, whose members are associated with magico-religious practices. Because of their tight organization and high prestige, as well as their close ties to economic life, these groups may have had a considerable impact on traditional society.

THE ASSESSMENT OF MISSION IMPACT

An evaluation of the role of the Christian missions in Africa in modern times is a task of enormous proportions. We are presently witnessing a transfer of responsibility from European and American mission outposts to an African clergy; consequently, although thorough research and systematic study of the information contained in innumerable archives and the publications of the various missionizing organizations has only begun, reflections on the role of the missions in shaping modern Africa have become more frequent and more critical.[27]

Under these circumstances we can make only a few general suggestions as to the significant lines of development that are becoming visible through research into this scramble for Africa called "mission."

We must first try to understand the impact of missions on religious processes, as distinct from other social phenomena. In other words, such obvious aspects of social change as the educational, medical, and, occasionally, economic enterprises linked to the missions concern us only insofar as they are tied to institu-

26. This aspect will gain further significance once the logical and historical connections between "secret societies" in traditional Africa and "prophetic-messianic movements" in the present are better understood. J. L. Comhaire was, to my knowledge, one of the first to point out such connections in "Sociétés secrètes et mouvements prophétiques au Congo Belge." *Africa,* XXV (1955), 54–59.

27. It should, however, be noted that attempts to systematize understanding of the missions (that is, of their operation, not just their history) were initiated more than a generation ago and have now attained academic status as "missiology."

As far as the social sciences are concerned, this kind of work may have an interesting outcome. The founders of the discipline of anthropology were often ridiculed by their immediate successors as being armchair scholars, relying on the reports of missionaries and a few explorers. "Field work" in an exotic country—made possible, of course, by the pacification of the savages under colonial rule and funds from interested institutions—became the sacred ritual of initiation into the trade. Today one is tempted to predict an imminent revalorization of armchair scholarship, for two reasons: the huge archival material on Africa awaits analysis, and "exotic" countries no longer provide what one might call laboratory situations—undisturbed observation of certain aspects of society while other aspects remain "controlled."

tions which center around religious beliefs and which, in their activities of various kinds, are directed toward the maintenance and propagation of those beliefs. If the problem with which we start is defined in such a way, it follows that an appraisal of the role of the missions in changing Africa must begin with an understanding of the belief systems involved, or, more exactly, with an understanding of the diversity of beliefs and goals and of the means chosen in the pursuit of these goals. Although the visible operations of the missions of all denominations may have been similar, and although the representatives of these missions were all white people with cultural and political links to the colonial powers, we must not assume that all missions played the same role and had a similar impact.[28]

Some of the differences would concern such things as (1) the theological foundations for the mission (and the sometimes very important differences in these foundations within a denomination); (2) the influences of different theological "schools," often tied to different nationalities, operating in different territories; (3) the specific methods and policies of missionizing, and the degree to which these were based on theological foundations and change; (4) theological views (often intimately connected with the history of the home country) concerning the relationship between church and state and, consequently, cooperation between mission and colonial (and post-colonial) administration; and (5) the involvement of missions in the colonial endeavor, and the ways in which colonial powers used mission societies in extending their influence.

We must take into account still another complicating dimension. Those who have had the opportunity to know missionizing churches both at home and abroad are often impressed by the fact that these institutions in addressing themselves to two different audiences tend to express varying intentions, purposes, and programs. We must therefore be critical in accepting the claims of these institutions to uniformity in intent and execution. "Mission" does serve different functions in the mother country and in the field. The organizational links are usually very tight because of the financial dependence of the field stations, but the flow of resources, personnel, and even "ideas" has not always been directed to the mission country, nor has it been directed to all mission countries equally. In Europe and the United States, "mission" often became an efficient incentive for fund raising and recruitment for vast educational enterprises of which actual mission work was only a part. For example, small Catholic orders struggling for survival opened token mission branches with the admitted aim of reviving interest in their particular functions in the home country.

On the other side, in the mission country the missionaries were often intellectually and socially isolated from the home order. Such isolation not only

28. Examples of such simplification are D. E. Apter, "A Critique of Missions: Changing Africa and the Christian Dynamic," mimeographed (Chicago: University of Chicago, 1960); and J. A. Onwumelo, "Congo Paternalism" (Ph.D. diss., University of Chicago, 1966).

implied a time gap in the diffusion of ideas, but it often resulted in a "materialization" of the activities of the mission (the church- and school-building syndrome). With improved communication in the last decade, conditions have changed considerably, but the pattern set at the height of the colonial era is still very influential.

The dual character of most missions, reflecting differences between belief systems and goals, makes it clear that the specific impact of Christian religious institutions on African society must be understood as the result of a complex interplay of independently variable aspects of these institutions.

Attention to these questions reflects our opinion concerning the "results" of mission efforts. There are impressive statistics of conversion, and reports on the progress of the various projects of mission work are available, but we have very few serious studies of what religious conversion has meant to the missionized African.[29] A paradoxical situation seems to be evolving. While we gather more and more information of good quality about separatist, sectarian, and charismatic-prophetic groups, there is to my knowledge no study available that would give us an empirically based analysis of the beliefs held by "orthodox" mission Christians. The assumption is, of course, that these beliefs are the same as those expressed in the official teachings of the churches—an assumption which should be put to a hard test.

RELIGIOUS PROCESS AND SOCIAL CHANGE

In this section, I will return to the proposition that there is an intrinsic relation between religion and change, and I will suggest more explicit evidence in support of my assumptions.

As we have seen, an attempt to assess the impact of missions, that is, religious institutions, on African society is necessarily inconclusive owing to the lack of adequate data and conceptual tools. It should now be made clear that such an outcome is in a certain sense inevitable. Most of the concepts used by sociologists and social anthropologists are designed to cope with patterns of action which are, if not stable, at least regular and predictable. To a great extent, these theories and methods are devised to deal with "normal" and repetitive aspects of social behavior, with clearly discernible "structures" and "functions." Under conditions which are in fact stable (as in certain periods of colonial rule) this approach has worked very well, and with regard to Africa it has produced

29. Mention should be made of the excellent work on the missionary factor produced by such authors as B. G. M. Sundkler, Roland Oliver, J. V. Taylor, Max Warren, G. A. Shepperson, and F. B. Welbourn. For general orientation and bibliographical references, see Welbourn, *East African Christian*.

analyses of traditional culture and society which are remarkable for their detail.

But what if we are confronted with a situation in which exceptions to established patterns of behavior become so frequent and so important that they cannot be disregarded? Max Weber, one of the great theorists of social science, introduced into our vocabulary a concept that was meant to deal with behavior and modes of social integration based on the "extraordinary," the non-everyday, the new and creative: *charisma.*[30] This concept is used by many observers of contemporary African religion, who despite differences in theoretical inclination tend to agree on the following points: (1) the ethnographic scene in Africa is increasingly dominated by the emergence of "religious movements" based on the acceptance of a prophetic message. Such a movement may take one of several forms, ranging from a separatist replica of a mission church to an original synthesis of traditional and Christian beliefs. (2) What unites these movements and connects them with others that are less specifically religious and less tangible in their social manifestations is the fact that in all of them religious ideas and religious language are used to interpret changed intellectual, social, economic, and political conditions and to give expression to the perceived change in such a way that action can be organized and directed.

French sociologist Georges Balandier is among those who recognized most clearly the importance of charismatic religion in the processes of change and progress.[31] He began to follow this line of investigation in the early 1950s. In 1962 he gave a short comprehensive presentation of his views under the title "Les Mythes politiques de colonisation et de décolonisation en Afrique."[32] In this work he examines the effect of, and the response to, colonization in African myths, legends, and rituals. He proposes to see the development as a process with three phases.

First, the "colonial fact" is recognized and incorporated into existing myths. As examples he quotes the Bwiti cult among the Fang (Gabon), various mask societies which incorporate Europeans into their symbolism, and other semiritual associations organized after the model of the colonial society and its hierarchy. It is characteristic of this phase that the material inferiority of the colonized is depicted in the myth as a curse.

Myths belonging to the second phase show an active reaction against the colonial domination. They imply a rehabilitation of African culture and the African

30. For a definition, see Max Weber, *The Theory of Social and Economic Organization* (New York: Macmillan, The Free Press, 1957), pp. 358 ff. Concerning recent utilization of the concept, see Johannes Fabian. "Charisma and Cultural Change," *Comparative Studies in Society and History,* XI (1969), 155–73; and R. C. Tucker, "The Theory of Charismatic Leadership," *Daedalus* XCVI (1968), 731–56.

31. See his *Sociologie actuelle de l'Afrique noire* (Paris: Presses Universitaires de France, 1955), and *Afrique ambigue* (Paris: Plow, 1957), 42–83.

32. *Cahiers internationaux de sociologie,* XXXIII (1962), 85–96.

way of life. Polygyny and the rules of kinship are revalorized, and often a direct connection between the people of Africa and the people of Israel or ancient Egypt is postulated. To this stage belong religious innovations of a revolutionary character, prophetic-charismatic movements whose philosophical content is somewhere between myth and political ideology. Although such movements may lead to popular revolts, the governing ideas are still placed on the level of the myth, that is, in a realm outside of historical time.

The last phase, that of the revindication of independence, comes about when these myths are used, in various ways, by a small elite as a means of mobilizing political action. The mythical roots remain visible in the "messianic" accent of modern politics in Africa.

Balandier's views may or may not represent an actual evolutionary sequence, but they do direct our attention to what we have called "religion as a process." They help us to understand that religion has had an impact on Africa not only in its fully institutionalized forms but also in the very process of institutionalization, that is, in the process of transformation between perception of reality in terms of ultimate categories and the orientation of action through the religious beliefs and norms in which this perception becomes symbolized.

In Africa these processes operate in characteristic ways. At the level of the individual there is the endeavor of Western-educated Africans to find a spiritual synthesis of Western and African world views. Such a synthesis can be the basis of an identity that incorporates their African cultural heritage and yet still allows them to communicate with, and contribute to, non-African intellectual life.

Some of these efforts at synthesis have come out of the new African universities, such as Makerere University College in Uganda or the University of Ibadan in Nigeria.[33] Others have been expressed in conferences or joint publications.[34] Another such synthesizing movement found its forum in the publications of Présence Africaine and has been identified with French-speaking Africans who rallied around the philosophy of negritude.[35]

The African clergy has exercised another type of integrating influence. These are the people who, by the nature of their education, have experienced the battle of the symbols most acutely and who have been under the most severe pressure to integrate their African identity with their function as representatives of the Christian message. It is no surprise that Catholic priests whose ties to a

33. Examples are F. B. Welbourn, *East African Christian* (London: Oxford University Press, 1965); and E. B. Idowu, *Towards an Indigenous Church* (London: Oxford University Press, 1965).

34. Examples are *The Church in Changing Africa* (New York: International Missionary Council, 1958); and Ram Desai, ed., *Christianity in Africa as Seen by Africans* (Denver: Swallow, 1962); and C. G. Baeta, ed., *Christianity in Changing Africa* (London: Oxford University Press, 1968).

35. See G. Deroy, "Présence africaine et christianisme," mimeographed (University of Louvain, 1966); and Abiola Irele, "Negritude—Literature and Ideology," *Journal of Modern African Studies*, III (1965), 499–526.

Western organization were strong became the most vociferous participants in this process of reorientation.[36] The African clergy has always been in close contact with the thinking of political ideologues, many of whom, it will be remembered, initially declared their programs to be "Christian socialism."[37]

One of the participants in the April, 1961, colloquium on African religions organized by the African Society of Culture in Abidjan was the Belgian Franciscan missionary, Placide Tempels.[38] He has played an important part in a movement which clearly illustrates the manner in which religion and religious syntheses have had a continent-wide impact on the emergence of a new African identity on the popular level.

Father Tempels is well known for his work *La Philosophie bantoue*, which is an attempt to give a systematic picture of the traditional world view of the culture in which he worked as a missionary (the Luba-Katanga, in what is now Congo-Kinshasa). The book was acclaimed by many Africans and many colonials, but it became so controversial that the authorities thought it wise to send Tempels back to Belgium. *Bantu Philosophy* (its English title)[39] was criticized by colonialists, who suspected that it might make the natives too self-conscious, as well as by anthropologists and philosophers, who disdained its amateurish methods.[40] What these critics failed to recognize was that Tempels' intent was essentially a "confession," that is, a reappraisal of his role as a missionary and of the dignity of the Africans he was supposed to convert. The machinations against the book and its author did not arrest its effect as a catharsis of the encounter between African and Western world views. Senghor expressed its importance as follows:

> We should all have in our libraries: *La Philosophie bantoue*, by Reverend Placide Tempels; *Dieu d'eau*, by Marcel Griaule; or simply, *Les Contes de l'Ouest Africain*, by Roland Colin. From these volumes we would learn that Negro-African philosophy, like socialist philosophy, is existentialist and humanistic, but that it integrates spiritual values.[41]

Father Tempels' role as an ideologue of the Bantu soul does not exhaust the influence of this remarkable man. When Tempels was allowed to return to

---

36. See A. Abble and J. C. Bajeux, *Des Prêtres noirs s'interrogent* (Paris: Présence Africaine, 1963); and R.-M. Tchidmbo, *L'Homme noir face au christianisme* (Paris: Présence Africaine, 1963).

37. As an example of the role of religion in African political ideology, see Léopold Sédar Senghor, *Pierre Teilhard de Chardin et la politique africaine*, Cahiers Pierre Teilhard de Chardin, III (Paris: Editions du Seuil, 1962), 13–65.

38. See *Colloque sur les religions* (Paris: Présence Africaine, 1962), pp. 219–23.

39. (Paris: Présence Africaine, 1959).

40. See F. Crahay, "Le 'Décollage' conceptuel: conditions d'une philosophie bantoue," *Diogène*, LII (1965), 61–84; and F. E. Boulaga, "Le Bantou problématique," *Présence Africaine*, LXVI (1968), 4–40.

41. Léopold Sédar Senghor, *On African Socialism*, trans. Mercer Cook (New York: Praeger, 1964), p. 49.

the Congo he began to preach his message and became, probably to his own surprise, the leader of a prophetic-charismatic movement, the Jamaa, which has spread throughout the Katanga and Kasai provinces and has attracted large numbers of previously indifferent mission Christians.[42]

The Jamaa movement can serve as a paradigmatic case for the formidable processes of reorientation and new syntheses which occur in popular religious movements throughout sub-Saharan Africa. These movements are increasingly receiving the attention of anthropologists and other interested observers, as evidenced in a recent bibliography which lists more than a thousand references to African religious movements.[43] Our understanding of these phenomena, however, is still in its beginnings. We still lack criteria for typological distinctions (for example, as between a merely sectarian proliferation of "churches" and truly creative attempts to formulate a new African religion). However, the frequency and number of followers of these movements are an impressive demonstration of our assertion that interaction on the level of religious and metaphysical beliefs continues to be one of the most powerful factors of change in Africa.

The problem of religion and change opens a wide field for stimulating research. Interest in change often arises from new situations in the field in which traditional methods of analysis no longer seem relevant. For this reason, an anthropologist concerned with religion and change will find it necessary to reexamine the theories and methods he has been accustomed to using. This essay, while pointing to the need for self-criticism, has attempted to draw some of the lines along which future research is likely to proceed. It has suggested that an analytical distinction between religion as an institution and religion as a process could enable the researcher to combine the approach and findings of earlier structuralist-functionalist anthropology with a new (or revived) interest in historical processes of continental rather than just colonial range. To suggest a combination of approaches is a *practical* conclusion derived from a review of past and present anthropological concerns with change and religion in Africa. This does not imply that *theoretical* progress in our understanding of Africa is dependent only on improved skills in handling available data and available methods.

It is probably true that for a majority of anthropologists African reality is still simply "available" and that it matters little what kind of orientations the researcher brings to the field as long as he is able to demonstrate the success of his methods and techniques in "accounting for" and hopefully "predicting"

42. See Fabian, "Charisma and Cultural Change"; and Johannes Fabian, "Dream and Charisma: 'Theories of Dreams' in the Jamaa-Movement (Congo)," *Anthropos*, LXI (1966), 544–60.

43. R. C. Mitchell and H. W. Turner, *A Bibliography of Modern African Religious Movements* (Evanston, Ill.: Northwestern University Press, 1966).

developments. This is the philosophy that guides research designs and the funding of projects. No one could deny the success of such studies in understanding and planning, for instance, economic and technological change, yet it should be equally clear that an approach geared to the scientific engineering of realities is, when extended to explanations of cultural change, inherently domineering and suggestive of an intellectual colonialism which is strongly resented by Africans. Progress in understanding the kind of change in which religion and world view are involved will come about only when anthropology outgrows its naïvete concerning the availability of "data." Ideas and religious beliefs are given to the researcher only in a context of communication and (usually) only through the medium of language. Consequently, information is never simply waiting there to be "picked up." It must be learned in very much the same way as one learns a language: by submitting to its rules, by thinking in its terms, and by sharing it with a community of speakers. Anthropology has just begun to realize the theoretical and methodological implications of a cooperative rather than domineering approach. The study of religious processes in Africa will contribute much to bring about this new awareness.

IV

Consolidation of
Nation-States

20

African Concepts
of Nationhood

JOHN N. PADEN

IN THE EUROPEAN CONTEXT, the term *nationalism* usually refers to those movements, feelings, and ideologies which demand that the basic political boundaries and identities of a people be contained within the framework of a sovereign state. *Sovereignty*, as the concept emerged in the nineteenth and twentieth centuries, reflects an international system wherein states are accorded complete autonomy on internal matters, legal equality and inviolability within the external (or international) context, and some precise delimitation of territoriality.

If a sovereign state is based on a single national identity we refer to it as a *nation-state*. A sovereign state which comprises several national identities may be called a *multinational* state. The idea of *nation* refers to a people, or *volk*, who regard themselves as sharing common values and goals, as sharing a common history and a common future, and as being somehow distinguishable in various ways from other peoples. Within the European context, the characteristics which have been used most frequently to distinguish different peoples have included the following: language, culture, proximity (or territorial identification), religion, political system, and economic interdependence. While none of these characteristics is necessarily essential to the consolidation of a nation-state, some combination of them is usually present.

The concept of a people sharing common values and a common identity clearly relates the issue of nationality (and nationalism) to the issue of ethnicity. *Ethnicity* may be regarded as communal (as opposed to associational) loyalty or identity and is usually accompanied by the claim of kinship or common origin (real or assumed). The notion of ethnicity does not necessarily require political independence, sovereignty, or territoriality. Ethnic groups, such as the Bakongo (Congo-Kinshasa) or the Tswana (Botswana), which have petitioned for separate political status are expressing what may be called ethnic nationalism. The terms *ethnic group* and *nationality group*, as van den Berghe points out in his essay in this volume, often have overlapping meanings. In general usage, however, an ethnic group is a smaller scale unit than a nationality group. Also, ethnic groups emphasize *kinship*, a notion which may be transmuted in various ways in the concept of nationality.

Nationalism need not preclude certain types of subnational loyalties, either in the nation-state context or in those cases of the multinational state where a sufficient commonality of interest reinforces the legitimacy of the national state (rather than the component nationalities) as the seat of sovereignty. Peoples usually have multiple identities or loyalties, each relative to different needs or situations. Thus, for example, within Germany the Bavarians and the Prussians (peoples associated with specific geographical regions, religions, and cultures) are significant subnational identity groups, but only if these peoples demanded secession from the nation-state of Germany would we regard this as nationalism in the fullest sense.

A conceptual category which relates the notion of nationality to that of sovereignty is *irredentism*. This would occur if an international (or sovereign-state) boundary divided a people or nation and the members of this nation were dissatisfied or frustrated enough to actively demand reunion. An irredentist movement usually originates with a minority group resident in a state neighboring their homeland state. Examples would include the Turks in Cyprus, the Ewe in Ghana, or the French in Alsace-Lorraine between 1870 and 1914.

In trying to explain how national identity emerges, a major branch of theory concentrates on definition by reference to the external context; a "we" group, for instance, is distinguished from a "they" group which is usually in relative proximity. Thus, to a certain extent, Polish nationalism emerged as a response to the Russians along Poland's eastern border and the Germans along its western border. Since nationality is ultimately a matter of social definition rather than of objective definition, the self-ascriptive identity processs and the external-ascriptive process are always interrelated. The question of what constitutes a "German," "Pole," or "Russian" will vary with the time context, the spatial context, and a variety of subjective perceptions. This process was clearly demonstrated when members of these European groups migrated to America where new (usually more general) categories of national identities were ascribed to them.

Another major process in the emergence of national identity is the extension of loyalties from smaller to larger scale units. Thus, the city-states of the Italian peninsula began to coalesce in the late nineteenth century into what finally emerged as the nation-state Italy. In cases where multinational empires have broken up, as with the Hapsburg Empire and the Turkish Ottoman Empire after World War I, and with the various colonial empires after World War II, the resultant components may regroup themselves into units smaller than the original empire but larger than the individual components. Thus Yugoslavia was formed after World War I from several peoples, such as the Croats, Serbs, Macedonians, Slovenes, and Montenegrins.

THE SCOPE OF AFRICAN NATIONALISM

Three stages of nationalism accompanied the emergence of African states from colonial rule. These included the early proto-nationalistic phenomena, the drive to independence, and the post-independence period of nationalism and supranationalism.

Proto-nationalism

The idea of African proto-nationalism has been developed in recent years as a category for discussing phenomena related to demands for political autonomy (as opposed to sovereignty) in the period prior to the organization of African nationalist movements. In most African states this generally occurred in the time period from 1900 to 1935. The distinguishing feature of these phenomena was active rejection of the establishment and legitimacy of alien rule. Major manifestations of proto-nationalism have been resistance movements, rebellions, and individual protests.

Resistance movements usually occurred at the time of colonial conquest. Thus, the Fulani battle at Burmi (Northern Nigeria) in 1903 was a clear effort to resist alien (British) rule. The Ashanti wars of 1899 and the Islamic wars of Samory Touré were in a similar category.

Rebellions, or revolts, usually occurred shortly after the occupation of an area. They constituted early attempts to throw off alien rule once such rule had been established. Examples would include the Maji Maji rebellion (Tanganyika) against the rule of the Germans and the Zulu rebellion (South Africa) against the British in 1906.

Individual protest movements have taken a variety of forms. Frequently they involved leaders from the African Christian churches (such as John Chilembwe of Malawi, who, in Nat Turner style, was willing to "strike a blow and die"). Other protestors were leaders of nascent labor unions (as in the Copperbelt) or of ethnic voluntary associations (such as Harry Thuku of Kenya) who were willing to go to jail for petitioning against heavy taxation, poor work conditions, and land alienation. Nationalist literature of a later period has accorded these men both a real and a symbolic role in the independence movements.

The Independence Movements

African nationalism can be clearly identified in the period 1945 to 1960. In the late 1930s urban organizations began to emerge, often drawing on the new,

Western-educated, professional and skilled classes. These organizations raised the issue of increasing African participation in the civil service, administration, government, and in the modern economic sector. An example of such an organization would be the Lagos Youth Movement (Nigeria), founded in 1934, which later became the springboard for nationalist leaders such as Nnamdi Azikiwe.

During World War II the African colonies provided manpower and staging bases for the Allies, especially in the North African campaigns against Italy and Germany. In return for this assistance, Britain and France promised major reforms in the colonial system. But as a result of the war, the myth of European infallibility was broken, and the universalistic concepts of freedom, democracy, and justice, which had been part of the rhetoric of the Allied confrontation with fascism, were interpreted by the educated class of Africans as applicable within the African context.

With regard to this question of principles and values, Thomas Hodgkin comments on the political vocabulary of early African nationalists:

> The theoretical weapons with which African nationalists make their revolutions have been largely borrowed from the armouries of the metropolitan countries. Much of the political thinking of contemporary African leaders is bound to be derivative. They are themselves the products of European schools and universities. They are asserting claims of a kind that have already been asserted by Europeans, around which a European sacred literature has been built up. And they have to state their case in a language that will be intelligible to their European rulers. . . . [Three strains of Western thought stand out: 1] the Christian idea of human brotherhood and the specifically Protestant conception of an "Elect"; [2] the traditional democratic belief in "the right to choose our own governors . . . "; and [3] the Socialist (not necessarily Marxian) conception of a society in which "economic exploitation," poverty and unemployment are abolished, and rewards are related to work.[1]

Within a brief period of approximately fifteen years following World War II, African political parties were formed, self-government was demanded, and independence was won in most African states. The speed of change does not mean that the task was easy. In almost every case, the colonial power offered major resistance of some sort. It is a tribute to the organizational skill, and often charismatic inspiration, of the pre-independence African nationalists that they were able to mobilize enough support to enforce their demands and to do so, in nearly all cases, without resort to violence.

Nationalism and Supranationalism

The territorial units within which the nationalist movements developed were, for the most part, the colonial units. During the pre-independence nationalist

---

1. *Nationalism in Colonial Africa* (New York: New York University Press, 1957), p. 170.

period, however, a matter of considerable debate among nationalist leaders was the question of the most appropriate boundaries for future nation-states in Africa. In a few cases, it was suggested that units smaller than the existing colonial units, consisting primarily of ethnic nationalities, be the basis of nationhood in Africa. In most cases, however, the idea of using ethnic nationalities as a basis for future nationhood was rejected by the elites in favor of political groupings which were larger than the existing colonial units. The arbitrary nature of the inherited colonial boundaries militated against their acceptability to nationalist leaders who were intent on promoting a new order of things. But the acquired identities of the peoples constituting the former colonies, as well as objective factors such as the intracolonial structure of communications systems, tended to reinforce the originally arbitrary boundaries, and the viability of the former colonial boundaries has been stronger than had been anticipated. As Zolberg points out in his essay in this volume, in the immediate post-colonial nation-building period the major source of national unity in almost every case turned out to be the legacy of the nationalist party of the independence movement.

Yet certain pre-independence concepts of nationalism extended beyond the imposed framework of colonial boundaries associated with the inherited national state systems. It may be that when the birth pains of the new African states have lessened, the reservoir of ideas generated in the pre-independence period will regain importance in African nationalism.

In this essay, we will identify six categories of nationalism which posit emergent communities larger than those existing within the inherited national boundaries of the new states of Africa. Some categories of nationalism proposing political communities, either larger or smaller than the existing states, are based on various types of traditional loyalties. The most important of these are ethnic nationalism (in the case of large groups of people such as the Fulani or Hausa or Ibo) or religious nationalism (which would include religious denominations, both Christian, as in Ethiopia, and Islamic, as in Mauritania, Morocco, or the Somali Republic).[2] We will be examining here, however, only the large-scale territorially or ideologically based political nationalism.

The six "suprastate" categories of nationalism which will be considered in this essay reflect the thought of African leaders during the pre-independence period. This range of alternative bases of nationalism in Africa is in contrast to patterns of nationalism in Europe, where state boundaries emerged after the development of national loyalties. The six categories to be discussed include

2. See John N. Paden, "Urban Pluralism, Integration, and Adaptation of Communal Identity in Kano, Nigeria," in *From Tribe to Nation in Africa,* ed. Ronald Cohen and John Middleton (San Francisco: Chandler Press, 1970); for a discussion of the circumstances which tend to produce ethnic nationalism, see also John N. Paden, "Situational Ethnicity in Urban Africa with Special Reference to the Hausa" (Paper presented at the meeting of the African Studies Association, New York, November 2, 1967).

Eur-Africanism, Marxism-socialism, negritude, Pan-Africanism, Third-World-ism, and African regionalism.

THE IDEA OF A EUROPEAN-AFRICAN COMMUNITY

Under the Fourth Republic (1946–58) France governed its colonies and territories through an organization called the French Union, which was made up of metropolitan France (including Algeria and Corsica), the overseas departments, the overseas territories, and the associated territories. But in 1958, with the inception of the Fifth Republic, the French Union was replaced by a new governmental system called the French Community. The French Community was designed to provide for the continuing political and economic association of the African member states with metropolitan France and the remaining overseas departments and territories.

Prior to 1958, many African deputies to the French National Assembly found ideological, as well as political and economic, justification for the continuing relationship with France through the proposed multinational French Community. In July, 1957, Félix Houphouet-Boigny, of Ivory Coast, outlined this position. He is quoted at length to illustrate the major elements of this argument:

> . . . I think I have the right to consider myself the authentic spokesman of millions of African men and women who have chosen, in preference to the type of independence just acquired by the neighboring state of Ghana, a Franco-African community founded on liberty, equality and fraternity.
>
> In considering where the real interests of the colored peoples of the French territories in Africa lie, we do not begin with a blank slate. The relations which prevail between Frenchmen of the mother country and Frenchmen of Africa already exist in an historical complex of events lived in common, in which good and bad memories mingle. . . .
>
> As a preliminary, we must remove the aura which the concept of independence holds in our imaginations. Why do we not demand independence? To answer this question, I can only ask another: What is independence? Industrial and technical revolutions are making peoples more and more dependent on one another. . . .
>
> . . . What countries are self-sufficient? Not even the United States. Indeed, the countries of Europe in the Coal and Steel Community, in Euratom and in the Common Market are prepared to relinquish a part of their sovereignty, that is to say, a part of their national independence. Why, if not to bring about, by association and mutual aid, a more fully elaborated form of civilization which is more advantageous for their peoples and which transcends a nationalism that is too cramped, too dogmatic and by now out of date? . . .
>
> We know what France asks of us — to share in her institutions and to share in

them as equals. The right of citizenship has been granted without restriction to all the inhabitants of the French Union, and all the electors, whatever their origin, are gathered in a single college. . . .

. . . Territorial assemblies are endowed with broad deliberative powers allowing them to adopt autonomous laws distinct from legislation which applies to the mother country. They have an executive responsible to them, to whom is entrusted the direction of territorial affairs with the exception of foreign relations, defense and security, which remain in the hands of the central power. It is in some degree self-government, but it maintains essential links with the Republic, and is not without analogy to the federal structure of the United States of America.

What makes it certainly unique, however, among various relationships that have existed in modern times between a mother country and its dependencies is the participation of overseas populations in the central government of the Republic. . . .

. . . We feel at home in [the French Union]. We participate in family discussions. Nothing is hidden from us — neither hopes nor dangers. How could we better preserve the interests of the Negro people who for so many years have put their confidence in us again and again? It is this awareness of a comprehensive interdependence of mutual interests which has permitted the creation of a Franco-African community based on equality. It is expressed by autonomy in the management of local affairs and intimate association in the management of the general interests of the Republic. . . .

The presence of the French in Africa is the result of military conquests or of peaceful penetrations which go back to the end of the last century. France has suppressed slavery wherever it existed and has put an end to the quarrels which set different ethnic groups against one another; it has given its education to the African masses and its culture to an élite; . . . In French ranks, in turn, we have poured out our blood on the battle fields for the defense of liberty, and we have won a place in the history of France and of the free world. We do not want to abandon this recent heritage by trying to go back to our origins. . . .

. . . in a world where interdependence has become the supreme rule, outbreaks of fanaticism and nationalism accomplish nothing and run the risk of merely increasing misery. . . .

. . . It is important that the Franco-African community — egalitarian, humane, and fraternal — appear to all nations not only as an example to be emulated but also as an element of international stability on which a sure future can be built.

In our view, that community is an act of faith in this future, also an act of human solidarity. It enables us to bring our stone to the world edifice without losing either our national identity or the French citizenship which we have earned and acquired worthily."[3]

In short, Houphouet-Boigny suggested that the purposes of a Franco-African community would be to ensure the economic and social interests of the black

3. From "Black Africa and the French Union," *Foreign Affairs*, XXXV (July 1957), 593–99; excerpted by special permission from *Foreign Affairs*, copyright 1957 by the Council on Foreign Relations, Inc., New York.

peoples of Africa and to further a civilization drawn from the best of both African and French culture. He deplored nationalism as a means to these ends and was prepared to relinquish elements of sovereignty in favor of an interdependence which would be in the "true" interests of both France and Africa. The African, according to Houphouet-Boigny, has found himself at a unique stage in history—one in which the notion of "nation-state" is losing its significance. Hence the African nationalists should bypass the nation-state epoch in the interests of more rational groupings of peoples. The objections which were raised against this Eur-African concept generally focused on the need to establish a national identity prior to a merging of identity into more extended forms of association.

During the 1958 election for ratification of the Fifth Republic constitution, French African colonies were given the option of becoming member states in the French Community. In each case (with the exception of Guinea, which opted for complete independence), the territorial assemblies became legislative assemblies and the executive councils became national governments. Article 86 of the constitution of the Fifth Republic allowed member states to opt for complete independence at a later date (which all eventually did). Thus, initally considerable autonomy and identity were accorded to each unit within the French Community. The actual division of powers within the Community, however, was not markedly different from that of the former French Union. The African legislatures were still excluded from full control over their own foreign policy and defense, economic and financial policy, general organization of external and common transport and telecommunications, higher education, and justice. Furthermore, the "overseas" states of the Community did not have treaty-making powers. Ironically, the remaining ("residual") powers in the African states were made to look like sovereignty itself.

In its essentials the Community was a federal scheme in which one of the federating units (France) predominated, but in which the federal authority did not extend to the local affairs of the federating units, each of which considered itself to be a "republic." The president of the Community was the president of the French Republic (Charles de Gaulle), the executive council consisted of thirteen prime ministers, and the senate was composed of 284 delegates elected by the respective assemblies (186 of these delegates were representatives of metropolitan France).

Today the French Community has been modified beyond recognition. This process of transformation began in December, 1959, when the Mali Federation (consisting of Senegal and Mali) inquired whether it could opt for complete independence and still remain in the Community. This trend reached its culmination in 1960 when most of the French-speaking African states achieved independence. Nevertheless the rationale for a commonwealth type of community (that is, primarily an economic and cultural association rather than a strong political association) continues to be essentially that which was outlined earlier by Houphouet-Boigny. Such a conception of nation and multination is still implicit in much of the economic planning in French-speaking Africa.

THE IDEA OF A MARXIST-SOCIALIST COMMUNITY

The idea of the solidarity of working-class elements in all sovereign states had long been a prime tenet both in European socialism and Soviet communism. Partly because of the "working-class" status of most farmers and laborers in the African context, and partly because of the wartime alliances between the French Communist Party (CPF) and other resistance elements in France (including de Gaulle), the immediate postwar period was one of considerable rapport between the CPF and many French-speaking African leaders.

In July, 1948, however, French Communist leader Raymond Barbé sent a letter to the various African Communist study groups warning them against ideological nationalism and urging that they stress instead the idea of class struggle. The African reaction to this policy position was largely negative. The major break in relations, however, occurred in 1950, when the transnational West African party (RDA), severed its connections with the French Communist Party.

At about this same time in North Africa, a similar break was beginning to occur, largely as a result of French Communist support for the French government position against the nationalists in Algeria. In 1954 the Algerian national liberation movement (FLN) had taken control of the labor unions and had warned the workers against divided loyalties. Aimé Césaire, a leading West Indian black nationalist (and poet), summarized this disenchantment in his 1956 letter of resignation to Maurice Thorez, secretary-general of the French Communist Party:

> The colonial question cannot be treated as a subsidiary part of some more important global matter, as a part over which others can patch up compromises. . . . Here it is clear that I am alluding to the French Communist Party vote on Algeria, the vote by which the Party granted the Guy Mollet-Lacoste government full powers for its North African policy. In any case, it is patently established that our colonialism, the struggle of coloured peoples against racism, is much more complex, indeed, it is of a totally different nature than the struggle of the French workers against French capitalism. . . . I think I have said enough to make it plain that it is neither Marxism nor Communism I repudiate; the use certain people have made of Marxism and Communism is what I condemn. What I want is that Marxism and Communism be harnessed into the service of coloured peoples, and not coloured peoples into the service of Marxism. . . . There will never be any African communism because the French Communist Party conceives its duties towards colonial peoples in terms of a tutorship to be exercised, and because the

French communists' very anti-colonialism yet bears the stigmata of the colonialism they are combating.[4]

Conversely, it became clear to French Communists that some types of nationalist leaders in Africa might be opposed to international "proletarian" interests. Stalin had anticipated this confrontation:

> The revolutionary nature of the national movement does not necessarily imply the existence of proletarian elements in the movement, the existence of a revolutionary basis for the movement.[5]

The case of the Tunisian labor movement bore out this suspicion, for the general union of Tunisian labor (UGTT) became associated with the conservative Neo-Destour Party. Subsequently the Tunisian labor movement was denied affiliation in the Communist-led World Federation of Trade Unions (WFTU).

The estrangement of African labor movements from European Communists continued to the point where eventually most of the African unions disaffiliated from the WFTU. Under the leadership of Sékou Touré of Guinea, most of the French-speaking West African unions regrouped into the general union of labor in Black Africa (UGTAN).

Yet the values and identities of Marxism-socialism continued to serve as a potential basis of community and political grouping. Much of the vocabulary of nationalist protest, especially that directed against colonial political and economic systems, continued to be phrased in Marxist-socialist terms. This terminology frequently lost much of its precise meaning and was increasingly adapted to African problems and conditions. Thus, for example, when the leader of the conservative opposition party in Ghana, J. B. Danquah, claimed to be a "socialist liberal," it was apparent that the concept of socialism was being used more in a symbolic sense than as a basis for any particular political community.

In retrospect, there seem to have been three categories of persons in Africa during the pre-independence period who identified themselves as Marxist-socialist: (1) a small assortment of "neo-Stalinists," who faded in importance after 1956; (2) a variety of former Communist trade unionists who had renounced ties with European communism but still espoused a revolutionary class struggle in Africa; and (3) an increasing number of African leaders who counted Marx as one of their spiritual fathers but aligned themselves with a more specifically African notion of socialism. These three groups will be considered in more detail below.

4. *Letter to Thorez* (Paris: Présence Africaine, 1956).
5. Joseph Stalin, *Marxism and the National and Colonial Question*, 2d ed. (London: Lawrence and Wishart, 1936), p. 8.

Neo-Stalinists

Brief mention must be made of Soviet theories of African nationhood current in the early postwar period. Stalin had laid the framework by writing:

> A nation is an historically evolved, stable community of language, territory, economic life, and psychological make-up manifested in a community of culture. . . . The nation is not a racial or tribal, but an historically constituted community of people.[6]

Within French-speaking Africa, there was probably only one group which approximated a neo-Stalinist position regarding African "nationhood": the African party of independence (PAI). This group was formed in Dakar in 1956 after the Loi Cadre reforms were instituted. The PAI espoused "scientific socialism" and sought to enlist the support of the urban proletariat of Dakar and Saint-Louis. Its leadership included students, teachers, chemists, dentists, and other white-collar workers. The secretary-general of the PAI, Majhemout Diop, was a Dakar bookseller who had spent several years in Eastern Europe as a member of the secretariat of the International Union of Students. His writings tried to reconcile Marxism-Leninism to the African situation. The result might be interpreted as a sort of neo-Stalinism, at least on the question of nationalities. A major work by Diop in 1958 summarized this position on "the national question":

> In Black Africa there does not exist a single nation, but several are certainly in formation. . . . The non-existence, however, of nations, or of a single Black African Nation, does not mitigate our claims for freedom. . . . In the world today, there exist multi-national states, including the most powerful of states such as the Soviet Union. There are several types of nations. The Socialist nations are the consequence of socialist revolutions, while bourgeois nations appear with capitalism and die with it. Just as Marxists are not for the negation of the nation, they are against all national political egoism, which tends to overestimate the interests of one nation to the detriment of others. To the nationalism of the bourgeoisie we propose international proletarianism. . . . Proletarian nations have their right to freedom. Lenin has said "Complete equality of nations and the union of workers of all nations is the national program assigned to the workers of Marxism." Stalin has written: "The countries of the Soviet consider that each nation, large or small, has particular qualities or specific characteristics not found in other nations. It is these particularities of each nation which consitute the culture of the world . . . no nation is more important than another."[7]

6. *Ibid.*, p. 5.
7. Majhemout Diop, *Problèmes politiques en Afrique noire* (Paris: Présence Africaine, 1958), p. 183 [my translation].

With regard to the equality of nations and the definition of nationhood, Diop is quite clear, yet at no point does he focus his analysis on the characteristics of the nation or nations in Africa. Speaking only in general terms regarding "the future of nations," Diop offers a dialectic of historical development:

> Marxism affirms that the disparity between nations will only be overcome after a long period. All during this period, nations will be born and develop themselves, others will fuse. Yet still it is necessary that nations first be bourgeois and then be transformed into socialist nations.[8]

The rejoinder to this notion of nationhood and dialectic of history was expressed most forcefully by Aimé Césaire:

> We are offered solidarities with the people of France; with the French proletariat, and, via communism, with all the world's proletariats. I don't make light of these solidarities, I don't deny them. But I don't want to see them blown up into metaphysics. There are no allies thrust upon us by place, by the moment, by the nature of things. But if our alliance with the French proletariat bars us from contracting any other, if it tends to make us forget or retreat from other necessary and natural, rightful and fertile alliances, if communism pillages our most vivifying friendships, wastes the bond that weds us to West Indian islands, the tie that makes us Africa's child, then I say that communism has served us ill in having us swap a living brotherhood for what looks to have the features of the coldest of all chill abstractions.[9]

The plea for Africanization of ideology came to characterize most of the remaining African Marxists. Yet even this group was divided over the issue of class formation and class struggle in African society.

Class-Struggle Afro-Marxists

The "Afro-Marxist" position incorporated fierce nationalism and Pan-Africanism with an insistence on Marxist tools of class analysis. It is exemplified by trade unionists such as Diallo Seydou. Implicit concepts of the nation in much of the writing of this group focus on a unified Africa consisting of peasants and workers and led by a vanguard of workers and intellectuals. This group of nationalist thinkers was increasingly undermined by the political elites of the new African states, who regarded class-struggle theory as a threat to political stability.

African Socialists

African socialism was a strong influence on nationalist thought in both the colonial and post-colonial periods. It may be illustrated from the writings of

8. *Ibid.*, p. 202.
9. *Letter to Thorez.*

President Senghor of Senegal. Senghor was especially concerned with what he considered to be the alienation of modern Africa from its source of values. In interpreting Marx, Senghor regarded him primarily as a sociologist of alienation. But economic alienation was closely related, for Senghor, to spiritual and cultural alienation. Thus in 1959 he wrote:

> Socialism [means] return to original sources. . . . Can we integrate Negro African cultural values, especially religious values, into socialism? We must answer that question once and for all with an unequivocal *yes*. . . .
>
> The Atheism of Marx can be considered as a *reaction of Christian origin against the historical deviations of Christianity.* It impaired the essence of religion all the less because the idea of *alienation* is of religious origin. We find the equivalent of this in Mohammedanism. . . .
>
> Negro African philosophy, like socialist philosophy, is existentialist and humanistic, but . . . it integrates spiritual values.[10]

In a sense Senghor echoed the chords of Rousseauian protest against the industrial disruption of the "natural harmony" of men and things, the moral disruption, the alienation from meaning and roots—alienations which characterize a society in the transitional process of modernization. The values to be restored would form the basis of political community.

Senghor specifically challenged the "class-struggle" Marxists on a number of points. He was insistent that the moral community was not to be found either in the division of society into classes or in the totalitarian state system of the Communist countries. He contended that, first, the class struggle was more complex than Marx thought. Second, Marx was wrong on peasant theory. He was also wrong on theory of capitalist concentration. He was wrong on periodic economic crises in capitalist countries. Furthermore,

> in the Communist countries, the "dictatorship of the proletariat," contrary to the teachings of Marx, has made the state an omnipotent, soulless monster, has stifled the natural freedoms of the human being, and has dried up the sources of art, without which life is not worth living.[11]

To Senghor, the state should be a moral agent whose purpose and function are to overcome all forms of alienation. Cultural and spiritual matters are included in these functions. The purpose of the state is to promote or restore the moral autonomy of people. Just as the proletariat of the nineteenth century "were estranged from humanity, the colonized people of the twentieth century, coloured peoples, are even more estranged, and similarly alienated."[12] The peoples with which Senghor was most concerned were those of

10. Léopold Sédar Senghor, *African Socialism: A Report to the Constitutive Congress of the Party of African Federation,* trans. and ed. Mercer Cook (New York: American Society of African Culture, 1959), pp. 13, 22, 32.

11. *Ibid.,* p. 17.

12. *Ibid.,* p. 3.

Black Africa; he regarded them as a potential nation which could be brought into being through the state. "The state is the expression of the nation: it is primarily a means of realizing the nation."[13] This process of cultural reassertion was at the heart of Senghor's nationalism. Senghor would both make a nation out of African peoples and find a nation in Negro values. "We must assure a cultural base for the future Nation, by defining essential characteristics of traditional Negro African Civilization which, blending with European and French contributions, will undergo a renaissance."[14]

NEGRITUDE AND NATIONHOOD

Senghor based his notion of African nationhood on the assumption that there is a commonality of values characteristic of traditional Black Africa. This conceptual category of nationalism with its racial parameter was known as negritude. Three distinct varieties of this category seem to emerge which are relevant to our discussion of nationalism: (1) the general espousal of black African values and personalities; (2) the assertion that black skin color is in itself a positive thing; and (3) the assertion that black people everywhere share a common soul (or unconscious).

Black African Values

In the first instance, negritude was a political and cultural assertion by Africans in Paris that assimilation into French culture was absurd and that Negro-African values could make a positive contribution to universal civilization and at the same time provide a means of personal identification for the intellectuals involved. The black populations of the French West Indies (for example, Guadeloupe and Martinique) also participated in this reaction against French assimilation. In fact, it was a West Indian, Aimé Césaire, whose poem "Cahier d'un retour au pays natal" (written in 1939) set the scene for the postwar literary movement of negritude as outlined by Wilfred Cartey in his essay in this volume. This literary movement included a number of writers and poets who were also nationalists, including Rabemananjara of Madagascar; Senghor, Birago Diop, and David Diop of Senegal; Roumain of Haiti; Paul Niger of Guadeloupe; and Leon Dalmas of Guiana. Their rejection of assimilation was based on the disillusioning experiences of black people in metropolitan France.

Later, certain English-speaking intellectuals joined at least peripherally in the movement. The American writer James Baldwin, who attended the First Congress of Black Writers and Artists held at the Sorbonne in 1956, summarized

13. *Ibid.*, p. 12.
14. *Ibid.*

the mood and consensus of the assembly as follows:

> It became clear as the debate wore on, that there *was* something which all black men
> held in common, something which cut across opposing points of view, and placed
> in the same context their widely dissimilar experience. What they held in common
> was their precarious, their unutterably painful relation to the white world. What
> they held in common was the necessity to remake the world in their own image, to
> impose this image on the world, and no longer be controlled by the vision of the
> world, and of themselves, held by other people. What, in sum, black men held in
> common was their ache to come into the world as men. And this ache united peo-
> ple who might otherwise have been divided as to what a man should be.[15]

By the time of the Second Congress of Black Writers and Artists, held in
Rome in 1959, the emphasis had shifted from a simple rejection of white culture to the issue of the responsibilities of black intellectuals in aiding the "rediscovery" of African culture.

Black Skin Color

The second conception of negritude as a basis for group identity had little to
do with cultural values or the notion of a return to the "homeland." It is concerned with the dignity of black skin coloring. It asserts that "black is beautiful,"
without trying to justify an elaborate set of common cultural values. This type of
assertion tends to emerge only in a biracial context and has been less characteristic of French-speaking Africa than of Brazil, for instance. In fact, negritude
as defined by skin color became a form of Brazilian subnationalism. It was initiated in Latin American literary circles as a reaction against the claims of mulat-
toism—that is, the assertion that it was good to be neither black nor white, but
brown. (It will be noted that other Afro-American movements in Brazil incorporate the cultural values argument. Thus religious sects called *Candomblês
Sangões* formed a federation of African sects which sends members to Nigeria
to be initiated into Yoruba religious associations.)

Black Soul

The third variety of negritude related to group identity asserted that black
people throughout the world share an unconscious experience which distinguishes them from other men. This is more than a rejection of oppression, or
a reassertion of African cultural values, or a pride in black skin coloring. It is a
view of culture not as a product of environment or a learned set of behavior
traits, but as a genetic inheritance, less on a level of conscious thought and behavior than on an unconscious level. Senghor has elaborated this view in combination with the two other classes of negritude mentioned above. Thus:

15. James Baldwin, *Nobody Knows My Name* (New York: Dial Press, 1961), pp. 28–29.

> We could assimilate mathematics or the French language, but we could not strip off our black skins nor root out our black souls. And so we set out on a fervent quest for the Holy Grail: our *Collective Soul.* And we came upon it. . . . *Negritude is the whole complex of civilised values—cultural economic, social and political—which characterize the black peoples.* . . . All these values are essentially informed by intuitive reason. . . . This sentient reason . . . expresses itself emotionally through self-surrender, coalescence of subject and object; through myths, by which I mean the archetypal images of the collective soul; above all through primordial rhythms, synchronised with those of the Cosmos. . . . In other words, the sense of communion, the gift of myth-making, the gift of rhythm, such are the *essential elements of Négritude*, which you will find *indelibly stamped on all the work and activities of black men.*[16]

Senghor has on occasion attempted to demonstrate that the writings of black Americans such as Richard Wright manifest not only the *force vitale* of the African but even the specific forms of expression. He argues that "collective soul" is transmitted by heredity and that the cultural manifestations of black soul are similarly transmitted. Thus:

> As certain biologists point out, the psychological mutations brought about by education are incorporated in genes, and are then transmitted by heredity. Hence the major role played by culture.[17]

Although the scientific basis of this assertion is questioned by modern geneticists, in a way Senghor's argument rests less on whether temperament can be transmitted by chromosomes than on the notion of archetypal patterns of existence. Thus it is asserted that peoples and civilizations have developed archetypal patterns of personality which are distinctive and which characterize the modal sector of their populations. It should be noted, however, that Senghor draws heavily on the writings of the French Catholic priest Pierre Teilhard de Chardin and espouses the principle that "all things converge," that is, that eventually European, African, and other archetypes will contribute to the emergence of a new "phenomenon of man" in the global context.

Cultural and Historical Assertions of Negritude

French-speaking African scholars within the mainstream of ideological negritude reacted against several aspects of Western scholarship on Africa—especially those aspects which focused on the differences between African societies rather than on the similarities. The intellectual elite of negritude sought a historical and cultural basis for black African unity. One of the foremost African scholars along this line has been Cheikh Anta Diop. In 1956, Diop wrote:

16. "What Is Negritude?" *Negro Digest* (April 1962), p. 4 (Reprint of a speech given at Oxford University, 1961, italics added).
    17. *Ibid.,* p. 5.

When we have created . . . a sovereign, continental and multinational state, we shall have to, whatever one may say, endow it with an ideological, cultural super-structure which will be one of its essential ramparts of security. That means that such a state will have to be, as a whole, aware of its past, which presumes the elabo-ration of a general history of the Continent, embracing the particular histories of particular nationalities.[18]

Diop has attempted to synthesize such African commonality in his own re-search. His major work, *The Cultural Unity of Negro Africa*, compares African and "Aryan" civilization.[19] He suggests that the world is divided into two cultural groupings: Aryans, including Semites and Asians, and meridional peoples (*méridionaux*), including black Africans. Negro African culture is traced from its original linkage with civilization in Egypt. Diop's concept of the nation envisages a multinational, federal Africa. The exact basis for nationality, however, is not clearly delineated.

A second theme in the cultural nationalism of negritude has been the unity of black African philosophy and religion. At the Second Congress of Black Scholars and Writers, one resolution stated:

[The Commission] urges that the African philosopher should learn from the tradi-tions, tales, myths, and proverbs of his people, so as to draw from them the laws of a true African wisdom complementary to the other forms of human wisdom, and to bring out the specific categories of African thought. . . . It is highly desirable that the modern African philosopher should preserve the unitary vision of cosmic reality which characterises the wisdom of traditional Africa.[20]

The Congress also outlined what it considered to be the essence of all black African religious systems:

—a fundamental faith in a transcendental Force from which man draws his origin, upon which he depends and towards which he is drawn.
—the sense of a vital solidarity ("*solidarité*"), a French word which seems to us the least removed from the Fulah *neddaku*, the Bambara *maya*, the Madagascan *fi-havana*, and others, and which comprises a series of moral and social virtues, such as Ancestor worship, the veneration of Elders, hospitality, the spirit of tolerance, etc.
—the vital union between spiritual and practical life.[21]

A German writer, Janheinz Jahn, attempted to draw together the various aca-demic studies of African religion and, by focusing on similarities, to demonstrate

18. Cheikh Anta Diop, "Apports et perspectives culturelles de l'Afrique," *Présence Africaine*, VIII–X, special issue (1956), 342 [my translation].
19. (Paris: Présence Africaine, 1962).
20. Quoted in Colin Legum, *Pan-Africanism* (New York: Praeger, 1962), p. 217.
21. *Ibid.*

the existence of a black African religious philosophy which emerged from the fundamental elements in various African traditional religions.[22] While generally criticized by Western scholars, his effort elicited support from many of the disciples and spokesmen of negritude. According to one African reviewer of Jahn's work:

> More important than to the Africanist and anthropologist is this book to the young African nationalist. For the last fifteen years or so we have been talking a lot about the African personality, without being very sure what we mean by it. At the basis of it was a rejection of the increasing tendency to assimilate European culture. . . . Now here Mr. Jahn in his book *Muntu* offers a solution: a new-African culture which is inspired by the common elements in our traditions. . . . The experts will tear it to pieces, but it will remain an important pioneering work.[23]

A more sober consideration of some of the theoretical aspects of comparative African values, world systems, and societal organization is found in the work of Louis-Vincent Thomas of Dakar.[24] The major difficulty for an African intellectual of the negritude persuasion, however, is the problem of differentiating the loyalties and identities of ethnic communities, national communities, and racial communities.

The Diaspora and Negritude

Since one tenet of negritude is the commonality of all black persons, the question of the relationship of black Africans to black people in the New World is of considerable importance to the negritude concept of nationhood. Two apparently mutually exclusive positions seem to have characterized African nationalist thought on this issue: (1) some form of Black Zionism, or espousal of return to the motherland, Africa; and (2) a "spiritual" nationalism, comparable perhaps to certain conceptions of Judaism which do not espouse a return to a homeland.[25] In a sense, this is the issue of irredentism, that is, of scattered minorities living outside the homeland. Continuing the analogy, those black Africans who were forcibly removed from their homeland and resettled throughout various parts of the world have come to be known in some literature as the African Diaspora.

The African Diaspora, especially in the Americas, has played an important role in negritude concepts of nationhood. (Aspects of Afro-American attitudes toward Africa are explored in James Turner's essay in this volume.) The chal-

22. Janheinz Jahn, *Muntu, The New African Culture*, trans. Marjorie Gren (Dusseldorf: Eugene Diederichs, 1958; London: Faber & Faber, 1961).

23. Omidiji Arabbalu, reviewing *Muntu*, in *Black Orpheus* (November 1959), p. 57.

24. See "A General Outline of the Schedule of Theoretical Studies," *Présence Africaine*, IX (1961), 115.

25. See Simon Dubnow, *Nationalism and History, Essays on Old and New Judaism* (Cleveland: World Publishing Co., Meridian Books, 1961).

lenge of negritude to Afro-Americans was considerable, yet as late as 1962 a black American professor, E. Franklin Frazier, could still write, "The question of integration and assimilation of the American Negro has not been considered or raised by American Negroes but by African intellectuals."[26]

Certain proponents of Black Zionism, such as Marcus Garvey[27] and later (temporarily) Malcolm X, have advocated some type of return to Africa. The countervailing position has been a recognition that the Afro-American is a synthesis of both Africa and the West. American novelist Richard Wright wrote in 1956:

> My position is a split one. I'm black. I'm a man of the West . . . I see and understand the West; but I also see and understand the non or anti-Western point of view. . . . This double vision of mine stems from my being a product of Western civilization. Being a Negro living in a White Christian society, I've never been allowed to blend in a natural and healthy manner with culture and civilizations of the West. . . . I'm not non-Western. I'm no enemy of the West. Neither am I an Easterner. When I look out upon these vast stretches of this earth inhabited by brown, black and yellow men . . . my reactions and attitudes are those of the West. I see both worlds from another and third point of view.[28]

The process and elaboration of "synthesis" by Afro-American intellectuals (who until recently included only a relatively few black Americans, self-consciously regarding themselves as products of both Africa and the West) has taken a variety of forms. One early spokesman for the synthesis point of view was W. E. B. Du Bois. (It is of historical interest, however, to note that both Wright and Du Bois eventually chose to take up permanent residence in Africa, more specifically in Ghana.) According to Du Bois in 1903:

> The history of the American Negro is the history of this strife—this longing to attain self-conscious manhood, to merge his double self into a better and truer self. In this merging he wishes neither of the older selves to be lost. He would not Africanize America, for America has too much to teach the world and Africa. He would not bleach his Negro soul in a flood of white Americanism, for he knows that Negro blood has a message for the world.[29]

Negritude and Nationhood

There have been many different intellectual positions taken on the issue of the "community" implications of negritude. The relevance of negritude to African nationalism and/or theories of nationhood has been considerable. The assertion of black African values and culture was intended by some writers to

26. "The Failure of the Negro Intellectual," *Negro Digest* (February 1962), p. 28.
27. See Edmund Cronon, *Black Moses* (Madison: University of Wisconsin Press, 1962).
28. "Tradition and Industrialization," *Présence Africaine*, VIII–IX (1956).
29. *The Souls of Black Folk* (Greenwich, Conn.: Fawcett Publications, 1961), p. 17.

provide a basis for a black-Africanism, with potential political implications. The assertion that blacks throughout the world are tied by a common collective unconscious may provide a basis for either a spiritual or political nationalism (the latter, particularly, in the form of irredentism) which is transcontinental in scope. The notion of diaspora, then, becomes especially relevant.

The racial criteria of nationhood have been in direct confrontation with concepts of Pan-Africanism which look for a geographical/cultural basis for solidarity between black Africans and North African Arabs and Berbers. (It should be noted, however, that the assertion "black skin color is good" is compatible with a variety of other nationalisms and need not in itself be suggested as a basis for political nationhood.)

The sharpest criticisms of race as a basis for nationhood have come from black African nationalists themselves, many of them Muslims. Mamadou Dia, while deputy premier of Senegal, may have reflected the Islamic point of view when he wrote, "We must discard racist theories that claim to base the national vocation on the race or the people."[30]

Within Senegal, which is 85 per cent Muslim, there has been considerable criticism by young Muslim intellectuals writing in Arabic of Senghor's notion of negritude. An alternative transnational concept for such writers has been Pan-Africanism.

PAN-AFRICANISM AND NATIONHOOD

Pan-Africanism seeks a continental rather than a specifically racial basis for unity. Perhaps the outstanding spokesman for Pan-Africanism was Kwame Nkrumah when he was president of Ghana. In a sense, Nkrumah accepted Senghor's notion of unconscious archetypes but asserted that the African continent contained three major civilizations which, he argued, should synthesize identities into a new, distinctively African, "consciencism." These three civilizations were "traditional Africa, Islamic Africa, and Euro-Christian Africa." According to Nkrumah:

> African society has one segment which comprises our traditional way of life; it has a second segment which is filled by the presence of the Islamic tradition in Africa; it has a final segment which represents the infiltration of the Christian tradition and culture of Western Europe into Africa, using colonialism and neo-colonialism as its primary vehicles. These different segments are animated by competing ideologies. But since society implies a certain dynamic unity, there needs to emerge an ideology which, genuinely catering for the needs of all, will take the place of the competing ideologies. . . .

30. *The African Nations and World Solidarity* (New York: Praeger, 1961), p. 5.

Such a philosophical statement will be born out of the crisis of the African conscience confronted with the three strands of present African society. Such a philosophical statement I propose to name *philosophical consciencism*, for it will give the theoretical basis for an ideology whose aim shall be to contain the African experience of Islamic and Euro-Christian presence as well as the experience of the traditional African society."[31]

The translation of ideas of African civilizations and geography into ideas of African nationhood seems to have taken two major forms: (1) assertion that nationhood is a "collective vocation," that is, a working together of peoples with common purposes; and (2) assertion that the continent of Africa, because of her internal historical development, has in some usually undefined way endowed her inhabitants with a personality which is *African* rather than *black*.

Pan-Africanism as a Collective Vocation

The first conceptualization is summarized by Mamadou Dia of Senegal:

One might define the nation as a collective vocation, depending on a common scale of values, common institutions, and, finally, common aims. . . .

Increasingly numerous are the examples of historically and ethnically heterogeneous groups that share a collective national vocation. It is to be hoped that this process may become general, thus settling certain frightful dramas and making new nations centers of humanism, by the diversity of the human elements assembled. . . .

As a vocation the nation cannot be a rigid framework for activities: it is a stimulus. Its frontiers cannot be those of dwarf states that try to atomize it. . . .

. . . The nation as a collective vocation within African dimensions necessarily groups diverse countries and peoples. Hence the stupidity of certain border disputes that seem to excite African or Arab leaders who lack neither culture nor political realism. They act as if it were a question of fixing a definite form to this vast movement that will continue to seek an equilibrium not yet attained. . . .

The Venetian and Florentine national vocations, although clearly expressed, were no less happily merged in a wider and more authentically national collective vocation—the Italian vocation.[32]

Dia has both asserted a criterion for nationhood and given examples of national vocations. He makes this concept even more explicit in his recurrent rejection of racialism:

Nationalism in this sense is something quite different from a theory founded on racial or religious ideology. Nationalism with a racial or religious basis is an irrational construction depending not so much on a national conscience as on the collective folly of the crowd, on the destructive force of exasperated instincts. . . .

31. *Consciencism* (London: Heinemann Educational Books, 1964), pp. 68, 70.
32. *The African Nations*, pp. 5–7.

> This is why those African nations destined to play any historic role whatsoever will neither be Negro, Berber, or Arab nations, nor Christian, Moslem, or animist nations . . . but . . . if they are to be anything at all—a synthesis, or let us say, a civilization.[33]

Dia cites examples of multiracial national vocations which include the Soviet Union, India, and "the forthcoming confederation of Independent States of the Franco-African Community."[34]

Dia is explicit in his rejection of certain types of suprastate nationalism, particularly international proletarianism:

> On the other hand, one cannot refuse the various national vocations the right to exist, on the pretext of unification or supranationality. . . . Western socialists who urge colonized people to abandon their national vocation in favor of socialism—without, however, renouncing their own nationalism—have to be shown the firm desire for nationhood. . . . Nothing is less certain than the contention that class is a higher form of integration than nation.[35]

The idea of collective vocation is not dissimilar to the notion of manifest destiny which gave impetus to nineteenth-century American consolidation of nationhood within a geographical context that could not claim racial, historical, or even religious homogeneity. It is a future-oriented nationalism, rather than a past-oriented concept.

Pan-Africanism as Cultural Synthesis

The second concept of Pan-Africanism would attempt to establish a sense of history and mystique which characterizes the continent as a whole. It may be either more or less inclusive than the notion of collective vocation.

Pan-Africanism began its historic life "not in the 'homeland' but in diaspora,"[36] as did the literary aspects of negritude. Until recently, Pan-Africanism was largely a phenomenon of English-speaking areas, just as negritude was largely a phenomenon of French-speaking areas. The First Pan-African Congress, held in London in 1900, was sponsored by H. Sylvester Williams (Trinidad) and W. E. B. Du Bois (United States). Although the Second Congress was held in Paris (1919) with the cooperation of Blaise Diagne (Senegal), it was dominated by Du Bois. The Third Congress (1921) was held in both London and Brussels, and the Fourth (1923) in London and Lisbon. The Fifth Congress (1927) was the last to be led by Du Bois.

The Sixth Congress (1945) was entirely different in character and representa-

---

33. *Ibid.*, pp. 9–10.
34. *Ibid.*, p. 9.
35. *Ibid.*, p. 7.
36. Legum, *Pan-Africanism*, p. 14.

tion. Convened by English-speaking West Indian George Padmore in Manchester, England, it included young, English-speaking Africans who were not satisfied with the slow pace of colonial reform. These included many who were to be in the forefront of African nationalist movements: Kwame Nkrumah, J. Annan, E. A. Ayikumi, Edwin J. dePlan, Dr. Kurankyi Taylor, Joe Appiah, and Dr. J. X. de Graft Johnson (all from the Gold Coast, which was to become the independent state of Ghana); Chief H. O. Davies, Magnus Williams, Chief S. L. Akintola (all from Nigeria); plus Jomo Kenyatta (Kenya); Wallace Johnson (Sierra Leone); Dr. Raphael Armatoe (Togo); and Peter Abrahams (South Africa). A major issue at that time, as mentioned in Ali Mazrui's essay in this volume, was whether to use physical force in the anti-colonial struggle.

These postwar nationalists did not base their appeal for self-determination on concepts of negritude. Of the eight independent African states which met in Accra in 1958 for the First Conference of Independent African States, only Ghana and Liberia represented Black Africa; five states were Arab. Yet, according to Colin Legum, "The Accra Conference immediately proved the validity of one of the concepts of Pan-Africanism: a bond of color did exist between former colonial peoples."[37]

"Color," however, is to be distinguished from "negritude"; color in this context refers to non-white, rather than specifically to black. As if to demonstrate this non-racial concept of African continental solidarity, President Nkrumah of Ghana married an Arab woman from Egypt.

Although there was no mention at the First Conference of Independent African States of the formation of a "United States of Africa," the All-African Peoples' Organization, which also met in Accra in 1958, did draft a resolution calling for an eventual "commonwealth of free African States." It will be noted that African leaders from the French colonies did not participate in these early discussions.

To summarize, the basic goal of Pan-Africanism has in most cases been continental solidarity or nationhood, with the prospect of a nation stretching from the Cape to Cairo, and from Dakar to Mogadishu.

THE THIRD WORLD

The premise of African interracial continental solidarity is perhaps only one step removed from a bond between African states and other new nations in the former colonial empire zones. Because these new nations were not part of the Western or the Communist blocs, they are often referred to as the Third World (*Tiers-Monde*). The common shared experiences include a legacy of

37. *Ibid.*, p. 42.

colonialism, relative poverty, and "skin color." Basing his ideas on the economic reasoning of Gunnar Myrdal,[38] Dia speaks of the "Proletarian Nations,"[39] that is, those Asian and African countries with per capita incomes of about $100 per year. These nations not only constitute a third bloc in world politics but are characterized by involvement in the "anticolonialist revolution."[40] This is part of their "collective vocation."

The Bandung Conference (1955) was the point in time when these common interests were first apparent to the various nationalist leaders (although it will be noted that the only African state participating was Ethiopia; the Gold Coast sent observers). Certain African political exiles during the colonial period, however, had found haven in Cairo. Cairo too was much involved in the Afro-Asian solidarity movement, the first conference having been held there in December, 1957. Colin Legum interprets the basis for Third World solidarity:

> Although blacks identified themselves emotionally with their skins, they were always intellectually willing and able to identify themselves with peoples of other colours who were in the same boat as themselves — victims of white superiority, of colonialism, of imperialism, and of discrimination. Black regeneration was one aspect of the struggle for emancipation; the wider struggle against colonialism and injustice demanded wider alliances.[41]

After African nationalists had intensified their drive for independence, however, the wider alliance or identity with other poor states began to fade into what Césaire earlier described as "fleshless universalism." Poor states were seen to be economic competitors in agricultural production and for import capital. The problem which demanded the full energies of the African leaders was that of national integration within their inherited state boundaries. Even the notion of Pan-Africanism began to appear grandiose as a starting point. The French-speaking African states therefore began to turn their attention to the more immediate possibilities of suprastate regionalism.

THE IDEA OF SUPRASTATE REGIONALISM

Some of the most important attempts at suprastate regionalism have occurred in French-speaking Africa. During most of the colonial period (1904–58) there existed a formal federation of states in French West Africa. Loyalty toward such a suprastate organization may be distinguished from loyalties to other political

38. Gunnar Myrdal, *Economic Theory and Under-Developed Regions* (London: Duckworth, 1957).
39. *The African Nations*, p. 34.
40. *Ibid.*
41. Legum, *Pan-Africanism*, pp. 40–41.

groupings. Three early sets of experiences influenced postwar political thinking on this type of regional association: (1) the creation of transterritorial political parties, (2) the creation and dissolution of the Mali Federation, and (3) the attempt at a Ghana-Guinea-Mali union (Union of African States).

Transterritorial Political Parties

Apart from the founding in Senegal of a branch of the French Socialist Party (SFIO), in the late 1930s, most of the French West African parties were formed after the war. Of these, two were regional in scope: the Rassemblement Démocratique Africain (RDA) and the Indépendants d'Outre Mer (IOM).

After the initial referendum defeat of the Fourth Republic Constitution in May, 1946, several African leaders called for a "united front of all worker, cultural and religious movements in Black Africa to fight 'revival of colonialism.' "[42] A conference was called at Bamako (Mali) in October, 1946, and over 800 delegates from all parts of French Africa attended. Houphouet-Boigny announced that the purpose of the RDA, which was set up at the conference, was the union of Africans and their alliance with French democrats. (Lamine Guèye and Yacine Diallo had failed to attend the conference and other socialist leaders had withdrawn.) In the 1946 elections, the RDA gained six deputies to the French National Assembly, five senators, and seven councilors of the French Union. The association of the RDA with the French Communist Party and their eventual split has been mentioned above.

The electoral reforms of 1951 extended the franchise in French West Africa to a conservative rural element, to the disadvantage of the more radical parties such as RDA. Yet by 1956 Houphouet-Boigny had reoriented himself to less radical policies and joined the Mollet government in Paris as a cabinet minister. The RDA at that time held nine National Assembly seats in Paris.

The IOM was not a political party in the strict sense, but rather a grouping of African parliamentarians which was formed in late 1947. Membership in IOM was not incompatible with membership in territorial parties, but it included elements which were not represented in the RDA or SFIO. The IOM congress in 1953 at Bobo-Dioulasso (Upper Volta) advocated a federal republic for French-speaking West Africa. Shortly thereafter Senghor proposed dividing French West Africa into two parts: one centered at Dakar (Senegal) and the other at Abidjan (Ivory Coast), each with a premier and local parliament.

By the first half of 1956, leaders from the IOM, RDA, and SFIO were all stressing the need for regional unity. Labor leaders such as Bakary Djibo were appealing to Senghor and Houphouet-Boigny to follow labor's attempt at unification. The IOM was succeeded early in 1957 by the Convention Africaine

42. Virginia Thompson and Richard Adloff, *French West Africa* (London: Allen & Unwin, 1958), p. 84.

(CAF), and this was succeeded in 1958 by the Parti du Regroupement Africain (PRA), which united all of the non-RDA parties (with the exception of the parties in Mauritania). The reconciliation of the socialist party, SFIO, and IOM had occurred earlier when the socialists broke their ties with the French parent party. During this period, both the PRA and the RDA were advocating some form of federal government for French West Africa. When the 1958 referendum occurred, most of the West African parliamentarians supported, in one form or another, the concept of regional community.

Thus, under the Fourth Republic, a number of transterritorial or suprastate political relationships were developed. French-speaking West Africa was considered to be a likely candidate for a federal structure which would link up the eight component states. The actual pattern as it evolved, however, provided for independence on an individual state basis, with the exception of Senegal and Mali, and a continuing association with metropolitan France through the French Community.

The Experience of the Mali Federation

The Mali Federation was conceived on January 17, 1959. Forty-four representatives from the states of Senegal, Dahomey, Sudan (Mali), and Upper Volta met at Dakar to regroup into a "Mali Federation." The conference resulted in a constitution with sixty-two articles, which stipulated Dakar as the capital, French as the official language, and the four participating states as the member states. There was to be a federal president who would choose two cabinet ministers from each member state. A federal legislative assembly was to be elected for five years which would consist of twelve delegates from each of the four member states. For various reasons, however, Dahomey and Upper Volta withdrew from the arrangement. On March 25, 1959, the Mali Federation, consisting of Senegal and French Sudan (Mali), was established within the French Community, and a new party, Parti de la Fédération Africaine (PFA), was set up to accommodate the merger.

The subsequent dissolution of the Mali Federation in the summer of 1960 was probably caused by several factors, Senegal preferred a loose federation, reflecting perhaps the fact that most of the wealth was in that region, while French Sudan (Mali), with its larger population, wanted a unitary state. Also, Senegal had closer links with France (25,000 Frenchmen actually lived in the city of Dakar), while French Sudan had strong Islamic linkages and was closer to Guinea than to Senegal in its political propensities.

From the dissolution of the Mali Federation came a greater realization of the nature and problems of nationhood. The concepts of nationhood held by the nationalists during the brief experience of federation are most instructive in retrospect. Thus, Senghor remarked to the PFA constituent assembly:

We have made a good start in Mali by uniting populations whose natural characteristics—climate, soil and blood, language and customs, art and literature—are similar. Senegal and the Sudan constitute, moreover, a rather homogeneous and relatively rich economic ensemble. . . .

And yet, in the interest of Black Africa and of France, our aim must be to unite, within the Mali Federation, all the states of the old A.O.F. . . .

The reconstruction, on new bases, of the old French West African federation is in the political interest of the Africans; this is clearly in line with our concept of "Nation." The Upper Volta and Niger are grassland, prairie countries, like Senegal and the Sudan. The fact that the Ivory Coast and Dahomey are mostly forest offers an additional reason for not separating them from the other countries. They are complementary to the others.[43]

Senghor further elaborates his notion of black African unity with regard to English-speaking African states:

Nor do we intend to forget our African neighbors who speak English. But let us be frank: they should not ask us to leave the Community while they remain in the Commonwealth. Horizontal inter-African solidarity will gradually be established, by beginning at the beginning with economic and cultural relations.[44]

The failure of the Mali Federation had noticeable effects on African regionalist thinking. Certain conservative nationalists felt disillusioned with political unification and began to focus on economic cooperation. Others, more radical, turned to ideological groupings. The ex post facto evaluation by Senegalese leaders of the causes of failure of the Federation is of interest. According to Mamadou Dia,

In our fight against Balkanization, we failed to consider the precolonial fact that is territorialism. Our mistake has been our failure to pay sufficient attention in our analyses to this phenomenon, a fruit of colonialism and a sociopolitical fact that a theory of unity . . . cannot abolish. We allowed ourselves to be lured by the mirage of the most intellectually satisfying construction. . . .

. . . The Senegalese masses adopted the Mali mystique only because they were attached to their leaders. . . . Senegalese territorialism was still alive, all the more so because the Sudanese presence in Dakar was too indiscreetly manifest to let the people forget it. . . . the rupture of the Federation was welcomed with relief by the masses. . . . The Sudanese . . . were no less territorialists. . . . They thought Sudan and reacted above all as Sudanese. With a slant less Malian than Sudanese they studied problems that were properly Malian, especially problems related to defense, justice, education and the Africanization of cadres.[45]

43. *African Socialism*, pp. 4–5.
44. *Ibid.*, p. 46.
45. *The African Nations*, p. 140.

On the question of "federalism," Dia continued:

> Marx, who was scientific, readily yielded to the rigors of facts and did not hesitate, whenever it became necessary, to revise his position on a given political problem of his time. First, an antifederalist—for reasons that half-baked Marxists today pick up and transpose *mutatis mutandis*—he quickly qualified his opinion and admitted the federal solution along with the right of self-determination. Why should others not be allowed, by the force of events, to change from an acceptance of federalism to the rejection of federalism, at least temporarily?[46]

Partly as a result of this misadventure in territorial federalism, a new type of regionalism appeared in West Africa; this might be termed *ideological regrouping*.

The Ghana-Guinea-Mali Union

The Ghana-Guinea-Mali union, called The Union of African States (UAS), was announced by communiqué on December 24, 1960. It was probably conceived as a reaction to the Brazzaville bloc, led by Senegal and Ivory Coast. Furthermore, the Republic of Mali needed a route to the sea and was perhaps reacting to the recent failure of the Mali Federation. The UAS charter provided an embryonic confederal framework. While sovereignty was to reside in each of the member states, the heads of state were to consult quarterly, diplomatic representation was to be coordinated, and permanent ideological and economic committees were set up; the supreme executive organ was to be the Conference of Heads of States.

One point of focus in this essay has been the identification of the ideological justifications for various types of nationalism and concepts of nationhood. In the case of the UAS there was to a marked extent a similarity of political ideas on means and ends of the state. This means-and-ends criterion is not dissimilar to Dia's collective vocation, or common goals. President Sékou Touré of Guinea has summarized this concept:

> If the laws of development lead to the regrouping of societies, and in consequence to the enlargement of existing entities and their transformation into multi-national entities, it is still necessary that each element should find itself in identical conditions, should have similar means available, and should use these means to the same ends.[47]

President Keïta of Mali elaborated on the prerequisite of ideological sympathy to the regrouping of African states:

46. *Ibid.*, p. 143.
47. *The Political Action of the Democratic Party of Guinea*, Vol. III (Conakry: Imprimerie Nationale, 1960).

We are convinced that the states of Africa will never be independent, in the full sense of the word, if they remain small states, more or less opposed to one another, each having its own policy, each taking no account of the policy of the other. Our Constitution, therefore, provides for a total or partial abandonment of sovereignty in favor of a grouping of African states, but such an abandonment of sovereignty demands an identity of views with our fellow states. One cannot build a complete whole without contradictions. Certain common viewpoints on international policy and on economic policy are absolutely necessary, together with an understanding of the contradictions contained in economic planning, and the necessity for each state to consider its economy within the framework of one large African economy, if it is to constitute an entity with the other states. For this reason we recognize that this abandonment of sovereignty necessitates an identity of views with our partners, both in foreign and domestic policy. The Republic of Mali has decided to cooperate in all fields with all the African states, whatever may be their political, economic, or social set-up. This means, however, that we envisage a political organization in cooperation with the other African States only in so far as they have identity of views with us in the field of international policy, and also in the field of internal economic policy. But this does not preclude us from cooperation with all the African States, whatever their alignment in international policy, and whatever may be their political or economic system.[48]

In summary, even though there has been a long history of regionalism and regionalist thought in French-speaking West Africa, the difficulties of establishing suprastate political communities have been considerable. (Perhaps the most successful example of African regionalism in practice has been the more recent phenomenon of the entente consisting of Ivory Coast, Dahomey, Niger, and Upper Volta.) In the immediate post-colonial period, criteria for regional unity or multinational community formation included economic interdependence, congruence of political values, and personal rapport between political elites.

NATIONHOOD AND POLITICAL COMMUNITY

The six categories of potential suprastate political communities outlined in this essay may be grouped into those with relatively static boundaries, and those with changing, or mutable, boundaries.

Concepts of Static Community Boundaries

The boundary line between Black Africa and North Africa, although to some extent indistinct, tends to be defined by the historic location of peoples along the

48. Address at Chatham House, London, May 17, 1961; published as "The Foreign Policy of Mali," *International Affairs*, XXXVII (1961), 432–39.

Sudanic belt. A number of national states straddling this "line" are faced with the problems of biracialism. Such states include Mauritania in the west and the Republic of Sudan in the east, both with a light majority (Arab/Berber) and a black minority. The Central Sudanic states, such as Chad, reverse these racial proportions. In most cases, there has been an attempt to build a nationalism and to develop concepts of nationhood which do not depend on racial classifications.[49] (Islam has influenced this non-racial thought.) African nationalists who have espoused political union of Black Africa, however (with or without diaspora), would presumably seek a political redistricting along racial boundaries.

The most static and most inclusive boundary line, of course, is the geographical definition of the continent of Africa. Pan-Africanism has subsequently sought to find or develop cultural homogeneity within these continental boundaries.

Concepts of Mutable Community Boundaries

The idea of a Franco-African community is essentially an ideological concept based on notions of French citizenship, culture, and political interests. Basic acceptance of a defined value system is necessary to such a community of like-minded states. Racial distinctiveness, however, tends to underlie such concepts, and hence the concept of a European-African community may be partly in the static category.

The concept of international proletarianism is probably ideological at core since class membership is usually a matter of ideological perception. These perceptions will change, both over time and space, as is evident in the difference between the class-struggle Afro-Marxists and the African socialists.

Even the idea of a Third World is essentially an ideological concept. The experiences which are felt to provide a commonality between states are related to perceptions of colonialism, relative deprivation, and non-Western value systems.

In the immediate post-colonial period, the temporary alignment of African states into a Casablanca group and a Monrovia group was primarily ideological. Both groups consciously rejected racial boundaries. Thus, the locational identity of the "radical" group (Casablanca) was in a non-black area (Morocco), while the chairman of the "conservative" group (Monrovia) of associated labor organizations was an Arab. It is of further significance that when these two organizations dissolved in about 1963, they jointly established a Pan-African organization (Organization of African Unity), which has emerged as the dominant supranational grouping in contemporary Africa. The headquarters for this organization are located in Addis Ababa, an area which symbolically links non-black peoples with Black Africa.

49. For a sample of such concepts of nationhood in Mauritania, see Alfred G. Gerteiny, "The Political Thought of a Modern Muslim African Statesman: Moktar Ould Daddah" (Paper presented to the International Congress of Africanists, Dakar, 1967).

The Future of African Nationalism

The loyalties, values, and identities of the different types of African national-ism and concepts of nationhood will continue to demand the attention of African leadership. The three major levels of nationalism will probably turn out to be subnational ethnic loyalties, sovereign-state nationalism, and some combination of regionalism and Pan-Africanism. The accommodation of such multiple loyal-ties in the future will require the reevaluation of many of the issues which were first raised in the pre-independence and early post-colonial period.

The political units which achieved independence were not predestined to emerge in any particular form or number. In certain areas (for example, Ni-geria), relatively autonomous units were fused into a larger federation. In other areas (for example, French West Africa), a federation was broken down into component parts. The decisions which determined these results were to some extent based on European and African concepts of nationalism and nationhood. Future reorientations and reorganizations will likely be informed by these same sources.

21

Patterns
of Nation-Building

ARISTIDE ZOLBERG

FOR THE PURPOSES OF CLARITY, large-scale political changes such as the ones which have occurred in recent decades in Asia and Africa can be sorted into several components: (1) changes in the size of the political community; (2) changes in the fundamental ideas, or culture, governing behavior related to politics; and (3) variations in development, that is, the degree to which these cultural changes are in fact institutionalized, or transformed into norms, structures, and roles. These aspects of change are not bound to any particular historical period and can be used to discuss the transformation of the Roman Empire into feudal Europe as easily as the transformation of contemporary societies in Africa into new states.

The concept of modernization is historically much more specific but involves changes in many spheres of social action besides the political. Within the political sphere itself, usually as the result of cultural diffusion and the emergence of new elites which are the bearers of new ideas, modernization entails the appearance of a new culture of politics which stresses certain institutional arrangements for government and a specific range of relationships between the rulers and the governed within a nation. To this extent, nation-building is a part of modernization.

One of the major problems in the literature dealing with the processes of development, modernization, and nation-building has been the tendency to extrapolate from specific research to high levels of generalization which then appear to reveal patterns of the past, the present, and the future. The study of how a specific traditional system is being transformed into a relatively modern one in a particular place at a particular time is taken to be a paradigm of how *the* traditional system is being transformed into *the* modern system. Yet we know on the basis of common-sense observation that "political development," "modernization," and "nation-building" can refer to very different processes, and that the combination of circumstances may vary greatly. In one case, national communities may be carved out of large empires which are based on a universal system such as religion. An ideology such as religious reformism thus may bridge a sharp differentiation in status between urban elites, who control the land, and peasant masses, under the leadership of a component of the urban elite. In another case, national communities may emerge from situations where many small societies devoid of sharp status differentiation are being amalgamated into arbitrarily defined larger units under the leadership of a group of recently educated men who are drawn more or less evenly from the societies that constitute the country and who act according to the precepts of a pragmatic, secularist ideology.

The analysis of nation-building in a particular part of the world therefore requires us to pay attention first to the available building materials, and then to the characteristics of the architects, contractors, and their crew, as well as to the blueprints they are utilizing. It then becomes possible to discuss what sorts of obstacles the nation-builders are likely to encounter in pursuing their goals and to evaluate their chances of success.

NATION-BUILDING IN SOCIETAL PERSPECTIVE

The starting point for political analysis must be a consideration of the societies which serve as the environment for African political systems.[1] Usually, political scientists who speak of political systems have in mind, at least implicitly, the context of an identifiable, concrete society, be it contemporary Great Britain or a small tribe of northern Togo. It is more difficult, however, to take as given the existence of a "society" which encompasses all the individuals living within the territorial confines of any contemporary African country. A century ago, or less, there existed on the African continent, within the area encompassed today by any single country, a fairly large number of societies varying in size, in social structure, and in culture, each with a corresponding political system. These societies ranged from relatively undifferentiated ones, in which political and kinship structures were almost inseparable, to highly differentiated ones, usually referred to as "states." These societies did not exist in isolation from one another, but constantly interacted as regional systems.

About a century ago, however, certain of the European states, hitherto only peripherally involved on the African continent, extended the boundaries of their own political communities to include some of these societies. The creation

1. For the concepts "environment" and "political system" as used here, see the works of David Easton, especially *A Systems Analysis of Political Life* (New York: John Wiley, 1965).

of new political boundaries did not, of course, automatically result in the creation of new societies within these territories. At least initially, the various societies caught within the colonial administrative nets retained their identities.
Although the new colonial units provided a territorial mold within which social,
economic, political, and cultural changes occurred, we are becoming increasingly
aware that these processes, although related, did not necessarily occur at the
same rate, and that the rates of change varied not only between countries but
also between regions of the same country. If we construe the original African
societies as sets of values, and norms, and structures, it is evident that they survived to a significant extent everywhere up to the time of independence, even
where their existence was not legally recognized, as in the most extreme cases
of direct rule. Furthermore, the new set of values, norms, and structures which
constituted an incipient national center did not necessarily grow at the expense
of the older African societies. For example, although many individuals left the
rural areas for the new towns, they did not necessarily leave one society altogether to enter into a new one; instead, the behavior of a given individual continued to be governed by norms from the social, ethnic, and economic systems
which defined his multiple roles and which may have mixed to define a particular role.

Because the new national centers in Africa had not developed at the time of
independence, we cannot characterize an African country today as a single
society, with a relatively integrated system of values, norms, and structures.
Since the new African states do, however, encompass in a single territory two
sets of values, norms, and structures — the "new" and the modified "traditional,"
the latter often subdivided into distinct subtypes — it is useful to think of these
sets as forming a particular type of *unintegrated society* which can be called "syncretic." Thus, when compared to other Third World clusters, the African states
in general are characterized by extremely weak national centers with a periphery of societies which have until recently been self-contained. Also typical are
levels of economic and social development close to the lowest limits of international statistical indexes of development. Comparative data for 1965 and
1966 rank Africa as the lowest of four Third World areas (Africa, East Asia,
Latin America, Near East/South Asia) in total GNP, annual growth of GNP,
electric power per capita, life expectancy, physicians per capita, literacy, and
percentage of pupils in the population. Africa was tied with one other area for
bottom place in several other indicators, and ranked relatively high only in
acres of agricultural land available per capita.[2]

The extreme weakness of national centers in African states suggests that those
responsible for nation-building can apply only very limited political leverage to

2. See United States Agency for International Development, *Selected Economic Data
for the Less Developed Countries* (Washington, D.C.: Government Printing Office, 1967).
The data are for 1965 and 1966.

bring about the desired transformation of the society. They must first create the tools of change — political institutions. But the process of state-building is itself conditioned by the societal environment; it would be expected, therefore, that the builders would experience many setbacks. The initial edifice of a government may be fragile. If such is the case, it might also be expected that some African countries might not be able to hold together as political units. If they do endure, their political life will be characterized by irregular events and a high incidence of conflict. A consideration of the creation of political institutions and of political conflict will therefore enable us to grasp two complementary aspects of African political processes. Another problem faced by the nation-builders in their attempt to transform African societies is that of integrating their constituent units, usually referred to as "tribes" or "ethnic groups." An examination of this process will give us a sense of what nation-building in emergent Africa might be like.

THE CREATION OF POLITICAL ORDER

Political architects who engage in nation-building need blueprints.[3] Thus the period of African independence witnessed the proliferation of more or less explicit and systematic statements of political means and goals, usually called "ideologies." Since the architects shared similar circumstances, it is not surprising to find that, despite the apparent diversity of ideological orientation, there appeared many persistent and similar themes related to nation-building; there has been a great deal of ideological borrowing from the experiences, or the assumed experiences, of older nations. Beyond this, there has been adaptation and invention by African statesmen to define more precisely what the nation means in the African context.

The first important dimension of the nation is territory, and Africans have usually accepted without question the territorial boundaries which they inherited from the colonial period. Other foundations of national identity which have derived from the historical experiences of older nations are more problematic. With very few exceptions, as in Tanzania, African countries do not have a single dominant language; French or English may be used in elite circles, but these languages remain unknown to a substantial proportion of the population. Ethnicity as a unifying principle is too restrictive, since on the whole the ethnic unit is smaller than the nation-building unit. Religion is also usually related to smaller units, except where Islam is dominant or in the few cases where Christianity has become truly indigenous and widespread. The ideology of

3. Some of the ideas discussed in this section have been elaborated on in Zolberg, *Creating Political Order: The Party-States of West Africa* (Chicago: Rand McNally, 1966).

Africanness, whether in the French-speaking tradition of negritude or in the English-speaking version of "African personality," was very serviceable during the period of nationalist struggle, but less so at the time of independence. Although the concept facilitated the development of unity within the continent, it could not serve to distinguish Africans of one country from those of another country.

Hence, in the absence of broadly based unifying principles, African leaders came to identify as a major foundation for nationhood the experience of loyalty to the political movement which came closest to representing the country during the period of decolonization. The most obvious cases were those in which a single political organization was able to transform itself from a pre-independence nationalist movement into a dominant political party, as in Ghana, Tanzania, Guinea, and elsewhere. In such countries, the party was the widest, best-known membership group which had political meaning for the inhabitants of the country. The national community thus came to be defined in partisan political terms. Support for the party and its ideas was therefore a way of entering into a sort of social contract, of participating in a nascent national community. As a community, the party was not exclusive. Membership, on the whole, tended to be vaguely defined and primarily required non-involvement in any other political organization which opposed the party. The ideological paradigm might go as follows: the people are one, as demonstrated by the existence of a single party; acting through the party, which directs the state, the people build the nation. The party is the basis of the legitimacy of all other institutions; ultimately it *is* the people, it *is* the nation. Therefore, it *must* be one. Political opposition is to be resisted because by its very existence it denies the unity of the nation.

Not all African countries, of course, came to independence with a dominant party which could claim to speak for the nation in the above sense. In the less-developed French-speaking African countries, as well as in Sierra Leone and Kenya, for example, mass organizations never developed, and political participation remained very limited until after independence. In most of these cases, however, the African rulers who were in office at the time of independence were able to create at least the semblance of a one-party state. Their justification for doing so was very much in line with the reasoning outlined above. The major exceptions to the one-party trend were Nigeria, Congo-Kinshasa, and Uganda. In these states strong regional differentiations, based in part upon the continued existence of relatively large-scale traditional political units, made dominance by a single organization impossible. Significantly, in these exceptional cases, no explicit blueprint of nation-building seemed to emerge. Federal arrangements, embedded in the constitution established at the time of independence and as a condition of independence in Nigeria and in Uganda, *could* have been used as the starting point for a nation-building blueprint. This was not the case, mainly because other institutional prerequisites of federalism, including appropriate leadership groups, did not exist. From the very beginning, insurmountable problems were apparent in these countries. In Congo-Kinshasa one political group did internalize a "mass-party" ideology similar to that discussed above, but the circumstances of decolonization and a series of acute crises at the time of independence resulted in the destruction of the party.

The prevalence of the single-party ideology is confirmed by the later experiences of many of the countries which did not initially reflect that ideology. There are now indications that African military leaders have internalized an ideology of nation-building very similar to that of the one-party rulers. Hence, in the long run, the one-party ideology is not to be analyzed in terms of the existence of a dominant party, but rather in terms of the existence of an administrative framework directed by an oligarchy, whether civilian or military, which views itself as indispensable to the building of the nation. Mass parties have tended to decline in the post-independence period, and the importance of bureaucracies has increased. There is a general consensus in Africa today that nation-building presumes the existence of a state. The emergent ideology is one which attributes overwhelming importance to state-building. Although economic and social development remain important goals, they tend to be viewed as means of fostering a stronger state rather than as goals in themselves.

THE INSTRUMENTS OF NATION-BUILDING

Within the general framework discussed above there were significant variations in the degree of institutionalization of national centers in different African countries around the time of independence. To continue our metaphor, there were variations in the effectiveness of the instruments available for the pursuit of nation-building. The first of these variations relates to the characteristics of the ruling groups. Absolute size and cohesion of a ruling group may be difficult to estimate, but it is relatively simple to recognize certain variations. In Ghana, for example, there was a sizable body of experienced politicians and administrators who were fairly well educated and had been involved in the running of public policy for the better part of a decade before independence, while in Congo-Kinshasa the training of elites began only shortly before the rapid acceleration of decolonization and the process of institutionalizing political participation of Africans occurred within a period of two or three years and was not completed by the time of independence. These differences between African administrative elites were not due exclusively to the political policies of the respective colonial powers. There were also general economic and geopolitical factors which facilitated or hindered the development of a personnel infrastructure. A policy variable in this respect, however, was the extent to which secondary education, rather than primary or higher education, was developed.

But even the most apparent variations in political arrangements at the time of independence, such as differences between mass-party states, "no-party" states, and multiparty federal states, tended to be exaggerated by observers because insufficient attention was paid to the extent to which these arrangements were in fact institutionalized. An examination of political parties, the most widely studied and documented feature of the African political scene, reveals a large gap between the organizational model from which the leaders derived their inspiration and their capacity to implement such models. The very use of the word "party" to characterize such structures may involve a dangerous reification. African "parties" which have adopted a Leninist model, for example, seldom function in the way in which European "vanguard" organizations have functioned to establish control over various sectors of the society. Rather than controlling society, African parties tend to reflect social structure and to merge with it.

These comments may be extended to include constitutional arrangements which, in the absence of legitimation derived from norms and institutions indigenous to the society, seldom had reality beyond their existence as the written word. Constitutional arrangements, therefore, could easily be modified from year to year, or maintained as part of a ritualistic adherence to accepted practice but ignored in relation to the realities of the political process. In most African countries, there is some sort of "civil service"; but this is so rarely governed by bureaucratic norms that it is perhaps better to speak of "government employees," a term which does not imply the notion of administrative neutrality associated with civil service. Likewise, "trade unions" are bodies which seldom exhibit the expected organizational characteristics. They often consist of aggregates of employed and unemployed townsmen intermittently mobilized for a temporary purpose, such as a street demonstration or a strike. Finally, African armies, which have come to play an increasingly important political role, exhibit to only a limited degree the discipline and hierarchical organization we normally associate with military institutions. Instead, they often consist of an assemblage of armed men with very limited skills who may or may not obey their officers. The officers themselves are less a cohesive group than a fluid coalition of factions.

Given this view of African society, we should expect to find that the operations of even the most modern institutions in Africa are not always *institutionalized* and often are governed by values and norms that stem from both the "new" and the "residual" sets. The societal environment shared by all new African states thus imposes severe initial limits upon the range within which significant variations in regime can develop. Here we face a paradox: although the widespread image of African society and politics is one of very great change, it can be argued that very little is changing. This paradox involves an analytical distinction between levels of the political system. While there may be rapid change of "authorities," leadership elites, and even regimes, there is very little change at the normative level, that is, in the relation of political institutions to the society. The processes involved in such developmental changes cannot occur independently of the characteristics of the society itself. Hence, the creation of political order through the organization of modern political institutions at the time of independence tended on the whole to be unsuccessful. We shall consider below some of the political consequences of the failures.

POLITICAL CONFLICT AND NATION-BUILDING

African countries which contain unintegrated ethnic communities and which are characterized by a low degree of institutionalization of political structures related to the national center may actually break into smaller components. A few, indeed, have been on the verge of doing so since they became independent. The fact that most do persist as territorial states cannot be attributed exclusively to the operations of internal factors, such as a sense of community and the ability of authorities to enforce cohesion. Persistence may also reflect an inertia with regard to the instruments of government inherited from the colonial period. It may also reflect the absence of effective external challenges and the protection provided by a contemporary international system which, more often than not, guarantees the existence of even the weakest of sovereign states.

Yet those states which hold together in spite of disintegrative forces are likely to experience a high incidence of internal political conflict.[4] Although the occurrence of conflict may be random in time and space, it is not random in structure. The societal constraints which define patterns of integration and limit the extent of institutionalization also shape conflict into discernible patterns. An examination of these patterns complements our understanding of the processes of institutionalization. In the following discussion one aspect of the expression of political conflict will be considered in some detail: the *coup d'état*. It will be suggested that in Tropical Africa the *coup d'état* has become part of the normal political process, while revolutions are likely to fail and civil wars will seldom occur.

The coup can be viewed as a normal pattern in African politics on statistical grounds, in that it has become the modal form of governmental change. More significantly, however, coup behavior is the normal consequence of direct confrontations between incumbent governments and opposition elements in situations where the military force at the disposal of the government is very limited. This condition is widespread in African countries; yet it tends to prevent actual civil war because a government usually falls before extensive mobilization of

4. For a more detailed analysis of political conflict, see Zolberg, "The Structure of Political Conflict in Tropical Africa," *American Political Science Review*, LXII (1968), 70–87.

support by both sides can occur. Governments may even prefer to withdraw peacefully rather that fight. Coups determine who will rule, at least temporarily, but do not in themselves affect the structure of the political system. The scope of the conflict is usually limited in relation to the society as a whole; it may be accompanied by brutality, but it seldom entails more strategic forms of violence. The occurrence of coups appears to be random in relation to most of the classificatory variables applicable to African states, such as indexes of social and economic modernization, type of regime, or ideological orientation of the incumbents or of their opponents. Yet coups arise from similar processes and are remarkably similar in their course.

The legitimacy of the new African regimes was probably highest at the time when nationalist leaders first assumed responsiblity for the central executive in their respective countries, usually a few years before independence. At that time the new leaders were still viewed as champions of the oppressed, and they could rely on the techniques of machine politics, institutionalized in the form of broadly based coalitions with one or more governmental parties. The expansion of the bureaucracy during the period of welfare state colonialism absorbed many job claimants. A few bridges, roads, hospitals, and schools were being built by the departing colonial power, and the general pace of development appeared to be high. At the same time, the coercive apparatus, which usually remained under the control of expatriate officials until the last moment, was a neutral instrument of control in the hands of the colonial government. In most new states these psychologically advantageous circumstances were carried over into the immediate post-independence period, but in country after country this political capital was rapidly frittered away by the new regimes in meeting contingencies.

Although the circumstances varied, these contingencies were associated with three general processes. First, there was a growing gap between the ideological aspirations of the leaders and their capacity to implement the policies these aspirations entailed. Hence, governments with a very limited capability tended to overextend their resources. Second, most regimes were faced with the consequences of the rapid extension of political participation. When, as a result of the introduction of universal suffrage, political entrepreneurs attempted to mobilize individuals with the least exposure to modern political institutions, primordial sentiments became manifest and interethnic cleavages were often exacerbated. The result was an escalation of the demands made by ethnic groups to the center. Third, all African countries have experienced an inflationary spiral of demands formulated by modern sector personnel. This group includes civilian employees of government, who overlap with the bulk of the membership of labor unions in many countries; the second- and third-generation elites, who find that the highest positions in various institutional spheres have been filled by relatively young men and that the period of rapid expansion is over; and members of the uniformed services (army, gendarmery, and police).

The demands made upon the central government during the post-independence period thus increase without a concomitant increase in government capability, and indeed often with a net decrease in capability as the result of structural factors. Under the impact of these processes, the center's weakness is unmercifully exposed. As Talcott Parsons has indicated, such situations are analogous to a run on a bank. He has suggested that the system's response can be twofold:

> First, an increasingly stringent scale of priorities of what can and cannot be done will be set up; second, increasingly severe negative sanctions for non-compliance with collective decisions will be imposed.[5]

But the greater reliance on force as a technique of government, as has occurred in most of post-independence Africa, tends to have results opposite to those intended. First, governments which rely on coercion tend to become less adept at discriminating between danger signals and may tend to approach even the smallest disturbance by expending a great deal of force. However, since the reserve is small, as the available force becomes dispersed the government's vulnerability to more serious threats is increased.[6] Second, the relative legitimacy of political institutions undergoes a sort of deflation; the value of any organization capable of wielding force, whether in an institutional form, such as the army and the police, or through the manipulation of bodies of men by means of civil disobedience, riots, and strikes, is increased, Third, the use of force by the government to overcome deteriorating legitimacy paradoxically undermines this legitimacy in the eyes of those to whom the implementation of force must be entrusted—that is, the army. Fourth, attempts to resolve this problem by building up countervailing institutions (such as a presidential guard or a gendarmery to offset the army) often exacerbate the situation by engendering dissatisfaction among those services whose relative status has been lowered. Finally, potential opponents who are deprived of opportunities to express demands through institutionalized political channels must resort to force to make their demands felt. But since the government's coercive capability is a limited resource, its credibility is lessened over time in the eyes of potential challengers.

The atmosphere in which a coup is likely to occur can be created by almost any type of conflict situation, originating almost anywhere in the social structure, within the ruling group or outside of it; but not every kind of confrontation is likely to lead to the government's downfall. A government has to be threatened physically, which means that the challengers must be able to deploy force in the capital city. Hence, successful coups usually involve two bodies of manpower:

5. Talcott Parsons, "Some Reflections on the Place of Force in Social Process," in *Internal War*, ed. Harry Eckstein (New York: Macmillan, The Free Press, 1964), pp. 59–64.

6. This proposition is related to David Apter's suggestion that there is "an inverse relationship between information and coercion in a system" (*The Politics of Modernization* [Chicago: University of Chicago Press, 1965], p. 40).

labor unions (or, more properly, aggregates of employed and unemployed townsmen) and members of uniformed services. These groups are related asymmetrically: the unions cannot bring about the downfall of a government without the active support or at least the acquiescence of the army and the police, while the uniformed services can carry out a successful coup without securing outside alliances. In the final analysis, then, the role of the uniformed services is determinative, regardless of its size or degree of professionalism. There were successful interventions by the Togo army of 250 men in 1963 and by the Central African Republic's army of 600 men in 1966, each of which was the smallest military establishment on the African continent at the time of its coup.[7]

Military interventions have been escalated to straightforward takeovers from strike-mutinies, in which armies acted like any other grievance organization, and from referee actions, in which the army intervened after conflict had been initiated by others. Several of these takeovers occurred after earlier referee actions failed to bring about the desired change. In other cases a referee action was transformed into a takeover when civilian politicians failed to meet the army's expectations. All coups have been facilitated by the contagion of a successful military intervention in a neighboring country. But even the establishment of military regimes does not seem to lessen the probability of future civilian or military coups, since African armies share the structural characteristics of other institutions. The solidarity of their leadership, the control they have over their own organization, and the degree of leverage they can exert over the society are not likely to be much greater than what existed in the government they replaced.

Those structural features of African societies which ensure the frequency of coups also ensure that more strategic forms of internal conflict, such as revolutions and civil wars, will be rare. Since existing national centers are weak, they will not be able to withstand attempts to modify the political community, as in regional secession movements. At most, the antagonists will become involved in a protracted but low-key struggle, in which bloodshed may increase significantly but in which there will be no clear-cut evidence of changes in the capabilities of either side unless external powers intervene. Revolutions are unlikely to occur because on the one hand, governments fall too easily, and on the other hand, alternative elites do not have the degree of ideological and organizational solidarity required to effect structural changes. The exceptions are those few countries which, deviating significantly from the African societal structure discussed

7. On the African military, see M. J. V. Bell, "Army and Nation in Sub-Saharan Africa," *Adelphi Papers*, No. 21 (August 1965); and David Wood, "The Armed Forces of African States," *Adelphi Papers*, No. 27 (April 1966) in the series published by the Institute of Strategic Studies, London. See also Zolberg, "Military Intervention in the New States of Tropical Africa," in *The Military Intervenes: Case Studies in Political Development*, ed. Henry S. Bienen (New York: Russell Sage, 1968).

above, approximate the plural society model (such as Rwanda and Zanzibar).[8] The cases which best approximate recognizable revolutionary situations are Congo-Brazzaville following the coup of mid-1963 and the several rebellions in Congo-Kinshasa which began in 1964. Both of these cases contained some of the elements of the "second revolution," the truly new beginning, prophesied by Frantz Fanon.[9] One took an urban form; the other, especially in the Kwilu region, took a rural form. But after four years the Brazzaville regime (initially responsive to an anti-Western urban youth movement) seemed to have settled down into the usual party-state mold; the Kwilu uprising in the western Congo was for the most part contained by military action before the end of 1964, having been unable to establish links with Congolese dissidents in the east.

Growing tensions and the recurrent availability of desperate leaders may contribute to the emergence of similar movements elsewhere. These movements may generate relatively large-scale sporadic violence. Yet it is unlikely that such movements will be able to translate their revolutionary aspirations into the institutionalization of a new regime and of new social structures. Since the new African states do not have a strong center, they cannot be turned inside out; attempts to do so bring about only slight shifts in the relative positions of various groups, while the society as a whole remains very much as it was before. If revolutionaries gain control of a government, they will encounter the same constraints upon their attempts to mobilize as did the first wave of radical-minded leaders. Recurrent unsuccessful attempts to change the African world may well give rise to a vendetta morality and to full-scale secession movements.[10]

THE PROCESSES OF NATIONAL INTEGRATION

Nation-building involves not only the creation of political institutions capable of maintaining peace and order and of pursuing policies which foster social and economic development, but also the transformation of the syncretic societies of contemporary African countries into national societies. Nation-building thus involves what has come to be called "national integration." This entails

> the aggregation of independently defined, specifically outlined traditional primordial groups into larger, more diffuse units, whose implicit frame of reference

8. See M. G. Smith, *The Plural Society in the British West Indies* (Berkeley and Los Angeles: University of California Press, 1965).

9. *The Wretched of the Earth* (New York: Grove Press, 1965); and the discussion in Zolberg, "Frantz Fanon: A Gospel for the Damned," *Encounter*, XXVII (November 1966), 56–63.

10. See, for example, E. J. Hobsbawm, *Primitive Rebels* (New York: W. W. Norton, 1965).

is not the local scene but the "nation"—in the sense of the whole society encompassed by the new civil state.[11]

The most problematic aspect of national integration in Tropical Africa has been, and remains, "tribalism." But tribalism is a very inadequate concept with reference to a very complex reality. Africans cannot be assigned to mutually exclusive classificatory units of similar character called "tribes" or "ethnic groups." Increasingly, it is recognized that while an ethnic group or tribe usually suggests a closed, ascriptive group based on descent from a common ancestor, such a group is in practice defined by the theory its members hold of themselves. The identity to which they refer involves not only the fact of descent, but many other elements such as exploitation of the soil, history, religion, and spatial organization; and everywhere these groupings have been modified over centuries by social changes.[12] The concept of ethnicity constitutes a moving rather than a static pattern of identities; interaction between the old and the new does not occur once and for all when "tradition" encounters "modernity," but continues in a process of change.

The interaction of the old and the new to constitute patterns of incipient national integration can be illustrated by comparing two cases from West Africa: Ivory Coast and Mali.[13] The two countries are contiguous; they shared the same colonial experience for over half a century and were administered as provinces of a common larger unit; their dominant political organizations were, for a period of almost fifteen years after World War II, subunits of a larger, interterritorial party, the Rassemblement Démocratique Africain (RDA); and many members of their first-generation elites shared a common secondary socialization through education and occupation and had established close ties of personal friendship. The two countries went through exactly the same steps of constitutional development from 1945 to 1960 and became independent at the same time, with the same formal institutions.[14] Yet, approaching the end of the first decade of independence, their paths appear to be diverging toward what may

11. Clifford Geertz, "The Integrative Revolution, Primordial Sentiments and Civil Politics in the New States," in *Old Societies and New States,* ed. Clifford Geertz (New York: Macmillan, The Free Press, 1963), p. 153.

12. For useful discussions of the concept "tribe" and "ethnic group," see Immanuel Wallerstein, "Ethnicity and National Integration in West Africa," reprinted in *Comparative Politics,* ed. Harry Eckstein and D. E. Apter (New York: Macmillan, The Free Press, 1963), esp. p. 666; Paul Mercier, "Remarques sur la signification du 'tribalisme' actuel en Afrique noire," *Cahiers internationaux de sociologie,* XXXII (1961), 61–80; and Jean Gallais, "Signification du groupe ethnique au Mali," *L'Homme,* II (1962), 106–29.

13. An elaboration of these case studies with detailed references can be found in Zolberg, "Patterns of National Integration," *Journal of Modern African Studies,* V (1967), 449–67.

14. For the political history of French-speaking West Africa, see Ruth Schachter Morgenthau, *Political Parties in French-Speaking West Africa* (New York: Oxford University Press, 1964).

eventually become opposite poles in a continuum of African patterns of national integration.

An approximation of the significant features of their respective societal landscapes can be achieved with the aid of an old-fashioned construct, the ethnographic, or culture, circle. Ivory Coast can be divided into four of these, none of which accounts for more than one-third of the population; furthermore, none of the four constitutes any sort of cultural core with a center in the Ivory Coast itself; and there was in the past relatively little interaction among these circles toward the middle. The self-image of Ivory Coast, internalized by Africans from the perceptions of European explorers and administrators, is one of very great fragmentation. Little in their experience challenges this view.

The Mali pattern is very different. A single core of related peoples, which Mali shares with Guinea, contains more than half of the population; a second accounts for about one-fifth; and the remainder is divided among three other culture circles. The largest group is not merely an ethnographic construct but is a unity defined with reference to the historical tradition of the Empire of Mali. This provides important links between the Mali population and peripheral groups with whom they have lived in close relationship, ranging from mutual conquest and coexistence within a large-scale state to symbiotic economic life. There have been conflicts, but a sense of "belonging to Mali" has persisted, reinforced by nearly universal adherence to Islam. The most distinctive pattern of traditional culture in Mali was the existence of a network of trading towns which served as the foci of regional culture. These towns were ethnically heterogeneous; a town's immigrant population was amalgamated into a core urban culture through a process which involved a shift from an ethnic to a residential identity. Hence, traditional Mali consisted of a shifting coalition of regional political communities with urban and rural components.

Recent social changes have reinforced these contrasts. In Ivory Coast, which underwent fairly rapid economic transformation after World War II, the major effect of cash-crop agriculture was to reinforce fairly sharp divisions between those different parts of the country which coincided with the distinct culture circles. There developed poorer and richer ethnic groups, a pattern which reinforced earlier differentiation. At the same time, there was large-scale migration of certain economic groups from one part of the country to another, thus creating a sudden confrontation between immigrants in the new towns. The tendency has been for these immigrant groups to create urban voluntary associations based on ethnic links, thus fostering the transformation of the country into a society of ethnic segments with a rural and an urban component. Concurrently, these social and economic changes contributed toward an increasing rate of transactional integration at the national level.[15]

15. *Transactional integration* refers to the process discussed by Karl W. Deutsch in various works; see, in particular, "Social Mobilization and Political Development," reprinted in Eckstein and Apter, *Comparative Politics*, pp. 582–603.

Mali has not undergone the same experience. The country remained an
economic backwater, and the colonial system invested very little in the development of an economic and social infrastructure. Much of the population is still
involved in the traditional market economy, and there are fewer opportunities
for the sort of sudden ethnic confrontation that is typical of the new Ivory Coast
towns. Hence, there is less interference with integrative patterns typical of the
older Malian urban culture.

Political leaders in both countries started with the same model of mass-party
organization, inspired by the continental European left. In attempting to in-
stitutionalize these organizations, however, they have necessarily adapted them
in a manner congruent with preexisting societal patterns. In Ivory Coast, the
movement which eventually became the dominant political party was erected
on the basis of a vast ethnic coalition founded on the network of ethnic associations in the capital city, themselves linked with the rural areas and towns of the
hinterland. Much of the postwar political history of Ivory Coast can be understood in terms of a process of fragmentation and recombination of this coalition;
opponents have necessarily defined their own organizations in ethnic terms as
well. The ethnic criterion is prominent in all representative institutions, in a
manner familiar to students of urban political machines in the United States.
The dominant party's success can be attributed to its ability to hold the ethnic
coalition together. This is accomplished by distributing benefits to second-tier
leaders in the form of offices and general economic rewards, while maintaining
a relatively high level of prosperity for the country as a whole. This prosperity
was the result, initially, of the high prices for tropical commodities during and
immediately after the Korean War. The maintenance of these prices afterward
was assured by a deliberately pro-French policy on the part of Ivoirien leadership.

In Mali, during the equivalent postwar period, a significantly different process
developed. From 1945 to 1959, there were two poles of political organization,
neither of which could be clearly identified as an ethnic coalition. They resem-
bled the heterogeneous bipolar factions often observed in Malian towns. The
primacy of one of these groups toward the end of the period can be attributed
to a variety of factors, including a more forceful ideological appeal, greater concern with organizational detail, occasional assistance from the interterritorial
parent organization in Ivory Coast, and, less tangibly, the fact that its attitude
was congruent with the historical coalition which prevailed in the area. Although
there were variations in regional support for one or the other of these two national coalitions at various times, neither of them could be identified as an *ethnic*
coalition, as were their counterparts in Ivory Coast. The only clearly ethnic parties in Mali were peripheral ones, involving groups which were traditionally at the
edge of the central political arena, such as the Dogon. The growth of the one-
party state tended to take on the appearance of a confederacy of urban-domi-
nated regions represented by ambassadors at the center. In the absence of an

economic boom, the party organization's distributive capacity was limited to
rewarding its followers with political and administrative offices.

Around the time of independence, Mali and Ivory Coast shared the characteristic approach to nation-building discussed above. This involved, at the ideological level, a commitment to "oneness," and, at the institutional level, a reliance on the administrative and coercive apparatus inherited from the colonial government and sustained by the dominant party. But the relationship between these instruments was weighted in favor of the party in Mali and in favor of the administrative apparatus in Ivory Coast. If one considers the party alone, it appeared that the center was exerting much more leverage on the national society in Mali than in Ivory Coast. But if party and administrative instruments are considered together in each country, as structures by means of which the national center is attempting to transform society, then the situation may well be reversed. As of 1968, the Malian party seldom effectively reached beyond the country's administrative centers. Its cadre was composed primarily of government employees (including schoolteachers), often the only literate adults in an area, for whom party activity was a supplementary obligation in the same sense that participation in civic affairs is an obligation for corporation executives in the United States. The party's main contribution was the performance of administrative tasks such as the relaying of information concerning governmental decisions. In Ivory Coast, the party cadre includes mainly "old militants" whose orientation is almost exclusively local; hence, the party is not a major instrument used by the center to effect change, but rather an instrument used to elicit local support. The national center has invested heavily in the national administrative apparatus. The bureaucratic ranks were initially filled by highly skilled French administrators whom France was willing to maintain and Ivory Coast was willing to retain; but increasingly these men are being replaced by well-trained Ivoiriens. The country's resources enable the government to create specialized administrative structures to carry out development programs, thus freeing the general administrations, patterned after the continental prefectoral system, for the performance of political tasks.

In the final analysis, however, a focus on institutions alone would mask the emergence of profound differences of purpose and of ultimate orientation which are related to the societal patterns discussed above. The constraints imposed upon the leadership by the availability of means, and the choices they have made within the range available to them, are determined to a large degree by the societal environment. In Ivory Coast, where development is progressing at a remarkable rate, one senses that the leadership is counting on the long-run beneficial effects of transactional integration. The one-party state serves to hold political conflict in abeyance, almost in a Gaullist sense, while the consequences of these modernizing processes become more firmly established. The network of ethnic associations referred to earlier remains the basis for political management while the population is being assimilated into a new Franco-African culture which derives little or no inspiration from the past. In Mali, non-political factors cannot be relied upon to bring about the integrative transformation. The Malian party-state stressed a territorial federalism combining the major regions, all connected by Islam and the area's historical traditions. Reinterpreted to fit a Marxist-Leninist linguistic mold, this party-state was not merely a temporary arrangement, but rather the contemporary avatar of an older polity which defines the very order of society itself.

Whether the processes that are discernible in these two countries and elsewhere in Africa will result in the kind of societal wholeness that we can call "integration" cannot be seriously foretold. Although Ivory Coast and Mali have already moved further along the difficult path to national integration than many countries, the institutional patterns sketched above are still extremely precarious. In 1968, both countries belonged to that dwindling group of African states which had not experienced a *coup d'état.* It would be foolish to attribute this apparent stability to structural factors which distinguish these two countries from their neighbors. There had been near misses in both cases, and the failure of attempted coups can be accounted for only in terms of circumstantial events.[16]

CONCLUSIONS

In this essay, no attempt has been made to rank-order the African states with regard to degree of success in nation-building. This might be done by developing a new typology of African states based not on similarities and differences among formal political institutions, but rather on similarities and differences in social structures more generally. From this point of view, it is clear that a small number of countries, such as Ivory Coast and Ghana, stand out from the rest and are on the verge of reaching a threshold of societal development which may be labeled "incipient modernity." These states are exceptional in the contemporary African scene and are likely to become even more so as the effects of incipient modernization become infused into every sphere of social life, including the political. At the other extreme, there is a fairly large group of countries, such as the Cen-

16. Mali experienced a military coup on November 19, 1968. A precipitating factor was military resentment against the activities of a "popular militia" patterned after the Red Guards. According to available information, there was no bloodshed; the president was arrested when he stepped off the river boat on which he was traveling at the time of the coup. Other party and government leaders, as well as officers who opposed the coup, were arrested. The officers established a Military Committee of National Liberation headed by Lt. Moussa Traore, leader of the coup. This committee in turn established a mixed military-civilian government headed by Capt. Yoro Diakite which included several technical specialists who had been members of the Modibo Keïta government. Although it is too early to evaluate the new regime's orientation, greater attention appears to be paid to economic efficiency.

tral African Republic or Upper Volta, which are among the least developed in the entire world. Unfortunately, they are likely to remain at their present level for a long time; it has become evident that wherever there was *some* potential for relatively rapid modernization, it was brought out during the colonial period. In between are countries with some potential for modernization but with a complex of problems which has so far prevented the potential from developing. It is not necessary to view politics as merely epiphenomenal to suggest that the general characteristics of the social structure, and especially the nature of primordial solidarities and the overall degree of modernization, impose limits within which variations of regime can occur.

The approach followed here, which might be called "comparative macro-analysis," stresses the identification of broad structural patterns obtained inductively but inspired by general theoretical considerations. In its present form, this method cannot achieve a very high degree of empirical precision or theoretical elegance. But it is, on the whole, suitable for the task at hand, which is to explore a world that is essentially unknown, not only to us but also to those who live within it. In that sense, it is very much like an early map; it does not constitute a sure guide, but it does identify salient features of the terrain which can be used for orientation.

22

Political Systems Development

CRAWFORD YOUNG

From experts on African questions,
Deliver us, O Lord![1]

AFRICAN POLITICS IS A GRAVEYARD of typologies and predictions. The compressed temporal space of African independence encompasses two distinctive phases, marked by sharply contrasting approaches to understanding. The era of nationalist triumph, culminating in 1960, was ushered in with confidence, optimism, and euphoria, an attitude shared by African statesmen and "experts on African questions."[2] In the wake of the accumulating frustrations of an independence which often fell short of the towering expectations, a dramatic shift in style and tone has occurred. In the language of observers, "political decay" replaced "political development"; "charismatic heroes" became "charming rogues"; the warning by René Dumont that "Africa is off to a false start" became the savage pessimism of Albert Meister's question "Can Africa take off?"[3] The African poet who wrote the epigram cited above might well repeat his lament today, nearly two decades later. Is not today's analysis operating in as cramped a perspective as that of the yesterday of independence? Are we freezing the swing of

1. Bernard Dadie, "Litanie d'un sujet français," *Afrique débout!* (Paris: Pierre Seghers [1950]), p. 25, quoted in Ruth Schachter Morgenthau, *Political Parties in French-Speaking West Africa* (New York: Oxford University Press, 1964), p. xxii.

2. Major contributions capturing the spirit of the times were Thomas Hodgkin, *African Political Parties* (Baltimore: Penguin Books, 1961); Immanuel Wallerstein, *Africa: The Politics of Independence* (New York: Random House, Vintage Books, 1961); and Morgenthau, *Political Parties in French-Speaking West Africa.*

3. Samuel P. Huntington, "Political Development and Political Decay," *World Politics,* XVII (1965), 386–430; W. Arthur Lewis, *Politics in West Africa* (London: Oxford University Press, 1965); Dumont, *L'Afrique noire est mal partie* (Paris: Editions du Seuil, 1962); Meister, *L'Afrique peut-elle partir?* (Paris: Editions du Seuil, 1966).

the pendulum of political development in mid-arc by projecting conclusions drawn from an exceedingly narrow segment of African history, the handful of years since independence?

Perhaps we can escape the constraints of cross-sectional analysis by viewing the development of political systems in a time-series framework. The unit of analysis is the contemporary territorial state; therefore, the base point is necessarily the colonial state. For analytical purposes, we may characterize political systems at any given stage in terms of the key sources and vehicles of power. Our central assumption is that the contours of the system at any given stage limit the number of possible outcomes at the succeeding stage. This, of course, assumes that alterations in the environment are only partial, and that no apocalyptic transformations of the context of African political systems occur. But let us stress the modesty of our aspiration. We seek only a conceptual device for illuminating the process and direction of change, for understanding where we now stand in the politics of independence, and for offering a framework for reasoned speculation (not prediction) concerning the range of conceivable alternative patterns of development in the immediate future.

The analytical phases we would suggest are four: (1) the colonial political system; (2) the nationalist political sector arising as a substitute for the colonial system and becoming in some cases a virtual anti-state; (3) the independence political formula; and (4) the second-stage post-independence regime, already present in the majority of independent African states. We propose to sketch a paradigm of the political system at each stage, to examine the transition from each phase to the next, and to consider the range of observed variation in outcome.

Our universe is composed of the thirty-nine African states which were independent as of January, 1968. South Africa, however, as a state based upon a racial caste system and ruled by a white oligarchy, presents such special circumstances that most of the generalizations we suggest do not really apply. Two other special cases worth noting in passing are Liberia and Ethiopia, examples of historic African states which avoided prolonged colonial subjugation.[4]

THE COLONIAL POLITICAL SYSTEM

The colonial political system was, at its zenith, a nearly perfect model of a bureaucratic regime. After the initial period of quelling resistance from those African kingdoms having the military and political capacity to oppose European penetration, and the subsequent suppression of widespread rebellions which

4. Liberia (or its coastal settlements) was under the nominal tutelage of the American Colonization Society from 1822 to 1847, and Ethiopia was briefly under Italian rule from 1936 to 1941.

arose in both stateless and centralized societies when the first consequences of colonial overrule became apparent, the elite corps of colonial administrators constituted a mandarinate whose authority was virtually unrestricted.[5]

There were, it is true, different emphases in the theoretical dogma which arose as prescriptive rationalization of the administrative practice emerging in the first decades of colonial practice. But the basic requirements were everywhere the same: to impose colonial order, to generate sufficient local revenue to make colonial administration self-supporting, and to assure the security of the missionaries (except in Muslim areas) and trading companies who sought to follow the flag (or even precede it) into the hinterland. After colonial hegemony was established, some kind of accommodation with traditional elites was necessary in most areas. The personnel and means available to the colonial state were initially very small; for example, in the first decade of colonial rule in the Congo, when King Leopold's authority was being established, there were never more than 120 Europeans in the army of conquest. Delavignette gives a vivid description of the role of 60 French administrators in Niger in the interwar period, governing one million people in an area half the size of France.[6] All colonizers had to find a formula by which a small expatriate elite could meet the goals of the colonial state.

The colonial mandarinate created a state in which political power was exercised by a central bureaucracy of Europeans in the territorial capital, with a field corps of district officers who enjoyed wide latitude in maintenance of order within their areas. A residual area of local power and influence often remained with the African intermediaries, especially where they were the legitimate heirs of established centralized systems, such as in the Buganda kingdom in Uganda, the Hausa-Fulani emirates of Northern Nigeria, Barotseland in Zambia (formerly Northern Rhodesia), the Bayaka region in southwestern Congo, or the Wadai sultanate in northern Chad. But the African chiefs, legitimate or imposed, had a restricted orbit of influence and had very little impact on decision-making at the territorial level. At the top the colonial state was susceptible to pressures from expatriate interest groups, such as settlers, corporations, or missions. But even in dealing with these groups the colonial bureaucracy enjoyed a substantial degree of freedom. The respective metropolitan governments set only broad guidelines to direct the colonial decision-making elite. In the case of former British territories, colonial governors were, until World War II, fairly immune from London directives if they did not demand Exchequer subsidies and if they could prevent any crisis situation from inviting public attention. In the French case, despite the façade of centralization, colonial legislation was delegated to

5. For portraits of the three main colonial bureaucratic systems, see Robert Heussler, *Yesterday's Rulers* (Syracuse, N.Y.: Syracuse University Press, 1963); Robert Delavignette, *Freedom and Authority in French West Africa* (London: Oxford University Press, 1950); and Crawford Young, *Politics in the Congo* (Princeton: Princeton University Press, 1965).
6. *Freedom and Authority.*

the Ministry of Colonies; in practice, effective control was in the hands of the territorial governors and the two governors-general in Dakar and Brazzaville. In the Belgian territories, only in the rare case of a strong minister of colonies was much real authority exercised from Brussels. In short, to a remarkable degree the heart of the colonial state was its local European bureaucracy, which had very few effective constraints on its operation, from either above or below. This was the structure of power to which nationalist movements responded, and which provided the grid within which social change occurred at an accelerating pace.

In the years following World War II, nationalist movements arose in antithesis to the colonial system. The colonial mandarinate came to recognize—slowly— that its hegemony could not be perpetual. The metropolitan powers, caught up in the environment of cold-war competition for the Third World, began to participate more actively in colonial administration, laying down policies which provided opportunities for African organization. The social changes which came in the wake of colonial penetration—emergence of important urban centers, development of a modern educational system, diffusion of the cash economy— produced an elite capable of organizing an effective challenge to the colonial system.

THE NATIONALIST POLITICAL SECTOR

The character of the nationalist response was shaped to an important degree by the nature of the transitional mechanisms. For the most part, in former British, French, and Belgian territories, these were determined by the constitutional norms of the colonial powers. The withdrawing power, if it had to go, was determined to do so with honor. Colonial self-respect required that a political sector be introduced to parallel the bureaucratic mechanisms which had run the colonial state. The colonial administrators assumed that the African personnel to succeed to power would emerge from the electoral procedures which had been enshrined as the model of good government at home. Thus the British evolved a sequence for devolution of power that entailed gradual conversion of legislative councils, which before World War II had been advisory bodies with little if any African membership, into elected parliaments. Colonial department heads were gradually replaced with African ministers who were ultimately responsible to the legislature. In the French case, African political participation was made available on a limited scale in the French National Assembly. In 1956, provision was made for fully elected territorial assemblies with ministers responsible to them. In the former Belgian Congo, when the sudden decision was made for immediate independence in 1960, a faithful replica of the Belgian constitution was produced and the full apparatus of the Belgian parliamentary state erected in less than six months.

The definition of legitimacy in terms of the arithmetic of parliamentary democracy had important consequences. To win control of the state, African nationalists had to begin by seizing the political sector. The vehicle for achieving this goal was the political party, organized for electoral competition. The party, however, did not control the colonial bureaucracy; in fact it usually penetrated rural areas by aggregating the manifold grievances focused upon the European administration. Two interacting, partially competing power systems developed — the colonial bureaucracy, which managed the formal, authoritative institutions of government, and the nationalist parties, which derived their force from their ability to organize the people for elections and to mobilize them for other specific manifestations of opposition, such as boycotts, demonstrations, and strikes.

Under the mandate to permit African political organization, the first response of the colonial administration was frequently to encourage the formation of parties subject to its manipulation. The French were particularly prone to this policy; in the words of one pro-French writer: "The administration had no choice. The elections, since they were mandatory, had to be rigged."[7]

Administrative parties were launched by the administrations in Morocco, Algeria, Chad, Ivory Coast, and elsewhere, especially in the late 1940s. The Belgian administration banked heavily on the fate of its creature in the Congo, the Parti National du Progrès.

But the colonial bureaucracy was not really equipped to compete with the growing nationalist forces in a political arena where its particular skills and resources were not relevant. The metropolitan government placed growing pressure on the colonial administration to respect its rules of decolonization; for example, the 1951 elections in former French Africa were cynically rigged, whereas the 1956 elections, except in Algeria, were relatively honest. Also, the mandarinate faced the growing ability of nationalist parties to organize rural areas. For example, the Belgian administration in the Congo had been in a position to exercise a decisive influence in many parts of the countryside as late as the end of 1959. However, in the May, 1960, national elections to designate the successors to the colonial regime, the administration party won a meager 15 out of 137 seats.

In this phase of development there emerged two main types of parties, "mass" and "patron," and two types of party systems, single and competitive. Mass parties were characterized by the aspiration to penetrate every village, hostility toward traditional authority structures, an aggressive style of total opposition to the colonial administration, a radical, Marxist-Populist flavor to its ideological rhetoric, and an organizational framework modeled on European parties of the left.[8] Patron parties were inclined to build a national alliance

7. Michael Clark, *Algeria in Turmoil* (New York: Praeger, 1960), p. 48.
8. Important questions have been raised by Zolberg and others on the accuracy of the "mass" party model, but it is retained here as a useful ideal type, especially for the

founded upon existing local authority structures; they were less belligerent in style and more moderate in program pronouncement. Where the mass-party model was approximated, there was a strong tendency toward the voluntary or forced absorption of all competing groups. The more ideological character of these movements, plus the tendency to identify the party with the nation, implied that no legitimate political activity could occur outside the party. As former president Kwame Nkrumah declared of his party, the "CPP is Ghana." Under these circumstances no one could stand outside the party. However, where the patron-party style predominated, or where mass movements had become identified with ethnic nationalism, the alien control over the electoral process frequently permitted the emergence of a competitive party system. The classic examples of the outcome of the mass single party in the terminal colonial period are Guinea, Mali, Tunisia, Ivory Coast, and Tanganyika. Competitive parties developed in Uganda, Sudan, Lesotho, Congo-Kinshasa, Nigeria, and Sierra Leone. It should be noted that where competition did occur, it tended to follow religious (as in Uganda and Sudan) or ethnic (as in Congo and Nigeria) cleavages.

There were, however, areas where the nature of the colonial system was such that it tended to obstruct the process of devolution of power upon the African. A factor in these areas was the presence of a large and powerful settler population, which saw any change in the electoral rules of the colonial power as a direct threat to its survival. Another such factor was the existence of a vision of empire which precluded separation of the overseas territory. The cases in point are Algeria, the Portuguese territories, Rhodesia, and, for a time, Kenya. The same factors encouraged the emergence of a nationalist elite. It became evident, however, that access to power through electoral processes was not going to be possible—in Algeria and Rhodesia because the settler element controlled the legal processes, and in the Portuguese possessions because both elections and decolonization were beyond the pale of political practice. A guerrilla army rather than a political party was required by the situation. This in turn implied utterly different organizational skills, and dictated different techniques of relating the movement to the population. The most effective revolutionary movements, in the phase of organizing resistance to the colonial system, were those of Algeria and Portuguese Guinea.[9] In Kenya, the Mau Mau revolt at a time when settler sway seemed unshakable was highly instrumental in eventually committing the metropolitan government and colonial administration to the enforcement of an

---

terminal colonial period, even if extant parties probably fell further short of the model than was generally acknowledged at the time. See Aristide R. Zolberg, *Creating Political Order* (Chicago: Rand McNally, 1966).

9. On the little-known Portuguese Guinea uprising, see John A. Marcum, "Three Revolutions," *Africa Report*, XII (November 1967), 8–22; William Zartman, "Guinea: The Quiet War Goes On," *ibid.*, 67–72; and Basil Davidson, " 'Portuguese' Guinea: Seeing for Oneself," *West Africa*, No. 2631 (1967), pp. 1417–19.

orthodox, constitutional electoral devolution of power to the African majority.[10]

Whether by guerrilla war or constitutional politics, a common occurrence was the coalescence within the territorial state of nationalist political forces. This led to an escalation of demands upon the system, above all for a shortening of the independence timetable. The very fact that this political force was outside the inner sanctum of colonial power, the bureaucracy, yet was increasingly an authoritative spokesman for the population, created impossible dilemmas for the colonizer. Margery Perham, her hand on the pulse of colonial policy formulation in Britain, states the problem succinctly:

> Power cannot be held in suspense. Once it was known that it would be transferred, the position of the colonial government could become so weak, and that of its still irresponsible successors so strong, that the interim period of uncertainty could become intolerable, if not dangerous.[11]

Thus, the alternative power system developing through political parties secured its control over the newly established institutions of the political sector before much effort was made to decolonize the bureaucratic sector. The mandarinate had established criteria for entry which greatly restricted African access in view of the very limited opportunities for secondary and higher education until the 1950s. A political career had no prerequisites; politicians did not need diplomas. But after World War II a university degree was essential for entrance to the senior cadres of public service. The figures on this are eloquent. In 1939, in Nigeria, there were only 23 Nigerians in the senior service; in 1947, the number was still only 182.[12] In Ghana, Africans composed only 13.8 per cent of the senior service in 1949, and still only 38.2 per cent in 1954.[13] In Kenya, the public service was not opened to Africans until 1955. At the end of 1960, of 1,600 professional-level functionaries, only 42 were Africans. In Tanganyika, the first African entered the senior service in 1951. In 1958, of the 4,000 top posts, only 5 were held by Africans.[14] In Morocco in 1955, the French held two-thirds of all civil service jobs; there were no less than 40,000 French civil servants.[15] In Ivory Coast in 1956, not a single African held a decision-making position in the senior

10. For the thesis that Mau Mau is best interpreted as a revolutionary nationalist movement, see Carl G. Rosberg, Jr. and John Nottingham, *The Myth of Mau Mau: Nationalism in Kenya* (New York: Praeger, 1966).

11. *The Colonial Reckoning* (London: Collins, 1961), p. 80.

12. James S. Coleman, *Nigeria: Background to Nationalism* (Berkeley and Los Angeles: University of California Press, 1958), pp. 312–14.

13. Dennis Austin, *Politics in Ghana, 1946–1960* (London: Oxford University Press, 1964), p. 158.

14. Meister, *L'Afrique*, pp. 266–67.

15. Douglas E. Ashford, *Political Change in Morocco* (Princeton: Princeton University Press, 1964), pp. 109–221.

administration.[16] In the Congo (Kinshasa), at the moment of independence in 1960, of the 4,642 top slots, only 3 were filled by Africans.[17]

A crucial aspect of this phase of political development was the nature of the mass-elite relationships, which experienced a major metamorphosis after independence. The accumulated privileges of the exercise of power tended to be concentrated within the expatriate group. In many territories, the European minority received more than half the national income. The nationalist counter-elite did not bear the onus of actual exercise of governmental power. Whether the struggle was electoral or armed, the nationalist leadership had an absolute need for the support of the countryside. Numbers were critical; whether the tactic was appealing directly to villagers, or stitching together a series of alliances with local or regional notables and chiefs, the keys to the political kingdom were in the ballot box. Rewards for support came through promissory notes for the future. In most cases no mortgage payments needed to be met until independence arrived. Both the continuing needs of party organization and the focused requirements of electoral campaigns compelled a sustained effort at building linkages between elite and mass.

THE INDEPENDENCE POLITICAL FORMULA

Independence symbolized the assumption of full authority by the nationalist political counterpart to the colonial bureaucratic system. It represented a fundamental transformation of relationships, and it had the ineluctable consequence of a swift liquidation of the expatriate mandarinate. The rules of the political game were redefined. Power for the triumphant nationalist elite now derived from its control of the state, rather than from access to potential backing from the countryside. Prestigious positions in the bureaucratic hierarchy were key rewards for the elite faithful; swift Africanization was also dictated by the desire to assume full control of the state machinery, and was reinforced by the sheer logic of nationalism. In the aftermath of independence, nationalist ideology was given further elaboration in the form of African socialism, which gave impetus both to the role of the state and to the urgency of Africanization.

This third phase in the development of African political systems may be labeled the independence political formula.[18] The dominant political forms were

16. Aristide R. Zolberg, *One-Party Government in the Ivory Coast* (Princeton: Princeton University Press, 1964), p. 101.

17. *INCIDI, Staff Problems in Tropical and Subtropical Countries* (Brussels: 1961), p. 174.

18. A useful compendium which in fact derives its generalizations by extrapolating from this cross-section is James S. Coleman and Carl G. Rosberg, Jr., *Political Parties and National Integration in Tropical Africa* (Berkeley and Los Angeles: University of California Press, 1964).

TABLE 7
AFRICAN POLITICAL SYSTEM TYPES, INDEPENDENCE AND AFTER*

Country	Phase 3: Political Formula at Independence	Phase 4: Second-Stage Post-Independence Regime (as of mid-1969)
Algeria	revolutionary liberation movement	military regime
Botswana	dominant patron party	party-state
Burundi	dominant patron party	military regime
Cameroon	dominant patron party	party-state
Central African Republic	mass party	military regime
Chad	dominant patron party	party-state
Congo-Brazzaville	dominant patron party	party-state
Congo-Kinshasa	competitive party	military regime
Dahomey	competitive party	military regime
Ethiopia	no party traditional	no party traditional
Gabon	dominant patron party	party-state
Gambia	competitive party	competitive party
Ghana	mass party	military regime
Guinea	mass party	party-state
Ivory Coast	mass party	party-state
Kenya	dominant patron party	party-state
Lesotho	competitive party	party-state
Liberia	dominant patron party	party-state
Libya	no party traditional	no party traditional
Madagascar	dominant patron party	party-state
Malawi	mass party	party-state
Mali	mass party	military regime
Mauritania	dominant patron party	party-state
Morocco	dominant patron party	no party traditional
Niger	dominant patron party	party-state
Nigeria	competitive party	military regime
Rwanda	dominant patron party	party-state
Senegal	dominant patron party	party-state
Sierra Leone	competitive party	military regime
Somalia	dominant patron party	competitive party
South Africa	competitive party	party-state
Sudan	competitive party	military regime
Tanzania	mass party	renewed mass party
Togo	dominant patron party	military regime
Tunisia	mass party	renewed mass party
Uganda	competitive party	party-state
UAR	dominant patron party	military regime
Upper Volta	dominant patron party	military regime
Zambia	mass party	party-state
Totals:	mass party = 9 dominant patron party = 18 competitive party = 9 revolutionary liberation movement = 1 no party traditional = 2	party-state = 19 renewed mass party = 2 military regime = 13 competitive party = 2 no party traditional = 3

*Readers should exercise proper caution in interpreting this table. The categories are not susceptible of rigorous definition and therefore are rather imprecise at the margins; the totals, however, give a useful indication of the overall distribution of system types. Because the basepoint for Phase 3 varies with the country, the time interval between Phase 3 and Phase 4 varies substantially in some cases. (For example, Lesotho and Botswana only became independent in 1966, while the modern Egyptian state gained its sovereignty in 1922.) The Republic of South Africa, with its racial caste system, obviously is a very special case, and some may prefer to exclude it from the tabulations.

political parties, which swiftly moved to consolidate control by imposing restrictions on opposing groups and by inducing voluntary fusion into the ruling group.[19] The salient political form appeared to be a single-party system. The application of the categories of mass party and dominant patron party to specific countries is bound to raise objections and endless debate on given cases, as few real parties fully match the abstract paradigms. However, useful indications can be given on orders of magnitude by a rough classification. The analysis in Table 7 shows that of the thirty-eight independent African states (excluding South Africa), at the moment of independence nine were led by reasonable approximations of a mass single party. In eighteen other cases, there was a dominant patron party.[20] Nine instances of competitive party systems survived the terminal colonial electoral processes (including three — Nigeria, Congo-Kinshasa, and Uganda — where no party achieved an electoral majority). Two states (Ethiopia and Libya) had traditional no-party systems, and Algeria achieved independence behind the revolutionary military Front de Libération Nationale (FLN).

SECOND-STAGE POST-INDEPENDENCE REGIME

The assumption by the nationalist parties of the reins of government provided the means for transition to another phase. Africanization of the bureaucracy and the exercise of power through formal institutions of government led to a tendency toward partial fusion of party and state.[21] The nationalist elite, encumbered with the boundless promises of the drive for independence, faced enormous difficulties in maintaining the relationships with the countryside which had developed in the terminal colonial period. There were agonizing limitations imposed by the uncertainties of export prices, the high cost of the administrative infrastructure of the state, and the dependence on the developed world for both markets and finance. The central concern silently shifted from organization to control. Political personnel who had devoted years to the hardship of agitational politics had been absorbed into the machinery of government. Africanization and independence had offered substantial satisfactions to the incumbent generation of leadership; however, the growing numbers of new post-independence university and secondary school graduates, the urban workers, and the rural peasantry were out of power. The nationalist elite and

19. Martin Kilson, "Authoritarianism and Single-Party Tendencies," *World Politics*, XV (1963), 262–94.

20. Three special cases arise out of the attachment of small units with already established parties to larger territories with single parties: Tanzania (Zanzibar), Somalia (British Somaliland), and Cameroon (West Cameroun).

21. The emergence of the "party state" is set forth as the central trend in post-colonial West Africa by Zolberg, *Creating Political Order;* see also Henry Bienen, "One-Party Systems in Africa," mimeographed (Princeton University, 1968).

functionaries benefiting from Africanization had become a political-administrative middle class; new lines of social division and conflict became evident.

The range of possible outcomes was limited by the nature of the independence
political formula and the new context of change within which the dominant
power-holders operated. The mass parties faced a particularly acute dilemma,
as their whole style of operation was totally altered by success in gaining power.
The essential skill developed by the mass party had been solidarity-making;
the role of governance compelled them to adopt, to some extent, an administrative-technocratic orientation.[22] The arteries of communication hardened; the
shriveling party structure became simply a transmission mechanism for directives and official exhortation. The excitement of political rallies promising more
abundant life was supplanted by exhortations for harder work. The most dramatic demonstration of the total erosion of a once potent party, with mass support in a substantial part of the country, was the complete evaporation of the
Convention People's Party in Ghana with the overthrow of Nkrumah in February, 1966. The CPP had become nothing more than the projection of the political
personality of Nkrumah. The elimination of one man caused the party to vanish
with hardly a trace.

The mass party, as it stood in the independence political formula, was an
unstable form. The change in its role generated a strong tendency toward
atrophy of its mass character; the mass party eroded into an oligarchic machine
or, in the extreme case illustrated by the final days of the Nkrumah regime,
simply into an agent of personal rule.[23] Only two of the mass-party regimes,
Tunisia and Tanzania, appear to have been able to maintain their momentum;
an examination of these cases may shed light on the mechanisms available to
revitalize mass parties.

The Cases of Tanzania and Tunisia

In the case of Tanzania, one may point to a specific political mechanism which
has provided the dominant party, TANU (Tanzanian African National Union),
with renewed vitality.[24] One of the most interesting political innovations of the
contemporary world is the one-party electoral system devised to preserve both

22. The dichotomy between "administrators" and "solidarity-makers" is developed
with particular skill by Herbert Fieth, *The Decline of Constitutional Democracy in Indonesia*
(Ithaca, N.Y.: Cornell University Press, 1962). See also S. N. Eisenstadt, "Breakdowns of
Modernization," *Economic Development and Cultural Change*, XII (1964), 345–67. The
"mass" character of competitive parties in an opposition role was better maintained; the
APC in Sierra Leone is an example.

23. Henry Bretton, in *The Rise and Fall of Kwame Nkrumah* (New York: Praeger, 1966),
argues that the Nkrumah regime was always an illustration of personal rule rather than
of a mass party.

24. TANU operates only in mainland Tanzania (formerly Tanganyika). These re-
marks do not apply to Zanzibar, where the dominant Afro-Shirazi party has not sought
any means of revitalization.

democracy and a single-party framework in Tanzania. The system was constructed on the premise that some form of competitive mechanism had to be built into the party itself to replace competition from outside. It was devised after a special presidential commission carefully examined ways and means of building a democratic one-party state.[25] The crux of the procedure was to offer a contest between two candidates in the 107 single-member districts into which mainland Tanzania was divided. A petition with twenty-five signatures was sufficient to enter the race. The TANU district executive committees then selected two candidates, with the TANU Central Committee having an opportunity to screen the nominations. The campaign took place under rather stringent restrictions. Candidates spoke at formal gatherings organized by the party; they were not permitted to hold their own campaign meetings. Use of Swahili was obligatory; discussion of race, ethnic group, or religion was prohibited. Wide areas of government policy were also out of bounds, including matters such as the development plan, the role of Tanzania's Asian community, nonalignment, and East African cooperation.

Despite these limitations, there can be no doubt that the September, 1965, elections, the first to be conducted under the new rules, had a therapeutic effect on the regime. A dramatic demonstration of both the impact of the elections and the need for them was the high turnover of parliamentary seats; less than one-fourth of the incumbents won reelection. Two ministers and six junior ministers were defeated at the polls. The government did not interfere to assure the reelection of its top personnel, and the evidence from these carefully studied elections is that the populace did find them a meaningful opportunity for political participation.[26] The turnover rate is all the more remarkable when one recalls that the parliamentary salary is, for many deputies, far greater than that of alternative forms of employment. Politicians have a high personal stake in their political careers. The content of the campaign speeches was dominated by local issues, partly because most other issues were proscribed. In a number of constituencies, there is evidence that the visual political symbols by which candidates were identified to the many illiterate voters (a house or a hoe, assigned by lot) had some effect on the results. But the 1965 elections remain a crucial moment of renewal and rebirth for the mass-party system in Tanzania. They compelled the elite to rebuild a link with the countryside; the turnover demonstrated how badly it had been eroded.

The 1965 elections are not the sole explanation of the relative success of TANU in sustaining itself. The nature of the leadership of President Julius Nyerere is of central importance as well. The recognition by Nyerere of the

25. Government of Tanzania, *Report of the Presidential Commission on the Establishment of a Democratic One-Party State* (Dar es Salaam: Government Printer, 1965).

26. A team of researchers covered every aspect of the elections and reported very favorable findings; see Lionel Cliffe, ed., *One Party Democracy* (Nairobi: East African Publishing House, 1965).

necessity to build into his system constraints on the party in order to maintain its vitality is suggestive of a political style very different from that of Nkrumah. In many other ways, Nyerere demonstrated a concern for preserving an open society and active rural support. However, it is important not to exaggerate the distinctions we are suggesting between party systems containing renewal mechanisms and obligarchic machines; Tanzania and TANU fall some distance short of the mass-party model,[27] while other systems endowed with leaders of broad political vision, such as those in Zambia or Senegal, are not entirely dissimilar from Tanzania.

Tunisia has found rather different mechanisms for maintaining the momentum of the mass party, the Destour Socialist Party. Elections per se have not played a major part in this instance. The processes of revitalization in Tunisia are more subtle and elusive, yet the contrast between the Destour Socialist Party, after more than a decade of independence, and most African ruling parties is dramatic.

Part of the answer lies simply in the greater historic depth of Habib Bourguiba's Destour party. The movement was already well established in the 1930s, unlike sub-Saharan parties. Its internal structures were created in the perspective of a long-range struggle, rather than in the context of the swift achievement of the primary goal of independence. The party developed a whole family of ancillary organizations, such as UGET (students), UGTT (workers), UNFT (women), and UTICA (traders). These have enjoyed a degree of autonomy; but there has been continuing political conflict between the ancillary organizations and the party on the boundaries of legitimate dissent. The creative tension thus sustained is one of the sources of regeneration. The homogeneity of society and culture in Tunisia has assured that tensions are not translated into ethnic or religious confrontations and escalated beyond the point where the system can manage them.

Since independence, the Destour Socialist Party has been able to transform successive challenges into revitalizing impulses. A classic example was the process of Tunisia's commitment to planning and socialism. In 1956, Bourguiba engineered the removal of trade union leader Ben Salah because his economic doctrines were judged too radical for the regime. Five years later, Ben Salah was dramatically returned to grace as Minister of Planning. The mounting pressures from a younger generation of militant intellectuals for a redirection of Tunisia's economy was converted into new strength as Bourguiba adopted the program of a potential opposition force.[28]

The renewal process in Tunisia partly occurs through the cooptation of in-

27. Henry Bienen gives excellent treatment of the necessary qualifications for the description of TANU as a "mass party" in *Tanzania: Party Transformation and Economic Development* (Princeton: Princeton University Press, 1967).

28. For a useful study of Bourguibism in theory and practice, see Clement Henry Moore, *Tunisia since Independence* (Berkeley and Los Angeles, University of California Press, 1965).

dividuals. A careful analysis of the career lines of top Tunisian leaders would show many who first became visible as articulate critics of what they felt to be the inadequate forward momentum of the regime. The ablest protagonists were disarmed by the offer of responsibility within the system and scope for converting their bill of indictment into the Destour Socialist policy.

As in the Tanzanian case, the style and character of the leadership from the top, especially from Bourguiba, is a significant dimension. A cyclical pattern is discernible; periods of stagnation in the late 1950s, and again in the middle 1960s, were visible. But each time the regime has been able to generate a renewed sense of momentum, and, from this, a refurbished legitimacy. Challenge has been met with a political response, rather than with increased application of coercion.

Parties, Elections, and Military Takeover

For mass-party states which failed to find a formula for renewal, and for patron-party states generally, the initial outcome was an oligarchic party-state. The metamorphosis was less spectacular in the latter case, as the contrast is less marked between the patron party and the oligarchic party-state. But the same forces operated; the sources of power were now in the capital, and a network of rural allies was less vital.

Competitive-party systems have proved very difficult to sustain. The tensions generated by a genuinely open electoral contest, when the outcome threatens the existing distribution of power among ethnic groups or regions, can be enormous. Elections of this nature, since 1960, have been held in Sierra Leone, Burundi, Congo-Kinshasa, Nigeria, Somalia, and Sudan. Only in Somalia were the results fully accepted; a remarkably deviant case, Somalia has had three peaceful, constitutional changes of government since independence. In Sierra Leone, elections in 1967 that were free enough for the opposition party to win led immediately to an army coup. In Burundi, open elections were held in 1965; the results led to a sharp shift away from Watutsi hegemony over the numerically superior Bahutu. A series of coups ensued which eliminated the Bahutu threat and restored Watutsi overrule under army auspices.

In Nigeria, the national general elections in 1964 became a massive confrontation between regional parties. So high were the stakes believed to be by the participants that all felt it necessary to rely heavily on intimidation and coercion.[29] The poisonous atmosphere of distrust which these elections left behind was a mortal blow to the competitive-party system in Nigeria. The *coup de grâce* came the following year when regional elections in the Western Region were conducted under even more deplorable conditions. Not long after, in January,

29. A fictionalized version of these elections, and of post-independence politics in Nigeria generally, conveys admirably the flavor of the situation; see Chinua Achebe, *A Man of the People* (Garden City, N.Y.: Doubleday, 1965).

1966, a group of army officers assassinated the leader of the government party and ended the independence political formula.

In Congo-Kinshasa, the national elections held in 1965 were rendered almost meaningless by the entirely ephemeral character of the political groups contesting them. A new coalition movement knitted together by Prime Minister Moise Tshombe fell apart shortly after winning an apparent electoral triumph. Voters were totally unable to discern any relationship between their voting choice and subsequent political outcomes. In this instance, the sheer anarchy of a parliament with no control over political conflict made the results so capricious and unpredictable that a military coup occurred in November, 1965, to forestall a genuine risk of breakdown at the center. Thus the very nature of competitive parties, and the strong tendency for them to reflect communal or ethnic divisions, meant that an open fight tended to pit community against community. A competitive-party system as an independence political formula was also, in general, unstable and tended toward either a fusion of parties into an oligarchic party-state or a military coup.

The fate of the single case to date of a revolutionary movement achieving power merits notice, although one cannot properly draw inferences from a single outcome. In Algeria, during the epic eight-year armed struggle for independence, the insurgent movement appeared to grow from weakness to strength. The revolutionary core was very small when violent action was unleashed on November 1, 1954, but by 1956 it was able to hold at bay a French army approaching 500,000. The potent sense of nationalist identity born of common hardships, the transcendent character of the struggle, and the inspiring vision of the future seemed to most observers the guarantee of a regime of exceptional dynamism. A peasantry which had endured the trauma of the Algerian revolution could not fail to have the *élan* and the commitment to transformation which would create a new Algeria.[30] But the outcome was to be utterly different. The first symptom visible to the world was the appearance of direct factional conflict between two armed groups for control of the government at the moment of independence. Six weeks passed before the Ben Bella group consolidated its control over Algiers. Subsequently, a whole array of competing groups became evident. The commanders of the six *wilayas* (military districts) appeared to regard their areas as personal fiefs. The external armies which had been based in Tunisia and Morocco had factional interests to promote. Traces of Kabyl-Arab tension surfaced. The imprisoned leaders differed sharply from those who had supervised the government in exile. The Algerian revolution drifted into an incoherence which culminated in a military coup in June, 1965.[31]

Thus, as the African independence political formula moved into a post-

30. This thesis in its most memorable formulation was advanced by Frantz Fanon, especially in *L'An V de la révolution algérienne* (Paris: F. Maspero, 1960); and Fanon, *The Wretched of the Earth* (New York: Grove Press, 1965).

31. David Gordon, *The Passing of French Algeria* (London: Oxford University Press,

independence stage, new rules governing access to power produced a limited range of outcomes. The most frequent were the erosion of mass or patron parties into either an oligarchic party-state or a military regime. The competitive-party formula exhibited a strong tendency to move toward one of the same two outcomes. Other possibilities were the preservation of a mass-party regime through the evolution of mechanisms for political renewal (as in Tunisia and Tanzania) and, in rare instances, through the maintenance or emergence of a competitive-party system (as in Somalia and Kenya). The range of possible outcomes arising from a military system will be discussed below. We have already considered the nature of renewed mass parties; we turn now to a consideration of the character of the oligarchic party-state and the military regime.

The Oligarchic Party

The key political resources for the elite of the oligarchic party-state were the security apparatus of the state, offices of government commanding allocation of funds or other goods, and, in certain cases (especially former French territories such as Senegal, Ivory Coast, and Gabon), significant external support. The ability to serve as spokesman for a large or strategically located regional group was another valuable asset. Zolberg has suggested that the oligarchic party-state is analogous to the American urban machine. Although it is not genuinely democratic, he argues, "it tends to avoid senseless cruelty." Zolberg continues:

> By shunning serious commitment to a very demanding ideology, the machine maintains solidarity among its members by appealing to their self-interest while allowing for the play of factions and for recurrent reconciliation. It can easily provide for the formal and informal representation of a multitude of relatively modern and not-so-modern groups in the society, including those based on explicit economic or political interests.[32]

A useful example of the oligarchic machine was the Binza caucus group which dominated Congo politics from 1961 to 1964. The membership of the network suggests the types of political resources which were aggregated into effective power. Key members are shown in Table 8.

This shadowy caucus brought together leaders situated in strategic positions. Bomboko, Nendaka, and Mobutu had been politicians prior to independence, while Ndele and Kandolo had a more administrative-technocratic background. Each had at least a modest regional clientele. It was to some extent an invisible

---

1966); and Arslan Humbaraci, *Algeria: A Revolution That Failed* (London: Pall Mall Press, 1966).

32. *Creating Political Order*, pp. 160–61.

TABLE 8
BINZA CAUCUS GROUP, 1961–64, CONGO-KINSHASA

Name	Position	Region of Origin
Justin Bomboko	Minister of Foreign Affairs	central Congo
Victor Nendaka	Director of the Sûreté (special branch)	northeast Congo
Joseph Mobutu	Commander, Armée Nationale Congolaise	northern Congo
Albert Ndele	Director of National Bank	lower Congo
Damien Kandolo	Permanent Secretary, Ministry of Interior	east-central Congo

political machine rather than a party; indeed, subsequent efforts of the group to form a political party failed.

A pervasive aspect of the oligarchic party-state is the importance of personal ties. Politics is a highly complex matrix of interacting patron-client networks. Personal ties can be based upon kinship, common ethnic origin, membership in the same religious brotherhood, or, among members of the elite, shared educational or professional experiences. If a service is required from government, an individual will make an effort to introduce his demand through a network to which he is attached. If there is none available, it is very likely that, anticipating failure, the individual will abandon his request. Patron-client networks involve a set of mutual obligations; the client is expected to support his patron and be governed by his political wishes. In return, the client is entitled to distributive benefits—favored access to employment, or lodgings, or emergency financial support. The vintage politician is a man who succeeds in weaving together a large series of subnetworks. The need for access to substantial resources is axiomatic; the reward system is fundamental to the patron-client network. Rewards are not always material. In Senegal, for example, the most extensive patron-client networks are built around the Muslim brotherhoods; the *marabout*, or holy man leading an order, is able to distribute supernatural rewards through his exceptional piety and presumed ability to fathom and manipulate occult forces.

In the absence of non-governmental institutional structures, the oligarchic party-state exhibits great fluidity as alliances of patron-client networks form and dissolve. Costs and benefits of coalitions are under continuous recalculation, which results in frequent shifts.[33] The patron-client networks are critical in the political communication process. Mass media play a relatively small role in most

33. The extant literature on micro-politics in Africa lends abundant support for these generalizations; indeed, the interaction of networks is more readily visible at this level. For a penetrating and suggestive analysis of this phenomenon at the local level in India, see F. G. Bailey, *Politics and Social Change: Orissa in 1959* (Berkeley and Los Angeles: University of California Press, 1963).

African states; political information passes through the patron-client network by word of mouth. This diffusion process involves a heavy dose of selective perception as knowledge of a political event is diffracted in passing through the patron-client prism.

System mutations arising out of the oligarchic party-state appear to move primarily toward a military regime. There is as yet no instance of a mass movement arising in antithesis to an oligarchic party-state. The administration is unlikely to permit the formation of such a movement, and an open electoral framework for a movement of radical opposition is highly improbable. A large part of the potential leadership of such movements is absorbed into oligarchic coalition politics. The nearest approximation to a revolutionary opposition seeking to mobilize on a mass scale was the Congo rebellion of 1964–65. It proved subject to fragmentation; in choosing the path of violence the initiating elite found itself unable to direct or control the forces unleashed.[34]

Military Rule

The military coup as a form of political change was almost totally unanticipated at the hour of African independence, although in retrospect it is not difficult to see why armies are able to seize power from oligarchic party machines with little opposition. Initially, the military was restrained in the majority of cases by the presence of expatriate officers at top levels. Not until Africanization of the major command posts had occurred was the army in a position to intervene. The first military takeover took place in 1952 in the United Arab Republic; the former Wafd oligarchic party-state had completely lost its momentum and legitimacy. Sudan followed in 1958, although six years later the army relinquished power. Through 1969 sixteen states had experienced successful military coups. The coup is generally triggered by some particular impasse in the affairs of the oligarchic party-state. A recurrent underlying cause is simply that the consumption requirements of the patron-client network coalition outstrip the available resources of the state.

It is important to note that the regimes installed by the military are by no means wholly staffed by the army. The more general pattern is for a large percentage of the positions to be held by members of the political-administrative elite who had controlled the previous government. What has altered is the visible basis of power and legitimacy. All political actors recognize that the army is ultimately the basis of the regime and that any direct challenge to its authority will be dealt with by military means. This is a significant change in the ground rules, but the change often merely sets a new framework for the continuation of previous patterns of network interaction.

34. For details on the rebellion, see especially Benoit Verhaegen, *Rébellions au Congo*, Vol. I (Brussels: Centre de Recherche et d'Information Socio-politiques, 1966); and Charles Anderson, Fred von der Mehden, and Crawford Young, *Issues of Political Development* (Englewood Cliffs, N.J.: Prentice-Hall, 1967).

Military regimes are unlikely to enjoy indefinite power; one of the more important open questions about African politics is the range of alternatives possible after military rule. Experience to date suggests the following possibilities: (1) a return of power to the previous dominant political groups, as in Sudan in 1964; (2) a coup by younger officers, or by a different army faction, as in Dahomey in 1967; or (3) an effort to politicize and invest the regime with non-military symbols, as in UAR and Congo-Kinshasa. Only the last of these outcomes constitutes a real innovation. It merits further consideration.

In both UAR and Congo, the military elite has tried to construct from the top a political movement capable of offering a means for political organization of the countryside and support for the regime. In UAR, the movement has been through several incarnations, its latest designation being the Arab Socialist Union. The initial undefined nationalism of the Nasser regime has been replaced by a relatively specific set of ideological commitments. In both UAR and Congo the military antecedents of the government have been deemphasized. Congo President Mobutu quietly replaced his uniform with a Tanzania-style tunic and a leopard-skin cap. All previous political parties were dissolved, and the regime launched its own party: the Mouvement Populaire de la Révolution (MPR). The MPR was constituted on a basis entirely different from earlier Congo parties; rather than being founded upon the regional clientele of local political notables, it was imposed from the top. In adopting the radical vocabulary of earlier mass parties elsewhere, it clothed itself in a populist garb. Regional party leaders were appointed from the center and operated primarily on the basis of resources made available from it. Officials were forbidden to work in their home territories where they might have an opportunity to develop a personal following. The MPR and the Arab Socialist Union faced a similar dilemma. Both, in the final analysis, were designed as control mechanisms, to foster regime supports rather than to elicit and process demands. The burden of generating support for a regime which lacked the capability to meet the expectations of the countryside was a major constraint upon effectiveness and legitimacy. No doubt military regimes elsewhere will be tempted to try changing their spots as a means of increasing longevity.

CONCLUSIONS

In the immediate future, then, African political systems seem likely to be predominantly of the oligarchic party-state or military regime types. A military regime may then lead to a regime-imposed single-party system (see Table 9). But African economies are unlikely to expand rapidly enough to provide adequate resources for any of the existing systems to enjoy stable development. There are many constraints upon the range of political outcomes which have

TABLE 9

TIME SEQUENCE OF AFRICAN POLITICAL DEVELOPMENT

Phase 1: *Colonial*	Phase 2: *Nationalist*	Phase 3: *Post-independence*	Phase 4: *Second-stage Post-independence*	Phase 5: *Future*

Colonial bureaucratic state → Nationalist anti-state

Mass single party → Renewed mass party

Patron single party → Oligarchic party-state

Competitive parties → Military regime

Revolutionary liberation movement

Military regime → Party-state restoration

Reshuffled military

Imposed single party

not been given adequate attention in this essay. Increasing numbers of university graduates will appear on the scene, and those who do not find satisfying outlets are likely to place high ideological demands on the system. The spread of political consciousness in many states is likely to intensify ethnic nationalism. If a large and self-conscious ethnic group believes itself excluded from the distribution of power and rewards, it is likely to contemplate the option of secession, as Biafra has attempted in the Nigerian context. Active separatist movements which have resorted to armed revolt since independence, in addition to Nigeria, have appeared in Congo-Kinshasa, Uganda, Kenya, Ethiopia, Sudan, and Chad.

Yet unrelieved pessimism regarding the development of African political systems would be as misplaced as the unbridled optimism of ten years ago. Within the limited range of available alternatives, the majority of African states have maintained a standard of government which is quite creditable. There is no African equivalent of *Tonton Macoute* in Haiti, nor are African military regimes really comparable to the rapacious nineteenth-century Latin American dictatorships. Although authoritarian practices are widespread, use of coercion is in most cases quite limited. African states have neither the coercive capacity nor the apparent intention of moving in the direction of totalitarian models, such as Hitler's Germany or Stalin's Russia. African political development may well reach maturity to the extent that fundamental contextual problems can be resolved. By any standards, states at the upper end of the performance scale, such as Tanzania and Tunisia, have rendered an excellent accounting for their first decade of independence. If due weight be given to the magnitude of problems and limitation of resources, most states can lay claim to a political balance sheet which shows perhaps modest, but nonetheless positive, results for the initial phase of self-management.

23

Legal Systems Development

ROLAND YOUNG

ONE OF THE SIGNIFICANT DEVELOPMENTS in Africa during the last century has been the introduction of new legal systems, with the consequent modification of the force of customary law for controlling society and regulating human relationships. With the introduction of new legal systems, procedures and institutions have been established by which old law can be changed and new law created.

Perhaps we can achieve a clearer picture of this momentous development by viewing African law in its historical context. Three aspects should be stressed: customary law, foreign law, and the new national legal systems. Customary law is a concept with many shades of meaning, but it is used here as a general category embracing all types of traditional law. Law as a method of resolving disputes was not unknown in the pre-colonial period; and, indeed, many writers have commented on the litigious nature of traditional societies. Although customary law has been modified in content, in procedures, and in methods of enforcement, it continues to control many aspects of African life. In rural areas, in particular, customary law still has considerable potency in regulating property, descent, and marriage. For purposes of this chapter, customary law is extended to include Islamic law, Hindu law, and the ancient law of Ethiopia as expressed, say, in *Fetha Negast* ("Legislation of the Kings").

A second aspect of African legal development has been the introduction, or reception, of foreign legal systems, comprising a corpus of interrelated concepts and following established systematic procedures for litigating disputes. The new, colonially induced legal systems and the old, traditional systems have some points in common, but they are not the same. Among the newer ideas is the belief that law can be created by a positive act of government—normally by the legislative branch. At the close of the Middle Ages, this idea had a considerable impact on the growth and modification of law in the Western world, and it now has a modern parallel in the development of law in Africa.

473

A third aspect of jurisprudential development has been the growth of a more unified national legal system, embracing all categories of people and all types of law. As systems of national law develop, it becomes possible to carry on inter-related activities over extensive areas. An obvious example is found in the economic field (commercial transactions, contracts, and sales, for instance). In a similar fashion, the application of national standards of criminal justice and criminal procedure makes it possible to establish the conditions of peaceful life over large areas. The varieties of law become integrated through a common system of courts. It is this newer national legal system which is now in the process of development. One may still refer to legal pluralism as a characteristic of African law; but the multiplicity of laws are now being integrated into an inter-related system, particularly at the national level. Part of this law is customary or modified customary, part has been received, and part has been developed, or "made."

On a still broader scale, the new nations of Africa have been confronted with the problem of establishing legal relations with one another and with the rest of the world. Here the field of public international law provides many of the categories, concepts, and procedures which are being followed in Africa.

Law has many meanings, and in considering the nature of law in Africa one is immediately faced with the problem of developing categories and definitions. In fact, it is not easy to define Western-type law, for the definition of law, Roscoe Pound has said, "has been the battle-ground of jurisprudence."[1] It is even more difficult to develop a pluralistic and transcultural definition of law, one which encompasses the various types of African customary law, the law found in Western legal systems, and the law as expressed in the newer unified state systems. Western law makes certain assumptions about the nature of the society to be regulated, as does African law; both perform a similar function, albeit using different procedures and different conceptual frameworks.

Law serves as a unifying regulator within a community, and with the development of a legal system the various segments of law can be related to one another. In Western terms, some aspects of the law are of local application only, perhaps the result of a referendum or the verdict of a jury. Other aspects have a wider applicability, such as a tax law which extends to state or nation. Still other aspects, such as procedural rights found in the expression "due process," are of a more transcendent nature, embracing cultures and civilizations. In Africa, much of the traditional law is of a local nature, based on the family or community. The newer law is based on broader, more comprehensive standards and tends to form a more or less coherent body of rules which create the basis of order in a community.

---

1. Roscoe Pound, ed., *Readings on the History and System of the Common Law*, 3d ed. (Rochester, N.Y.: Law Library, 1927).

Paul Bohannan has defined law in terms of "double institutionalization," a definition which can be applied both to customary African law and to Western legal systems. He writes that customs

> are norms or rules . . . about the ways in which people must behave if social institutions are to perform their tasks if society is to endure . . .

and the law is a body of binding obligations

> which has been reinstitutionalized within the legal institution so that society can continue to function in an orderly manner on the basis of rules so maintained.

Reciprocity is the basis of custom; law rests on the process of double institutionalization. Law, he says, is never a mere reflection of custom; it is

> always out of phase with society, specifically because of the duality of the statement and restatement of rights. . . . Thus, it is the very nature of law, and its capacity to "do something about" the primary social institutions, that creates the lack of phase. . . . It is the fertile dilemma of law that it must always be out of step with society, but that people must always (because they work better with fewer contradictions, if for no other reason) attempt to reduce the lack of phase.[2]

Law, then, is an institution which regulates relations within society; it prevents certain types of harmful activity; it supports a certain type of order by the process of "double institutionalization"; it recognizes an "ought" element which "is culturally determined and may change from society to society and from era to era." Certain aspects of legal institutions are not shared with other institutions of society. Legal institutions "must have some regularized way to interfere in the malfunctioning (and, perhaps, the functioning as well) of the nonlegal institutions in order to disengage the trouble-case." They are concerned with two kinds of rules: procedural laws, which govern the activities of the legal institution, and rules of a substantive nature, which are "substitutes or modifications or restatements of the rules of the nonlegal institution that has been invaded."[3]

With the introduction of new systems of law in Africa, a certain confusion, or lack of phase, may arise because different standards can be applied to similar cases. Thus, the growth of law, or of legal systems, has been accompanied by growing conflicts of law, with attempts being made to harmonize the various systems, and by the use of law for new purposes, including the legitimation of a national government.

2. "The Differing Realms of Law," in *Law and Warfare: Studies in the Anthropology of Conflict*, ed. Paul Bohannan (Garden City, N.Y.: Doubleday, Natural History Press, 1967), pp. 47–49.
3. *Ibid.*, pp. 45–47.

AFRICAN CUSTOMARY LAW

It is not possible in this essay to treat in any detail the various types of African customary law. In most cases, customary law was unrecorded until recently, and it is difficult to reconstruct it in its earlier forms. The Kupers have made the following comment on African customary law:

> The legal systems of "traditional" African societies are extremely diverse. In some there are no units or offices that coincide with the Western concept of a judiciary. In others, only the religious aspect of power is institutionalized, and it provides the main sanction for public activities. Yet in others there are elaborately conceptualized and verbally defined distinctions, a separation of legal from other institutions.[4]

African law may be described in such a manner as to show the existence of a system, but the nature of the system revealed may in fact be determined by the categories selected for analysis. As Allott and Cotran have remarked, many apparent differences between African legal systems

> are created by or aggravated by the different legal training and background of those who write about or administer them, and by differences in legal terminology. It has often been remarked that when a French lawyer writes about customary law, he naturally attempts to fit it into French legal categories and the English lawyer into English categories.[5]

Recent writings on customary African law include discussions of ordeals, moots, feuds, criteria of "reasonableness," compensation to "restore the equilibrium," negotiations outside the court system, witchcraft, and self-help.[6]

A discussion of some of the main characteristics of African law may be useful in providing background for sections of this essay which are concerned with the interrelationships of customary law and received law. One makes generalizations

---

4. Hilda Kuper and Leo Kuper, "Introduction," in *African Law: Adaptation and Development*, ed. Kuper and Kuper (Berkeley and Los Angeles: University of California Press, 1965), p. v.

5. A. N. Allott and Eugene Cotran, "A Background Paper on Restatement of Laws in Africa," mimeographed (University of Ibadan, 1964).

6. Esther Warner, "A Liberian Ordeal," in Bohannan, *Law and Warfare*, pp. 271–75; James L. Gibbs, Jr., "The Kpelle Moot," *ibid.*, pp. 277–89; Daryll Forde, "Justice and Judgment among the Southern Ibo under Colonial Rule," in Kuper and Kuper, *African Law*, pp. 76–96; Max Gluckman, "Reasonableness and Responsibility in the Law of Segmentary Societies," *ibid.*, pp. 120–46; Gluckman, *The Judicial Process among the Barotse of Northern Rhodesia*, 2d ed. rev. (Manchester: Manchester University Press, 1967); Gluckman, *Idea in Barotse Jurisprudence* (New Haven: Yale University Press, 1965); S. F. Nadel, "Reason and Unreason in African Law," *Africa*, XXVI (1956), 160–73; Paul Howell, *Manual of Nuer Law* (London: Oxford University Press, 1954); P. H. Gulliver, *Social Control in an African Society: A Study of the Arusha Agricultural Masai of Northern Tanganyika* (London: Routledge & Kegan Paul, 1963); Jan Vansina, "A Traditional Legal System: The Kuba," in Kuper and Kuper, *African Law*, pp. 97–119; and Paul Bohannan, "Drumming the Scandal among the Tiv," in Bohannan, *Law and Warfare*, pp. 263–65.

on African law with some diffidence, for customary law tends to be parochial and particular rather than general and uniform. Nevertheless, there seems to be a basic difference between African law and Western law on the concept of abstract, individual rights which arise from, and are inherent in, the legal system. In Western law a person has rights that are created by the legal system and are enforceable through the legal system; but it is not at all clear that African societies conceive of rights within a legal system or, indeed, of rights in any abstract sense. The evidence suggests otherwise; and a more appropriate summation (as suggested by Ronald Cohen) would seem to be that African societies conceive of law not in terms of abstract rights but in terms of concrete role relations with other people, particularly members of the family, which can be transferred. It might be said, then, that customary law is an amalgam of specific relationships, not a system of abstract rights. To a large degree, therefore, African customary law is governed by status relationships.

This fundamental difference between Western and African law poses the issue of comparability: Is it permissible to use Western legal concepts in describing the African legal process? Different views on this subject are expressed in the approaches to African law followed by Paul Bohannan and Max Gluckman. In his work on the Tiv (Nigeria), Bohannan states that he has tried *not* to explain or translate the Tiv system of jural control in terms of the Western legal system, which, he says, "would do violence to the Tiv ideas and folk systems."[7] As an example he cites the Tiv use of the word *jir* as a key legal concept, a notion possibly covered by the English word "counteraction":

> Tiv see their tribunals, both courts and "moots," with a single set of concepts. The two have different internal structuring, but in the long run both are *jir* and the purpose of both is to "repair the *tar*," to make the community run smoothly and peacefully. The elders of the moot also repair the *tar* ceremonially. Tiv see the ceremony and the *jir* as two aspects of the single task of repairing the *tar*: what we might call the government aspect and the religious aspect of social welfare.[8]

Bohannan illustrates the difference between European and Tiv ideas about law in his interpretation of the establishment of colonial legal structures, that is, the Native Authority tribunals:

> The European folk system sees the Native Authority tribunal basically as a court which, within established limits, applies "native law and custom." Tiv, in their folk system, see the same organization as a *jir* which arbitrates disputes brought before it. "Native law and custom" as a "corpus" of "law" which can be "sure," is simply not a Tiv idea. Neither is it a Tiv idea that a "court" may have "authority" to carry out its "decisions." Rather, Tiv believe that a right answer exists to all

---

7. Paul Bohannan, *Justice and Judgment among the Tiv* (London: Oxford University Press, 1957), p. 6.
8. *Ibid.*, p. 213.

disputes; they take disputes before the *jir* in order to discover that answer, and the principals to the dispute must concur in it when it is discovered.[9]

A different approach to the study of customary law has been followed by Gluckman. Using procedures and concepts which are essentially Western, he finds similarities in the legal approach of the West and that followed by the Barotse or Lozi of Zambia. On the whole, he finds that

> the Lozi judicial process corresponds with, more than it differs from, the judicial process in Western society. Lozi judges draw on the same sources of law as Western judges—the regularities of the environment, of the animal kingdom, of human beings; and customs, legislation, precedent, equity, the laws of nature and of nations, public policy, morality. They assess evidence in the same way. They manipulate the different types of legal rule which can be applied to a particular situation, and the ambiguity of the concepts which make up the legal rules, in a similar attempt to achieve justice according to their lights. . . . The dominant factors which produce important differences are the comparatively egalitarian and undifferentiated nature of social relations, the absence of pleadings and counsel and complex procedure, and the unwritten state of the law.[10]

Gluckman finds that the Lozi courts use concepts familiar to Western law, including the reasonable man—"the man on the Clapham omnibus," as one judge expressed it:

> The standards of right behavior against which the behavior of the parties is assessed to see if they have acted rightly or wrongly are those of "the reasonable and customary man." This exists as a distinct concept in the Lozi language, though it is not always explicitly stated by the judges.[11]

These different approaches illustrate some of the difficulties of understanding African law in Western legal terms. Concepts are, to an extent, a method of classifying material, and material can usually be classified in different ways. Bohannan cites the Tiv concept of "debt" (*injo*), which is used as a major category for classification:

> Many torts have debt aspects; most contracts have debt aspects. Tiv "classify" on the notion of debt, as it were, not on the notion of "tort" and "contract." It is not for us to say that Tiv do not understand tort or contract; neither is it for Tiv to say that the English do not understand debt.[12]

A legal concept that has created considerable misunderstanding in Africa is the Western idea of ownership, particularly the ownership of real property.

9. *Ibid.*, pp. 212–13.
10. Gluckman, *The Judicial Process among the Barotse*, p. 357.
11. *Ibid.*, p. 358.
12. Bohannan, *Justice and Judgment*, p. 212.

Traditional African societies had notions of control over land, particularly where land was in short supply, but the Western concept of freehold and lease-hold are not necessarily applicable, nor is the ambiguous concept of "communal" ownership. In the parts of Africa where shifting agriculture was practiced, the peasant cultivator would move from one area to another as the land wore out. In such a situation, the concept of permanent possession or ownership over a precisely delimited piece of land would be clearly inappropriate. With regard to the practice of shifting agriculture, it would be nearer the mark to refer to a corpus of ambulatory relationships that are applicable regardless of what land is considered or where it is located. The relationships remain constant as the peasants move from one area to the other, but the object of control is continually changing. The situation is similar, say, to soldiers on the march who bivouac at a different place every night. The relationship of the soldiers to each other and to a camp remains constant, but the site of the camp changes.

Another major difference between African and Western law includes legal procedures. The procedures of the Western court system are highly regularized and depend for their successful operation on a trained profession of judges and lawyers who are bound by a common professional tradition. The distinctive features of the system include judicial precedents, jury trial, prerogative writs (including habeas corpus), a hierarchy of courts, and independence of judges. An African scholar describing Western legal procedure writes as follows:

> The basis of the system is that every court is absolutely bound by the decisions of all courts superior to itself, but the highest court of the land holds itself bound by its own previous decisions.[13]

Gluckman has noted in African courts "the absence of pleadings and counsel and complex procedure, and the unwritten state of law." The jury system, for instance, was not an aspect of customary African law, and from the date of its introduction in West Africa more than a century ago the system has been criticized as "inappropriate." In Sierra Leone, for instance, it was alleged that

> an Akoo jury will never convict an Akoo, and that they will never acquit a white man or a Timmanee, and that the verdict of an Akoo is generally agreed upon out of court before the trial comes on.[14]

A modern commentator, with a similarly low opinion of the jury, has stated that

> to entrust the defendant's liberty to a jury on these terms is not democracy; . . . it is the despotism of small, nameless, untrained, ephemeral groups, responsible to no one and not even giving reasons for their opinion.[15]

13. W. C. Ekow Daniels, *The Common Law in West Africa* (London: Butterworth, 1964), p. 175.
14. *Select Committee Report*, Vol. 5, p. 50, quoted by Daniels, *The Common Law in West Africa*, p. 197.
15. Glanville Williams in *The Listener*, August 24, 1961, p. 280.

Prior to European influence, the customary laws of Africa were normally unwritten, and hence there was no written body of case law to serve as precedents in future cases. There were, however, two exceptions to this statement. One exception was Islamic law, which has prevailed in North Africa for centuries and has penetrated southward with various degrees of saturation. In some parts of English-speaking Africa, Islamic law and customary law were treated as largely identical. These areas included Ghana, Sierra Leone, Uganda, and Nyasaland (Malawi). In other areas Islamic law was regarded as a third system, alongside received law and indigenous law. These included Somaliland, Kenya, Zanzibar (now part of Tanzania), and Zambia. Between these two categories fall Gambia and Tanganyika (now part of Tanzania).[16] The second exception is the *Fetha Negast,* a compilation of canon and civil law dating from about the thirteenth century, which was for some three hundred years the only legal code in Ethiopia.[17]

WESTERN INFLUENCE IN AFRICAN LAW

During the historical period following the establishment of European rule in Africa, the laws of Africa were greatly changed, partly by the introduction of new legal systems and partly by the establishment of methods for making new law and modifying the old law. The English legal system, including common law and equity, was introduced into Africa, as were systems of codified civil law of continental Europe (French, Belgian, Portuguese, Spanish, Dutch). The new legal systems included a hierarchy of courts which not only provided new methods for adjudicating disputes but also helped to adjust the law to changing times. Legislatures and bureaucracies, which could create positive law in the form of legislation, orders, and regulations, were also established. Constitutional law, creating the structure of government, was also included in this category, but will not be dealt with in this essay.

The pattern of induced legal changes was not identical in the various colonies. Nor have the new nations of Africa followed the same course in promoting further legal change. Nevertheless, one can identify the pattern of change. New systems of law, based on commonly held legal assumptions, are being created in the various African countries. Part of that process has included the increased international interaction on legal development. No one need be surprised to find West African lawyers, trained in the English Inns of Court, serving as judges in East Africa, or to find American lawyers teaching law in Ethiopia, or

16. J. N. D. Anderson, "The Future of Islamic Law in British Commonwealth Territories in Africa," in *African Law: New Law for New Nations,* ed. Hans W. Baade (Dobbs Ferry, N.Y.: Oceana Publications, 1963), pp. 89–90.

17. *Encyclopaedia Britannica,* 1968, s.v. "Ethiopia, Ancient: The Silver Age and the Decline of Geᶜez."

Australian lawyers teaching law in Tanzania. Such developments have been possible because of the similarity of concepts, processes, and methods of legal reasoning found in Western legal systems—despite their differences in detail. They have also been possible because of the similarity of legal issues found in modern society, again despite the differences in detail in resolving them.

The trend toward the development of unified national legal systems in Africa has been uneven, and nowhere has this goal been reached. The complete unification of law would, in fact, presuppose considerable internal adjustments in those nations composed of mixed societies. The unification of marriage laws, for instance, would be a step of momentous significance in a country where both monogamy and polygamy are practiced and where these practices are sanctioned by ethnic tradition or by religion. A similar momentous change would be the unification of land law on, for example, a leasehold or freehold basis. On the other hand, the unification of commercial law might be accomplished relatively easily and would meet with little resistance from traditional groups. We should note, however, that changes of law by legislation may not indicate a real change in legal practice. The abstract standard and the concrete fact may be far apart; law and society may be "out of phase."

The change that has taken place in the law of Africa has been gradual and can be illustrated by the lengthy and complex introduction of the English common law into Africa. The system of common law was alien to Africa. It developed in England from feudal law, and after a long process it was so modified that it could be applied to a highly industrialized society, with considerable emphasis placed on rights, procedures, and "constitutionalism." The transfer of common law principles to a territory outside England was not without precedent. Several of the American states had adopted English common law; for instance, the constitution of the state of Illinois, enacted in 1818, provided that

> the common law of England, so far as the same is applicable and of a general nature, and all statutes or acts of the British Parliament made in aid of and to supply the defects of the common law, prior to the fourth year of James the First, . . . and which are of a general nature and not local to that kingdom, shall be the rule of decision, and shall be considered as of full force until repealed by legislative authority.

In a similar fashion, an ordinance of 1876 relating to the Gold Coast (now Ghana) provided that

> the common law, the doctrines of equity, and the statutes of general application which were in force in England at the date when the colony obtained a local legislature, that is to say, on the 24th day of July, 1874, shall be in force within the jurisdiction of the court.[18]

18. Gold Coast Supreme Court Ordinance, No. 4 of 1876, quoted by Daniels, *The Common Law in West Africa*, p. 121.

In commenting on the transfer of the common law to Africa, Lord Denning made the following comment:

> Just as with an oak, so with the English common law. You cannot transplant it to the African continent and expect it to retain the tough character which it has in England. It will flourish indeed but it needs careful tending. So with the common law. It has many principles of manifest justice and good sense which can be applied with advantage to peoples of every race and colour all the world over; but it has also many refinements, subtleties and technicalities which are not suited to other folk. These off-shoots must be cut away. In these far off lands the people must have a law which they understand and which they will respect. The common law cannot fulfill this role except with considerable qualifications. The task of making these qualifications is entrusted to the judges of these lands. It is a great task.[19]

The English common law was introduced into Africa on an eclectic basis. All aspects of the law were not included; it did not apply to everyone, even those living within the same "jurisdiction"; and the vast bulk of the peoples continued to live under customary law, in whole or in part. But customary law was in turn modified indirectly by the new legal system, with its different concepts and procedures, and by the procedures followed by the new courts.

The common law system was extended gradually over time, in some cases by including people within the jurisdiction of the new courts who were otherwise "outside" the law, and by increasing the number and kind of offenses. An early example of the extension of the system to include people not within the settled areas is found in the West African Offences Act, 1871, which provided that

> the inhabitants of certain territories in Africa [adjoining the settlements of Sierra Leone, Gambia, Gold Coast, Lagos, and adjacent protectorates] not being within the jurisdiction of any civilized government, and crimes and outrages having been and being likely . . . to be committed within such territories against British subjects and persons resident within any of the said settlements, [it was requisite] to provide for the trial and punishment of such crimes and such outrages. [Crimes or offences committed within twenty miles of the boundaries of the settlements] or by persons not subjects of any civilised power [against British subjects or persons resident within the settlements] shall be cognizable in the superior courts exercising criminal jurisdiction within any of the said settlements [and shall be tried, prosecuted, and punished in] the same manner as if the crime or offence had been committed within such settlements.[20]

The introduction of English common law was normally accompanied by two types of reservations, called respectively the "residual clause" and the "repugnancy clause," each of which has played its part in developing, modifying,

19. *Nyali Ltd.* v. *A.-G.*, [1955] 1 All E.R., 646, 653.
20. Daniels, *The Common Law in West Africa*, p. 33.

preserving, transforming, and expanding the laws of Africa. The two clauses were expressed in various forms, but the purpose was the same—to provide a degree of flexibility in the application of the common law. In the British Settlements Act, 1843, the residual clause provided that such laws and courts should be established "as may be necessary for the peace, order and good government" of the territories concerned. In Sierra Leone, the Courts Ordinance provided that where no rule was applicable to a matter in controversy, "the court shall be governed by the principles of justice, equity, and good conscience."[21] An explanation for the inclusion of a residual clause was given by Justice Brandford Griffith in the Nigerian case of *Cole v. Cole* (1898):

> These words show that the legislature was well aware that it could not lay down specific rules as to where native law and custom was to apply and where it was not to apply. It was aware that cases must arise for which it could not possibly provide, accordingly it framed the section in very general terms, expressly specifying one particular class of transaction in which natives should not take advantage of native law and custom, and finally giving the court large discretionary powers.[22]

The repugnancy clause was also expressed in various ways. A Gambian ordinance provided that no person should be deprived of any law or custom existing in Gambia, "such law or custom not being repugnant to natural justice, equity, and good conscience." Judges in the Cape Coast (in what is now Ghana) were to observe "such of the local customs . . . as may be compatible with the principles of the law of England." Other expressions included "not repugnant to Christianity or to natural justice," or "natural justice and morality," or "natural justice and humanity." The French used the expression "*coûtumes compatible avec la civilisation occidentale*." In Belgian and Portuguese territories, "indigenous laws which were prejudicial to the *ordere publique*" were denied recognition.[23]

Several cases illustrate the use of the repugnancy clause. In *Gwao bin Kilimo v. Kisunda bin Ifuti* (1938),[24] Mange, a government clerk, was convicted for converting another's money to his own use. The respondent brought an action against Mange for the return of the money. In executing the judgment given in his favor, the respondent attached property belonging to Gwao, Mange's father. According to the evidence presented, it was the practice of the Wanyaturu, in certain cases, for a father to pay compensation voluntarily for cattle stolen by his son or he could be compelled to do so. The issue was thus posed: Was customary law applicable in this case, in which event Gwao's property could perhaps be taken in execution of the judgment against his son; and if applicable, was the custom "repugnant to natural justice, equity, and good conscience"? The judge thought it was not right to take away a man's property in order to compensate

21. *Ibid.*, pp. 120–21, 291.
22. 1 N.L.R. 15, at 21, 22 (1898).
23. Daniels, *The Common Law in West Africa*, pp. 254, 267.
24. (1938) 1 T.L.R. (R), 403.

a party injured at the hands of the man's son. "It is against our general ideas of justice," he said, "that a man should suffer or be punished directly either in person or in property for some wrong which he has not done himself." Thus, one of the understood principles of customary law, the legal responsibility of kinship groups for individual behavior, was overruled.

In another case, the procedures followed in deposing a chief were declared void because they did not follow "principles of natural justice." These were here interpreted to mean "rules of procedure so fundamental in any system of law that their observance is obligatory on every court of law." The plaintiff, who had held the title of chief for some ten years, "was 'drummed out' of the Iwarefa body by his fellow Iwarefa chiefs in a way which amounted to taking matters into their own hands."

The repugnancy clause was also used by the court to defeat stale claims. In the case of *Ado* v. *Wusu*, the defendant claimed that he and his family had been undisturbed in occupation of land for nearly 200 years without paying tribute. The plaintiff claimed, however, that his ancestor had permitted the defendant's ancestor to settle on the land in dispute and that it was now his land. The plaintiff won the case in the lower court, but the decision was reversed on appeal. The court reasoned as follows:

> We accept the finding and entirely agree that in accordance with strict native law and custom the plaintiff remains the owner. But there is a long series of decisions in which it has been laid down that the courts will not allow the strict native law and custom to be invoked in such cases as this when the effect is, in equity, unjust.[25]

The same rule against stale claims has been developed in Kenya, but according to one commentator it has not found acceptance with the people:

> In so far as customary land law is concerned, the rule or observation by the Kenya Court of Review that to allow stale claims for possession is repugnant to justice, equity and good conscience, is not regarded by the law consumers as part of their customary law. As a result litigation after ligitation concerning the same problem occurs. In this one may be led to believe that these judicial pronouncements intended to reform a rule of customary law tenure have no effect among the people they are intended to guide. Here the judicial rule is not working.[26]

The fact that a court finds a particular practice "repugnant" does not necessarily modify the custom or even make it illegal. In the words of Lord Atkin, the court can reject a customary law but it "cannot itself transform barbarous custom into a milder one."[27] W. C. E. Daniels has said that the declaration that a custom is repugnant

25. (1938) 4 W.A.C.A., 96.
26. L. L. Kato, "Methodology of Law Reform," in *East African Law and Social Change*, ed. G. G. A. Sawyerr (Nairobi: East African Publishing House, 1967), p. 293.
27. *Eshugbayi Eleko* v. *Government of Nigeria*, A.C. 662, at 673 (1931).

does not imply that it is illegal. In fact the practice can still go on publicly, after a judge's decision in a particular case. What it does imply is that the High Court will not allow itself to be made the instrument to observe, or enforce the observance of, a customary law which is repugnant.[28]

An analogous question is whether the court should apply native law and custom even though it is not repugnant. In the nineteenth-century case of *Cole* v. *Cole*, the issue was raised whether the succession to the property of a Christian African, who was married by Christian rites outside the colony, was governed by the Marriage Ordinance of Nigeria, the English law of succession, or customary law. The judge held that the case was governed by the English law of succession:

> When the court has before it a matter which is purely native, or where all the circumstances to be taken into account are connected with native life, habit, or custom, then undoubtedly native law and custom should apply. . . . Does this mean that the court is bound to observe native customs or to allow native customs to apply in every case of a native where the custom is not repugnant to natural justice, etc., . . . nor incompatible with any local Ordinance? I think not.[29]

CRIMINAL LAW

The Western system of criminal law is highly rationalized and specific, the product of a particular type of political organization. When we think of criminal law we tend to think in terms of Western criminal law. Criminal law makes certain assumptions about the kind of behavior which must be suppressed and the agency responsible for suppressing it. Certain offenses are "crimes" and are subject to prosecution by the "state"; other offenses are "torts" and are subject to "civil action." This distinction — a fine one at times — between a crime and a tort has been developed historically, the product of much controversy, litigation, and the application of moral standards. A further fine distinction has developed between the abstract state and a concrete person with abstract rights. In modern times, criminal law is always written, an exception to the common law practice of "finding law" by referring to past cases; and the process for bringing criminal prosecutions is highly proceduralized. So the following question can be raised: It is possible for something called "criminal law" to exist in a society not organized in the form of a "state"? The answer, of course, depends on how one defines the relevant categories of criminal law. There are some analogies between African and Western criminal law, but the "fit" is not always precise.

The argument has been advanced that in many African societies all wrongs

28. *The Common Law in West Africa*, p. 286.
29. (1898) 1 N.L.R. 15, at 21.

are penal, or again that wrongs treated in Western law as crimes, such as murder and theft, are treated in some African societies as matters for private redress. There is no one standard to follow. Eugene Cotran, who has examined traditional law in many African societies, has concluded that "most African societies do make a distinction between crimes and civil wrongs."[30] He quotes Schapera, who wrote (in *Tswana Law and Custom*) that Tswana law (of contemporary Botswana), in practice if not in theory, "is divided by the people themselves into two main classes. These may quite conveniently be termed 'civil law' and 'criminal law' respectively although their categories are by no means identical with those of European systems of law." He also draws on Haydon, who wrote (in *Law and Justice in Buganda*) that in ancient Buganda it is probable that

> certain crimes such as treason against the Kabaka, witchcraft, incest, sexual perversions, adultery with the royal wives or chief's wife, theft and cowardice in war were classed as crimes against the State and were punished with death or at the least mutilation. Other offences were dealt with as torts and were settled by the payment of compensation to the injured party.

Although there is evidence that such a distinction exists, Cotran says,

> it is more difficult to put forward a general definition of what are regarded as crimes for all African societies. Different societies may have different bases for distinguishing between crimes and torts: (1) trial may be in different courts adopting different types of procedure, e.g., criminal offences before the chief or counsellors, and civil before clan or family elders; (2) sanctions may be different, e.g., capital punishment, banishment, social ostracism and public ridicule, mutilation and flogging for crimes; reconciliation, restitution and compensation for civil wrongs; (3) crimes are wrongs contrary to the basic beliefs of the community, whilst civil wrongs are directed against the individual.[31]

In modern times, far-reaching changes have been made in the field of criminal law. The procedures and substance of Western law have largely replaced customary law with regard to criminal matters. The introduction of criminal law is another example of how written codes may be more easily transferred between systems than abstract principles of law based on precedent. For instance, the present Criminal Code of Ghana was based on an Ordinance of 1892, which in turn was based on a criminal code drafted in 1877 for Jamaica. Although the code was not adopted in Jamaica, it eventually became law for St. Lucia, British Honduras, St. Vincent, Grenada, and the Gold Coast (Ghana). The Nigerian Criminal Code Ordinance of 1916 was modeled on the Criminal Code Act of Queensland (Australia), 1889, which in turn was based on the draft of the

---

30. "The Position of Customary Law in African Countries," in Sawyerr, *East African Law and Social Change*, p. 14.
    31. *Ibid.*, p. 15.

English Criminal Code of 1879 and on the penal codes of Italy and of the state of New York. The Penal Code Law of Northern Nigeria, adopted in 1959, is based on the Sudan Penal Code, which in turn was adopted from the Indian Penal Code. The latter has been described as "the criminal law of England freed from all technicalities and superfluities systematically arranged and modified in some few particulars . . . to suit the circumstances of British India."[32]

ISLAMIC LAW AND ETHIOPIAN LAW

Islamic law in Africa is of major significance in the inland Sudanic belt, stretching from Senegal to the Republic of the Sudan. J. N. D. Anderson has remarked that

> Islam has penetrated, or is still penetrating, many parts of the continent, and the influence of Islamic law has been widely spread, superficially at least, through Muslim merchants and members of the religious orders. As a result the indigenous customary law has been leavened, in certain areas, by Islamic principles and precedents—to a degree which differs widely, of course, from place to place. In certain areas, moreover, it has been virtually displaced by the law of Islam, particularly where a native ruler has attempted to impose this law upon his people. But nowhere in tropical Africa has the imposition been complete, for traces of the customary law survive even in the most rigidly Muslim areas.[33]

Anderson has raised the question of whether an authoritative law, which is regarded as firmly based on divine revelation, can so adapt itself, or be adapted, as to enable it to resolve the typical conflicts of an industrial society. His answer in affirmative, based on the fact that Islamic law has changed not only in Africa but in other Muslim countries as well. In criminal and commercial law, in the law of evidence and procedure, and in large parts of the civil codes, "Islamic law has been quietly put on one side."

There has been less change in the sphere of Islamic family law and succession. Matters dealing with divorce, inheritance, adoption, and marriage are still largely guided by the tenets of Maliki law, the predominant Islamic legal school in West and North Africa. In such cases, there is often a National Shari'a Court of Appeals to adjudicate such civil disputes on the highest level. In only one African state with an important Muslim minority (Ivory Coast) has national legislation curtailed the Islamic practice of legally allowing four wives.

32. *History of Criminal Law of England*, III, 300, quoted by Daniels, *The Common Law in West Africa*, pp. 249–50.
33. "The Future of Islamic Law," p. 89.

The process by which Islamic law, particularly Islamic criminal law, has come to be modified in the modern period is summarized by Anderson:

> Muslim countries have contrived to effect reforms in what purports (at least) to be still Islamic law by a variety of ingenious devices. One is a procedural device, by which parts of the Islamic law are simply precluded from judicial enforcement (or even recognition). Another, which has been given the widest possible application, consists in an eclectic selection of principles for which some support can be found among the heterogeneous Muslim authorities of the past, and the promulgation of these principles in the form of statute law. Yet another, which has received less acknowledgment, represents a reinterpretation of the ancient texts in a manner more acceptable to contemporary opinion. And each of these is at times reinforced by statutory regulations which are represented as augmenting, rather than contradicting, the sacred law.[34]

Turning to the other major body of customary codified law in Africa, Ethiopian law, a similar process of revision is evident. Indeed, one of the most singular developments in African law has been the adoption by Ethiopia of six basic codes which now constitute the body of law in that country. The adoption of these codes provides Ethiopia with one of the most modern legal systems in Africa. The six new codes are the Penal Code of 1957 (amending the Penal Code of 1930); the Civil Code, the Maritime Code, and the Commercial Code, all of 1960; the Criminal Procedure Code of 1961; and the Civil Procedure Code of 1965.

The new codes supplanted the body of customary law, which had not been unified or codified. According to one observer,

> The principal origins of law were the *Fetha Negast*, for the Coptic-Christian populations of the ancient provinces; the Moslem law, for the populations of Harrar and the coastal areas of the Red Sea; and the customary law, for the other regions of the country which are considered more "African" in the popular sense.[35]

The preamble of the 1930 Penal Code pointed out that

> the principles of the modern European Codes used as models are still often very close to those which are found expressed in the *Fetha Negast*. "Whether common sources had been transmitted by way of Rome, as in Europe, or by Alexandria, as in Ethiopia, on many points the Roman-Occidental conception, reflected in the Ethiopian tradition, joined together and easily allowed the modernization of the work on this ground."[36]

34. *Ibid.*, p. 96.
35. Jean Graven, "The Penal Code of the Empire of Ethiopia, 1959," in *Materials on Comparative Criminal Law as Based upon the Penal Codes of Ethiopia and Switzerland*, ed. Steven Lowenstein (Addis Ababa: Faculty of Law, Haile Sellassie I University, 1965), p. 57.
36. *Ibid.*, p. 59.

THE GROWTH OF AFRICAN STATUTE LAW

We have noted earlier the significance for African law of the introduction of new institutions capable of creating law, that is, the legislature and the bureaucracy. Both types of institutions have initiated extensive legal changes. The introduction of new machinery for making law is reminiscent of the development of the legislative function of Parliament in the sixteenth century. Thomas Smith, writing in 1583, gave his impressions of this development, where, in his words, the Crown in Parliament "can make and unmake law, can change rights and possessions of private men, legitimate bastards, establish religions, condemn or absolve (by its attainders, etc.) whomsoever the Prince will."[37] Legislation has been used for many purposes, including the modification of customary law. Slavery has been abolished by statute; trial by ordeal became an offense against the Criminal Code.

At the local level in Africa new assemblies made it possible to adapt customary law to modern needs. In Ghana, for instance, the power of chiefs to abolish inequitable custom is regulated by the Chieftaincy Act (1961): "If the law is uncertain or it is considered desirable that it should be modified, or assimilated by the common law, the Council is empowered to make representations to the House of Chiefs having jurisdiction over the area." The chiefs can also "draft a declaration of what in their opinion is the customary law relating to any subject in its area or any part thereof."[38]

Legislatures have also been used to modify "received law." An example of this is found in the idea proposed in Ghana of incorporated private partnerships. The Gower Report stated:

> The principal weakness of the present type of partnership as an organisation for African business is that the firm has no separate existence and that the partnership is automatically dissolved on the death or retirement of any partner. Under this Bill, a distinction is drawn between the *partnership* relationship and the *firm*. The former is dissolved on the death or retirement of any partner. But the firm (the business itself) on registration of the partnership becomes a separate legal entity capable of permanent survival and its life is not destroyed by a change in the constitution of the partnership.[39]

In Tanzania, to give another example, freehold tenure has been abolished and freehold has been converted to ninety-nine years held by the government. Legislation has given boards and commissions extensive control over land held under customary law. An act relating to rights of occupancy makes

37. *De Republica Anglorum* [1584], quoted by T. F. T. Plucknett, *A Concise History of the Common Law*, 5th ed. (Boston: Little, Brown, 1958), p. 263.
38. Daniels, *The Common Law in West Africa*, p. 290.
39. L. C. B. Gower, *Final Report on Company Law in Ghana* (Accra, 1961), p. 308.

far-reaching changes in the rules relating to ownership and holding interests in the land. Where the law is unclear or open-ended, as it is in many places, it is an administrator or an administrative tribunal which is charged with the duty of giving it coherent meaning and not a court.[40]

The Range Development and Management Act of 1964 had the effect of enclosing land against pastoralists:

> [It] is designed to create a legal framework for the conversion and development of range areas—specifically so for the Masai district. . . . The Minister, after consultation with a commission, may make rules prohibiting and restricting entry into the area, providing that certain categories of persons must have residence certificates to be able to reside in the area, and empowering the Commission to issue permits of entry and erect road barriers to control entry into the area. . . . All these rules, orders, and measures are taken on the basis that customary law still applies to the land in the range development area, but clearly their effect will often be to alter or make redundant some of these rules, and this alteration is being done by an administrative body which has no standing in the traditional society and which is not under any obligation to investigate the existence or content of customary rules governing the same matters before acting.[41]

There is a highly abstract character to some of these legislative enactments, and it may be another case where statute law and the living law are "out of phase."

INTEGRATION AND INTERRELATION OF LEGAL SYSTEMS

The trend in modern Africa is clearly toward the integration of law within a unified national legal system. This is the goal, however slow or fast the pace or whatever the approach. The integration of law has been considered part of the process of nation-building, and in some states, such as Tanzania and Ethiopia, integration has been promoted as a device for increasing national unity. The complexity of national integration as a background for legal integration is summarized by Robert B. Seidman:

> This, then, was the matrix for the law of English-speaking Africa at independence: a dichotomous society, sharply split between the subsistence economy with its associated culture and law and the commercial-industrial private, Westernized sector; a pluralistic legal order; demands upon the legal orders that implied fundamentally irreconcilable jural postulates—status, contract, and plan; and a governing elite

40. J. P. W. B. McAuslan, "Control of Land and Agricultural Development in Kenya and Tanzania," in Sawyerr, *East African Law and Social Change,* p. 184.
41. *Ibid.*, pp. 187–88.

for whom law was more frequently a restriction to be avoided than a tool for the rational application of state power.[42]

The place of customary law in the process of national integration is highly controversial. On the one hand it may exacerbate ethnic societal differences, but on the other hand it may be necessary to placate the various ethnic groups. From the viewpoint of modern planning, A. Arthur Schiller writes that customary law is

> generally dismissed as of minor importance by the lawyer immersed in the legal problems of economic development, characterized as antiquarian by the policymaker, and surrendered to the anthropologist, who normally attempts to reconstitute the pristine, primitive law untainted by contact with Western ways and modern life.[43]

Seidman, for instance, whose interests are in legal planning, gives grudging recognition to the place of customary law:

> Perhaps the only valid generalization that can be made about customary law in Africa is that, in all its diversity, it has been reasonably apt to answer the problems thrown up by the subsistence economy and the existing level of technology.[44]

The unification of African customary law is being brought about through various devices, such as the "restatement projects" and codification, or, as in Ethiopia, by a series of codes which have replaced the older law. A parallel trend is found in the development of unified national court systems, with the courts having jurisdiction over all types of cases, regardless of the nature of the litigants or the type of law involved.

If customary law is brought into the legal system and thus becomes part of the "law of the land," it is necessary that the law be raised to a level of abstraction where useful principles can be deduced from a case to be applied to subsequent cases. L. T. Fallers, who has studied customary Soga law (Uganda), has described some of the problems involved in relating the Soga system to the national legal system:

> [The legal reality] for the vast majority of village-dwelling Africans is the traditional ethnic group, . . . [and the] relevant boundaries between bodies of law are not the familiar political frontiers shown on most maps but rather the many times more numerous boundaries between traditional tribes and kingdoms which appear on the maps of anthropologists.[45]

42. "Law and Economic Development in Independent, English-Speaking, Sub-Saharan Africa," in *Africa and Law: Developing Legal Systems in African Commonwealth Nations*, ed. Thomas W. Hutchison, *et. al.* (Madison: University of Wisconsin Press, 1968), pp. 27–28.
43. "Introduction," in Hutchison, *Africa and Law*, p. ix.
44. "Law and Economic Development," p. 9.
45. "Customary Law in the New African States," in Baade, *African Law*, p. 72.

This customary law is still important, according to Fallers, because "it continues to order relations among members of the community." He would like to see customary law remain vigorous and made flexible, incorporated in the national legal system and equipped with tools for further evolution, rather than "sweeping it away in a burst of legislative enthusiasm."

In Busoga, the two systems of law, customary and modern, are interrelated and may be used to reinforce each other. Marriage, for example, may be contracted under the national Marriage Ordinance, but a large majority of the Soga continue to contract customary marriages as well, through the payment of bridewealth. Fallers has found, however, that the local courts have failed to develop generalized principles and precedents as guides to future cases, and that they tend not to translate norms into more abstract principles. He writes as follows:

> The clear statement and communication of a precedent-setting decision in response to a new problem requires, if such decisions are not to be random departures from tradition, much more explicit formulation of what is being done.

At present, judges have not made such formulations. An observer must examine the whole body of testimony to get the full implications of a decision. What is required, according to Fallers, is a corps of judges and clerks who are trained in court procedure but also "in somewhat more analytical modes of reasoning":

> The writer found judges unwilling or unable to discuss abstract rules of law, generally responding to questions by saying that a rule could not be stated in the absence of all the facts of the case.[46]

An early effort toward simplifying and unifying customary law was promoted by the late Hans Cory, the former government sociologist of Tanganyika, who, in a series of *barazas* (conferences), sounded out chiefs in various parts of the country on the rules which were followed in settling local disputes. Cory hoped to secure a measure of agreement on the appropriate customary rules to be followed in various types of cases and thus to build up a body of doctrine that would assist judges in their deliberations. At the same time, it was thought that an understanding of the content of the law would make it less necessary for the judges to rely on the advice of elders and assessors who themselves might have a personal or family interest in the outcome of the case.

A later and more far-reaching development is the Restatement of African Law project, sponsored by London University, under the direction of A. N. Allott. The sponsors of the project have argued that there is a need for a restatement, or rearrangement, of African law, inasmuch as the territorial legal systems in the former British territories "are an uneasy and uncertain amalgamation of rules derived from the law of England, and rules elaborated on the spot by legislation and interpretation."[47]

46. *Ibid.*, p. 82.
47. Allott and Cotran, "A Background Paper," p. 4.

The Restatement of African Law project involves customary law as well as general law, so there is concern that legal "harmonisation or even integration with the customary and other personal laws would be promoted or achieved."[48] The project favors restatement over codification or "piecemeal judicial interpretation." Those administering and changing the law should know precisely what elements are being integrated and harmonized.

Within the African context, the restatement of law has been taking place through court decisions, where descriptions of customary law are often made in legal English. According to Allott,

> The judge is naturally tempted to accommodate African conceptions in English categories. Thus the institution of family property may be described by an English or English-trained judge in terms of joint tenancy, or corporations, or trustee-beneficiaries, or of agency—all conceptions of the English law which have to be adapted or stretched to fit the African institution.

The reverse may also take place, where legal terms are stretched to fit another legal system:

> Whenever a native court, or an African speaking an African language, has tried to apply the concepts or rules of English law to a legal situation before it or him, it is possible that such reverse restatement may take place, and the English law will be "africanised" in consequence.[49]

The restatement of African law follows certain general guidelines, which include the following: (1) inconsistencies and doubts in existing law should be removed; (2) local divergencies should be resolved, or at least noted and compared; (3) the applicable law should be stated in as precise language as possible; (4) restatements of one kind of law must employ a uniform terminology; (5) the restatements must have as much authority as scientific scholarship can give; and (6) there must be arrangements for periodic revision to conform to new interpretations and the changing society in which the law operates.[50]

In theory, at any rate, the unification of law has gone further in Tanzania than in any other African state. Schiller has commented on this development:

> The restatement of the customary law in Tanzania was from the start a first step towards the unification of the law. Nyerere called for a unified code as a vital element in the building of a nation state. Government officials met with tribal representatives chosen by district councils in order to ascertain the rules applicable in the fields of family law and succession throughout the Bantu patrilineal tribes of the country. They prepared uniform statements of the law and submitted these draft pronouncements to local authorities. Although in many instances the rules

48. *Ibid.*, p. 8.
49. *Ibid.*, p. 9.
50. *Ibid.*, p. 10.

proposed varied considerably from the local practice, these declarations were accepted by the district councils and were promulgated as rules of law binding upon the courts. Hence, unification of the customary law of most of the Bantu peoples of Tanzania has been accomplished, at least in the printed notices issued as supplements to the official gazette.[51]

UNIFICATION OF AFRICAN LAW THROUGH COURTS

African law has also been unified through the development of a national system of courts. When foreign legal systems were introduced into Africa there was a tendency to create specific courts having jurisdiction over specific peoples or laws. Local courts, for the most part, applied customary law and had jurisdiction over Africans. The newly created courts, if not the law, were a foreign import and provided a new form into which the old law would have to fit. Whether the new local courts were in fact "native courts" depended in part on the perspective from which they were viewed. Writing in 1957, Bohannan said:

> There are today two folk systems operative in Tivland. There is that scheme of looking at social institutions which characterizes the tribal Africans and which includes their views not merely of "indigenous institutions" but also of European inspired and dominated institutions. There is also the scheme of looking at things which characterizes a colonial administration and is shared more or less fully by other local Europeans; it includes views not merely of governmental and mission institutions, but also of other African institutions into which the Europeans do not enter directly. The two systems are seldom congruous.
>
> Therefore it is not surprising that administrative officers and other Europeans living in Tivland refer to those bodies officially termed "Grade-D courts" as "native courts," while the Tiv refer to them as "government courts".[52]

With the passage of time and the increased mobility of the people, it has been necessary to develop a legal system with greater flexibility. The present trend points toward a unified legal system, with the courts having jurisdiction over all types of persons and cases. The rationalization for this development was made in 1951 in a report which stated:

> As any modern secular state develops, if it is to keep free of communal or racial strife, there comes a time when special courts for particular classes of inhabitants must give way to general courts for all manner of men. We think the time has come now in this country, and we therefore recommend that local courts should have authority . . . over all persons.[53]

51. "Introduction," in Hutchison, *Africa and Law*, p. xiii.
52. Bohannan, *Justice and Judgment*, p. 7.
53. *Korsah Report of Native Courts in the Gold Coast* (Accra, 1951), p. 24.

Concomitant with the development of a common court system is the attempt to introduce, in the English-speaking countries, English procedures and rules of evidence. The result is that customary procedure is being assimilated by the English court system. In Ghana, customary law has been assimilated with the common law, to be applied where applicable; but it would not be applied where the "proper law" of a transaction was a non-customary law. A law case, in other words, might contain elements of customary law, common law, and legislation, and it would be heard by courts in a single system rather than by courts created for the type of law they are to administer.

In Uganda the unification of courts is well advanced. According to G. F. A. Sawyerr,

> Magistrates' courts of all grades are now empowered to apply one body of law with many components—local statutes, the received English law and customary law—each component applied presumably in an appropriate case.[54]

The concept of "membership of a customary community," Sawyerr writes, has in some places replaced the term "native" or "African," but this concept of community in turn raises new legal problems, such as the types of acts which make one a member of the community, and the question of acceptance or rejection by the community.

In Tanzania, where extensive integration of law courts has taken place, the Magistrates Courts Act of 1963 established a single hierarchy of courts, consisting of primary courts, district courts, resident magistrates' courts, and the High Court. The primary courts were given general civil jurisdiction

> over causes of action governed by customary or Islamic law, and certain other matters in respect of which jurisdiction was specifically conferred by statute. Original jurisdiction over marriage, guardianship and inheritance under customary law, and certain types of immovable property was confined exclusively to Primary courts.

Although the jurisdiction of the primary courts is concerned mainly with matters controlled by customary law, "It is not limited to these and . . . it is not defined by reference to the race of the parties."[55]

The development and systemization of African law has not been completed and its further development will require additional effort by all segments of the new African states. The training of judges, lawyers, and legislators with proper expertise, the explanation of the law to the people, and the enrichment of ideas concerning rights, legitimacy, and due process are items of concern. Research is also necessary in developing a unified and interrelated legal system and in learning how the law affects the life of the people. One of the most

54. "Internal Conflict of Laws in East Africa," in Sawyerr, *East African Law and Social Change*, p. 141.
55. *Ibid.*, pp. 118–19.

important areas of research in the development of African law is that relating to the conflict of law, or, in lay language, the interrelationship of legal systems, when more than one system of law is involved in a case. This problem has been stated by Sawyerr:

> Due to the constant intercourse between peoples subject to these various laws, it is inevitable that from time to time cases coming before the courts will raise issues which, because of the identity of the parties or the nature or form of a transaction, have contacts with more than one of these systems of law. In such circumstances a court may be called upon to select the particular system by the rules of which to decide the issues.[56]

Internal conflict of law may occur, in Allott's words,

> when a judge is required to choose between two or more systems of law which are not territorially distinct, i.e., which apply concurrently and without spatial separation within a single territorial jurisdiction. There is thus an overlap between one system and another, which cannot be removed merely by drawing a boundary on the ground.[57]

Conflict may occur between general law and customary law, between different systems of customary law, between customary law and Islamic law, between schools of Islamic law, and between different national systems of law.

Another area of research relates to the impact of legal change on the people. Is the new law accepted, or do the litigants resolve their disputes outside the legal system? There is the possibility that legal change will be little more than an exercise in conceptualization and that legislation or even judgments will not represent the actual living law. In the words of L. L. Kato:

> Law reform is the process whereby the "desired free law" may take the form of "formal law" like a statute or a precedent. It is the incorporation of the practices and desires of the law consumers into a legally recognized category. . . . The problem of law reform involves a re-examination of the working of the concept of justice, i.e., the justice of an individual rule or decision as well as the justice of the legal system as a whole.[58]

Schiller has sounded a word of caution on the dangers of separating law from its popular base:

> If future judgments are rendered by magistrates who are strangers to the community, and if they are based upon principles dictated by the central government and at odds with well-established and recognized rules of the local customary law, there is good reason to expect less resorting to the state judiciary. For these de-

56. *Ibid.*, p. 110.
57. A. N. Allott, *Essays in African Law* (London: Butterworth, 1960), p. 154.
58. "Methodology of Law Reform," pp. 279, 281.

cisions would have little or no weight in enhancing one's position in the give and take leading towards settlement. A diminution in the use of the courts means an increase in the number of traditional arbitral hearings. The nullification of the judicial process on the part of a substantial element of the rural population is a serious danger. It is a giant step back on the road to tribalism.[59]

The problems of African legal development are considerable. They include the conceptual framework of the law itself. In addition, the creation of legal institutions and the training or retraining of personnel are formidable tasks. It is of significance that much of the recent political instability of African states has not affected the embryonic legal systems. The future of African legal systems rests more directly with the processes of adapting law, whether customary or Western, to the needs of national states which are ever bending under the winds of change.

59. Schiller, "Introduction," in Hutchison, *Africa and Law*, p. xviii.

24

Economic Systems Development

ARNOLD RIVKIN

AN OVERVIEW OF ECONOMY-BUILDING IN AFRICA

GENERALLY SPEAKING, the colonial territories in Africa have come to independence with dual economies—that is, economies with a traditional and a modern sector. Most of the new states have relatively small modern sectors in which production is for the market and the exchange of goods is achieved through the use of currency. Most also have large subsistence sectors in which production is primarily for home consumption, and such exchange of surplus goods as occurs is largely unplanned and frequently carried on through barter, with only limited use of currency. The two sectors converge or intersect at various points—such as the withdrawal of labor from the subsistence sector by the modern sector, and the remittance of cash wages by migratory labor in the modern sector to their families in the subsistence sector—but by and large the economic circuits and links between the two sectors are circumscribed and limited. Thus, every African state is confronted with the need for developing new economic structures, that is, for extending the market sector or monetizing the subsistence sector. What is required is the development of economic structures that involve the production of goods for the market, to be distributed through established marketing channels, with payment in currency or through credits extended by recognized banking institutions.

Most of the modern economic structures in Africa have been overwhelmingly concerned with primary production of agricultural and mineral products for the export market. There has been a tendency throughout the colonial period and into the first decade of independence for African countries to emphasize production for the export market almost to the total exclusion of rational cash-crop agriculture and industrial production for the domestic market. This tendency is understandable. Since the advent of the European presence in

498

Africa the export market has accounted for, and still accounts for, the largest part of Africa's vitally needed foreign exchange; this, in turn, is used for financing imports and also, more recently, for financing national development plans and the growth of the domestic private sector. The tendency has, however, increasingly resulted in the unnecessary use of foreign exchange to finance the import of foodstuffs to feed growing urban areas and of the types of consumer goods which would logically provide the starting point and impetus for internal industrialization.

Thus, notwithstanding the growth of economic activity directed toward the export market, the rationalization and modernization of complementary economic activity to produce cash crops and consumer goods for the expanding domestic market has tended to lag. What is required is the extension of the market-sector structure of African economies to accommodate production of cash goods for the domestic market as well as for the export market in combinations appropriate to the circumstances of the various African countries. Similarly, private foreign investment needs to be thought of as a source of financing not only modern production for the African export market (for example, exploitation and plantation agriculture) but also the development of production for the domestic market.

Frequently, too, African production has been of a single-crop or two-crop variety. Many African states have been, and remain, dependent on the production of a single agricultural commodity for 60 per cent or more of their foreign exchange earnings (for example, the dependence of Ghana on cocoa, Senegal and Gambia on peanuts, Dahomey on palm kernels and palm kernel oil, Sudan on cotton, Ethiopia on coffee, and Somalia on bananas). In several instances African countries have been similarly dependent on the production of a single mineral for 75 per cent or more of their foreign exchange earnings (for example, the dependence of Zambia on copper and Libya on petroleum). In only a few instances have African economic structures been based on multiple crops or on a combination of agricultural and mineral output (for example, Nigeria and Congo-Kinshasa).

In some instances the production of semiprocessed and processed primary agricultural and forest products has been gaining in importance in the export earnings of African countries, as in the extraction and refining of peanut, palm, and palm kernel oil; and washing, grading, and packaging of coffee; and the processing of hardwoods and the manufacturing of plywood. There has also been an increase in some African countries (for example, Nigeria and Gabon) in the refining of crude oil with a corresponding increase in export earnings or import savings. There has been mounting pressure to expand the processing of crude ores within African countries in order to increase the value of exports: plans are now under way to provide more refining capacity for copper in Zambia; and in a few countries, such as Guinea, the processing of bauxite into the intermediate product of alumina has been introduced. Industrial production has generally played a very small part in African export earnings, with the exception of the Republic of South Africa and, to a lesser degree, Rhodesia, which has been a key industrial supplier to Malawi and Zambia; but in a growing number of cases, industrial production for the domestic market has been expanding to include commodities such as processed and canned foods, textiles and clothing, cigarettes, soft drinks and beer, light household utensils and pottery, and building goods.

There is thus a widespread need in African countries to diversify production by enlarging the range of primary products produced, by increasing the degree of processing of these commodities, and by introducing industrial production on an increasing scale to serve both growing internal and, in the long run, external markets. The Yaounde Convention, which, through May, 1969, governed the association of eighteen African states with the European Common Market, provided for a special productivity and diversification fund of $230 million to help African states to meet these needs.

In addition to these basic structural changes involved in African economy-building, the new states are confronted with major philosophical decisions as to the type of economy they want to build. Should it be an economy with a larger or smaller state-controlled sector? Should it be an economy which encourages private investment, local and foreign, and seeks to develop a significant private sector? Should it be an economy which encourages independent voluntary institutions, such as trade unions, agricultural cooperatives, chambers of commerce, and smallholder farmers' groups, and permits them to share in economic decision-making?

The new states have tended to assign a major role in economy-building to the government and to minimize the role of private entrepreneurs and independent institutions. To some extent this trend is an inevitable consequence of the shortage of capital in the hands of private individuals and, in some areas, of the lack of experience and cultural tradition conducive to economic activity involving production for the market. In part it has grown out of the psychological compulsion of the new African states to catch up with the world's modern affluent states, as well as from the need to carefully allocate scarce resources.

In addition, an ideological preference has made itself manifest for a vague but fairly common economic objective frequently called "economic independence" and for an equally vague but common philosophy called "African Socialism." These terms are seldom defined but have been employed to describe both heavily state-dominated economies, such as those of Guinea, Mali, and Tanzania, and relatively open economies, such as those of Senegal and Kenya. Frequently what is meant by both terms is reduction of the once predominant role of the former colonial power in the trade, investment, and aid patterns of the recently independent African state or dilution of that role through the introduction of trade, investment, and aid patterns with states other than the former colonial power. These objectives have required an increase in state participation and control over the country's economy. In some cases, as in Guinea and Mali, egalitarian concepts of developing (or "preserving") classless societies have been associated with the terms "economic independence" and "African Socialism"; and sometimes, as in Tanzania, concepts of "communalism" with respect to ownership and organization of production have been read into the meaning of the two terms; perhaps most often, as in Senegal, Tunisia, and several other states, the concept of a more equitable and even distribution of income and wealth in society than has traditionally prevailed has been implied in the use of the two terms.

Finally, as Crawford Young observed in his essay in this volume, state-dominated economies with large public sectors have been associated with oligarchic or authoritarian one-party states. It would seem contradictory to seek to centralize and control all political power and at the same time encourage and sanction the development of independent economic power outside the control of the single, comprehensive political party. The dominant party inevitably feels the need to avoid competitive or conflicting poles of power and to control economic units or groups, such as trade unions, cooperatives, and trade associations, which, although they may be economically motivated, dispose of significant political power. At any rate, this has been the trend. The evolution of Ghanaian one-party authoritarianism before the military coup of February, 1966, was accompanied by just such an evolution of government combined with party control of the country's economic structure. There are many examples of comparable situations.

In only a limited number of cases have African countries sought to develop large private sectors which have substantial local as well as foreign investment and participation. Nigeria prior to the 1966 coup was perhaps the outstanding example (with the exception of South Africa) of an African country with an important and growing private sector involving an increasing number of indigenous as well as overseas investors and personnel. In lesser and varying degrees the oligarchic party-states of Ivory Coast and Kenya have also had growing private sectors, attributable in large part, however, to foreign private investment. It would be difficult to predict what would happen in these countries if and when significant numbers of indigenous investors and personnel become involved in the economy and develop vested interests in the growing private sectors. Will the restrictive political format of the oligarchic party-state be flexible enough to accommodate the development of independent and non-party-controlled foci of economic and political power? Or will the state *cum* party control over economic activity expand the economy with a corresponding growth of the state sector but at the expense of the private sector? In other words, sooner or later, at some critical juncture, the oligarchic party-state structures, in attempting to nurture the growth of large private sectors, will inevitably be confronted with a major dilemma. Should they extend their authority over the private sectors, and in so doing transform them into public or quasi-public sectors? Or should they refrain from extending state authority over the private sectors, thus diluting their monopoly of political and economic power but possibly preparing the way for their transformation into states with multiple sources of such power, as frequently obtains in Western state systems?

AFRICAN ECONOMIC GROWTH SINCE INDEPENDENCE: OVERALL TRENDS AND PERFORMANCE

During the first half of the Decade of Development – 1960–65 – the average rate of growth of per capita real gross domestic product in Africa was among the lowest in the world, 1.4 per cent per annum. This compares with the average rate of growth for all underdeveloped countries of 2.3 per cent per annum. It also compares unfavorably with the average rate of growth of 2 per cent per annum for the period 1955–60, and of 1.8 per cent per annum for the period 1950–55. Thus, Africa in its first decade of independence has been experiencing a decline in the average rate of growth of real per capita GDP. There has also been a decline in the average rate of growth of annual GDP, from 3.9 per cent in 1950–55, and 4.2 per cent in 1955–60, to 3.6 per cent in 1960–65. There has been only a modest increase in the average rate of growth of population from 2.1 per cent in the periods 1950–55 and 1955–60, to 2.2 per cent in the period 1960–65.[1]

An average annual per capita growth rate of 1.4 per cent does not allow for more than a modest increase in consumption levels on a continent where in most countries the average annual per capita income is $100 or less (in some it is as low as $40 to $50). Furthermore, it must be noted that an average such as Africa's 1960–65 per capita growth rate of 1.4 per cent conceals extremes. In fact, a large number of African countries have been stagnating at dead center, hardly keeping pace with their estimated 2.2 per cent average annual rate of growth of population and even experiencing a decline in average annual per capita income. This is not revealed by the continental average, which also includes the relatively high growth rates of the handful of countries with greater economic potential. See Table 10 which sets out the per capita GNP of all the independent African states as of 1965. The table also reveals the sharp contrast between the economies of all the independent African states outside of South Africa (thirty-eight in number) on the one hand, and South Africa on the other.

1. International Bank for Reconstruction and Development, *World Bank and IDA Annual Report 1966/67* (Washington, D.C.: Government Printing Office, 1967), p. 26. Sources other than the one used as a basis for the foregoing computations place the average rate of growth of African population at levels as high as 2.5 to 3 per cent. Obviously, if the average rate of population growth exceeded the 2.2 per cent used here, then the average rate of growth of per capita GDP would be correspondingly lower.

TABLE 10
INDEPENDENT AFRICA:
POPULATION AND GROSS NATIONAL PRODUCT PER CAPITA, 1965
(IN U.S. DOLLARS)

Ranking (by population size)	Country	Population (Est. mid-1965)	GNP per Capita (Est. end 1965)
1	Nigeria	57,500,000	80
2	United Arab Republic	29,600,000	150
3	Ethiopia	22,600,000	55
4	South Africa (incl. South-West Africa)	18,441,000	520
5	Congo, Dem. Rep. of	15,627,000	65
6	Sudan	13,540,000	95
7	Morocco	13,323,000	180
8	Algeria	11,871,000	210
9	Tanzania	10,515,000	70
10	Kenya	9,365,000	85
11	Ghana	7,740,000	230
12	Uganda	7,551,000	100
13	Malagasy Republic	6,420,000	80
14	Cameroon	5,229,000	110
15	Upper Volta	4,858,000	50
16	Mali	4,576,000	60
17	Tunisia	4,414,000	200
18	Malawi	3,940,000	40
19	Ivory Coast	3,835,000	210
20	Zambia	3,710,000	200
21	Guinea	3,500,000	75
22	Senegal	3,490,000	170
23	Niger	3,328,000	70
24	Chad	3,307,000	65
25	Burundi	3,210,000	45
26	Rwanda	3,110,000	50
27	Somalia	2,500,000	55
28	Sierra Leone	2,367,000	140
29	Dahomey	2,365,000	60
30	Togo	1,638,000	90
31	Libya	1,617,000	490
32	Central African Rep.	1,352,000	75
33	Liberia	1,070,000	180
34	Mauritania	1,050,000	150
35	Congo (Brazzaville)	840,000	120
36	Lesotho	838,000	55
37	Botswana	559,000	55
38	Gabon	463,000	250
39	Gambia	330,000	75

Source: International Bank for Reconstruction and Development, *World Bank Atlas* (Washington, D.C., 1967), pp. 3–4.

It explains why South Africa is increasingly grouped with countries that have developed economies.[2]

The foregoing brief outline of the economic growth status of African countries during the first half of the Decade of Development — the first ten years of African independence — reveals the almost awesome magnitude of the economic development task confronting *all* of the recently independent African states (as well as the older states of Ethiopia and Liberia). It also reveals worrisome trends of stagnating and declining average annual growth rates of overall GDP and per capita income. This is true despite the frequently proclaimed national objective of economic development and the near universal adoption of economic development plans for achieving this objective throughout independent Africa.

Although rudimentary economic development plans existed in African countries prior to independence (for example, in Congo-Kinshasa and Nigeria), with independence they took on a new importance and mystique. Ghana, which achieved independence early in 1957, set the trend in development planning. Plans became the hallmark of post-independence economic status and activity in one new African state after another.[3] Unfortunately, as the foregoing growth trends show, the early experience with development planning has not been particularly successful. Few, if any, African countries have been able to come within striking distance of achieving the goals of their plans. There are many reasons for this apparently poor performance. Some plans, frequently prepared with outside assistance, have been totally lacking in realism with respect to their assumptions, scope, and goals (for example, those of Morocco, Ethiopia, Somalia, and Sierra Leone). Others were equally unrealistic in being far beyond the capability of the country to execute (for example, Ghana, Guinea, and Mali). Still others, not necessarily lacking elements of the foregoing weaknesses, fell prey to internal political instability and violence (for example, Nigeria, Sudan, and other states which have experienced military *coups d'état* since 1963). There were many other reasons for the disappointing performance, such as limitations on availability of foreign aid and foreign private investment and on foreign exchange earnings in trade. The scarcity of foreign exchange was due partly to the level of African exports and partly to the adverse movement of terms of trade against producers of certain primary products.

THE PROBLEMS OF DEVELOPMENT PLANNING

For a long time experts have been debating how much and what kind of economic development planning is appropriate for African countries in their

2. IBRD, *Annual Report*, p. 24, n. 1.
3. It should be noted, however, that Ethiopia's first five-year development plan dates from 1955.

present circumstances. Some strongly recommend what has frequently been termed comprehensive planning. This approach seeks to plan for the total economy, the private as well as the public sector—to establish not only planning objectives and goals but also quantitative targets, frequently including production targets. Another school of experts, who are in effect "anti-planning" planners, would restrict African planning to the identification of a handful of priority projects in the public sector. In between these two extremes there are planners who would seek somehow to impart a sense of order and priority to the use of resources, particularly in the public sector.

Notwithstanding the controversy among the planners, there can be little question that the formulation of a correlated and realistic series of development goals, priorities, policies, and approaches is urgently required. There can, for example, be little argument about the need for officials to make a systematic assessment of their country's situation in order to evolve a set of reasonable development goals that are within their country's capacity to achieve. There can also be little dispute about the need to develop reasonable guidelines for the type of technology, institutions, and manpower availabilities each of the new states should seek to develop in its circumstances and in light of its decisions concerning its development goals and policies.

Independent African states frequently have adopted development plans which have not served their principal needs. Many plans have been too elaborate and often irrelevant to the realities of the states in question; others have been ill-conceived and, although avoiding the pitfalls of the *folie de grandeur* school of planning, have been little more than "shopping lists" for external aid.

Among the most difficult planning problems confronting the African states has been that of identification and selection of development priorities and thus decisions regarding allocation of resources. Primarily, there has been the problem of determining priorities among the three major sectors: the productive sector (agriculture and industry); the infrastructural sector, or "economic overhead" (transportation, telecommunications, power, etc.); and the social welfare sector, or "social overhead" (education, health, social amenities, etc.). Within these major sectors, the problem is that of determining priorities among subsectors (for example, between agriculture and industry within the productive sector). During the period under consideration most African countries have tended to give investment priority to the non-productive sectors; that is, investment has gone into economic and social overhead. There has been considerable investment in "bricks and mortar"—public buildings, transportation, and urban improvements. There has also been considerable investment in education and welfare projects. Finally, there has been a widespread tendency within the productive sector to favor investment in industry over agriculture, with results often leading to uneconomic industrial enterprises and stagnating or declining agricultural output. The latter pattern has frequently resulted in increasing imports of food and a declining share in world trade.

Although there may not be anything intrinsically wrong with investment priorities and allocations of the foregoing type, the overallocation of resources to non-productive sectors accounts in significant part for the limited, stagnating, or declining growth rates in many African countries. Frequently the timing for such investment has been premature; often the scope and magnitude of such investment have outstripped need or capacity to maintain it; generally it has led to unbalanced investment patterns without adequate concentration on generating productive resources either for further investment or for defraying the costs of social services on a continuing basis.[4]

Closely related to the problems associated with investment priorities and re-source allocation is performance with respect to the crucial problem of mobiliza-tion of domestic resources for development. As the foregoing discussion implies, the failure to select appropriate priorities and the overallocation of resources to non-productive sectors have resulted in modest growth rates and limited generation of new domestic resources for further investment in development. They have also served to limit private savings and the possibilities for domestic private investment in profitable economic undertakings. Failure to expand the growth rate significantly has also limited the possibility for increasing the size of the wage-earning labor force, the income of self-employed persons, and the income of agricultural smallholders. Thus, expansion of the domestic tax base has been correspondingly limited, and import revenues have also tended to be limited as the result of restricted or falling domestic demand and/or restricted availability of foreign exchange with which to meet domestic demand.

The inability to significantly increase the internal mobilization of resources has often coincided with a growth in ordinary budget costs, that is, in "recur-rent public expenditure" as opposed to "development expenditure." There have been several causes for this; among them are the costs of achieving and exercising sovereignty and the insistent pressure by the populations on their political lead-ers to redeem their pre-independence campaign pledges, such as "more educa-tion, more health facilities, more sound amenities, better wages, and more and better fringe benefits." In addition, recurrent budgets may be used to support prestige and politically motivated expenditure on such things as state-operated airlines, television networks, military establishments, and public stadiums, con-ference halls, and buildings.

Expenditure on military establishments has been of growing importance in many African countries. This not only has affected economic development priorities and absorbed growing amounts of recurrent expenditure in largely non-productive areas, but also has become a political factor reflected in the large number of military coups and resultant military governments in African

4. For a full discussion of development priorities, resource allocation, and the rela-tionship of industry and agriculture in the productive sector, see Rivkin, "The Role and Scope of Industrialization in Development," in *Industrialization in Developing Countries*, ed. Ronald Robinson (Cambridge: Harvard University Press, 1965), pp. 54–66.

states. In the same way that maintenance of a costly foreign service is considered indispensable in today's world, so too is the maintenance of a modern military force. Unquestionably, self-defense is the inherent right of every state. During the colonial period in Africa, the colonial power by definition had a monopoly of force and generally did little or nothing about developing indigenous armed forces until independence was imminent. Frequently, new states have had to develop military forces from scratch. Some countries, such as Gambia, Sierra Leone, Niger, and Tunisia, have done this with considerable restraint, developing modest forces to maintain internal law and order, control smuggling, help collect import and export duties, and prevent illegal immigration. Many, however, have raised armed forces as a prestige symbol, a source of national pride and identity, and a potential source of power in inter-African affairs. In these countries there has been an attempt to develop not only light infantry forces but also tank and artillery battalions and even small navies and air forces. In Somalia, Ethiopia, Congo-Kinshasa, Morocco, and Algeria, for example, a growing part of the recurrent budgetary expenditure (to say nothing of development or "capital" budget expenditure) goes for military purposes — perhaps as much as 35 per cent in the case of the first two, and probably not much less in the other cases. Military and paramilitary expenditure was an important factor in the economic and financial difficulties which brought pre-coup Ghana to the brink of bankruptcy in 1964–66.

There have also been non-productive expenditures in the productive sectors. In many instances, economic development has been equated with the size of the factory chimney. Poor investments have been made in plants which are too large by any standards for foreseeable needs, or too automated in the given circumstances of capital scarcity and large-scale unemployment or underemployment, or inappropriate in terms of technology, the availability of skilled staff, or the supply or raw materials. The desire to have the outward trappings of economic development has thus been an important factor limiting the discretion and circumscribing the freedom of action of the political leaders of the new states in their economy-building policies.

In summary, overall economic growth trends and performance since 1960 have been modest to poor, with the partial exception of a handful of the more promising economies of such countries as Nigeria (pre-civil war), Ivory Coast, Kenya, and Tunisia. The growth trends over an even larger period have not been encouraging, and experience with planned growth has left a legacy of major development problems.

INTERNATIONAL TRADE AND INVESTMENT IN AFRICA

International trade is normally the principal source of foreign exchange income for most underdeveloped countries. Private foreign investment and public foreign aid are the other main sources. External capital inflow has generally financed on an average less than 20 per cent of gross investment of underdeveloped countries. The financing of such development in Africa, however, has been considerably higher, averaging about 30 per cent—among the highest in the world.[5] Hence the role of external capital inflows is a crucial one for African economic development and must remain a principal consideration in African development planning.

Some countries with known or promising mineral resources attract unusually large investment of private foreign funds (for example, oil exploration and exploitation in Libya and Nigeria and iron ore exploitation in Liberia and Mauritania). Under a variety of special circumstances, many other countries receive unusually large amounts of foreign aid from multilateral or bilateral sources. The eighteen African Associate Members of the European Economic Community, for example, received some $500 million during the first five-year funding of the European Development Fund and are scheduled to receive another $730 million during the current five-year funding period (that is, $1,230 million between 1957 and 1969, including the two-year carry-over period between the expiration of the Overseas Territories Implementing Convention under the Treaty of Rome of 1957 and the ratification of the Yaounde Convention of Association of 1964).

The contribution of international trade, however, cannot be neglected. Given the present situation, it is likely to remain of central importance for African economic development for a long time to come. For most African countries the export sector serves as the "engine of growth." According to a World Bank report,

> Despite the uncertain price outlook over the medium term, it is likely that the African continent will continue to expand its export-type output. The relative lack of alternative investment opportunities in a number of countries, an ample labor supply and the availability of natural resources for exports . . . , make such an outcome probable.[6]

During the period 1960–65 there seems to have been a close relationship between economic growth rates and the expansion of trade of African countries. Areas which have achieved more rapid growth have also had fairly high rates of increase in exports and imports. Conversely, many African countries which have been lagging in the growth of GDP have also been lagging in the growth of their external trade.

Although exports of underdeveloped countries to developed countries in-

5. IBRD, *Annual Report*, p. 26.

6. D. Avramovic, "Postwar Economic Growth for Low-Income Countries," mimeographed (Washington, D.C.: International Bank for Reconstruction and Development, Economic Development Institute, 1963), p. 20.

creased from $27 billion to $42 billion during the period 1959–66, they did not keep pace with the growth of exports of developed countries among themselves and with the expansion of world trade generally. Thus the share of underdeveloped countries in world trade during the same period fell from 27 per cent to 23 per cent.[7] For ten selected African countries for which comprehensive data are available,[8] accounting for 38 per cent of African GDP, exports in the period 1960–65 increased 4.9 per cent compared to an average of 7.3 per cent for forty selected underdeveloped countries (including the ten African countries) during the same period.[9]

In African countries generally during the 1960–65 period, imports rose faster than the relatively slow growth of GDP. For the same ten selected African countries, imports during the period rose at an annual average rate of 6.1 per cent — significantly in excess of the 1.7 per cent average annual GDP growth rate and also at a rate in excess of their 4.9 per cent average annual export growth rate.[10] During the same period, the average price level of primary commodities, which form the bulk of African exports, did not change. In contrast, however, there was a rising trend in the average prices of manufactured goods — a significant part of African imports. Hence, the net result of these trends in the terms of trade was detrimental to the economies of most African countries.[11]

In light of the rate of increase in imports, as compared to the growth rate of GDP and exports, and the adverse movement of the terms of trade, it is not surprising that many African countries have had increasing difficulty in mobilizing domestic resources for development. Compare the following figures for the ten selected African countries and the group of forty selected underdeveloped countries respectively (each figure represents a percentage of GNP averaged for the period 1960–65): gross investment rate — 14.2 to 17.5; savings rate — 9.7 to 14.4; current accounts deficit — 4.5 to 3.1.[12] Thus, the ten African countries lagged behind the average for the forty underdeveloped countries in the important gross investment and savings rates categories, while running a larger current account deficit. In sum, there seems to have been a close relationship in African countries during the 1960–65 period not only between a low growth

7. G. D. Woods, *Development: The Need for New Directions* (Washington, D.C.: Government Printing Office, 1967), p. 9.

8. Ethiopia, Ghana, Kenya, Malawi, Morocco, Nigeria, Sudan, Tanzania, Tunisia, and Uganda.

9. IBRD, *Annual Report*, p. 27. If exports of certain African countries not included in the selected ten for which comprehensive data are available (such as petroleum from Algeria and copper from Zambia) are added in, the African average for exports would be increased. On the other hand, if exports of other countries not included in the selected ten (such as those of landlocked countries — Mali, Niger, Upper Volta, Chad, Central African Republic, Rwanda, Burundi, etc.) are added in, the African average for exports would be decreased.

10. *Ibid.*

11. *Ibid.*

12. *Ibid.*

rate and lagging external trade, but also between a low growth rate with comparatively low rates of gross investment and savings and a comparatively high rate of growth in current account deficit.

A significant portion of Africa's current account deficit was offset during the period 1960–65 by favorable official and private capital flows. For example, in 1965, the most recent year for which comprehensive statistics are available, the current account deficit of about $1.695 billion was offset by a combined official and private capital flow of just over $2 billion.[13] The importance of external capital flows has therefore been made more crucial as a result of the relatively poor performance of most African countries in achieving overall economic growth and in maintaining, let alone expanding, their share of world trade.

INTERNATIONAL AID AND CURRENCY RELATIONS

The flow of private foreign investment to the underdeveloped countries, particularly to those with per capita annual incomes of $250 or less (that is, most African countries), declined sharply during 1966. The Development Assistance Committee (DAC) of the Organization for Economic Cooperation and Development reported a decrease of $600 million in the flow of private foreign investment to underdeveloped countries from its fifteen members (the principal capital-exporting countries of the world).[14]

The flow to all underdeveloped countries of official capital assistance in the form of disbursements rose slightly in 1966. However, this obscured the declining trend of such assistance generally, and to Africa particularly. The declining trend is also obscured by the time lag in disbursements of foreign trade within African countries, thus creating a full "pipeline" which is still feeding in outside capital. There has also been an increase in official aid flows from the smaller DAC aid-givers, such as Austria, Canada, Denmark, Japan, and Sweden, which has augmented the general flow to underdeveloped countries. Despite expanding national incomes in developed countries, however, official aid to underdeveloped countries, including African states, reached a plateau in 1962. In fact, insofar as Africa is concerned, the largest aid-giver, France, reduced its absolute level of aid. This is mainly the result of its reduction of aid to North Africa; its aid to Africa south of the Sahara has remained fixed at roughly $275 million annually. The other three principal Western aid-givers to Africa—the United Kingdom, the United States, and Germany—have also reduced the relative level of their aid to Africa in relation to the growth in their national income. In absolute terms, however, the level of aid to Africa was maintained or was

13. *Ibid.*, p. 29.
14. *Survey of International Development,* IV (August 15, 1967), 1.

increased slightly in the period 1960–66. This was due in part to the pipeline lag, and in part to factors such as the growth in aid of some of the smaller DAC aid-givers, the maintenance of roughly the same level of aid by the four principal aid-givers (without regard to the growth of national income), and a growth in multilateral aid from the Overseas Development Fund of the EEC and the World Bank Group (the International Bank for Reconstruction and Development and the International Development Association).

Taking into account, however, rising prices and the practice of giving aid which is "tied" to the donor country (that is, restricting the use of aid to financing imports of goods and services from the specific aid-providing country), there has probably been no increase, and perhaps there has even been a decline, in the level of effective aid to African countries in the last few years.[15] In the years immediately ahead, given the trend of declining authorizations and/or commitments of new aid from France and the United States, among others, as distinct from the flow of aid already in the pipeline, official aid from the principal bilateral Western aid-givers is likely to decline somewhat.

Eur-African trade, investment, and aid are the most distinctive and important aspects of Tropical Africa's economic presence in world affairs. Almost without exception, the new states continue to deal with their former colonial rulers as the principal source of trade, investment, and aid. Most have retained their membership in the currency zones to which they were linked before independence.

Various African countries have tried to diversify their external economic relations and, in particular, to develop new trading partners and new sources of external aid. Nigeria, Congo-Kinshasa, Tunisia, and Kenya have been developing new economic ties with the United States. Others, such as Guinea and Mali, have developed new economic relationships with the Soviet bloc and Communist China. A fair number of countries in the area have also developed expanding economic relationships with Israel and Japan. By and large, however, the Eur-African ties remain paramount and have been consolidated for the eighteen African states which are associate members of the EEC. Under the original Treaty of Rome, signed in 1957, and the more recent Yaounde Convention of Association of 1964, these states have developed a series of preferential trade, aid, and investment relations with the six European countries of the EEC.[16]

Only Mali and Guinea have terminated their membership in the French franc

15. See IBRD, *Annual Report*, pp. 33–35; *La Politique de coopération avec les pays en voie de développement, Rapport de la Commission d'Etude* (Paris: Documentation Française, 1963), Vols. I–II; I. M. D. Little, *Aid to Africa* (New York: Macmillan, 1964); Teresa Hayter, *French Aid* (London: Overseas Development Institute, 1966); and *U.S. Overseas Loans and Grants, July 1, 1945–June 30, 1965* (Washington, D.C.: Government Printing Office, 1966).

16. See Arnold Rivkin, *Africa and the European Common Market*, 2d ed. rev. (Denver: Denver University, 1966), p. 67, for a full discussion of the importance of the trade, aid, and investment arrangements established between the "European Six" and the "African Eighteen."

zone. As a result, lacking gold and hard currency reserves to back their respective national currencies, both have found themselves with inconvertible and
deteriorating currencies which are increasingly unacceptable both in international trade and as a means of exchange internally. This loss of value and
confidence in the Malian and Guinean currencies has resulted in severe shortages of imported goods (capital and consumer), extensive smuggling of exports
through neighboring countries for hard currency or consumer goods, losses of
foreign exchange and public revenue, growing internal inflation, mounting
budgetary deficits, falling agricultural and cattle production, and other at-
tendant economic and financial ills. In 1967, after some five years in the monetary wilderness, Mali prepared to reenter the franc zone via the West African
Monetary Union, pursuant to the terms of two sets of economic and financial
accords with France. As qualifying steps for reentry—presumably during 1968—
Mali adopted an austerity budget, underwent a 50 per cent devaluation in the
value of the Malian franc, and initiated a reorganization of the twenty-odd public
enterprises whose annual losses have been a major continuing drain on its recurrent budget. Only Guinea now remains completely outside the French franc
zone.

The three ex-Belgian colonies, Congo-Kinshasa, Rwanda, and Burundi, all
severed their formal ties with the Belgian franc. All three, but particularly the
Congo, have experienced a continuing depreciation in the value of their currency. The Congolese franc has been devaluated three times since independence, most recently in 1967 by the overwhelming rate of 240 per cent. Many of
the Congo's financial and economic ills have been closely related to the declining value and confidence in its currency as an acceptable medium of exchange, and all have been related to the more basic political problems of the
area.

In these three instances—Mali, Guinea, and Congo-Kinshasa—the dual nature
of their economies has tended to act as a buffer to the more direct and acute
impact that deteriorating and inconvertible currencies usually produce in more
developed countries. Their large subsistence sectors have been less directly
affected by the decline in imports and the fall in international and domestic
trade than their market sectors. The former were able to turn inward to subsistence production of food and other basic necessities and to barter transactions, and thus were more readily able to do without consumer and other
goods which can be acquired only with money. Although subjected to stresses
and some outbreaks of violence as a result of consumer shortages and curtailment of illegal trading and currency transactions, the subsistence sectors of the
three countries have been able to absorb and blunt the sharp edge of much
economic discontent. By way of contrast, in the somewhat more sophisticated
economy of Ghana, which severed connections with the sterling zone during the
Nkrumah regime, the subsistence sector was not able to perform the buffer role
to the same degree. This lesser capacity, in combination with other political and

economic factors, contributed to the military *coup d'état* and overthrow of the Nkrumah government in February, 1966. It is pertinent to note that in 1967 the military regime found it necessary to devalue the deteriorating Ghanaian currency by some 30 per cent.

Liberia, which has no colonial history, uses the United States dollar as a medium of foreign exchange and is thus the only African member of the dollar area. Ethiopia's currency is independent and backed by Ethiopian reserves of gold and hard currencies. Both Liberia and Ethiopia have important trade and aid ties with the United States. There are also United States investments in Liberian rubber plantations and iron-ore mines.

One more special currency area in Africa should be briefly noted – the South African rand area. With the independence of Botswana and Lesotho in 1966 and the independence of Swaziland in 1968, the South African rand, which is the currency in these countries, must now be viewed as a separate monetary zone. The monetary relationship of the three small "enclave" countries with the Republic of South Africa is reinforced by a customs union, trade patterns, transportation links, labor migration, and many other interlocking economic ties. The Republic of South Africa's official aid to, and private investment in, the three new states are also likely to reinforce the economic and financial links of the four countries.

To summarize, in the international context Africa is not a major area for trade or investment. With a few exceptions, it does not loom large in terms of the total trade and investments of the European powers. The Belgian trade and investment relationship with Congo-Kinshasa is an exception. As for France, only its dealings with Ivory Coast, Senegal, and Gabon have any particular significance. South Africa, despite its racial policies, is the only African country of major importance to the United Kingdom for trade and investment. Rhodesia (which is in a state of "rebellion" against the U.K.), Zambia, and Nigeria are economically of significance to the United Kingdom, but trade relations with these countries are not of the order of magnitude of those with South Africa. To the United States and the Soviet Union, Africa is an area of minor economic significance. South Africa is the principal trading partner and area of American investment in Africa, despite official U.S. acceptance of the United Nations boycott of selected exports to South Africa.

In the foreign-aid field, Africa has been the principal recipient of French foreign aid and an important recipient of British foreign aid. The Development Fund of the European Economic Community, to which the six European members contribute, has, as we have noted, also been a major source of external aid. Of the many geographic areas which have been recipients of United States aid, Africa has received the smallest amount. Likewise, Africa has received only limited aid from the Soviet Union. In individual cases the United States has provided important quantities of aid – to Nigeria for its first post-independence economic development plan, to Guinea in order to counter ties to the Soviet bloc, and to Congo-Kinshasa as a consequence of the continuing crisis in that country. Similarly, the Soviet Union has provided significant quantities of aid to such countries as Guinea, pre-coup Ghana, and Somalia; Communist China has also committed aid to Algeria, Tanzania, Guinea, Congo-Brazzaville, and Mali.[17]

The economic importance of Africa internationally can be expected to increase in time. Trading and investment opportunities have been opening up in more countries and are likely to grow. In view of the widespread political instability and internal economic difficulties of the area, however, a dramatic change in Africa's economic importance is not likely to occur in the near future.

PROBLEMS OF AFRICAN ECONOMIC DEVELOPMENT

Most countries of Africa have achieved "international sovereignty." They are members of the U.N. and have diplomatic relations with other states. But in most cases, the task of state-building—that is, of constructing stable governmental structures—remains to be accomplished. During the colonial period, government structures were primarily designed to maintain law and order; to provide the minimal services required by the bulk of the population to function at a subsistence level, and by the small European colonial populations to function at a modern level; and to accommodate limited economic activity, generally related to the export sector. In only a few instances were governmental structures adapted to carrying on nation-building programs, launching sustained and correlated programs of economic development, developing and maintaining the economic and social infrastructure required for expanding economic activity, providing the promised enlarged programs of social services, conducting foreign relations, maintaining military forces, and discharging the countless other functions which nation-states in the twentieth-century world are now called upon to perform. The lack of defined and organized levels of government and established channels of communication between the center, intermediate regional, and local levels has frequently frustrated the operations of one new government after another.

Second only to the fundamental problem of state-building in Africa is that of nation-building. The new states have come to independence with little or no sense of national identity. All are confronted with the problem of welding together populations divided by ethnic, cultural, religious, and regional differences. In almost every instance, the new states have to create national loyalties which transcend, but at the same time are compatible with, traditional and local loyalties to tribe, religion, and region. In cases such as the unification of the

17. Alexander Eckstein, *Communist China's Economic Growth and Foreign Trade* (New York: McGraw-Hill, 1966), p. 307.

former British Southern Cameroons and the French-speaking Republic of Cameroon, and the union of former British Somaliland with the U.N. Trust Territory of Somalia, the problem of heterogeneous populations has been complicated by the vastly different cultural, linguistic, juridical, political, and economic heritages from the colonial period.[18]

In the larger African countries the problem of fusing together the disparate population is complicated by vast distance and limited transportation and communication links. In countries like Ethiopia and Mali, the problem tends to be aggravated by natural barriers such as mountains and deserts; in others, such as Gambia and Malawi, by their odd geographic configurations; and in still others, such as Chad and the Central African Republic, by their isolated, land-locked locations.

In many African countries the political systems have been unable to cope effectively with the problems of state-building and nation-building, and there has been widespread political instability. This is evident from the twenty military *coups d'état* which have occurred since January, 1963. For the most part, the military governments, although they have to some degree provided a measure of law and order, have not yet shown much more aptitude than the civil governments for inducing meaningful participation by their people in political and economic development programs. The resulting context for development has been anything but favorable in such countries as Dahomey and Upper Volta.

A third problem common to, and implicit in, state-building and nation-building is that of institution-building. Although many factors have been singled out by one observer or another as crucial to development, the cumulative African experience in the first decade of the independence era suggests that whereas these several factors may be of varying importance, no one, or combination, of them has sufficed to sustain an integrated program of African political and economic development in the absence of an appropriate institutional structure. The African states have not been lacking in the political skills and organizations so often associated with the requirements of national political development (such as political parties, charismatic leadership, national political symbols, and so on); yet there has been little or no development of accepted (legitimate) state structures or political systems and even less growth of political stability.

ECONOMIC INSTITUTION-BUILDING

At the economic level Africa has appeared to have many of the factors necessary for its development. Country after country has adopted a national de-

18. I. M. Lewis, "Integration in the Somali Republic," in *African Integration and Disintegration*, ed. Arthur Hazelwood (London: Oxford University Press, 1967), pp. 251–84; and Edwin Ardener, "The Nature of the Reunification of Cameroon," *ibid.*, pp. 285–338.

velopment plan, and some have had several plans since their independence. Many have begun to develop and exploit more effectively their resource base. Those countries fortunate enough to come to independence with substantial reserves or with access to significant external aid have stepped up their rate of investment. Several of the new states, regardless of their reserves or aid, have increased their rate of investment in particularly favored sectors. Some African states have made efforts to reorient the monetary, investment, trade, and/or aid patterns of their economies away from those which existed during the colonial era and toward the Communist bloc, or toward non-colonial Western powers and other developed countries. Thus African countries have not been lacking in the presence of important economic factors often associated with the requirements for economic development; yet there has been little institutionalization of growth, and, more often than not, even where growth has taken place, little real development.

Economic institutions to build modern economies in Africa have been lacking, to even a greater degree than state and political institutions. Very few African states had developed, until recently, under the pressure of outside stimuli, economic institutions which consciously sought to induce greater production of a wider variety of commodities and products for more than the subsistence needs of the producing unit, the family. Traditionally there has been little or no impetus for market production or for an exchange economy.

Almost everywhere in Africa there is an absence of the institutions required to formulate plans and, equally important, to execute them. Most governments lack essential knowledge about the physical features of their countries and do not have the facilities and personnel needed to acquire and develop the necessary information and data. Statistical services and research bodies are needed for economic planning or programming, as are services such as geological and topographical units to map and explore the resource base and test the soils, and meteorological and hydrological services to record rainfall and locate surface and subsurface water. Crucial institutions are needed for transferring data to producers and potential producers (agricultural extension services, industrial advisory services, manpower training institutions); for carrying out the physical elements of development projects (public works departments, soil conservation services, and reforestation units); for mobilizing internal resources (savings institutions, commercial banks, development banks, home-loan and mortgage institutions, domestic money markets, and stock and bond markets); and for marketing (commodity markets, trading centers, and storage and grading centers). The list is almost endless. The gap between what exists and what is needed is tremendous. The capacity to develop the institutions is limited. Traditional subsistence society did not provide the incentive or create the need for the types of individuals and institutions that economy-building requires. There is now a desperate race in Africa to set up institutions and to create the skilled and semiskilled personnel that is required to span the gulf between subsistence and market production.[19]

Intimately related to institution-building as a precondition for economy-building is the associated problem of technological modernization. Africa presents the striking incongruities of the most modern, automated equipment and the most primitive, backward technology at one and the same time. Hence, side by side, one finds the machine-drawn plow and the crude digging stick, the dial telephone and the talking drum, the modern hospital and the medicine man, the jet airplane and the human beast of burden.

Africa lacks a hierarchy of technology. It lacks a technology developed in response to its contemporary needs and purposes. It lacks the supporting institutions for adapting imported technology, for rationalizing and developing it, and for training staff to use and maintain it. Often, on a continent with surplus or underutilized manpower, one finds no particular philosophy or system of labor-intensive investment and production. At the same time, on a continent with scarce capital resources, one finds no particular philosophy or approach to capital-intensive investment and production.[20]

A final problem to be taken into account, one which is intimately related to modernizing a country's technology, is manpower development. In the same way that technological development must take place within the framework of a country's national development plan and within the constraints imposed by an absence of basic institutions, so too must it relate to the state of skilled, trained, and experienced manpower in the country. The new states are lacking or are seriously deficient in the skilled manpower necessary for establishing and sustaining a modern economy. Manpower development in turn presupposes appropriate training institutions and national planning goals to accord priorities and establish targets.

Manpower planning in African countries, which are just embarking upon programs of economic development, is in its infancy. There are few guidelines (and even less hard data) on manpower requirements and availabilities. It is necessary to make the best estimates of current needs and availabilities, then to make projections based on national planning objectives, taking into account the country's institutional capacity for training. Thus, manpower planning has a direct bearing on size, volume, and content of a country's educational effort. It also has a direct bearing on the establishment of realistic development objectives or goals for all of the sectors of a country's economy. It does no good to establish goals for the expansion of agricultural output if the facilities for training extension workers, agricultural technicians, and marketing specialists to help

19. Arnold Rivkin, ed., *Nations by Design: Institution-Building in Africa* (Garden City, N.Y.: Doubleday, 1969).

20. Arnold Rivkin, *Africa and the West* (New York: Praeger, 1962), pp. 148–72.

achieve the goals cannot conceivably keep pace with the manpower requirements for attaining the expected rate of increase.

There is, therefore, a direct need to phase manpower development planning to institution-building, to development goals, and to a country's technological modernization program. African states are confronted with multiple inter-related major problems which require simultaneous solution if the net result is to be development. All too often one or another of the problems has been faced, perhaps successfully, while the larger development situation has not improved and may actually have deteriorated.

Also, African states generally tend to be overextended in terms of social welfare standards or practices left over from the colonial period, which they find extremely difficult, if not impossible, to discard. French-speaking African states, for example, have inherited a costly program of *allocations familiales* (family allowances); the French developed this program to meet the population problem of metropolitan France after World War I and subsequently extended it to Africa, although population growth in the African colonies was hardly a crucial problem.

Even more universal, however, than the inherited social welfare practices are the universally distorted wage and salary structures bequeathed to most African countries. Developed to meet the needs of the colonial period—that is, to attract Europeans to staff the public services and the private sectors—a structure of premium wage-rates with generous fringe benefits was developed for the expatriate serving in Africa. At the same time, regardless of the level of productivity of the African employee, the salary and the wage structure for manual, unskilled, and semiskilled African labor tended to be depressed. In short, the ceiling was highly inflated and the floor was very low indeed; there was no graduated ladder of salaries and wages.

With independence, Africans have tended to move into the senior positions in government and the private sector vacated by departing Europeans, frequently without regard to skills and experience but at the inflated expatriate salary and fringe-benefit scale. And because the floor was so low, pressures to increase salaries and wages, to retain existing social welfare practices and fringe benefits, and to add new ones have been extremely strong. Instead of closing the wage gap by lowering the ceiling and developing an intermediate ladder, the tendency has often been to raise not only the floor but also the ceiling. Hence, wage inflation has become a common phenomenon, affecting the cost of both public services and industrial production. The potential for developing the primary symbol of progress, a growing industrial sector which would be competitive with industry elsewhere in the world, is handicapped by the perpetuation of these legacies from the colonial period. Thus, African countries are confronted with major problems of rationalizing and adapting inherited welfare practices and wage and salary structures to the needs and capabilities of their economies.[21]

21. Arnold Rivkin, *The African Presence in World Affairs* (New York: Macmillan, The Free Press, 1963), pp. 67–94, 118–29.

THE OUTLOOK FOR AFRICAN
ECONOMIC DEVELOPMENT

The outlook for the development of modern economic systems and the prospects for accelerating the rate of economic growth in Africa over the next several decades are most uncertain. The development of productive economic structures and suitable growth rates are both dependent on an involved complex of internal and international factors.

Internally, as we have seen, the development nexus — political stability and a sound economic structure — is the crucial factor. The need to build an appropriate constitutional and political structure to house a productive economy is basic; so too is the corollary need to develop a modern, dynamic, and productive economic system to sustain the political and constitutional structure. Although conceptually separable, in Africa today the achievement of political stability and a modern economic structure must proceed hand in hand. The premium is on sound political and economic performance to face and then cope with the basic economy-building and development problems already discussed.

Internationally, the problems of the volume, value, and terms of trade, the flow of official economic assistance, the volume and quality of foreign private investment, the state of the world economy, and, more generally, the patterns of world affairs are the basic factors which will affect African economic development. They will interact and influence favorably or adversely the internal state of affairs and the domestic effort of all African countries. What, then, are reasonable economic growth goals for African countries to seek over the next several decades?

Slogans such as "catching up" and "closing the gap," which are now part of the African development vocabulary, should be recognized as propaganda goals which divert energy and resources from more meaningful development efforts. African countries with per capita incomes of $50, $75, and $100 per year — even those with per capita incomes of $250 per year — are not going to be able to "close the gap," let alone "catch up" with the developed economies with per capita incomes ranging from $1,000 to $3,000 per year.

The improbability of "closing the gap" is most sharply illustrated by a single comparison. The United States alone, growing by between 5 and 6 per cent a year, adds over $40 billion to an annual GNP which is now over $730 billion, thereby acquiring each year, as an extra, about as much as the entire GNP of Africa.[22] Stated in other terms, the "poverty line" in the United States is now set at a family income of $3,000 or less, or roughly 15 to 30 times what might be estimated to be the family income of an *average* African family. Rates of growth even higher than that of the United States in developed economies with annual per capita GNPs of $2,000, $1,500, and $1,000 also vividly highlight the

22. Woods, *Development*, p. 11.

improbability of African countries "catching up" with developed economies in the foreseeable future.

What is possible, however, is a significant and steady growth in the absolute per capita incomes of African countries so that the standard of living can be improved for the existing generation and certainly for the next generation. Much can be done to improve the diet, clothing, housing, education, and immediate material requirements of individual Africans by the steady improvement in the growth rate; and much could be done to generate resources so that these improvements are sustained for future generations. This does not mean catching up, nor does it preclude the possibility that the existing gap between developed and underdeveloped economies in per capita income will not grow greater. Nonetheless, absolute improvement in the standards of living of Africans and the increasing participation of more and more Africans in productive modern economic efforts would not only be worthwhile goals in and of themselves but would also serve in an important way to enhance the nation-building programs of African countries.

What, then, are the prospects for Africa in the world economy over the next several decades?

The prospects are difficult to assess in light of the trends already discussed. Assuming improved internal performance in growth rates and export availabilities, it seems likely that African countries generally will expand the volume and value of their participation in world trade. It is not clear, however, that they will be able to hold or increase their relative share of world trade without various types of international assistance to improve their access to and income from world markets.

Of the many schemes now actively under study or consideration, it seems clear that Africa will need a combination of most, and perhaps all, of them if it is to hold its own and go beyond this minimal goal and augment its share of world trade. Many African countries for the balance of the 1960s and most of the 1970s are likely to remain producers and exporters of primary products (agricultural and mineral). This is particularly true of most of the former French territories and a good many of the former British territories—for example, Gambia, Sierra Leone, and Malawi, as well as countries such as Somalia, Rwanda, Burundi, and Ethiopia. These countries will need help in the form of access for their primary products to developed markets. This would include some combination of tariff preference of the type the eighteen African Associated States of the European Common Market now receive, commodity stabilization arrangements of the type now in effect for coffee but not yet for cocoa, price supports of the type France has made available (and, now on a reduced scale, the EEC) to Senegal and Niger for groundnuts and groundnut oil, reduction of those excise and other internal taxes which discourage the consumption of coffee and tropical products in developed countries (as in West Germany), and compensatory financing of the type proposed in a recent World Bank Staff Study for UNCTAD.

By the mid-1970s some of the more developed African economies may also have need of preferential entry and tariffs for their semiprocessed, processed, and manufactured goods, of the type now afforded by the EEC to the eighteen African Associated States and of the type being sought by underdeveloped countries generally under various proposals agreed upon at the Algiers Conference of 1967 and put forward at the second United Nations Conference on Trade and Development in New Delhi in February, 1968.

All African states will have need of more public assistance and private overseas investment. This implies a reversal in the current trend of declining flow of official bilateral assistance and private overseas investment to Africa and/or a marked increase in multilateral assistance. Recently the World Bank reaffirmed earlier staff studies indicating that underdeveloped countries "could use effectively $3–4 billion *more* per year in external capital during the next five years than they are now receiving."[23] African countries obviously could use a fair share of any such increase, to say nothing of the need to halt the present trend of declining external capital flows to Africa.

The needs are quite clear; the prospects for meeting them, however, are far less so. What is clear with regard to meeting the needs is that African prospects will be considerably enhanced if the factors under African control are handled in a satisfactory manner and the domestic development nexus is effectively established. The external factors are likely to be more responsive and to interact more favorably under these conditions.

On the international level, the relevant factors are likely to show some improvement. This is apt to occur partly as a result of the efforts of the African states in the international arena, partly as a consequence of the efforts of developed states to aid the development of African states and to improve their trade and economic relations with them, and partly as the outcome of the efforts of the United Nations Conference on Trade and Development and other international organizations, the efforts of producing and consuming states with respect to compensatory financing and commodity stabilization, and the efforts of the world community generally to augment world trade.

23. I. S. Friedman, "Statement to the UN Economic and Social Council," at Geneva, July 13, 1967, mimeographed (Washington, D.C.: International Bank for Reconstruction and Development, 1967), p. 3.

25

Developments
in Technology

RAYMOND A. KLIPHARDT

INTERACTION BETWEEN ENGINEERING and the natural sciences on one hand and the social sciences on the other is necessary for human progress in all societies, but it is perhaps most urgently needed in the developing countries, where an accelerated rate of change is required. Throughout the world, ecological patterns and the distribution of natural resources show no regard for international boundaries. In Africa, however, the division between the have and have-not states is more pronounced than it is in either America or Europe. This places a premium on ecological engineering as one means of correcting the imbalance in resources, both between and within countries, and of ensuring more efficient utilization of existing resource potential.

WATER TECHNOLOGY

Water supply is the critical factor that determines habitability or limits human activity in most of Africa. Water, however, is in short supply in at least 75 per cent of Africa south of the Sahara.[1] The importance of water supply may be emphasized by the enumeration of six major categories of use. (1) Domestic use by man and his animals: this is a rather limited usage, although husbandry is usually the main occupation of people who live in dry countries. (2) Irrigation: it is estimated that from 4,000 to 13,000 gallons per day per acre are needed for various crops, and in many areas this must come entirely from irrigation. (3) In-

1. E. B. Worthington, *Science in the Development of Africa* (London: Commission for Technical Cooperation in Africa South of the Sahara, 1958), p. 114.

dustry: industrial development draws heavily on water supply, and it can readily pollute that supply. (4) Fisheries: inland fisheries are normally found on lakes and rivers, but reservoirs of dams offer additional opportunities. (5) Transport: the topography of Africa does not allow easy water transportation, despite an extensive network of lakes and rivers, because of discontinuities at waterfalls and rapids. (6) Hydroelectric power: the same vertical irregularities that hinder water transport offer exceedingly favorable opportunities at many locations in Africa for hydroelectric power, particularly in the Congo Basin.

There are important local variations and climatic cycles, but the greatest changes in availability of water are due to man's intervention in natural conditions. Destruction of vegetation increases runoff, reduces penetration of rainfall through the soil, and results in the disappearance of streams and springs during the long dry season. The tapping of underground water by sinking wells for the domestic supply of villages is a positive human endeavor, provided it is coupled with a means of assuring adequate replacement by checking runoff. It has been found, for example, that the use of water from effluent streams, wells, and boreholes in the drainage basin of Lake Naivasha in Kenya has resulted in a general lowering of the groundwater table (that is, level of water in the soil) in that area and to the overall lowering of the lake itself. Runoff can be checked, however, by the construction of large dams which affect populations and areas many miles from the site, and catchment projects on small streams, collecting from drainage basins of a few hundred acres. A notable American project, the Tennessee Valley Authority, is looked to by many as a prototype for the efficient use and control of water resources. Experience gained directly at the TVA has supplied some basic principles, applicable on large and small scales, of dealing not only with water supply directly, but with waste treatment and disposal as well.

The drainage pattern in Africa is dominated by a series of large river systems, each of which covers hundreds of thousands of square miles. Almost invariably, therefore, the larger African rivers (the Nile, Congo, Niger, Zambezi) are international waterways. Furthermore, since their watersheds also span political boundaries, efficient water resource development, even on most of the smaller streams and tributaries, is a venture which requires international cooperation. A dam on the Niger River, for example, will involve not only the country in which it is located but will have an impact on all areas downstream, and its functioning will be closely related to activities in areas farther upstream. Occasionally a dam may be constructed in one country by, and primarily for, another, as in the case of the Jebel Aulia Dam on the White Nile, which was built by the United Arab Republic in the Republic of the Sudan.

The Nile Basin provides several examples of how scientific and technological research may become subordinated to national politics and how the activities of one government may greatly alter conditions in another country. A long stretch of the White Nile passes through the Sudd, a vast swampy area between Juba and Malakal in Sudan. During its slow and tortuous passage through this extremely flat region, an estimated 50 per cent of the Nile's water is lost by evaporation. In an attempt to cut this evaporation loss, a 300-mile-long canal has been proposed to carry half the river's flow from Jonglei (north of Juba) around the Sudd to rejoin the main river south of Malakal. Coupled with this proposal is the plan to store water in Lake Albert so that the major flow of the White Nile at Khartoum would occur when the flow of the Blue Nile, which joins it at that point, is at its lowest. Although the major benefit would accrue to the United Arab Republic, the Jonglei Canal would be built in Sudan, and the Lake Albert Reservoir would be on the border of Uganda and Congo-Kinshasa. Further complicating the matter is the fact that Lake Albert contains chemical salts which are largely removed by natural activity as the water flows through the Sudd. The Jonglei Canal would greatly reduce this effect, possibly with a detrimental effect on agriculture in Egypt.

Another problem involving the Nile system as a waterway relates to the increasing growth of water hyacinth in the White Nile south of Khartoum. Development has been undertaken for spraying equipment and for a sawing system to enable spray boats to penetrate the solid mats of plants that block the river during high water. But White Nile water is used to irrigate extensive cotton-raising projects, and the chemical (2, 4-D) sprayed on the water hyacinth is believed to have a damaging effect on the cotton. A detailed study of stage and dose factors in the chemically caused damage to cotton has been initiated.

Overall, the technological studies concerned with water supply in Africa are increasingly trying to relate conservation of this natural resource with control of runoff, evaporation, and transpiration of plants (estimated to be three or four times that of evaporation in swampy areas). Work is being done on the problems of artificial rain-making, waste treatment, and optimum utilization of water for irrigation, fish-farming, transportation, and generation of electrical power.

FOOD PRODUCTION TECHNOLOGY

Increased food production is another important factor in the development of African states. Here, again, there is a great need to expand research on man's influence on his physical environment. The clearing of a forest to cultivate a garden or the burning of many square miles of savanna to provide improved pasture may so upset the balance of nature as to change the natural vegetation and climate. Africans have long recognized that too frequent tilling of the soil causes deterioration, and they have attempted to counter this by a system of shifting cultivation (sometimes called rotational bush fallow). In some areas of Africa the population lives permanently in the same place and cultivates surrounding plots in rotation; in others, the whole village site is changed every few years. When there are significant increases in population, however, the shifting agricultural system frequently breaks down, and substitutes need to be found. But what are the optimum patterns of rotation and the necessary crop-to-fallow ratio? Studies are being made to establish systems of fixed cultivation using rotation of crops, mixed cropping, green manuring, composting, and fertilizers in the effort to solve these problems.

Rotation of crops is a procedure whereby the subplots of a garden plot are planted with different individual crops in sequential order. Mixed cropping is a plan of growing two or more crop plants on the same ground at the same time, generally a leguminous crop and a grain crop. The African farmer usually plants the crops in relation to their growing periods and can thus distribute the labor of harvesting. Research conducted at numerous places in Africa, however, indicates that the system of mixed cropping is applicable only where low yield is acceptable. Work at the Moor Plantations' Research Station at Ibadan indicates that in the southern part of Nigeria two crops can be grown per year by using green manures (a crop such as beans or clover plowed under while still green) to revitalize the soil and thus improve the crop-to-fallow ratio from 1:7 to 1:2 (that is, one year of cropping to two of fallow per subplot). Other studies are more cautious regarding the benefits of green manuring in the humid tropics. Composting has not yielded general success, as the African farmer seldom takes the necessary pains to water frequently and to turn the composting materials; furthermore, water may be in short supply. In Kampala (Uganda), however, refuse has been composted in a manure which is used by the banana growers in the area. In some areas regeneration of the soil is accomplished quickly by planting elephant grass. Studies in Rhodesia showed that after breaking the natural veld (grassland) and applying nitrogen fertilizer, cultivators could plant elephant grass which would grow to a height of ten feet or more and could be cut for a two- to three-year supply of silage. The land may then be grazed for a year or two, and subsequently plowed and cultivated to yield two or three heavy arable crops, mostly maize, before repeating the rotation. Thus instead of ranching beef animals on the natural veld at the rate of one animal per thirteen acres, the same land with a little irrigated pasture will graze one animal per three acres averaged through the rotation, and will yield feed for other purposes.[2]

Research on African crop plants will have more far-reaching significance than studies of local cultivating techniques. Most research has been done on the cultivated plants whose products are exported; cotton, tobacco, and rubber are notable examples. Continuing work on the problems of improving the food supply of the continent will relate to producing strains which maximize desirable characteristics when the plants are grown in a wide range of conditions and to studying optimum climate and soil conditions for each plant, the nutrition of

2. *Ibid.*, pp. 271–73.

plants as concerns growth and reproduction, and resistance of plants to disease and depredations from birds. Such research has been and continues to be applied to such crops as the sorghums, the millets, maize, rice, wheat, pulses, groundnuts (peanuts), sesame, palm oil, palm fruits, soybeans, cassava, ordinary potatoes, yams, coffee, tea, cocoa, fruits, sugar, ginger, and cloves.

Rice provides the main diet for most people in Sierra Leone and was a large import until 1935, when it became an export commodity as a result of the development of swamp-grown rice in the Scarcies area. The Republic of the Sudan has been importing up to a thousand tons of rice per year but has started experimenting with the raising of various strains from India.

Important problems relate to the supply of meat. The Food and Agriculture Organization of the United Nations reported in 1950 that the continent of Africa, with 23 per cent of the world's land surface and only 8 per cent of the human population, had 26 per cent of 'the goats, 15 per cent of the sheep, and 11 per cent of the cattle. Meat supplies are often short, however, and improvement of stock has been hindered by social and religious traditions, in which social status is determined by the size of flocks and herds, and by marriage customs involving the transfer of domestic animals. It is not uncommon for Africans to suffer from protein deficiencies in their diet while maintaining more animals than their land can support.

Current research in the production of protein may well be significant in many African areas. Harold B. Gotaas, an internationally known sanitary and environmental engineer of Northwestern University, has developed proposals to grow and harvest algae on ponds of sewage to provide high-protein feed for fowl and livestock. He states that, at best, an acre of high-protein crops will yield less than a ton of protein, whereas an acre of sewage in a moderate climate would yield twenty tons of protein. It is further estimated that, depending on the land, algae is 100 to 300 times more efficient than grazing in producing protein for beef cattle.

TRANSPORTATION TECHNOLOGY

Increased quantity, quality, and efficiency of food production are of no avail without adequate internal transportation. The relatively weak and unintegrated development of transport in Africa is one of the continent's most pressing problems. One part of an African country occasionally imports from foreign sources the same commodity that is going to waste in another part of the same country. Most of the coastal and capital cities have more effective economic links with other African, European, or Asian centers than with interior areas of their own country.

Table 11, based on statistics compiled in 1960, offers striking comparisons

TABLE 11
RAILWAYS AND COMMERCIAL VEHICLES: 1960

Country	Miles of railway per thousand square miles of territory	Miles of railway per ten thousand population	Number of commercial vehicles per ten thousand population
Nigeria	5.2	2.7	7
Sierra Leone	11.1	1.2	13
Ethiopia	1.6	0.3	4
Italy	87.6	2.0	93
France	113.5	5.3	359
U.S.A.	60.3	12.1	676

Source: Data derived from Wilfred Owen, *Strategy for Mobility* (Washington, D.C.: The Brookings Institution, 1964), pp. 210–12, 216–17.

between various African countries and some of the more developed areas of the world.

Many of the social, economic, and political implications of inadequate transport in Africa have been explored in Chapter 18 of this volume. It is important to note here, however, that from the standpoint of research in transport engineering and planning a "systems approach" must be maintained. In other words, efforts must be made to view transportation as part of a larger network of relationships between people and their cultural and physical environment. According to Wilfred Owen, a leading transport economist:

> For every case in which transport has produced notable social and economic impacts, there seems to be another in which the effect of transport on levels of living has been limited. Sometimes high standards of mobility have been achieved at the expense of higher standards of living. For transport affords unparalleled opportunity to make mistakes, including errors of location, technology, design, timing, or the mistake of investing in transport at all.
>
> A good case can be made, however, that appropriate transport facilities are the key to development. For without transport, supply and demand are restricted by the high cost of moving, and by ignorance of whether goods can be sold and for how much. Improvement in living conditions is dependent on the ability of people to communicate and on their capacity to trade.[3]

TECHNICAL TRAINING AND RESEARCH FACILITIES

All branches of science and engineering are making important contributions in African countries. Undergraduate and graduate collegiate studies in African

3. Wilfred Owen, *Strategy for Mobility* (Washington, D.C.: The Brookings Institution, 1964), pp. 18–19.

universities are being expanded as fast as they can be supported. Various programs funded by African and/or foreign nations are bringing research talent together to work on the problems of water supply, food production, transportation, topography, cartography, geology, meteorology, bioclimatology, public health, and various aspects of industrialization and technological development. The faculties, increasing in number and competence, are distributing their research activities between matters of immediate relevance to the local scene and wider professional concerns, with an interest in being represented in the international journals and the mainstream of academic thought.

In 1962, when Sudan was planning to spend approximately $100 million of its own funds to attract private investments, it requested assistance from the United Nations Special Fund for an industrial research institute and a food-processing research center. The Fund's managing director retained the services of the Stanford Research Institute to assist in the evaluation of the projects and their potential impact on the industrial development of Sudan. Considerations with regard to the proposed industrial research institute related to the feasibility of establishing a center that could ensure a supply of technically trained personnel to study indigenous problems and provide technical assistance to government and industry. Regarding the food-processing research center, SRI suggested a central food-processing training and demonstration center near Khartoum, with more remote stations limited to simpler packaging, grading, and processing until more local competence could be developed. They also suggested air transport for certain perishable, high-priced commodities, and agricultural transfer to non-perishable crops in areas with inadequate transport. Lockheed Aircraft International recently conducted an extensive two-and-one-half-year transportation study in a major African developing country using systems analysis techniques. Included in this research was a physical road survey for the purpose of developing a master plan for growth of the country's transportation systems; a study of soil and drainage conditions in order to subdivide the country into homogeneous areas in terms of costs of road construction, road maintenance, and vehicle operation; and the training of local nationals in the techniques used in the study.

In 1967, a group of thirty-four engineering educators and other specialists from nine African and four other nations met in Kumasi (Ghana) to discuss the special characteristics of engineering education in Africa and their consequences in the educational system. Specifically, a staff was chosen to collect and disseminate information related to curriculums, postgraduate programs, and engineering materials for use in secondary schools. Technical reports on topics such as rainfall, soils, tropical woods, and small industry were also collected and distributed, as was information on common research activities, exchange of students and faculty, and sharing of opportunities offered by visiting lecturers and expert consultants. The Kumasi conference agreed to urge all engineering and science personnel to participate as advisers in their governments' economic, social, and educational planning, especially in science and technology at the pre-university level, and to serve as advisers in relevant technical aspects of public projects. Strong encouragement was given to cooperative research programs with organizations outside the university and between universities, including non-African institutions, to the ends that available local capability be addressed to problems of local and regional importance and that recruitment of foreign specialists be implemented. Plans are in force for convening this conference every two years.

The interaction of technology and natural sciences with the social sciences in Africa's future development is of vital importance. Progress in improving material aspects of the living experience and the longevity of human beings will surely depend upon a hard core of research and application in engineering and science. But in an area with such a rich and enduring heritage of cultures, an understanding of human institutions and patterns is clearly needed to bring about an accommodation of people and projected changes.

Africa and the Modern World

African International Relations

ALI A. MAZRUI

THE WORLD IN WHICH AFRICAN STATES EMERGED after World War II seemed one of almost symmetrical alignments and allegiances. To the north of Africa lay Europe, the chilly home of imperial powers. In the southern tip of Africa itself lay the Union of South Africa, the most institutionalized case of racism in the world. In other words, both the north and the south symbolized for African nationalism targets of opposition and foci of political antagonism. Acute imperialism flowed from the north, and acute racism flourished in the south.

By contrast, to the east lay the continent of Asia and the comradeship of the Indians, the Chinese, and other fellow sufferers of the colored world. To the west of Africa lay the Americas. Latin America later came to be included in the comradeship of the Third World and to be regarded as an area which shared the indignity of indigence. North America consisted of Canada, the most liberal influence in the British Commonwealth, and the United States, with a tradition of anti-imperialism and with the liberal credo which was carried by American Negroes into the heart of early Pan-Africanism.

We may therefore say that for the African nationalist both the Asian East and the American West carried the warmth of friendly allegiance against colonialism, while the European North and the Afrikaner South symbolized the cold forces of colonialism and racism. With the attainment of independence in Africa this political symmetry was disturbed by a new alignment of forces and new patterns of friendship and enmity. But before discussing these changes we should examine more carefully the golden age of symmetrical African alignments—when north-south was a meridian of antagonism and east-west a connecting line of alliance.

532

THE ETHICS AND THE TACTICS

To discuss patterns of development in history is to indulge in generalizations. As one such generalization, we might say that African nationalism borrowed ideas from the Americas and Europe and strategies and tactics from Asia. Wilsonian notions of self-determination, liberal ideals of individualism, and the concept of one man–one vote were part of the package of philosophical norms which Africa inherited from the Western world. But strategies and tactics such as Gandhian passive resistance, Nehru's policy of non-alignment, and Mao Tse-tung's modes of revolutionary opposition were all part of the heritage which Africa received from the Orient. To some extent this differential legacy from the Orient and the Occident has elements of historical irony. After all, the Orient is supposed to be a wellspring of universal values and religious systems. Most of the major religions of the world have come from the Asian continent and its perimeter. The Occident, on the other hand, is supposed to be the home of techniques and skills, of industrial strategy and mechanical methods. Even the miracle of Japan's rapid industrialization and Westernization was described by the Japanese themselves as a case of adopting "Western techniques" while retaining "Japanese spirit." Time and again, in other words, Asia has been regarded as the fountainhead of spiritual values, while Europe has been regarded as the great source of practical techniques. Yet here was African nationalism borrowing techniques of social protest from contemporary Oriental experience, while adopting some of the political values of the Western world.

Among the important African borrowings from Asia during the colonial period was the Gandhian concept of passive resistance. Gandhism had been operative in India for more than a decade before the technique really captured the imagination of African nationalists. In West Africa the Gandhian torch was taken up by Kwame Nkrumah, the leader of nationalism in the Gold Coast. By June, 1949, Nkrumah had launched the strategy of "Positive Action," designed to harass the British authorities into granting one concession after another to the nationalist movement. Nkrumah viewed positive action as

> legitimate political agitation, newspaper and educational campaigns, and, as a last resort, the constitutional application of strikes, boycotts and non-co-operation based on the principle of absolute non-violence, as used by Gandhi in India.[1]

Later, Nkrumah was to say: "We salute Mahatma Gandhi and we remember, in tribute to him, that it was in South Africa that his method of non-violence and non-co-operation was first practised."[2]

In retrospect, it is clear that many early African nationalists were convinced

1. Kwame Nkrumah, *Ghana, the Autobiography of Kwame Nkrumah* (Edinburgh: Thomas Nelson, 1959), p. 92.

2. James Duffy and Robert A. Manners, eds., *Africa Speaks* (Princeton: D. Van Nostrand, 1961), p. 50.

that Gandhism would always be successful. At the 1958 All-African Peoples Conference, however, one of the major debating points was whether violence was or could be a legitimate instrument of the African nationalist. The Algerians—then struggling against the French—put up a spirited case in defense of armed insurrection, but Black Africa was divided in its opinion. The chairman of that conference in 1958 was Tom Mboya of Kenya. By 1963, Mboya would observe cautiously in his autobiography that "even those African leaders who accept Gandhi's philosophy find that there are limitations in its use in Africa."[3] By the time the Organization of African Unity came into being in May, 1963, Africa could actually think in terms of establishing a liberation committee to aid insurrectionist movements in the remaining colonies on the continent. Far from being against the use of force, the Organization of African Unity actually encouraged insurrection in the Portuguese territories and, later, in Rhodesia after Ian Smith's Unilateral Declaration of Independence.

But what had happened to the Gandhism which had once animated and inspired many African nationalists? There were a number of reasons for the greater militancy assumed by independent African states. One important factor in the shift in African mood was the action taken by India against the Portuguese colony of Goa on the Indian subcontinent. This was the first instance of a former colony taking direct military action to eject an imperial power from a neighboring territory. China had contributed indirectly in Indochina to the humiliation of the French at Dien Bien Phu, but China had never been colonialized in the same sense as India and Africa. The victory of the Vietnamese at Dien Bien Phu was substantially a victory of the Vietnamese themselves—much as Algerian independence ultimately came through the efforts of the Algerians themselves. India's military action against the Portuguese regime in Goa was, thus, in a class by itself. Accomplished with ease and confidence, it was a display of Asiatic power against the imperial arrogance of a European country. It was the first case of a former colony successfully intimidating one of the oldest empires of the era of European expansionism.

The impact of this event on Africa was greatly accentuated by the fact that Portugal's remaining empire was now in Africa itself. Tom Mboya was soon saying in Kenya that he was "strongly in favor" of India's action over Goa. And on the west coast of Africa the man who had once been described as the "Gandhi of Ghana," Kwame Nkrumah, was now declaring, "I am most happy about India's annexation of Goa which I consider long overdue."[4]

This then was the paradox of India's ideological impact on African nationalism. The country which had once inspired African nationalists to a non-violent approach to liberation had now set the precedent of a military confrontation with a colonial power.

3. *Freedom and After* (Boston: Little, Brown, 1963), p. 45.
4. This point is discussed more fully in Mazrui, *Towards a Pax Africana* (Chicago: University of Chicago Press, 1967), pp. 209–10.

DIPLOMACY AND REBELLION

In addition to the techniques of passive resistance, India contributed to African nationalism the concept of non-alignment, which served as the basis of African diplomacy on attainment of independence. In a sense, the doctrines of non-violence and non-alignment are closely related, and were developed sequentially in the Indian context. One school of African thought had adopted Gandhi's concept of passive resistance, and almost all African countries borrowed Nehru's doctrine of non-alignment. As Uganda's President Milton Obote put it in his tribute to Nehru on his death: "Nehru will be remembered as the founder of non-alignment . . . the new nations of the world owe him a debt of gratitude in this respect."[5]

Independence is a time when a newly created state has to seek direction for its diplomacy. The experience of conducting international relations as a sovereign state is entirely new. The idea of a foreign policy is also relatively new for such a state. The concept of non-alignment was therefore a useful guideline for the newly decolonized states of Africa. Non-alignment was essentially a policy of pragmatic non-committal. By eschewing commitment to alliances in the early post-independence period, and by rejecting the notion of automatic alignment in the cold war, the non-aligned countries gave themselves time to think. Non-alignment as a policy was well suited to a period of experimentation. It enabled the new states to try out relations with countries in both the Western bloc and the Eastern bloc, to seek direct knowledge and direct contact with a diversity of other countries, and to find out for themselves what the rest of the world was like. Commitments to only one bloc on attainment of independence would have limited the experience of diplomatic relations, particularly with the Eastern bloc. The opening of embassies is expensive, and if the policy of non-alignment had not required contact with both sides, it might seem wasteful to establish embassies among Eastern countries by a small power already committed to the West. This sort of reasoning was clearly manifest in a number of new states, including several in French-speaking Africa.

Non-alignment on the pattern formulated by Nehru set the stage for a period of diplomatic maturation. It allowed new states a period of trial and error in a diversity of relationships. Of course, there was always the risk of having one's fingers burned. It has been suggested that India's faith in Chinese good intentions, stemming in part from the policy of non-alignment, resulted in her unreadiness to meet the Chinese invasion in 1962. If this interpretation were true, it could still be argued that burning one's fingers as a result of direct trial and error is part of the process of growing up in the world of diplomacy.

India is not the only Asian country to have contributed strategies and techniques to African nationalism. Communist China, as a model, has also had an

5. *Uganda Argus* (Kampala), May 29, 1964.

impact on several of the new African states. It might be said that whereas India bequeathed non-violence as a method of changing imperial relationships, China bequeathed revolutionary violence as a method of social transformation. Admiration for China in this regard goes back at least to the Mau Mau insurrection in Kenya. One of the leaders of the Mau Mau movement was even called "General China." The Chinese established relationships with people like Felix Moumie, the rebel leader of Cameroon, and Abdulrahman Babu, a leading radical of revolutionary Zanzibar. The Simba rebels of the Congo seemed to have established a special revolutionary comradeship with the Chinese Communists.

It seems likely that because of the diplomatic costs incurred through their identification with opposition political forces in many African states, the Chinese are becoming more circumspect in their involvement in Africa. But this might merely result in more subtle ways of extending support to African revolutionaries, as the Chinese will probably continue to "offer themselves as the allies of oppositionists, rebels, and power-seekers." To use the words of Colin Legum, "In this field they have virtually no competition — neither the West nor the Russians will openly support movements against the *status quo*."[6]

These are some of the ways in which the Orient has provided a source of oppositionist techniques for African nationalists and African radicals. These techniques came from the East, but, as we have said, some of the animating values of contemporary African politics came from the West. It is to the latter phenomenon that we now turn.

DIPLOMACY AND IDEOLOGY

We have described Europe as one of the targets of the African nationalistic offensive. This was inevitable, since it was from Europe that imperialism had come to Africa. But Senegal's Mamadou Dia grasped an essential paradox when he described Europe as "mother of nationalism and, at the same time, by a strange destiny, mother of colonialism."[7]

This was an exaggeration on both counts, but there is some truth in the suggestion. Liberal democratic notions such as individual freedom and universal suffrage, as well as socialist and Marxist concepts such as class struggle and economic exploitation, found their way from Europe to the African continent where

6. He has also observed, "The Chinese are liberal in their payments to individuals selected by them as useful allies . . . large sums have been paid to individual politicians in Zanzibar." See Colin Legum, "Peking's Strategic Priorities," *Africa Report*, X (January 1965), 21. More recently, there have been indications or allegations about Chinese financial support for some of the domestic opponents of the Kenyatta regime in Kenya.

7. *The African Nations and World Solidarity*, trans. Mercer Cook (New York: Praeger, 1962), p. 3.

they were Africanized to some extent before they were adopted by African radicals.

The United States also contributed some of the political norms of contemporary African politics. The role of American education for Africans is one important link in this regard. As a Nigerian student dramatically put it in the 1940s, "The first skirmishes in the struggle for political freedom of the 21,000,000 people of Nigeria are being fought in the colleges of the U.S."[8]

This too, is a romantic exaggeration. But it is substantially true that Africans who were educated in the United States have tended to be more single-minded in their nationalism than Africans educated in, say, Great Britain. Perhaps it was not accidental that the radical leadership in Ghana passed from the British-educated elite to the primarily American-educated Nkrumah. Nor was it entirely a coincidence that the father of modern Nigerian nationalism was Nnamdi Azikiwe, also a product of American education.[9]

Another source of Western values for African statesmen was the United Nations. It is true that the United Nations is by intention a world body and its values ought not to be related to any single cluster of states, but in reality the United Nations Charter was greatly influenced by European values.[10]

The U.N. Charter contributed some of the values and some of the rhetoric which came to characterize African nationalism. Indeed, the U.N. Charter developed into the ultimate documentary confirmation of the legitimacy of African aspirations, although it is probably safe to say that very few African nationalists had in fact read it. Those who had were less interested in the specific procedures for assuring world peace than in the reaffirmation of "faith in fundamental rights, in the dignity and worth of the human person, in the equal rights of men and women and of nations large and small."[11] In spite of this limited or selected grasp of what the U.N. Charter was all about, it became a kind of documentary expression of natural law and a global bill of rights. Demands for liberation by both Asian and African nationalist movements came to be increasingly based on the principles of human rights "as set forth in the Charter of the United Nations . . . and of the Universal Declaration of Human Rights as a common standard of achievement for all peoples and all nations."[12]

8. Prince Okechukwu Ikejiani, "Nigeria's Made-in-America Revolution," *Magazine Digest* (January 1946), p. 57, cited in James S. Coleman, *Nigeria: Background to Nationalism* (Berkeley and Los Angeles: University of California Press, 1960), p. 244.

9. For some of the reasons which contributed to the greater radicalism of American-educated as compared with British-educated Africans, see Mazrui, "Borrowed Theory and Original Practice in African Politics," in *Patterns of African Development*, ed. Herbert J. Spiro (Englewood Cliffs, N.J.: Prentice-Hall, 1967), pp. 98–101.

10. In this case the term "European" includes the Soviet Union as well as the New World as cultural extensions of European civilization.

11. This quotation is taken from the opening lines of "Re-Affirmation of the United Nations Charter."

12. See, for example, the final communiqué of the Bandung Conference of 1955. Text is given in Robert A. Goldwin with Ralph Lerner and Gerald Sourzh, eds., *Readings in World Politics* (New York: Oxford University Press, 1959), p. 539.

The United Nations became a liberating factor in practice as well as in principle. Yet in this process it exhibited two paradoxical capacities: that of a collective "imperialist" with trusteeship responsibilities of its own, and that of the grand critic of imperialism at large. Indeed, as early as 1953, exasperated voices were already complaining that "perhaps the term 'self determination' should be dropped, now that the United Nations is called upon to do the determining."[13]

PAN-AFRICANISM AND RACIAL SOVEREIGNTY

After independence the theme of liberation remained important in African diplomatic activity, both in the United Nations and in other areas of debate and action. The Organization of African Unity devised methods of giving moral, and sometimes material, support to insurrectionists in the remaining colonies of Africa. African states were often strongly united in a mood of denunciation on issues such as that of Rhodesia after the 1965 Unilateral Declaration of Independence. Unity in action, however, was less common than unity in mood. When the African states passed a resolution to break off diplomatic relations with Britain over the Rhodesia issue, only nine fulfilled that resolution. Even the support for freedom fighters from the Portuguese territories has at times been a subject of disagreement between African states within the Organization of African Unity. Notwithstanding these divergent policy preferences, the fact remains that the newly independent African countries have found a major unifying political conviction to be the shared commitment to the liberation of the rest of the continent.

Anticolonialism, however, is second to opposition to white racism as a unifying and unanimously supported cause in Africa. While there is a pervasive feeling that foreign rule is morally reprehensible, there are, in fact, a number of cases where African countries do not react strongly to the phenomenon of foreign rule as such. For example, there is very little African antipathy toward Chinese imperialism in Tibet. And even within Africa there has often been acceptance of the need for colonial rule as a transition to independence. In 1958 the bulk of French-speaking African countries voted in the referendum arranged by de Gaulle for a continuation of French colonial rule. This referendum was a striking case of colonialism by consent. Even on the issue of Rhodesia, many African countries are demanding the end of the illegal independence and the restoration of British control over the country. The issue here is racism,

13. See, for example, Clyde Eagleton, "Excesses of Self-Determination," *Foreign Affairs*, XXXI (1953), 592–604. This point is also discussed more fully in Mazrui, "The United Nations and Some African Political Attitudes," *International Organization*, XVIII (1964), 449–520.

not colonialism. Even if Ian Smith had legally formed the government of an independent country, the majority of African states would still demand that this independence be terminated and British colonialism restored. Why? Simply because with Smith in control the principle of racial sovereignty is violated in Rhodesia. The legitimate sovereignty of Africans is being violated by the racist rule of a white minority. This is regarded as a greater breach of African aspiration than is traditional British control from London. Here then is a case in which African antiracism is a stronger motivation than African anticolonialism.

At present much of the sentiment of Pan-Africanism is focused on these twin areas of antiracism and anticolonialism. The idea of Pan-Africanism as a quest for continental integration has considerably subsided since the early days of Nkrumah's militancy. Regional organizations such as the East African Community or the Organization of States on the Senegal River are very much a part of interstate relations in Africa; but the idea of a continent-wide unification movement has receded into the limbo of obscure romanticism since Nkrumah's fall from power in 1966. Today the issues of antiracism and anticolonialism stir deep responses in Africa and constitute two major bonds of empathy among Africans.

Finally, there is a widespread feeling that African political problems ought to be solved by African effort and exertion. This feeling lies behind the strong disapproval of the use of mercenaries in African civil wars like that of Nigeria or, earlier, of the Congo. To employ mercenaries in a war of Africans against Africans is regarded as a violation of racial sovereignty. It is also a violation of the principle of *Pax Africana*, a principle which dedicates itself to the ideal of creating a state of affairs in which the peace of Africa would be maintained and protected by Africa herself.[14]

JOHN F. KENNEDY AND MAO TSE-TUNG

Pan-African sentiments and policy preferences are by no means the only major areas of African diplomatic activity. Africa has to deal not only with herself, but also with countries and continents elsewhere. We have already discussed the heritage of non-alignment which Africa received from India. In the first few years of independence the policy of non-alignment was neatly balanced in its operation. After all, the cold war was a bipolar phenomenon, with the Western bloc and the Eastern bloc relatively homogeneous in their diplomatic postures. The world of the non-aligned could therefore be made to appear something of a Third World, operating within the chasm which separated the world of communism from the world of Western values. But this golden age of non-alignment was only too brief.

14. These ideas are discussed more extensively in Mazrui, *Towards a Pax Africana.*

The days when the East and the West were neatly divided, while the newly independent states were acting in mediating roles, was a period of history which came to an end late in 1962, though its demise was disguised for a year or two longer. Two people had a great influence in the decline of non-alignment as a major factor in global calculations. One was John F. Kennedy, after he was elected president of the United States in 1960; the other was Mao Tse-tung, chairman of the Chinese Communist Party. By a strange destiny these two vastly different world leaders jointly contributed to a major change in the world scene: the role of the non-aligned was transformed, as were a number of other things in international politics.

The three years of the Kennedy administration had a decisive impact on the nature of non-alignment in both Asia and Africa. Kennedy's influence on the future of non-alignment took two main forms. The first was simply greater American acceptance of neutrality in the cold war as a legitimate stance for the new states. The second important influence on non-alignment resulted from the Cuban crisis of October-November, 1962, and its effect on Soviet-American relations. The confrontation of the giants over Cuba helped to rescue non-alignment from its own crisis of confidence following China's invasion of India at about the same time. How were these crises interrelated?

According to at least one view at that time, a basic assumption of non-alignment was that it was possible for a country without an alliance to be left alone militarily by *both* blocs. All that was needed, therefore, to invalidate non-alignment was an invasion of a non-aligned country by a member of one of the blocs. Mao Tse-tung fulfilled this condition when he attacked neutralist India. In other words, Mao apparently succeeded where John Foster Dulles had failed — the sanctity of non-alignment was destroyed, at least temporarily. The *Times* of London had a curt editorial to celebrate the explosion of the myth of neutralism.[15] On November 11, 1962, the *New York Times* even managed to collect quotations from Africans allegedly disillusioned with non-alignment. On the night of December 3, 1962, a professor from the London School of Economics commented over the BBC upon "the end of the neutralist myth." This interpretation of the significance of the Chinese invasion of India was fairly representative of Western opinion.

The *New York Times* might have been right in its reference to a mood of disenchantment in the ranks of the African non-aligned. There might indeed have been a moment of agonizing doubt as to the meaningfulness of the diplomatic stance they had so far fondly cherished. But among the implications of the Cuban crisis — when the worst was over and people could reflect afresh — was

15. Important editorials in the *Times* during this period included "India's Eddies," November 1, 1962; "China's Gain and Loss," November 22, 1962; and "Wooing the Neutrals," December 1, 1962. See also the article by the Delhi correspondent of the *Times* entitled "India after the Fighting, I: Need to Reconsider Non-Alignment," December 31, 1962.

a *vindication* of non-alignment. The humiliation of Cuba in 1962 arose because a foreign nuclear base was permitted on Cuban soil—a contravention of one of the basic tenets of Afro-Asian neutralism. In a letter to U Thant on October 27, 1962, Fidel Castro said that his country flatly rejected "the presumption of the United States to determine what actions we are entitled to take within our country, what kind of arms we consider appropriate for our defense, what relations we are to have with the U.S.S.R., and what international policy steps we are entitled to take."[16] Yet Castro's ally, Nikita Khrushchev, capitulated to Kennedy's demands with little pretense at consultation with Castro. The moral was not lost to the non-aligned in Africa: if an African voice was to be marginal in influencing big events, it had better be marginal outside the blocs. The experience of little Cuba was a warning against allowing oneself to be used in a global nuclear strategy by one of the big powers. The crisis of confidence which China's behavior had created among the non-aligned was resolved by the new sense of fearful vindication which emerged from the Cuban confrontation.

Indeed, even while the Cuban crisis was going on, African states participated in the search for a solution. Ghana and the United Arab Republic submitted a joint draft resolution to the Security Council on October 24, 1962, urging the parties in the dispute to refrain from further aggravating the situation while the search for a modus vivendi was in progress.[17] The Union of African and Malagasy States (the old UAM) submitted a set of proposals on the immediate steps to be taken to reduce the danger of war. It was clear that the survival of humanity was an issue which concerned all states, and Africa asserted her right to have a say in a matter so grave.[18] Africa's freedom from military involvement with either of the big powers did not appear to be a diplomatic handicap at such a moment.

The Cuban crisis strengthened the case for non-alignment, but indirectly it also weakened the impact of non-alignment on world affairs. The Cuban confrontation was the great turning point in Soviet-American relations. The intense ideological competitiveness between the two countries was replaced by a more sober relationship. The Soviet Union was humbled over Cuba. This by itself had a major impact on the Third World. But at least as important was the use to which John F. Kennedy put his triumph. He did not gloat over Khrushchev's capitulation. On the contrary, he congratulated him on his statesmanship.[19] Before long the "hot line" between Washington and Moscow was established. The Soviet-American détente was born.

16. United Nations, Press Release (SG/1359), October 27, 1962, pp. 2–3.
17. (S/5190), p. 1.
18. For the UAM proposals, see United Nations, Security Council, Letter (S/5195), October 25, 1962, pp. 1–2.
19. "I welcome Chairman Khrushchev's statesmanlike decision to stop building bases in Cuba. . . . This is an important and constructive contribution to peace"—Kennedy on receipt of Khrushchev's letter of capitulation on October 28, 1962 (U.S. Department of State, *Bulletin*, Vol. XLVII, No. 1220, November 12, 1962, p. 745).

This détente helped to reduce what little status Africa had had as a "crisis area." For as long as non-alignment had been regarded as dangerously near to communism, Africa had a chance of being regarded as "critical." The Soviet-American scramble to buy the ideological souls of Africans began to lose its momentum. Cuba had strengthened the case for non-alignment, but it had also helped to reduce its rewards. The Clay Report on U.S. foreign aid was presented to Kennedy soon after the Cuban confrontation. The year 1962 was, in fact, a peak year of American aid to Africa. But in the fiscal year 1963 the economic assistance program for Africa began to drop back. From 12.5 per cent of the AID figure, Africa's share dropped to 10.4 per cent in 1963 and then to 8.8 per cent in 1964.[20] Although there was an overall global reduction of American foreign aid, this reduction might itself have been influenced by the change in the tempo of the cold war following the Soviet-American détente. With that change Africa was reduced even further in status as a "security risk" for the United States.[21]

It was not only the Western hemisphere which was changing the globe. Transformative influences were also coming from the East. In 1923, writing on his deathbed, Lenin had linked three countries together and assessed the impact of their populations. He said:

> In the last analysis the outcome of the struggle will be determined by the fact that Russia, India, China, etc., account for the overwhelming population of the globe. And it is precisely that majority that, during the past few years, has been drawn into the struggle for emancipation with extraordinary rapidity.[22]

Lenin saw in this fact an assurance of the complete victory of socialism. For a while in the 1950s it did seem that Russia, India, and China, the three most populous countries in the world, intended to remain on sufficiently friendly terms to exert a shared influence on the rest of the world. Alternative possibilities began to be discernible. If China and Russia remained together, communism would retain a powerful alliance. If India and China remained together, something approaching "Pan-Asianism" would continue to exert a shared in-

20. AID loans and grants, $315,000,000; Food for Peace program, $108,400,000; Export-Import Bank loans, $67,600,000. Agency for International Development, *U.S. Overseas Loans and Grants and Assistance from International Organizations, Obligations and Loan Authorizations; July 1, 1945–June 30, 1963* (Washington D.C.: Government Printing Office, 1964). See also Agency for International Development and the Department of Defense, *Proposed Mutual Defense and Development* (Washington, D.C.: Government Printing Office, 1965), Table 2. See also "U.S. Economic Aid to Africa, 1950–1964," *Africa Report*, IX (December 1964), 8–12. A new peak of $212.1 million was reached in 1966. I am grateful to Rupert Emerson for bibliographical guidance.

21. See Usha Mahajani, "Kennedy and the Strategy of Aid: The Clay Report and After," *Western Political Quarterly*, XVIII (1965), 656–68; see also Arnold Rivkin, "Lost Goals in Africa," *Foreign Affairs*, XLIV (1965), 111–26.

22. In Edgar Snow, *The Other Side of the River: Red China Today* (New York: Random House, 1962), p. 646.

fluence on diplomatic events in the world, and could constitute a collective leadership of the colored peoples of Asia and Africa.

Yet for a while it was India rather than China which was the effective leader of the new states. One factor which helped India to retain this leadership for a decade was the general diplomatic isolation of Communist China, including her exclusion from the United Nations. But by the time Nehru died, non-alignment in the old sense had already been rendered impossible by Communist China. The two most populous members of the old community of Afro-Asian states had each played a crucial role in the history of non-alignment—one, India, had virtually invented it; the other, China, had virtually destroyed it.

But, as we have indicated, it was not the Chinese invasion of India that destroyed non-alignment; at most what the Chinese invasion imperiled was *India's* non-alignment. Even if that invasion had eliminated non-alignment from the rest of eastern and southern Asia as well, it could conceivably still have left Africa and the Middle East as the last and defiantly enduring bastions of non-alignment in the world.[23]

What destroyed non-alignment in the old sense was not China's conflict with India, but China's dispute with the Soviet Union. The old non-alignment that Nehru had bequeathed to Afro-Asians had been based on the assumption of a bipolarized cold war. Its whole conceptual framework postulated a dichotomy between East and West—and sometimes between communism and capitalism. China's dispute with Russia suddenly rendered such dichotomies too simple. Reluctantly, but with increasing tempo, African states saw themselves having to cope not only with archaic contests between Russians and Westerners, but also with competition and hostility between the Russians and the Chinese.

CONCLUSION: GROWTH AND COMPLEXITY

The birth of African diplomacy and its evolution to the present time is a process whose pattern so far can be only roughly discerned. Much of the dust of history will have to settle before the full picture of Africa's diplomatic growth in the first decade of independence can be adequately comprehended. Nevertheless, in this essay we have attempted to trace some of the main outlines of that growth and some of the patterns which suggest themselves for analysis. Inevitably there are a number of oversimplifications in this discussion, but excessive fear of generalizations can stifle perception and inhibit discernment of the broader movements of history.

We have tried to demonstrate that the Orient was one of the great sources of techniques and tactics for African protest movements, and that the Occident

---

23. This point is discussed more fully in Mazrui, "The United Nations and Some African Political Attitudes."

has been a major source of some of the political values which animated African political and diplomatic behavior in the closing stages of colonial rule and the opening days of African sovereignty. India bequeathed to Africa some elements of Gandhian passive resistance, as well as the whole doctrine of non-alignment as a basis for small-power diplomacy. From the Western world and the United Nations came some of the ideas and the rhetoric of the liberal ethos, ranging from principles of universal suffrage to the whole conception of self-determination as a basis for individual freedom.

But changes have occurred in the world of African political behavior since independence. Some of the old ideas of Pan-Africanism as a movement for broader integration have declined in importance, while the older commitments to antiracism and anticolonialism have persisted right down to Ian Smith's Unilateral Declaration of Independence and beyond.

The doctrine of non-alignment has itself responded to the fluctuations of political meteorology on the world scene. Preeminent among those who effected this change, and with it the international role of the new African states, were two individuals—John F. Kennedy and Mao Tse-tung. We have attempted to demonstrate that Kennedy's contribution to the emergence of a Soviet-American détente reinforced the effects of Mao Tse-tung's alienation from Russia. The world neatly divided between Communists and anti-Communists receded into the background of history. In some respects the Soviet Union had become closer to the United States than to Communist China, and the context of foreign relations for the non-aligned states became more complex than ever. President de Gaulle of France contributed his own share toward this complexity as he appeared to transform France into a European non-aligned power. It might even be said that the triumvirate of Kennedy, de Gaulle, and Mao Tse-tung wrote the epitaph to bipolarity as a basis of alignment in the world. No longer could the West and the East be considered "blocs" in any real sense.

In like manner, the old symmetry of African affiliation and orientation had sustained a disintegrative shock. It could no longer be said convincingly that to the north lay the enemy imperialism; to the south, among the Afrikaners, the enemy racism; to the east, the source of techniques of resistance; and to the west, the fountain of political values. The universe of Africa's political behavior was now rescued from this symmetrical simplicity.

But complexity is always the companion of growth and maturation. As the patterns of African diplomatic affiliation and diplomatic behavior have become more complex, so has the depth of African maturity in international politics. The old behavior of people suffering under foreign rule must now give way to the conduct of sovereign peoples engaged in foreign relations.

27

Africa and
the Islamic World

IBRAHIM ABU-LUGHOD

AFRICA HAS CONSTITUTED AN IMPORTANT PART of the Islamic world for over one thousand years. It is, therefore, justifiable to speak of the interrelationship of Africa and the Islamic world and to try to assess the relative importance of a universal religious system as a determinant of the kind of secular relations that may prevail between the two. One may also try to assess the implications of such a common bond in terms of international politics. These questions may indeed be crucial both for the student of international politics and for policy-makers engaged in shaping foreign policies. The task in this essay, therefore, will be to explore the nature of the common bond and to assess its influence, not only upon the historical development of African states but also upon the way African society has related to a larger world.

SKIN COLOR AND THE SAHARAN BRIDGE

Until very recent times, students of Africa and many others made a clear distinction between Black Africa, or Africa south of the Sahara, and North Africa. While the factors making for such a clear distinction varied, an under-lying assumption was the fact of color. It was assumed that skin pigmentation, so significant an element in Europe's social thought throughout the nineteenth century, could be used as the basis for the division of Africa into at least two undifferentiated wholes. Yet North Africa, by nineteenth-century European standards, was probably not considered white; the ambiguity of how to classify North Africa along the skin pigmentation continuum is apparent in European works of the nineteenth century. Despite the confusion in ascribing a skin color to North Africans, many writers of that period nonetheless referred to color as the differentiating factor between the two Africas. (This distinction excluded the unique problem of "white" South Africa.)

Today, the weight of historical, cultural, and political evidence militates against this kind of distinction. To take skin pigmentation as the significant variable introduces more problems than it solves. Even in contemporary times, with the sovereign state system firmly established in Africa and with human movements greatly constrained by the "closed" frontiers of that system, it is enormously difficult to draw a meaningful boundary between the two Africas on the basis of skin pigmentation. Any observer would immediately notice the gradual shading of color as one moves southward. The tremendous mixture of peoples, stirred by great population movements in the history of the continent, has given rise to an infinite variation in skin color. A traveler in North Africa would immediately be struck by the variation in skin pigmentation in all regions, from the Atlantic to the Red Sea.[1]

The distinction between the two Africas is frequently linked to the existence of what seems to be a natural barrier, namely, the Sahara, the vast and inhospitable desert separating Black Africa and North Africa. But the geographic separation, while true in modern times, was more apparent than real prior to the nineteenth century. Until the advent of the European colonist the great Sahara was actually the organic link between the two Africas, and historically it has served as a bridge between them. Peoples have always moved back and forth across the Sahara, and trade and culture have been transported with them. The variations in skin pigmentation which exist today in Africa reflect a history of extensive contact and interpenetration throughout the entire northern half of the continent, cutting across, rather than being compartmentalized by, the Sahara.

The view of the Sahara as a barrier is a reflection of the ethnocentrism of our present age. Until very recent times the Sahara did indeed serve as an effective barrier — but against the European, rather than the African. The European approach to Africa has always been by sea rather than overland; but for the African, the caravan routes connecting Africa south and north of the Sahara have been traveled for countless centuries.[2]

The reorientation of these trade routes toward the Atlantic to the south of the Sahara and along the Mediterranean borderlands to the north was a direct consequence of the Europeans coming to Africa. Even with this reorientation, however, the trade routes traversing the Sahara never really died; they simply receded in importance. One of the questions that remains to be answered is whether these functional linkages between North Africa and Africa south of

1. This question is lucidly discussed by L. C. Brown, "Color in North Africa," *Daedalus*, XCV (1967), 464–80.

2. See E. W. Bovill, *The Golden Trade of the Moors* (London: Oxford University Press, 1958); see also I. William Zartman, "The Sahara: Bridge or Barrier," *International Conciliation*, No. 541 (January 1963), pp. 3–13.

the Sahara that were weakened by the European invader can be re-created — links that are increasingly important to the political ties envisioned by Africa's leadership.

Given the minimal importance of color to the separate identity of Africa either south or north of the Sahara, and reemphasizing the crucial historical function of the Sahara as a bridge between the areas, it is necessary to ask whether the distinction between the two Africas can still be maintained with any degree of seriousness. We have suggested that the Sahara acted as a link in terms of the movements of people and goods between the two regions. But it acted in an equally significant way as a bridge for the transmission of ideas and cultural patterns, the most important of which, for our purposes, were those associated with the spread of Islam. This resulted in the emergence of cultural patterns which further linked the two areas.

To the extent that Islam and its resulting cultural imprints became a yard-stick which could measure the differences as well as the similarities between regions, it has become increasingly necessary to differentiate between those portions of Africa that were affected historically and socially by the Islamic system and those that remained outside of its cultural matrix. To the extent that Africa could be differentiated along religious lines and subdivided according to the geographic boundaries of religious influence, the criteria of color and environmental barriers must be relegated to the background. Until the advent of Christian missions one would have been justified in dividing Africa along the religious dimension on the grounds that the religious system of Islam gave rise to specific patterns of social and political life that were at great variance with those of pagan areas. In recent times one might be justified in speaking of three divisions along this dimension: Islamic, Christian, and pagan.

There is no doubt that the introduction of Islam into Africa was of great importance to the later development of the continent. If for no other reason than to understand the religious affirmation of many citizens within contemporary African states, an affirmation that may be of political significance in the future, the Islamic factor in African life ought to receive its due from the student of modern Africa. It is to this element that we shall now turn our attention.

MUSLIM COMMUNITIES AND STATES
IN MODERN AFRICA

It is almost impossible, even today, to obtain a clear picture of Africa's population in terms of religious affiliation. What is being made more evident, however, particularly in those African states committed to systematic census enumeration, is that the proportion of Islamic adherents has been significantly under-estimated. In some cases these findings may have put an entire political system in jeopardy, as was the case in Nigeria. For many years it was commonly assumed that Muslims constituted approximately one-third of the total population of Nigeria, and the federal structure of the Nigerian state was shaped partly in accordance with that ratio, although the official basis for the regional division of Nigeria was territorial rather than religious. In the 1962 census it was reported that the Muslim population was considerably larger than the politicians who had framed the federal structure thought it to be. The consequence was felt immediately. Among politicians and bureaucrats the validity of the entire census was called into question; and on a popular level, riots and demonstrations broke out which foreshadowed political pressures toward constitutional revision. The integrity of the entire federal structure was challenged and the attempted secession of the Eastern Region of Nigeria from the federation in 1966 may have been in part a response to fear of Northern Muslim domination. It is not improbable that the fear of similar consequences in other areas of Africa where religious affirmation of citizens may be translated politically leads to an implicit acceptance of existing myths and prevents the carrying out of an up-to-date census. The complete lack of any formal census in Ethiopia may reflect this fear.

The student of modern Africa is therefore compelled to use outdated and often inaccurate data regarding religious distribution patterns. Authoritative sources such as the *Demographic Yearbook* of the United Nations are at best outdated and at worst grossly incorrect. For certain African areas the demographers of the United Nations project the population figures on the basis of 1946 data, which even then were known to be wrong. The information presented in this essay is based on all existing resources, and with recognition of the serious problem of establishing validity.[3]

Taking the continent as a whole, it is reasonably safe to state that at least one out of every three Africans is Muslim. These individuals believe, to one degree or another, in the basic tenets of Islam, practice certain of its rituals, and identify themselves with a community of believers within their immediate society as well as in Africa generally and beyond. These Muslim populations are unevenly distributed; and religious tensions, with consequent political tensions, also vary from one area to another. If one were compelled to draw a line below which Islam becomes a relatively minor facet of African life, that line would be drawn just above the tropical rainforest belt and would stretch from the Atlantic to the Indian Ocean (see map on page 549).

While gross numbers may be misleading in terms of political implications, almost half of Africa's independent states (fifteen out of thirty-eight) contain

3. My estimates are based on several sources, including Louis Massignon, *Annuaire du monde musulman* (Paris: LeRoux, 1962); J.-C. Froelich, *Les Musulmans d'Afrique noire* (Paris: Editions de L'Orante, 1962); United Nations, *Demographic Yearbook* (New York: United Nations, 1963); Vincent Monteil, *L'Islam noir* (Paris: Editions du Seuil, 1964); and *The Europa Yearbook*, 40th ed., Vol. II.

ISLAMIC AREAS

Muslim majority

Significant Muslim minorities

a majority population that is clearly Islamic in identity.[4] Five other states contain Islamic minorities of sufficient strength and numbers to exert strong pressure on the political system for concessions which would guarantee the continued
viability and importance of the Islamic groups to the system as a whole.[5] While
this is not the place to indicate the significance of religion as a factor in the
political life of the community, it is important to remember that the question
assumes greater relevance here precisely because historical Islam has been more

---

4. Algeria, Chad, Gambia, Guinea, Libya, Mauritania, Mali, Morocco, Niger, Nigeria,
Senegal, Somalia, Sudan, Tunisia, and the United Arab Republic.

5. Ethiopia, Tanzania, Upper Volta, Ivory Coast, and Cameroon.

than a spiritual system regulating the relations of man to his Creator; it has given rise to a social and political system and to an emergence of distinct cultural patterns, as well as intellectual trends, that continue to affect the modern political life of the community. To some extent, Africa's political formulation of its goals of independence and the type of social and political order that was and is desired by its articulate leaders have been affected by this Islamic factor. As has been suggested elsewhere, much of Africa's ideology, while derived from Western political and social theory, has drawn on indigenous sources of ideas and patterns that were decidedly Islamic in nature.[6]

The fact that nearly half of Africa's independent states contain Muslim majorities does not necessarily qualify them for designation as Islamic states. For such designation, constitutional provisions would be needed to translate the religious affirmation of people into concrete state commitments, goals, and principles. Upon examination of the various constitutional documents of the African states, one finds that approximately one-fourth classify themselves officially as Muslim states.[7] By their definition, they include an article in the basic law of the country to indicate to the world at large that they are indeed Islamic states; precisely what this means is a different problem altogether. But for symbolic affirmation, for purposes of official holidays, and perhaps for purposes of law and legislation, such states may indicate a preference for those policies which are perceived to be compatible with their Islamic identity. That such a course of action is neither simple nor clear-cut is obvious from an examination of the various policies carried out by the states that designate themselves as Islamic.[8]

Another group of independent states, while containing Islamic majorities, acknowledge their identification with Islam in a cultural sense only.[9] Their constitutional documents and the public pronouncements of their leaders affirm the basic secular orientation of the state by refusing to insert a constitutional provision for an official state religion. While thus affirming their commitment to a secular course of public policy, a commitment to Islamic goals results from the pressure exerted by their Muslim constituencies. Thus far, the public behavior of these states has not been significantly different from those states that have affirmed their commitment to Islam through their constitutional documents.

It is perhaps significant to point out that those states which have inserted a

6. Ibrahim Abu-Lughod, "The Islamic Factor in African Politics," *Orbis*, VIII (1964), 425–26.

7. Algeria, Libya, Mauritania, Morocco, Somalia, Sudan, Tunisia, United Arab Republic.

8. See Vernon McKay, "Islam and Relations among the New African States," in *Islam and International Relations*, ed. J. H. Proctor (New York: Praeger, 1964), pp. 164–66. The ambiguous implications of Islam for the politics of countries with Muslim majorities are discussed in Abu-Lughod, "Islamic Dilemmas of Arab Politics," *Review of Politics*, XXVIII (1966), 447–76.

9. Chad, Gambia, Guinea, Mali, Niger, Nigeria, Senegal.

religious clause in their constitutions are easily identifiable as Arab or Arab-influenced. Where Arab influence has been minimal, African states have apparently opted for a more secular orientation. We will come to this point later on when a typology of Islamic penetration is analyzed.

One would expect that in societies undergoing the process of modernization, as are most African societies, religion would play a more important role in politics than in societies that have been modernized and tend to be secular. One would suspect that in premodern societies the religious affiliation of the majority of the people would play a critical role in the election of high public officials. While in general this may prove to be the case, Africa presents interesting contrasts indeed. Senegal is a country in which the majority of people are Muslim; yet the president is Roman Catholic and his Muslim competitor was deserted by coreligionists on other than religious grounds.[10] Eventually, the religious affiliation of a majority may translate itself politically by their refusal to accept a head of state who is not Muslim. This is one of the imponderables of religion and politics in Africa. All we can say at this point is that a Muslim majority does not guarantee an Islamic system, nor does it necessarily lead to the emergence of such a system. Economic, social, and political factors have to be taken into consideration before we can assess the potential of religion as a factor in the political life of new African states.

THE EARLY FORMS OF ISLAM IN AFRICA

While one may postpone final judgment concerning the centrality of Islam in contemporary Africa until more concrete and authentic data become available, it is important at this stage to determine the process by which Islam became a factor in African life.

It will be recalled that Islam emerged as a universal religious system in the seventh century A.D. in Arabia. At that time, the Prophet Muhammad, living in Mecca, received revelations from God (Allah), which were recorded as the Koran, or Holy Scripture. These revelations did not repudiate the Scriptures of the Hebrew Old Testament or the Christian New Testament, but rather asserted themselves as a further, and final, addition to all previous revelations contained in the Judaeo-Christian heritage.

The subsequent diffusion of Islam was multidirectional and to some extent followed the routes that were already familiar to the Arab disciples of the Prophet. Africa's contact with Arabia certainly predated the emergence of

---

10. The significance of the discrepancy between the religion of the president and that of the majority of the citizens in a country like Senegal is discussed in Ali A. Mazrui, "Islam, Political Leadership and Economic Radicalism in Africa," *Comparative Studies in Society and History*, IX (1967), 274–91.

Islam; it is well known that the Arabs of the Arabian Peninsula had carried on trade relations with Africa, having settled on the east coast of Africa long before Islam emerged. The same is true of the North African populations before they were Arabized and Islamized. Yet with the emergence of Islam something new developed in the nature of the contact and interaction which characterized Arab-African relations. From the seventh century on it was the self-appointed task of the traders, the settlers, and others to share their belief systems with the African populations with which they had contact.

To the extent that Islam made its appearance in Africa contemporaneous with its emergence in the Arabian Peninsula, we are indeed justified in speaking of it as one of the indigenous African religious systems. The fact that the earliest adherents of Islam were external to Africa, although including Africans living in the Arabian Peninsula (it will be recalled that the first Muslim prayer-caller, Bilal, was an African resident in Mecca at the time of the Prophetic Mission), does not militate against the indigenousness of Islam to the African continent. Therefore it should not surprise the student of religious systems to find specific African manifestations of the Islamic system which to some extent differentiate it from its Asian counterpart and perhaps explain some of the underlying reasons for its successful expansion in Africa.

In tracing the expansion of Islam, and with it the Islamic community in Africa, it becomes evident that expansion was not steady, nor was it accomplished through uniform methods. Yet one can chart its progress through the centuries and at the same time chart the type of carriers who made Islam a factor in African life. The first spurt of activity corresponds to the period of early expansion from the Arabian Peninsula. It will be recalled that the Arabs, as part of the Semitic community of the Arabian Peninsula, had experienced historical movements of expansion that took them into the Fertile Crescent and into Egypt. But this demographic expansion, instead of leading to the ethnic absorption into the populations among whom they settled, resulted instead in the cultural and religious conversion of the host populations. The expansion of the Arab population into the adjacent areas, accomplished at first through the military conquest of already decaying political and military powers, placed the Arabs in a position of political control over these areas. Their adherence to Islam, the ideology which inspired their expansion, made it subjectively possible for them to offer the populations a choice of equal treatment and full participation in the new social and political system. The result was the Islamization and the Arabization of the host populations. This was the process which established an Arab-Muslim community throughout the North African coast. Within a relatively short period of time the entire area of North Africa, stretching from Egypt to Morocco, came under Arab control; and with that control went the establishment of Islamic centers of worship, education, and public law that marked North Africa indelibly as an Arab-Islamic territory. Had North Africa not been won to the incipient Arab-Muslim community, conceivably the history of West Africa would have been quite different; for subsequent West African history was to a large extent determined by activities and movements emanating essentially from North Africa. This is a point to which we shall return in a later section.

The relatively rapid entrenchment of Islam and the Arabs in North Africa resulted in two simultaneous processes: the use of Arabic became widespread, and centers of learning were established in North Africa which were in meaningful interaction with other intellectual centers concerned with language, law, theology, and history in Egypt, Iraq, and elsewhere in the Arab world. Eventually Arabic language and literature gave North Africa its ultimate identity as an Arab area. A process of Arabization had taken place which resulted in the linguistic and, to some extent, ethnic transformation of the host population. On another level, although the Arabs who settled in the area were numerically insignificant, the simultaneous process of Islamization was taking place.

Arabization and Islamization were equally significant in North African history, and each of these two factors had different implications for the region. Arabization meant that subjectively the North Africans, regardless of historical justification for such a classification, viewed themselves as an integral part of the Arab community. While during the medieval period this ethnic factor was not particularly critical, it became of central importance once the system was transformed into a modern one in which justification for ethnic and linguistic nationalism was sought. While the factor of Arabization drew North Africa into the vortex of Arab politics and in modern times introduced itself into the problems of international relations, the Islamization of North Africa made it part and parcel of a community that was universal in its belief system and transnational in its aspiration. Some tension between the two identities was perhaps inevitable under certain conditions, and eventually North Africans had to stress one or the other. A stress on the Arab identity might lead to negative consequences in terms of internal social and political organization, while a stress on the Islamic identity might help in the expansion of certain norms and ideals. Historically, the North Africans were to use both factors selectively to the advantage of the expanding community. The positive and negative effects of this kind of selective use of both processes will be dealt with in a later section to illustrate its importance for contemporary African relations with the Islamic world.

The point should be made, however, that although North Africa became increasingly Arab and Muslim and, in cultural and political terms, began to interact more intensely and positively with the rest of the Islamic world (which had its epicenter in the Arab world), there was never a reduction in the amount of interaction between Africa north and Africa south of the Sahara. What was affected was the type of interaction, with cultural and ideological interchanges playing an expanding role. Up to the time of the Islamization of North Africa the interaction was for the most part economic in nature. The caravan routes traversing the African continent were the means by which goods, gold, and other commodities were shipped from areas south of the Sahara to a North African terminus. The three most frequented caravan routes ended in Morocco, in Algeria, and in Tripolitania (modern Libya). Forms of interaction other than trade were also present. Historians and archaeologists know that certain cultural implements—ideas, art, and other forms of expression—were transmitted by these trans-Saharan routes, but the extent of this cultural transmission is open to question. A visit to a North African museum will indicate the extent to which North African aesthetic expression was influenced by its counterpart in Africa south of the Sahara. This aspect of cultural exchange, then, while not initiated at the time of Muslim ascendance, did intensify and became more central in the period following North African conversion.

THE EXTENSION OF ISLAM IN AFRICA

The successful Islamic penetration of sub-Saharan Africa was largely dependent upon the vitality of North Africa, for soon after its conversion the latter's Muslim community began to introduce its new system of values and norms to the population with whom it had always interacted.[11] Historians are prone to attribute the Islamic expansion into the interior of Africa to the hard work and devotion of the traders and peripatetic missionaries. There is no doubt that some areas of Africa were exposed to the Islamic faith through these individuals, but the historical evidence quite clearly reveals the fact that major acts of conversion of substantial portions of Africa, especially on the west coast, were primarily the result of sustained religious-military efforts on the part of newly converted African peoples. This use of military conquest as a technique for spreading the faith constitutes one of the most interesting chapters in the history of Islamic penetration into Africa (see map on page 555).

11. There are a number of studies of the growth and development of Islamic communities in all parts of Africa, although none is completely authoritative: J. Spencer Trimingham, *Islam in the Sudan* (London: Oxford University Press, 1949); Trimingham, *Islam in Ethiopia* (London: Oxford University Press, 1952); Trimingham, *Islam in East Africa* (Oxford: Clarendon Press, 1964); Trimingham, *Islam in West Africa* (London: Oxford University Press, 1959); J. N. D. Anderson, *Islamic Law in Africa*, Colonial Research Publication 16 (London: H.M.S.O., 1954); Lyndon Harries, *Islam in East Africa* (London: Universities' Mission to Central Africa, 1954); N. A. Ziadeh, *Sanusiyah: A Study of a Revivalist Movement in Islam* (London: E. J. Brill, 1958); S. F. Mahmud, *A Short History of Islam* (Karachi: Oxford University Press, Pakistan Branch, 1960); I. W. Arnold, *The Preaching of Islam*, 3d ed. (Lahore: Institute of Islamic Culture, 1961); George Delf, *Asians in East Africa* (London: Oxford University Press, 1963); H. J. Fisher, *Ahmadiyyah: A Study in Contemporary Islam on the West African Coast* (London: Oxford University Press, 1963); M. Brelvi, *Islam in Africa* (Lahore: Institute of Islamic Culture, 1964); J. M. Abun-Nasr, *The Tijaniyya: A Sufi Order in the Modern World* (London: Oxford University Press, 1965); and I. M. Lewis, ed., *Islam in Tropical Africa* (London: Oxford University Press, 1966).

Arab

Berber

Black African

Asian (mainly Indo-Pakistani) settlements

0   500   1000

Scale in Miles

AGENTS OF ISLAMIZATION

The process of conversion started in significant and systematic fashion about the tenth century A.D. By then, much of the interior of the North African region had been won to the new faith. The interior and mountainous regions of this area were inhabited by a population ethnically different from that found along the Mediterranean coast. Whereas Arabs continued to settle on the coast and to interact chiefly with the Arab world and with southern Europe, the peoples of the interior still looked southward for their contacts. It is reasonably well known that the human links between sub-Saharan Africa and Mediterranean Africa were provided by the Berber communities which inhabited much of the region between coastal North Africa and the Western Sudan. Strategically located at the termini of the trade routes, traditionally warlike and mobile, the Berber tribes often intruded into both areas of Africa. By the tenth century they had been won to the Islamic faith. Yet their conversion, while creating a religious bond with the rest of the inhabitants of the region, did not eliminate the ethnic tension between the Berbers and other groups. Furthermore, their residential isolation and traditional mode of life made them suspicious of the increasing encroachment of the cultural superstructure of the urban Arab Muslims. Despite these tensions and suspicions, however, the religious bond became increasingly viable and a kind of unity prevailed.

Such symbiosis and integration as occurred was largely the product of a new movement within the Islamic system that emerged essentially to bridge the gaps existing between indigenous communities and the urban-based, formalistic Islam which was associated with a power elite dominated by Arab Muslims. Historically, what brought about this increased integration became known as the Sufi (mystic) movement; Sufism was one of the movements in North Africa that assumed a dominant role not only in cementing the relationship between the Berber communities of North Africa and the Arab dwellers on the coast but also in facilitating the large-scale conversion of other areas of Africa. By the eleventh century, a Sufi order known as al-Murabitun (the Almoravids) assumed total control of the entire region of northwest Africa and from that position pushed in both directions—northward into Spain and southward into the interior of Africa. What is significant about al-Murabitun, aside from the fact that it represented the first significant movement in the history of the Islamic community in which the political leadership was either dominated or inspired by an organized Islamic fraternal order, is that its dynasty was Berber-dominated, that it seriously thought in African terms, and that it actively sought the conversion of Africa.

It accomplished its early objectives not through the normal historical contacts, but by a large-scale military offensive, admittedly inspired by religious zeal, against Ghana, an established African state. The Ghanaian state then was ruled from A.D. 1076 to 1088 by a Berber dynasty originating in North Africa. This pattern of interaction was to continue throughout the succeeding centuries. The conversion, peaceful or otherwise, of individual groups of Berbers, and, later, of black Africans, resulted in the political and military dominance of those groups which, soon thereafter, assumed the responsibility of expanding the frontiers of the faith. For the most part, that expansion had to be accomplished at the expense of an already existing state structure in which the dominant elite was pagan. The displacement of that elite placed the new Muslim elite—whether Berber or black African—in a position of control, and it was through that political and military control that other aspects of Islamic culture were established. No sooner had the displacement succeeded than the religious counterpart of the military-political elite began to function effectively. The setting up of an Islamic legal system, one of the most important aspects of Islamic culture, and of an educational system centered around the mosque became questions of paramount importance. Ultimately, of course, it was these institutional structures that became significant in implanting Islam as a faith throughout the regions that were controlled militarily or politically.

Three aspects of the Islamization process of the interior of Africa ought thus to be noted. In the first place, the agents who carried it to the interior were, ethnically, indigenous Africans, whether Berber or black African. At no point did the Arabs of the North play any significant role in the Islamization of any area in the interior. In the second place, this indigeneous factor is responsible to some extent for the relative political independence of the African Muslim communities. At no point in the history of the Islamic world did any non-African Islamic state attempt to intrude deep into the African interior; it is doubtful that any such attempt could have succeeded. In the third place, the strong connection between religious and political power (exemplified by the control by the religious order of the political movements which carried Islam into the interior) gave African Islam a characteristic not common in the rest of the Islamic world—throughout history, African areas were to a large extent controlled by the Sufi religious orders, which in turn competed effectively with the established political elite. The history of many West African areas can be viewed as the periodic eruption of these Sufi religious orders in search of political control.

These characteristics of African Islam had given rise not only to the political independence of African areas and their isolation from the mainstream of the Islamic world, but also to a cultural independence that aided and occasionally hindered the political independence of these areas. No sooner had religious orders succeeded in setting themselves up as the mainstays of orthodoxy in the areas of their control than they established indigenous cultural centers to serve the particular religious and cultural needs of the community. Whereas the original African Muslims had sent their sons to Cairo, Fez, and other North African areas to be educated, in due course local centers of education and learning under the control of local leadership and supported by existing political dynasties of African states south of the Sahara were established. And it was these institutions that ultimately produced a distinct intellectual leadership for the African community that could deal with the problems of adaptation of Islam to the African interior. The centers of learning at Timbuktu and Jenne eventually assumed an importance for Africa equal to those at Cairo and Istanbul for other Islamic areas.

The cultural and political independence of large areas of Africa did not necessarily mean the total severance of all ties with the Islamic community outside the continent. On the contrary, links continued to be fostered; pilgrims traveled to Mecca (Arabia), performing their religious duties and traversing the Islamic world, and scholars continued to exchange ideas across "national" frontiers. Yet, the vitality of African Islam was not dependent upon what was going on elsewhere. The relationship of Africa to the Islamic world was that of equals, united by a common profession of faith and subordination to a common set of values and norms.

The penetration of Islam into areas other than the Western and Central Sudan provides interesting contrasts indeed. For one thing, Islam never reached very far inland from the coast of East Africa, nor did it affect the lives of as many Africans, or to the same extent, as it did in the West African areas. Furthermore, and perhaps equally significant, the agents of Islamization were decidedly different and, as a consequence, the nature of the Islamic system on the east coast of Africa was quite different from that of West Africa.

We indicated earlier that the east coast of Africa was quite well known to the Arabs of the seventh century. It could be expected that once Islam became established in their society they would make some attempts at conversion; yet the evidence indicates that the early efforts at conversion, if any, were rather unsuccessful. Apparently the Arab settlers and merchants, long accustomed to trade and interaction with other Africans on the east coast, continued, even in their new-found identity as Arab Muslims, to conduct their relations with the host population just as their predecessors had done in previous periods. Insofar as we can determine, there was no serious endeavor on the part of the Arab-Muslim traders of the seventh century to convert the host population to their new religion.

Conversions did take place, however, although somewhat more gradually and less dramatically than in North or West Africa. Equally important, such gradual conversion occurred as a result of an ethnic settlement of fresh immigrants from the Arabian Peninsula who came to Africa in search of a haven from the religious persecution that periodically erupted in Arabia. The first such settlement took place sometime in the eighth century A.D. At that time a group of Arab Muslims crossed to East Africa for political and physical safety; they were escaping from pressures exerted by the ruling Islamic dynasty, the Umayyads (whose capital was in Damascus), against the followers of the fourth Islamic Caliph, 'Ali, who supported a rival claimant to the institution of the Caliphate. They had been designated heretics by the orthodox followers of the Umayyads. At the time these Arab followers crossed to East Africa, the banner of disobedience was carried in the name of the grandsons of the Caliph 'Ali. These immigrants, who became known as the Zaydiyyah, established themselves as a separate, and almost self-sustaining, community of believers, and generally refrained from actively proselytizing among those Africans with whom they came into contact.

This group was followed by another wave of migrants who crossed into East Africa by the tenth century. Unlike the first migrants, who were classified as heretics, or Shiá, the second group was largely composed of orthodox Muslims. Although the two migrant communities were united by a common belief system, they were also set against each other by their political allegiances and theories of legitimacy. Their political beliefs were sufficiently at variance to generate a good deal of tension between them so that they remained separate communities with a certain degree of residential isolation. In time, the two communities clashed, and the earlier wave was compelled to move southward, gradually being incorporated by the African Bantu-speaking peoples. The victorious Sunni (orthodox) community established a closely knit social and political system which eventually engendered the distinctively urban Islamic system so common elsewhere in the Islamic world. It was the second community that succeeded in establishing urban centers, such as the present city of Mogadishu. Yet despite its victory and its settlement, the second community also refrained from active proselytism. Accordingly, the African converts to Islam on the east coast of Africa were the result of types of processes other than those of proselytism or military conquest. But because of the smallness of the community and its abstinence from active involvement with the inner workings of the African system, it continued to depend on the active cultural and economic life of the Arabian Peninsula. For many centuries to come both East Africa and the Arabian Peninsula remained the "home" of this East African Arab-Muslim community.

A third wave of migration issued later from the Persian city of Shiraz, and these migrants became known as the Shirazis. Like the first wave, they were heterodox Muslims. Their encounter with the already established Sunni community was therefore one of tension. The difficult relationship compelled them to set up a separate communal settlement which served only to exacerbate the existing tension characteristic of the orthodox-heterodox relationship. Zanzibari Arab politics until the Revolution of Zanzibar in 1964 were largely shaped by the historical conflict between the Sunnites and the Shirazis; pre-Revolution Zanzibari political parties to some extent also reflected this historical schism. This third group of migrants adhered to the tradition of its predecessors and refrained from any overt act of proselytization.

Although the successive waves of Arab-Muslim migrants to East Africa failed to produce an indigenous African-Muslim community, in due course such a community did emerge, mostly through a slow process of interaction and intermarriage with Africans. The result has been the Swahili people in East Africa and the much more widespread Swahili language—primarily a combination of Arabic and Bantu. This mixed Swahili community, however, remained relatively small and was confined primarily to the narrow strip along the eastern coast of Africa from Somalia to present-day Tanzania. A final wave of migration, that of Sunni Muslim Arabs from the present territory of Musqat and Oman, took place in the nineteenth century when the Omanis succeeded in assuming control over the coast of East Africa.

Although the Arab Muslims in East Africa did not actively proselytize, there is at present a large and influential Islamic community on the east coast of Africa. It includes Arabs (or Arabized Africans), Indians, Swahili, and several other groups of African Muslims. The black African Muslims now outnumber all other Muslim groups as the result of an important stimulus from new immigrants from the Indian subcontinent who throughout the twentieth century have assumed a most active and systematic role in converting Africans. In East Africa this conversion has been accomplished primarily by the Ismailis under the overall leadership of the Aga Khan. In West Africa the Ahmadiyya of Pakistan have served the same function in this century. Although the Islamic community of the east coast is substantial in number, it is divided within itself in terms of basic doctrines, attitudes, orientation, and background. While the original settlers may have had good reasons to be antagonistic toward each other, instead of gradually working out a social and cultural compromise in their new milieu they opted to perpetuate the original schisms; this had significant social implications. For example, the original communities tended to segregate themselves spatially and occupationally, interacting with one another only in narrowly limited roles. Not only did they maintain this pattern of social interaction among themselves but, in essence, they transferred their initial and personal schisms to the new African converts. In due course, Africans were incorporated through marriage into clans of the Arab settlers and, on the basis of such incorporation, claimed descent from some ancient Arabian tribe and inherited its traditional attitudes and values. Thus, the initial dispute became rooted in new soil among people who had no connection either with the ethnic origin of the community or with its ideological dispute.

This brief discussion of the Islamization of East Africa sheds light on a number of significant points. In the first place, the "Arab" orientation of this area is self-evident. The Arab settlers in coastal East Africa continued to look to the Arab homeland for guidance and inspiration. At no point did they develop a positive African outlook. It is precisely in these African areas that social or religious movements originating in the Arabian Peninsula found fertile soil. In part, this "Arab" outlook may explain the early interest of Somalia in receiving aid and assistance from a country like Egypt. It also helps to explain why Egypt has succeeded thus far in playing a larger role in the affairs of some East African states than in the affairs of the West African states.

Second, and more important, in East Africa Islam remained essentially an Arab religion. Almost all Africans who were converted to Islam were *ipso facto* Arabized or absorbed into the mixed Swahili community. Historically, this meant the spread and use of the Arabic language and technology. The moderate success of the Wahhabi movement (which established the conservative "Saudi" Arabian state) on the east coast is explained partly by the "Arab" character of this area.

Finally, the later conversions of Africans accomplished through the organized activities of the Ismailis and others, while enlarging the community numerically, added to the hostility implicit in their relations with it. These movements for the most part had their origin outside the Arab world, derived their strength and support primarily from the Indian subcontinent, and were consequently viewed by orthodox Muslims with ambivalence and suspicion. In their communal existence in Africa today, they tend to perpetuate Indian or Pakistani patterns, to segregate themselves from other Muslims, and to organize their community life separately. Educationally, economically, and socially they remain aloof from their coreligionists.

This enumeration of divisive factors must not obscure the positive contribution of Islam to the area. The spread of Islam on the East African coast, as elsewhere, introduced a unique system of law, provided a basis for a cohesive social order, and furnished its adherents with an identifying ideology and culture which could, when properly manipulated, form the basis of a separate "national" existence (as among the Somali).

AFRICAN ISLAM IN THE COLONIAL ERA

The advent of European colonialism in the latter part of the nineteenth century affected Islamic areas of Africa differently.[12] First of all, paradoxically, the Europeans inadvertently assisted the spiritual expansion of Islam while weakening its political control. Second, the European presence unwittingly contributed to the decline of traditional Islamic forces and assisted radical Islamic reform and leadership. Finally, it contributed substantially to the modernization of Islamic areas.

It will be recalled that when the Europeans advanced militarily into Africa they clashed with the existing political and military orders. In many parts of West Africa these political systems were controlled by the Islamic religious orders, which had effected a successful alliance with the political elite. These existing regimes were no match for the modern European powers, and in some cases they had already lost a great deal of legitimacy and support. Political control rested to a large extent on a feudal basis of social organization, on an arbitrary system of government, and on an ideational system that was decidedly medieval in character. In the initial phases of the European confrontation, the established elites offered considerable resistance, but gradually they were defeated everywhere in Africa.

It was at this point that the European powers had to evolve a policy to contend with indigenous elites in the future. During the initial stages of European colonialism, the pre-existing elites were thought to constitute a threat and,

12. Virginia Thompson and Richard Adloff, *French West Africa* (London: Allen & Unwin, 1958), pp. 571–79. See also, Roland Oliver, *The Missionary Factor in East Africa* (London: Longmans, Green, 1952); Reginald Coupland, *East Africa and Its Invaders* (Oxford: Clarendon Press, 1956); and J. Spencer Trimingham, *The Christian Church and Islam in West Africa* (London: Sudan Christian Mission, 1956).

accordingly, the European powers evolved hostile policies that were calculated to bring them to an end. In time, however, a more effective approach commended itself to the colonial powers, largely through the observations of officers *in situ* who recognized that the religious orders and their political counterparts had an extensive network of contacts, controlled large-scale social organizations, and were in communication with large sectors of society. If these orders could be satisfied and won over, they could perform invaluable services and could assure a certain degree of stability and tranquillity.

By the end of the nineteenth century and the early part of the twentieth, colonial policies toward Muslim elites became quite clear. The elites were to be encouraged and assisted, provided they were willing to collaborate with the European powers. Certain of the Muslim religious elites opted for this alternative, perhaps out of their own weakness or for anticipated gains. This collaborationist response had been common, with minor exceptions, to all Islamic elites in Africa. Two of the exceptions involved the Sanusi religious order, which had its origin in Libya, and the Mahdi movement of the Sudan. In both cases, the European powers found it necessary to defeat them totally. Both movements had emerged in response to internal tensions and had aspirations to displace pre-existing corrupt elites. Both movements were reformist in nature and aspired to extend their doctrinal and political control over other Islamic areas. Their zeal and ideology made it imperative for them to carry out the struggle against the European occupation to the bitter end; consequently, they were almost destroyed. With their eclipse, however, no national elite emerged to collaborate with the European powers and their reputation remained untarnished. Ironically, before the military coups of 1969, the descendants of these two movements had returned to political power.

This early pattern of interaction between the European powers and the Islamic elites had three important consequences for the later evolution of Africa. First of all, the spiritual expansion was facilitated by the European powers, who looked with favor upon it as long as it did not pose any kind of political threat. Second, Muslim settlers and merchants began to propagate their faith in areas hitherto prohibited to them by constant insecurity. This was made possible by European "pacification" of the interior of Africa. Third, a convenient escape for energies was provided by this outlet for religious enthusiasts; otherwise, these energies might have been harnessed for politically disruptive activities in the central areas where colonial control was most entrenched.

Thus, this type of interaction made it possible for Islamic religious orders to undertake missionary tasks successfully and thereby expand the frontiers of Islam at the expense of the ethnic religions. That these Islamic orders in effect competed with Christian missionaries seeking the conversion of Africans in no way disturbed the colonial administrations. Their major concern was the successful pacification and acquiescence of the population, and this was partly effected by colonial support for expansion of the orthodox Islamic religious orders.

It should perhaps be observed that this pattern of interaction was typical of both British and French areas. It is conveniently assumed that the two types of control effected by the powers, namely, the "indirect" control adopted by Britain and the "direct" French control, resulted in different policies insofar as Islamic religious orders were concerned. The actual events, however, turned out to be much the same for both areas. Where the indirect principle was applied, the colonial state provided sanction and legitimacy for the feudal religious-political center, exercised by the chiefs and emirs; this was quite clear in the pattern of Northern Nigeria. Where the direct principle was applied, authorities often exercised control directly on behalf of the religious elites and suppressed political challenges to those religious leaders.

This pattern of interaction between the colonial powers and the dominant Islamic religious groups—those whose control was perpetuated by the colonial powers—had important implications for the development of nationalist movements in Islamic areas. It became more and more obvious to those who were seeking political autonomy for their areas that a serious obstacle presented itself in the form of an entrenched elite which anticipated a weakening of its own power in the event of relaxation of external control. By the same token, the colonial powers often saw any nationalist challenge to the entrenched religious elite as an indirect challenge to its own authority; a weakening of the control exerted by the traditional religious elite would have meant an increase in the power of organized groups that derived their legitimacy and support from the secular base of society. An examination of practically all African areas with Islamic constituencies would reveal quite clearly that the challenge to external control automatically meant a challenge to the internal traditional elite which collaborated politically with the colonial power. Thus when a modern group, not overtly political in nature, advocated an internal reform such as the establishment of a secular school system based on modern principles, it was opposed by the established system of administration, often at the behest of the traditional religious-political elite. This kind of symbiosis resulted, in the end, in the emergence of nationalist movements that were antiforeign as well as antireligious in tone. The secularist trend of a country like Guinea or Senegal or Mauritania cannot be understood without reference to this early symbiosis between the traditional religious authority and the European power.

In areas where Muslims were not in the majority, the story differs somewhat but not greatly. While the nationalists evolved programs of political action and vision that were designed to transcend the fragmentary system (in which the fragmentation was based on a tribal, ethnic, linguistic, or religious basis), they did so in order to marshal public support for independence. But independence would have meant a reorganization of the entire political structure and the abolition of those privileges that had been granted individuals or groups; in the end it would have given rise to a group whose cohesion would have sprung from territorial loyalty. The Muslim groups, supported by the colonial power, saw in the emergence of such an independent polity a threat to their existing autonomy and privilege and perhaps feared that independence would bring about a curtailment of their internal power. There is no doubt that such would be the case if the state were organized on the basis of secular principles. Accordingly, Muslim groups in Nigeria or Ghana were in the main hostile to the young nationalist movements and, perhaps as a result of negative pressure, postponed the day of independence. Once independence was attained, such Islamic minorities continued to present special problems for the new polities.

The antinationalist stance of Islamic groups and their lack of contribution to the nationalists' struggle for independence did not mean, however, that the Islamic community did not contribute to the process of independence. This contribution was often made indirectly and mostly on the bases of the Islamic ideology. It will be recalled that the successful struggle for independence in Islamic areas required large-scale political organization with effective networks in important areas where the struggle was launched. What happened, in fact, was that secular organizations with political and economic programs for the future succeeded in enlisting a good measure of public support. These secular organizations succeeded in forging effective links among the various citizens of the community for secular ends. But it must be remembered that the members of the community had already been prepared for collective endeavor, largely through the Islamic religious orders. They were long accustomed to the discipline and organization necessary for collective action. The secularist leadership did provide a new program, but it relied on the existing organizational base. It should also be remembered that the communal emphasis and solidarity already present for the Muslims had succeeded in giving rise to distinct communities on the basis of law and education that were markedly different from other communities, whether African or European. The basis of solidarity was used and manipulated by the nationalist leadership for secular and more programmatic ends. Unlike non-Islamic areas of Africa, the principle of self-definition did not consume much of the energy of the Islamic nationalists and they utilized the existing principles of solidarity for further political action. Where other areas had to struggle to forge a link between diverse ethnic groups, the Muslim community was already there. What they needed was a program to which the population could commit itself for the establishment of a new order.

Finally, it should be stated that the nationalist agitation for independence in Islamic areas differed from that of other areas in what it chose to emphasize. Non-Muslim African areas often emphasized the racial bond and conceived of the colonial struggle in racial or anti-European terms. In Islamic areas the struggle, when not waged in secular terms of an economic or political nature, was waged in the name of the Islamic community. For Muslims, the world is divided; but the division is on the basis of faith, not color. (Thus, Europeans are thought of as "Christians" rather than as "white men.") The racial tensions so characteristic of African areas are notably absent in the Islamic culture zones.

On the whole, colonialism was disruptive to the Islamic communities in Africa, territorially, culturally, and ideationally. Yet, it is obvious that there were certain gains. Increasing proselytism attracted new members to the faith and augmented the number of believers. At the same time, colonialism facilitated the movement of peoples across continents. The presence of the Ahmadiyya, the Ismailis, and other Asians in Africa can be attributed to the colonial system. While their presence has ultimately had an adverse effect on ethnic and national cohesion, it has at the same time increased the internationalism of African Islam. An increasing dependence of African Islam on Islamic communities elsewhere has become a factor of importance throughout the continent. The lines of communication among Muslims, regardless of their nationality and locale, have thus been opened; the use and effect of these links will have implications for the entire Islamic world.

AFRICAN ISLAM IN THE POST-INDEPENDENCE ERA

The emergence of the independent African states reflects the successful culmination of the nationalist struggle for the separate units demarcated by the former European colonial powers. These units, as is well known, were carved out without regard to traditional cultural geography, that is, ethnic groupings, language, economy, or religion. Territorially, then, they had no exact previous counterparts; culturally, they represent diverse backgrounds and efforts. Yet, as separate units, each has had its own history and development. Over the years, these colonial units which have become the new African states have built certain affinities and exhibited certain patterns that may ultimately prove to be too strong and viable to give way to efforts at wider integration.

Common to all of the new states, however, are a number of factors that are important for the determination of the Islamic element in their political and social life. They were all subjected over a period of time to an intensive process of modernization, urbanization, and development inspired or carried out largely as a result of European control. These had the effect of disrupting certain of the traditional institutions, of undermining some of the traditional norms and values and replacing them by others. The emergence of secularist trends, in part as a result of these large-scale processes of modernization, is perhaps of critical relevance to our discussion. Such trends of secularization are evident throughout Africa and the rest of the Islamic world and they have had an important effect not only on the value system of the believers but additionally, and perhaps more importantly, on the institutional bases of society.

Partially as a result of these processes, the new African states with Islamic majorities have tended to assume a secularist stance. They are likely to conceive of their future in secular terms, subordinating religion to the exigencies of social and political development. On internal levels such a development may be desirable. But at the same time, the African states have been struggling to bring about greater national integration and unity; in doing so they may utilize religious factors which underlie the system and which may aid the process of national unification. It is at this level that the religious factor has assumed a certain importance. Although no uniform practice holds true for all African states, it is quite clear that religion has played an important role in the political life of states such as Algeria, Somalia, and the Sudan. National development and the attempt to bring about a greater degree of national cohesion in these states have been significantly affected by increasing reliance on the Islamic factor.

Yet Islam may play another role, given the appropriate conditions. Many of the African states, Islamic or otherwise, have attempted (thus far unsuccessfully) to bring about greater unity on the supranational level. Their commitment to some kind of broader unity has resulted in a number of regional attempts at unification. The Organization of African Unity is in part a response to this commitment to restructure the presently fragmented map of Africa. Regional confederations may eventually prove to be the most feasible means to this end. It is in the context of regional unification that Islam may prove to be a factor of importance, for here the Islamic bond among adjacent states may be emphasized and used as the basis for regional units. The ideological commitment of North African states to closer union is in part explainable by their common religious affiliation. Whether it will take place is, of course, dependent upon other factors.

The immediate relevance of Islam to international politics has been noted by several of the Islamic states, and their recognition of that relevance prompted them to reinforce their identity with one another in religious terms. Thus, for example, Egypt began its activities in Africa with a built-in asset, namely, its identity as an Islamic modern national community. It has assisted morally and materially in the effort of other Islamic communities in Africa to utilize religion as a justifying factor, though obviously helping to gain political advantages as a result.

One may note another important use of Islam in African developments: its role in the submersion of an otherwise explosive ethnic division in the population. It will be recalled, for example, that North Africa's population is in part divided into the Arab and the Berber groups. Ethnicity historically had been a divisive factor that was conveniently utilized by the colonial powers. The North Africans themselves recognized the divisive ethnic element and in its place emphasized their solidarity on the basis of the common Islamic faith. Thus far this emphasis has succeeded in maintaining the national integrity of the countries in question, but as the process of modernization gains greater momentum it may be that the religious element will not prove viable and ethnic tension may reassert itself.

At this point in history, it is difficult to foresee the precise role which Islam will play in the development of internal and regional African politics. Whether the international efforts represented by such groups as the World Islamic Congress will ultimately succeed in giving rise to a community of independent states united by religion or with some degree of coordination in their policies is also an open question. At this juncture, one simply ought to note that the Islamic factor is present in Africa, and that it will have considerable effect on future internal and external developments throughout the continent.

28

Confrontation in Southern Africa

GWENDOLEN M. CARTER

AFRICA'S MOST SERIOUS INTERNATIONAL PROBLEM lies within its own borders. The division between independent African-controlled states and the colonial and white-minority-controlled territories of southern Africa splits the continent ideologically, politically, and strategically. To African-controlled countries, the racial discrimination and minority white domination in the Republic of South Africa and Rhodesia and the Portuguese colonial control of Angola and Mozambique are open affronts to their principles of non-racialism and independence under majority rule. To the dominant white groups, on the other hand, their political control is the safeguard of a highly privileged economic and social position whose continuance they justify on grounds of development and stability and which they are prepared to maintain by force.

In terms of area and population, the African-controlled states of the continent have the vast advantage. In terms of capital resources, economic development, and external lines of trade, the balance swings as decisively to the advantage of white-controlled southern Africa. Although the white population of southern Africa numbers less than 4.5 million in territories whose total population is over 38 million and in a continent of about 300 million people, the resident whites and colonial administrators (in the Portuguese territories) control the political, economic, and military sources of power within their respective countries. Moreover, these countries form a contiguous block of territory extending across the southern end of the continent and up its flanks as far as Congo-Kinshasa on the west and Tanzania on the east, with the keystone of this white-controlled area the Republic of South Africa. Thus white domination in southern Africa has two significantly related aspects: regional control over the resources, development, and character of life of a large, strategic, and relatively wealthy area; and internal control, within state boundaries, of majority populations which suffer discrimination and are exploited as cheap labor.

SOUTHERN AFRICA'S WHITES

Whites came to southern Africa from 1652 on and slowly but steadily spread out from the original Dutch settlement at Capetown. (Since the closing of the Suez Canal Capetown is once more a crucial refueling and reprovisioning port between Europe and the Far East.) After the Cape was ceded to the British at the end of the Napoleonic Wars, English-speaking settlers were established around Port Elizabeth and subsequently in Durban, while Afrikaners (descendants of Dutch, Huguenot French, and German settlers) trekked north into the Orange Free State and the Transvaal in a vain effort to escape British imperial influence and missionary liberalism. Kimberley diamonds and, in the 1880s, Witwatersrand gold drew in many more European entrepreneurs and settlers, as well as the funds for development. As Cecil Rhodes schemed for an all-British route from the Cape to Cairo, whites penetrated to Rhodesia in 1890, pushing the boundaries of white settlement farther north. As Mbata notes in his essay in this volume, South African whites quickly created a network of discriminatory provisions that impeded or prevented the African majority, the Coloured (mixed blood), and the Asians (who came as indentured labor or subsequently as traders) from achieving the share of power that their numbers and importance to the economy would have justified. In other words, whites created and maintained a rigorous system of domestic colonialism, that is, coercive rule by one racial group over others within a single country. In a modified form the same system developed in Rhodesia.

The domestic colonialism of the Republic of South Africa and Rhodesia is more discriminatory and more difficult to change than was traditional colonialism. Those in control in domestic colonialism live side by side with those they dominate. They depend on African labor for the unskilled and semi-skilled services performed throughout their countries, and they believe that their affluence and even their safety depend on retaining full political and coercive control. In South Africa,[1] by far the most developed country, both industrially and commercially, on the African continent, whites and Africans interact in the economy to such a degree that white leaders can exploit at will the latent fear of the white urban lower class that African economic competition might undercut them. Indeed, the 1920s saw a massive migration from drought-stricken farms into the largely English-dominated towns by poor-white, or potential poor-white, Afrikaners with few skills and fewer prospects. What threatened to be the world's worst poor-white problem was mitigated by the development of new jobs through a state-controlled iron and steel industry,

---

1. *South Africa* refers throughout this essay to the Republic of South Africa. *Southern Africa* refers to the region comprising South Africa, South-West Africa, Lesotho, Botswana, Swaziland, Angola, Mozambique, Rhodesia, Malawi, and Zambia (although Zambia is increasingly oriented toward the north and east, its history and economic associations still link it to the southern African grouping).

but it was solved chiefly by government and trade union efforts to carve out areas of the economy and administration reserved for whites at inflated scales of pay. Thus political control is used as the safeguard of economic privilege.

Fears of economic competition and of submergence by the superior numbers of the non-white majority, as well as a Calvinistic sense of elitism and mission, were factors in the development of the intense sense of nationalism that still characterizes Afrikaners today. Afrikaner nationalism was also fired in the strife of the Anglo-Boer War at the turn of the century and politicized by the tardy recognition that their combined votes can make their will decisive in the all-white national parliament. Since the National Party electoral victory of 1948 (repeated with increasing majorities in successive elections), the old Afrikaner fear of domination by the English-speaking whites has been replaced by an obsession with the spectacle of African political control spreading southward in the continent and an increasing fear of the potential power of South Africa's own African majority. Moreover, English-speaking whites, although by and large continuing their electoral allegiance to the opposition United Party, have confirmed their basic support for the South African system of racial discrimination.

SOUTH AFRICA'S STRENGTHS AND WEAKNESSES

Compared to any other area in Africa in which whites have settled in considerable numbers, the percentages and absolute numbers of whites in South Africa are high. Algeria, scene of prolonged and bitter fighting before France relinquished control in the early 1960s, had just over a million *colons*, 10 per cent of the total population (some sixty thousand now remain). South Africa, however, has 3.75 million resident whites (60 per cent Afrikaans-speaking and 40 per cent English-speaking), forming 20 per cent of its 18 million people. In addition, South Africa's former mandate, South-West Africa, which it continues to dominate despite a United Nations vote that it has lost the right to do so, has nearly 75,000 whites, 16 per cent of that huge territory's 500,000 people.

South African whites have long boasted that the standards of education and skills of their non-white populations are higher than those in other African countries. Though these claims can now be disputed, it is true that there have long been South African non-whites with professional and industrial skills and middle-class status. Politically, however, the qualifications they have secured have been used against them. As more Africans in the Cape Colony qualified for the franchise under the technically color-blind voting provisions prior to South African Union, literacy and additional economic provisions were introduced to restrict their votes. The provisions of the South Africa Act, under which that country received its independence in 1910, perpetuated the exclusion of non-whites from the franchise in the Free State and Transvaal as a means of bridging the division between English- and Afrikaans-speaking peoples and the four territories linked by Union. Moreover, the constitution provided that only whites could sit in Parliament.

The process of increasing restrictions continued after Union. In 1936, Africans who had been qualified for the vote in Cape Province (the only one in which they had the franchise) were removed from the common roll and placed on a separate roll where they were able to elect only three white members to represent them in the 159-member Parliament. In 1956, after a six-year constitutional battle, the Coloureds were similarly removed from the common roll to a separate one to elect four whites. In 1959 the African parliamentary franchise was abolished. The only offices (other than urban advisory boards) for which Africans can now vote are in the Transkei, which since 1963 has possessed a partially elected African legislature, the model for other semiautonomous Bantustans (African rural territories with special status) to be established within South African borders.

In 1960 the international community was shaken by news of the panic shooting at Sharpeville of unarmed Africans demonstrating against the hated pass system. Ensuing African stay-at-home work boycotts were broken by force; a state of emergency was declared in which sympathetic whites, as well as Africans, Coloureds, and Asians, were jailed or detained; and the two African nationalist organizations were banned. These were the African National Congress, since 1912 the historic standard-bearer which had swelled in size to over one hundred thousand with the passive resistance campaign of 1952–53, and its breakaway of 1958, the Pan-Africanist Congress. Neither has been legal since that time.

Moreover, subsequent attempts both by liberal whites and by Africans to force change through violence have been effectively countered by steadily tightening coercive methods of control. A network of paid African informers, long periods of detention without trial on suspicion of knowledge or association, and the use of torture have enabled police to identify potential leaders and to thwart emerging organizations.

The residential segregation of most urban Africans in townships separated from white areas by open land that is easily controlled by machine guns and helicopters provides the physical framework for constant control. Water and food come from the white centers. The buses and trains which carry Africans to and from their town-based jobs are easy to supervise. While it is not impossible that a violent antiwhite outburst could take place in a white residential or commercial area, the knowledge of the odds against successful defiance and of the scope and severity of the punishment serve as powerful deterrents.

Thus South African whites possess extraordinary sources of power. Their numbers constitute approximately four-fifths of all resident whites on the continent. Their government has ruthlessly reacted to internal threats to its control and has refused to listen to appeals to ameliorate disabilities. The country they dominate occupies a strategic position at the southern end of the continent with easy access to, and established lines of trade with, the most developed countries of the world. South African trade with the United Kingdom provides a significant surplus to the latter's balance of payments. The South African military and police establishments are strong, well armed, and well trained, particularly for riot control and for coping with guerrilla incursions.

Still more significant for the South African position vis-à-vis independent African-controlled states is the pervasive character of its economy. The southern portion of the African continent forms, in practice, an economic and geographical subsystem of communications, commercial transactions, and mutual interaction that makes all countries in that sphere more or less dependent upon the highly developed South African economy. The three enclaves of African-controlled territory that lie within southern Africa—Botswana, Lesotho, and Swaziland—are particularly dependent on South Africa for employment for their migratory labor, markets for their products, and their supply of manufactured and imported goods. Their current lack of economic independence is underscored by the fact that they are included in the South African customs zone and use South African currency.

But even more striking than the economic dependence on South Africa of these three weak countries whose total population is only 1.7 million (of whom 16,000 are white) has been the evidence of South Africa's economic significance for Malawi and even Zambia, which potentially has the strongest economic base of any African-controlled country. Malawi, with slight economic potential of its own and apparent unconcern by its President Banda over working with white-controlled states, has welcomed the benefits of its *de facto* economic vassalage to South Africa and Rhodesia. In contrast, Zambia has made a mammoth and heroic effort to turn its trade and communications routes away from Rhodesia since the latter's unconstitutional attempt to declare its own independence on November 11, 1965, but has had to replace Rhodesian goods by South African.

Yet there are also elements of potential weakness in the situation of South African whites. The African majority within the country is cowed, but it has sources of strength, notably its indispensable role in the South African economy through its skills and numbers; its links (however weak at the moment) with militant groups outside; the long-established sense of nationalism among its better educated and more skilled members, and their basic sense of determination ultimately to secure a dominant voice in the management of the whole country; and the pervasive sense of bitterness that militates against satisfaction with purely economic returns. The international community shares in large measure the African resentment of and opposition to discriminatory provisions based on color. South Africa's buffer states, which are less strong than it is, are under international pressure to change their racial policies, and Rhodesia, in particular is already subject to international sanctions. Guerrillas frequently probe the boundary zone between white-controlled and African-controlled states. All these factors need to be analyzed before coming to more conclusive evaluations regarding the growing confrontation in southern Africa.

SOUTH AFRICA'S BUFFER STATES

South Africa's buffer states — Rhodesia, Angola, and Mozambique — have relatively small white populations, both in absolute numbers and in percentages. Rhodesia has only about 220,000 whites, little more than 5 per cent of its total population of 4.25 million. Angola, abutting on South-West Africa, has approximately the same number of whites as Rhodesia, but over a million more Africans. Mozambique, which adjoins South Africa on the east side of the continent, has far fewer whites, about 100,000, in a still larger total population of about 8 million. Thus, where South Africa has approximately 3.75 million whites living side by side with over 14 million non-whites, most of them Africans, the whites in the buffer states number little more than half a million among nearly 18 million Africans.

The controlling elements in these situations are the presence of army and police units, pervasive and effective administrations, scattered and divided African ethnic groups, and South African support. In Angola and Mozambique there are Portuguese army units of considerable size; in Rhodesia there is a small, permanent, well-trained defense force now supported by South African planes and mobile units. Official notice has been given that there are regional defense arrangements between these countries.

In opposition are international pressures, guerrilla activities, and growing nationalist sentiment among local Africans.

INTERNATIONAL PRESSURES FOR CHANGE
IN SOUTHERN AFRICA

South Africa's racial practices have been criticized and condemned in the United Nations since the establishment of that body. Since 1958 the United States has voted in support of such resolutions. In 1963 the United States took an important further step by imposing an arms ban on South Africa for any type of weapon or equipment that could be used against its non-white majority, an action preceding by several months the United Nations vote to establish such a ban. This ban has had relatively little effect in practice, however, owing to a rapid increase in the production of armaments within South Africa and to the fact that France and a number of other countries continue to sell it arms.

The strongest steps taken through the United Nations to influence the course of development in southern Africa have been with regard to Rhodesia. The British government under international law still retains sovereignty in that territory, and following the unconstitutional Unilateral Declaration of Rhodesian Independence on November 11, 1965 (a status which no government, including that of South Africa, has recognized), the United Kingdom requested United Nations members to enforce sanctions, at first on a voluntary basis and subsequently in the spring of 1968 on a mandatory basis. These sanctions have the objective of forcing Rhodesia's white-controlled government to accept the six conditions that the British have insisted must precede a constitutional grant of independence. The most significant of these conditions, and the one that the Rhodesian whites resist most strongly, is that a gradual but irreversible extension of political rights, and thus potential power, be guaranteed to the African majority, which, as we have seen, includes nearly 95 per cent of the population of Rhodesia. The six points also include the requirement that steady progress be made in eliminating racial discrimination and the condition that any constitutional settlement must secure majority approval.

The principle the British government is seeking aid to enforce is the one it has followed since World War II in regard to granting independence to other colonies. This principle is that there must be a popularly supported national government, which has won an election on an open franchise, before ultimate political control is transferred to local hands. Reinforcement for this insistence in regard to Rhodesia is provided by the South African record of steadily diminishing political rights for Africans since independence. In the light of this experience, white Rhodesian claims that they could best "advance" their own Africans ring hollow.

Sanctions have created a slow but steady attrition in the Rhodesian economy despite large-scale and continuous assistance from South Africa, lesser aid from the Portuguese, and skillfully operated schemes to evade the bans on movement of materials in and out of Rhodesia. Yet white control remains unshaken, for despite vehement pleas by African countries, particularly Zambia, the British have refused to use military force to change the situation in Rhodesia.

LIBERATION MOVEMENTS AND CONFRONTATION

The only groups applying force, though still in small and sporadic efforts, are guerrillas. Since 1963 FRELIMO has worked out of southern Tanzania to secure a base in northern Mozambique. This effort has been successful to the degree that by 1968 its operations were being carried on entirely within that territory. A serious blow to FRELIMO came with the assassination in Dar es Salaam of its distinguished and liberal leader, Eduardo Mondlane, who had pursued a non-racial policy in his relations with Portuguese settlers in northern Mozambique.

FRELIMO continues under less moderate leadership in its efforts to free Mozambique from Portuguese control.

Other guerrilla activities affect the northern sector of white-held southern Africa. The Portuguese have had the heaviest engagements. They are harassed in several areas of Mozambique, they are fighting against three substantial and mobile liberation forces—GRAE, MPLA, and UNITA—in Angola, and they face constant attacks in Portuguese Guinea in West Africa as well.

Guerrilla action in Rhodesia has been spasmodic. In September, 1967, African liberation forces engaged in hand-to-hand fighting with Rhodesian troops in the Zambezi Basin. They clashed again in May, 1968, and infiltration continues. On the ground that these guerrilla forces include Africans from South Africa as well as from Rhodesia, and that in this sense the Zambezi is South Africa's frontier, South African police and ultimately military units have been sent to support Rhodesian troops. There are unconfirmed rumors that South Africans also have been sent into Mozambique to the area of Cabora Bassa where a mammoth dam is being constructed with the aid of South African capital.

Without exaggerating the extent of the harassment from the north or the present commitment of the South Africans to support all of white-held southern Africa, these engagements epitomize the confrontation that forms Africa's most crucial international issue. Whites are apprehensive that their entrenched positions could be dangerously shaken by a powerful external thrust coordinated with an internal uprising. Africans in turn fear that the superior force and economic power of the white-controlled states might be used to push north the boundaries of *de facto* white control. Their recollection of the effectiveness of white South African and Rhodesian mercenaries who operated in the Congo reinforces such fears.

POSSIBLE FUTURE DEVELOPMENTS IN BUFFER ZONES

In the light of the manifest strength of white-controlled regimes and the inherent weaknesses of those under African rule (because of ethnic divisions, economic underdevelopment, and lack of capital resources), can there be said to exist a genuine confrontation in southern Africa? The answer is affirmative because of the intensity of feeling on both sides of the division: From the Africans there is a combination of factors—determination to force change, bitterness, and fear of white power; and from the whites there is a determination to maintain the privileged position they have by whatever means are necessary. How this confrontation will develop is problematic, but there are a number of possibilities that should be considered.

It seems likely that the South African government would have favored a settlement between Ian Smith's government in Rhodesia and the United Kingdom, both to limit Rhodesia's ever increasing economic demands on South

Africa and to reduce the international attention focused on southern Africa because of sanctions. Such a settlement might have been along the lines proposed by Prime Minister Wilson when he met with Ian Smith on the battleship *Fearless*; his suggestions greatly modified the previously adopted British stand of NIBMAR (no independence before majority rule) but reasserted the need for guarantees of irreversible progress in extending African franchise rights and for securing general acceptance of whatever constitutional provisions are agreed upon by the two governments. But the June, 1969, vote in Rhodesia in favor of establishing a republic put an end to such discussions and widened the division between Rhodesia and the United Kingdom.

If serious African resistance were to develop within Rhodesia in the future, some observers believe that South Africa's success in dealing with its small neighbors—Botswana, Lesotho, and Swaziland—and with Malawi suggest that it might prefer to have Rhodesia governed peacefully by an African government if it would maintain good relations with its powerful southern neighbor rather than existing in a state of disorder under a shaky white regime. But so far the regime is not shaky, nor is internal resistance visible.

Others anticipate that Mozambique will be the weak point in white control because of its overwhelmingly high proportion of Africans and because of the degree to which it impinges on three independent African-controlled states, Tanzania, Zambia, and Malawi. As noted, however, considerable South African private capital is being poured into the building of the Cabora Bassa Dam on the lower Zambezi with the expectation that its power can be tapped for industrial development of the Witwatersrand. Moreover, the long-established and substantial labor commitment from Mozambique for the Transvaal mines is economically important to South Africa, as is the Transvaal's outlet through the port of Lourenço Marques. It is possible that the South African government considers continued Portuguese control of southern Mozambique to be even more important to its own strategic interests than is white control in Rhodesia.

And what of South-West Africa, the huge territory on the Atlantic that South Africa long controlled as a mandate? The United Nations declares that South Africa has now forfeited whatever rights it may have had there because it failed to administer the territory in the interests of its inhabitants. Indeed the territory has been renamed Namibia and has been technically placed under United Nations trusteeship as a step toward independence. Here too there are nascent liberation movements and a long history of efforts through the United Nations and the International Court of Justice to shake South African control. However, as with southern Mozambique, South African security is directly involved. With or without right, South Africa controls South-West Africa, profits by its wealth of diamonds, precious metals, and karakul, and administers it virtually as part of its own territory. South-West Africa is also on South Africa's air route to Europe, much of which is over Portuguese or Spanish territories since independent African states do not permit

South African planes to overfly their land. Short of massive force, it is difficult to envisage a change, in the near future, in the control of South-West Africa.

POSSIBILITY FOR CHANGE WITHIN SOUTH AFRICA

In any case, whatever possibilities exist for inducing or forcing change in South Africa's border states, African nationalists and their supporters will not be satisfied until there is radical change in race relations in the present heartland of racial discrimination, the Republic of South Africa itself. This most developed of all African states has great internal sources of strength, as we have seen, through its economic growth and prosperity, ruthless political and administrative controls, overseas links through trade and finance, and, because of its buffer states, current remoteness from any overt attacks. Yet at the same time, as we have also seen, South African whites have within their own borders a degree of interaction with the non-white majority that goes far beyond that of any other African state.

In a very real sense South African whites face a dilemma in relation to their non-white majority. The latter are integrated into the production process that assures the country's wealth. Africans have developed a bourgeoisie of professionals and skilled workers in secondary industry (although they are far from equally compensated with whites in grade and pay); in addition, they hold approximately 75 per cent of the semiskilled jobs throughout industry and a still higher proportion of the unskilled occupations in every field. In 1960 Africans outnumbered whites in every town and city in the country except Pretoria and Capetown, and non-whites formed a majority in nearly every urban center. Yet the basic principle on which the dominant regime operates is that the country must be run for the benefit of its white inhabitants and that non-whites, particularly the Africans, are not regarded as participating members in a common society but as sojourners without guaranteed rights even to remain in urban areas where they were born.

The philosophy developed to justify this position is that each group in South Africa basically has its own center and its own lines of development. The whites have approximately 87 per cent of the total land in the country. The remaining 13 per cent, called reserves, has been set aside for African occupancy. In the official view these reserves provide the "homeland" for each major African group regardless of whether a majority of the Africans from that group are in that territory or not. If Africans live outside their "homeland" (because of birth, training, employment, or for any other reason), their relation to this "homeland" is supposed to be provided primarily through their right to vote for elected representatives for the legislature of the "homeland" once that area has achieved Bantustan status.

So far only the Transkei has an elected minority of members in its all-African legislature. The Ciskei, also composed of Xhosa-speaking Africans, and Tswana-land have been given appointive legislatures and executive committees as the last stage before the establishment of semielective ones. So has Ovamboland in the northern part of South-West Africa. A similar development is being pressed in Zululand in northern Natal, despite the reluctance of some leading Zulus, and also in other predominantly African areas. Only those already named, however, have consolidated or near-consolidated areas (there are more than 250 separate parcels of land making up the reserves). In any case the partial jurisdiction exercised by any African legislature is only over rural areas and is subject to the overriding jurisdiction of the white-controlled national parliament and adminis-tration.

The South African government's purpose in instituting the Bantustan pro-gram was to provide an alternative to African nationalist objectives, once formu-lated as securing an equitable share in the political, economic, and social systems of the country but increasingly aimed at a dominant role in South African life. The original formulation of the program by Prime Minister Hendrik Verwoerd suggested the ultimate goal of independence for each of these territories. But very little, if any, progress has been made in this direction in the Transkei despite the support of some members of its legislative assembly. Moreover, although the chief minister, Kaiser Matanzima, has urged white capital to invest in the Transkei now that the original government ban on such investment has been lifted there has been slight response.

There are probably a number of reasons why territorial separate development within South Africa is proceeding so slowly and with so little effect. There is good reason to believe that the program had been designed to divert international criticism, but the initial fanfare over "South Africa's answer to the racial prob-lem" created far less international enthusiasm than had been expected. In practice, as observers have pointed out, the Bantustan program as implemented in the Transkei has not yet moved beyond an early stage of colonial representa-tion such as was common in African countries in the 1950s.[2] In the period since the Transkei has had its partially elected legislature, that is, since December, 1963, Basutoland (Lesotho), Bechuanaland (Botswana), and Swaziland have achieved independence. It is possible that the degree of international concern for these three new countries, small as it is, has acted as a deterrent to permitting the Transkei to acquire independence. Lesotho, Botswana, and Swaziland have Peace Corps volunteers, for example, and Botswana has been visited by World Bank and UNESCO missions and all have been able to apply directly to non-African countries for technical aid.

In addition to these external factors, Africans within the Republic of South

2. Gwendolen M. Carter, Thomas Karis, and Newell Stultz, *South Africa's Transkei: The Politics of Domestic Colonialism* (Evanston, Ill.: Northwestern University Press, 1967).

Africa have shown little enthusiasm for the Bantustan development. While most African nationalists, inside and outside the country, have ceased to be outspokenly negative about territorial separate development, this is not because they see it as an acceptable alternative to a decisive role in the whole country; rather, it is because they feel that the Bantustans might offer some opportunities for mobility in an otherwise tightly controlled situation. Moreover, it is questionable whether even Africans, like Chief Kaiser Matanzima, who have cooperated with the South African government envisage restricting their interests and activities over a long period of time to such limited areas as the Bantustans can comprise.

Thus the Bantustan program has failed to satisfy the major purposes for which it was devised and, in addition, the apparently insatiable though uneven white demand for labor continues to pull Africans in large numbers out of the so-called homelands, which in any case are incapable of supporting them and their families. Thus while the South African government continues to move slowly to establish structures for African rural reserves which appear to extend them a measure of autonomy, it is not with the objective of subdividing power in a federal system or through a genuine partition.

The question then arises as to whether the South African government can maintain its control indefinitely in a situation in which Africans, Asians, and Coloureds are broadly intermeshed with whites in an expanding economy. The fact that increasing non-white participation in the economy has always been more than counterbalanced by increasing coercive restrictions has convinced most opponents of the system that only internationally enforced economic restrictions coupled with ultimate use of force, both internal and external, will break the system. Others hold that at some point, possibly to be reached in a sudden expansion of economic activity, the restrictions maintained by coercive laws, administrative regulations, and vigilant police action, supported by the network of African informants, will collapse by the sheer weight of economic demand. However, neither course appears to be a strong possibility at this point.

CONCLUSIONS

The confrontation of black and white within southern African countries is an old story whose essential form has not changed. Unlike the whites in Kenya and Ivory Coast who ultimately accepted the logic of numbers and the appropriateness of African control, those in South Africa and Rhodesia have responded to the internal and external pressures for African advance by tightening restrictions and attempting to divert African aspirations from a share in national decisions to the management of ethnically defined, impoverished rural areas.

Viewing Africa as a whole, by 1964 the boundaries of contiguous African-controlled states had spread to Zambia and Malawi, which border "the white redoubt." In this perspective, racist policies can no longer be looked at solely in relation to a particular country, for they have become part of a regrouping of countries within an international zone of potential bitter conflict. The spasmodic stabbing southward by guerrillas and countermeasures to consolidate white economic influence over small or compliant African states are early moves in what has become an international as well as internal struggle between black and white for control of southern Africa.

What is the significance of this fact for the West, and particularly for the United States? At the moment the situation may seem less pressing than other international issues, but potentially the confrontation in southern Africa could create the most dangerous of all conflicts: an open struggle between black and white. In such a case, black numbers and populist values would be pitted against economic and military predominance marshaled by a ruthless determination to preserve the privileged position of the whites. Such a struggle, infused on both sides with the ferocity born of desperation, would inevitably split American opinion and create counterpressures on policy-makers that could dangerously escalate our own internal racial tensions.

The U.S. government has maintained as consistent a stand as it has in support of sanctions against Rhodesia because of several factors: the minimal economic sacrifices involved; the size and growth of American private industry's stake in African-controlled countries, which by some estimates is now larger than that in white-controlled southern Africa; the awareness, however dim as yet, that the United States effort to establish a color-blind society at home requires a commitment to that principle in international relations; and the hope that a progressive change in Rhodesian race relations would have a constructive influence on South Africa's racial policies. That sanctions appear to have had so much less effect than was expected does nothing to justify a relaxation of efforts to maintain them unimpaired.

The same consistency should be followed by the United States in mounting pressure on the Portuguese government to ameliorate race relations in Angola, Mozambique, and Portuguese Guinea, and to move them steadily toward control by their own African majorities. The United States should also exert pressure on South Africa, both diplomatically and at the United Nations, to persuade it to accede to requests for U.N. representation in South-West Africa and to permit that territory to move toward independence.

Surveying the total picture in southern Africa, it is both feasible and highly desirable that the maximum amount of constructive economic aid and diplomatic support should be extended to those states that seek to maintain harmonious and non-discriminatory racial policies: Zambia, Tanzania, Botswana, Lesotho, and Swaziland. Yet decisive change in that area will not take place until the racial situation in South Africa conforms to those same standards.

Thus at the heart of the confrontation in southern Africa stands its strongest, most discriminatory regime, whose transformation is the ultimate goal of those seeking fundamental change in the world's last major stronghold of traditional and domestic colonialism.

29

Contemporary African Literature

WILFRED CARTEY

THE LITERATURE OF A REGION, of a people, charts the vibrations of that region and captures the rhythms of that people. In contemporary African literature, as writers attempt to apprehend the total reality of their vast continent, the vibrations are multiple, the rhythms plentiful. The literature draws its creative sap from the earth of Africa, its variations from the diverse rhythms of the African peoples. Vibrations spool backwards, echoing the mythic, the folkloric, the traditional; rhythms resound, probing immediate social and political circumstances. Times coalesce, traditions and myths are actualized, historicity and contemporaneity shade together. Man and his circumstance correspond, motifs interlock, themes crisscross. This commingling of forms and of circumstances gives a totally social dimension to the literature.

On the larger structural level, two converse yet complementary movements give continuity and duration to African literature: a movement away from the traditional and a symbolic return to it. The movement away, the falling apart of things, the dissonant vibrations, may result from an inherent weakness in the structure of the traditional; or it may result from the collision of well-organized indigenous social structures with a foreign culture, the corollary to intense racial and social conflicts, colonialism, and apartheid. The symbolic return is the validation of tradition by some African writers, the questioning of tradition by others.

AUTOBIOGRAPHY

The autobiographical novel, one of the dominant forms in recent African literature, recounts the author's growth, especially his emotional development and increasing awareness of his social circumstances. In this type of novel the motifs of mother and earth bind together to form a single symbol. This symbol recurs as a dominant motif throughout. Many writers of the autobiographical statement turn to childhood to recall the bliss and easy circumstances of life, as in *L'Enfant noir (The Dark Child)* by Camara Laye, and *Kossoh Town Boy* by Robert Cole. *L'Enfant noir* becomes a nostalgic re-creation of life cushioned from the thrust of historical or political upheavals. When life is troubled and chaotic, writers invoke quiet moments in which they are cushioned by the mother from the full force of adverse social conditions. Movement away from the mother—"thrusting her aside"—is movement away from Africa.

James Ngugi in *Weep Not Child*, Ezekiel Mphalele in *Down Second Avenue*, Peter Abrahams in *Tell Freedom*, and Cheikh Hamidou Kane in *Ambiguous Adventure* focus their attention on the political surroundings and, using a selective process different from that of Camara Laye and Robert Cole, present the stresses of growth and the harsh encounters with colonial administration and apartheid. The plot of these novels delineates the protagonist's growth from childhood to manhood and his ever increasing awareness, through education, of his circumstance. But any education, any growth of awareness, demands its proper sacrifice. Such is its nature: to create a contrast so startling that the past must be abandoned in favor of the future it promises, or the reality it so starkly reveals.

This new awareness often leads the protagonists into struggle or active conflict, embitterment, loss of hope, and finally escape. Confusion and perplexity often assail them, and, with the possible exception of Robert Cole in *Kossoh Town Boy*, they all suffer loneliness. And so in spite of love of the land, in spite of nostalgia, in spite of Africa, Mother Africa, many move away—some inevitably through the process of growth and across the cycle of initiation into life, others because of the compulsion of growing alienation and disaffection from the realities which surround them.

THE CONFRONTATION OF BLACK AND WHITE

A falling away from the kind of unity and certainty portrayed in the world of *The Dark Child* is inevitable. The movement away from one's spiritual heritage, the breakup of old beliefs, may result from the natural and gradual growth of boy into man, or it may be brought about by the thrust on the individual of external forces. Colonialism is perhaps one of the most powerful of these external forces, and the concomitant conflict between individuals, generations, and groups becomes the moving force in these novels.

The plots of novels such as *Une Vie de boy* and *La Vieux Nègre et la médaille* by Ferdinand Oyono, *Le Pauvre Christ de Bomba* by Mongo Beti, *The River Between* by James Ngugi, *Batouala* by René Maran, and *Things Fall Apart* by Chinua

Achebe treat the theme of colonialism and the clash of cultures. In the course of colonial imposition many indigenous social structures were shattered, family groupings destroyed, and individuals plunged into disillusionment and despair. It is the reverberations of this breakup, this destruction, this increasing disillusionment, which resound in these novels.

The naïve black, the resisting black, the black middleman, the newly arrived white, the white missionary, and the white administrator who has discovered his power are all types which appear in this group of novels, and their interaction provides the character conflict. The initial deceptions and subsequent development of knowledge are the moving impulses. The movement away from a source is an unavoidable consequence of the clash of two worlds in which all the heroes seem to move from a certainty of effort and position to uncertain striving and disillusionment.

In these novels we follow the African through his awakening to the meaning of the white man's presence. Inability to comprehend, and thus to sympathize, is perhaps the most significant cause of tension and conflict in any human relationship. The novelistic statement reveals a nearly complete void of penetration and understanding between Africans and Europeans, blacks and whites. Like the African, the white man also misrepresented and naïvely misinterpreted the characteristics of those he encountered. Throughout the novels, the white man regards the black man as subhuman, as at best a child, a simpleton worthy of tolerance and condescension. There is neither sympathetic penetration into the African's psychological reactions to the white imposition nor comprehension of his defensive gestures.

Given mutual misconceptions and fears, conflict and struggle between the two races could not be avoided. The application of force by the white colonizer to produce desired actions is the material of this group of novels. The physical destruction of life and property by the white man is paralleled by the psychological destruction of the African and his mode of being. Presentation of the clash inherent in the various exploitative situations gives structure to the novels, all of which have a deep sense of the pathetic and a tragic inevitability about them.

ALIENATION

The movement away from the spiritual heritage of a people leads to disintegration of traditional patterns, and when things fall apart the rhythms of life are broken and disillusionment ensues. The works in English dealing with alienation are almost all South African: *Blame Me on History* by Bloke Modisane, *And a Threefold Cord* and *A Walk in the Night* by Alex La Guma, *The Quartet* by Richard Rive, and *The Living and the Dead* by Ezekiel Mphalele. The realism is not shot through with historical analysis, but rather becomes a contemporary representation of immediate social situations wherein the writer is often actor, moving through the total environment of his art.

The system of apartheid and the resultant overwhelming alienation of the black man is the essential subject of these South African novels. As the writers daub their canvases in stark colors, they depict the dual realities of the all-pervading, all-controlling outer society—the dominant white ruling minority—which chokes and strangles the inner society—a black, Coloured, Asian majority. It is the play of the former on the latter and the total reactions of the latter which constitute the essential elements of these works. The outer society and its social institutions have a corrupting historical legacy to which all of the writers attribute the alienation of their protagonists. Writers postulate that, by a converse application of justice, violence sanctioned by all the institutions of South Africa becomes a "given."

It is not surprising that the outer society exploits, and seems at times to enslave, the inner society. Economic control is ensured by a brutal system of migratory labor with all its consequent disruptive forces and suffering. In this literature, which is primarily located in an urban complex, migrant workers, effectively controlled by pass and influx laws, are brutalized, even as they carry the work-burden of the society. It is this system of economic exploitation that supports the white population and simultaneously enfeebles and threatens the ultimate survival of the blacks.

Enfeeblement and destruction, however, may also result from imprisonment or from the brutality of the police, who appear throughout these works. The police, who are the executors of the legally unjust social system, are a constant motif in all of this literature and are drawn by all of the authors with unsympathetic slashes of the pen. Curfews and raids, jailings and beatings, truculent calculations, and the use of weapons make the police the agents of the outer society, the hunters of the inner society, whose members are sought out and destroyed like animals. Thus the police seem to control every gesture, every action, almost every thought process of many of the characters.

Even those whites who are not represented as having fears of being haunted by blacks, even those "liberal" whites who "know" the blacks—when not unsympathetically portrayed—are ironically presented. Few truly liberal whites appear in these works; when they do appear, an all-pervasive stereotyping of one group by another is operative. Everyone is suspect and true feelings are not easily perceived. The reality of the South African social order is presented in all its diversification: its unsavory outer material aspects, its corrosive and cramping emotional stresses, its atmosphere of abandonment and decay, all of which induce an immense alienation and compel a desire to flee. The inner society feels that the outer seeks its total absorption, seeks to suck from it its very marrow and matter.

The inner group, however, remains and perseveres in spite of the hostility of the outer group; it continues to survive in spite of the decay and abandonment in which it lives. All the authors present, as a "given" of the inner group, a total sense of the material and physical horror brought on by an ever present, inimical exterior, omnipresent also in its hostile advances. Thus it is that all elements of nature, of society, and of man seem to be enemies of the inner group. We are given, then, a total, realistic interpenetration of cause and effect and all of its extensions. Realism is of two kinds: the immediate presentation of the lives of the characters—and often of the authors themselves—and a material presentation of the outward circumstances controlling these lives. The outward features are ugly, the lives often creatural. The presentation is a baroque compilation of unwholesome elements—a continuous repetition of degrading incidents—to the point where the canvas becomes an exposition of horror. We note the apparent hostility even of nature to the lives of this group, the poverty and decay in many of the living quarters, and the shabby communal gathering places of the lower classes of society.

In all these works an insistent feeling of alienation enshrouds the various types and characters. The outer group—the white world—is a point of reference, always controlling and goading reactions which end in alienation from self and group, or in the ultimate alienation in death.

THE POLITICAL KINGDOM

Many characters in the novels which attempt to apprehend the urban political realities of contemporary Africa experience a state of anxiety as they search for a course of action and a way of relating to these realities. In the cities, where values are shifting and codes of behavior are amorphously evolving, protagonists are unable to cope with the newness of this African circumstance. In novels such as *No Longer at Ease* and *A Man of the People* by Chinua Achebe, *A Night of Their Own* and *A Wreath for Udomo* by Peter Abrahams, *Jagua Nana* and *People of the City* by Cyprian Ekwensi, and *Les Bouts de bois de dieux* by Sembene Ousmane, the portrayal of the social and political dilemmas becomes a shifting, all-pervasive background. The resolution of problems, economic or moral, which beset the characters of these novels becomes the action; characters who are coincident to the convoluted social circumstances often become convoluted and twisted.

Many characters attempt to comprehend the immediate reality of heterogeneous societies by exploring current problems and searching for moral solutions in a transitional world. We receive the political and social emanations of this transitional world caught in upheavals and cataclysms which bring with them violence and moral decay. On the political level, the exploration of historical dynamics becomes the novelistic presentation of the inner workings of political parties—a searching for political kingdoms.

In their search for approaches to the political kingdom, many characters arc imbued with the poetry of action. The situation which confronts those who search for the political kingdom may advocate its own justification and, by creating its own ethic, give validity to all action. At times, therefore, the argument of means and ends disappears in that of causal situation and resultant action. In the quest for political freedom, to act is to hope and to exist; but to act is often to be alone. Many of the protagonists in these novels feel the weight of aloneness when called upon to arrive at decisions leading to involvement. The immediacy of the situation gives larger significance to the analyses of action, to the discussions of methods of approach, to the realization of political goals. Planning is necessary to offset the newness of a political situation which might produce an inherently destructive power struggle.

Thus the novelists debate the expediency of action and often discuss the process of political development. The novels, though they pose political questions, are not structured around a series of polemical dialogues. Rather, the questions give direction to the actions of the characters. The novelists, pushing the characters through immediate problematical political action, continually confront them with choices: how does a leader act in order to consolidate gains which will lead to the realization of political ideas?

In this search for the political kingdom most of the novelists seem to suggest that each and every ally is acceptable, that all sectors of the population may be mobilized to achieve political ideals. These novels are constantly involved in the dialectic of action, between choice of action and effect, decision and result. The characters are often caught in a historical moment, socially and politically indeterminate, which can be decided through action. Through all the novels we are presented with a sense of historical causation and social determinism which dictate the progress of the novel and the formation of its characters. Pre-independence action, of necessity more destructive and violent, is distinguished from post-independence decisions, by nature more constructively problematic.

But the characters are not simply social or political refractions; rather they are people caught in the violent flux of social forces which sweep through Africa today. The outward social and political circumstances are not simple contributing factors—they become controlling forces in the lives of the main characters. The political scene is not simply a political scene—it pulses with life. The urban scene is not simply urban—it, too, has a will and a way of its own.

The political climate within these novels, the game of practical politics, is cynically delineated. There is little idealism in this portrayal; it is stark, with greed, corruption, and violence prevailing. Participation in politics exposes one to danger and often brings with it a brutal end. And so the political scene is surfeited with corruption and bribery, is heavy with threat and violence, and reels under the debilitating effects of opportunism. In the urban political reality corruption has become a way of life, all-pervasive, all-encompassing, and totally acceptable.

It is clear, therefore, that the political and social realities in which action is to be carried out are completely subversive to ideals and actions stemming from poetry. Inevitably dreams are lost and goals are obliterated by the overpowering presence of formless ferment in heterogeneous transitional societies. Some of the characters in the novels resist bribery and refuse to sink into corruption, persisting in their search for the political kingdom. Disillusionment or heroic death often awaits them, even as disillusionment and violent death confront those overwhelmed by the force of politics and the city. At times the pull of tradition and the peace of rural circumstances are romantically presented by the novelists as a point of rest—a hiatus before the final disillusionment. But tradition becomes nostalgic and the movement back to it illusory. And so many of those who have moved away return, bent on resolving the problems and the dilemmas that both drove them away and brought them back. Often their search condemns them, and their deliberations ostracize them.

THE POETS OF NEGRITUDE

The loss consequent on colonialism and the alienation deriving from the movement away from rural traditions to urban political realities are in one way or another reflected in the thesis of the negritude poets: Léopold Sédar Senghor, Aime Césaire, Leon Damas, Bernard Dadié, David Diop, Tchicaya U Tam'si. To return symbolically to the source, to abnegate the loss, the alienation, the confusion, is the prime intention and motive of the negritude poets as they search through their single selves for a communal African authenticity. Thus, things remembered (that is, things lost) and the reentry into infancy (that is, something past) link them, even as they seek a rebirth, to the beginnings of things. And since the child is, in African ontology, ever akin to and close to the ancestor, to recall the ancestors is but a short step away from the plunge into those elements which lie at the beginning—at birth. Infancy and ancestry, recalling and re-identifying, exile and return—these are themes which color the works of the negritude poets.

Negritude becomes a ceremony ritualizing the earth of Africa and the life of its peoples. Its poets, grasping the external world, revitalize life through the cogency of pure memory, through the power of the poetic word. Negritude for the poet is not superficial, exterior, facile, and shallow; it is a descent into the heart of the matter. What was tense or dammed up flows; what lay dormant or shrouded in past times becomes present and dynamic. The belief in the primacy of life, in its enduring quality, leads the poet of negritude to offer his poetic power to the service of all mankind.

In the search for the poetic absolute, time and space for the negritude poet must be uninterrupted and continually flowing. It is the desire of all poets to seek the absolute in the midst of chaos. To find the quality of endurance of a person, a people, is to show the quality that abides in all things, to show that all things are in a state of constant becoming, that time flows, detoured, yet never interrupted. To accept the duration of all things is to capture the essence of all things. In attempting to capture the essence of their people, these poets release a rhythmic flow, delving deep into their furthest beginnings, into the nearer past, the immediate present, and the future of tomorrows unwinding to an infinity. Time, space, and memory flow together to the rhythms of the elements or to the rhythms of life. Timelessness becomes a constant motif, symbolizing the duration of a race, of a people. Entry into the extensions of space, into the center of time, is at the heart of the poetry of negritude.

The poets of negritude ascribe force and curative strength to rivers and waters, accepting the rhythmic pulsations of all elements, each force concatenating with another force to form an essential unity. They accept the unbroken convergencies of all things and give a total sense of the organic and inorganic. A restorative power, a cleansing and abiding vision, invoke their poetry. And so the poet hymns with rhythmic cadences the purity, eternal motion, and power of waters. Man is united to the elements, transformed by them, invigorated by them; from the earth mother, he receives life.

Negritude for the poet explores only essences, seeks only essentials, but essences and rhythms move together, bringing with them spontaneous abandon and freedom, the power to dance all things, thereby performing a ceremony to life. Such ceremony is no mere happening; it becomes charged with a deeper significance, with a presentiment which produces illusions and contorts ideas. Drugged nights, years of exile—exile from self, exile from childhood and natural instincts, exile from homeland, exile from race—all become too long, too arduous, and are converted by the negritude poet into a point of symbolic return.

At the heart of the poetry of negritude is return from exile, rejection of Europe, reclamation of the oppressed peoples of the world, and the acceptance of and identification with those who still live close to the earth. Thus, negritude opens out, redeeming not only those who live close to the soil of Africa, but all people who work the land. Negritude seems to postulate that man is not sufficient unto himself, that he receives regenerative force from without. Thus do the poets of negritude appeal to forces outside themselves for strength and for inspiration.

THE NATURE OF MAN

Some writers, however, question the relationship of man to forces outside himself, doubt the primacy of return to tradition, and wonder at the relationship of man to the pull of the earth. Can single man, still linked to the sources of the fountain and tied to his guardian angel, extricate himself even when the bells of exile sing softly and the time for worship has begun? Man is an ontological being set in a qualitatively historic and mythic time, controlled by worship and belief, family and ancestry, sacrifice and meditation. Man is linked to all the forces of the earth, affecting and being affected by them, seeking his own mask, his own destiny, and often his own tragic fulfillment. The question that is reiterated in the plays of Wole Soyinka and John Pepper Clark and in the novels of Amos Tutuola is whether man can be at one and the same time linked to the earth mother and yet not controlled by her.

The final optimism which we discern in Soyinka is nowhere present in the plays of John Pepper Clark. In Soyinka, man, through some act of defiance, interrupts the cycle of unending history and brings to an end an inherited and tragic destiny. Clark holds out no such optimistic end to the tragic pull of man's inheritance, sees no solution through action to the destructive force of the curse which may have befallen a man, a race. Therefore, Clark's vision of history is based on the uninterrupted continuity of man's tragic destiny. His treatment of phenomena, too, differs in one basic way from that of Soyinka. In Clark, man's tragic destiny is not only presaged by phenomena, but is totally reflected in their various manifestations.

In the kaleidoscopic world of Amos Tutuola's novels, all realms flow together, all varying manifestations of reality merge and coalesce. Yoruba myths, customs, and manners synchronize with Western artifacts, bringing about a concretization of concepts and a tautness of imagery. All details are foreground, illuminated by the author's total experience. There is no inherent clash of cultures, for all cultures are his domain and from all of them he derives his material. This material is transmuted through the author's imagination, and the fusion gives to reality a sense of otherness and to myth a veracity.

Much in Tutuola is mythic and folkloric, but much springs from ordinary, everyday, lived reality. Only after being fortified by juju and prepared by sacrifice do his heroes cross over into an imaginary realm contiguous to their own real world to pursue their searches and go on their wanderings. Indeed, Tutuola's novels are the ultimate expression of return to acceptance of tradition in all its varying manifestations. All things flow together, movement away leads to movement back, return follows exile, a new day follows the agony of night.

The literature of a people should be consonant with the rhythms of the life of that people; the literature for the vast continent of Africa should reflect the throbbing complexities of that continent and its thrusting hopes. Many problems beset the African writer. In what language should he write? In that of the people who imposed their ways upon him? Or should he use his own vernacular? What reality must he apprehend and to whom should his writing be directed? Can he, by the use of African imagery, capture the local psychology through known symbols and images and give it a definition distinctively African?

African writing cannot be other than social, for the writer is caught in the vibration of the region and the rhythms of its peoples. In many parts of Africa, the rhythms are broken; a region may be caught in internecine conflict. The continent is still searching for its own pattern of development, striving toward its own future fulfillment. In all of these affairs, it is not only incumbent on the writer, but indeed demanded of him, to explore circumstances, to offer prognoses, to bring about the consonance of African man and his circumstance.

30

Afro-American
Perspectives

JAMES TURNER

THE TERM *Afro-American* is increasingly used with reference to Americans of African descent. A widespread and growing knowledge of Africa and a developing sense of pride in African origins have allowed black Americans to recognize Africa as an ancestral homeland. In the past, however, Africa and race derived their importance for black Americans mainly from the fact that they were symbolic of the slavery and oppression which black men endured in this country. Escape from this painful status resulted in a psychological rejection of both Africa and black skin color. Rupert Emerson and Martin Kilson summarize this symbolic role of Africa:

> Africa, in one form or another, has always been a part of the reality of Americans of African descent. The relationship has often been tortuously ambivalent and confused, but given the segregated frame of Negro acculturation to American standards and the influence of white supremacist values, this was not surprising. . . . [Black people] have been shaped in their behavior and self-definition by the standards of the politically dominant white populations.[1]

THE CHANGING IMAGE OF AFRICA

In the New World, as in Europe, Africa was reputed to be a land of savage black men, unbearably hot, infested with insects and wild animals, overrun with jungle, and with no culture above the very primitive. Stories of cannibalism were

1. "The American Dilemma in a Changing World: The Rise of Africa and the Negro American," in *The Negro American*, ed. Talcott Parsons and Kenneth Clark (Boston: Houghton Mifflin, 1966), p. 638.

592

invented by white novelists, and the myth of Tarzan (the invincible white man who could paternalistically protect the simple-minded natives) persists to some extent in American life today. In short, the negative image of Africa became an argument for the "inferiority" of black people, and this premise, in turn, justi- fied the status of black people in the New World. Charles E. Silberman elaborates this phenomenon:

> Against this debasing picture of "the African" the Negro . . . had no defense; he had no way of knowing that the picture happened to be false. On the contrary, this "evidence of the black man's inferiority," as Isaacs puts it, "was borne in upon him with all the weight and authority of the all-knowing, all-powerful, all-sur- rounding white world," thereby confirming the sense of his own worthlessness that white attitude and actions had already established.
>
> In the interviews with a hundred and seven leading Negroes that formed the basis of *The New World of Negro Americans*, Isaacs found that "in nearly every in- stance" the early discovery of the African background had been "a prime element" in shaping the individual's knowledge of and attitude toward himself and his world—so much so that the subjects could recall the details, and the names of the texts, with agonizing clarity forty, fifty and even sixty years later!
>
> In general, therefore, Africa served to alienate the Negro not just from America, but from the whole human race. In self-defense, he tried to dissociate himself from Africa.
>
> The key word was black. For a Negro to dissociate himself from Africa meant, after all, to dissociate himself from the African's color, hair, features—from the Negroidness that stared at him from the pictures in the public-school textbooks and that assaulted his senses from the movie screen. But in the last analysis, dis- sociation was impossible, the pervasive fact of color remained. And so the Negro's rejection of Africa was, at bottom, a rejection of himself.[2]

It was within this historical and social-psychological context that black na- tionalism emerged in the New World as an ideology. Its meaning and relevance to the social conditions of the Afro-American are derived directly from the legacy of the persisting stigma of race and ancestry. St. Clair Drake, a sociologist, explains that Negroes

> are "victims" of one persisting legacy of the slave trade—derogation of "negroid- ness." The idea that a dark skin indicates intellectual inferiority is rapidly passing, but at the esthetic level derogatory appraisal of thick lips, kinky hair and very dark skin is still prevalent. That many Negroes reject their own body image is evident from advertisements for skin lighteners in the major Negro publications. . . . The ever-present knowledge that one's Negroid physiognomy is evaluated as "ugly" lowers self-esteem and, therefore, weakens self-confidence.[3]

2. *Crisis in Black and White*, (New York: Random House, 1964), pp. 168–69.
3. "Social and Economic Status," in Parsons and Clark, *The Negro American*, p. 33.

The emergence of sovereign states in Africa, however, seems to have changed in varying degrees the self-image of increasing numbers of Afro-Americans, as well as their vision of their place in the world. The contemporary recognition and respect being accorded Africa are allowing Afro-Americans to see Africa in a new light and to identify with their African past. Many Afro-Americans seem to realize that to deny black men a place in history was a means of keeping them down. They seek to construct a new understanding of the African past and to relate this history to Africa of the present. In so doing they hope to erase the stigma of race.

The denial of this past-present relationship has been central to Afro-American self-contempt. The attempt to construct a new relationship with Africa is explained by John Davis, president of the American Society of African Culture, as the effort

> to bring to the American Negro . . . an understanding of the continuing value of our gifts and a pride in our origins, so that we may join other Americans who feel secure in the traditions of their past and their contributions.[4]

BLACK IDENTITY AND AFRO-AMERICAN NATIONALISM

Harold Isaacs contends that the "African identity" is a strong prospect for a wider identity, because it offers a context for solidarity of black skin color and provides the Afro-American with an equivalent of what other Americans could boast of or disavow: a homeland.

The possibility of a "wider identity" was raised at the American Negro Leadership Conference on September 29, 1964, in a speech by Chief S. O. Adebo, permanent representative of Nigeria to the U.N.:

> A great many of the things that happened to you here, which you thought happened to you because you were a minority people, happened to us in Nigeria. . . . I no longer think simply as a Nigerian; I no longer think simply as an African. I think more as a person of color. And the objective of all of us is to restore to the man of color, wherever he may be, whether in Nigeria, or in the United States, or in Moscow, or in Brazil, the dignity of a human being. That is why we are involved in the same struggle in Africa, here, and elsewhere.[5]

The issue of identity is inescapable, and pride in race must play a crucial part in the new identity. It no doubt will continue to lead to a considerable degree of racial self-consciousness, indeed, to some extent, to race chauvinism. Black men and women are not struggling to become free simply in order to disappear.

4. "An Editorial Statement," *African Forum*, I (Summer 1965), 3.
5. Emerson and Kilson, "The American Dilemma," p. 651.

Contrary to the liberal argument that the race problem can be solved in this country only by total integration and complete assimilation and eventual miscegenation, there are Afro-Americans who do not want to disappear and who seek to preserve specifically Afro-American values and cultural traits.

Robert Penn Warren recalls a conference session at Howard University in 1959 at which this feeling was expressed:

> The auditorium had been packed — mostly Negroes, but with a scattering of white people. A young girl with pale skin, dressed like any coed anywhere, in the clothes for a public occasion, is on the rostrum. She is . . . speaking with a peculiar vibrance in a strange irregular rhythm, out of some inner excitement, some furious, taut élan, saying: "—and I tell you I have discovered a great truth. I have discovered a great joy. I have discovered that I am black. I am black! You out there — oh, yes, you may have black faces, but your hearts are white, your minds are white, you have been whitewashed!"[6]

This sense of newly discovered identity is a conscious experience of "an increased unity of the physical and mental, moral and sensual selves, and a oneness in the way one experiences oneself and the way others experience us."[7]

Much of academic research, as well as analysis of the race relations situation during the past three decades, seems to accept the liberal assumption of historian Kenneth M. Stampp that "Negroes are, after all, only white men with black skins, nothing more, nothing less."[8] But black men in America are not simply carbon duplicates of white men — to contend that they are is misleading. Differences in skin color, hair texture, and physical features constitute a fact. However, the issue is not whether differences exist, but what they mean socially:

> Identified as a Negro, treated as Negro, provided with Negro interests, forced, whether he wills or not, to live in Negro communities, to think, love, buy and breathe as a Negro, the Negro comes in time to see himself as a Negro . . . he comes in time, to invent himself.[9]

The Afro-American subculture maintains a subterranean and private world of rituals, symbols, and motifs. Rupert Emerson and Martin Kilson in a discussion of black nationalism make the following observations:

> The Black Muslims still represent, at the level of the Negro's subterranean world, a force of ultimate significance. This is found in its influence upon the new stage in the Negro's self-definition. This stage, moreover, has been reinforced by the rise of more rational black nationalist concepts than those represented by the Black

6. *Who Speaks for the Negro?* (New York: Harcourt, Brace & World, 1965).

7. Erik H. Erikson, "The Concept of Identity in Race Relations," in Parsons and Clark, *The Negro American*, p. 232.

8. *The Peculiar Institution* (New York: Random House, Vintage Books, 1964).

9. Lerone Bennett, Jr., *Negro Mood* (Chicago: Johnson Publishing Co., 1964), p. 49.

Muslims, and all of them have been affected by the debut of African nationalism on the international scene. . . . There are, however, many other groups of this sort, and they are likely to have a more sustained influence upon the Negro's new thrust for self-realization . . . than the Black Muslims. Unlike the Black Muslims, these organizations are secular in orientation, intellectually capable of coping with the modern world; and they reject naive political goals.[10]

According to St. Clair Drake, "Increased identification of educated Negroes with some aspects of the Negro subculture and with the cultural renaissance taking place in Africa may become the norm."[11] It is not unusual to find people in the larger urban ghettos who were previously wary about identifying themselves with Africa now proudly proclaiming their blackness and developing interest in African politics, art, and literature. Among the well educated, and even the less educated, discussions of negritude are becoming commonplace. Among many young people there is a certain reverence for the memory and image of such men as Patrice Lumumba (Congo-Kinshasa), Kwame Nkrumah (Ghana), and Jomo Kenyatta (Kenya), to name a few. These men are looked up to as black heroes and idols, and as role models. It is interesting to note, in this regard, that the late Medgar Evers—slain NAACP civil rights field director for the state of Mississippi—had named one of his sons Kenyatta. Ordinary black men and women who a short time ago were using hair-straighteners and skin-bleaches are now wearing the new "Afro" and "natural" hair styles, as well as African-style clothing. Some are even taking African names and are learning to speak an African language.

Erik H. Erikson explains such social-psychological phenomena as the development of a consciousness of identity:

> Identity here is one aspect of the struggle for ethnic survival; one person's or group's identity may be relative to another's; and identity awareness may have to do with matters of an inner emancipation from a more dominant identity, such as the "compact majority."[12]

Writer John O. Killens comments on the function and value of the new identity:

> One of the main tasks of Black consciousness is to affirm the beauty of our blackness, to see beauty in black skin and thick lips and broad nostrils and kinky hair; to rid our vocabulary of "good hair" and "high yaller" and our medicine cabinets of bleaching creams. To de-niggerize ourselves is a key task of Black consciousness.[13]

The same mood is conveyed by another of the present generation of new writers, William K. Kgositsile:

10. "The American Dilemma," pp. 640–41.
11. "Social and Economic Status," p. 33.
12. "Concept of Identity in Race Relations," p. 230.
13. "The Meaning and Measure of Black Power," *Negro Digest* (November 1966), p. 36.

Thus the Black artist who embarks upon a search for new standards and values for his salvation must, among other things, discard the tools presented to him by the social order which has proved to be the number one enemy to his sensibility and conscience . . . if he is committed to his people [he] looks elsewhere for new standards and values, for new identification and allies.[14]

The fundamental question raised by black nationalism is whether integration is really desired, or, more specifically, whether Afro-Americans "should" want integration:

In the whole history of revolts and revolutions, "integration" has never been the main slogan of a revolution. The oppressed's fight is to free himself from his oppressor, not to integrate with him.[15]

Black nationalist ideology molds a new image of the dominant group. This is the other side of the coin and may be radical in its implication as black men redefine themselves and, of necessity, reevaluate "the white man." Many black intellectuals today seek to diminish the importance of being white—that is, they reject the idea that men of one skin color are ordained to determine the lives of men of a darker skin color. The objective of this process is to wrest the black man's image from white control; its concrete meaning is that white men should no longer tell black men who they are and where they should want to go, and that black men must no longer be bound by white men's definitions. This is partly a response to the control of communications media by the dominant white group.

Historically, black men have reacted to white control of their image in a variety of ways. According to Bennett:

In the past, some Negroes attempted to define themselves by becoming counter-contrast conceptions, by becoming, in short, opposite Negroes, opposite, that is, to what white men said Negroes were.[16]

This process has been described by one sociologist as

the backfire of the dynamics of American assimilation which gave rise to an increased sensitivity, on the part of Black people, in reacting to the institutionalized nature of bigotry . . . a subsequent development of a more positive regard for Black culture and community, and a determination to reconstitute the basic processes to U.S. life as they affect Black people.[17]

He further contends that "the most pervasive trend for today's young Black intellectuals is their vigor and degree of self-consciousness about being Black."

---

14. "Has God Failed James Baldwin?" *Liberator*, VII (January 1967), 11.
15. Killens, "Meaning and Measure of Black Power," p. 33.
16. *Negro Mood*, p. 55.
17. Gerald McWorther, "Negro Rights and the American Future," *Negro Digest* (October 1966), p. 20.

Growing militant ethnic assertion of Afro-Americans is a twofold process. On one level it is a psychological response to the social and political conditions of subordinate status and rising expectations, and on another level it is a fervent quest for new social values and political orientation. The economic exploitation and social discrimination which define persons of African descent as a social category give many of its members an avid sense of race consciousness. The conversion of a social "category" into a cohesive social group has broader theoretical and empirical implications. One proposition would suggest that when an aggregate is categorically defined and uniformly treated it will eventually — on the basis of its externally defined commonness — transmute itself into a conscious group. Subsequent internal interaction will evolve a movement to define the boundaries of the group and make demands for relations with other groups on new terms. This minority group formation process may precipitate a review of the core values of the dominant group, since some of these values are likely to be dysfunctional for the newly articulate minority. This may lead some minority group members to reject or call into question the legitimacy of the social system. I would suggest that this is precisely the development taking place among increasing numbers of Afro-Americans.

The following comments by Stokely Carmichael are illustrative of this point:

> Our concern for black power addresses itself directly to this problem, the necessity to reclaim our history and our identity from the cultural terrorism and depredation of self-justifying white guilt.
>
> To do this we shall have to struggle for the right to create our own terms through which to define ourselves and our relations to the society and to have these recognized. This is the first necessity of a free people, and the first right that any oppressor must suspend.[18]

The current Black Power movement, which is fundamentally a form of black nationalism, is an ideological movement of social-psychological as well as political importance. Although the militancy of black nationalism is an explicit response to a real situation, it is primarily a symbolic value assertion, and secondarily a political impetus or perspective. Black nationalism seeks to affirm and accentuate group and individual identity with Africa as a central symbol in the configuration of a new "psychosocial identity." Lerone Bennett, social historian and a leading contemporary black intellectual, writes in an unpublished essay of this fundamental change among Afro-Americans:

> In the most essential sense our people are engaged in two revolutions in America: a revolution in the streets and a revolution in the winding corridors of the mind.
>
> These two revolutions are proceeding at the same time on different levels, and they are complementary facets of the same reality: the historical explosion of a

18. "Toward Black Liberation," *Massachusetts Review*, VII (1966), 639–51.

people in the sudden labor of self-discovery, self-determination and self-legitimization. In short it is a total struggle: for without the revolutionary range in images, symbols, and ideas, in sum the revolution of the word, the struggle for freedom and dignity can not fulfill itself. Black people have been told that they must love others at all cost, but I suggest we must come to a point of appreciating ourselves and loving ourselves, and understanding the great beauty that is us and the glory of our magnificent history and heritage. So that we can begin to re-knit together the separate parts of a people fractured by the burden of evil social and historical experiences into a whole and regenerating identity. For the Black race must be free of white-value domination and racial exploitation which have made us a race of culturally frustrated people.

AFRO-AMERICAN IDENTITY
IN HISTORICAL PERSPECTIVE

One of the foremost advocates of a reclamation of Africa as a way of refurbishing the image of the black man was Marcus Garvey, whose efforts spanned the first quarter of the twentieth century. The legacy of Garvey is not so much political as it is symbolic. Perhaps more than any other person of his time or before him, he was able to fire the hearts and minds of black people with his bold vision of the rise of Africa and the reality of Black Power. Garvey preached the gospel of a united Africa under the rule of black men, and in the process he developed a mass movement among Afro-Americans, particularly in the New York area. He made Africa the center of consciousness for black Americans, and relation to it the major political question of his day. Bennett says Garvey's achievement was based on two essential components: (1) "He went to the heart of the race problem by ripping away the shame and inferiority that were stunting the growth of black men"; and (2) "He focused attention on Africa when black nationalism was dormant."[19]

Many black leaders and intellectuals of the time were unalterably opposed to Garvey and his African scheme. His principal protagonist was W. E. B. Du Bois. Du Bois, however, was also concerned with the freeing of Africa from the stranglehold of colonialism. He figured prominently in the early Pan-African movement as its spiritual and intellectual mentor and as convener of the earliest Pan-African conferences. Garvey and Du Bois were not the only Afro-Americans with deep interest in Africa, nor were they the first to explore the significance of Africa for black men in America. Much of the work of black creative writers during the Harlem Literary Renaissance, which developed almost parallel with the Garvey movement, centered on the question of the meanings of African heritage for their art. Notable examples are the sonnets of Claude McKay: "Africa,"

19. Lerone Bennett, Jr., "Who Was Marcus Garvey?" *Negro Digest* (July 1962), p. 4.

"Outcasts," "Enslaved"; "The Negro Speaks of Rivers" by Langston Hughes; "Georgia Dusk" by Jean Toomer; "Heritage" by Countee Cullen; and "Stars of Ethiopia" by Lucian B. Watkins. Contemporary black writers and intellectuals have formed the American Society of African Culture (AMSAC) to assess their relationship to their African roots. AMSAC is the counterpart to the Society of African Culture formed originally by French-speaking West Africans in Paris.

With regard to the historical origins of Afro-American consciousness, Richard B. Moore, historian and political analyst, contends that before Garvey, Harlem had become Africa-conscious and to a considerable degree had related this consciousness to its own oppressed condition. He argues that Garvey seized the opportunity to "harness this upsurge against oppression and to direct the existing consciousness of Africa into a specific organized movement under his leadership." He concedes that "the Garvey movement did heighten and spread the consciousness of African origin and identity among the various peoples of African descent on a wider scale than ever before."[20] Together, Du Bois and Garvey, more than any others, made black Americans aware of and interested in their African origins. Du Bois was to say, upon taking Ghanaian citizenship in the post-colonial period:

> My great-grandfather was carried away in chains from the Gulf of Guinea. I have returned that my dust shall mingle with the dust of my forefathers. There is not much left for me. But now, my life will flow on in the vigorous, young stream of Ghanaian life which lifts the African personality to its proper place among men. And I shall not have lived and worked in vain.[21]

As early as 1787, the freed slaves of Newport, Rhode Island, formed the Free African Society to promote group cohesion and repatriation to Africa. African societies were formed in other parts of the northeast section of the country, uniting members on the basis of their mutual African origin and previous condition of servitude, as well as on the common experience of the threat and violence of their environment.

In 1815, Paul Cuffee of Boston, a well-to-do entrepreneur, piloted himself and a boatload of other ex-slaves and their descendants to Sierra Leone in West Africa. *Walker's Appeal to the Colored Citizens of the World*, by David Walker, appeared in 1820 and was followed, slightly more than a decade later, by Henry Highland Garnet's "Address to the Slaves of the United States" and, in 1843, by his *Call to Rebellion*. In 1852, Martin R. Delany, Harvard-educated physician, writer, editor, and theoretician, published his book, *The Condition, Elevation, Emigration and Destiny of the Colored People of the United States Politically Con-*

20. "Africa Conscious Harlem," *Freedomways*, III (1963), 321.
21. Quoted in Cameron Doudu, "The Return of a Prophet," *Drum* (June 1963), p. 7.

sidered, which was a statement of the doctrine which today is called Black Zionism. Delany proposed an expedition to the "Eastern Coast of Africa" for the purpose of eventual settlement there. It is worthwhile to quote a few passages from this book because of the enduring relevance of the sentiments it conveys:

> Every people should be the originators of their own designs, the projectors of their own schemes, and creators of the events that lead to their destiny—the consummation of their desires.
>
> We have native hearts and virtues, just as other nations; which in their pristine purity are noble, potent and worthy of example. We are a nation within a nation. . . .
>
> But we have been, by our oppressors, despoiled of our purity, and corrupted in our native characteristics, . . . leaving us in character, really a "broken people." Being distinguished by complexion, we are still singled out—although having merged in the habits and customs of our oppressors—as a distinct nation of people.[22]

It is interesting to note the essential parallel between this statement and the following comment of W. E. B. Du Bois, one of the most outstanding of the early Afro-American scholars and intellectuals. Hollis Lynch, a West Indian scholar who has done specialized research in Africa and the Americas on the subject of Pan-Negro nationalism, contends that early black nationalists were, compared to most of their peers, "well educated, economically well-off, and proud men of immense race pride."[23] Du Bois, from the latter part of the nineteenth century through the first half of the twentieth century, was a major exponent of such feeling:

> We are Americans, not only by birth and by citizenship, but by our political ideals, our language, our religion. Further than that, our Americanism does not go. At that point, we are Negroes, members of a vast historic race. . . . We are the first fruits of this new nation, the harbinger of that black tomorrow which is yet to soften the whiteness of the Teutonic today. . . . As such, it is our duty to conserve our physical powers, our intellectual endowments, our spiritual ideals; as a race, we must strive by race-organization, by race solidarity, by race unity to the realization of that broader humanity which freely recognizes differences in men, but sternly deprecates inequality in their opportunities of development.[24]

22. Quoted in Bill McAdoo, "Pre-Civil War Black Nationalism," *Progressive Labor* (June–July 1966), p. 40.

23. "Pan-Negro Nationalism in the Nineteenth Century" (Lecture given to the Program of African Studies, Northwestern University, January 23, 1967).

24. *American Negro Academy Occasional Papers*, No. 2 (1897), pp. 10–12, quoted in E. U. Essien-Udom, *Black Nationalism* (Chicago: University of Chicago Press, 1962), pp. 28–29.

AFRICA AND THE AFRO-AMERICAN
IN CONTEMPORARY PERSPECTIVE

The quest for new values thus leads the black nationalist to the belief that self-definition and self-determination are one and the same, and his new self-perception must of necessity be predicated upon terms that are divergent from white Western values. An essential development of this new identity is that the association of the "black race" with Africa acquires a new meaning. Instead of being a source of shame, Africa becomes a source of pride and an important referent in this new orientation. This is an essential end of black nationalism. The social-psychological function of this orientation is to permit open and unashamed identification with the continent, a kind of poetic sublimation of those associations which constitute for most Afro-Americans a source of conflict in their relationship with white Western culture: a process of self-avowal and self-recognition.

Neither Garvey nor Du Bois was the first to visualize a strong and independent West Africa, although they gave the idea new urgency and a tremendous impetus. Garvey's efforts had been preceded by Bishop Henry McNeal Turner, the Africa-oriented leader of the African Methodist Episcopal Church. Bishop Turner, the chief prophet of black nationalism, urged his people to go back to Africa. Turner, like his contemporary Edward Wilmot Blyden, who emigrated to Liberia, traveled widely in Africa. He symbolized the early phase of black nationalism in this country. According to Edwin S. Redkey:

> Among the various Negro responses to their American ordeal, the least known and understood is "black nationalism." It has embraced many forms. . . . it has existed in one form or another among Afro-Americans since before the Civil War.[25]

With regard to the organizational aspects of black nationalism, W. E. B. Du Bois, describing his split with the National Association for the Advancement of Colored People (NAACP) in 1934, wrote in his autobiography:

> I proposed that in economic lines, just as in the lines of literature and religion, unified racial action should be planned and organized and carefully thought through. This plan would not establish a new segregation; it did not advocate segregation as the final solution of the race problem; exactly the contrary; but it did face the facts and faced them with thoughtfully mapped effort. . . . What was true in 1910 was still true in 1940 and will be true in 1970.[26]

Commenting on this remark, Wallerstein suggests, "It is not fanciful to see here

25. "Bishop Turner's African Dream," *Journal of American History*, LIV (1967), 271–72.
26. Quoted in Immanuel Wallerstein, "Du Bois and Padmore," *Africa Report* (May 1968), p. 51.

the intellectual roots of black power ideology."[27] The conceptual parameters of Black Power ideology are still, to a certain extent, in the formative stages. Yet the thinking of Du Bois has been a foundation upon which much of this ideology will rest.

In recent times Malcolm X has been the single most influential personality and thinker in the growing Black Power movement and Pan-African orientation among Afro-Americans. After his split with Elijah Muhammad and the "Nation of Islam," he traveled widely in Africa, staying with African leaders. He envisioned a relationship with Africa that involved what he considered "an intellectual, cultural and psychological attachment to Africa, a sort of spiritual adjustment to the fact of African heritage."[28] He claimed for Afro-Americans an identity of interest with Africa. He planned a world-wide unity of black men with Africa as the focus or frame of reference for political guidance. His was truly a dream of the Black Diaspora. Though he was assassinated while on the threshold of political maturity, his legacy has spawned a new epoch for the black masses as well as for the leadership class. The demand now is for economic development and control of the black community, for self-determination, and for the establishment of independent cultural institutions and the legitimacy of black creative expression. The mood of Afro-America is one of disenchantment with the present socioeconomic system and a determination for a change in status. It urges neither integration nor accommodation with white society.

For many sensitive Afro-Americans the American dream is a façade, a cruel illusion that has created a nightmare of humiliation and oppression built upon broken hopes and unfulfilled promises. They are uncertain about their place in the larger white society and about where their loyalties should be. For some, their allegiance is to their people, to black people wherever they may be. Some black militants and revolutionaries, like Stokely Carmichael and H. Rap Brown, talk of preparation for the role Afro-Americans must play in the coming black liberation struggle in South Africa as well as in Harlem. However, for others, a rapprochement with Africa is not without difficulty and ambivalence. As they begin to ask who they are and where they belong and where they should be going, they feel certain that their destiny cannot be realized in America—at least as it is presently constituted. But there is not, on the other hand, a credible or practical bond to the continent of their ancestors. Black writer Julian Mayfield, organizer of the AMSAC conference on "The Afro-American Writer and his Roots," comments on the dilemma of the black man in America:

> The likelihood is that the Negro people will continue for several decades to occupy, to a diminishing degree, the position of the unwanted child who, having been brought for a visit, must remain for the rest of his life.[29]

27. *Ibid.*
28. Malcolm X, *The Autobiography of Malcolm X* (New York: Grove Press, 1965).
29. "Into the Mainstream and Oblivion," *The American Negro Writer and His Roots* (New York: American Society of African Culture, 1960), p. 34.

Over the time and distance that separate Africa from her American descendants, real cultural differences have emerged. Richard Wright, the great Afro-American writer, eloquently relates the anguish of culture conflict in his attempts at resettlement in Africa. There are other problems. Perhaps more than other Americans, Afro-Americans have accepted the myths and distortions about Africa, and have internalized the false images and stereotypes of the "dark" continent. Many Afro-Americans are left with the feeling that they are victimized because of an inglorious past; consequently, they often feel a deep sense of confusion, injustice, and bitterness at the fond attention given African students and diplomats in the United States, precisely because the same society has derogated the African past for so long. There are also semantic misunderstandings: when an African, for instance, proclaims that he is not a "Negro," Afro-Americans may interpret this behavior as a rejection of kinship and common identity.

Nonetheless, there is an increasing belief within all levels of the black community that African and Afro-American will ultimately be drawn to each other by what James Baldwin designated as a "need to recreate the world in their own image." "What in sum they hold in common," he concludes, "is their ache to come into the world as men."[30]

30. *Nobody Knows My Name* (New York: Dell Publishing Co., 1961), p. 35.

Epilogue

31

Social Science
and Africa

JOHN N. PADEN

THIS CONCLUDING ESSAY will draw on the preceding essays to illustrate aspects of social-science research in Africa. Five major themes will be explored: the language of social science, as it has come to be used in African studies; interdisciplinary research priorities in Africa; methods of observation, especially techniques used frequently in the African context; major types of social-science analysis in African studies (comparative and developmental); and a discussion of problems of social-science research in Africa.

Social science refers to the systematic study of those aspects of human experience which are manifest in observable behavior.[1] While observation and analysis focus primarily on behavior in the broadest sense, they are also concerned with the sets of meaning (*cognition*) attached to behavior, and with the emotions (*cathexis*) which attach to both behavior and meanings. Such inquiry is "scientific" to the extent that it follows repeatable rules of observation, establishes a vocabulary capable of operational definition, and establishes frequency, probability, or sequential relations between units and events. Although social science is often distinguished from the "humanities" or "arts," it is clear that music, painting, or literature may be studied systematically as types of human behavior.

In a world of different cultures the necessity for a social-science approach is twofold: cross-cultural communication requires a common set of symbols and meanings (language), and the tendency toward ethnocentrism in the perception of other culture groups requires strict attention to the process of observation itself.

---

1. For a useful introduction to social science, see Johan Galtung, *Theory and Methods of Social Research* (New York: Columbia University Press, 1967).

THE LANGUAGE OF SOCIAL SCIENCE

Basic to social-science inquiry is the notion of *definition*. A definition proposes the essential characteristics of a thing. Criteria for good definitions include common usage, precision, utility, and parsimony. Basically, however, definitions are arbitrary, or stipulative, although we try to justify them by their utility in approximating reality. There are several types of definitions, among them demonstrative, negative, paradigmatic, and operational (the latter including a set of rules by which we can measure a variable or concept).

Concepts are systems of definitions which are interrelated by the logic of their elements. Thus, concepts are essentially definitional and may be arbitrarily established. The concept of "elite," for example, might be posited as follows: "An elite is a segment of a social system which by reason of status or class is regarded as having influence or authority within that system."

The authors of the essays in this volume have used specialized vocabulary from their own disciplines, but have tried to define such concepts for the general reader. Thus, for example, Dalton refers to social money, redistribution, transactional mode, and reciprocity. Soja refers to transaction, circulation systems, and information. Berry uses the linguistic concepts of lingua franca, vehicular language, phonological transformation, ideophone, syllabary, logography, and glottochronology. In the Cohen essay on traditional society a series of definitions regarding matters of kinship and marriage is proposed.

Definitions also form part of a specialized vocabulary, or "language," common to social science as a whole. Major definitional tools of analysis include the concepts of variable, correlation, hypothesis, theory, model, and system. Each of the social-science disciplines may use these concepts in a slightly different way, but certain usages appear to be widely shared. A *variable* is commonly regarded as a characteristic of a unit within a universe (or context). This characteristic may take on different values for different units of the same generic category, and hence is not constant. For example, age or educational levels of an elite would constitute variables. *Correlation* refers to the degree to which two variables share a common patterning in that variations in one correspond to variations in the other.

A *hypothesis* makes a statement about the expected value of a concept or variable. For example, a hypothesis may make a statement about the specific age of an elite ("all political leaders in Africa are male and over twenty-one"). A *theory* is a statement of the anticipated relationship between sets of hypotheses or variables based on some logic of causality. Thus, we may theorize that if the average age of political elites is sixty-five or over, political instability may result among the contenders for power. In this case, there is an implied relationship between the two hypotheses. A *model* is a statement of anticipated relationship or correlation on the operational level which need not have a theoretical base. A *system* is a context within which component parts are interrelated.

Within a system, changes in the characteristics of one unit cause changes in other units. For example, in the African context, if the international price of cocoa decreases, certain types of social tension within a country may increase. Or, as some types of urbanization increase, certain types of traditionalism may decrease.

The units within the context being examined may be individuals, groups, institutions, or other types of entities. Cities, countries, and regions are often taken as units of observation. Psychological or historical studies may focus on individuals as the units of observation. Anthropological or political studies may select groups as the relevant units. Groups involve individuals with interrelated roles and a common frame of reference. Units are comparable when they share certain similar defining characteristics. Thus, nation-states may differ in size and complexity, but all share the defining characteristic of international sovereignty.

The types of interactions between units have been distinguished by a variety of concepts, such as conflict, coordination, and cooperation. The functionally specialized social sciences (such as political science, economics, linguistics, sociology, and anthropology) examine types of interactions which deal with particular functions within society. Thus, linguistics may deal with communications functions, and economics with production and exchange of goods and services. The crosscutting social sciences, by contrast, are organized around dimensions such as space or time. Thus geographers may consider communications, exchange, or other functions of society, but they will stress the ways in which these functions are expressed within a particular area and how they affect the flow and movement of people, goods, and ideas over space. Historians stress social patterns in time sequences.

If social systems may be defined in terms of their functions, it must be recognized that functions are usually purposive, and, in fact, reflect the values of the individuals involved. Within social science the term *value* is used in two ways: it may be regarded as a broad orientation toward goals (such as equality or justice) or it may be regarded as a set of preferences. Apart from the discipline of sociology, there seems to be an increasing use of "values" in the sense of "preferences." By extension, moral values would deal with preferences as to appropriate behavior between human beings.

The concept of *belief*, or belief system, usually refers to the assertion that something is true rather than false, whether it is preferred or not. Cohesiveness or compatibility of beliefs is necessary if they are to be combined into a belief system.

The concept of *culture* refers to the modal patterns of values, beliefs, and behavior which characterize a particular social group, and usually entails a cohesive world view. This concept is closely related to the notion of *ideology*, which asserts certain propositions as being true and of value. Ideology, however, includes the additional notion of an imperative to a course of action. The notion of culture and/or world view is especially important in the study of non-

Western society. Willett, in his essay, makes a special plea for examining African sculpture as a reflection of world views. Albert, in her essay, suggests systematizing cognitive research in the form of a new discipline: ethnoscience, or ethno-philosophy.

An important concept in the study of values and cultures is that of *symbol*. A symbol may connote an array of meanings. This point is illustrated in Fabian's essay on religion and change in which he discusses the meanings attached to the symbolic gestures of conversion and baptism. A symbol of ethnic identity may be circumcision; a symbol of generational identity may be length of hair; the symbol of an African political party may be a crowing rooster or a palm tree. That people will fight and die for symbols is well known, and this fact points to the importance of getting beyond the outward manifestations of cross-cultural behavior into the range of meanings and emotions which are associated with such behavior.

In summary, there is an ongoing process within social science of trying to establish a language of observation and analysis. In this process, there is a constant give and take on the matter of definitions and concepts, but the establishment of a truly international language of social science which could be used appropriately by any social-science discipline within any cultural or geographical context remains a hope for the future. It is of interest to note, however, that much of the impetus for such a language has come from social scientists who are working in the non-Western world, a significant number of whom have been working in Africa.

INTERDISCIPLINARY RESEARCH PRIORITIES

Although social scientists are working toward the development of an objective language of analysis, the initial selection of problems and/or units for analysis is still a matter in which the values or preferences of the researcher may, and should, enter. It is only after the issues or problems are selected that an attempt toward objectivity is undertaken. Increasingly, research priorities are being suggested by the African states themselves or by the emergent university communities in Africa (including those at Ibadan, Makerere, Legon, and Dakar). While a distinction is sometimes made between social-science research and policy-science research, this does not mean that social science is oblivious to the basic research needs of Africa. The discussions by Pierre van den Berghe on problems of racism and economic exploitation, Aristide Zolberg on problems of nation-building, and Gwendolen Carter on racial confrontation in South Africa clearly indicate broad issues of major importance to African statesmen.

In the past, many of the priorities in social-science research have been determined by the traditional academic division of disciplines. This maintenance of rigid boundaries within social-science disciplines seems at last to be dissolving. The work by Dalton on social and political factors in economic development, the basically societal approach of Willett to the study of African art, and even the interest of physical scientists such as Kliphardt in adapting technical developments to societal needs — all these seem to point to the necessity for even further interdisciplinary research. Whether such research is to be undertaken by individuals or by teams may increasingly become a matter for consideration.[2]

The interdisciplinary nature of most problems in Africa has encouraged the growth of new disciplines which overlap existing boundaries. Furthermore, since disciplines tend to be organized around functions, there is no logical justification for their existence in examining societies where functions are not clearly differentiated. These points may require some elaboration.

The development of "boundary line" disciplines may be illustrated by the example of political science in Africa. First, there are scholars working in areas other than political science who are concerned with African political phenomena in relation to their own disciplines. Examples would be the work by Soja (geography) in political geography, Cohen (anthropology) in political anthropology, LeVine (psychology) in political psychology, Berg (economics) in political economics, Apthorpe (sociology) in political sociology, Rotberg (history) in political history, Whiteley (linguistics) in political linguistics, and Fernandez (anthropology) in political aspects of religion.[3]

Second, a number of political scientists specializing in Africa are working in

2. For an excellent example of coordinated studies, see P. C. Lloyd, A. L. Mabogunje, and B. Awe, eds., *The City of Ibadan* (Cambridge: At the University Press, 1967).

3. Edward W. Soja, *The Geography of Modernization in Kenya* (Syracuse, N.Y.: Syracuse University Press, 1968); Soja, "Communications and Territorial Integration in East Africa: An Introduction to Transaction Flow Analysis," *East Lakes Geographer*, IV (1968), 39–57; Ronald Cohen, "Political Anthropology: The Future of a Pioneer," *Anthropological Quarterly*, XXXVIII (1965), 117–31; Marc J. Swartz, Victor W. Turner, and Arthur Tuden, eds., *Political Anthropology* (Chicago: Aldine, 1966); Ronald Cohen and John Middleton, *Comparative Political Systems: Studies in the Politics of Pre-Industrial Societies* (Garden City, N.Y.: Doubleday, Natural History Press, 1967); Robert A. LeVine, "The Internalization of Political Values in Stateless Societies," *Human Organization*, XIX (1960), 51–58; LeVine, "Political Socialization and Culture Change," in *Old Societies and New States*, ed. Clifford Geertz (New York: Macmillan, The Free Press, 1963), pp. 280–304; Elliott Berg, "The Economic Basis of Political Choice in French West Africa," *American Political Science Review*, LIV (1960), 391–405; Raymond Apthorpe, "Political Change, Centralization, and Role Differentiation," *Civilisations*, X (1960), 217–23; Robert I. Rotberg, *Political History of Tropical Africa* (New York: Harcourt, Brace & World, 1965); Wilfred Whiteley, *Swahili: The Rise of a National Language* (London: Methuen, 1969); and James Fernandez, "Politics and Prophecy: African Religious Movements," *Practical Anthropology*, XII (1965), 71–75.

areas which lie outside of traditional political science: Mazrui's work in literature, Abernethy's work in education, and Johnson's work in language policy would illustrate this trend.[4]

Third, certain political scientists are working in the broader societal context in which the political system functions. This concern with "political culture" parallels the earlier societal focus characteristic of social anthropology.[5] In addition, some political scientists are working on problems which are inherently interdisciplinary, where there is no clear disciplinary claim to priority: "modernization," "integration," and even "nation-building" defy the existing perimeters of academic classification.[6]

Almost all of the social-science disciplines in Africa have been concerned with these broader, problem-oriented topics. Yet a process such as "modernization" may have a unifying conceptual basis which crosscuts several disciplines. Writers such as Eisenstadt, Shils, Banton, Almond, Rosberg, Parsons, and Coleman would suggest that such a basis is the phenomenon of "role differentiation." The processes of "urbanization," "secularization," and "division of labor" are all based on the notion of role differentiation.

If modern-sector studies can be handled only through cooperation between existing social-science disciplines, traditional-sector studies (which because of the diffuse nature of society often require an inquiry into the totality of societal relationships) necessarily go beyond any particular discipline. The discipline of anthropology has historically served to unify such studies, but in the future an even broader perspective may be necessary. The priorities of "development" entail consideration of rates and degrees of change in the functional differentiation of society. The frequent existence of ethnic pluralism within a given context requires social scientists to construct ways of evaluating multiple subsystems with varying degrees of internal differentiation.

The debate as to the primacy of any particular dimension (for example, political, economic, social) in African societal development is irrelevant to the extent that social behavior is multifunctional. However, given the process whereby societal sectors become increasingly distinct, the plea for a social-science

4. Ali A. Mazrui, "Some Socio-political Functions of English Literature in Africa," in *Language Problems of Developing Nations*, ed. Joshua A. Fishman, Charles A. Ferguson, and Jyotirindra Das Gupta (New York: John Wiley, 1968), pp. 183–98; see also John N. Paden, "Kano Hausa Poetry," *Kano Studies*, No. 1 (September 1965), pp. 33–38; David B. Abernethy, *The Political Dilemma of Popular Education* (Stanford: Stanford University Press, 1969); Willard Johnson, *The Cameroon Federation: Political Integration in a Fragmentary Society* (Princeton: Princeton University Press, forthcoming); and Johnson, "African-Speaking Africa: Lessons from the Cameroon," *African Forum*, I (1965), 65–77.

5. See, for example, Lucien Pye and Sydney Verba, eds., *Political Culture and Political Development* (Princeton: Princeton University Press, 1965).

6. David Apter, *The Politics of Modernization* (Chicago: University of Chicago Press, 1965); Joseph S. Nye, Jr., *Pan-Africanism and East African Integration* (Cambridge: Harvard University Press, 1965); and Brian Weinstein, *Gabon: Nation-Building on the Ogooue* (Cambridge: M.I.T. Press, 1966).

approach is not intended to mitigate the need for disciplinary bases. Yet, for both practical and theoretical reasons, the disciplinary scholar who intends to work within the African context should be equipped to act in the broader capacity of "social scientist." Whatever the difficulties of social-science research in Africa,[7] they are less than those of narrow confinement to a particular discipline. A clear alternative to the strictly disciplinary approach is the problem-oriented approach.

The problem-oriented approach has already resulted in a proliferation of "institutes" which cut across disciplinary boundaries. Institutes of urban affairs and international relations are common on African and American campuses, and in the future we may also see institutes of modernization, national integration, cultural engineering, and social change. In Kano, Nigeria, an institute of Hausa studies is being established, which will include linguistic, historical, and cultural aspects of research.

Priorities of research in Africa will vary according to whether a disciplinary or a problem-oriented approach is employed. Such priorities will probably emerge as a compromise between the interests of the social-science community as a whole, the interests of the host-country peoples and governments, and the interests of the individual researchers.

METHODS OF SOCIAL-SCIENCE OBSERVATION

There have been historic differences between and within academic disciplines with regard to the credibility of different types of evidence. The blurring of disciplinary boundaries in African research has included not only substantive but also methodological boundaries. In most cases, the methods and techniques within particular disciplines have counterparts in other disciplines. To a certain extent the process of establishing social science as a legitimate base for inter-disciplinary research will depend on the degree to which those scholars utilizing counterpart types of methods can agree on some standardization of the rules of evidence.

In all approaches to methodology, two problems exist: *verification* and *validity*. Verification refers to the processes by which the accuracy, or *reliability*, of the recorded observation may be checked, and validity refers to the processes by which variables are allocated to the appropriate conceptual categories.

As mentioned earlier, the need for strict attention to the methodology or procedure of observation is partly the result of problems of ethnocentrism, whereby an individual scholar or observer may find that his perceptions are colored by his own cultural or personal experience. Within the African context,

7. For a discussion of these difficulties, see Kenneth Thompson, "Social Sciences in the Developing Nations," *Background: Journal of the International Studies Association*, X (1966), 163–76.

this problem exists whether the observer is a white American or European, a black American, an African from a different cultural unit than the one under observation, or an African from the cultural unit being studied.

One goal of social science, then, is objectivity with regard to the study of cross-cultural phenomena. Many scholars, however, are fully aware of the intellectual arguments of phenomenology—that is, the belief that all reality is subjective.[8] Rather than dismiss the possibility for intersubjective communication and understanding, some scholars have attempted to refine techniques such as participant observation, whereby the observer himself experiences the phenomena under observation. In fact, within the African context, the methodology of participant observation has become, along with interviews, survey research, experimental tests, and documentary analysis, one of the major techniques of data collection.

Participant Observation

Participant observation is based on the premise that firsthand observers of a situation may influence that situation, i.e., that persons who observe are noticed and may affect the course of events. Techniques of participant observation have been evolved to assess the impact of an observer on a situation and to establish procedures for reporting personal experiences.

Participant observation may entail different degrees of involvement. In the case of complete involvement, the observer is also *partisan*. Participation, however, may be *partial*, as in cases where the observer is obviously an "outsider" but is interacting in significant ways with the persons in the group under observation. Finally, participation may be *passive*, as in cases where the observer does not have a role in the unit under observation but where his mere presence may influence the actors involved. The technical and ethical problems implicit in this approach will vary according to the type of participation.

The theoretical implications of participant observation are elaborated in the work of Bruyn, and the methodological aspects are discussed in the work of Becker.[9] One of the best-known applications of participant observation can be found in Whyte's *Street Corner Society*,[10] but Africanist scholars, especially anthro-

8. For a theoretical discussion of phenomenology and social science, see Alfred Schutz, *Collected Papers I: The Problem of Social Reality*, ed. Maurice Natanson (The Hague: Martinus Nijhoff, 1967), esp. pp. 118–50; for methodological implications, see Harold Garfinkel, *Studies in Ethnomethodology* (Englewood Cliffs, N.J.: Prentice-Hall, 1967).

9. Severyn T. Bruyn, *The Human Perspective in Sociology: The Methodology of Participant Observation* (Englewood Cliffs, N.J.: Prentice-Hall, 1966); Howard S. Becker, "Problems of Inference and Proof in Participant Observation," *American Sociological Review*, XXIII (1958), 652; Howard S. Becker and Blanche Geer, "Participant Observation and Interviewing: A Comparison," *Human Organization*, XVI (1957), 28–32.

10. William Foote Whyte, *Street Corner Society*, 2d ed. (Chicago: University of Chicago Press, 1955).

pologists such as Laura Bohannan and Hortense Powdermaker,[11] have also contributed to the overall understanding of participant observation methods and experience.

Drawing on the experience of the contributors to this volume, it is possible to illustrate the different types of participant observation. James Turner is a full participant in the Afro-American movements and perspectives of which he writes. Likewise, J. Congress Mbata has been active in South African nationalist movements. Wilfred Cartey may be regarded as a partial participant in the realm of creative contemporary black literature insofar as his role is primarily that of a critic rather than an author. The field work of contributors such as Jack Berry, Klaus Wachsmann, Ethel Albert, Johannes Fabian, and Ronald Cohen illustrates the notion of passive participation, observing at close hand and over long periods selected aspects of particular social systems. It should be noted, however, that insofar as Berry has contributed to governmental discussions within Africa concerned with the directions of national language policy, he may be regarded as a partial participant, or, at times, as a full participant.

Interview Data

Interviews, in which the researcher talks in depth with a respondent either following a fixed set of questions or in a more open-ended manner, are a primary means of gathering data. The techniques of interview may vary with each discipline and each problem. Oral data, which are essentially interview data, may be used to re-create aspects of the history of a preliterate society. John Rowe and Jeffrey Holden have used this technique in their work in Buganda (Uganda) and Futa Toro (Senegal), respectively. A useful description of oral-data techniques.is found in Vansina's description of his work in the Congo.[12]

With regard to content, some interview techniques have been developed which attempt to re-create affective or cognitive patterns rather than mere behavior patterns. One example of such techniques is the *focused* interview, which attempts to elicit the respondent's feelings toward, and interpretations of, a set of historical events which are known to both the interviewer and the respondent. There are special techniques to correct for errors in memory or other distortions.[13]

---

11. Laura Bohannan [Elenore Smith Bowen], *Return to Laughter* (Garden City, N.Y.: Doubleday, Natural History Press, 1954); Hortense Powdermaker, *Stranger and Friend: The Way of an Anthropologist* (New York: W. W. Norton, 1966).

12. Jan Vansina, *Oral Tradition; A Study in Historical Methodology*, trans. H. M. Wright (Chicago: Aldine, 1965).

13. See Robert K. Merton, Marjorie Fiske, and Patricia L. Kendall, *The Focused Interview: A Manual of Problems and Procedures* (Glencoe, Ill.: The Free Press, 1956). See also W. H. Hunt, W. W. Crane, and J. C. Wahlke, "Interviewing Political Elites in Cross-Cultural Comparative Research," *American Journal of Sociology*, LXX (1964), 59.

Survey Research

Much of survey research is essentially a form of interview. However, instead of concentrating on individual depth interviews, teams of interviewers administer standardized questions which can be coded and, usually, machine processed.[14] Survey research in Africa has for the most part dealt with attitudes and background characteristics. Census enumeration can be a form of survey research to the extent that it asks questions regarding background characteristics of a population. Attitudinal research may try to elicit responses to real or hypothetical questions. The major problems in survey research include maintenance of uniformity among the various members of the interview team, the matter of selecting a sample, and the possible exclusion of areas of information because of the need to produce comparable (and/or machine readable) types of answers. The advantage of survey research is its breadth of coverage.

Remi Clignet and Akin Mabogunje have used survey research techniques in Africa in their respective studies of Ghanaian and Ivoirien schoolchildren and Nigerian urban migrants. Any research that deals with very large numbers of respondents will probably employ some techniques of survey research. To date in Africa there has been only limited use of this technique due to problems of financial resources and of training large survey-research teams.

Experimental Testing

Experimental tests may be used to elicit reactions to certain specified stimuli, usually in small group or individual studies. One example is the Thematic Apperception Test (TAT), in which a respondent is given a set of pictures that he interprets. The use of these techniques is often limited to psychologists who can work intensively with small groups of persons. Student groups and hospital patients are frequently used as bases for experimental samples.

Ronald Cohen and Robert LeVine have used experimental testing in some of their work in Africa—LeVine in his study of achievement motivation among schoolboys in Nigeria, and Cohen in his work on marriage and divorce in Bornu.[15] Cross-cultural use of stimulus-response experiments, however, is usually difficult to interpret unless this technique is combined with other observational methods. LeVine and Cohen, for example, spent considerable amounts of time engaged in participant observation prior to the experimental tests.

14. For technical details of survey research see C. H. Backstrom and G. D. Hursh, *Survey Research* (Evanston, Ill.: Northwestern University Press, 1963); for an evaluation of survey research in non-Western contexts, see J. M. Stycos, "Sample Surveys for Social Science in Underdeveloped Areas," in *Human Organization Research*, ed. R. N. Adams and J. J. Preiss (Homewood, Ill.: Richard Irwin, Dorsey Press, 1960), pp. 375–88.

15. See, for example, Robert A. LeVine, *Dreams and Deeds: Achievement Motivation in Nigeria* (Chicago: University of Chicago Press, 1966); and Ronald Cohen, *Dominance and Revolt: A Study of Marriage and Divorce among the Kanuri of Bornu* (forthcoming).

Documentary Analysis and Content Analysis

Content analysis refers to the processes by which written materials are systematically analyzed and classified.[16] Documentary analysis is less concerned than content analysis with problems of sampling.[17] In fact, in documentary analysis a single manuscript may be used as the basis of an urban history, as the *Kano Chronicle* has been used in Nigeria until recently. Content analysis is more systematic in its method insofar as the focus is likely to be on patterns of communications rather than on the subtleties of substantive matter. Quantitative content analysis may even engage in word counts or concept-frequency counts.[18] To date, documentary analysis has been more extensively used in Africa than has content analysis.

The essays by John Paden and Roland Young both reflect the use of documentary analysis. In the former, writings by African leaders are examined with regard to concepts of nationhood; in the latter, legal discussions and documents are examined with regard to precedents and concepts of jurisprudence. Other scholars have undertaken content analysis of African newspapers or parliamentary debates for indications of government policy. At the same time, historians are discovering documents in Africa (in European, North African, and vernacular languages) which, when carefully analyzed, may open new doors on the past.

The Idea of Methodology

In short, the purpose of methodology in data collection is to establish rules of evidence. This is necessary not only to establish the credibility of the claims to knowledge made by scholars but also to establish the foundations upon which cross-cultural data analysis may be undertaken. By making explicit the methodology of observation and the procedures of data gathering, a scholar is in effect suggesting that any other scholar who followed the same procedures would come up with the same observations and conclusions. Such potential for duplication of research is usually called *replicability*, and may be regarded as an essential premise of all science.[19]

16. See Robert C. North et al., *Content Analysis: A Handbook with Applications for the Study of International Crisis* (Evanston, Ill.: Northwestern University Press, 1963).

17. See James S. Coleman, "Documentary Research," in *Studying Politics Abroad: Field Research in the Developing Areas*, ed. R. E. Ward (Boston: Little, Brown, 1964), pp. 72–102; also J. H. Madge, *The Tools of Social Science* (Garden City, N.Y.: Doubleday, 1965), Chap. 2, "Documents."

18. For an account of quantitative content analysis, see P. J. Stone et. al., *The General Inquirer: A Computer Approach to Content Analysis* (Cambridge: M.I.T. Press, 1966).

19. For a preliminary discussion of replication, see Stanley Schachter, "Interpretative and Methodological Problems of Replicated Research," *Journal of Social Issues*, X, No. 4 (1954), 52–60.

The utilization of particular types or combinations of data-gathering techniques will depend on the nature of the research problem and the type of analysis which is intended. But it is important to recognize that there is no essential difference in the methodological approaches of the various social-science disciplines. The techniques of observation used in linguistics are much the same as those used in sociology. Survey research in economics is essentially the same as that in geography. It is the interdisciplinary nature of social-science methodology which contributes both to the unity of social science and to the permeability of disciplinary boundaries.

MAJOR TYPES OF SOCIAL-SCIENCE ANALYSIS

Analysis refers to the assessment of data patterns after the data have been gathered through any of the methods mentioned above. Types of analysis may be categorized by several criteria: the number of units involved (e.g., comparative analysis of many units *vs.* developmental analysis of a single unit); the number of variables involved (e.g., bivariate *vs.* multivariate analysis[20]); or the nature of the data involved (e.g., nominal, ordinal, or interval data[21]). Comparative and developmental analysis will be discussed below.

Comparative Analysis

Comparative, or synchronic, analysis is concerned with analyzing the similarities and dissimilarities of units which are regarded as sharing certain defining characteristics. Such units may be nation-states, urban areas, ethnic societies, individuals, or any other set of units. Comparative analysis of such units may be *cross-sectional*, insofar as a functionally defined portion of such units may be isolated for comparative purposes. The comparisons may also be cross-cultural or cross-national. A comparative study of political parties in Africa, or even a typologizing of regimes, as is undertaken in Crawford Young's essay, would illustrate this approach. The comparative approach (in contrast to the case-study approach) of both Cohen and Dalton, with reference to the characteristics of kinship patterns and economic patterns respectively, has only quite recently become common among anthropologists concerned with ethnic societies.

20. *Multivariate analysis* refers to the assessment of interactive effects between more than two variables. This is frequently done through computer techniques. See, for example, Irma Adelman and Cynthia Taft Morris, *Society, Politics, and Economic Development: A Quantitative Approach* (Baltimore: Johns Hopkins Press, 1967).
21. *Nominal data* refers to the naming of a thing, with no rank order implied (for example, Crawford Young's typology of regimes). *Ordinal data* refers to a scale which consists of approximate rank order, usually in more-than/less-than terms (for example, the relative complexity of a legal system as suggested in Roland Young's essay in this volume). *Interval data* refers to a scale which consists of precise numerical specifications of quality or quantity (for example, GNP per capita as used in Arnold Rivkin's essay in this volume).

Although the essay by Crowder does not compare a large number of units, it is essentially comparative in its assessment of the British and French colonial systems. When the analysis focuses upon a specific comparison of areas or places and the patterns of interaction within and between them, it may be termed *spatial*, as in the examination of circulation systems by Soja. This distinctively spatial approach to comparative social-science analysis, although frequently implicit in many studies, is only beginning to receive widespread attention in Africa.

Sometimes the comparative analysis is undertaken by a single researcher, such as LeVine in his comparison of Hausa, Yoruba, and Ibo achievement motivation in Nigeria, or Crawford Young in his discussion of Tunisia and Tanzania in his essay in this volume, or Zolberg in his analysis of Ivory Coast and Mali.[22] In other cases, the comparison is carried out by scholars who draw their original data from case studies conducted by other persons, as Coleman and Rosberg have done in their analysis of African political parties, or Carter in her series on African political development.[23] One of the most monumental comparative efforts in African studies, building on the case studies of many scholars, is Murdock's analysis of ethnic patterns in Africa.[24] The major difficulty with comparative analysis based on Murdock is that the original case studies vary in quality and even in the variables selected. However, an impressive demonstration as to how scholars may build on one another's work in comparative analysis is the recent study by Barrett of six thousand syncretistic religious movements in Africa, which draws on Murdock's data for ethnic coding.[25] By contrast, the comparative analysis of the linguistic patterns of Africa by Greenberg,[26] as presented in the Berry essay, was based on original sampling of word forms from a systematically selected sample base.

22. LeVine, *Dreams and Deeds;* Crawford Young has also done comparative analysis of Congo-Kinshasa and Uganda; Aristide R. Zolberg, "Patterns of National Integration," *Journal of Modern African Studies*, V (1967), 449–67.

23. James S. Coleman and Carl G. Rosberg, eds., *Political Parties and National Integration in Tropical Africa* (Berkeley and Los Angeles: University of California Press, 1964); Gwendolen M. Carter, ed., *National Unity and Regionalism in Eight African States* (Ithaca: Cornell University Press, 1966); see also Carter, ed., *African One-Party States* (Ithaca: Cornell University Press, 1962); and Carter, ed., *Five African States: Responses to Diversity* (Ithaca: Cornell University Press, 1963).

24. George Peter Murdock, *Africa: Its Peoples and Their Culture History* (New York: McGraw-Hill, 1959). In a later work, *Ethnographic Atlas* (Pittsburgh: University of Pittsburgh Press, 1967), Murdock presents coded data on 239 African societies, grouped into 85 "clusters." He uses such variables as subsistence economy, mode of marriage, family organization, marital residence, community organization, patrilineal kin groups, matrilineal kin groups, jurisdictional hierarchy, etc. Most of the Murdock data is nominal, but some is ordinal.

25. David B. Barrett, *Schism and Renewal in Africa: An Analysis of Six Thousand Contemporary Religious Movements* (London: Oxford University Press, 1968).

26. For a discussion of methodology, see Joseph H. Greenberg, *Anthropological Linguistics: An Introduction* (New York: Random House, 1968).

Developmental Analysis

The idea of developmental analysis (also called longitudinal, time-series, or diachronic) is based on the assumption of change within a single unit over time. This is basically the historical approach. The single unit may be the entire international system, as is illustrated in Mazrui's description of the impact of Africa on international patterns of alignment and non-alignment. Or the single unit may be the national state, as is implicit in the time projections on economic data in the essay by Rivkin. The unit of observation may also be the overlap zone between two groups, such as the European and African groups in South Africa described by Mbata. The boundaries of the unit itself may undergo change, as Abu-Lughod and Hammond suggest in their respective descriptions of the expansion of the Islamic community in Africa and the extension of the African community to the New World. The transport networks outlined by Soja and the urban systems described by Mabogunje may also be charted in terms of their change over time.

Whatever the type of unit, time-series data constitute the core of developmental analysis. After an initial baseline is selected, a rate of change can be calculated. In the African context, that baseline may be the date of independence (see Crawford Young), the dates of the colonial period (see Crowder),[27] some standard unit of time (see Mabogunje in his use of vital statistics for urban and rural areas, or his charting of African urban growth in ten-year periods), or some locally relevant date (in Mabogunje's essay, for example, 1947 is given as a baseline year in looking at urban craftsmen in Morocco).

Developmental analysis does not necessarily need to be bound by standardized time periods or even precise data. It is the general direction of change which is important rather than some precise quantity of change over time. The essay by Mbata on racial policy in South Africa and the essay by Turner on Afro-American identity formation both stress the emergence of patterns within an overall time framework, without strictly adhering to internal compartmentalization of time units. It should be noted, however, that any form of developmental analysis is distinct from a literary or artistic rendering of time, which is often dealt with as a subjective phenomenon, particularly in autobiographical literature.[28]

It should be clear from the above examples that an analysis may be both comparative and developmental. Crawford Young's suggestion that the various African regimes have gone through four distinct time phases is perhaps the

27. See also Michael Crowder, *West Africa under Colonial Rule* (Evanston, Ill.: Northwestern University Press, 1968).

28. For examples of such autobiographical literature, see Wilfred Cartey, *Whispers from a Continent: The Literature of Contemporary Black Africa* (New York: Random House, 1969).

clearest example of this combination. Another example is Rivkin's discussion of comparative rates of economic change.

The merits of developmental analysis ultimately focus on the possibility of projecting time-series data into the future and hence achieving some degree of predictability. The merits of comparative analysis rest in its ability to predict system characteristics in an unknown unit if that unit is similar to a known unit in other significant respects. For example, an urban center known to have a low average age level and a disproportionate percentage of male to female inhabitants may well serve to predict certain other social characteristics, such as patterns of urban instability.

PROBLEMS OF SOCIAL-SCIENCE RESEARCH

The purpose of this essay has not been to suggest that social science holds, even potentially, all the answers regarding ways of understanding the African experience. Social-science research at the moment is often inadequate by its own standards, which may in fact prove to be visionary. In the effort to establish standards, however, it is important to recognize certain problems in social science, most of which are clearly illustrated in the African context.

The first problem is identifying appropriate units for analysis. Should individuals, ethnic groups, urban centers, national states, or other units be selected as the focus for such problem-oriented research as modernization or social change? Also, comparative analysis of any sort requires comparability of units. It has been partly in response to this requirement that the unit of "tribe" is being used less frequently by scholars to refer to the range of traditional societies in Africa. It has become clear that such societies may be fundamentally different types of units—for example, kinship groups, language groups, religious groups, ecological groups—and that to mix them together may violate the unit comparability requirement of social science.

The second problem is that of missing data. In many cases within the African context, it is not possible to obtain systematic information on a subject. Hence, a researcher must devise some technical means of dealing with missing data or he must be willing to make qualitative judgments regarding the probable characteristics of such data. In all of the essays in this volume, the authors have continually stressed the difficulty of obtaining continent-wide data to sustain generalizations about Africa as a whole. When generalizations are made— and the demand for such generalization is one reason for undertaking this volume—it is important to recognize whether propositions are based on data, extrapolation, or subjective judgment.

A third area of weakness in social science, especially within the African context, is the tendency to concentrate on behavioral analysis to the exclusion of value or cognitive analysis. In certain respects behavioral analysis is less difficult to undertake, but the necessity for interpreting behavior within a framework of meaning appropriate to the African context should not be forgotten. The essays by Fabian and Albert, for example, emphasize the need for a more comprehensive view of symbols and values.

Fourth, there is often a tendency in social science to deal with the known rather than the unknown. This problem is the challenge which the African experience clearly presents to social science, as well as to the hundreds of societal systems in Africa that are trying to bridge the culture gaps between themselves. The greatest service social science could render Africa may well be to remain sensitive to the unique, the unknown, the emerging, the ambiguous, rather than to engage in the rigid application of techniques and problem orientations which may have proved useful or appropriate in the Western world.

Finally, there has been the problem that research priorities in Africa have often been established in a haphazard manner, or perhaps even to serve colonial ends. It is clear today, however, that African social scientists (such as Ali Mazrui, who is dean of social sciences at Makerere University, or Akin Mabogunje, who is dean of social sciences at the University of Ibadan) will be taking the lead in blending the priorities of the social-science community with the needs of the African countries. It is also becoming evident that Afro-American scholars in the United States (such as James Turner, who is director of the Africana Studies Program at Cornell University, or Wilfred Cartey, who is chairman of the Black and Puerto Rican Studies Department at the City College of New York) may propose new criteria of relevance for research on the African experience. But, and perhaps more important, Africa—the probable birthplace of mankind—will increasingly attract research designed to explore patterns of the human experience which transcend any single continental setting.

The Contributors

IBRAHIM ABU-LUGHOD is Professor of Political Science and Associate Director of the Program of African Studies at Northwestern University. Born in Palestine, he received his doctorate from Princeton University. His publications include *Arab Rediscovery of Europe*: *A Study in Cultural Encounters* and *The Arab-Israeli Confrontation of June 1967*.

ETHEL M. ALBERT is Professor of Anthropology at Northwestern University. Born in Connecticut, she received her Ph.D. in philosophy from the University of Wisconsin. She has written extensively on Rwanda and Burundi. She is co-editor of *The People of Rimrock*: *A Comparative Study of Values and Social Systems in Five Cultures*.

JACK BERRY is Professor and Chairman of the Department of Linguistics at Northwestern University. Born in Leeds, England, he received his doctorate from the University of London. He is author of *An English-Twi-Asanti-Fante Dictionary* and *A Dictionary of Sierra Leone Creole*. At present he is co-director of a survey of multilingualism in Accra, Ghana.

GWENDOLEN M. CARTER is Director of the Program of African Studies at Northwestern University and is Melville J. Herskovits Professor of African Affairs. Born in Canada, she received her Ph.D. from Radcliffe College. She is a former president of the African Studies Association. Her publications include *The Politics of Inequality: South Africa since 1948* and *South Africa's Transkei: The Politics of Domestic Colonialism*.

WILFRED CARTEY is Professor of English and Comparative Literature and Chairman of the Black and Puerto Rican Studies Department at the City College of the City University of New York. Born in Trinidad, he received his Ph.D. from Columbia University. He is literary editor of *African Forum* and is the author of *Whispers from a Continent: The Literature of Contemporary Black Africa*.

REMI CLIGNET is Associate Professor of Sociology at Northwestern University. Born in Reims, France, he received his doctorate from the University of Paris.

His publications include *The Fortunate Few: A Study of Secondary Schools and Students in the Ivory Coast* and *Many Wives, Many Powers: Authority and Power in Polygynous Families.*

RONALD COHEN is Professor of Political Science and Anthropology at Northwestern University. Born in Canada, he received his doctorate from the University of Wisconsin. His publications include *The Kanuri of Bornu* and *From Tribe to Nation in Africa.*

MICHAEL CROWDER is Research Professor and Director of the Institute for African Studies, University of Ife, Nigeria. Born in England, he received his B.A. at Oxford University. He is the author of *A Short History of Nigeria; Senegal: A Study in French Assimilation Policy;* and *West Africa under Colonial Rule.*

GEORGE DALTON is Professor of Economics and Anthropology at Northwestern University. Born in New York City, he received his doctorate from the University of Oregon. He is co-author of *Growth without Development: An Economic Survey of Liberia* and is co-editor of *Markets in Africa.*

JOHANNES FABIAN is Assistant Professor of Anthropology at Northwestern University. Born in Glogau, Germany, he received his doctorate from the University of Chicago. He is preparing for publication his field research on the Jamaa, a prophetic-charismatic movement in Katanga.

PETER B. HAMMOND is currently Senior Post-Doctoral Fellow and Faculty Research Associate of the Institute of Southern History, The Johns Hopkins University. Born in California, he received his Ph.D. from Northwestern University. He is the author of *Yatenga: Technology in the Culture of a West African Kingdom* and is editor of a two-volume work, *Physical Anthropology and Archaeology* and *Cultural and Social Anthropology.*

JEFFREY HOLDEN is a Research Fellow of the Institute of African Studies at the University of Ghana, and has been a visiting professor in African History at Northwestern University. Born in England, he received his M.A. at Oxford in modern history. His research has focused on pre-colonial Islamic state formation in West Africa.

RAYMOND A. KLIPHARDT is Professor of Engineering Sciences at Northwestern University and former director of the Northwestern University – University of Khartoum Cooperative Project. Born in Chicago, he received his M.S. in mathematics from the Illinois Institute of Technology. He is the author of *Program Design in FORTRAN IV.*

ROBERT A. LeVINE is Professor of Human Development and Anthropology at the University of Chicago. Born in New York City, he received his doctorate from Harvard University. He is currently conducting work in Nigeria as Director of the Child Development Unit, Ahmadu Bello University. His publications include *Nyasongo: A Gusii Community in Kenya* and *Dreams and Deeds: Achievement Motivation in Nigeria*.

AKIN L. MABOGUNJE is Professor of Geography and Dean of the Faculty of Social Sciences at the University of Ibadan, Nigeria, and has served as visiting professor of geography at Northwestern University. Born in Kano, Nigeria, he received his doctorate from the University of London. He is the author of *Yoruba Towns* and *Urbanization in Nigeria* and is co-editor of *The City of Ibadan*.

ALI A. MAZRUI is Professor of Political Science and Dean of the Faculty of Social Sciences at Makerere University College, Uganda, and has been a visiting professor at Northwestern University. Born in Mombasa, Kenya, he received his doctorate from Oxford University. His publications include *Towards a Pax Africana: A Study of Ideology and Ambition* and *On Heroes and Uhuru-Worship: Essays on Independent Africa*.

J. CONGRESS MBATA is Associate Director of the Program of Afro-American Studies at Cornell University and has been a Research Associate at the Northwestern University Program of African Studies. Born in Johannesburg, he received his diploma at the University of South Africa. He has served as Field Officer for the South African Institute of Race Relations and was the founder and former editor of the *Sharpeville Times*.

JOHN N. PADEN is Assistant Professor of Political Science at Northwestern University. Born in Boston, he received his Ph.D. from Harvard University. He has prepared for publication a study of the influence of religious elites on political culture and community integration in Kano, Nigeria, and is currently conducting research in West Africa on problems of national integration.

ARNOLD RIVKIN was Development Adviser for the International Bank for Reconstruction and Development, specializing in African area problems of economic development and external aid. He received his L.L.B. from Harvard Law School and is the author of *Africa and the West*; *The African Presence in World Affairs*; and *Nations by Design*.

JOHN ROWE is Assistant Professor of History at Northwestern University. Born in Binghamton, New York, he received his doctorate from the University of Wisconsin. He is the author of *Revolution in Buganda: 1856–1900* and is editor and co-author of *A History of Africa*.

EDWARD W. SOJA is Associate Professor of Geography at Northwestern University. Born in New York City, he received his doctorate from Syracuse University. He is the author of *The Geography of Modernization in Kenya: A Spatial Analysis of Social, Economic, and Political Change*.

JAMES TURNER is Director of the Program of Afro-American Studies at Cornell University. Born in New York City, he did his graduate work in sociology at Northwestern University. He has participated in the leadership of Afro-American organizations and has written extensively on black studies in the United States.

PIERRE L. van den BERGHE is presently Professor of Sociology at the University of Washington. Born in Lubumbashi, Congo, he received his doctorate from Harvard University. He edited *Africa: Social Problems of Change and Conflict* and is author of *South Africa: A Study in Conflict* and *Race and Racism.*

KLAUS WACHSMANN is Professor of Ethnomusicology at Northwestern University. Born in Berlin, he has served as the curator of the Uganda Museum in Kampala and of the Wellcome Collection of Primitive Art, now at UCLA. He has been the chairman of the ethnomusicology committee of the Royal Anthropological Institute and is currently President of the Society for Ethnomusicology.

FRANK WILLETT is Professor of Archaeology and African Art at Northwestern University. Born in Lancashire, England, he was Research Fellow at Nuffield College, Oxford University. He has been archaeologist to the federal government of Nigeria and curator of the Ife Museum. Among his publications is *Ife in the History of West African Sculpture.*

CRAWFORD YOUNG is Associate Professor of Political Science at the University of Wisconsin and is currently Associate Dean of the Graduate School. Born in Philadelphia, he received his doctorate from Harvard University. He is the author of *Politics in the Congo* and co-author of *Issues of Political Development.*

ROLAND YOUNG is Professor of Political Science at Northwestern University. Born in Colorado, he received his doctorate from Harvard University. He is co-author of *Smoke in the Hills: Political Conflict in the Morogoro District of Tanganyika* and is currently studying problems of African legal systems on a Guggenheim Fellowship.

ARISTIDE ZOLBERG is Associate Professor of Political Science at the University of Chicago. Born in Brussels, he received his Ph.D. from the University of Chicago. His publications include *One-Party Government in the Ivory Coast* and *Creating Political Order: The Party States of West Africa.*

Index

Aba Women's riots, 247

Abeokuta (Nigeria), 173, 336

Abidjan (Ivory Coast), 316, 319, 321, 347, 365, 373

Abraham, W. E., 278

Abrahams, Peter, 41, 586

Accra (Ghana), 253, 347, 350, 363, 365, 368, 373, 425

Acephalous polities, 54–56. *See also* Political systems, traditional

Achebe, Chinua, 583, 586

Acholi (people), 285, 289

Adebo, Chief S. O., 594

Addis Ababa (Ethiopia), 350, 432

Afars and Issas, Territory of: French rule in, 4; population of, 26; regional grouping of, 32

Africa: area, 8, 25; circulation regions, 369 (map); climate and vegetation, following 20 (map), 23–25; demography, 259–60, 347–52; ecological zones, 21–25; languages, number of, 8, 80; literacy rates, 263; political units, number of, 3, 8, 34; physiographic features, 20–25, following 20 (map), 22 (map); population, 8, 25–27, following 20 (map), 26 (table), 276 n, 503 (table); population concentrations, 25, 27, 260; population growth, 27, 259–60, 502, 502 n; racial groups, 28–31; regions, 31–34; river and drainage system, 21, 523; sociocultural environment, 280–81

African Data Bank, 43 n

African Diaspora, 174, 420–21, 422, 603

Africanisms. *See* African survivals

Africanité, 256

Africanization, 315; of army, 469; of bureaucracy, 459, 461, 518; in education, 310–11, 325; of management, 327, 353, 518; of school curriculums, 325

African law. *See* Law, African, 476

African Methodist Episcopal Church, 602

African National Congress (ANC, South Africa), 225, 229, 230, 571

African nationalism. *See* Nationalism, African; Nationalist movements

African personality: as adaptation to environment, 282; assumptions about, 276–77; in characteristics of agricultural societies, 298–99; and conceptual systems, 99–100; and cultural values, 41; described as central tendency, 279, 281; described as trait psychology, 39, 281, 284; effect of, on entrepreneurial initiative, 78; limitations of concept of, 283; perpetuation of idea of, 277; as a philosophy, 277, 438; popular stereotypes of, 277–78; and sociocultural environment, 280–81; studies of, 278; terms used in studies of, 279; and uniformities in behavior, 283–97. *See also* Behavior, African; Interpersonal relations

African socialism, 269, 412, 414–16, 432, 459, 500–501. *See also* Marxist-socialist ideology

African states and kingdoms: administrative structures in, 113, 189–90; artistic production in, 113; centralization of authority in, 193–94; legitimation of authority in, 186; maintenance of authority in, 189–91; European ignorance of, 238; finance and taxation in, 190; formation of, in East and central Africa, 179–80; formation of, in Western Sudan, 182–84; oral tradition in, 159–61; population concentration in, 25; rise and fall of, 252; ritual leadership in, 187–88; trade patterns in, 183, 335. *See also* Centralized state systems; Chieftaincy; Kingship; Political systems, traditional; *and names of individual states:* Akan, Ashanti, Axum, Benin, Bono-Mansu, Bornu,

Buganda, Dahomey, Ewe, Ghana, Hausa-Fulani, Ife, Kanem-Bornu, Kongo, Kush, Lozi, Lunda, Mali, Merowe, Monomotapa, Ngola, Oyo, Rwanda, Sokoto, Songhai, Wadai, Zimbabwe

African studies: and Afro-American studies, 7, 209; curriculum development in, 61; growth of, 5–8, 154; in 1960s, 7, 77, 164; programs of, 4, 157, 622

African Studies Association (ASA), 6

African survivals: in aesthetic forms, 205; in Caribbean area, 201; factors determining degree of, 206; in language, 206, 208; in literature, 205; in religion, 204–5, 208, 417. *See also* Creole languages

African universities, 74, 156, 527–29, 610. *See also* Ghana, University of; Ibadan, University of; Makerere University College

Africa script, 88

Afrikaans churches, 213

Afrikaner National Party (South Africa), 210, 226

Afrikaners: ancestry of, 569; nationalism of, 570

Afro-Americans: cultural survivals among, 201, 205, 206, 208, 417; economic position of, 207; emergence of black nationalism among, 593–94; historical perspective on, 599–601; and image of Africa, 592–94; need for studies of, 7; political participation of, 207–8; and racial conflict in South Africa, 580, 603; rejection of Africa by, 208, 592–93, 604; religious syncretisms among, 208; repatriation movements among, 208, 420–21, 600–601; subculture of, 204–6, 595; West African origins of, 195, 196–98, 203–4. *See also* African Diaspora; Black identity; Black nationalism; Slavery, New World; Slave trade

Afro-Asiatic language group, 83

Afro-Portuguese ivories, 126

Afro-Shirazi Party (Zanzibar), 462

Agades (Niger), 335

Aga Khan, 560

Age: of African individuals, 317; segregation by, 285

Age-set organizations, 56, 57, 90, 269

Agriculture, African: characteristics of, 66, 280; in cocoa farming, 242–43; criteria of efficacy in, 103; cash crops in, 70, 240–42, 268–69, 364, 447; declining output of, 505; and development planning, 505; and domestication of plants, 170; ecological dependence of, 66; effect of, on political organization, 50; as evidence of Bantu migration, 171; export products of, 499; in introduction of Asian and American crops, 171, 253; land tenure in, 71–72, 272–73, 353 (*see also* Land-tenure systems); research on, 524–26; shifting, 479, 524–25; subsistence farming in, 72, 266–67, 269, 512. *See also* Economies, African

Ahmadiyya, 560, 565

Air transport, 367, 373, 576. *See also* Transportation systems

Ajami script, 89

Akan (people): population, 27; music among, 142

Akan (state), 160

Akintola, Chief S. L., 425

Akoo (people), 479

Albert, Lake, 524

Alexandria, 349, 350

Algeria: administrative parties in, 456; caravan routes in, 554; Chinese aid to, 514; colonial policy in, 233; competing groups in, 466; economic exploitation of, 268; French conquest of, 254; Front of National Liberation (FLN) in, 411; GNP per capita in, 503; independence of, 534; independence political system of, 460; insurgency movements in, 457, 466; Islam in, 549–50, 550 n, 566; literacy in, 263; military in, 507; population of, 26, 503; regional grouping of, 32; revolution in, 411, 466; settler population in, 272, 457, 570; social change in, 259; urban concentration in, 333

Algiers (Algeria), 350

Algiers Conference (1967), 521

Alienation, theme of, 584–86, 588

All African Convention (South Africa), 229–30

All-African Peoples' Conference (1958), 425, 534

Allocations familiales, 518

Almoravid empire, 124, 184–85, 556

American Colonization Society, 453 n

American Society of African Culture (AMSAC), 594, 600

Amharic (language), 89, 91

Ancestor worship, 198, 280

Anglo-Boer War, 221, 223, 570

Angola: circulation region of, 371; Portuguese control of, 236; 268; 568; 573; liberation movements in, 272, 575; political institutions in, 257; population of, 26; regional grouping of, 33; white population of, 457, 573

Ankole (state), 270

Apartheid policy, 210, 255, 585
Arab: culture, 552–53; expansion under
    Isalm, 336, 552; occupation of North
    Africa, 334; settlements in East Africa, 180,
    558–60
Arabic documents, 174, 181
Arabic language, 82, 553, 559; literature in,
    44, 91; script in, 89, 181; spread of, 560
Arab Socialist Union, 470
Art, African: aesthetic considerations, 117,
    119–21; and the artist, 122; characteristics
    of, 120–21; context of, 117; demand for,
    126; environmental and social influences
    on, 112–115; external influences on,
    124–26; investment of value in, 121;
    generalizations about, 114–15; painting as
    a form in, 108; Pitt-Rivers Collection of,
    109; religious purpose of, 115–16; social
    purpose of, 116; souvenir trade in, 126;
    and Western education. *See also* Masks;
    Sculpture
Art, African, study of: aesthetic approach to,
    109–110; the artist in, 110;
    data available for, 111–112; degeneration
    theory in, 109; ethnological approach to,
    109; field work in, 111, 112, 114;
    functionalist approach to, 114–15; through
    institutions, 113; radiocarbon dating in,
    122–23; research needs in, 115
Ashanti (Akan) people: music of, 149;
    population, 27
Ashanti (state), 252, 335; centralization of
    power in, 173; oral tradition in, 160–61;
    social stratification in, 270
Ashanti Wars (1899), 405
Askia Muhammad, 185, 187, 188, 189, 190,
    193
Assimilation policies, 245, 256, 305, 307–8,
    345, 410, 416
Ateso (language), 136
Atlantic Charter, 236
Authority relations. *See* Political authority
Avoidance relations, 50, 284. *See also* Social-
    distance patterns
Axum (state), 172, 179, 252
Azikiwe, Nnamdi, 406, 537

Back to Africa movements, 208, 404, 420–21
    600–601. *See also* Black Zionism
Baganda (people), 88, 295
Bahima (people), 142
Bahutu (people), 465
Bai Bureh, 239
Bakongo (people), 403
Bakri, al-, 186, 188, 190

Balandier, Georges, 395–96
Baldwin, James, 416, 604
Baluba (Luba) people, 252, 270, 397
Baluhya (Luhya) people, 287, 378–79
Bamako Conference (1946), 427
Bambara (language), 89
Bambara (people), 144
Bamum script, 89
Bandung Conference (1955), 426, 537 n
Bantu languages: characteristics of, 85, 88,
    95, 559; classifications of, 82–86, 84 (map),
    86 (map), 171; literary tradition among, 91;
    survey of, 94
Bantu migration, 29, 30, 171
Bantu Philosophy (Tempels), 397
Bantu-speaking peoples, 29, 219, 385–86, 397
Bantustan program: African attitudes
    toward, 578–79; African political
    participation in, 571, 578; failure of,
    578–79; purpose of, 221, 577–78, 579. *See
    also* Native Reserves
Barbe, Raymond, 411
Barotse (people), 270, 478
Barotseland Protectorate (Zambia), 454
Basin-and-swell structure, 21
Basle missions, 163, 309, 310
Basuto (people), 219
Basutoland, 33, 173, 222. *See also* Lesotho
Baule (people), 144–45
Bayaka (people), 454
Beatrice, Donna, 387
Bechuanaland. *See* Botswana
Bedouins, 56
Behavior, African: absence of separation
    anxiety and related affects in, 294–96, 299;
    adjustment to intergenerational differences
    in, 301; adjustment to mobility in, 299;
    affective reactions in, 294–95; competitive
    striving for resources in, 290, 293;
    concreteness of thought in, 296–97;
    dependence on kinship structure in, 300;
    emphasis on material transactions in, 288;
    functional diffuseness of relations in,
    290–92; hierarchical ordering in, 286;
    response to economic incentives in, 301;
    social-distance patterns in, 284; tendency
    to blame and fear others in, 292–93, 297,
    302; trait clusters in, 39; variations in, 297–
    99. *See also* African personality; Hostility;
    Interpersonal relations
Beira (Mozambique), 365, 370
Belgium: colonial rule in the Congo, 454;
    decolonization policies of, 455, 56;
    education policy in the colonies, 311–12
Bello, Muhammad, 181

Bembe (people), 118
Ben Bella group, 466
Benguela (Angola), 363
Benin (city-state), 113, 238, 252, 335; Afro-Portuguese ivories in, 126; bronze-work in, 111, 118, 123; excavation of, 124; social stratification in, 270
Bennett, Lerone, 595, 598
Ben Salah, 464
Berber (people), 90, 555–56
Beti, Mongo, 583
Biafra, 373, 472, 539. *See also* Nigeria
Bidonvilles, 268, 338, 347, 355, 356
Bilateral descent systems, 20, 265
Bilingualism, 81, 82
Binza caucus group, 467, 468 (table)
Birth rates, 349, 350 (table)
Black Africa, 32, 432, 545, 546–47
Black Frenchmen, 307. *See also* Assimilation policies
Black identity: and Afro-American nationalism, 594–99; as assertion of collective unconscious, 418, 421–22; and black soul, 417–18; and changing image of Africa, 592; expressed at 1958 Accra Conference, 425; and Garvey movement, 599–600; identification with Africa in, 421–22, 594–99, 602–4; in philosophy of negritude, 416–22; symbols of, 610. *See also* Afro-Americans; Black nationalism; Negritude
Black Muslims, 595–96
Black nationalism, 594–99; and Black Power movement, 598; early leadership of, 601; Garvey's role in development of, 599–600; and identifications with Africa, 594–99; ideology of, 597; militancy of, 598; as quest for new values, 598, 602, 603; roots of, 593, 602–3; Turner as prophet of, 602. *See also* Afro-Americans; Black identity; Negritude
Black Power. *See* Black nationalism
Black Zionism, 420, 421, 601. *See also* Back to Africa movements
Blyden, Edward Wilmot, 602
Boas, Franz, 109
Bobo-Dioulasso (Upper Volta), 427
Boer War. *See* Anglo-Boer War
Bonny (Nigeria), 363
Bono-Mansu (state), 160
Bornu (state), 187, 252. *See also* Kanem-Bornu
Botswana: communications and transport network in, 370; economic dependence of, 513, 572; GNP per capita in, 503; independence political system in, 460,

578; as labor reservoir, 267; population of, 26, 503; racial policies in, 580; regional grouping of, 33; South African relations with, 576
Boundaries: colonial, changing function of, 16; colonial, circulation systems within, 365, 366; colonial, OAU resolution on, 15; colonial, retention of, 14–16, 407, 565; colonial, and supranational communities, 15, 431–32; community, in traditional Africa, 52; national, establishment of, 258, 407, 437; national, concepts of mutability of, 432–33; national, concepts of static nature of, 431–32
Bourguiba, Habib, 464–65
"Brain drain," 263–64, 304
Brazil, 201, 204, 206, 417
Brazzaville, 33, 371
Brazzaville bloc, 430
Brideprice, 280, 281, 289
Bridewealth, 46, 265, 266
British East Africa: administrative policy in, 33, 372; literature of, 92
British Emancipation Act (1833), 218
British Settlements Act, (1843), 483
British West Africa: administrative policy in, 33, 247; educational policy in, 245, 308–11, 314, 322; indirect rule in, 240, 563; legislative councils in, 247; literature of, 92. *See also* Great Britain
Bronze casting, 111, 118, 123
Brown, H. Rap, 603
Burundi, 372
Buganda (kingdom): colonial administration in, 454; criminal law in, 486; historiography in, 162, 168; music in, 143, 147–48, 151; oral tradition in, 160; regalia instruments in, 145–46; reign of Mutesa in, 162; as secondary empire, 173
Bulawayo (Rhodesia), 337, 368, 370
Burden texts, 142, 147
Burmi, battle of, 405
Burundi: circulation systems in, 372; currency depreciation in, 512; elections in, 465; exports of, 520, 509 n; GNP per capita in, 503; independence political system in, 460; population concentration in, 27; population of, 26, 503; regional grouping of, 32–33; social stratification in kingdom of, 270
Bushman (language), 83–84
Bushmen (people), 30, 112, 258, 269

Cabora Bassa Dam, 576
Cairo, 349, 350, 426, 557

Calabar (Nigeria), 363

Cameroon, Federal Republic of: circulation network of, 373; GNP per capita, 503; German rule in, 233–34; ideological influence of China in, 536; independence political system in, 460; interurban linkages in, 368; Islam in, 549 n; linguistic diversity of, 80; music in, 150; population of, 26, 503; rainfall in, 23; regional grouping of, 32, 33; unification of, 514–15

Cameroon, Mount, 23

Carmichael, Stokely, 598, 603

Catholic church: and missions, 393; and slavery, 201; syncretisms of, in slave communities, 204–5

Cape Coloureds, 30, 217, 347, 569

Cape Province: 221–22, 225, 569, 571

Cape settlement: Dutch East India Company in, 210–12; partition scheme in, 214; slavery in, 212–13, 215

Capetown, 213, 337, 347, 350, 365, 370, 569, 577. *See also* Cape settlement

Cape Verde Island, 26

Capital investment, 273, 517

Carthage, 333

Casablanca (Morocco), 350

Casablanca group, 34, 432

Cash-crop agriculture, 70, 240–42, 268–69, 364, 447, 498–99

Cash economies, 242–43, 267, 301, 319, 357, 365

Cave paintings, 108, 125

Censuses, 259, 548

Central Africa (region); early urban centers in, 337–38; extent of, 32

Central African Economic Union, 34

Central African Federation, 33

Central African Republic: birth and death rates in, 350; circulation region of, 371; in East African Economic Community, 372; economy of, 451; exports of, 509 n; GNP per capita in, 503; independence political system in, 460; 1966 military takeover in, 444; natural barriers in, 515; population of, 26, 503; regional grouping of, 32

Centralized state systems, 55, 57–59; in colonial period, 234, 454; communications in, 190; consolidation of power in, 193; development of, 172–73; forms of, 186; kingship in, 58; maintenance of authority in, 193–94; payment of tribute in, 75; and problems of political organization, 58; trade patterns in, 172. *See also* African states and kingdoms; Political systems, traditional

Cesaire, Aime, 411, 414, 416, 426, 588

Chad: administrative parties in, 456; circulation network of, 373; exports of, 509 n; GNP per capita in, 503; independence political system in, 460; Islam in, 549–50, 550 n; natural barriers in, 515; population of, 26, 503; racial composition of, 432; regional grouping of, 32; separatist movement in, 472

Chad Basin, 21

Chagga (people), 91

Chieftaincy, 57–59; in colonial period, 454; deposition procedures in, 484; in French West Africa, 240–41; role diffuseness of, 290. *See also* Kingship

Childbearing, 290

Childrearing: behavioral differences among societies, 298; relations between parent and child, 295

Chilembwe, John, 405

China: aid to African states, 514; ideological influence of, on emerging nations, 535–36; as proponent of revolutionary violence, 536; and the Third World, 543–44

Chokwe (people), 124

Christianity: and African clergy, 396–97; and education, 262; in Ethiopia, 179, 252; ideology of change in, 255–56; and indigenous religions, 384; influence of on African art, 125–26; in Kongo kingdom, 387; and manumission of Cape slaves, 213; number of adherents to, 261; in towns, 246. *See also* Churches, African; Missions; Separatist church movements

Chronology, problem of, 168–69

Churches, African, 179, 228, 262, 405, 619

Circulation systems: effect of colonial boundaries on, 366, 373; in the Congo Basin, 371–72; consolidation of, 366–67; defined, 360, 374; in development of internal networks, 367; in development of modern networks, 362–68; in East Africa, 372; growth of trading ports in, 363–64; and interethnic linkages, 361–62; Lockheed study of, 528; in the Maghrib, 374; in the Nile Basin, 374; in penetration of the interior, 364–66; rural-urban interaction in, 380; in the South African region, 370; subnetworks of priority linkage in, 367–68; in supranational integration, 377; in traditional societies, 360–62; and transportation technology, 526–27; in West Africa, 372–74; in the Zambezi region, 370

Ciskei, 578

Cities. *See* Urban centers; Urbanization
City-states. *See* African states and kingdoms
Clark, John Pepper, 590
Clientage, 51
Climate, of Africa, 23–25
Codified law. *See* Criminal law; Ethiopia;
     Islamic law; Law, Western;
     Legal systems
Cognatic descent. *See* Bilateral descent
     systems
Cold War, 535, 539–43
Cole, Robert, 583
Collective vocation, in nationalist theory,
     421–25
Colonial administration: administrators in,
     240–42, 384, 454, 584; Africans in,
     458–59; civil service in, 440; goals of,
     454, 514; systems of, 33, 240–41, 454; as
     theme in African history, 173
Colonialism: in Americas, 201; and
     "civilizing mission," 255; and the
     colonial mentality, 249; economic liabilities
     of, 268; economic and political motives
     for, 237–38; domestic, in Southern Africa,
     569, 570–72; as ideology of change, 254;
     in literature, 584; paternalism in, 238,
     254–55; rationalization of, 237–38, 239;
     religion as symbolic medium in, 383–388;
     resistance to, 176, 236 n, 239–40, 247,
     395–96, 405, 452, 534, 537; secular
     influence of, 565–66; in socioeconomic
     change, 70; in Southern Africa, 568–69,
     570–72; and traditional status systems,
     271. *See also* Colonial administration;
     Colonial period; Colonial powers
Colonial period: bias in historical accounts
     of, 234; compartmentalization of services
     in, 366, 368; dates of, 236–37;
     development of cash crops in, 240–41;
     development of transportation network
     in, 243; economic exploitation in, 242–43;
     education policy in, 305–12; effect of, on
     agriculture, 242–43; effect of, on African
     life, 240–42; effect of, on African
     economies, 242–45, 267; effect of, on
     education, 245–46; effect of, on Islamic
     communities, 565; end of, 3–4;
     establishment of European cities during,
     346–47; establishment of export
     economies in, 367; ethnic pluralism in,
     12–13; evaluation of, 248–49; Islam in,
     561–65; legal systems in, 477; missionaries
     in, 261–62; partition of Africa in, 254;
     paternalism in, 235, 238; political
     systems in, 453–55; prewar and postwar,

compared, 236–37; political and economic
     legacy of, 258–59; resilience of traditional
     societies in, 257; standard of living in,
     242; wage and salary structures in, 518;
     zones of colonial organization in, 33. *See
     also* British East Africa; British West
     Africa; Boundaries; Colonial
     administration; Colonialism; Colonial
     period; Decolonization; Education;
     French Equational Africa; French West
     Africa; Nationalist movements;
     Resistance movements; Social change;
     White settlers
Colonial powers, 233; civilizing mission of,
     237–38; economic exploitation by,
     242–43, 267–68; patterns of rule of,
     233–34; spheres of influence of, 5 (map);
     policies of, 240–41, 561–62. *See also*
     Colonial administration; Colonialism;
     Colonial Period; Belgium; Germany;
     Great Britain; France; Portugal
Common law: introduction into Africa,
     481–83; repugnancy clause in, 482–85;
     residual clause in, 482
Communications: and ethnicity, 378–79;
     growth of modern systems of, 368–74;
     research in, 380; theory of, 374–76;
     Western innovations in, 359. *See also*
     Circulation systems; Mass media
Comoro Islands: population of, 26;
     regional grouping of, 33
Competitiveness. *See* Interpersonal
     relations
Competitive-party systems, 457, 465–66.
     See also Political parties
Conakry (Guinea), 365
Conference of Independent African States,
     425
Conceptual systems: assumed consistency of,
     106; concept of belief in, 609; in
     consciencism, 422–23; and cultural
     logics, 105; defined, 99; expression of, in
     art and literature, 112, 198; new-
     African culture in, 420; secularization
     of, 565; studies of, 99, 100, 107, 622;
     synthesis of Western and African world
     views in, 396; systematic view of, 100–101;
     techniques for understanding, 102.
     See also Alienation; Cultural system; Islam;
     Religions; Values
Congo Basin: as circulation system, 371;
     colonial administrations in, 371; physical
     features of, 21; population of, 27; trading
     systems in, 362
Congo (Brazzaville): Chinese aid to, 514;

circulation region of, 371; GNP per capita in, 503; independence political system in, 460; population of, 26, 503, regional grouping of, 32; revolutionary situation of, in 1963–64, 445

Congo (Kinshasa): administrative parties in, 456; Africans in colonial administration of, 459; Belgian trade with, 513; Binza caucus group in, 467; birth and death rates in, 350; circulation system of, 371; colonial exploitation of, 268; colonial rule in, 454; competitive party system in, 457; coppermining in, 267; currency depreciation in, 512; decolonization policies in, 439; development plans in, 504; and East African Economic Community, 372; economic relations of, 511; economic structures in, 499; 1960 elections in, 456; 1965 elections in, 465, 466; game population in, 390; GNP per capita in, 503; ideological influence of China in, 536; independence political system in, 460; military regime in, 470, 507; 1965 military takeover in, 466, 469; political parties in, 438; population of, 26, 27, 503; problems of federalism in, 438–39; rainfall in, 23; regional grouping of, 33; and regional unification movements, 371; revival of theories of divine kingship in, 391; revolutionary situation of, in 1963–64, 445; separatist movements in, 472; Simba rebels in, 536; subsistence sector in, 512; urbanization in, 349; U.S. aid to, 514

Congo River, 371

Consciencism, philosophy of, 422–23

Conseils-generaux, 248

Convention Africaine (CAF, Senegal), 427

Convention People's Party (CPP, Ghana), 457, 462

Copperbelt (Zambia), 40, 337, 368, 405

Coptic denominations, 179

Coups d'état. See Military takeovers

Co-wife relations, 46, 48, 49, 284, 290, 293

Craft industries: adaptation of, to modern production processes, 343–44; in African cities, 338–39; goods produced by, 340; guild system in, 339–40; and immigrant labor, 354; revival of, 342–43; structure of, 338; undermining of, 341–43

Creole languages, 87, 206–7, 208

Criminal law, 485–87. *See also* Law, African

Cross-cultural data, Murdock's, 280

Cullen, Countee, 600

Cultural bias: in colonial attitudes, 237–38; in education, 308; of European

administrators, 254; in historiography, 161, 162–63, 163–64; in music, 129, 134–35, 150 51; and rationalizations of colonialism, 237; in research, 101, 102, 162, 607, 613–14

Cultural logics. *See* Conceptual systems

Cultural system, 131–33, 138–39, 143–46. *See also* Conceptual systems; Social life, traditional; Traditional societies

Culture, concept of, 609

Culture contact: between North and sub-Saharan Africa, 3, 361, 546, 553–54; study of, 382. *See also* Circulation systems; Pre-colonial contact; African survivals

Currency: coinage of, 337; deteriorating, 512; introduction of, 243; relations, 511–13; use of, 498; zones, 511–12

Customary law. *See* Law, African

Dadie, Bernard, 588

Dahomey: birth and death rates in, 350; circulation network of, 372, 373; 1967 coup in, 470, 515; GNP per capita in, 503; and Mali Federation, 428; independence political system in, 460; New World cultural survivals from, 201, 204; oral tradition in kingdom of, 160; palm oil in, 499; population of, 26, 503; railways in, 373; regional associations of, 431; regional grouping of, 32; returned slaves in, 306; slave-trading in kingdom of, 174; social stratification in kingdom of, 270

Daima (Nigeria), excavations at, 123

Dakar (Senegal), 33, 347, 350, 364, 365, 368, 373, 428

Damas, Leon, 588

Dan (people), 117, 118, 120

Dance, 140, 144, 198

Danquah, J. B., 412

Dar es Salaam (Tanzania), 364, 365, 370, 372

Data collection. *See* Research methodologies

Dating: use of King lists in, 169; problem of, 168–69; radiocarbon, 122–23; secession systems in, 169; solar eclipses in, 169

Death rates, 350 (table), 351

de Gaulle, Charles, 410, 411, 538

Decolonization: mechanisms for, 455–59; policies for, 458, 574; processes of, 442; shortening of timetable in, 458

Degeneration theory, 109

Demographic patterns, 345, 349–52, 548. *See also* Population

Descent systems, 42–45, 45 (map), 265, 266, 280. *See also* Bilateral, Matrilineal,

Patrilineal, Unilineal descent systems;
Kinship groups
Destour Socialist Party (Tunisia), 412, 464
Development, economic. *See* Economy-
building
Development planning. *See*
Economy-building
Dia, Mamadou, 423, 426, 429–30, 536
Diaspora. *See* African Diaspora
Dieu d'eau, 100
Diglossia, 82. *See also* Multilingualism
Dinka (people), 30
Diop, Cheikh Anta, 418–19
Diop, David, 588
Diop, Majhemout, 413
Diplomacy. *See* International relations
Discographies, 128
Divine-kingship, 187, 391, 391 n
Divorce, 47 n, 47–48
Djibouti (Somalia), 365
Documents: analysis of, 617; Arabic, 174,
181, 617. *See also* History, African, study of
Dogon (people): field work among, 111;
growth of one-party state among, 448–49;
masks and ancestor figures of, 114, 116,
118; music of, 128; world view of, 100
Douala (Cameroon), 368
Drakensberg Escarpment, 23
Drum: personification of, 134;
as mnemonic device, 145
Drumming: imitation of speech sounds in,
142, 146–47; instruction in, 149;
melismatic techniques in, 149; pitch in,
138
Du Bois, W. E. B., 421, 424, 599–600, 601,
602, 603. *See also* Pan-Africanism
Durban (South Africa), 350, 365, 370, 569
Dutch East India Company, 210–12, 220
Dutch settlement, 210–14, 215, 569

East Africa: Arab character of, 560; Arab
community in, 558–60; Arab and Persian
control over, 253–54; early Arab
settlements in, 552; area of, 32;
British administration of, 372; circulation
system of, 372; coastal ports of, 364; early
urban centers in, 336–37; expansion of
Islam, 336; Indian influence on, 561;
Indian settlement in, 179–80; Islamic
community in, 559–60; Islamization of,
558; and long-distance trade, 361. *See also*
British East Africa
East African Economic Community, 34,
372, 539
Economic anthropology, 62–63

Economics: analytical concepts for study of,
73–76; comparative studies of, 78–79;
conceptual vocabulary of, 74
Economies, African: absence of machine
technology in, 66–68, 69–70; absence of
market organization in, 68–69; and cash
crop revolution, 242; characteristics of,
63–66, 73; in colonial period, 77,
267–69; compared to industrialized
economies, 64–66; data on, 62 n; dual
nature of, 70, 498–99; ecological
dependence of, 66, 69; effect of colonial
transport network on, 344, 367;
interpenetration of economy and society in,
69, 71; isolation of, 70; low productivity
of, 69; prestige sectors in, 75; problems
of, 269–70, 502–4; production processes
in, 71–73; reciprocal transactions in,
74–75; redistribution processes in, 75;
role relations in, 71; scale and diversity in,
63–66; social context of, 69–73; social
sanctions in, 70; underdevelopment of, 38,
266–67, 268–69, 313, 502; in West
Africa, 197. *See also* Agriculture;
Circulation systems; Craft industries;
Economies, modern sector; Economy-
building; Modernization; Plantation
economies
Economies, modern sector: development
of cash crops in, 242–43; European
commercial firms in, 243, 244, 353;
growth trends in, 502–4; institutional
infrastructure of, 515–18; legacy of
colonial administration to, 258–59; market
expansion in, 367; patterns of trade, aid,
and investment in, 507–14; resource
allocation in, 505–7. *See also* Economy
building; Modernization
Economy-building, 498–500; and
development as an ideology of change,
255; development plans in, 499, 504–7,
516; diversification of production in, 500;
establishment of development nexus in,
519–21; and growth rates, 502–4, 506;
"growth without development" in, 268;
impact of colonialism on, 242–45;
incentives in, 516; institution-building in,
515–17; and investment in infrastructure,
505–6; legal problems of, 491; and levels
of economic and social development, 436;
literature of, 434; manpower in, 517–18;
mobilization of domestic resources in, 506;
neo-colonialism in, 255; and population
growth, 260; priorities in, 505–6;
private and public-sector development in,

500–502; problems of, 514–15; resource allocation in, 505–6; role of government in, 500; traditional and modern elements in, 38; in urban centers, 379–80; effect of urban problems on, 358; at village level, 77, 79. *See also* Capital investment; Cash economies; Circulation systems; Economies, modern sector; Foreign aid; Foreign investment; Modernization

Education: achievement motivation in, 245, 330; Africanization of, 310–11, 325; as agent of socialization, 326; American, influence of, 537; and changing values, 329–30; colonial impact on, 245–46; demand for, 309, 320–21; and development, 264, 307, 311, 313; in Dutch settlements, 212; and economic growth; 328–29; elitism of, 264; and elite formation, 312, 326, 439; and elite unemployment, 263; European curriculums in, 264, 314; facilities for, 328–30; and independence movements, 254, 537; languages used in, 98 n, 264, 307, 308, 309; and levels of aspiration, 309, 319, 321, 328–30; and location of schools, 324–25; and mission schools, 256, 308–10, 314, 325; numbers involved in, 245, 263, 311; and occupational aspirations, 326–27; and occupational structure, 310, 312, 313–14; Phelps-Stokes report on, 310–11; post-independence development of, 315; in pre-colonial period, 263; and religious conversion, 262; postwar reorganizations of, 307; and psychological tests, 317; pyramidal system in, 264; and recruitment of teachers, 324, 328; and technical training programs, 527–29; resistance to, 312; and social class, 271, 273–74; in underdeveloped economies, 316; urban, contrasted to rural, 321; and urbanization, 246; as vocational training, 306–7, 309, 310, 314, 353–54, 357. *See also* Education policies; Elites, modern; Mission schools; School enrollments

Education policies: Belgian, 311–12; British, 245, 308–11, 314, 322; French, 245, 305–308, 314, 322; in post-independence period, 315–16, 328

Efik script, 89

Egypt. *See* United Arab Republic

Egypt (kingdom), 333, 560

Ekwensi, Cyprian, 586

Electoral processes, 456, 457, 462–64, 465–67

Elijah Muhammad, 603

Elites, modern, 273–74; access to senior service, 458–59; administrative, 327, 439, 459, as beneficiaries of independence, 274; and economic development, 304; and education, 310, 312, 326–29; formation of, 329–30, 439, 455; increase in number of, 328; as a meritocracy, 264; and nationalist counter-elite, 459; psychological differences of, 297–98; and educational selectivity, 316–320, 321–23; second- and third-generation, 442; socialist ideologies of, 274; as technocratic intellectuals, 274; unemployment of, 263, 307, 313, 328; in urban areas, 258, 330; values of, 330

Elites, traditional, 193, 259, 271

Elmina (Ghana), 363

Empires, African. *See* African states and kingdoms

English (language): in African literature, 92, 93; as lingua franca, 248; use of, in schools, 264, 309

Enugu (Nigeria), 368

Equatorial Guinea (Fernando Po and Rio Muni): regional grouping of, 32; population of, 26.

Ethiopia: American lawyers in, 480; at Bandung Conference, 426; circulation system of, 374; codification of law in, 488, 491; coffee in, 499; currency in, 513; development plans in, 504; exports of, 509 n, 520; GNP per capita in, 503; independence political system in, 460; integration of legal system in, 490; Islam in, 549 n; lack of census in, 548; military in, 507; natural barriers in, 515; population of, 26, 27, 503; racial types in, 30; regional grouping of, 32, 372; religious nationalism in, 407; separatist movements in, 472; social stratification in early empire of, 270; traced from Axum, 179; traditional elite rule in, 259

Ethiopian Church (South Africa), 228

Ethiopian Highlands, 21, 27

Ethiopic script, 89

Ethnicity: changing boundaries of, 12, 378, 379, 436, 446; and communications, 378; defined, 11–14, 59–60, 403–4; in educational selectivity, 318; and ethnic nationalism, 407, 472; as a legal reality, 491; and occupational aspirations, 326; situational, 436; and social differentiation, 320; and tribalism, 12; in voluntary associations, 346

Ethnic pluralism: and colonial boundaries, 15, 258, 366, 368; in colonial period, 12–14; influence of Islam on, 566–67; in nation-building, 13, 435–36, 514; in Nigerian civil war, 248; and centralized state systems, 58
Ethnocentrism. *See* Cultural bias
Ethnomusicology: cultural bias in, 133; methods of, 133; regional studies in, 132
Ethnopharmacology, 103–104
Ethnoscience: defined, 103; in study of cultural technologies, 103; and uses of linguistic anthropology, 103–5. *See also* Conceptual systems
European Common Market, 500, 520
European Development Fund, 508
European Economic Community, 508 511, 520, 521
Europeans in Africa, 272, 584. *See also* Missionaries; Pre-colonial contact; White settler populations
Ewe (kingdom), 335
Ewe (people), 378, 404
Ewondo *populaire* (language), 80
Export trade. *See* International trade

Faidherbe, General, 305
Family life: co-wife relationships in, 46, 48, 49, 284, 290, 293; and divorce, 47–48; domestic cycles in, 49; domestic slavery in, 51; factors determining size of domestic group, 40, 49–52; fostering in, 51; male role in, 49; and marriage, 47; role obligations in, 50; sex segregation in, 285–86; sibling relationships in, 48; social distance patterns in, 284–286; social stratification in, 287–88; traditional patterns in, 47–49, 197. *See also* Household organization; Social life, traditional; Traditional societies
Fang (people) 395
Fatalism: as a world view, 106; relation of, to change, 107; Western misinterpretations of, 106
Fernando Po. *See* Equatorial Guinea
Fez (Morocco), 339, 557
Fingo (people), 219, 222
Food and feeding, significance of, 288–89
Fon (people), 115
Foreign aid, 17, 504, 510–12
Foreign investment, 269, 355, 499, 504, 507–10, 511–12
Forest belt. *See* Rainforest

Fostering, 51
France: aid to Africa, 510, 513; arms sales to South Africa, 573; colonial policies of, 233, 322, 454–55; colonial policies of, compared to British, 240–41; decolonization policies of, 455, 456; colonial education policy of, 305–8, 314, 322 (*See also* Assimilation policies); French Fifth Republic, 408–10; and "Overseas France," 235; in slave trade, 201. *See also* French Equatorial Africa; French West Africa
Frazier, E. Franklin, 421
Free African Society, 600
FRELIMO,574–75
French Communist Party (CPF), 411, 427
French Community, 408, 410–11, 428. *See also* Assimilation policies
French Equatorial Africa: administrative structure of, 33; colonial policy in, 233; education policies in, 306; regional grouping of, 32
French (language): as lingua Franca, 248; in literature, 93; in schools, 264, 307
French National Assembly, African deputies to, 408, 427
French Socialist Party (SFIO), 427–28
French Somaliland. *See* Afars and Issas, Territory of
French Sudan. *See* Mali
French Union, 408, 410
French West Africa, 426–31; administrative structure of, 33, 247; *conseils-généraux* in, 248; education policy in, 245, 306; elections in, 427, 456; as a federation, 426, 433; historiography in, 162; literature of, 92; political participation in, 247; 1958 referendum in, 410, 428, 538; regionalist thought in, 432; role of chief in, 240–41; transterritorial political movements in, 427–28. *See also* Assimilation policies; Education policies
Front of National Liberation (FLN, Algeria), 411
Fulani Jihad, 174, 255
Fulani (language), 80, 83–84, 90
Fulani (people), 27
Futa Toro, 186, 188

Gã (language), 82
Gabon: aid to, 467; French trade with, 513; GNP per capita in, 503; independence political system of, 460; oil in, 499; as oligarchic party-state, 18; political

institutions of, 257; population of, 26, 503; rainfall in, 23; regional grouping of, 32

Gamba (king), 385

Gambia: British in, 236; circulation network of, 373; education in, 308; GNP per capita in, 503; independence political system of, 460; Islam in, 549–50, 550 n; Islamic law in, 480; military in, 507; natural barriers in, 515; peanuts in, 499; population of, 26, 503; primary product exports of, 520; regional grouping of, 32; use of repugnancy clause in, 483

Gandhism, 533–34

Garvey, Marcus, 421, 599–600, 602

Gao (Mali), 253, 335, 363

Geꞌez (language), 89, 91

Genealogy, 42–43

Germany, colonial policies of, 233–34

Ghana: Africans in colonial administration, 458; "brain drain" from, 263–64; circulation network of, 373; cocoa in, 244, 499; Criminal Code of, 486; currency depreciation in, 513; development planning in, 504; W. E. B. DuBois in, 421; economy of, 267, 268; exports of, 509 n; GNP per capita in, 503; independence of, 154; independence political system in, 460; interurban linkages in, 368; Islamic law in, 480; legal system in, 495; linguistic diversity in, 82; literacy in, 263; migrant labor in, 40; military and paramilitary expenditure in, 507; 1966 military takeover in, 501, 513; modernity of, 450; Muslim groups in, 564; nationalist leaders in, 425; nationalist movements in, 438; population of, 26, 503; positive action in, 533; railways in, 373; regional grouping of, 32; and resolution on Cuban crisis, 541; ruling group in, 439; schools in, 308, 309, 310, 318, 319, 322; single-party system in, 501; social change in, 259; Soviet aid in, 514; subsistence sector in, 512; in Union of African States, 430; urban population in, 349. *See also* Ghana Empire; Gold Coast; Nkrumah, Kwame

Ghana Empire, 3, 184–85, 238, 252; administrative structures in, 189; Berber conquest of, 556; centralized authority in, 184; Islam in, 188; king as ritual ruler in, 187; origins of, 184; recruitment of elite in, 193; taxation in 191; titles of ruler of, 187; trade network of, 183. *See also* African states and kingdoms

Ghana-Guinea-Mali Union, 430–31

Ghana, University of, 63

Gift-giving, 74, 74 n, 288, 299–301

Glen Grey Act, 217

Glottochronology, 95

Gola (people), 134

Gold Coast: British in, 236; cash crops in, 240; cocoa production in, 242, 244, 247; English common law in, 481; gold in, 244; pre-colonial trade in, 336, 363

Gonçalo, Don, 385–86

Gondwanaland, 20

Gray, Sir John, 162

Great Britain: abolition of slave trade, 216, 218; aid to Africa, 513; colonial administration, policies of, 33, 233, 247, 454, 458; colonial policies of, compared to French, 240–41; colonies as liabilities to, 268; decolonization policies, 455; education policy in the colonies, 245, 308–11, 314, 322–23; in New World slave trade, 201; and occupation of the Cape, 216; position on Rhodesian UDI, 538, 574–76. *See also* British East Africa; British West Africa

Great Dyke region, 337

Great Lakes region, 23, 27, 32, 362

Great Trek, 218, 569

Greenberg, Joseph H., 85, 97, 104; on Bantu migration, 171; language classifications of, 82–86

Gross national product per capita, 503 (table), 520

Guerrilla organizations. *See* Liberation movements; Resistance movements

Guild system, 339–40, 341, 343, 345, 353

Guinea: birth and death rates in, 350; bauxite in, 499; Chinese aid to, 514; circulation network in, 373; currency deterioration in, 511; development plan in, 504; economy of, 500, 501, 511; French colonial policy in, 233; GNP per capita in, 503; independence political system in, 460; Islam in, 549–50, 550 n; nationalist movements in, 438; population of, 26, 503; rainfall in, 23; regional grouping of, 32; 1958 referendum in, 410; single-party system in, 457; social change in, 259; Soviet aid to, 514; subsistence sector in, 512; traditional religious authority in, 563; and Union of African States, 430; U.S. aid to, 513

Guinea Coast, 25

Guianas, the: 204, 206, 208

Gun War, 222

Gusii (people), 298

Gurage (people), 144

Haiti, 201, 204, 206, 208
Hamitic language group, 83
Handy Man (*Homo Habilis*), 170
Hansberry, Leo, 154 n
Harlem Literary Renaissance, 599
Hausa (language), 80, 81, 89, 90, 257
Hausa (people), 27, 48, 147, 362, 613
Hausa-Fulani emirates, 192, 270, 454
Herodotus, 157, 158, 161
Herskovits, Melville J., 91, 110
Hertzog Bills, 225, 229
Hierarchy, social. *See* Social stratification
High Commission Territories, 33
Historians: African Christian writers, 162–63;
    armchair scholars, 161, 392 n; colonial
    administrators, 161–62; contemporary
    African scholars, 165; earliest, 157; Gray,
    162; *Griots,* 146, 160, 161, 163, 183;
    Herodotus, 157, 158, 161; ibn-Khaldun,
    158–59; Johnson, 163, 239; Kagwa, 145,
    162; Leo Africanus, 191, 335; Strabo, 157,
    158; Vansina, 94–95, 166–67, 615
History, African, study of: acorn approach
    in, 164 n; administrator-scholars in,
    161–62; Arabic manuscripts in, 166, 174,
    181, 617; archival sources in, 181;
    armchair scholarship in, 161, 392 n;
    cultural bias in, 161; current themes in,
    170–76; documentary analysis in, 166, 617;
    and early travelers' accounts, 157; and the
    empire builders, 161–62; European-
    oriented studies in, 161; interdisciplinary
    approach in, 156; and local histories,
    161–62; Marxist interpretations in, 177–78;
    missionary bias in, 162–63; nationalist
    bias in, 163–64; objections to, 155; oral
    tradition in, 166; place of ibn-Khaldun in,
    158–59; in post-independence period,
    155, 156, 164–65; in pre-twentieth-century
    period, 157–61; problem of chronology
    in, 168–69; radiocarbon dating in, 122–23;
    research techniques in, 164, 165–69; 253;
    role of Africans in, 162–63, 165; Vansina's
    influence on, 167; Western interpretations
    in, 177–78; Western Sudan in, 181–82.
    See also Historians; History, African,
    themes in; Oral tradition; Research
    methodologies
History, African, themes in: Bantu
    migration, 171; bureaucratic structure,
    173; Islamization, 174–75; literacy, role
    of, 173; military organization and
    technology, 173; resistance movements,
    175–76; secondary empires, 173; slave
    trade, 173–74; state-building, 172–73;
    social and cultural history, 175; trade, 172.

    See also History, African, study of
Holland, trade routes of, 201, 210
Horn of Africa, area of, 32
Hostility, manifestations of, 293, 296, 298.
    See also Interpersonal relations
Hottentot (people): in Cape area, 210; as
    labor supply, 216; racial type of, 30;
    relations with Dutch settlers, 211–12,
    214–15; rights to land, 214; subjugation of,
    217
Hottentot (language), 83–84
Houphouet-Boigny, Felix, 308, 408, 427
Household organization, 49–52, 69–70, 352.
    See also Family life; Social life, traditional
Hughes, Langston, 600
Hunting and gathering bands, 54
Hydroelectric power, 523

Ibadan (Nigeria), 336, 339, 346, 350, 364,
    368, 523
Ibadan, University of, 396, 622
Ibibio (people), 118
Ibn-Battuta, 111, 186
Ibn-Khaldun, 158–59, 161
Ibo (people), 27, 118, 239, 248
Ife (city-state), 113, 123
Ifni, 26, 32
Igbo Ukwu (Nigeria), 123
Ijebu (city-state), 113
Ile-Ife (Nigeria), 335
Immigration, 246, 312, 349
Income, per capita, 502, 519
Independants d'Outre Mer (IOM), 427–28
Independence: British conditions for, 574;
    patterns of, 6 (map); political formulas at,
    459–61; shortening of time table for, 458.
    See also Decolonization; Independence
    movements; Independence period
Independence movements: centered in
    towns, 246; and earlier rebellions, 175–76;
    impact of education on, 245–46; influence
    of Christianity on, 246; and liberalization
    of colonial policies, 248; militancy in, 534;
    and messianic movements, 262;
    role of education in, 254; stance of
    Islamic groups in, 563–64. *See also*
    Nationalist movements
Independence period: characteristics of
    new nations in, 436; economic growth in,
    502, 508–10; non-alignment policy in, 535;
    phases of, 452. *See also* Independence;
    Independence movements; Nationalist
    movements
Indians: as agents of Islamization, 560–61;
    in East Africa, 559, 561
Indigénat, 242, 247, 293

Indirect rule, 240, 563

Industrialization: and capital ownership in colonial era, 273; and cultural change, 256–57; similarities between countries in, 256–57; under colonial rule, 244. *See also* Industry, modern

Industry, modern: adaptation of traditional crafts in, 343–44; concentration of, 356; and development, 505; employment in, 356–57; requirements of, 357; small-scale, 344; and urban development, 357

Industry, traditional. *See* Craft industries

Initiation rites, 57

Institute of African Studies (Ghana), 174

Integration, racial, in U.S., 595, 597

Interdisciplinary research, 97, 104, 156, 528–29, 610–13

Interlacustrine region. *See* Great Lakes region

International African Institute (IAI), 88, 94, 150

International proletarianism. *See* Marxist-Socialist ideology

International relations: concept of non-alignment in, 535, 540; public law in, 474; themes of, 543–44

International trade: African export earnings, 499–500, 520; export market, 498–99, 520; export trade, 242, 244, 367, 507–10

Interpersonal relations: avoidance customs in, 50; competition for scarce resources in, 290, 293, 296, 301, 302; emphasis on material transactions in, 288–290, 297, 299, 300, 301, 302; expressions of deference in, 287–88; lack of intimacy in, 286; significance of food and feeding in, 288–89; social stratification in, 286–288. *See also* Behavior, African; Hostility

Inter-Tropical Convergence Zone (ITCZ), 23

Ironworking, 170, 171, 179, 183, 336

Irredentist movements. *See* Back to Africa movements

Islam: African manifestations of, 552; Arabic and Hausa literature on, 174; colonial policy toward, 561–62; and control of traditional political systems, 561; and educational institutions, 557; educational system in, 557; effect of colonialism on, 561; effect of, on political systems, 548–51; emergence of, 551; entrenchment of, in North Africa, 552–53; extent of, 548–50, 549 (map); in Ghana Empire, 190; ibn-Khaldun as historian of, 159; in fourteenth century, 159; indigenousness of, to the African continent, 552; influence

of, on art, 113, 124; influence of, on literature, 91–92; and intellectual leadership, 557, in Mahdi movement, 562, and Muslim communities, 564–65; in national integration, 447; and nationalist movements, 563; number of adherents to, 261, 547–48; and penetration of sub-Saharan Africa, 252, 554–61; and political authority, 187–88, 262; political theory in, 186–88; in the post-independence era, 565–67; process of conversion in, 262; reform movements in, 175, 255; religious orders in, 234, 468, 561–62, 563, 565; and secularization of social systems, 565–66; social and political system of, 253, 550; spread of, 31, 174–75, 261–62, 336, 551–54, 555 (map), 562–63; spread of, through military conquest, 554–56; spread of, associated with trade patterns, 172; and states with Muslim majorities, 549; in Sudanic state formation, 181; toleration of traditional practices in, 262; in towns, 246; in the Western Sudan, 188. *See also* Religious orders, Islamic

Islamic law, 487–88; adaptability of, 487; codification of, 192–93; and establishment of legal systems, 556; Maliki legal school in, 487; modification of, 488

Islamization, 31, 174–75, 261–62, 336, 551–54, 555 (map), 562–63

Ismailis, 560, 565

Iteso (people), 147

Ituri Forest, 30

Ivory Coast: administrative parties in, 456; Africans in colonial administration of, 458; aid to, 467; "brain drain" from, 263–64; and Brazzaville bloc, 430; cash crops in, 240; circulation network in, 373; cocoa production in, 242; coffee production in, 242; colonial legacy in, 258; economy of, 267, 507; education in, 308, 317, 318, 319, 321, 322, 324; ethnic coalitions in, 448; ethnic pluralism in, 447; French colonial policy in, 233; GNP per capita in, 503; independence political system in, 460; Islam in, 549 n; legislation against polygyny in, 487; modernity of, 450; national integration in, 446–50; pacification of, 236 n; party system in, 18, 448, 449, 457; population of, 26, 503; private sector economy in, 501; pro-French policy of, 448; regional associations of, 431; regional grouping of, 32; ruling class in, 274; and trade with France, 513; white settlers in, 579

Iwarefa (people), 484

Jamaa movement, 398
Johannesburg (South Africa), 347, 349, 350
Johnson, Reverend Samuel, 163, 239
Judicial systems. *See* Legal systems

Kaduna (Nigeria), 368
Kaffir languages, 83
Kaffir Wars, 219, 220
Kagwa, Apolo, 145, 162
Kainji Dam, 243 n
Kalabari (people), 114, 117, 118
Kalahari Basin, 21
Kalahari desert, 24, 30, 50
Kampala (Uganda), 368, 372, 525
Kanem-Bornu (kingdom), 190, 191, 192,
    193, 252
Kano (Nigeria), 192, 335, 346, 362, 363,
    364, 368
Kano Chronicle, 617
Kanuri (people), 40, 42, 44, 45 n, 48
Kanuri (language), 89
Kasavubu, Joseph, 391
Katanga, Province of, 172, 371, 337
Katsina (Nigeria), 335, 345, 363
Keïta, Modibo, 430, 450 n
Kennedy, John F., 540, 541
Kenya: Africans in colonial administration
    of, 458; colonial legacy to, 258; distribution
    of power in, 272; economy of, 267, 500,
    501, 507, 511; exploitation of, 268;
    exports of, 509 n; GNP per capita in,
    503; independence political system in,
    460; interurban linkages in, 368;
    Islamic law in, 480; Mau Mau movement
    in, 536, 457; party system in, 18, 438, 467;
    population of, 26, 379, 503; regional
    grouping of, 32, 372; resistance to colonial
    system in, 457; ruling class in, 274;
    separatist movements in, 472; urban
    population in, 349; water supply in, 523;
    white settler population in, 272, 457, 579
Kenya Highlands, 21, 27, 372
Kenya, Mount, 21
Kenya Peoples' Union, 18
Kenyatta, Jomo, 425, 596
Khartoum (Sudan), 350, 524, 528
Khoisan language group, 84
Khoisan peoples, 30
Kikuyu (people), 175, 378
Kilimanjaro, Mount, 21, 172
Kilwa (Tanzania), 180, 337, 364
Kimberley (South Africa), 569
Kingdoms, African. *See* African states and
    kingdoms
King-lists, use of, 169
Kingship, 58–59; accumulation of wealth in,

191–92; disappearance of, 272;
    legitimation of authority in, 262; and
    protection against rivals, 193–94; reciprocal
    responsibilities in, 75; ritual aspects of,
    187–88; slave trade in, 199; techniques of
    increasing power in, 193; tribute in, 75.
    See also Chieftaincy; Divine kingship
Kinshasa (Congo), 350, 351
Kinship groups, 42–49; categories of
    relations in, 42–45; characteristics of,
    264–65; classification of, 43; corporate
    responsibility in, 40, 484; as economic
    units, 69, 300; family organization in, 47;
    in industrializing societies, 265; and land
    tenure, 71–72; marriage forms in, 46–47;
    material transactions in, 289; number of
    dependents in, 40; obligations of members
    in, 299–301; and occupational specializa-
    tion, 40, 338, 352; political alliances of, 56;
    as political units, 51; polygynous societies
    in, 280; preservation of, 300; prevalence of
    patrilineal descent in, 44–45; unlineal
    descent as determinant of, 265; in
    urbanizing society, 300, 352; in West
    Africa, 197; Western types of, 265. *See
    also* Descent systems
Kongo (kingdom), 125, 134, 175, 180, 252,
    387–88
Kotoko (people), 147
Kumasi (Ghana), 364, 368, 528
Kung Bushmen, 52
Kush (kingdom), 179, 252
Kwilu uprising, 445

Labor: availability of, 340, 357; expatriate,
    269; migratory, 40, 405, 498; and trained
    personnel, 356–57; in small-scale industry,
    344; in South Africa, 267, 370; as
    substitute for machinery, 357; unskilled,
    269
Lagos (Nigeria), 253, 347, 350, 352, 363,
    364, 365, 368, 373
La Guma, Alex, 584
Land-tenure systems, 71–72, 272–73, 353,
    479, 481, 484, 489–90
Language: culture-bound distortion in
    study of, 101–102; in music, 96, 135–36,
    147; and physiology, 105; and rhythm,
    141–42; Senghor's philosophy of, 141,
    149; social context of, 143–44; in
    social-science, 608–10; in study of
    conceptual systems, 105; and thought,
    104–5. *See also* Linguistics
Languages, African: characteristics of, 87–88;
    classifications of, 82–87, 83 n, 84 (map),

86 (map), 171; in education, 98 n, 310; as lingua francas, 81, 143, 198, 248; in literature, 89; multiplicity of, 8, 65–66, 80–82; New World survivals of, 206–7, 208; surveys of, 94; tonal, 96; in West Africa, 198; place of vernaculars, 97; written tradition in, 88–89. *See also* Language; Linguistics; Multilingualism; Sociolinguistics

Latin America: African survivals in, 204–6; impact of Europe on, 257; religious syncretisms in, 205; slavery in, 202; slave settlements in, 201

Law, 474–75. *See also* Common law; Criminal law; Law, African; Law, Western; Islamic law; Legal systems

Law, African: compared to Western law, 476–80, 485–87; creation of new systems in, 480–81; criminal law in, 485–87; customary, 473, 476–80, 492; and growth of national legal systems, 474; growth of statute law in, 489–90; and impact of legal change, 496–97; introduction of codified law into, 480; introduction of English common law into, 481–83; introduction of foreign legal systems into, 473, 475, 480, 494; pluralism of, 474–75; repugnancy and residual clauses in, 482–85; and restatement of African law project, 492–93; and statute law, 489–90; unification of, 494–95; Western Influence in, 480–85. *See also* Islamic law; Legal systems

Law, Islamic. *See* Islamic law

Lawrence, T. E., 159 n

Laws of the Indies, 212

Law, Western: compared to African law, 476–80, 485–87; criminal law in, 485–87; court system in, 479. *See also* Legal systems

Laye, Camara, 583

Lebanese, in West Africa, 244

Lega (people), 121

Legal systems: colonial, 477; conflict of law in, 496; courts in, 494–95; English, 480; *indigénat* as, 241–42, 247, 293; integration of, 490–97; and jurisdiction of courts, 494; Islamic, 556; Western, 480–81. *See also* Common law, Islamic law, Ethiopia, law in; Law; Law, African; Law, Western

Legislative councils, 247

Lenshina, Alice, 262

Leo Africanus, 191, 335

Leopoldville. *See* Kinshasa

Lesotho: communications and transport network in, 370; competitive party system

in, 457; economic dependence of, 572; GNP per capita in, 503; independence of, 578; as labor reservoir, 267; political system in, 460; population of, 26, 503; population concentration in, 27; racial policies in, 580; South African relations with, 272, 513, 576

Levirate, 50

Liberation movements, 534, 574–75; FRELIMO, 574–75. *See also* Resistance movements

Liberia: and American Colonization Society, 453 n; Americo-Liberian regime in, 259, 272; circulation network of, 373; in dollar area, 513; GNP per capita in, 503; independence political system in, 460; iron ore in, 508; population of, 26, 503; Poro Society in, 113; rainfall in, 23; regional grouping of, 32

Libya: GNP per capita in, 503; independence political system in, 460; Islam in, 549–50, 550 n; petroleum in, 499, 508; population of, 26, 503; regional grouping of, 32; Sanusi order in, 562

Lineage systems. *See* Kinship groups; Descent systems

Lingua francas, 81, 143, 198, 248

Linguistic anthropology, 103

Linguistics: American influence on, 94; early work in, 93; in ethnoscience, 103; heuristic value of, 105; in historical studies, 95, 96; interdisciplinary research in, 94; in investigation of place names, 96; in oral history, 94; Sapir-Whorf hypothesis in, 105; research possibilities in, 96; in the study of Africa, 93–98; in the study of conceptual systems, 102–103; World War II studies in, 94. *See also* Language; Sociolinguistics

Literacy, 173, 263

Literature, contemporary: and Afro-American writers, 599–600; allegorical novel in, 91; autobiographical novel in, 582–83; theme of alienation in, 584–86; theme of confrontation of black and white in, 583–84; theme of man's nature in, 589–91; theme of negritude in, 588–89; theme of political kingdom in, 586–88

Literature, traditional, 89–93; Arabic influence on, 91; and colonial educational policies, 92; European influence on, 92–93; as linguistic evidence, 91; and music, 141, 142–43; and musical instrument, 146–47; New World survivals of, 205; oral tradition

as, 92, 96; praise-poems as, 90, 142, 143, 147; prose-narratives as, 90–91; proverb and the riddle as, 91, 142–43; Senghor's philosophy of, 141, 149; song-texts as, 90; Swahili tradition in, 91; unwritten, 89; vernacular and European languages in, 93
Lobito (Angola), 365, 370, 371, 372
Lourenço Marques (Mozambique), 365, 370, 576
Lozi (kingdom), 172
Lozi (people), 478
Luanda (Angola), 363
Luba (people). *See* Baluba
Luganda (language), 65, 136, 145, 147–48
Lugard, Lord, 161
Luhya (people). *See* Baluhya
Lumpa sect, 262
Lumumba, Patrice, 596
Lunda (state), 252
Luo (people), 142
Lusaka (Zambia), 368

Macroanalysis, 451
Madagascar. *See* Malagasy Republic
Maghrib, 32, 158
Mahdi movement, 562
Mai Idris Alooma, 193
Maji Maji rebellion, 176, 405
Makerere University College, 396, 622
Malagasy Republic: GNP per capita in, 503; independence political system in, 460; people of, 30; population of, 26, 30, 503; rainfall in, 23; regional grouping of, 33
Malawi: colonial legacy in, 258; economic dependence of, 572; exports of, 509 n; GNP per capita in, 503; independence political system in, 460; as labor reservoir, 267; natural barriers in, 515; population of 26, 503; population concentration in, 27; primary-product exports, 520; protest movements in, 405; regional grouping of, 33; relations with Mozambique, 576; relations with South Africa, 576, 580
Malawi, Lake, 21
Malcolm X, 421, 603
Mali: birth and death rates in, 350; circulation network of, 373; Chinese aid to, 514; currency deterioration in, 511; development plans in, 504; economy of, 500, 501, 511; ethnic pluralism in, 447; exports of, 509 n; GNP per capita in, 503; growth of one-party system in, 448–49, 457; independence political system in, 460; Islam in, 549–50, 550 n; in Mali Federation, 410; national

integration in, 446–50; natural barriers in, 515; 1968 military coup in, 450 n; population of, 26, 503; regional grouping of, 32; social change in, 259; subsistence sector in, 512; in Union of African States, 430
Mali Empire, 179, 238, 252; administrative structures in, 189; caste system in, 94; conquest of, 179, 185; historiography in, 162; regalia in, 186; state structure of, 185; trade network in, 183
Mali Federation, 410, 427, 428–30
Maliki law, 487
Malinke (language), 81, 82, 89
Malinowski, Branislaw, 95, 382
Mambwe (people), 40
Mande (language), 89, 181
Mande (state). *See* Mali Empire
Mandingo (people), 146
Manpower planning, 517–18
Matanzima, Chief Kaiser, 578, 579
Mao Tse-tung, 533, 540
Marriage, 46–47; bride-price in, 280, 281, 289; bridewealth in, 46, 265, 266; endogamy in, 52; husband's obligations in, 299; importance of fertility in, 290; law of, 481, 492; prevalence of certain types of, 280 n; polygynous, 46, 265, 280, 281, 487; sex segregation in, 285; stability of, 47. *See also* Family life
Marxist-Socialist ideology: and African conditions, 269; and African socialism, 432; and class-struggle Afro-Marxists, 414; followers of, 412; and interpretations of African history, 177–78; in nationalist movements, 411–16, 536; and neo-Stalinism, 413–14; rejection of, 424. *See also* African socialism
Masai (people), 175, 269, 285
Masai (language), 83–84
Masks: context of, 109, 117; functions of, 118–19; painting of, 114; in Poro Society, 118; rank of, 119; and social prestige of owner, 119; spirit occupation of, 114
Mass media, 367, 368, 373, 374–76, 379
Mass parties, 462–65
Mass-elite relationships, 459
Matadi (Congo-Kinshasa), 365, 371
Matrilineal belt, 44
Matrilineal descent systems, 43, 44, 266, 318
Maran, René, 583
Mau Mau revolt, 457–58, 536
Mauritania: biracialism in, 432; circulation network of, 373; GNP per capita in, 503;

independence political system in, 460; iron ore in, 508; Islam in, 549–50, 550 n; political parties in, 428; population of, 26, 503; regional grouping of, 32; religious nationalism in, 407; traditional religious authority in, 563

Mauritius, 26

Mboya, Tom, 534

Mecca, 551, 552, 557

Mediterranean zone, 24

Merowe (state), 171, 172, 179

Messianic movements. *See* Separatist churches

Metallurgy, 170, 253. *See also* Ironworking; Bronze casting

Methodology. *See* Research methodologies

Migration patterns: of Arab-Muslims, 552, 559; Bantu, 29, 30, 171; into cities, 346, 351, 354, 355, 358; and desiccation of the Sahara, 183; in pre-colonial period, 76

Mineral resources, 244

Military establishment: characteristics of, 440; development of, 507; expenditures on, 506; mercenary soldiers in, 539; as theme in African history, 173

Military regimes, 470, 472

Military takeovers, 18–19, 441–44; causes of, 275, 443–44, 469; in Congo-Kinshasa (1965), 466, 469; contagion effect in, 444; effect of, on development, 17, 504, 506–7, 513, 515; in Ghana (1966), 501, 513; labor unions in, 444; in Mali (1968), 450 n; in Nigeria (1966), 272, 466; number of, 469; patterns of, 17; and political change, 441–42, 469–70; in Sierra Leone (1967), 466

Mining, 201, 244, 337, 508

Missiology, 392 n

Missionaries: and African art, 125; as diplomatic agents, 173; early, 199, 384; influence of, on historiography, 162–63; in literature, 584; in northern Nigeria, 245; political motivations of, 200, 385

Missions: dual character of, 394; evaluating history of, 384; links of, to mother country, 392–93; in kingdom of Kongo, 387–88; Portuguese, 383–388; pressures of, on colonial administrations, 454; role of, in shaping modern Africa, 392–94; and social change, 392; in South Africa, 228; and witchcraft, 302. *See also* Missionaries; Mission schools

Mission schools, 309, 314, 325; in British West Africa, 245, 308–10; development of African leadership in, 256, 262; African

languages in, 310; European languages, in, 309; organization of, 308

Mixed marriages, 212–14

Mnemonic devices, 145, 160

Mobility-stability continuum, 52–53

Modernization: concept of, 77, 434; economic development in, 61, 498; interdisciplinary studies of, 612; intergenerational differences in, 301; irreversibility of, 269; receptivity to innovations in, 301; religious element in, 566–67; rural and urban, 358; social and economic integration in, 78; technology in, 533; and territorial fragmentation, 366, 368; of traditional economies, 77. *See also* Economy-building; Industry, modern; Social change; Technology; Westernization

Modisane, Bloke, 584

Mogadishu (Somalia), 336, 364, 559

Mondlane, Eduardo, 574

Monomotapa (kingdom), 180, 385, 385–87

Monrovia group, 34, 432

Morocco: Africans in colonial administration of, 458; birth and death rates in, 350; caravan routes in, 554; craft organization in, 341, 342 (table); development plans in, 504; exports of, 509 n; French colonial policy in, 233; GNP per capita in, 503; handicraft products of, 343 (table); independence political system in, 460; Islam in, 549–50, 550 n; military in, 507; population of, 26, 503; regional grouping of, 32; religious nationalism in, 407; trade groups in, 352; traditional elite rule in, 259

Mossi (people), 40

Mouridiyya, 234

Mouvement Populaire de la Revolution (MPR, Congo-Kinshasa), 470

Movimento popular de Libertacão de Angola (MPLA), 575

Mozambique: communications and transport network in, 370; FRELIMO activities in, 575; guerrilla war in, 272; and commitment of labor to South Africa, 576; population of, 26, 503; Portuguese army in, 573; Portuguese control of, 568; relations in Southern Africa, 576; regional grouping of, 32, 33; trading stations in, 364; white population of, 573

Mphalele, Ezekiel, 584

Multilingualism, 65–66, 80–82; and language attitudes, 81; and lingua francas 81, 143, 198, 248; and military conquest, 80; in nation-building, 437; in social relations, 82. *See also* Languages, African

Music: analysis of, 130 (figure); bio-basic factor in, 131, 133; and language, 96; and religion, 198; Senghor's philosophy of, 129, 135, 141, 146, 149; study of, 129, 132; use of instruments in, 134. *See also* Music, African; Musical instruments; Rhythm

Music, African: American religious syncretisms of, 205; characteristics of, in West Africa, 198; cultural system in, 131–33, 138–39, 143–46; double phenomenon in, 148–49; foreign influence on, 133; innovation in, 139, 151; language in, 135–36, 141–44, 146–48; notation of, 148; pitch and timbre aspects of, 138; relation of cultural system and language in, 143–44; relation of cultural system and musical instrument in, 143–46; relation of instrument and rhythm in, 148–50; relation of musical instrument and language in, 146–48; relation of rhythm and language in, 135–36, 141–43; rhythm in, 135–43, 150–51, 150 n; secret language in, 144; social context of, 134, 136, 139–40, 143; in teaching language, 144; terminology in, 148; trend toward synthesis in, 130; tunings and scale in, 149–50. *See also* Musical instruments

Musical instruments: cultural bias in definition of, 135; defined, 133–34; imitation of speech by, 147; origins of, 146; as regalia, 145; in social context, 134, 145; tuning and scale of, 150; voice as, 136. *See also* Drums; Music, African

Musical time. *See* Rhythm

Musqat and Oman, 559

Nairobi (Kenya), 350, 364, 368, 372, 379

Namib, 24

Namibia. *See* South-West Africa

Natal, 27, 217, 219, 221–22, 225, 578

National Association for the Advancement of Colored People (NAACP), 596, 602

National identity: and black identity, 594; emergence of, 404–5; found in political party, 438; foundations of, 437–38; Islam in, 566–67. *See also* Black identity; Ethnic pluralism; Nationalism, African

National integration: defined, 445; development and integration of legal systems in, 481, 490–94; Islamic factor in, 566–67; need for communication network in, 373–74; processes of, 445–50; in immediate post-colonial period, 407. *See also* Ethnic pluralism; National identity; Nationalism, African. Nation-building

Nationalism, African: forms of, 423–25; alternative bases of, 407; compared to European, 14; defined, 403–4; as ethnic nationalism, 472; and experience of Mali Federation, 428–30; future of, 433; ideology of negritude in, 416–22; and independence movements, 405–6; India's ideological impact on, 533–35; in Islamic areas, 564–65; levels of loyalties in, 15; and proto-nationalism, 405; race as a basis for, 422; Senghor's philosophy of, 415–16; stages of, 405–8; in South Africa, 230, 577, 578; Soviet theories of, 413–14; effect of urbanization on, 357; values and rhetoric of, 533–38; Western philosophical norms in, 533. *See also* Black nationalism; Boundaries; National integration; Nationalist movements; Supranationalism

Nationalist movements, 455–59; and assimilation policies, 308; assumption of power in, 461; and changing basis of power at independence, 461–62; coalescence of, 458; development of, 405–6; in Islamic areas, 563–64; limitations of Ghandism in, 533–34; Marxist-Socialist terminology in, 412, rise of, 455; strategy of positive action in, 533; in South Africa, 230, 577, 578; transformation of, into political parties, 438; Western ideologies in, 536–37. *See also* Nationalism, African

Nation-building: approach to, 445–50; political institutions in, 440–41; communications systems in, 375–77, 380; concept of, 434–35; defined, 376; economic problems in, 514–15; example of Ivory Coast, 446–50; example of Mali, 446–50; ideologies of, 437; institutionalization of political structures in, 439–41; and political conflict, 441–45; problems of, 435–37; processes of national integration in, 445–50; and rise of nationalist political sector, 455–59; role of education in, 315; role of institutions in, 515; in societal perspective, 435–37; territory in, 437; traditional society in, 436; transactional integration in, 449; weakness of national centers in, 436. *See also*

Boundaries; Economy-building; Ethnic pluralism; National identity; National integration; Nationalism, African; Political systems, modern
Nation of Islam.
See Black Muslims; Black nationalism
Native Reserves (South Africa), 214, 218, 221, 268, 273, 370, 577. *See also* Bantustan program
Natives Land Act (South Africa), 225, 229
Natives Representative Council (South Africa), 226, 230
Ndebele (people), 270–71
Ndembu (people), 390
Negritude: and Afro-Americans, 596; as assertion of black African culture, 421–22; as nationalist ideology, 438; concepts of, 416; defined by Senghor, 418; Muslim criticism of, 422; as reaction against assimilation policies, 256, 589; as theme in literature, 588–89. *See also* Black identity
Nehru, 533, 535
Neo-colonialism, 255, 327. *See also* Foreign Investment
Neolithic revolution, 252
Neutralism. *See* Non-alignment policy
Ngola (kingdom), 180
Ngugi, James, 583
Niger: circulation system of, 373; exports of, 509 n; French administration in, 454; GNP per capita in, 503; historiography in, 162; independence political system in, 460; Islam in, 549–50, 550 n; military in, 507; population of 26, 454, 503; price supports in, 520; regional associations of, 431; regional grouping of, 32
Niger Basin, 21
Niger Bend, 21
Niger-Congo language group, 41
Nigeria: Africans in colonial administration of, 458; "brain drain" from, 263–64; Cash crops in, 240; 1962 census in, 548; circulation network in, 373; city states in, 113; civil war in, 373, 472, 539, 548; cocoa production in, 242; competitive party system in, 438, 457, 465; criminal code in, 486–87; development plans in, 504; economy of, 267, 499, 507, 511; elections in, 465–66; ethnic pluralism of, 15; exports of, 509 n; GNP per capita in, 503; historiography in, 162; household organization in, 51; independence political system in, 460; interurban linkages in, 368; Islam in, 549–50, 550 n, 564; literacy rate in, 263; 1966

military takeover in, 271, 272, 466; minerals in, 244; Muslim majority in, 548; nationalist leaders in, 425; oil in, 499, 508; political institutions in, 257; population of, 25, 26, 503; private-sector economy in, 501; problems of federalism in, 433, 438–39; rainfall in, 23; regional grouping of, 32; S.M.A. craft centers in, 125; and U.K. trade, 513; U.S. aid to, 513
Niger River, 21, 252, 523
Nile Basin, 32, 374
Nile River, 157, 252, 523
Nile Valley, 1, 21, 25, 332–34
Nkrumah, Kwame, 41, 259, 422, 425, 457, 462, 533, 534, 537, 596
Nok culture, 123, 170, 171
Non-alignment policy, 539–43; concept of, 535; effect of Mao Tse-tung on, 540; impact of Kennedy administration on, 540–41
North Africa: Arab identity of, 552–53; extent of, 32, 545; French aid to, 510; ideological unity of, 566; Islamization of, 552–53; links to Black Africa, 546–47; pre-colonial urban centers in, 333–34; skin color in, 545–47
Northern Rhodesia. *See* Zambia
Nubia, 125
Nuer (people), 30, 47, 53, 269, 300
Nupe (people), 124, 339
Nyakyusa (people), 56, 285
Nyasaland. *See* Malawi
Nyerere, Julius, 259, 463–64

Obote, Milton, 535
Occupational: aspirations, 313, 326–27; structure, 314, 328, 351, 353, 357; training, 40, 338, 339–40, 341
Odinga, Oginga, 18
Ogotemmeli, 100
Olduvai Gorge, 170
Oligarchic party-states, 18–19, 465, 467–70, 501–2. *See also* Political systems, modern
Oral tradition: in African kingdoms, 159–61; limitations of, in historiography, 166, 167, 615; as literature, 90; and musical instruments, 145–46; selective memory in, 161, 183–84; set down by African Christian writers, 162–63; song texts in, 143; telescoping of events in, 184; Vansina approach to, 94–95, 156, 166–67; as unwritten history, 96, 156, 325, 359. *See also* History, African, study of
Oran (Algeria), 350

Orange Free State, 225, 569, 571
Orange River, 21
Organization Commune Africaine et
    Malgache, 34
Organization of African Unity (OAU), 15,
    34, 432, 534, 538, 566
Organization for Economic Cooperation
    and Development, 510
Organization of Senegal River States, 373,
    539
Osmania script, 89
Ousmane, Sembène, 586
Overseas Development Fund, 511
Overseas Territories Implementing
    Convention (1957), 508
Oyo (kingdom), 238, 252, 335, 345
Oyono, Ferdinand, 583

Pan-Africanism, 422–25; antiracism and
    anticolonialism in, 539; concept of
    collective vocation in, 423–24; concept of
    cultural synthesis in, 424–25; concept of a
    "United States of Africa" in, 425; Du Bois's
    role in, 599. *See also* Supranationalism
Pan-Africanist Congress (PAC), 231, 571
Parti Africain de l'Indépendance (PAI,
    Senegal), 413
Parti de la Fédération Africaine (PFA,
    Senegal), 428
Parti du Regroupement Africain (PRA,
    Senegal), 428
Parti National du Progrès (Congo), 456
Passive resistance, 533–34
Pass laws, 216, 223, 227, 231, 229, 347, 571,
    585
Paternalism, in colonies, 235, 238, 254–55,
    584, 593
Patrilineal descent systems, 43, 44–45, 56,
    280, 281
Patrilocality, 280, 281
Patronate, 385, 385 n
Patron-client networks, 468–69
Pawning, 50–51
Pax Africana, principle of, 539
Periplus of the Erythraean Sea, 336
Personality, 282–83. *See also* African
    personality; Behavior, African
La Philosophie bantoue (Tempels), 397
Phoenicia, 157
Pidgin English, 80
Plaatje, Solomon J., 225
Plantation economies, 201, 202, 209
Plural societies. *See* Ethnic pluralism
Poetic traditions, 90, 588–89
Political authority, legitimation and

maintenance of, 189–94, 291–92; court
    ceremonials in, 186; through elite
    recruitment, 193; through Islam,
    187–88; law in, 475; in nation states,
    459; oral tradition in, 160; by ritual
    sanctions, 187–88; by theories of divine
    kingship, 187
Political conflict, 441–45. *See also* Military
    takeovers
Political instability, 16–19, 259, 457. *See also*
    Military takeovers; Political conflict
Political parties: administrative parties, 456;
    as basis for party-state, 18; in competitive-
    party systems, 456, 465–66; in
    development of alternative systems, 458;
    in French West Africa, 438; at
    independence, 440–41, 460 (table), 461;
    mass party regimes, 456, 462–65;
    in military regimes, 19, 470; in nationalist
    period, 407, 456; in oligarchic party
    state, 465, 467–69; patron, 456–57; in
    single party systems, 456; transformation
    of nationalist movements into, 438;
    transterritorial, 427–28. *See also*
    Oligarchic party states; Single-party
    systems; *and names of parties*
Political systems, modern: African
    participation in, 406, 578; colonial, 453–55;
    constitutional arrangements in, 440;
    creation of institutions for, 440–41; effect
    of Islam on, 548–51; at independence and
    after, 460 (table); influence of religion in,
    566; interdisciplinary studies of, 611–12;
    Islamic elites in, 561; leadership in, 464;
    legacy of colonial administrations to, 258;
    messianic character of, 396; military
    regimes as, 469–70; and party systems,
    438–40; patron-client networks in, 468–69;
    post-independence party regimes in,
    459–72; predominant types of, 470;
    power bases of, 461–62, 465; reliance on
    force in, 443; religious power in, 557;
    in rise of nationalist sector, 455–59;
    sequence of, 471 (table); stages for analysis
    of, 453; and state dominated economies,
    501; statute law in, 489–90; study of,
    452–53; as a theme in literature, 586–88;
    unsuitability of colonial models to, 258–59.
    See also Oligarchic party-states; Political
    parties; Single-party systems
Political systems, traditional: in
    acephalous polities, 54–56; administrative
    structures in, 189–90; authority patterns
    in, 291; in centralized states, 57–59; 172;
    compared to modern nation-state systems,

64; and displacement of elites, 271; descent group as core of, 56; diffuse structure of, 54; effect of slave trade on, 253; effect of agriculture on, 50; framework of, 182; hereditary succession to office in, 281; in hunting and gathering bands, 54; impact of colonialism on, 246–47; in Islamic states, 550; and mobility of the population, 55; "Oriental despotism" in, 177, 189, 190; ritual leadership in, 187–88; transitional stages of, in early empires, 192; in West Africa, 197. *See also* African states and kingdoms; Chieftaincy; Centralized state systems; Kingship; Political authority
Poll tax, 217, 259
Polybius, 157
Polygyny, 265, 280, 281, 487
Population: of African states, 261 (table), 503 (table); of the continent, 260; data on, 548; in demographic cycle, 259–60; density, 260; growth of, 331, 349, 354, 502; patterns, 25–27, 347–52, 358; in traditional communities, 53
Population movements. *See* Migration patterns
Poro Society, 113, 118
Port-cities, 363–64, 365, 370, 372
Port Elizabeth (South Africa), 350, 569
Port Harcourt (Nigeria), 347, 364, 365, 368, 373
Port Sudan (Sudan), 365
Portugal, 201, 202, 236, 268
Portuguese Guinea: guerrilla war in, 272; population of, 26; regional grouping of, 32; resistance to colonial system in, 457
Portuguese territories: army in, 573; effect of action in Goa on, 534; historiography in, 162; liberation movements in, 272, 574–75; settler population in, 457, 573. *See also* Angola; Mozambique; Portuguese Guinea
Post-independence period: demands upon governments in, 443; dynamics of class formation in, 271–72; failures of new regimes in, 442–43; legitimacy of the new regimes in, 442; major political patterns in, 18; political and economic problems in, 442; social mobility in, 274. *See also* Political parties; Political systems, modern
Praise songs, 90, 142, 143, 147
Pre-colonial contact, 157, 199, 252–53. *See also* Missions; Trade; Slave trade
Pretoria (South Africa), 347, 350, 577
Principé. *See* Saõ Tomé and Principé
Proverbs, 91, 142–43, 297

Psychological tests, 317, 325
Public health facilities, 351
Pygmies, 30

Quatre Communes (Senegal), 233, 247

Race: adaptive characteristics of, 28–3; culturally perceived myths regarding, 31; defined, 28. *See also* Skin color
Racialism: absence of, in Islamic culture zones, 565; in academic treatises, 277–78; and African antiracism, 538–39; in black identity, 594–95; in colonial period, 235, 271; in East Africa, 272; and national boundaries, 432; in nationalist thought, 432; in philosophy of negritude, 416–22; in post-independence period, 272; as rationalization of colonialism, 237; as rationalization of slavery, 202; rejection of, in nationalist theory, 423–24; in residential segregation, 345–46, 347; in South Africa, 210–14; in South African churches, 213–14; in urban development, 337
Racial sovereignty, principle of, 538–39
Radiocarbon dating, 122 n, 122–23
Railways: construction of, 337, 340; in development of circulation systems, 364; effect of, on traditional economies, 367; effect of, on urban development, 344; miles of, 527 (table); role of, in urbanization, 364–65; systems of, 368, 370; in West Africa, 373
Rainfall, following 20 (map), 23–24
Rainforest belt, 23, 113, 334–36
Rash Dashan, 21–23
Rassemblement Democratique Africain (RDA), 427–28, 446
Reciprocal transactions. *See* Gift-giving
Reduplication, 87
Regional associations, 34, 426–31. *See also* Supranationalism
Regional groupings: Black Africa, 31; Central Africa, 32; Horn of Africa, 32; North Africa, 32; Southern Africa, 33; Sudan, 182; West Africa, 32; Western Sudan, 179. *See also* Circulation systems
Regionalism: colonial patterns of, 33; concept of ideological regrouping in, 430; concept of territorial federalism in, 430; criteria for groupings in, 34; defined, 31; economic unions in, 34; language as criteria of, 33; and transterritorial regional parties, 427–28. *See also* Supranationalism
Religion: in acephalous polities, 55–56;

anthropological study of, 382, 389; ancestor worship in, 198; as battle of symbols, 383; Christian message in, 384; and converts to Islam and Christianity, 261; as a cultural system, 383; and immigrants, 246; as basis for division of Africa, 547; and change, 388, 390; music and dance in, 140; in New World slave communities, 204–5, 208; and political development, 551, 557, 566; prophetic charismatic movements, 395–96; and sedentary populations, 56; in segmentary societies, 56; spirit worship in, 198; supernatural beings in, 198; unity of, 419–20; variety in, 261; in West Africa, 198. *See also* Christianity; Islam; Separatist church movements

Religious nationalism, 407, 419–20

Religious orders, Islamic: Ahmadiyya, 565; missionary activities of, 562; and nationalist movements, 563–64; political power of, 557, 561–62; Tijanniyya, 234; Sanusi, 562; Sufi, 556, 557, 562

Repatriation movements. *See* Back to Africa Movements

Research in Africa, 77–79; in case studies in economic development, 78; in comparative studies in economics, 78–79; disciplinary approach to, 611, 613; interdisciplinary approach to, 611–12; interdisciplinary methodology in, 618; and need for study of legal systems, 495–96; and lack of data on conceptual systems, 101; errors of Western terminology in, 101; priorities in, 610–13, 622; reaction of African scholars to, 418; problems of, 621–22; problem-oriented approach to, 613, 621; by teams, 611; types of social-science analysis in, 618–21, 622. *See also* Cultural bias; History, African, study of; Interdisciplinary Research; Research methodologies; Social science

Research methodologies: content analysis, 617; data in, 62 n, 62–63, 621; documentary analysis, 617; experimental testing, 616; macroanalysis, 451; participant observation, 614; problems of verification and validity in, 613; purpose of, 617; survey and interview techniques in, 168, 615; survey research, 616. *See also* History, African, study of; Research in Africa; Social science

Resistance movements, 175–76: Aba Womens' riots, 247; Ashanti Wars, 405; of Bai Bureh, 239; Battle at Burmi, 405; Gold Coast cocoa holdup, 247; Gun War, 222; Kaffir Wars, 219, 220; Mahdi movement, 562; Maji Maji rebellion, 176, 405; Mau Mau revolt, 457, 536; Sanusi order in, 562; Sierra Leone railway strike, 247; Zulu rebellion, 405. *See also* Liberation movements

Retief, Piet, manifesto of, 218

Réunion, 26, 33

Rhodes, Cecil, 161, 569

Rhodesia: agricultural research in, 525; British NIBMAR policy in, 576; domestic colonialism in, 569; economy of, 574; economic exploitation of, 268; extension of political rights to Africans in, 574; international sanctions in, 572; international sanctions against, 574; interurban linkages in, 368; military in, 573; population of, 26, 503; regional grouping in, 33; 1897 revolt in, 176; South African troops in, 573; 575; trade with United Kingdom in, 513; 1965 Unilateral Declaration of Independence in, 3, 538, 572, 574; urbanization in, 337; U. S. position on, 580; white settlers in, 272, 457, 569, 573; Zimbabwe complex in, 123

Rhythm: defined by Hornbostel, 150; defined by Senghor, 141–42, 149; relations of, to language, 135–36, 141–43; in African music, 135–43, 150–51, 150 n, 72; relation of, to musical instrument, 148–50

Rift Valley system, 21

Rio Muni. *See* Equatorial Guinea

Rive, Richard, 584

Road transport, 367, 368, 373. *See also* Circulation systems

Robert, Shaaban, 92

Roman colonists, in North Africa, 333–34

Rumfa, Muhammad, 192

Ruwenzori Mountains, 21

Rwanda: anti-Watutsi revolution in, 217, 272; circulation systems in, 372; currency depreciation in, 512; exports of, 508 n; GNP per capita in, 503; independence political system in, 460; oral tradition in, 160; population in, 26, 27, 503; plural society in, 445; "premise of inequality" in, 100; primary product exports in, 520; Pygmies in, 30; regional grouping of, 32, 33, 372; social change in, 259

Rwanda (kingdom), 270

Sahara: as a barrier, 546; as a bridge, 546; desiccation of, 171, 183; effect of, on domestic units, 50; and reorientation of trade routes, 546; and trans-Saharan trade,

334–35, 361. *See also* Culture contact; Trade

Saint Helena, 26

Saint Louis (Senegal), 236, 363

Salisbury (Rhodesia), 337, 350, 364, 368

Sanusi religious order, 562

Saõ Tomé and Principé, 26, 33. *See also* Portugal

Sapir-Whorf hypothesis, 105

Sardauna of Sokoto, 271

Savanna racial type, 28–29

Savanna zone, 24

School enrollments, 245, 263, 310, 311; selectivity by age, 317–18; selectivity by ethnic group, 318; selectivity by family educational characteristics, 320; selectivity by family occupation, 319; selectivity by geography, 318; selectivity hypothesized, 321–22; selectivity by sex, 316–17; selectivity by urban-rural origin, 318–19. *See also* Education

Scramble for Africa, 155, 237, 254, 258

Scripts, used in African languages, 89

Sculpture: aesthetic considerations in, 119–21; Afro-Portuguese ivories, 126; techniques for dating, 122–23; as expression of conceptual system, 112; and missionary iconoclasm, 125; Nok terracottas, 122–23; proportion in, 114; reduced demand for, 126; "Sao" terracottas, 123; spirit occupation of, 114, 116; in West Africa, 120, 198

Secondary empires, as theme in African history, 173

Secret societies, 52, 391–92, 392 n

Segregation customs. *See* Social-distance patterns

Sekondi (Ghana), 363

Senegal: birth rates in, 350; "brain drain" in, 263–64; Brazzaville bloc in, 430; circulation network in, 373; colonial legacy in, 258; colonial policies in, 233; economy of, 500, 501; education in, 306; education policy in, 305–6; external support in, 467; GNP per capita in, 503; historiography in, 162; independence political system in, 460; interurban linkages in, 368; Islam in, 422; 549–50, 550 n; in Mali Federation, 410, 428; as oligarchic party-state, 18; party system in, 464; patron-client networks in, 468; peanuts in, 499; and political expression in colonial period, 247; population in, 26, 503; price supports in, 520; *Quatre Communes* of, 233; regional grouping in, 32; religious

pluralism in, 551; ruling class in, 274; and trade with France, 513; traditional religious authority and European power in, 563

Senegal River Basin, 373

Senghor, Léopold Sédar: on French West African federation, 429; language philosophy of, 141, 149; music philosophy of, 129, 135, 141, 146, 149; negritude philosophy of, 397, 418; poetry of, 588; on proposed division of French West Africa, 427; socialist philosophy of, 415–16

Separatist church movements: Barrett's analysis of, 619; and Donna Beatrice, 387–88; Ethiopian, 228; Jamaa, 398; Lumpa sect, 262; in New World slave communities, 205; as response to social change, 262; in South Africa, 228; syncretistic and messianic movements in, 262; Zionism, 228

Sex segregation. *See* Social-distance patterns

Seychelles, 26

Sharpeville riots, 231, 571

Sherbro (Sierra Leone), 126

Shirazis, 559

Sierra Leone: British in, 236; British conquest of, 239; circulation systems in, 373; competitive party system in, 457; Courts Ordinance in, 483; development plans in, 504; development of rice in, 526; elections in, 465; GNP per capita in, 503; independence political system in, 460; Islamic law in, 480; military in, 507; 1967 military takeover in, 465; minerals in, 244; nationalist leaders in, 425; political parties in, 438; population in, 26, 503; primary product exports in, 520; railway strikes in, 247; rainfall in, 23–24; regional grouping of, 32; returned slaves in, 83, 600

Simba rebels, 536

Single-party systems: analysis of, 439; in ideology of nation-building, 438; at independence, 438, 461; and military regimes, 470; in pre-independence period, 457; in Tanzania, 463. *See also* Political systems, modern

Skin color, 28–31; division of Africa in terms of, 545–47; in philosophy of negritude, 417. *See also* Race

Slavery, African: and caste system in early empires, 191–92; in colonial period, 239, 271; in kingdom of Dahomey, 174; in Hausaland, 192; in Kanem-Bornu, 193; in maintenance of ruler's authority, 192; in the Mediterranean World, 199; in traditional societies, 24, 51, 199, 280, 312

Slavery, New World: and American economic development, 207–9; and cultural effects of slave system, 203; economic consequences of, 206–7; family patterns in, 203; and leadership in slave communities, 205; nucleation of slave society in, 203; numbers involved in, 173, 195, 200–201; political consequences of, 207–8; rationalization of, 200, 202; religion in, 204–5; and returnees to Africa, 174, 306, 600–601; social consequences of, 207–8, 598; and social structure in slave community, 203; status of free Negroes in, 204; status of slaves in, 201–3; as symbol of Africa, 592; and technology, 202–3; in West Indies, 199. *See also* Afro-Americans; Slave trade

Slave trade: abolition of, 216, 218; economic motives for, 250; effect of, on African economy, 267; effect of, on traditional political systems, 253; as emotional issue, 174; European and African slavers in, 200; European states involved in, 201; as impetus to social change, 253; numbers involved in, 173, 195, 200–201; origins of slaves in, 196, 201; as theme in African history, 173–74; as triangle trade, 200–201; *See also* Slavery, New World

Social anthropology, 133, 381–82; 394–95

Social change: adaptation to, 299–303; charismatic religion in processes of, 395; colonialism as agent of, 70, 76–77; and creation of political institutions, 437; demographic patterns in, 259–60; and economic change, 266–69; in education, 263–64; effect of colonial boundaries on, 366; effect of communications and transport on, 365; equated with Westernization, 256; family and marriage patterns in, 264–66; and income distribution, 259; in pre-colonial period, 175, 253; communications and transport technology in, 360; religious institutions and, 388–92; religious process and, 261–62, 394–98; resistance of African cultures to, 257; role of communication in, 359; studies of, 175, 382; theoretical considerations in, 389–91. *See also* Urbanization

Social class. *See* Social stratification

Social-distance patterns: and absence of separation anxiety, 296; between persons differing in age and sex, 284–86; expressions of deference in, 287–88; maintained by prescribed interpersonal behavior, 286, 300. *See also* Behavior, African; Interpersonal relations

Social life, traditional, 38, 197–98; breakdown of traditional forms of, 352; and community patterning, 52–54; ideals of morality expressed in, 42; limited by lack of contacts, 359; marriage customs in, 46–47; urban patterns of, 345–46; *See also* Family life; Traditional societies

Social science: crosscutting, 609; defined, 607; functionally specialized, 609; interdisciplinary nature of methodology in, 618; language of, 608–10; methods of observation in, 613–18; problems of research in, 621–22; types of analysis in, 618–21, 622. *See also* Interdisciplinary research; Research methodologies

Social stratification, 269–75; by age and sex, 286–288; in allocation of work, 288, 291; in contemporary African cities, 353; and customary law, 477; and education, 291, 329–30; by racial castes in colonial societies, 271; and reciprocal expectations, 291–92; role of ethnic affiliation in, 320; and social mobility in modern Africa, 274; in traditional societies, 269–70; urban-rural, 273

Social welfare practices, 71, 518

Society, concept of, 38–39

Society of African Missions (S.M.A.), 125

Sociolinguistics, 97, 104

Soga (people), 491–92

Sokoto caliphate, 180, 181

Somali (language), 89

Somali (people), 44

Somalia: bananas in, 499; competitive-party system in, 467; dance in, 140; development plans in, 504; elections in, 465; Freedom songs of, 142; GNP per capita in, 503; independence political system in, 460; Islam in, 549–50, 566; military in, 507; 1969 military takeover in, 18; party system in, 18; population in, 26, 503; primary product exports of, 520; racial types in, 30; regional grouping of, 32, 372; relations of, with Europe, 560; religious nationalism in, 407; Soviet aid to, 514; Swahili community in, 559; unification of, 515

Songhai, 179, 181, 183, 185–86, 188, 191, 238, 252

Sororate, 50

South Africa: African bourgeoisie in, 577; African churches in, 228; African franchise in, 222, 224, 225, 570–71; African majority in, 568, 577, 579; African National Congress in, 225, 230, 571; African nationalism in, 223, 229, 256, 578;

African sources of strength in, 572–73; Afrikaner National Party in, 226; Afro-American attitudes toward, 603; All African Convention in, 229–30; arms ban on, 573; balance of payments in, 572; British liberalism in, 219; buffer states to, 573; Cape Provincial Council in, 226; class structure in 215; colonialism in, 233; communications and transport network in, 370; connections with Zambezi transport system of, 370–71; "Defiance Campaign" in, 230; discriminatory legislation in, 225–27; domestic colonialism in, 569; Dutch and German settlers in, 210–14, 215; economy of, 267, 502; Ethiopian movement in, 228; European settlement of, 210–12, 254; first partition scheme in, 214; Freedom Charter in, 230; GNP per capita in, 503; granting of responsible government to colonies in, 222; Great Trek in, 218; Gun War in, 222; Hertzog bills in, 225, 229; historical continuity of racial policies in, 210–14; ideology of white supremacy in, 210, 216; implications for U.S. racial conflict in, 580, 603; independence political system in, 460; international pressures in, 573–74; Kaffir Wars in, 219, 220; legislation of segregation in, 570–71; literacy rate in, 263; literature of alienation in, 584–86; military and police establishments in, 572; monetary zone in, 513; and Mozambique, 576; nationalist leaders in, 425; Native Reserves in, 214, 218, 221, 577–78; Natives Land Act in, 225, 229, 230; Natives Representative Council in, 226, 230; and non-white participation in the economy, 579; Pan-Africanist Congress in, 231; pass laws in, 223; pass system in, 216, 227, 229, 231, 571; pervasive economy in, 572; poll tax in, 217; poor-white problem in, 569; population of, 26, 503; position on Rhodesian UDI, 575–76; racial discrimination as government policy in, 570; racism as a rationale for slavery in, 202; regional groupings in, 32, 33; residential segregation in, 571; Sharpeville riots in, 231, 571; and slavery in Cape settlement, 211, 212, 213–14; sources of white power in, 570–71; South Africa Act in, 570; and South-West Africa, 576–77; trade with the United Kingdom in, 572; treason trial in, 230–31; *Umkhonto We Sizwe* party in, 231; Union constitution of, 224–25, 571; U.S. policy toward, 580; U.S.

trade and investment in, 513; white population in, 570; Zulu rebellion in, 217, 219. *See also* Bantustan program; Cape settlement; *and individual political units*

Southern Africa: circulation system of, 370; domestic colonialism in, 569, 570–72; early urban centers in, 337–38; area of, 33, 569 n; South African economy in, 572; population of, 568; South African buffer states in, 573; white minority control of, 259, 568

Southern Rhodesia. *See* Rhodesia

South-West Africa: African political participation in, 578; communications and transport network of, 370; economic relations of, with South Africa, 576; population of, 26; regional grouping of, 33; South African control of, 576; United Nations trusteeship in, 576; white population of, 570

Soviet Union, aid to African states, 514, 541–42, 545

Soyinka, Wole, 590

Spain, 201, 202, 206

Spanish North Africa, 26

Spanish Sahara, 26, 32

State-building, as theme in African history, 172–73

Status. *See* Social stratification

Strabo, 157, 158

Subsistence farming. *See* Agriculture, African

Sudan: agriculture in, 526; biracialism in, 432; competitive party system in, 457; cotton in, 499; development plans in, 504; early urban centers in, 334–36; elections in, 465; exports of, 509 n; GNP per capita in, 503; independence political system in, 460; Islam in, 549–50, 566; Jebel Aulia Dam in, 528; Mahdi movement in, 562; military regime in, 470; 1958 military takeover in, 469; Penal Code in, 487; population of, 26, 503; regional grouping of, 32, 372; separatist movements in, 472; UN research mission to, 528; White Nile in, 523–24

Sudan (region), 182. *See also* Western Sudan

Sudanic belt: Islamic law in, 487; population concentration in, 25; regional division of, 32; trading centers of, 335–63

Sudd, 21, 523–24

Sufism, 556, 557

Suku (people), 45 n

Sunni Ali, 185, 188, 189, 193

Sunni community, 559

Supranationalism, 406–8; in Afro-Asian solidarity movement, 426; assertion of black African values and culture in, 421–22; circulation systems in, 377; in economic unions, 34; Eur-African concept in, 410; and idea of suprastate regionalism, 426–31; ideology of negritude in, 416–22; Islam as unifying factor in, 566–67; Marxist-Socialist ideology in, 411–16; need for communication network in, 373–74; as Pan-Africanism, 422–25, 539; and Third World, 425–26; transterritorial political parties in, 427–28. *See also* Organization of African Unity; Regional associations

Survivals, African. *See* African survivals

Swahili (language), 81, 88, 89, 257, 559

Swahili literary tradition, 90, 91, 92

Swahili (people), 559

Swazi (people), 270–71

Swaziland: communications and transport network in, 370; economic dependence of, 513, 572; independence of, 578; as labor reservoir, 267; racial policies in, 580; population of, 26; regional grouping of, 33; South African relations with, 576

Syrian tradesmen, 244

Tanganyika: Africans in colonial administration of, 458; historiography in, 162; integration of law in, 492; Islamic law in, 480; regional grouping of, 32; single-party system in, 457. *See also* Tanzania

TANU (Tanzanian African National Union), 462 n, 462–64

Tanzania: abolishment of freehold tenure in, 489–90; Australian lawyers in, 481; Chinese aid to, 514; circulation systems in, 370, 372, 373; economy of, 500; 1965 elections in, 463; exports of, 509 n; FRELIMO in, 574; GNP per capita in, 503; independence political system in, 460; integration of courts in, 495; integration of legal system in, 490; Islam in, 549 n; mass-party regime in, 462–64; 467; nationalist movements in, 438; racial policies in, 580; population of, 26, 503; Range Development and Management Act of, 490; and relations with Mozambique, 576; religious ceremonies in, 172; regional grouping of, 32; social change in, 259; Swahili community in, 559; unification of law in, 493–94. *See also* Tanganyika; Zanzibar

Tariffs, 520–21

Ta'rikh al-Fattach, 185, 191

Ta'rikh al-Sudan, 184, 188

Taruga (Nigeria), 122

Tassili paintings, 112

Taxation, 190, 191, 241, 267, 301, 355, 506

Technical training, 527–29

Technology: absence of, in Africa, 66–68; as it affects culture, 66; available choice of, 356; borrowed, 257; as capital-intensive, 357; in colonial occupation, 235; in complex societies, 69; effect of, on traditional craft industry, 341–43; of food production, 524–26; incongruities in, 517; and introduction of modern production processes, 343–44; and introduction of transportation network, 344; lack of supporting institutions for, 515–17; limitations on, imposed by vocabulary, 104; preindustrial, in New World, 202–3; of transportation, 526–27; of water conservation, 523–24

Teilhard de Chardin, Pierre, 129, 418

Telecommunications. *See* Mass media

Tema (Ghana), 368. *See also* Accra

Tembu (people), 219, 222

Tempels, Placide, 397

Terminology, social-science, 608–10

Third World, 4, 330, 425–26, 432, 436, 455, 532, 539, 541

Thlaping (people), 390

Tijanniyya, 234

Timbuktu (Mali), 253, 335, 341, 345, 363, 557

Tiv (people), 53, 64, 477, 478, 494

Togo: circulation network of, 373; 1963 coup in, 444; German rule in, 233–34, 243; GNP per capita in, 503; independence political system in, 460; nationalist leaders of, 425; population in, 26, 503; railways in, 372; regional grouping of, 32

Tonga (people), 52

Toomer, Jean, 600

Toure, Samory, 239, 249, 405

Touré, Sékou, 259, 412, 430

Trade: and acceptance of colonial rule, 240; in African kingdoms, 180, 191–92; Arab, with East Africa, 336, 552; barter, 243, 498; in central Africa, 172; and communication patterns, 361; Dutch East India Company in, 210; and European exploitation, 237–38; and growth of ports, 363–64; items of, East Africa, 336; items of, West Africa, 334–35; penetration of the interior in, 364–65, 365 (table); reorientation of Saharan routes of, 546; shift in, in slave-trading period, 253; in

South African network, 371; in spread of Islam, 554; Sudanic, 335; Syrian middlemen in, 244; as theme in African history, 172; trans-Saharan, 361, 363, 546, 554; triangle pattern in, 200–201; with India, 337; with medieval Europe, 334; in Western Sudan, 183, 188. *See also* Culture contact

Traditional societies: boundaries of, 52; concept of, 37–39; central tendencies in, 280; communications in, 360–61; cultural and physical isolation of, 70; descent groups as political units in, 56; disruption of, 565; distinctiveness of, 280–81; diversity and smallness of scale of, 64–66; dynamic nature of, 252; interpenetration of economy and society in, 71; kingship in, 58–59; and kinship ties in urbanized areas, 265–66; mobility-stability continuum in, 52–53; as organic societies, 71; patterning of, 52–54; reciprocal transactions in, 75–76; religious activities in, 55–56; as repetitive systems, 389; resilience of, 257, 266; "social money" in, 75–76; social rights and welfare in, 71; social stratification in, 269–70. *See also* Economies, African; Family life; Political systems, traditional; Values, traditional

Transactional modes, in traditional economies, 74–75

Transkei, 571, 578

Transport systems, 243, 344–45, 355–56, 359, 360, 367, 368–74. *See also* Circulation systems; Railways

Transvaal, 244, 569

Tribe, concept of, 5, 12, 59, 60, 378, 446. *See also* Ethnicity

Tripolitania, 554

Tshombe, Moise, 391, 446

Tswana (people), 403, 486, 390

Tswanaland, 578

Tuareg (people), 48, 186

Tunis, 350

Tunisia: diversification of economic relations in, 511; economy of, 501, 507; exports of, 509 n; GNP per capita in, 503; independence political system in, 460; Islam in, 549–50 n; labor movement in, 412; literacy rate of, 263; mass party regime in, 462, 464–65, 467; military in, 507; population of, 26, 503; regional grouping in, 32; Destour party in, 412, 457, 464; urban concentration in, 333

Turner, Bishop Henry McNeal, 602

Tutuola, Amos, 590

Twi (language), 82

Uganda: Baganda in, 88; circulation system of, 372; competitive party system in, 457; economic development of, 268; economy of, 267; exports of, 509 n; GNP per capita in, 503; historiography in, 162; independence political system in, 460; interurban linkages in, 368; Islamic law in, 480; Makerere University College in, 396; music of, 143, 147–48; political parties in, 438; population of, 26, 503; problems of federalism in, 438–39; regional grouping of, 32; separatist movements in, 472; unification of courts in, 495. *See also* Buganda

UGTAN (Union Générale des Travailleurs de l'Afrique Noire), 412

UGTT (Union Générale des Travailleurs Tunisiens), 412

Umayyads, 558

Unemployment, urban, 354, 355, 356

UNESCO, 578

Unilateral Declaration of Independence (Rhodesia), 3, 370, 538, 574–76

Unilineal descent systems, 43, 44, 55, 665

Union of African and Malagasy States (UAM), 541

Union of African States (UAS), 427, 430

United Arab Republic (Egypt): activities in Africa, 566; GNP per capita in, 503; independence political system in, 460; Islam in, 549–50, 550 n; Jebel Aulia Dam in, 523; military regime in, 470; 1952 military takeover in, 469; population of, 25, 26, 503; regional grouping of, 32; resolution on Cuban crisis in, 541

United Nations, 236, 526, 537, 538, 543, 573, 576

United Nations Conference on Trade and Development (UNCTAD), 521

United Party (South Africa), 570

United States: aid to Africa, 513, 542, 542 n; influence of, on nationalist movements, 537; and international impact of Cuban crisis, 540–41; policy toward Africa, 542

Universal suffrage, 442

Upper Volta: circulation network in, 373; effect of coup on development in, 515; exports of, 509 n; GNP per capita in, 503; independence political system in, 460; Islam in, 549 n; and Mali Federation, 428; population of, 26, 503; regional association of, 431; regional grouping of, 32; resistance to French in, 236 n; underdevelopment of, 451

Urban centers: age and sex structure of, 351; birth and death rates in, 350 (table);

concentration of development in, 379–80; definition of, 347; demographic characteristics of, 351; in East African city-state system, 337; European cities, 346–47, 355–56; European influence on, 340; extended family in, 352; functional specialization in, 339, 347; limitations on growth of, 340; major contemporary, 348 (map); patterns in, typology of, 345–47; with population over 20,000, 348–49; with population over one million, 349; pre-colonial, 332 (map), 332–38; rejuvenated traditional cities, 345–46, 355–56; residential segregation in, 345–46, 347, 571; social mobility in, 353; socioeconomic characteristics of, 352–54; traditional cities, 67 n, 345, 362; unemployment in, 354, 356; Yoruba towns, 335–36. *See also* Urbanization

Urbanization: demographic patterns in, 260; and development of transportation network, 344; and early trade patterns, 335; and education, 318, 246; European impact on, 338; as a force for economic and social development, 357; impact of industrial Europe on, 340–45; and increase in witchcraft and sorcery accusations, 41, 302; and interethnic circulation, 362; and interurban linkages, 366, 367–68; kinship groups in, 265–66, 300; major African cities, 350; migration to cities, 351; and need for housing, 355; and overurbanization; and population increase, 347–52, 354, 358; provision of public utilities in, 355; rate of, 354, 358; role of industry in, 356–57; role of the railroad in, 364–65; and technical skills, 357; social effects of, 256; and social stratification, 273; sociopolitical problems of, 354–58. *See also* Urban centers; Voluntary associations

Usman dan Fodio, 181, 189, 255

U Tam'si, Tchicaya, 588

Vai script, 89

Values: defined, 609; effect of education on, 329–30; in philosophy of negritude, 416–22; political, 533–538, 542–44; traditional, 39, 41, 42, 415. *See also* Conceptual systems

van Riebeeck, Jan, 210, 214, 337

Vansina, Jan, 94–95, 166–67, 174, 615

Verwoerd, Hendrik, 578

Victoria, Lake (Nyanza), 23, 372

Vocational training. *See* Education; Guild system; Technical training

Voluntary associations, 246, 257, 346, 352–53, 405, 447

Wadai sultanate, 454

Wahhabi movement, 560

Water: categories of uses, 522–23; in Lake Albert reservoir, 524; supply of, 522; technology of conservation of, 523–24

Waterways. *See* Circulation systems

Watkins, Lucian B., 600

Watutsi (people), 272, 465

Wesleyan missions, 228, 308, 310

West Africa: aesthetic forms in, 198; circulation system of, 372–74; coastal ports in, 363; colonial rule in, 234–37; as cultural background of slaves, 196–98; ecology of, 196–97; extent of, 32; family organization in, 197; in independence period, 235; kinship patterns in, 197; languages in, 198; population of, 25; 374; slaves from, 196–98; traditional economy in, 197; traditional political systems in, 197; traditional religion in, 198; traditional social life in, 197; village boundaries in, 52. *See also* British West Africa

West African Monetary Union, 512

Westermann, Diedrich, 84

Westernization: and cultural relativism among Africans, 302; and colonial legacy, 256–59; equated with change, 256; and European cultural penetration, 257; and social status, 302; trend toward, 257; and urban elite, 258

Western Sudan: decline of empires of, 186; Islam in, 187–88; political authority in, 183–84, 189–94; region defined, 179; state formation in, 182–83. *See also* African states and kingdoms

Western Sudanic language group, 83–84

West Indies: criminal code of, 486; need for slave labor in, 199; reaction against French assimilation in, 416; slave trade in, 199, 201. *See also* African survivals

Westminster model, 259

White Nile, 523

White settler populations, 235, 272, 457, 514, 570, 573, 579

Whydah (Dahomey), 363

Witchcraft, 41, 101, 280, 283, 293, 298, 302

Witwatersrand, 27, 337, 370, 569, 576

Women, education of, 316–17, 320, 329

World Bank, 355, 511, 578

World Islamic Congress, 567

World view. *See* Conceptual systems

World War I, 236 n

World War II, 236, 406
Wright, Richard, 418, 421, 604
Written languages, 88–89, 181, 480

Xhosa (people), 219, 220, 222, 578

Yakö (people), 43
Yaounde (Cameroon), 368
Yaounde Convention (1964), 500, 508, 511
Yoruba (people), 27, 117, 120, 123, 148, 201,
  204, 234, 270, 298, 335, 366, 417, 590

Zambezi Basin, 362
Zambezi region, 370
Zambezi River, 21, 337, 523, 576
Zambia: copper in, 499; depletion of game
  population in, 390; economy of, 267;
  independence political system in, 460;
  interurban linkages in, 368; GNP per
  capita in, 503; and Mozambique, 576;

party system in, 464; population of, 26,
503; position on Rhodesian UDI, 574;
racial policies in, 580; regional grouping
of, 33, 372, 569 n; and Rhodesia, 572;
and South Africa, 580; trade orientation
of, 371; and trade with United Kingdom,
513; urbanization of, 337; urban
population of, 349. *See also* Cooperbelt
Zanzibar, 336, 364; anti-Arab revolution in,
271; historiography in, 162; ideological
influence of China in, 536; Islamic law in,
480; as plural society, 445; regional
grouping of, 32; 1964 revolution in, 559;
social change in, 259. *See also* Tanzania
Zaria Emirate (Nigeria), 339
Zaydiyyah, 558
Zimbabwe, 123, 180
Zionism, 228
Zulu (people), 47, 219, 270–71, 519
Zulu rebellion, 217, 219, 405